A Refreshing Spot. 1583197

WOOD COUNTY

SOME FACTS AND FIGURES

WOOD COUNTY, with a total of 4,357 farms in an area of 612 square miles, is distinctly a farm county. More than 91 per cent. of the entire area of the county is in its farms, and more than 70 per cent. is under cultivation. The farms are, as a rule, of more than average size, less than 4 per cent. being under ten acres. They are almost without exception profitable and correspondingly valuable. The farmers, as a class, are the most prosperous folks in the county. In view of the number of farmers, that is in itself a statement of the wealth of this section.

The farm population of Wood County is almost exclusively native-born white. There are but few foreign, and only one negro farmer in the entire county according to the most recent United States Government statistics.

It is interesting to note the number of farms in the county operated by their owners. Of this class there are 2,615 or 60 per cent. One thousand eight hundred and thirty-six or 70 per cent. of them are reported

3

free of mortgage debt. This is an exceptionally large percentage. Of the balance, the remarkably low mortgage indebtedness of only 29 per cent. of the entire valuation is carried. Even in the absence of other statistical figures, these mortgage statements alone would indicate exceptional prosperity among Wood County farmers.

The largest single crop, and the one produced most generally throughout the entire county, is corn, of which 4,463,745 bushels were produced in 1910, a notably bad crop year, but the latest for which authoritative figures are available. Following closely on this for quantity is oats, with a total of 2,620,974 bushels; wheat comes next, with 353,678 bushels, and potatoes fourth, with 185,525 bushels. The combined total value of these four crops was in excess of four million dollars.

Everywhere is an atmosphere of hard work. Everyone takes work seriously and as a matter of course. There is no false pride about it, and no failure to realize its importance and its necessity. Rich farmers' wives, and sons and daughters, take pride in their fine butter, their eggs, their vegetables, their chickens and their stock. The relations between the people of the farms and the people of the county seat are most cordial. The farmers deposit their savings in the local banks, and deal in the local stores.

This directory is published in the belief that it will serve to acquaint the residents of one end of the county with those of the other. We believe it to be accurate. We realize, however, that even in the most carefully compiled and printed books certain errors are bound to appear, and we apologize in advance for any such that may be found by our subscribers.

ISBN 978-1-5281-1607-7
PIBN 10906686

1 MONTH OF
FREE
READING

at
www.ForgottenBooks.com

By purchasing this book you are eligible for one month membership to ForgottenBooks.com, giving you unlimited access to our entire collection of over 1,000,000 titles via our web site and mobile apps.

To claim your free month visit:

www.forgottenbooks.com/free906686

English
Français
Deutsche
Italiano
Español
Português

www.forgottenbooks.com

Mythology Photography **Fiction**
Fishing Christianity **Art** Cooking
Essays Buddhism Freemasonry
Medicine **Biology** Music **Ancient
Egypt** Evolution Carpentry Physics
Dance Geology **Mathematics** Fitness
Shakespeare **Folklore** Yoga Marketing
Confidence Immortality Biographies
Poetry **Psychology** Witchcraft
Electronics Chemistry History **Law**
Accounting **Philosophy** Anthropology
Alchemy Drama Quantum Mechanics
Atheism Sexual Health **Ancient History**
Entrepreneurship Languages Sport
Paleontology Needlework Islam
Metaphysics Investment Archaeology
Parenting Statistics Criminology
Motivational

M. L. DONAHEY, President   B. C. HARDING, Cashier
H. G. HANKEY, Vice-President   G. W. FEARNSIDE, Asst. Cashier

FIRST
NATIONAL BANK

BOWLING GREEN, OHIO

---

4 PER CENT. ON SAVINGS
OR CERTIFICATES OF
DEPOSITS

DIRECTORS

M. L. Donahey	Henry Goodenough	M. B. Reider
H. G. Hankey	A. E. Cen	J. G. Starn
C. R. Nearing	J. F. Frost	B. C. Harding

THE FARM JOURNAL
RURAL DIRECTORY

OF

WOOD COUNTY

OHIO

(With a Complete Road Map of the County)

COPYRIGHT, 1916
BY WILMER ATKINSON COMPANY

PUBLISHED BY
WILMER ATKINSON COMPANY
PHILADELPHIA
1916

2

F

The Policy

of this Store
is Courteous
Treatment,
Satisfaction
and Full
Value for
Every Dollar

SPRAYING FORMULAS

FUNGICIDES.—Bordeaux mixture is made by taking three pounds of sulphate of copper, four pounds of quicklime, fifty gallons of water. To dissolve the copper sulphate, put it into a coarse cloth bag and suspend the bag in a receptacle partly filled with water. Next, slake the lime in a tub, and strain the milk of lime thus obtained into another receptacle. Now get some one to help you, and with buckets, *simultaneously* pour the two liquids into the spraying barrel or tank. Lastly, add sufficient water to make fifty gallons. It is safe to use this full-strength Bordeaux on almost all foliage—except, perhaps, on extra tender things, such as watermelon vines, peach trees, etc. For these it is wiser to use a half-strength mixture.

FORMALIN.—This is also called formaldehyde, and may be purchased at drug stores. Its principal use is to treat seed potatoes to prevent "scab." Soak the whole seed for two hours in a mixture of one-half pint formalin and fifteen gallons of cold water; dry the seed, cut, and plant in ground that has not recently grown potatoes.

BORDEAUX COMBINED WITH INSECT POISON.—By adding one-quarter pound of Paris green to each fifty gallons of Bordeaux, the mixture becomes a combined fungicide and insecticide. Or, instead of Paris green, add about two pounds of arsenate of lead. The advantages of arsenate of lead over Paris green are, first, it is not apt to burn foliage even if used in rather excessive quantities; and, second, it "sticks" to the foliage, etc., better and longer.

INSECTICIDES.—ARSENATE OF LEAD.—This is the best insecticide for chewing insects, and is for sale by seedsmen. Use about two pounds in fifty gallons of water.

WHITE HELLEBORE.—This, if fresh, may be used instead of Paris green in some cases—worms on currant and gooseberry bushes, for instance. (It is not such a powerful poison as the arsenites, and would not do so well for tough insects such as potato-bugs.) Steep two ounces in one gallon of hot water, and use as a spray.

FOR SUCKING INSECTS.—Now we come to another class of insecticides, suited to insects which suck a plant's juice but do not chew. Arsenic will not kill such pests; therefore we must resort to solutions which kill by *contact*.

KEROSENE EMULSION.—One-half pound of hard or one quart of soft soap; kerosene, two gallons; boiling soft water, one gallon. If hard soap is used, slice it fine and dissolve it in water by boiling; add the boiling solution (away from the fire) to the kerosene, and stir or violently churn for from five to eight minutes, until the mixture assumes a creamy consistency. If a spray pump is at hand, pump the mixture back upon itself with considerable force for about five minutes. Keep this as a stock. *It must be further diluted with water before using.* One part of emulsion to fifteen parts of water, is about right for lice.

CARBOLIC ACID EMULSION.—Made by dissolving one pound of hard soap or one quart of soft soap in a gallon of boiling water, to which one pint of *crude* carbolic acid is added, the whole being stirred into an emulsion. One part of this is added to about thirty-five parts of water and poured around the bases of the plants, about four ounces per plant at each application, beginning when the plants are set out and repeated every week or ten days until the last of May. Used to fight maggots.

WHALE-OIL SOAP SOLUTION.—Dissolve one pound of whale-oil soap in a gallon

6

of hot water, and dilute with about six gallons of cold water. This is a good application for aphis (lice) on trees or plants. For oyster-shell or scurvy scale use this spray in May or June or when the tiny scale lice are moving about on the bark.

TOBACCO TEA.—Place five pounds of tobacco stems in a water-tight vessel, and cover them with three gallons of hot water. Allow to stand several hours; dilute the liquor by adding about seven gallons of water. Strain and apply. Good for lice.

LIME-SULPHUR MIXTURE.—Slake twenty-two pounds of fresh lump lime in the vessel in which the mixture is to be boiled, using only enough water to cover the lime. Add seventeen pounds of sulphur (flowers or powdered), having previously mixed it in a paste with water. Then boil the mixture for about an hour in about ten gallons of water, using an iron but not a copper vessel. Next add enough more water to make, in all, fifty gallons. Strain through wire sieve or netting, and apply while mixture is still warm. A good, high-pressure pump is essential to satisfactory work. Coat every particle of the tree. This is the standard San Jose scale remedy, although some orchardists prefer to use the soluble oil sprays now on the market.

PYRETHRUM, OR PERSIAN INSECT POW-DER.—It may be dusted on with a powder bellows when the plants are wet; or one ounce of it may be steeped in one gallon of hot water, and sprayed on the plants at any time. It is often used on flowers, in greenhouses, on vegetables, etc.

BISULPHIDE OF CARBON.—This is used to kill weevils in beans and peas, etc. It comes in liquid form and may be had of druggists. When exposed to the air it quickly vaporizes into a poisonous and explosive gas which is heavier than air and which will destroy all insect life. (Caution.—Do not inhale the vapor, and allow no lights near.)

Tobacco stems, tobacco dust, kainit, soot, freshly-slaked lime, dust, etc., are often used as insect *preventives*—in the soil around plants to keep away grubs, worms and maggots, or dusted on to discourage the visits of cucumber bugs, etc. (Note.—The first four are excellent fertilizers as well as insect preventives.)

Crows and blackbirds frequently pull up planted corn. The best preventive is to tar the seed, as follows: Put the seed into a pail and pour on enough warm water to cover it. Add a teaspoonful of coal-tar to a peck, and stir well. Throw the seed out on a sieve or in a basket to drain, and then stir in a few handfuls of land plaster (gypsum), or air-slaked lime.

A NEW FUNGICIDE.—Some orchardists are now using the following self-boiled lime-sulphur spray, instead of Bordeaux, claiming that it is less liable to spot or burn fruit and foliage: Put eight pounds of unslaked lump lime in a barrel; add enough water to cover. When the lime begins to heat, throw in eight pounds of flowers of sulphur. Constantly stir and gradually pour on more water until the lime is all slaked; then add the rest of the water to cool the mixture. About fifty gallons of water, in all, are required. Strain. Two pounds of arsenate of lead may be added, if desired, to the finished mixture, which then becomes a combined fungicide *and* insecticide, and may be used in the same manner as advised for Bordeaux-arsenate of lead. (Special note.—The self-boiled mixture is *not* the same as the lime-sulphur advised for San Jose scale, which is too strong for trees in foliage.)

If you do not care to bother with making spraying mixtures at home, they can be purchased, already prepared, of seedsmen. For only a few trees or plants, the extra cost of these factory mixtures is not great.

7

SPRAYING CALENDAR

PLANT	FIRST APPLICATION	SECOND APPLICATION
APPLE .... (Scab, rot, rust, codling moth, bud moth, tent caterpillar, canker worm, curculio, etc.)	When buds are swelling, but before they open, Bordeaux.	If canker worms are abundant just before blossoms open, Bordeaux-arsenical mixture.
ASPARAGUS .... (Rust, beetles.)	Cut off all shoots below surface regularly until about July 1st.	After cutting ceases, let the shoots grow and spray them with Bordeaux-arsenical mixture.
BEAN .... (Anthracnose, leaf blight, weevil, etc.)	Treat the seed before planting with bisulphide of carbon. (See remarks.) When third leaf expands, Bordeaux.	10 days later, Bordeaux.
CABBAGE .... (Worms, lice, maggots, etc.)	Pyrethrum or insect powder.	7-10 days later, repeat.
CELERY .... (Blight, rot, leaf spot, rust, caterpillars.)	Half strength Bordeaux on young plants in hotbed or seedbed.	Bordeaux, after plants are transplanted to field. (Pyrethrum for caterpillars if necessary.)
CHERRY .... (Rot, aphis, slug, curculio, black knot, leaf blight, or spot, etc.)	As buds are breaking, Bordeaux; when aphis appear, tobacco solution or kerosene emulsion.	When blossoms drop, Bordeaux-arsenical mixture.
CURRANT GOOSEBERRY .... (Worms, leaf blight.)	At first appearance of worms, hellebore.	10 days later, hellebore. Bordeaux if leaf blight is feared.
GRAPE .... (Fungous diseases. Rose bugs, lice, flea, beetle, leaf hopper, etc.)	In spring, when buds swell, Bordeaux.	Just before flowers unfold, Bordeaux-arsenical mixture.
MELONS .... CUCUMBERS .... (Mildew, rot, blight, striped bugs, lice, flea beetle, etc.)	Bordeaux, when vines begin to run.	10-14 days repeat. (Note: Always use half strength Bordeaux on watermelon vines.)
PEACH .... (Rot, mildew, leaf curl, curculio, etc.)	As the buds swell, Bordeaux.	When fruit has set, repeat. Jar trees for curculio.
PEAR AND QUINCE .... (Leaf blight, scab, psylla, codling moth, blister mite, slugs, etc.)	As buds are swelling, Bordeaux.	Just before blossoms open, Bordeaux. Kerosene emulsion when leaves open for psylla, if needed.
PLUM .... (Curculio, black knot, leaf blight, brown rot, etc.)	When buds are swelling, Bordeaux.	When blossoms have fallen, Bordeaux-arsenical mixture. Begin to jar trees for curculio.
POTATO .... (Flea beetle, Colorado beetle, blight rot, etc.)	Spray with Paris green and Bordeaux when about 4 in. high.	Repeat before insects become numerous.
TOMATO .... (Rot, blight, etc.)	When plants are 6 in. high, Bordeaux.	Repeat in 10-14 days. (Fruit can be wiped if disfigured by Bordeaux.)

NOTE.—For San Jose scale on trees and shrubs, spray with the lime-sulphur mixture in autumn after leaves fall, or (preferably) in early spring, before buds start. The lime-sulphur

SPRAYING CALENDAR

Third Application.	Fourth Application.	Remarks.
When blossoms have fallen. Bordeaux-arsenical mixture.	8-12 days later, Bordeaux - arsenical mixture.	For aphis (lice) use one of the lice remedies mentioned elsewhere. Dig out borers from tree trunks with knife and wire. For oyster-shell scale, use whale-oil soap spray in June.
2-3 weeks later, Bordeaux-arsenical mixture.	Repeat in 2-3 weeks.	Mow vines close to ground when they are killed by frost, burn them, and apply a mulch of stable manure.
14 days later, Bordeaux.	14 days later, Bordeaux.	For weevils: Put seed in tight box, put a cloth over seed, pour bisulphide of carbon on it, put lid on and keep closed for 48 hours. Use 1 oz. to 4 bus. of seed.
7-10 days later, repeat.	Repeat every 10-14 days until crop is gathered.	Root maggots: Pour carbolic acid emulsion around stem of plants. Club root: Rotate crops; apply lime to soil; burn refuse; treat seed with formalin before planting.
14 days later, repeat.	14 days later, repeat.	Rot or rust is often caused by hilling up with earth in hot weather. Use boards for summer cro... Pithy stalks are due to poor seed; or lack of moisture.
10-14 days, Bordeaux.	Hellebore, if a second brood of slugs appear.	Black knot: Dark fungous-looking bunches or knots on limbs. Cut off and burn whenever seen.
10-14 days, repeat, if necessary.	2 to 4 weeks later, repeat.	Cane-borers may be kept in check by cutting out and burning infested canes.
When fruit has set, Bordeaux - arsenical mixture.	2 to 4 weeks later, Bordeaux.	For lice, use any of the lice remedies. For rose bugs, use 10 pounds of arsenate of lead and one gallon of molasses in 50 gallons of water, as a spray. Or knock the bugs into pans of kerosene every day.
10-14 days, repeat.	10-14 days, repeat.	Use lice remedies for lice. For striped bugs, protect young plants with a cover of mosquito netting over each hill. Or keep vines well dusted with a mixture of air-slaked lime, tobacco dust and a little Paris green.
When fruit is one-half grown, Bordeaux.	Note:—It is safer always to use half-strength Bordeaux on peach foliage.	Dig out borers. Cut down and burn trees affected with "yellows."
After blossoms have fallen. Bordeaux-arsenical mixture.	8-12 days later, repeat.	Look out for "fire blight." Cut out and burn blighted branches whenever seen.
10-14 days later, repeat.	10-20 days later, Bordeaux.	Cut out black knot whenever seen.
Repeat for blight, rot and insects.	Repeat.	To prevent scabby tubers, treat the seed with formalin before planting.
Repeat in 10-14 days.		Hand-pick tomato worms.

mixture is a fungicide as well as a scale cure, and if it is used the *first* early Bordeaux spray may be omitted.

Concrete

Concrete is made by mixing together Portland cement, sand and stone (or gravel). Various proportions of each are used, depending upon the use to which the concrete is put. About half an hour after mixing these materials together, the mass begins to stiffen, until, in from half a day to a day, it becomes so hard that you cannot dent it with the hand. By a month the mass is hard as stone—indeed, harder than most stones. The best way to buy cement is in cloth sacks. Manufacturers charge more for cement in cloth sacks, but allow a rebate for the return of the empty sacks. A bag of cement weighs 95 pounds, and four such bags make a barrel of 380 pounds.

It is important that your stock of cement be kept in a dry place. Once wet, it becomes hard and lumpy, and in such condition is useless. If, however, the lumps are caused by pressure in the storehouse, the cement may be used with safety. Lumps thus formed can be easily broken by a blow from the back of a shovel.

In storing cement, throw wooden blocks on the floor. Place boards over them and pile the cement on the boards, covering the pile with a canvas or a piece of roofing paper. Never, under any circumstances, keep cement on the bare ground, or pile it directly against the outside walls of the building.

Do not use very fine sand. If there is a large quantity of fine sand handy, obtain a coarse sand and mix the two sands together in equal parts; this mixture is as good as coarse sand alone.

Sometimes fine sand must be used, because no other can be obtained; but in such an event an additional amount of cement must be used—sometimes as much as double the amount ordinarily required. For example, in such a case, instead of using a concrete 1 part cement, 2½ parts sand and 5 parts stone, use a concrete 1 part cement, 1¼ parts sand and 2½ parts stone.

Besides being coarse, the sand should be clean. The presence of dirt in the sand is easily ascertained by rubbing a little in the palm of the hand. If a little is emptied into a pail of water, the presence of dirt will be shown by the discoloration of the water. This can be discovered also by filling a fruit jar to the depth of 4 inches with sand and then adding water until it is within an inch of the top. After the jar has been well shaken, the contents should be allowed to settle for a couple of hours. The sand will sink to the bottom, but the mud, which can be easily recognized by its color, will form a distinct layer on top of the sand, and above both will be a clear depth of water. If the layer of mud is more than one-half inch in thickness, the sand should not be used unless it is first washed.

To wash sand build a loose board platform from 10 to 15 feet long, with one end a foot higher than the other. On the lower end and on the sides nail a board 2 by 6 inches on edge to hold the sand. Spread the sand over this platform in a layer three or four inches thick, and wash it with a hose. The washing should be started at the high end and the water allowed to run through the sand and over the 2-by-6-inch piece at the bottom. A small quantity of clay or loam does not injure the sand, but any amount over 5 per cent. does.

Great care should be used in the selection of the stone or gravel. The pebbles should be closely inspected to see that there is no clay on their surface. A layer of such clay prevents the "binding" of the cement. If necessary, stone or gravel may be washed in the same way as above described for sand. Dust may be left in the crushed stone without fear of its interfering with the strength of the cement, but care should be taken to see that such dust is distributed evenly through the whole mass, and when dust is found in stone, slightly less sand should be used than ordinarily. As to the size of stone or gravel, this must be determined by the form of construction contemplated. For foundations or any large thick structure, use anything from ½ to 2½ inches in diameter. For thin walls use ¼ to 1-inch stone. The best results are obtained by the use of a mixture of sizes graded from small to large. By this means the spaces between the stones or pebbles are reduced and a more compact concrete is obtained. Moreover, this method makes it possible to get along with less sand and less cement.

Water for concrete should be clean and free from strong acids and alkalies. It may be readily stored in a barrel beside the mixing board and placed on the concrete with a bucket.

If you are at all in doubt about the purity of the water that you contemplate using, it would be well to make up a block of concrete as a test, and see whether the cement "sets" properly.

For ordinary work a very satisfactory concrete mixture is 1 part of Portland cement, 2½ parts of clean sharp sand, 5 parts of broken stone. In heavy foundation work, the quantity of cement can be considerably less. The important thing is to have the sand and cement thoroughly mixed, and to use only clean sand. Use only as much water as necessary. It is not well to work concrete in freezing weather.

Cold Storage Without Ice

Why not have a cold storage room somewhere on the farm? Winter apples may be kept in such a place until spring, thus avoiding the necessity of marketing the fruit at unprofitable times. A Pennsylvania farmer has such a place built in one part of his barn—a double-walled, double-doored, paper-lined space wherein he stores many hundred bushel crates of selected fruit. He says that the main essentials are to keep out heat and frost from the room. On cool nights he leaves the doors open, shutting them again when the sun begins to warm things up in the morning—the idea being to use cold air instead of ice for reducing the room's temperature. He aims to get the temperature in the room as low as possible without freezing the apples, and then hold it there. Night air is cheaper than ice, he says, and about as good.

How to Make and Use a Fireless Cooker

A saver of time, fuel and labor is the fireless cook stove, which can be made at home, absolutely without expense, and, though not adapted to all kinds of cooking, answers well for food that requires long, slow cooking to soften tissues, bring out flavors and conserve the juices, such as stews, pot roasts, soups, cereals, rice, tapioca, dried fruits, vegetables, etc. It consists of a kettle of agate or tin, inclosed in a box with insulating material between them to prevent the heat of the kettle from escaping. Food brought to the boiling point over a fire, and inclosed, still boiling, continues to cook. This is the whole principle. Choose a kettle with tight-fitting lid and a box large enough to allow six or eight inches of insulating material. Line the box, bottom, sides and hinged-on lid with stout packing paper, or several thicknesses of newspaper. Make a firm, cylindrical shape to fit easily around the kettle and fasten a circular bottom to it. This might be of asbestos paper, or paper soaked in alum water and dried. Then no matter how ·hot the kettle there would be no danger of scorching. Fill the bottom of the box with packing, which can be of cotton, wool, ground cork (in which imported grapes are packed and which grocers are usually willing to give away). Hay will answer, but does not pack so closely as these. Pack hard to a depth of three inches, place the cylinder, containing the kettle in the middle, and pack tightly around it, even with the top. The insulating material can be covered neatly with cloth, or a thin board with a round hole in the middle. A thick cushion will insulate the space between this and the lid, which must be fastened down tightly. If desired to cook several things at once it is best to have two or three such cookers, as the box should not be opened after the food is put in, except to reheat. Some persons prefer using a sort of double boiler, the inner kettle, containing the food, being placed in a larger one, partly filled with hot water. In this case the water in both kettles must be actually boiling. An additional vegetable can be put in the outside kettle, or water kept hot in it for dishwashing.

Ready-made cookers can be bought, but are rather expensive. Some of these will also bake and roast by means of thick disks of concrete which must be made very hot on the stove, then put under and over the kettle containing the food. The idea might be applied to the home-made cooker by heating soapstone griddles. These might be heated at the same time with a large iron pot. The meat or chicken, which should be seasoned, can be put in a kettle, a hot disk put in the bottom of the pot, the kettle set on this; the other disk put on top, then put the lid on the pot and bury in the cooker. The pot, however, should be inclosed in asbestos paper to avoid possible ignition. It would be interesting for each housekeeper to experiment and invent improvements on the central idea. The time required for cooking vegetables varies according to their age and fresh-

11

ness, so only the approximate time necessary can be given. There is little danger of their being overdone, or at least injured by long cooking, and if underdone it is always possible to take out the kettle, reheat, and return to the cooker, or if needed quickly, to finish on the range.

It is not worth while to use the cooker for food that takes but a short time to cook, such as corn, spinach, young peas, asparagus, etc., since the water for these must be brought to the boil anyhow, they can as well be cooked on the stove. Do not place the kettle next the flame but always have a lid under it.

POTATOES

Five minutes over fire, an hour in the box. Potatoes must not be left overtime in box or they become watery.

RICE PUDDING

Mix together in the kettle ½ a cupful of rice, a quart of milk, a tablespoonful of butter, ½ a cupful of sugar, a little salt and grated nutmeg. Boil on stove five minutes, in cooker six hours.

BREAD PUDDING

Soak ½ a pint of bread crumbs in a pint of milk, add a beaten egg, 2 tablespoonfuls of sugar and a pinch of salt. Beat with a spoon; heat on the stove till just short of boiling, stirring all the time. Put in the cooker an hour and serve with vanilla sauce.

CHICKEN FRICASSEE

Disjoint a chicken, roll in flour and brown in a little fat; as the pieces brown pack them in the kettle, and make some gravy in the skillet. Put this and a little water to cover the chicken. Boil twenty minutes, then put in cooker over night.

BOILED HAM

If wanted for 6 o'clock dinner, put ham weighing six pounds in kettle at 9 a. m. Cover with cold water and bring to a boil; boil briskly fifteen minutes. Put the lid on the kettle when it begins to boil and don't take it off till it is taken out of the hay box, in which it should be put while still boiling. At 2 o'clock take out, boil up again, put in a few cloves and 2 or 3 peppercorns. At 5.30 take out, skin, put in a pan, fat side up, stick in a few cloves, sprinkle slightly with sugar and plentifully with bread crumbs and bake in the oven till well done.

ONIONS

Of moderate size, boiled ten minutes on the range, should be tender after four hours in cooker.

STRING BEANS

Cut off the strings and slice down the middle; give five minutes over the fire, four hours in cooker.

CAULIFLOWER AND YOUNG CABBAGE

Five minutes over fire, five hours in cooker.

Cereals started over the fire at supper time and placed in the box should be ready for breakfast with just reheating. Half a cupful of cereal poured into three cupfuls of boiling water, with a teaspoonful of salt is about the proportion.

A fireless cooker can be used for things to be kept cold as well as hot. Ice cream, if frozen, then packed in a kettle with ice and sunk in the box will not melt, and butter if put in it cool and hard will keep in the same condition, as the air is practically excluded.

BOSTON BAKED BEANS

Soak 2 cupfuls of beans in cold water a whole day. At supper time drain, cover with fresh water, put over the fire and simmer slowly for half an hour; pour off the water, scrape a ¼ pound of salt pork, cut off a slice and push it down through the beans to the bottom of the pail; score the rest and put, rind side up, in middle of the beans. Mix a teaspoonful of salt, a tablespoonful each of sugar and molasses, just a dust of mustard, a half teaspoonful of baking soda and a cupful of boiling water. Add enough more water to come to the top of the beans. Cover, and boil ten minutes; then put in cooker. In the morning reheat for ten minutes, return to the box and about half past five in the afternoon take out, sprinkle a tablespoonful of sugar over the top, leave off the cover, put in hot oven for half an hour.

POT ROAST

Season the meat with salt and pepper, brown on all sides over a flame, and put in a stone jar, dry, no water whatever. Cover tightly. Put the jar in a kettle of hot water. Boil fifteen or twenty minutes. Place in a cooker for six hours. Even tough meat becomes tender and the juice at the bottom is very rich.

INDEX TO ADVERTISERS

NAME	BUSINESS	TOWN	PAGE
Acklin, Donald R.	Swine Breeder	Perrysburg	269
Adams, Henry J.	Garage	Fostoria	Third Cover
Aiken, J. A.	Grocer	N. Baltimore	282
Aller, E. L.	Lubricating Oils	Jerry City	298
Avery, A. E.	Coal and Builders' Supplies.	Bowling Green	264
Bailey, W. J.	Hardware and Implements.	Millbury	247
Baldwin, L.	Wagons and Carriages	Bowling Green	255
Banting Machine Co., The.		W. Toledo	292
Barakman, W. R.	Tinner.	Bowling Green	312
Barr & Snyder.	Real Estate Agents.	Bowling Green	306
Bender, Joseph	Cattle Breeder	Bowling Green	259
Beverstock, Edward	Lawyer	Bowling Green	247
Bike Shop, The	Bicycles and Motorcycles.	Fostoria	254
Blackburn, W. R.	Racket Store	Grand Rapids	270
Bloom, Earl D.	Attorney-at-Law	Bowling Green	248
Bolles Drug Store, The.	Druggist	Bowling Green	267
Bowers, E. J.	Gents' Furnishings and Dry Cleaning	Bowling Green	263
Bowman, S. W.	Attorney-at-Law	Bowling Green	248
Brink, George	Hardware	Custar	283
Brinkmeier, C. L.	Cattle Breeder	Dunbridge	263
Brim, Otto R.	Coal Dealer	Walbridge	268
Brown, M. E.	Real Estate and Insurance.	N. Baltimore	308
Buckey Paint-Varnish Co.	Manufacturers	Toledo	298
Burnham, J. E. M.D.	Physician	Prairie Depot	301
Caldwell, C. W.	Garage	Bowling Green	284
Campbell, A. R.	Attorney-at-Law	Bowling Green	250
Campbell Brothers	Hardware	Bowling Green	281
Campbell & Coller.	Plumbers	Bowling Green	303
Carr, E. T.	Machinery and Tractors.	Bowling Green	293
Chambers, J. W.	Drugs	Bays	300
Chidester Theater		Chidester	311
Citizens Banking Co., The.		Perrysburg	258
Citizens Savings Bank, The.		Pemberville	256
Clevenger Stores, The.	Dry Goods and Ready to Wear.	Bowling Green	269
Coen Brothers	Furniture	Bowling Green	273
Cole, E. A.	Physician	Bowling Green	299
Commercial Bank and Savings Co., The		Bowling Green	Fourth Cover
Comstock, Abel	Justice of Peace and Notary Public	Bowling Green	297
Conkey, Dr. W.	Veterinary Surgeon	Rudolph	313
Conklin, J. D.	Insurance Agent	Weston	297
Conn, G. H., D.V.M.	Veterinarian	Prairie Depot	312
Cramer, C. M.	Monuments	Bowling Green	295
Cranes Music Store.		Bowling Green	299
Cygnet Grain & Hay Co., The.	Grain Elevator	Cygnet	274
Danforth, H. J.	Insurance	Bowling Green	288
Davidson, P. M.	Ice Cream, Coal and Ice.	Bowling Green	265
Deck, J. F.	Undertaker	Bowling Green	312
Dickelman Mfg. Co.	Metal Specialties and Roofers.	Forest	16
Dicus Ladies' Furnishing Co.		Bowling Green	313
Dunipace, Wm.	Attorney-at-Law	Bowling Green	260
Dunnipace, Robt. L.	Cattle and Swine Breeder.	Bowling Green	248
Eberly, C. B.	Insurance and Real Estate.	Bowling Green	286
Eidson, J. W.	Hardware	Cygnet	284
Elliott & Beasley.	Grain	Stony Ridge	275
Elson, Dr. F. A.	Dentist	Bowling Green	266
Farmers' Lightning Protected Mutual Insurance Co., The.		Fremont	295
Farmers' Savings Bank Co.		Haskins	254
First National Bank		Bowling Green.	Front Fly Leaf

NAME	BUSINESS	TOWN	PAGE
Forney, A. & Co	General Store	Bowling Green	5
Fries & Hatfield	Attorneys-at-Law	Bowling Green	248
Fulton & Beckett	Insurance Agent & Garage	N. Baltimore	280
Gierke, Paul	Bakery	Grand Rapids	253
Gilbert & Tyler	General Merchandise	Walbridge	278
Ginder, Miss May	Millinery	Weston	295
Glenwood Farm	Cattle Breeders	Luckey	266
Goebel, Gus	Tinner	Bowling Green	311
Good, L. R	Grain and Coal	Bloomdale	271
Goodrick, J. M	Furniture and Undertaking	Prairie Depot	314
Gordon, Thomas C	Blacksmith	Bays	255
Gorsuch, G. A.	Physician	Bowling Green	300
Gorsuch, N. N. & Son	Garage	Grand Rapids	277
Gorrill, I. A	Attorney-at-Law	Bowling Green	249
Grand Rapids Garage Co		Grand Rapids	279
Hall, E. D	General Merchandise	Lime City	278
Hankey Lumber Co., The	Lumber	Bowling Green	Second Cover
Harrington & Dun	Attorneys-at-Law	Bowling Green	249
Hartman, W. W.	Blacksmith	Bowling Green	256
Haskins Hardware Co		Haskins	284
Helle, H. W.	General Store	Woodside	280
Herald, The	Newspaper	Weston	302
Hess, Mrs. N. O	Swine Breeder	Pemberville	268
Hoiles, C. H	Garage	Prairie Depot	281
Howe, Raymond R	Insurance Agent	Cygnet	290
James, Benjamin F	Attorney-at-Law	Bowling Green	250
Kander, H.	Second Hand Machinery and Scrap Material	Bowling Green	289
Kalmbach, Fred	Grain and Coal	N. Baltimore	276
Keener, Mrs. Jennie L	Milling and Poultry Raising	Weston	299
Kehler, Mayme	Abstracts and Loans	Bowling Green	247
Kelly & Hill	Attorneys-at-Law	Bowling Green	249
Knepper, W. I	Stock Raiser	Tiffin	275
Koch, Chas. L. Co., The	Lumber	Perrysburg	296
Ladd, Frank H	Department Store and Pianos	Bowling Green	246
Ladd & James	Attorneys-at-Law	Bowling Green	250
Lahman, Chas. E	Swine Breeder	Haskins	264
Lancashire, H. W.	Motor Cars	Toledo	251
Lang, Nelson & Co	Auctioneers	Weston	252
Lawrenz, O. R	Furniture & Undertaking	Grand Rapids	313
Lea, Thomas M	Dentist	Bowling Green	266
LeGalley, Charlie	Cattle and Poultry Breeder	Bowling Green	262
Lenhart & Easley	Insurance Agency	Bowling Green	291
Lincoln & Dirlam	Drug Store	Bowling Green	Third Cover
Linhart, S. A	Saw and Planing Mill	Bloomdale	293
Lockwood Electric Shop		Bowling Green	270
Longbrake, W. A	Garage	Milton Center	283
McKendree, M. & A. L	Physicians	Bowling Green	300
McMillen, W. H	Attorney	N. Baltimore	251
McStay, James	Insurance Agent	Cygnet	294
Mahr, F. L	Furniture	Perrysburg	275
Marleau, David	House Furnishings and Agricultural Implements	W. Toledo	286
Martin, Peter	General Merchandise	Millbury	278
Miller, Geo. F	General Merchandise	Walbridge	279
Milnor, W. W	Florist	Bowling Green	274
Mowry & Aumaugher	Swine Breeder	Amsden	260
Nearing & Sears	Insurance and Real Estate	Bowling Green	287
Nesmith, Rev. Dr. L. M	Chiropractor	Custar	261
Norris, C. E	Chiropractor	Bowling Green	261
Ott, Mrs. E. A	Milliner	Bowling Green	294
Observer, The	Newspaper	Prairie Depot	305
Page-Philipps Seed Co., The		Toledo	310
Painter, C. R	Attorney-at-Law	Bowling Green	249
Pelton, S. S	Life Insurance	Bloomdale	289
Perrysburg Banking Co., The		Perrysburg	259
Perrysburg Realty Co	Real Estate	Perrysburg	308
Petteys, D. J. & L. A	Swine Breeders	Grand Rapids	261
Phillips, J. S	Printer and Publisher	Cygnet	296

NAME	BUSINESS	TOWN	PAGE
Phillips, Wm. T., & Co	Seedsmen	Toledo	307
Place, Alfred W	Theatre	Bowling Green	311
Potter, Clarence & Son	Horse Breeder	Rudolph	272
Prieur, F. H	Hardware	Bowling Green	283
Rae, J. W	Physician	Bowling Green	300
Rager, Alf	Hotel and Restaurant	Bloomdale	306
Raubenolt & Lance	Furniture and Undertaking	Weston	315
Reid, Frank A	Attorney-at-Law	Bowling Green	250
Reider, M. B.	Miller	Bowling Green	272
Rickard, I. E.	Blacksmith	Tontogany	258
Riegle & Avery	Attorneys-at-Law	Bowling Green	Fourth Cover
Rossiter, J. W.	Veterinarian	Fostoria	314
Royce & Coon Grain Co., The	Mill and Elevator	Bowling Green	273
Sargent, Ed. O	Druggist	Bowling Green	268
Schaller, J. H.	Auctioneer	Tontogany	251
Schunk Hardware Co., The		W. Toledo	285
Seneca Company, Inc., The	Mfgrs. of Stock and Poultry Medicines	Tiffin	303
Shatzel, J. E	Attorney-at-Law	Bowling Green	250
Shepherd, W.	Bakery	Bowling Green	252
Sherwood & Gray	Carriage and Wagon Builders	Grand Rapids	257
Shroll, Wm.	Livery	N. Baltimore	288
Sibert, F. M. G.	Real Estate and Insurance	Weston	307
Smith, Wm.	Blacksmith	Lime City	257
Speck, Geo. H.	Publisher	Pemberville	302
Standard Garage, The	Garage	Prairie Depot	285
Stephens, James	Stock Dealer	Prairie Depot	270
Sterling, Frank L.	Physician	Cygnet	301
Sterling, Lou A.	Barber and Laundry Agency	Cygnet	253
Strong, T. D.	Coal Dealer	Bowling Green	267
Taber, C. M.	Dentist	Bowling Green	266
Thomas, Frank W	Newspaper	Bowling Green	297
Thompson, Chas. R	Gas Fitting	Bowling Green	304
Tontogany Banking Co		Tontogany	262
Wagner, Dell	Harness Maker	N. Baltimore	285
Walbridge Garage	Garage	Walbridge	276
Ward, Harley E.	Physician and Surgeon	Pemberville	301
Ward, Mrs.	Millinery	Bowling Green	294
Watkins, Mr. and Mrs. W. C	Furniture and Undertaking	Weston	315
Weston Elevator and Milling Co.		Weston	277
Weston Hardware and Implement Co.		Weston	282
Wiggins, S. T	Plumbing	Bowling Green	305
Williams, C. B.	Sanitarium and Hospital	Bowling Green	309
Williams, H. B.	Tailor and Dry Cleaner	Bowling Green	309
Wilson, George F.	Livery	Bowling Green	290
Wilson, Milo D.	Insurance	Bowling Green	287
Wolf, Ralph W	Bakery and Restaurant	Cygnet	255
Wood, E.	Nurseryman	Weston	271
Wood County Abstract & Loan Co.		Bowling Green	291
Wood County Insurance Agency		Bowling Green	291
Wood County Savings Bank Co.		Bowling Green	Back Fly Leaf
Yeager & Starn	Druggists	Bowling Green	271
Yonker, C. D.	Insurance Agent	Bowling Green	288
Young, D. W.	Undertaking	Bowling Green	2
Young Bros. Realty Co		Lansing	304
Zingg, Chas.	Farmer and Dairyman	Lime City	265

15

Main Street looking North, Bowling Green, Ohio.

WOOD COUNTY DIRECTORY

ABBREVIATIONS.—a, means acres; bds, boards; B tel, Bell telephone; 4 ch, 4 children; H&L, house and lot; Pbg 10, Perrysburg Township Road No. 10; O, owns; R1, Rural Route No. 1; ret, retired; T, tenant; 4h, 4 horses; 2c, 2 cattle.

The abbreviations used for the Townships of Wood County are as follows:

Bloom, Blo.	Liberty, Lib.	Portage, Por.
Center, Cen.	Middleton, Mid.	Ross, Ros.
Freedom, Fre.	Milton, Mil.	Troy, Tro.
Grand Rapids, Gr. Rs.	Montgomery, Mon.	Washington, Wash.
Henry, Hen.	Perry, Per.	Webster, Web.
Jackson, Jac.	Perrysburg, Pbg.	Weston, Wes.
Lake, Lake.	Plain, Pla.	

Names in CAPITALS are those of Farm Journal subscribers—always the most intelligent and progressive people in any county. No Tumbledowns, for no farmer can keep on reading the F. J. and being a Tumbledown, too. Many have tried, but all have to quit one or the other.

Abbot, Grant Weston Wes.

Abbot, Leander Weston Wes.

Abbot, Owen Weston Wes.

Abbott, Cathleen (dau Delbert) student Milton St Weston.

Abbott, Delbert (Clara) 3 ch stone cutter T H&L Milton Weston B tel.

Abbott, E. E. farmer O 40a 5h Bowling Green Lib 51 B tel.

Abbott, Frank RD North Baltimore Hen.

Abbott, Grant (Alice) 1 ch teaming & farming O 2a H&L 3h 1c High St Weston B tel.

Abbott, Owen 3 ch teaming O H&L 3h Weston B tel.

Abbott, Rollie (son Delbert) architect Milton St Weston.

Abbott, Ruth (dau E. E.) R1 Bowling Green Lib 51 B tel.

Abbott, Wm. (Isabelle) 5 ch farmer T 66a 4h 2c R1 Portage Lib 57 Ind tel.

Abel, C. J. (Mildred) 3 ch farmer O 40a 3h 2c R1 Prairie Depot Mon 44.

2

Abel, R Risingsun Mon.

Abke, Aaron (Minnie) 1 ch farmer T 186a 2h R1 Pemberville Fre 68 B tel.

ABKE, CHAS. (Marie) 3 ch farmer T 90a 3h 5c R4 Bowling Green Cen 115 B tel.

Abke, Frank (Carrie) 2 ch farmer T 90a 4h 4c R3 Pemberville Tro 60 B tel.

ABKE, HENRY (Edith) farmer T 80a 3h 3c R1 Pemberville Fre 62 B tel.

Abke, John H. farmer O 64a 2h R4 Bowling Green Cen 105.

Able, C. J. Prairie Depot Mon.

ABLES, TAYLOR G. farmer O 80a 3h R1 Pemberville Fre 84 B tel.

Achwab, L. J. (Samantha) 5 ch farmer T 80a 6h 3c R2 North Baltimore Hen 73.

Ackenberger, Geo. Walbridge Lake.

Ackenberger, J. W. Stony Ridge Lake.

Ackenberger, Simon Stony Ridge Lake.

Ackermann, Calvin (Jessie) 2 ch farmer T 80a 4h 4c R1 Hoytsville Jac 60 Ind tel.

Ackerman, Frank RD North Baltimore Hen.

Ackerman, Isaac (Ann J.) farmer O 200a 2h R1 North Baltimore Hen 123 B tel.

ACKLIN, DONALD R. (Imogen) 3 ch stock farmer O 160a 11h 5c R2 Perrysburg Pgb 2 B tel. See adv.

Acocks, A. L. Bloomdale Blo.

Adams, A. W. RD North Baltimore Blo.

Adams, Cathrine Custar Lib.

Adams, Celia R1 Prairie Depot Mon 105 B tel.

Adams, Chas. R. (Nell) 1 ch farmer T H&L 2h 1c R2 Prairie Depot Mon 35 B tel.

Adams, Cleon (Nellie) farmer T 60a 3h 4c R1 Prairie Depot Mon 38 B tel.

Adams, C. C. (Virene) farmer O 200a 11h 4c R2 Prairie Depot Mon 43 B tel.

ADAMS, C. C. (Pauline) 1 ch principal T H&L Second St Portage Por Ind tel.

Adams, C. E. RD North Baltimore Hen.

Adams, C. W. (Daisy) 2 ch farmer O 50a 5h 9c R1 Fostoria Per 123 Ind tel.

Adams, Earl school teacher Factory St Jerry City Por Ind tel.

Adams, Ellis Corp St Jerry City Por.

Adams, Miss Emma farmer O 6a R1 Pemberville Fre 66.

Adams, Eunice (dau S. R.) housekeeper R1 Deshler Jac 21.

ADAMS, FLOYD (Olive) 2 ch mail carrier O H&L 1h Main St Jerry City Por Ind tel.

Adams Frank (Edna) 2 ch harness shop O H&L Grand Rapids Gr Rs.

ADAMS, FRANK M. (Kate) 6 ch farmer O 50a 2h 6c R2 Prairie Depot Mon 47 B tel.

Adams, Frances A. Prairie Depot Mon.

Adams, F. B. (Mary) farmer O 60a 4h 4c R3 Prairie Depot Por 121 Ind tel.

Adams, G. A. (Frances) farmer O 120a 8h 2c R1 Prairie Depot Mon 118 B tel.

Adams, G. E. cattle RD Bowling Green Cen.

Adams, G. F. Jerry City Blo.

Adams, Harley RD North Baltimore Hen.

Adams, Hazel housekeeper Factory St Jerry City Por Ind tel.

Adams, Henry (Ella) ret blacksmith O H&L Grand Rapids Gr Rs Ind tel.

Adams, Henry ret R3 Prairie Depot Por 121 Ind tel.

Adams, H. M. (Myrtle) undertaker O H&L Main St Bloomdale.Blo B & Ind tels.

Adams, John RD Bowling Green Pla.

Adams, John L. (son G. A.) farmer R1 Prairie Depot Mon 118 B tel.

Adams, John M. 6 ch ret farmer O 1h 1c R1 Prairie Depot Mon 103 B tel.

Adams, J. W. (Catherine) 3 ch farmer T 160a 9h 13c R2 Custar Lib 35 Ind tel.

Adams, Mrs. M. 1 ch ret T H&L Comercial St Perrysburg Pbg B tel.

Adams, Madison (Ella) undertaker O 12a 2h Main St Jerry City Por.

Adams, Mrs. Matilda O H&L Factory St Jerry City Por Ind tel.

Adams, Mary E. West Milgrove Per.

Adams, Owen (Cora) farmer T 60a 3h 3c R2 Prairie Depot Por.

Adams, Olen J. cattle RD Prairie Depot Por.

Adams, Raymond W. (son G. A.) farmer R1 Prairie Depot Mon 118 B tel.

Adams, Russell (Chloe) 5 ch farmer O 20a 2h 3c R1 Deshler Jac 99 B tel.

Adams, R. R. (Jessie) farmer O 80a 8h 5c R3 Prairie Depot Mon 99 B tel.

Adams, Steward Hoytsville Jac.

Adams, Mrs. S. L. Freeport Mon.

Adams, S. R. (Susan) 10 ch farmer O 55a 1h 9c R1 Deshler Jac 21 Ind tel.

Adams, T. J. (Ida) 3 ch farmer O 140a 2h 5c R2 Prairie Depot Mon 35 B tel.

ADAMS, VIRGIL (son S. R.) farm hand R1 Deshler Jac 21.

Adams, Wayne (son G. A.) farmer R1 Prairie Depot Mon 118 B tel.

Adams, W. J. (Ada) laborer T H&L Hoytsville Jac.

Adamson, Wm. (Kitty) ret O H&L Front St Perrysburg Pbg B tel.

Adamson, W. P. Perrysburg Pbg.

Addler, Albert (son Christ) Custar Mil 44.

Addler, Christ (Mary) 8 ch farmer O 131a 4h 5c Custar Mil 44 B tel.

Addler, Katie (dau Christ) Custar Mil 44.

Addler, Mary (dau Christ) Custar Mil 44.

Addy, J. H. (Harriet) poultry dealer O H&L Main St Weston.

Adkins, Chas. (Lily V.) 3 ch drayman T H&L 2h Toledo St Bradner Mon.

ADKINS, CLIFFORD farmer O 40a 2h 1c Walbridge St Walbridge Lake 119 Ind tel.

Adkins, Edward (Julia) 2 ch gardener & farmer O 30a 3h 1c Station A East Toledo Ros 31.

Adkins, Ernest (son Fred) clerk R1 East Toledo Ros 23 Ind tel.

Adkins, Eva ret R1 East Toledo Ros 23 Ind tel.

Adkins, Fred farmer T 20a 2h R1 East Toledo Ros 23 Ind tel.

Adkins, Fred (Goldie) 2 ch engineer T H&L 1c Toledo Ave Bradner Mon.

Adkins, Mont. (son Fred) farmer R1 East Toledo Ros 23 Ind tel.

Adler, Adam (Mary) 8 ch farmer O 80a 5h 5c R1 Custar Mil 20.

ADLER, MISS EDITH R1 Custar Mil 17.

Adler, Frank (Rose) 7 ch farmer O 160a 4h 5c R1 Millbury Lake 120.

Adler, Frank, Jr. Custar Mil.

ADLER, GEORGE (Nellie) 1 ch farmer T 65a 3h 2c R2 Custar Mil 20.

Adler, Nick (Mary) hired man R1 Millbury Lake 120.

Aebell, Bert (May W.) dentist O 20a 2h R1 East Toledo Lake 132 Ind tel.

Affolter, Leon farmer T 40a 3h 1c Station A East Toledo Ross 31.

Agen, John (Maggie) 3 ch oil marker O H&L Mermill Por 19.

Agle, Ben farmer & laborer O 1a H&L R1 Stony Ridge Tro 7.

Agler, C. M. Millbury Lake.

Agner, Harry (Lucinda) 3 ch druggist T H&L Grand Rapids Gr Rs.

AIKENS, J. A. (Helen) 1 ch grocery T H&L 1h RD North Baltimore Hen.

Aikens, Maggie A. grocery O H&L RD North Baltimore Hen.

Akenberger, Fianna (dau J. W.) housekeeper R1 Walbridge Lake 91 Ind tel.

AKENBERGER, GEORGE (Almeda) 2 ch farmer O 80a 3h 5c R1 Walbridge Lake 20 B & Ind tels.

Akenberger, J. W. (Delia) farmer O 112a 3h 4c R1 Stony Ridge Lake 91 Ind tel.

Akenberger, Simon (Sofia) farmer O 164a 5h 9c R1 Stony Ridge Lake 90 Ind tel.

Alban, Wm. (Ina) 2 ch farmer T H&L 2h R2 Bowling Green Cen 5 Ind tel.

Albert, Geo. (Julia) 1 ch saw mill owner O H&L Luckey Tro Ind tel.

Albertson, S. B. RD North Baltimore Hen.

ALBRIGHT, LEWIS (Edith) 6 ch farmer O 80a 3h 4c R1 Millbury Lake 67 Ind tel.

Alcorn, Mrs. E. J. C. O H&L Tontogany Web Ind tel.

Aldrich, C. T. (Florence) 1 ch salesman T H&L R1 Rudolph Por 24½.

Aldrich, H. G. (Catherine) agent O H&L 1h R1 Rudolph Por 24½ Ind tel.

ALDRICH, THOMAS Haskins.

Aldridge, C. (Truda) 2 ch farmer R1 North Baltimore Hen.

Aldridge, T. (Mary) farmer O 82a 2h 5c R2 Haskins Wash 91.

Aldrige, S. O. (Delsia) farmer O 1c R1 North Baltimore Hen 69.

Aleshire, Ida 2 ch housekeeper R1 Portage Por 55 Ind tel.

Alexander, Earl (son H.) farmer R1 Pemberville Fre 70.

ALEXANDER, HARRY C. (Frances) 1 ch farmer T 80a 3h 5c R1 Tontogany Wash 26.

Alexander, Henry 2320 Fulton St Toledo Fre.

Alexander, H. oil producer O 240a 11h 5c R1 Pemberville Fre 70 B tel.

Alexander, John (Lottie) 6 ch laborer T H&L Third St Perrysburg Pbg.

ALEXANDER, MRS. MARTHA housekeeper O 80a R1 Tontogany Wash 26 Ind tel.

ALEXANDER, R. F. dairyman hired man Lime City Pbg 93 B tel.

ALEXANDER, WM. carpenter O H&L Pemberville Fre 40.

Alford, J. B. Grand Rapids Gr Rs.

Algyre, A. J. Rossford Ros.

Allduffer, Chas. Portage Lib.

Alleau, Fred farmer O 70a 2h 4c R1 Millbury Lake 111.

Allen, C. L. (Elsie) 6 ch laborer 1h R1 Weston Lib 49.

Allen, David cattle RD Jerry City Por.

Allen, E. G. (Cora) 1 ch farming O 110a 7h 6c R3 Weston Wes 56.

Allen, F. S. (Elma) 2 ch hardware T H&L 1h Prairie Depot Mon B tel.

Allen, James (Goldie) 2 ch teamster T H&L Second St Portage Por.

ALLEN, MRS. J. C. Pemberville.

Allen, Orvill (Eva) 1 ch farmer O 27a 3h 1c R3 Bowling Green Pla 87.

Aller, E. G. Weston Wes.

ALLER, E. L. lubricating oils Box 106 Jerry City. See adv.

Aller, Henry W. (Annie) 3 ch farmer O 160a 4h 4c R2 Custar Mil 29 Ind tel.

ALLER, LEROY (Alta) 5 ch oil salesman T H&L 2h 1c Cygnet Blo 2 Ind tel.

Allerman, Fred Millbury Lake.

Alsbauth, F. W. (Altha) 1 ch painter T Custar Mil Ind tel.

Alspaugh, Lucretia Weston Wes.

Alt, Geo. Lime City Pbg.

Alt, Grace Lime City Pbg.

Alt, Henry Lime City Pbg.

Alt, Louis Lime City Pbg.

Alt, Martin Lime City Pbg.

Alter, Catherine Corp St Portage Por.

ALTERMATT, W. M. farmer O 100a 5h 1c R1 Perrysburg Pbg 110.

Altman, P. S. Corp St Haskins Mid.

ALTMAN, RHENA Haskins.

Alwood, Chalmer B. (son Justin) laborer R2 Prairie Depot Por 118 B tel.

Alwood, Justin L. (Bertha) 3 ch laborer T H&L 1c R2 Prairie Depot Por 118 B tel.

Ambrose, Alley RD Fostoria Per.

AMELING, JOHN R1 Bradner Fre.

Ames, R. C. Perrysburg Pbg.

Amon, John (Agnes) 1 ch plumber T H&L Front St Perrysburg Pbg.

AMON, J. J. 3 ch hardware store O H&L Perrysburg Pbg B tel.

Amon, Mary ret O H&L Second St Perrysburg Pbg.

Amos, A. (Anna) 3 ch farmer O 145a 6h 6c R1 Portage Por 42 Ind tel.

Amos, Beatrice (dau A.) student R1 Portage Por 42 Ind tel.

Amos, Bert cattle RD Prairie Depot Por.

Amos, Calvin (Almeta) farmer T 80a 1h 1c R4 Bowling Green Cen 94 Ind tel.

Amos, Capp (Winifred) 1 ch farmer O 40a 6h 5c R1 Portage Por 50 Ind tel

Amos, Chas. (Hattie) 4 ch farmer O 181a 8h 6c R3 Prairie Depot Por 96.

Amos, Clinton (Olive) farmer T 1h 1c R3 Prairie Depot Por 96.

Amos, Curt (Merle) 1 ch farmer T H&L 3h Portage Por 6 Ind tel.

Amos, C. J. (Wealthy) 2 ch coal T H&L 2h 1c E Main St Portage Por Ind tel.

AMOS, C. R. (Maud) 2 ch farmer T 117a 5h 8c R1 Prairie Depot Mon 85 B tel.

Amos, Mrs. Delbert RD Bowling Green Cen.

Amos, D. A. (Herma) 1 ch farmer T 40a 7h 4c R1 Portage Por 50.

AMOS, E. B. (Austa) 6 ch garage T H&L Bowling Green Cen Ind tel. See adv.

Amos, Fred (Mary) 3 ch farmer O 121a 6h R1 Prairie Depot Mon 38 B tel.

Amos, G. W. (Mary A.) 2 ch farmer O 66a 3h 5c R4 Bowling Green Cen 103.

Amos, Henrietta (dau Jacob J.) housekeeper R1 Portage Por 39.

Amos, Jacob J. (Maggie) 4 ch farmer O 40a 4h 3c R1 Portage Por 39.

Amos, Jess (Florence) 3 ch farmer T 80a 3h 11c R1 Rudolph Lib 98 Ind tel.

Amos, J. M. (Matilda) ret farmer O 120a 2h 2c R3 Weston Mil 87 Ind tel.

Amos, Maggie RD Portage Por.

Amos, Matilda Weston Mil.

Amos, Michael (Emma) shipper Portage Por 6 Ind tel.

AMOS, PHILIP (Lydia) farmer O 134a 1h 8c R3 Prairie Depot Por 98.

AMOS, RALPH (Laura) 2 ch farmer O 40a 3h 1c R2 Weston Wes 16 Ind tel.

Amos, Trontous (son Jacob J.) farmer R1 Portage Por 39.

Amos, Vera (dau A.) student R1 Portage Por 42 Ind tel.

Amos, W. M. (Clara) 3 ch painter O H&L 1h R4 Bowling Green Por 95.

Amsler, Vernon C. (Lola E.) 4 ch oil man & pumping 1c R3 North Baltimore Blo 41 B & Ind tels.

Anderegg, F. J. (Lizzie) 1 ch farmer T 60a 2h 5c R1 Perrysburg Pbg 96 B tel.

Anderegg, Jacob (Mary) ret O 60a R1 Perrysburg Pbg 96 B tel.

Anderson, Abel (Matilda) 1 ch farmer O 160a 10h 14c R1 Fostoria Por 91.

Anderson, Axel RD Fostoria Per.

Anderson, A. Prairie Depot Mon.

Anderson, A. L. (Flora) 5 ch pumper T H&L 1h Prairie Depot Mon.

Anderson, A. T. (Inez) 2 ch farmer T 160a 2h 6c R1 Prairie Depot Mon 37.

Anderson, Mrs. Carrie 3 ch O H&2Ls Meyers St Jerry City Blo.

Anderson, Charles (Clara) 3 ch farmer O 20a 1h 2c West Millgrove Per 64.

Anderson, Clara M. West Millgrove Per.

Anderson, Dortha Margarete insulating for elect co R1 Tontogany Wash 40.

Anderson, Eulalie asst editor O H&L Pemberville Fre B tel.

Anderson, George (Mary E.) engineer O H&L 205 Maple St Rossford Ros.

Anderson, H. manager West Millgrove Per 64.

Anderson, H. M. ret Pemberville Fre.

Anderson, John U. (Anna) engineer T H&L 209 Maple St Rossford Ros.

Anderson, J. (Lola) ret O 30a H&L 1h 3c Prairie Depot Montgomery.

Anderson, J. H. Lemoyne Tro Ind tel.

Anderson, J. H. (Mary Elizabeth) 1 ch track foreman T H&L R1 Tontogany Wash 40.

Anderson, J. W., Sr. (Josephine) 9 ch blacksmith shop 1½a R1 Weston Lib 46.

ANDERSON, LEE (Pearl) 3 ch painter O H&L Meyers St Jerry City Blo.

ANDERSON, L. T. (Nellie) 2 ch farmer O 140a 7h R5 Bowling Green Cen 91 B tel.

ANDERSON, L. E. (Ola) 4 ch farmer T 80a 4h 2c R3 Prairie Depot Mon 99 B tel.

Anderson, M. S. (Lena) 2 ch clerk T H&L 5th St Perrysburg Per.

Anderson, Wm. (Nellie) 1 ch farmer T 80a 3h 8c R2 Weston Pla 3 Ind tel.

Anderson, W. A. Cygnet Blo.

Andress, Jesse L. breeder of horses O H&L 3h Main St Bloomdale Blo B tel.

Andrews, Laura Lemoyne Tro.

Androws, Andy (Blanche) 4 ch laborer O H&L 268 Walnut St Rossford Ros.

Andrus, Juston G. (son R. D.) 3h 2c 1701 Tracy St East Toledo Ros 14 B tel.

Andrus, R. B. (Maria) ret O 40a 1701 Tracy St East Toledo Ros 14 B tel.

Angel, Burr (son Dan.) grocer R1 North Baltimore Hen 69.

Angel, Daniel (Laura) 1 ch grocer O L 1h R1 North Baltimore Hen 69.

ANGEL, GEO. (Clara) 8 ch painter T H&L Pemberville Fre 40.

Angel, Ida RD North Baltimore Hen.

Angell, D. R. (Emma) 4 ch traveling man O H&L Maple Weston Ind tel.

Annis, W. S. (Edith) 1 ch driller O H&L 1h cor Walbridge & Washington Sts Cygnet Blo Ind tel.

ANTWINING, H. (Edith) 1 ch store keeper O H&L Haskins Mid 35 B tel.

Apel, Geo. RD Dunbridge Mid.

Apel, G. J. RD Weston Lib.

Apka, Galsat (Louise) 6 ch farmer O 60a 4h 3c R4 Bowling Green Cen 114.

Apple, A. F. Prairie Depot Blo.

Apple, Catherine Prairie Depot Blo.

Apple, Cristy (dau G. J.) RD Weston Lib 47.

Apple, Cloyce V. RD North Baltimore Hen.

Apple, C. H. RD North Baltimore Hen.

Apple, Fay (dau W. E.) Cygnet Blo 76 Ind tel.

Apple, G. J. (Mary) 4 ch farmer T 80a 3h 2c R1 Weston Lib 47.

Apple, G. W. (Mary D.) 1 ch farmer O 80a 5h 2c R1 North Baltimore Hen 14.

Apple, Harley (Pearl) 3 ch farmer T 160a 4h 2c R1 North Baltimore Hen 71 Ind tel.

Apple, J. H. (Ida) 1 ch ret O 267a RD North Baltimore Hen 69 Ind tel.

Apple, J. M. (Carolina) 1 ch carpenter O 12a H&L 1h 1c Jerry St Jerry City Blo.

Apple, Ober RD North Baltimore Hen.

Apple, O. L. Prairie Depot Blo.

Apple, V. E. (Ethel) 1 ch farmer T 80a 2h 6c R1 North Baltimore Hen 66 Ind tel.

Apple, W. E. 2 ch farmer O 140a 6h 4c Cygnet Blo 76 Ind tel.

Apple, W. S. (Esmerelda) farmer O 41a 1h 2c R1 North Baltimore Hen 69.

Arbuckle, W. F. (Nannie) 2 ch ret farmer O H&L 1h 1c R5 Bowling Green Cen 23 Ind tel.

Archer, Harvey (Grace) 1 ch farmer T 80a 3h 1c R1 Hoytsville Jac 91 B tel.

Archer, Henry RD North Baltimore Hen.

Archer, J. R. RD North Baltimore Hen.

ARGUE, THOMAS (Frances G.) 3 ch oil producer O H&L T 110a 1h Prairie Depot Mon B tel.

Aring, Anne 5 ch farmer O 160a 6h 7c R4 Bowling Green Cen 104.

Aring, Chas. R4 Bowling Green Cen 104.

Aring, Edward R4 Bowling Green Cen 104.

Aring, Henry cattle RD Bowling Green Cen.

Aring, John R4 Bowling Green Cen 104.

Arkelion, Harry RD East Toledo Lake.

21

Armbruster, Chas. A. (Anna) 1 ch farmer T 90a 4h 4c R1 Lime City Tro 13 Ind tel.

Armbruster, Frank RD Lime City Pbg.

Armbuster, Geo. (Mary) 2 ch farmer O 93a 5h 6c R1 Grand Rapids Gr Rs 43 Ind tel.

Armbruster, John (Mamie) 4 ch farmer T 100a 3h 4c R1 Lime City Tro 13 Ind tel.

Armbruster, Joseph ret O 100a 4h 4c R1 Lime City Pbg 50 Ind tel.

Armbruster, J. A. (Flora) 2 ch farmer O 83a 3h 6c R1 Lime City Pbg 52 Ind tel.

Armbruster, Raymond (son Joseph)) farmer T 100a 2h R1 Lime City Pbg 50 Ind tel.

Armbruster, William (Louisa) 4 ch farmer O 100a 1h 4c R1 Lime City Tro 13 Ind tel.

ARMBRUSTER, WM. F. (Rose) 2 ch farmer O 100a 5h 3c R1 Dunbridge Web 54 B tel.

Armitage, Elizabeth B. RD Bowling Green Pla.

Armitage, Fred (Bertha) 1 ch oil pumper T H&L 1c R2 Haskins Mid 37 B tel.

Armitage, John (Sarah) 1 ch farmer O 2a 1h R3 Bowling Green Pla 87.

ARMITAGE, J. F. (Jessie A.) 3 ch farmer T 80a 2c R2 Bowling Green Pla 97.

Armitage, Ray 3 ch oil pumper T H&L R2 Bowling Green Mid 41.

Armitage, Roy (Caroline) 3 ch oil pumper T H&L R1 Haskins Mid 38 B tel.

Armitage, S. H. Haskins Mid.

Armitage, Thomas (Louisa) farmer O 80a 4h 3c R2 Bowling Green Pla 97 B tel.

ARMITAGE, WM. (Elizabeth) farmer 21a 1h 1c R2 Haskins Mid 37 B tel.

Armitage, W. A. (Hattie) 3 ch farmer T 160a 5h 4c R1 Portage Por 51 Ind tel.

ARMSTRONG, J. L. (Lula ·E.) 2 ch farmer O 40a 6h 3c R2 Weston Wes 20 Ind tel.

Armstrong, N. C. (Franci) farmer O 40a 1h 2c R2 Weston Wes 28 Ind tel.

Arndt, Henry F. (Dorthea M.) farmer O 92a 4h 4c R1 Walbridge Lake 3 Ind tel.

Arnold, Mrs. Adelle ret 267 Walnut St Rossford Ros.

Arnold, Anna (dau Christ) R1 Stony-ridge Tro 10.

Arnold, Christ (Katie) 5 ch farmer O 8½a 1c R1 Stony Ridge Tro 10.

Arnold, E. laborer T 267 Walnut St Rossford Ross.

Arnold, Frank M. Grand Rapids Gr Rs.

Arnold, Jacob cattle RD Bowling Green Cen.

Arnold, Jas. W. (Mary E.) 2 ch farmer T 120a 5h 12c R1 Risingsun Per 93 Ind tel.

Arnold, J. H. (Minerva) 2 ch farmer O 20a 1h 2c R5 Bowling Green Cen 23 Ind tel.

Arnold, Lena (dau Christ) R1 Stony-ridge Tro 10.

Arnold, Verdon (son W. R.) student Hoytsville Jac.

Arnold, W. G. RD North Baltimore Hen.

Arnold, W. R. (Flora E.) 3 ch pastor church T H&L Hoytsville Jac.

ARNOULD; PLACID Rossford.

Arntz, Mary RD Fostoria Per.

Arr, C. A. Freeport Mon.

Arters, Albert Bradner Mon 17.

Arters, C. R. (Nellie) 4 ch pumper T 80a 2h 1c Bradner Mon 17.

Arters, Jay Bradner Mon 17.

Arters, T. H. (Letta Lenora) 6 ch oil producer T 78½a 2h 2c R1 Prairie Depot Mon 34 B tel.

Artz, Fred (Mary) 5 ch farming T 37a 4h 4c R3 Perrysburg Pbg 125.

Artz, Phillip Perrysburg Pbg.

Ash, B. F. (Catherine A.) 3 ch ret farmer O 4a 2h 3c R3 Weston Mil 86 Ind tel.

Ash, E. elevator Amsden Per B & Ind tels.

Ash, Glemn (Maud) oil driller T H&L Risingsun Mon.

Ash, Glem O. (son J. W.) confectionary store Risingsun Mon.

Ash, G. (Eleanor)˙ ret farmer O H&L Maple Weston Ind tel.

ASH, DR. H. E. bds Main St Box 4 Weston B & Ind tels.

Ash, Jesse (Sarah) 2 ch farmer O 71a 5h 7c R3 Weston Mil 86 Ind tel.

ASH, JOHN W. (Annie M.) oil con-tractor O H&L Risingsun Mon B tel.

Ash, Lyle E. (Maude) Risingsun Mon.

Ashenfelter, F. (May) 1 ch farmer O 40a 2h 3c R1 Grand Rapids Gr Rs 17.

Ashley, Mrs. Ellen 1 ch O H&L cor Crocker & Bell Sts Bradner Mon B tel.

Ashman, Lizzie Pemberville Fre.

Ashman, Wm. Pemberville Fre.

ASKINS, WEBSTER (Flora) 8 ch oil pumper T 4h 2c R1 Rudolph Hen 63 Ind tel.

Asmus, Anton (Eliza) 1 ch ret O 290a H&L Haskins Mid 35 B tel.

Asmus, Bertha (dau Anton) clerk Harkins Mid 35.

Asmus, Carl RD Haskins Mid.

Asmus, Chas. (Emma) 2 ch farmer T 80a 3h 3c R1 Haskins Mid 87 B tel

Asmus, Charley (Mary) 5 ch farmer O 150a 4h 10c R2 Haskins Mid 33 B tel.

Asmus, Edith (dau Anton) housekeeper Haskins Mid 35.

ASMUS, FRED (Edna) farmer T 84a 3h 10c R2 Haskins Mid 32 B tel.

ASMUS, F. F. (Emma) 2 ch farmer O 80a 5h 3c R1 Haskins Mid 43 B tel.

Asmus, Henry (Mary) 1 ch farmer O 104a 5h 5c R2 Haskins Md 89.

Asmus, Julia (dau Anton) housekeeper Haskins Mid 35.

Asmus, Mary RD Haskins Mid.

ASMUS, WM. (Eva) 1 ch farmer T 122a 4h 3c R1 Haskins Mid 53 B tel.

ASPACHER, JOHN (Ruth) 1 ch farmer T 80a 2h 2c R1 Stony Ridge Tro 10 Ind tel.

ASPACHER, WM. O R1 Dunbridge Web.

Aspacher, W. H. Dunbridge Web.

Atchley, Mrs. Barbara Hoytsville Jac.

Atchley, Isaac 3 ch farmer T 75a 2h 1c Hoytville Jac 116.

Atchley, Margaret farmer O 75a Hoytsville Jac 116.

Atkins, A. R. (Eva) 2 ch R R clerk O H&L Main St Weston.

Atkins, Gladys (dau A. R.) college student Main St Weston.

Atkins, Grace (dau A. R.) college student Main St Weston.

Atkins, Paul (Emma) 4 ch farmer T 160a 6h 4c R1 Jerry City Por 68 Ind tel.

Atwood, J. L. RD Prairie Depot Por.

Aubry, A. C. Custar Mil.

Audenkamp, Wm. (son E.) farmer 1h R4 Bowling Green Por 95.

Aufdencamp, Chas. RD Rudolph Lib.

Aufdenkamp, E. (Helena) 2 ch farmer O 59a 2h 4c R4 Bowling Green Por 95.

Aufderstrasse, Fred (Elizabeth) 3 ch carpenter O H&L Pemberville Fre 40.

Aufderstrasse, G. H. Pemberville Web.

AUFDERSTRASSE, H. F. W. (Louise) 3 ch farmer T 60a 3h 8c R2 Pemberville Web 39.

Aufderstrasse, J. H. (Mary) farmer O 50a 1h 2c R2 Pemberville Web 35.

Wood County. Is Noted for Its Fine Horses.

23

August, Ida 7 ch housekeeper O 20a 4c R2 North Baltimore Hen 59 B tel.

August, Mrs. W. S. RD North Baltimore Hen.

Augustine, Ray Pemberville Fre.

Ault, Bertha housekeeper R1 Lime City Pbg 53 B tel.

Ault, C. N. farmer O 40a 3h 3c R1 Jerry City Blo 70.

AULT, EDMUND farmer T 160a 3h 2c R1 Lime City Pbg 53 B tel.

AULT, FRANK farmer T 40a R1 Perrysburg Per 96.

Ault, Fred J. Lime City Pbg.

Ault, Geo. farmer T 80a 5h R1 Lime City Pbg 53 B tel.

Ault, Grace (dau Martin) housekeeper R1 Lime City Pbg 49.

Ault, John (Barbara) 3 ch farmer O 118a 1h 5c R3 Perrysburg Pbg 141 Ind tel.

Ault, John (Marilla) 1 ch farmer T 120a 5h 14c R1 Prairie Depot Mon 62.

Ault, Joseph farmer T 160a 3h 2c R1 Lime City Perrysburg 53 B tel.

Ault, Margaret Bradner Mon.

Ault, Martin (Elizabeth) farmer O 160a 6h 6c R1 Lime City Pbg 49 Ind tel.

Ault, Mary housekeeper R1 Lime City Pbg 53 B tel.

Ault, Wm. (Della) 5 ch farmer T 96a 3h 5c Bradner Mon 16.

AULT, W. H. R3 Prairie Depot.

Aumaugher, C. (Eliza) farmer O 7a 1h R1 Jerry City Por 76.

Aurand, Alice (dau M.) housekeeper R3 Prairie Depot Por 115.

Aurand, G. C. (Mary) physician & surgeon T H&L 1h Weston B & Ind tel.

Aurand, Harry L. (son M.) pumper R3 Prairie Depot Por 115.

AURAND, HARVEY M. (son M.) T R3 Prairie Depot Por 115.

Aurand, Jac E. (Clara A.) 4 ch farmer O 25a 1h 2c R3 Prairie Depot Mon 103.

Aurand, Michael farmer O 80a 3h 6c R3 Prairie Depot Por 115.

Aurand, S. E. (Rosie) farmer O 17a 3h 4c R3 Prairie Depot Por 120 B tel.

Aurand, W. H. (Sarah) 2 ch pumper O H&L 1h R2 Prairie Depot Por 114.

AUSTIN, A. C. ret O 40a 3h 3c R1 Bradner Fre 31 Ind tel.

AUSTIN, A. W. (Bertha) 3 ch farmer T 100a 6h 2c R3 Bowling Green Cen 82 Ind tel.

Austin, C. F. (Mary) 2 ch farmer O 20a 3h 2c R3 Weston Mil 2.

Austin, Fred (Margaret) 1 ch garage T H&L Bowling Green Ind tel.

Austin, Geo. L. (Lulu) 1 ch farmer T 60a 5h 9c R3 Bowling Green Pla 84.

Austin, Mary J. Weston Mil.

Austin, Roy Haskins Mid.

Austin, W. S. Haskins Mid.

Auverter, Chas. RD North Baltimore Jac.

Auverter, Emma J. RD North Baltimore Hen.

Auverter, Louis RD North Baltimore Hen.

Auverter, Michael RD North Baltimore Jac.

Auverter, Rachel RD North Baltimore Jac.

Auvester, Ardella RD North Baltimore Hen.

Averill, Arabel C. Perrysburg Pbg.

Averill, E. P. (May) ret O H&L Front St Perrysburg Pbg B tel.

Averill, Mrs. Henry E. 1 ch ret O H&L Front St Perrysburg Pbg B tel.

Avers, Fed (Elizabeth) 3 ch farmer O 76a R1 Pemberville Cen 121.

AVERS, JOHN H. (Katie) farmer 3h 5c R1 Pemberville Cen 121.

Avery, C. A. cattle RD Bowling Green Cen.

Avery, Elbert RD Bowling Green Pla.

AVERY, G. H. (Eva) 4 ch farmer O 10a 1h 1c R3 Bowling Green Pla 87 B tel.

Avery, John Bowling Green Lib.

Avery, J. N. (Susie) 6 ch farmer T 160a 6h 2c R3 Bowling Green Pla 87 Ind tel.

Avery, T. E. (Jennie) 4 ch farmer O 80a 4h 3c R1 Genoa Lake 44 B tel.

Avery, Violetta cattle RD Bowling Green Cen.

Avery, Wm. 1 ch farmer O 18a R2 Bowling Green Pla 91 B tel.

Avey, W. G. (Mary G.) 1 ch operator O H&L Union St Cygnet Blo 6 Ind tel.

Avokson, Wm. (Alta) 2 ch farmer O 40a 3h 4c R1 Weston Lib 47.

AYERS, ALBERT (Mary) 1 ch county commissioner O 65a 1h 1c R1 Millbury Lake 109 Ind tel.

Ayers, A. H. (Alla) farmer T 120a 5h 4c R3 North Baltimore Hen 88 Ind tel.

Ayers, Ella (dau A.) teacher R1 Millbury Lake 109 Ind tel.

Ayers, Frank Walbridge Lake.

24

Ayers, Oran ret O 40a 1h 1c R1 East Toledo Lake 112 Ind tel.

Ayers, Oliver H. (Emily E.) farmer O 40a R1 Millbury Lake 120.

Babcock, A. T. Prairie Depot Mon.

Babcock, E. E. (Clarinda) laborer T H&L Prairie Depot Mon.

Babcock, E. G. Prairie Depot Mon.

Babcock, S. M. (Alma) 3 ch farmer T 160a 5h 12c R2 Bloomdale Per 25 B tel.

Babel, Chris. (Catherine) farmer O 140a 1h 4c R1 Tontogany Wash 21 & 19 Ind tel.

Babione, Anna B. Luckey Tro.

Babione, D. D. Luckey Tro.

Bachman, Cra. (May) 2 ch trackman O H&L Taylor St Weston Wes Ind tel.

BACHMAN, J. (Jennie) 1 ch grocery store O H&L 2h Front St Cygnet Blo B & Ind tels.

BACHMANN, C. R. (Gertrude) 5 ch farmer O 80a 6h 6c R2 Dunbridge Cen 54 Ind tel.

Backus, H. R. Grand Rapids Gr Rs.

Backus, Jane Grand Rapids Gr Rs.

Bacome, William 3 ch ret farmer & soldier O H&L N Main St Weston B tel.

Bacon, H. C. Prairie Depot Mon.

Bacon, Laura A. Prairie Depot Mon.

Baer, Mrs. Bessie Hoytsville Jac.

Baer, Sam (Myrtle) 2 ch oil well cleaner O H&L 1h Cor Walbridge & Washington Sts Cygnet Blo 15 Ind tel.

Baggerly, Edward (Ella) 1 ch coal office O H&L cor Locust St Weston B tel.

Bahls, Frank (Louisa) 2 ch oil well driller O H&L 1h Luckey Tro Ind tel.

Bahls, Fred Latchie Lake.

Bahls, Louis Luckey Tro.

BAHMEN, HENRY (Kathryne) 7 ch farmer O 56a 4h 13c R1 Genoa Lake 42 B tel.

Bahmer, Mrs. Sarah 2 ch O H&L Oak St Weston B tel.

Bahnsen, Ben (Mabel) 1 ch railroader T H&L Walbridge Lake.

Bahnsen, B. (Minnie) 1 ch general merchandise O H&L 2h 1c Latchie Lake 83 B & Ind tels.

BAHNSEN, CHRIST (Emma) farmer O 15a 2h 3c Latchie Lake 95.

BAHNSEN, CHRIST (Eliza) 1 ch farmer O 47a 3h 5c R1 Genoa Lake 45 B tel.

BAHNSEN, CHRISTOFER ret T 20a Latchie Lake 95.

Bahnsen, Henry (Ella) 1 ch clerk T H&L 2h Latchie Lake 95.

Bahnsen, Herman (Matilda) 4 ch farmer T 40a 2h 2c R1 Genoa Lake 37 B tel.

Bahnsen, H. S. (Emma) 2 ch farmer O 60a 4h 9c Latchie Lake 96 B tel.

Bahnsen, Lewis (Maggie) 4 ch railroader O H&L Walbridge Lake.

Bahsen, Peter (Lena) farmer O 20a 2h 2c R1 Latchie Lake 85.

Baightel, George (Maud L.) 1 ch carpenter & contractor T H&L Grand Rapids Gr Rs Ind tel.

Baightel, Noah Grand Rapids Gr Rs.

Bailey, A. (Blanche) laborer O H&L Prairie Depot Mon B tel.

Bailey, Chas. (Bertha) 2 ch clerk H&L Millbury Lake.

Bailey, Elizabeth Jerry City Blo.

BAILEY, SIMON C. farmer O 78a 5h 7c R1 Jerry City Blo 60 B & Ind tels.

BAILEY, W. J. (Lucrecia) hardware & implements H&L Millbury Lake. See adv.

Baillet, John B. (Nellie) 2 ch glass worker O H&L 244 Maple St Rossford Ros.

Bair, Chas. J. (son Geo. A.) farmer R1 Prairie Depot Mon 86 B tel.

Bair, Geo. A. (Carrie) farmer O 160a 8h 3c R1 Prairie Depot Mon 86 B tel.

Bair, Jack (Addie) 3 ch quarryman T H&L Second St Portage Por.

Baird, A. J. 5 ch farmer T 240a 4h 10c R2 Bloomdale Per 19 B tel.

Baird, Charley (Elizabeth) 2 ch ret O H&L Sixth St Perrysburg Pbg B tel.

Baird, D. farmer Q 240a 5c R2 Bloomdale Per 19 B tel.

Baird, George (Lora) 7 ch laborer H&L Cygnet Blo 6.

Baird, Geo. W. cigar manufacturer T H&L Perrysburg Pbg B tel.

Baird, J. H. (Myrtle) farmer O 40a 5h 2c R1 Fostoria Per 60 Ind tel.

Baird, J. J. (Lorenda) T H&L Main St Bairdstown Blo.

Baker, Mrs. Adelia Weston Wes.

Baker, Amos West Millgrove Per.

Baker, Alice E. Bloomdale Blo.

Baker, A. (Mary) farmer O 80a H&L 1h 1c Prairie Depot Mon B tel.

Baker, B. C. Freeport Mon.

Baker, Chas. (Clara) 3 ch farmer T 80a 3h 6c R1 North Baltimore Hen 66 Ind tel.

Baker, C. E. (Alice A.) garage & agricultural implements O H&L N Main St Bloomdale Blo B & Ind tels.

25

Baker, C. E. (Vernie) farmer O 71a 1h 2c R1 Risingsun Mon 81.

Baker, Mrs. C. R. Tontogany Wash.

BAKER, DR. C. W. (Viola) 3 ch dentist T H&L Grand Rapids Gr Rs Ind tel.

Baker, C. W. RD North Baltimore Hen.

Baker, D. J. Cygnet Blo.

Baker, Edmund G., Jr. (son E. T.) farm hand R1 Lemoyne Tro 47.

Baker, Elizabeth 2 ch housekeeper R1 Stonyridge Tro 7.

Baker, Ethel (dau Maurice) West Millgrove Per 13.

Baker, E. L. (Marie) 2 ch garage T H&L Garfield St Bloomdale Blo B & Ind tels.

Baker, E. M. (Grace) 1 ch farmer O 60a 5h 9c R1 Fostoria Per 122 Ind tel.

Baker, E. T. (Linda H.) 3 ch farmer O 98a 4h 28c R1 Lemoyne Tro 47.

Baker, Foster A. (Eva) 2 ch electrician O H&L Walbridge St Cygnet Blo Ind tel.

Baker, Frank (Maggie) 7 ch laborer O H&L 1h 1c Luckey Tro.

Baker, Frank J. (Mary C.) farmer T 120a 8h 10c R1 Grand Rapids Gr Rs 21 Ind tel.

Baker, George (Beck) 4 ch bakery O 1a Main St Walbridge Lake.

BAKER, GEO. H. (Mae) 1 ch laborer T H&L Luckey Tro.

Baker, G. E. (Barbara) 6 ch laborer T H&L Jerry St Jerry City Blo 74.

Baker, Geo. W. (Mary) farmer O 50a 3h 5c R2 Weston Wash 7 Ind tel.

Baker, Harvey (Louisa) 2 ch farmer O 80a 4h 3c Stony Ridge Tro 12.

Baker, Hazel (dau Nellie) telephone operator Stony Ridge Tro.

Baker, Henry farmer O 20a R1 Walbridge Lake 26.

Baker, Herbert (son Frank) laborer Luckey Tro.

Baker, H. A. (Sena) 9 ch farmer T 320a 7h 40c R1 Fostoria Per 54 Ind tel.

Baker, Mrs. H. D. 3 ch O H&L N Main St Weston Ind tel.

Baker, Iona Marie (dau F. J.) housekeeper R1 Grand Rapids Gr Rs 21.

BAKER, JACOB (Susan) ret O 1a 1h R1 Walbridge Lake 15.

Baker, James G. (son Mrs. H. D.) N Main St Weston.

Baker, Jessie (dau Mrs. H. D.) N Main St Weston.

BAKER, JOSEPH (Bertha) 4 ch farmer T 80a 3h 2c R1 Walbridge Lake 99 Ind tel.

Baker, J. H. (Emma) novelty store O H&L & store RD North Baltimore Hen.

Baker, J. H. (Mary) farmer O 2a 1h Pemberville Fre 46.

Baker, J. M. Tontogany Wash.

Baker, J. W. (Anna) janitor O H&L Walbridge Lake.

Baker, Mrs. Leah ret O 62a R1 Stony Ridge Lake 32.

Baker, Levi (Louise) 8 ch laborer T H&L N Main St Bradner Mon B tel.

Baker, Lorissa T H&L Garfield St Bloomdale Bl.

Baker, Louis (son Harvey) farm hand Stony Ridge Tro 12.

Baker, Louis Walbridge Lake.

Baker, Louis H. Pemberville Fre.

Baker, L. A. RD North Baltimore Hen.

Baker, Mary Walbridge Lake.

Baker, Mary Edith (dau S. D.) postmistress & clerk Lemoyne Tro Ind tel.

Baker, Myrtle R. teacher Main St Weston Wes B tel.

Baker, Nellie 5 ch ret O H&L Stony Ridge Tro Ind tel.

Baker, Mrs. Nismier 2 ch farmer T 190a 8h 7c West Millgrove Per 13.

Baker, Purley R1 Weston Lib 47 Ind tel.

Baker, Ralph (son Sam) R3 Weston Wes 17.

BAKER, ROBERT (Grace) farmer & carpenter O H&L 1h 1c R1 Lemoyne Tro Ind tel.

Baker, R. L. Bloomdale Bl.

Baker, Sam (Rickie) 2 ch farmer T 200a 8h 2c R3 Weston Wes 17 Ind tel.

Baker, Mrs. Sarah 8 ch farmer O 9½a 1h 1c R1 Walbridge Lake 100 Ind tel.

Baker, Sidney W. (Elizabeth) 3 ch auto repairman T H&L R1 Walbridge Lake 15.

BAKER, S. D. (Asenath) 2 ch laborer O H&L 1h 1c Lemoyne Tro Ind tel.

Baker, S. R. Weston Wes.

Baker, T. C. RD North Baltimore Hen.

Baker, T. J. (Eva) 5 ch mail carrier O H&L Grand Rapids Gr Rs Ind tel.

Baker, Victor laborer N Main St Bloomdale Blo B & Ind tels.

Baker, Will 10 ch laborer T H&L N Main St Bradner Mon.

BAKER, WILLIAM (Elizabeth) 1 ch farmer T 30a 2h 1c R1 Walbridge Lake 19 Ind tel.

Baker, W. D. (Sofia) (farmer T 120a 5h 3c R1 Prairie Depot Mon 34.

Balazs, Joe (Elizabeth) 4 ch farmer T 60a 2h 6c R1 Stonyridge Lake 34.

Baldwin, A. B. (Fannie) 2 ch merchant O H&L Taylor St Weston Ind tel.

Baldwin, Ed. RD Weston Pla.

Baldwin, Edward Weston Mil.

Baldwin, Frank tool dresser Main St Jerry City Por.

Baldwin, Jane Elizabeth 3 ch ret O H&L Milton Center Mil.

Baldwin, John W. (Clara) 2 ch electrician O H&L 1c Box 172 Rossford Ros.

Baldwin, Leon laborer Main St Jerry City Por.

Baldwin, L. J. RD North Baltimore Hen.

Baldwin, W. F. (Minnie) 1 ch laborer T H&L Main St Jerry City Por.

Ball, Lon (Ada) 7 ch section hand T H&L Claron St Cygnet Blo 6.

Ballanbacher, Charles (Nellie) farmer O 2a 1h 1c R2 Weston Wes 45 Ind tel.

Ballantyne, A. Perrysburg Pbg.

BALLARD, F. M. Box 83 Rossford.

Ballard, Joe RD Tontogany Pla.

Ballmar, A. W. (Winifred) 1 ch thresher T H&L 2h R3 Weston Wes 13 Ind tel.

Ballmer, Lydie 4 ch T H&L Taylor St Weston.

Ballmer, O. C. R1 Bowling Green Lib 55 Ind tel.

Balls, Frank (Louise) driller O H&L Luckey Tro Ind tel.

BALTON, R. L. (Mae) 1 ch oil man O H&L 1h Harrison & Cherry Sts Bloomdale Blo B & Ind tels.

BALTZ, WM. (Lola) 3 ch farmer T 120a 7h 11c R3 North Baltimore Blo 17 Ind tel.

Bandeen, A. J. RD Bowling Green Mid.

Bandeen, Beryl R1 Pemberville Cen 114.

BANDEEN, H. G. (Maude) 3 ch farmer T 80a 3h 2c R4 Box 86 Bowling Green.

BANDEEN, LYLE farmer 1h R1 Pemberville Cen 114.

Bandeen, Mark R1 Pemberville Cen 114.

Bandeen, Wm. (Ida) 7 ch farmer O 80a 10h 3c R1 Pemberville Cen 114.

Bandy, Charles (Mella) farmer T 160a 1c R5 Bowling Green Web 19.

Banister, Chas. Weston Wes.

Banister, Sarah Weston Wes.

Bankey, August (Anna) 6 ch section hand O H&L Pemberville Fre B tel.

Bankey, Gust Pemberville Fre.

BANKEY, H. W. (Anna) 2 ch farmer T 120a 8h 38c R2 Prairie Depot Mon 43 B tel.

Banks, F. J. (Mary E.) 2 ch hardware merchant O H&L Main St Weston Ind tel.

Banks, George (Mary) 2 ch farmer O 4a 3h 5c R2 Weston Wes 45.

Banks, Helen (dau F. J.) trained nurse Main St Weston.

BANKS, MRS. MAUD Scotch Ridge.

Banks, Mary E. Weston Wes.

Banks, R. R. (Allie) farmer T 40a 7h 4c R2 Prairie Depot Por 81.

Banks, S. D. oil dealer O. H&L Main St Weston.

Banks, W. B. Scotch Ridge Web.

Bannister, Charles (Jennie) mason & carpenter O H&L Main St Weston.

Bannister, Emma (dau William) Sycamore St Weston.

Bannister, Hiram (Maria) 5 ch ret farmer O H&L Taylor St Weston.

Bannister, Sarah O H&L High St Weston.

Bannister, William (Frances) 3 ch farmer T 60a 3h Sycamore St Weston.

Barber, Albert Custar Lib.

Barber, Earl (Rose) laborer O H&L Grand Rapids Gr Rs.

Barber, Frederick R1 Rudolph Lib 36 Ind tel.

Barber, Harry Custar Lib.

Barber, George (Birdie) 4 ch handy man O H&L Weston.

Barber, George A. (son George W.) barber Weston.

Barber, Isabel M. Perrysburg Pbg.

BARBER, JONATHAN, SR. (Anna) 10 ch farmer T 320a 8h 23c R1 Rudolph Lib 36 Ind tel.

BARBER, J. J. R3 Grand Rapids.

Barber, Robert (Charlotte) 4 ch farmer O 60a 1h 1c R2 Custar Mil 39.

Barcherding, G. F. (Rhoda) farmer T 80a 2h 5c R1 Luckey Web 74 B tel.

Barcherding, Henry (Liza) 3 ch farmer O 225a 9h R1 Luckey Web 74 B tel.

Bard, O. W. (Annie) 2 ch farmer T 75a 2h 1c R1 Jerry City Blo 60.

Barger, Jacob RD North Baltimore Hen.

Barger, J. F. (Carrie) 2 ch farmer T 160a 8h 15c R1 Hoytsville Jac 101.

Barker, D. A. (May) 5 ch farmer T 65a 4h R2 North Baltimore Hen 21.

Barker, Rev. Ernest (Fern) T 2a 1h R1 Weston Pla 11.

Barker, W. H. (Verena) 1 ch farmer O 40a 3h 1c R2 Prairie Depot Mon 40.

Barman, Wm. (Melinda) mason O H&L Rudolph Lib 94.

Barnd, Jno. S. RD North Baltimore Hen.

Barnd, J. M. (Grace) 4 ch farmer T 80a 4h 4c R2 North Baltimore Hen 26 Ind tel.

Barnes, Wm. (Olive E.) janitor O H&L Haskins Mid.

Barnett, F. O. (Lucinda) 2 ch farmer O 195 2h Custar Mil 44 B tel.

Barnett, Lele (dau F. O.) school teacher Custar Mil 44.

Barnhisel, Mary S. Jerry City Blo.

BARNHISEL, P. S. (Mary S.) 3 ch farmer O 79a 3h 6c R1 Jerry City Blo 62 Ind tel.

Barnhisel, W. S. Bloomdale Blo.

BARNHOUSE, J. R. Bairdstown.

Barnum, Walter (Ida) laborer T H&L Luckey Tro.

Barr, A. D. (Bertha) 4 ch farmer T H&L 2h 1c R5 Bowling Green Cen 81.

Barr, Clarence W. (Alice E.) 4 ch farmer O 80a 4h 4c R3 Bowling Green Cen 45 Ind tel.

Barr, D. E. (M. E.) 7 ch farmer T 284a 8h 2c R5 Bowling Green Cen 81 Ind tel.

Barr, Dr. D. R. (Ida) physician & Surgeon O H&L Grand Rapids G Rs Ind tel.

Barr, Edward (Emma) 1 ch farmer O 40a 4h 3c R3 Bowling Green Cen 55.

Barr, J. F. (Emma) 1 ch laborer T H&L 2h 2c Jerry City Lib 68 Ind tel.

Barr, Wm. laborer T H&L Sugar Ridge Mid 69.

Barringer, Charles (Edna L.) 1 ch laborer T H&L Bairdstown Blo 48.

Barringer, Floe (dau O. J.) R2 Bloomdale Blo 124 B & Ind tels.

Barringer, John (Louisa) 1 ch farmer O 48 2-3a 2h 5c R2 Bloomdale Blo 124 B & Ind tels.

Barringer, O. J. (Alice M.) 6 ch farmer T 125a 1h 6c R2 Bloomdale Blo 124 B & Ind tels.

Bartelheim, Dora Luckey Tro.

Barterheim, John (Dora) 1 ch farmer 40a 3h 2c R1 Luckey Tro 28.

Barth, Herman (Caroline) 1 ch farmer O 65a 3h 10c R1 Pemberville Fre 59 B tel.

BARTH, H. E. (Edith) farmer T R1 Jerry City Por 28 Ind tel.

Barton, E. W. (Mary) 3 ch farmer T 10a 1h 1c R2 Weston Wes 23.

Barton, H. J. Weston Wes.

Barton, Jessie ret O H&L Second St Perrysburg Pbg.

Barton, Jno. Weston Wes.

Barton, R. P. (Lettia) 2 ch undertaker O H&L Perrysburg Pbg Ind tel.

Barton, S. R. (Nettie) ret gardener O 7½a 1h North Main St Weston.

BARTRUM, HARLEY J. (Metta M.) 3 ch farmer T 40a 4h 5c R1 Bloomdale Blo 61 Ind.

Bartz, Johanna RD North Baltimore Blo.

Bartz, Jno. J. RD North Baltimore Hen.

Bascom, M. C. (Ella) oil pumper) T Lot R1 North Baltimore Hen 65.

Bascom, Mrs. Nettie O H&L R1 Rudolph Lib 100.

BASEY, A. F. (Elsie M.) gen mdse O H&L Prairie Depot Mon B tel.

Bach, Augenette Haskins Mid.

Bash, Helen (dau J. C.) Weston.

BASH, J. C. (Ida) restaurant T H&L Weston B & Ind tel.

Bashore, Lucile 1 ch housekeeper R1 Luckey Web 74.

Bashore, A. G. T. (Minnie) 9 ch stave jointer T H&L Pemberville Fre Ind tel.

Bashore, Sherman (Minnie) 8 ch laborer T H&L Pemberville Fre Ind tel.

Bashore, T. Pemberville Fre.

BASHORE, W. E. school teacher Pemberville Fre Ind tel.

Baskem, Chas. RD Bowling Green Wash.

Bason, Frank Pemberville Fre.

Basor, Henry (Maria) ret O H&L Pemberville Fre.

BASSETTE, A. L. (Martha) 3 ch carpenter T H&L 1h 1c R7 Grand Rapids Wes 60 Ind tel.

Bassett, C. C. (son F.) farm hand R1 Hoytsville Jac 66 Ind tel.

BASSETT, C. D. (May) 2 ch farmer T 80a 3h 2c R1 North Baltimore Hen 12 B & Ind tels.

Bassett, C. F. (Alice) 4 ch farmer T 100a 5h 3c R1 Hoytsville Jac 66 Ind tel.

Bassett, C. S. Hoytsville Jac.

Bassett, Ray (Effa) telephone lineman O H&L Sycamore St Weston B tel.

Bassett, Sarah O 1a R1 Grand Rapids Wes 6.

Bassett, W. C. (son C. F.) farm hand R1 Hoytsville Jac 66 Ind tel.

Bateman, Clark 1 ch farming T 90a 5h 4c R2 Perrysburg Pbg 2 B tel.

Bates, Alfred (Josephine) laborer O H&L Risingsun Mon.

Bates, Ben (Frankie) 1 ch farmer O H&L Risingsun Mon.

Bates, Frank (Rose) farmer T 40a 2h 3c Custar Mil 12.

Bates, Geo. farm mgr R2 Custar Mil 43.

Bates, Heskel housekeeper R2 Custar Mil 43.

BATES, MRS. JENNIE R1 Risingsun.
Bates, Joseph farm mgr R2 Custar Mil 43.
Bates, Margaret ret O H&L Second St Perrysburg Pbg B tel.
Bates, Mrs. Mary J. 3 ch ret O H&L Risingsun Mon.
Bates, R. H. (Rebecca) 4 ch farmer O 30a 2c R5 Bowling Green Cen 100 Ind tel.
Bates, R. H., Jr. farmer 5h R5 Bowling Green Cen 110 Ind tel.
Bates, Susan ret O 40a 1h Custar Mil 12.
Bates, Sarah J. Custar Mil.
Bates, Tressie Risingsun Mon.
Bateson, Bert (May) 5 ch farmer O 40a 2h 4c R2 Prairie Depot Por 83.
Bateson, Cora student Walbridge Cygnet Blo.
Bateson, Effie 1 ch 2c R2 Prairie Depot Por 116.
Bateson, Chas. R. (Anna) 3 ch farmer T 80a 2h 4c R2 Prairie Depot Por 78.
Bateson, John R. (Nora E.) 5 ch farmer & oil producer T 76a 3h 6c R2 Prairie Depot Por 116.
Bateson, J. (Mary) general store O H&L 2h 7c R2 Prairie Depot Por 114 B tel.
Bateson, Lester laborer 1h R2 Prairie Depot Por 116.
Bateson, Mrs. M. J. 8 ch O H&L Walbridge Cygnet Blo.
Bateson, Nelson (Ida) 3 ch laborer O H&L Risingsun Mon.
BATEY, WM. (Lizzie) 3 ch farmer T 50a 3h 3c West Millgrove Per 68.

Bauerschmitt, Geo. Custar Mil.
Baugischmitt, Geo. (Lena) 8 ch farmer 74a 4h 4c R2 Custar Milton 43.
Baugischmitt, Leo. (son Geo.) farm hand R2 Custar Mil 43.
BAUM, GLENN (Enid) farmer T 28½a 2h 1c R1 Box 17A East Toledo Ros 27 Ind tel.
Baum, Guy W. (Mable) 1 ch farmer T 40a 2h 1c Station A East Toledo Ros 31.
Baum, William T. (Mary) ret O 28½a R1 East Toledo Ros 27.
BAUMAN, C. (Lora) 2 ch farmer O H&L 5h 1c Lime City Pbg 121 B tel.
Bauman, George (Bertha) 3 ch farmer T 80a 3h 3c R1 Dunbridge Web 52.
Bauman, Jacob (Anna) ret farmer O H&L R3 Perrysburg Pbg 74 Ind tel.
Bauman, Louis (Bertha) 1 ch farmer O 40a 2h 4c R4 Bowling Green Cen 112.
BAUMBERGER, GEO. (Catherine) 10 ch farmer O 10a 1c Custar Mil 97 B tel.
Baumen, Lewis Luckey Web.
Baumgardener, Coy (son W. A.) R3 Weston Mil 85.
BAUMGARDNER, C. L. (Grace) 3 ch farmer O 40 T 60a 5h 4c R3 Weston Mil 87 Ind tel.
BAUMGARDNER, C. R. (Hazel) farming T 2h R2 Weston Wes 41.
BAUMGARDNER, D. A. (Hattie) 2 ch farmer O 78a 3h 5c R3 Weston Mil 85 Ind tel.
Baumgardner, Earl (Ellen) farmer T 80a 2h 2c R3 Weston Mil 85 Ind tel.
Baumgardner, J. A. (Olivia) 4 ch farmer O 100a 6h 6c R3 Weston Mil 1 Ind tel.

"Goin' Fishin'?"

29

Baumgardner, S. Perrysburg.

Baumgardner, S. A. Weston Mil.

BAUMGARDNER, W. M. (Della) 2 ch farmer O 60a 3h 7c R3 Weston Mill 1 Ind tel.

Bausman, Fred (Mary) farmer O 120a 3h 5c R2 Pemberville Web 34 B tel.

Bausman, William (Dulcie) 1 ch farmer T R2 Pemberville Web 29.

Bausman, W. M. (Elsie) 1 ch laborer T R2 Pemberville Web 29.

Bavis, H. H. (Emma) 2 ch barber T H&L Findlay St Portage Por 2.

BAWDEN, WM. (Florence) 4 ch farmer O 40a 2h 3c R1 Dunbridge Web 54 B tel.

Bayer, Chas. (Helen) 6 ch harness shop O H&L 1c Perrysburg Pbg.

Bayer, Donald (son John) farmer R1 Perrysburg Pbg 110.

Bayer, John (Emma) 4 ch farmer O 180a 4h 5c R1 Perrysburg Pbg 110 B tel.

Bayer, Lulu (dau John) school teacher R1 Perrysburg Pbg 110.

Bayer, Merlin (son John) farmer R1 Perrysburg Pbg 110.

Bayliss, T. V. (Lettie B.) 4 ch oil man T H&L Bairdstown Blo 48.

Beach, Edward (Pauline D.) carpenter O 2a H Cherry St Perrysburg Pbg B tel.

Beal, W. E. (Clara) 1 ch salesman T H&L Main St Weston Ind tel.

Beals, H. B. (Alice) 3 ch farmer T 80a 7h 2c R1 Weston Mil 64 Ind tel.

Beam, Ethel (dau W. G.) housekeeper R1 Deshler Jac 38 B tel.

Beam, Geo. Bloomdale Blo.

Beam, Harry (Edna) 3 ch farmer T 50a 4h 5c Stony Ridge Tro.

Beam, J. 1 ch laborer T H&L East St Bradner Mon.

Beam, Mr. J. P. Bloomdale Blo.

Beam, Wesley (Annetta) 2 ch ret farmer O 50a 2c Stony Ridge Tro Ind tel.

Beam, William Gerald, Jr. (son W. G.) farm hand R1 Deshler Jac 38 B tel.

Beam, W. G., Sr. (Eliza) 4 ch farmer T 160a 7h 10c R1 Deshler Jac 38 B tel.

Beard, A. ret farmer T Dowling Mid.

BEARD, E. J. (Nettie) 2 ch farmer T 60a 2h 2c R2 Prairie Depot Por 113.

BEARD, J. M. (Stella) 5 ch farmer O 61a 4h 7c R1 Portage Por 10.

BEARRY, H. T. (Lillie May) 3 ch grocer O H&L & store Dowling Mid 76 B & Ind tels.

Beatty, Dr. E. R. (Veryl) 3 ch dentist O H&L Evans St Bradner Mon B tel.

Beatty, J. T. (Jane) farmer T 40a 4h 1c R2 Weston Wes 25 Ind tel.

Beatty, R. D. R2 Weston Wes 25 Ind tel.

Beaty, Wm. West Millgrove Per.

Beaverson, Frank RD Weston Pla.

Beaverson, Fred (Bertha) laborer O H&L Tontogany Wash.

BEAVERSON, JAMES (Bertha) 5 ch farmer T 83a 3h 2c R1 Weston Pla 7 Ind tel.

Beaverson, Jason RD Bowling Green Web.

Beaverson, Thomas (Mabel) 5 ch oil worker T 1c Bays Lib 106 Ind tel.

Bechstein, Henry Weston Lib.

BECHSTEIN, JOHN (Jessie) 3 ch farmer O 66¼a 6h 4c RD Weston Lib 1 Ind tel.

BECHTEL, F. A. (May) 4 ch laborer T 1c Cygnet Blo 7.

Bechtel, Horace RD North Baltimore Hen.

BECHTEL, R. W. (Hattie) laborer T H&L 1h 1c Cygnet Hen 8 Ind tel.

Bechtel, W. M. RD North Baltimore Hen.

Beck, C. C. (Ruth E.) 3 ch station agent T H&L Dunbridge Mid Ind tel.

Beck, F. G. (Lilly) 10 ch farmer T 75a 3h 6c R2 Bowling Green Pla 57 B tel.

Beck, Fred W. Pemberville Fre.

Beck, Mary A. RD North Baltimore Hen.

Beck, Mary J. O 130a 1h 4c West Millgrove Per 64.

BECK, TITUS (Lora E.) 12 ch farmer O 80a 4h 3c R2 Bowling Green Pla 63 Ind tel.

Beck, W. H. RD North Baltimore Hen.

Becker, Geo. (Maude) 8 ch farmer O 40a 3h 10c R1 Prairie Depot Mon 114 B tel.

Beckman, Cora Main St Cygnet Blo 6.

BECKMAN, DELBERT (Rose) 3 ch farmer O 8½a T 80a 3h 2c R1 Custar Mil 20.

Beckman, Geo. (Dora) 5 ch farmer O 80a 4h 9c Latchie Lake 130 Ind tel.

Beckman, H. Fred'k Millbury Lake.

Beckman, Joseph farmer O 50a 3h 2c R3 Bowling Green Cen 87.

Beckman, Lucien farmer T 80a 3h 1c R1 Tontogany Wash 21 Ind tel.

Beckman, Mary RD Bowling Green Cen.

Beckman, W. H. (Lena) farmer O 30a 8h 30c R1 Millbury Lake 126 Ind tel.

Beech, Nettie 2 ch R2 Pemberville Web 45.

BEECHER, WM. (Lillian) oil worker O H&L 1h 1c Brown St Jerry City Blo Ind tel.

Beeker, Edward (son Mrs. Frank) farmer R1 Pemberville Fre 68 B tel.

Beeker, E. L. (Gertrude) 1 ch farmer T H&L Bond St Pemberville Fre.

Beeker, Mrs. Frank 1 ch farmer O 186a 3h 8c R1 Pemberville Fre 68 B tel.

Beeker, Fred (Emma) 1 ch clerk O H&L Pemberville Fre 40 Ind tel.

Beeker, Geo. (Liza) laborer O H&L Pemberville Fre.

BEEMAN, E. L. (Alice) 2 ch manager elevator T H&L 1h 4c R2 Deshler Mil 15 B tel.

Beeman, W. E. (Hazel) 3 ch professor H&L Prairie Depot Mon B tel.

Beeson, Charley (Halley) 2 ch laborer R1 North Baltimore Lib 71 Ind tel.

Beettenok, H. (Louisa) 2 ch farmer O 36a 2h 4c R3 Bowling Green Web 14.

Behm, O. F. (Rosa) 1 ch oil pumper T H&L R1 Luckey Tro 53 Ind tel.

Beightol, B. M. Freeport Mon.

Beimwick, Mrs. Kathrine Pemberville Fre.

Beindick, Ed. (Lottie) 2 ch farmer O 118a 4h 12c R1 Pemberville Fre 73 B tel.

Beinert, Frank (Mina) 2 ch farmer O 115a 3h 6c R2 Haskins Wash 92 B tel.

Belford, Hannah C. Perrysburg Pbg.

Bell, Chester farmer T 40a 1h Jerry City Por 70 Ind tel.

Bell, Mrs. Geo. O 40a 3c Jerry City Por 70 Ind tel.

Bell, Geo. A. notary public O H&L Grand Rapids Gr Rs.

Bell, Laura school teacher N Main St Bradner Mon.

Bell, Mabel housekeeper O H&L Grand Rapids Gr Rs.

Bell, Myrtle D. housekeeper O H&L Grand Rapids Gr Rs.

Bell, Olive 1 ch O H&L N Main St Bradner Mon.

Bell, Tracy (Celia) farmer 1h Jerry City Por 70 Ind tel.

Bell, Urban (Hattie) 1 ch oil producer T H&L Factory St Jerry City Por.

Bell, Wm. (Sarah) farmer O 72a R1 Bradner Fre 89.

Bellmerl, Edward (Josephine) laborer O H&L Latchie Lake.

Bellville, L. E. Dunbridge Mid.

Beman, E. S. Haskins Mid.

BEMAN, GEO. (Garnet) 1 ch farmer T 120a 5h 2c R1 Haskins Mid 43.

Bemis, Chas. Haskins Mid.

Bemis, D. C. lawyer O H&L Haskins Mid.

Bemis, Fred (Susie) 1 ch butcher O H&L Haskins Mid 35 B tel.

Benard, Mrs. Orpha 1 ch housekeeper O H&L Risingsun Mon.

BENCH, EDWIN (Marie) 1 ch farmer T 80a 2h 5c R3 Perrysburg Pbg 69 Ind tel.

Bench, Julia ret O 80a R3 Perrysburg Pbg 69 Ind tel.

Bench, Wm. (Katie) 2 ch farmer O 65a 2h 3c R1 Walbridge Pbg 68.

Benchoter, Lewis (Alma) 1 ch veterinarian T H&L Grand Rapids Gr Rs Ind tel.

BENDER, JOSEPH (Thankful) 2 ch cattle breeder O 46a 4h 14c R4 Bowling Green Cen 25 B tel. See adv.

BENDER, W. P. 3 ch farmer T H&L 1c R4 Bowling Green Cen 25 B tel.

BENHAM, C. W. (Minnie) 6 ch painter O H&L 1c Stahl St Bradner Mon B tel.

Benham, Minnie B. Bradner Mon.

Benington, Catherine Dunbridge Mid.

BENLIEN, CHARLES (Elizabeth) blacksmith T L R1 North Baltimore Hen 70 Ind tel.

Benner, Chas. (Florence) 1 ch farmer T 80a 2h 6c Prairie Depot Mon 65 B tel.

Benner, John (Julia) 11 ch farmer T 80a 5h 6c R1 N Baltimore Hen 38.

Bennet, B. Corp St Portage Por.

Bennett, Chas. (Beatrice) 1 ch section foreman O H&L Second St Portage Por.

Bennett, G. F. RD North Baltimore Hen.

Bennett, W. S. (Dilla) general store T Main St West Millgrove Per B tel.

Benschoter, B. (Zilphia) farmer O 53a 5h 2c R2 Prairie Depot Por 124 Ind tel.

Benschoter, Douglas (son B.) farmer R2 Prairie Depot Por 124 Ind tel.

Benschoter, D. (Elizabeth) farmer O 50a 2h 2c R2 Prairie Depot Por 125.

Benschoter, Howard Grand Rapids Gr Rs.

Benschoter, Irvin (son B.) farmer 1h R2 Prairie Depot Por 124 Ind tel.

Benschoter, J. S. (Rachel S.) farmer O 132a 2h 2c R1 Grand Rapids Gr Rs 46 Ind tel.

Benschoter, Lucy (dau D.) housekeeper R2 Prairie Depot Por 125.

Benschoter, L. J. (Alma) 1 ch veterinarian T H&L 4h Grand Rapids Gr Rs Ind tel.

Benschoter, Quiros farmer O 35a R1 Jerry City Por 75.

BENSCHOTER, MRS. R. S. R1 Box 54 Grand Rapids.

Benschoter, Thos. (Mary) 3 ch farmer T 80a 11h 7c R2 Prairie Depot Por 66 Ind tel.

Benschoter, Victor (son B.) farmer 1h R2 Prairie Depot Por 124 Ind tel.

Benschoter, W. ret O H&L Grand Rapids Gr Rs Ind tel.

Benson, Daniel (Elsie) 1 ch skipper O H&L Prairie Depot Mon B tel.

Bentley, John (Alferta) 13.ch painter O H&L Third St Grand Rapids Gr Rs.

Bentley, Mrs. John 2 ch O H&L Grand Rapids Gr Rs.

Bentley, William (Bessie) 2 ch motorman T H&L 5th St Perrysburg Pbg B tel.

Benton, B. H. (Minnie V.) 5 ch blacksmith O shop H&L 1h 1c Bairdstown Blo 48.

BENTON, F. A. (Leah) hotel & restaurant T hotel Perrysburg Pbg Ind tel.

BERDUE, MARY Weston.

BEREHNING, HENRY F. W. (Emma) 2 ch farmer T 72a 3h 5c R1 Luckey Tro 51 Ind tel.

BERGE, ARTHUR (Carrie) 1 ch farmer T 40a 3h 7c R1 East Toledo Lake 71.

Berge, Mrs. Martha ret O 40a R1 East Toledo Lake 71 Ind tel.

Berger, H. C. Cygnet Blo.

Bergman, C. F. (Amanda) 2 ch farmer O 80a 6h 4c RD Deshler Jac 24 Ind tel.

Bergman, C. W. Rossford Ros.

Berkett, Sherm (Anna) carpenter O H&L 1h Grand Rapids Gr Rs Ind tel.

Berkmeyer, Carl Pemberville Fre.

Bernard, F. E. (Amy) 1 ch farmer O 85a 1h 13c Hatton Per 85 Ind tel.

Bernard, J. G. Weston Wes.

BERNARD, PHOEBE J. ret O Prairie Depot Mon.

BERNARD, W. E. (Orpha) 1 ch stationary engineer O H&L R1 Bloomdale Blo 114.

Berndt, Emil (Clara) farmer O 60a 3h 3c R1 Genoa Lake 42.

Berndt, Fred (Geraldine) 3 ch farmer T 80a 5h 6c R1 Stony Ridge Lake 85 B tel.

Berning, C. (Minnie) 3 ch butcher O H&L Luckey Tro Ind tel.

Berning, Florence (dau Thomas) 1 ch housekeeper Luckey Tro.

Berning, H. A. (Nellie) 2 ch barber O H&L Perrysburg Pbg B tel.

Berning, Thomas (Lilly) 2 ch laborer O H&L Luckey Tro.

Bernthisel, Chas. (Francis) farmer O 105a 3h Haskins Mid.

BERNTHISEL, HENRY (Blanche) 1 ch farmer T 105a 4h 8c R2 Haskins Mid 33 B tel.

BERNTHISEL, W. H. (Myrtle) confectionary & pool room T H&L Haskins Mid 35.

Bernthisel, W. W. Haskins Mid.

Berres, Elizabeth 6 ch farmer O 40a 2h 4c R1 Custar Mil 95.

Berres, John (son Elizabeth) farmer O 40a R1 Custar Mil 95.

Berres, Mathias Weston Mil.

Berres, Peter (Helena) 4 ch farmer O 40a 2h 5c R1 Custar Mil 95.

Berrgemier, Caroline housekeeper O H&L R1 Luckey Tro 51.

Berrgemier, John 2 ch farmer O 80a 2h 6c R1 Luckey Tro 51 Ind tel.

Barridge, S. A. 3 ch carpenter T H&L N Main St Bradner Mon.

Berry, A. W. ret farmer O 137a Custar Mil 44 B tel.

Berry, Elizabeth 5 ch ret O 46a 1c Custar Mil 44 B tel.

Berry, F. E. (Anna) laborer O 1a 1h Custar Mil 44.

Berry, H. E. RD Dowling Mid.

BERRY, JOHN (Mollie) 2 ch farmer O 10a 2h 2c R1 Bradner Fre 77 B tel.

Berry, Mrs. Jno. Custar Mil.

Berry, M. J. Bradner Fre.

Berry, Wm. (Hazel) 2 ch farm laborer R1 Rudolph Lib 37.

Berry, Wilda dressmaker Custar Mil 44 B tel.

Berry, W. W. Millbury Lake.

Bert, Frank (Jennie) 1 ch laborer T H&L Rossford Pbg 80.

Bessanson, Amelia ret O H&L 7th & Plank Sts Perrysburg Pbg.

BEST, JESS (Minnie) 1 ch pumper T 1h 1c R1 Rudolph Lib 71 Ind tel.

Bettenbrock, August Dunbridge Web.

Bettenbrock, Henry Dunbridge Web.

Betts, Henery (Philabina) ret O H&L 6th St Perrysburg Pbg B tel.

Beucler, Rev. J. J. RD North Baltimore Hen.

Beuth, Henry J. (Mildred) glass worker T H&L 94 Elm St Rossford Ross.

Bevelhymer, George (Mary) oil worker T H&L 1h Rudolph Lib 96 Ind tel.

Bevelhymer, Joe (Leana) 2 ch oil pumper T H&L Mermill Lib 94 Ind tel.

Bevelhymer, Joseph (Caroline) laborer .T R2 North Baltimore Hen 125.

Bevelhymer, John A. (Mattie) 3 ch laborer T Bays Lib 100.

Bevelhymer, P. RD North Baltimore Hen.

Beverly, Clarence (Mina) 1 ch laborer O H&L 6th St Perrysburg Pbg B tel.

Bevenson, Franklin (Emma J.) 3 ch farmer T 60a 4h 2c R1 Weston Pla 12 Ind tel.

Beverstock, A. J. RD Tontogany Wash.

Beverstock, Belle Tontogany Wash.

Beverstock, E. A. Weston Wes.

Beverstock, J. V. assist cashier O H&L Weston B tel.

Beverstock; May W. RD Tontogany Wash.

Bevond, W. E. Bloomdale Blo.

Bhaer, Sam Cygnet Blo.

Bick, Margaret 2 ch ret O H&L 3d St Perrysburg Pbg B tel.

Bickmyer, Frank Custar Mil.

Bickmyer, Fred (Susan) 1 ch farmer T 50a 2h 1c R2 North Baltimore Hen 59.

Bickmyer, Geo. implement O H&L Custar Mil.

Bickmyer, Matilda housekeeper Custar Mil.

Biddle, A. J. (Minie) 4 ch livery O H&L 3h Pemberville Fre B tel.

Biddle, Florence R1 Grand Rapids Wash 54.

Biddle, Gilbert (son A. J.) school boy Pemberville Fre.

Biehler, Augustus (Emma) 1 ch farmer T 80a 7h 20c R3 North Baltimore Blo 36 B & Ind tels.

Biehler, H. R. (Gertrude) farmer T 157a 10h 11c R3 North Baltimore Hen 111 Ind tel.

Biehlier, David (Anna) farmer O 160a 1h 20c R3 North Baltimore Hen 88 Ind tel.

Bierly, C. (Caroline) 3 ch ret O H&L Stahl Ave Bradner Mon B tel.

Bierly, H. B. ret O H&L Risingsun Mon.

Bigelow, Ray farmer R1 Rudolph Por 24 Ind tel.

Bigelow, Rolla (Viola) farmer O 57a 5h 3c R1 Rudolph Por 24 Ind tel.

Biggs, Dr. I. L. (Myrtle) 1 ch physician T H&L Custar Mil B tel.

Biggs, I. T. Custar Mil.

Bigley, Anna ret O H&L Risingsun Mon.

Bigley, A. L. (Mary) 3 ch oil marker O H&L Portage Lib 90 Ind tel.

Bihn, Albert (Laura) manager elevator O Sugar Ridge Tro.

Bihn, Edward (Viola) 8 ch farmer T 160a 1h 1c R3 Pemberville Fre 90 B tel.

Bihn, Frank Walbridge Lake.

Bihn, Frank (Della) 3 ch farmer O 47a 5h 16c R1 Stony Ridge Tro 7 Ind tel.

Bihn, John (Ferna) 2 ch well driller O H&L Stony Ridge Tro Ind tel.

Bihn, Joseph (Clara) 4 ch farmer O 101a 4h 3c R1 Millbury Lake 120.

Bihn, Lewis J. (Maria D.) 3 ch farmer T 120a 5h 10c R3 Pemberville Fre 34 B tel.

Biley, W. J. Millbury Lake.

Bill, Jacob B. Perrysburg Pbg.

Billheimer, Mrs. C. A. RD North Baltimore Hen.

Billings, Arthur (Maggie) farmer 68a 2h 4c R1 Luckey Tro 23.

Billings, H. W. (son William H.) barber Locust St Weston Wes.

Billings, William H. (Sarah) 5 ch barber T H&L Locust St Weston Ind tel.

Billingsley, Chas. (Elizabeth) 3 ch farmer T 200a 3h 3c R3 Prairie Depot Mon 96.

Billingsley, Edwin (Belria) 4 ch farmer T 200a 3h 3c R3 Prairie Depot Mon 96.

Billingsley, H. D. Prairie Depot Mon.

Billingsley, J. E. (Aldea I.) 3 ch farmer T 80a 3h 8c R3 North Baltimore Blo 21.

Billman, W. W. (Mary) farmer O 120a H&L 4h 10c R1 Bradner Mon 58 B tel.

Bilsky, Andrew (Anna) 2 ch glass worker O H&L Box 406 Rossford Ros.

Bing, Cap Tontogany Wash.

Binger, Geo. (Sina) 2 ch farmer T hired man 1c R9 Dunbridge Mid 81 Ind tel.

Binger, John (son John M.) farmer R2 Dunbridge Mid 81.

Binger, John M. (Eliza J.) 2 ch farmer T 35a 2h 1c R2 Dunbridge Mid 81.

Bingle, Geo. R1 Risingsun.

Biniker, Clarence (son Dencie) farmer R3 Perrysburg Pbg. 74.

Biniker, Dencie 6 ch farmer O 77a 3h 4c R3 Perrysburg Pbg 74 Ind tel.

Biniker, Fred L. (Elizabeth) farmer O 20a 5h 2c R3 Perrysburg Pbg 62 Ind tel.

Biniker, Nellie (dau Dencie) housekeeper R3 Perrysburg Pbg 74.

Birch, Wm. O. (Sara) 1 ch dealer O H&L 1h Front St Perrysburg Pbg B tel.

Bird, Dela farming Dowling Pbg 35 B tel.

Bird, Mrs. E. A. farming O 3½a Dowling Pbg 35 B tel.

3   33

Bird, George W. (Bessie) 4 ch gardening O 5a 1h Dowling Pbg 34.

Birkin, J. P. (Louise) 4 ch farmer O 100a 4h 12c R1 Perrysburg Pbg 37.

Birrie, Frank (Anna) 8 ch pattern maker O 4a 1c R1 East Toledo Lake 132.

Bisel, J. M. (Olive) farmer T 87a R2 Bloomdale Per 19.

Bisell, Cloyd Cygnet Blo 76 Ind tel.

Bisell, Forest Cygnet Blo 76 Ind tel.

Bisell, James Cygnet Blo 76 Ind tel.

Bisell, W. H. (Luzilla) 6 ch farmer T 80a 1h 6c Cygnet Blo 76 Ind tel.

Bisher, I. T. (La Vina) farmer O H&L Grand Rapids Gr Rs Ind tel.

BISHOP, ALBERT R3 North Baltimore 21.

Bishop, E. L. (M. E.) farmer T 90a 3h 5c R1 Weston Pla 12 Ind tel.

Bishop, G. E. (Laura) 1 ch farmer O 2a R2 Bowling Green Pla 91.

Bishop, Herbert (Nettie) 4 ch farmer T 160a 3h 3c R3 North Baltimore Blo 21.

BISHOP, RAY (son Wm.) laborer 1h R3 North Baltimore Blo 21.

Bishop, Wm. (Julia) farmer O 160a 4h 3c R3 North Baltimore Blo 21.

Bisbee, Chas. barber R2 Prairie Depot Por 114.

BISTLINE, B. O. Bradner Mon. 23.

BITTEN, RALPH (Bertha) farmer T 83a 3h 3c R1 Perrysburg Pbg 109.

Bitter, George (Julia) 5 ch farmer T 80a 4h 1c R1 East Toledo Ros 37 Ind tel.

Black, Dr. A. P. (Geneva) 5 ch O H&L Bradner Mon B tel.

Black, Ellie E. Tontogany Wash.

Black, G. W. RD North Baltimore Hen.

Black, Harold clerk East St Bradner Mon B tel.

Black, J. T. (Mary) 7 ch pumper O 5a R1 Rudolph Lib 70.

Black, J. J. Tontogany Wash.

Black, Laura (dau Lucy) dressmaker Scotch Ridge Web 35.

Black, Lucy housekeeper O H&L Scotch Ridge Web 35.

Black, Morris (Malinda) 2 ch laborer H&L Halton Per 84.

Black, R. Z. (Bertha) farmer T H&L R1 Rudolph Lib 77.

Blackall, M. J. RD North Baltimore Hen.

Blackburn, James (Alsina) 5 ch ret farmer O 3a H&L 2c Oak St Weston Wes.

BLACKBURN, W. R. (Clara) 3 ch racket store O H&L 2h Grand Rapids Gr Rs Ind tel. See adv.

Blacklock, R. J. 4 ch drayman T H&L 2h N Main St Bradner Mon B tel.

Blackman, C. J. (Julia) laborer O H&L Church St Bradner Mon.

Blackman, Edith housekeeper Jerry City Por 32 Ind tel.

Blackman, E. P. (Enola) 6 ch farmer & oil driller O 56a 2h 5c Jerry City Por 32 Ind tel.

Blackman, Frank (son G. E.) painter Jerry City Por 73.

Blackman, G. E. (Arvilla) farmer O 78a 4h 2c Jerry City Por 73.

Blackman, Harry (Liza) 3 ch painter T H&L Risingsun Mon.

Blackman, Ida (dau G. E.) Jerry City Por 73.

Blackman, L. (Sarah) 7 ch ret farmer O 3a 1h R1 Rudolph Lib 33 Ind tel.

Blackman, W. H. Bradner Mon.

Blain, Z. V. grocer O H&L 2h R1 East Toledo Ros 30 Ind tel.

BLAIR, ALBERT (Louise) restaurant, boarding & lodging T H&L Findlay St Portage Por Ind tel.

Blair, D. L. jeweler Main St Bloomdale Blo.

Blair, Jerry B. (Almina) farmer O 90a 2h 5c R1 Jerry City Blo 70 Ind tel.

Blair, Raymond A. (son Albert) student Findlay St Portage Por.

BLAKE, F. W. (Pearl) 3 ch farmer T 80a 7h 3c R1 North Baltimore Hen 53 Ind tel.

BLAKE, JAMES (Pearl) 5 ch superintendent school T 2h 1c R1 North Baltimore Hen 38.

Bland, J. A. (Anna) 5 ch farmer T 60a 3h 2c R1 North Baltimore Hen 35.

BLANDEN, GEORGE (Clara) 2 ch farmer O 60a 3h 2c R1 Walbridge Lake 118 Ind tel.

Blandin, Chas. I. (Emma) farmer O 53 1-3a 2h 3c R1 Walbridge Lake 4 Ind tel.

Blaney, Daniel Fredericktown Mon.

Blankertz, Wm. (Malsia) 1 ch clerk O H&L Front St Perrysburg Pbg.

Blasey, Mrs. C. M. housekeeper O H&L R1 Pemberville Fre 37.

Blasey, Elvena (dau Mrs. E. M.) school teacher Pemberville Fre 40.

BLASEY, H. W. (son Katherine E.) farmer T 20a 2h 2c R1 Pemberville Fre 37.

Blasingame, J. H. (Beunie) 1 ch farmer T 20a R1 Bradner Mon 54.

Blasingame, M. C. 4 ch farmer T 20a H&L R1 Bradner Mon 56.

Blasingame, W. H. 4 ch farmer T 40a 2h 1c R1 Bradner Mon 29.

Blasius, J. M. (Jessie) general store O H&L Milton Center Mil Ind tel.

Blasius, M. P. (Hermia) 3 ch farmer 50a 4h 3c R1 Custar Mil 13.

Blasius, P. N. (Lottie) 3 ch farmer & thresher T 60a 7h 9c RI Custar Mil 13 B tel.

BLECKE, FRED (Pearl) farmer T 8h RI Luckey Tro 20 B tel.

Blecke, John (Adelia) 1 ch farmer T 80a 2h 4c Luckey Tro 70 Ind tel.

Blecker, Harry RD North 'Baltimore Hen.

Bleckley, Christ RD North Baltimore Hen.

Blessing, Celia ret O H&L Risingsun Mon.

Blessing, Fred (May) 6 ch field foreman T H&L Crocker St Bradner Mon B tel.

Blessing, Geo. (Sarah D.) 1 ch farmer T 15a 2h 2c Risingsun Mon 73 B tel.

Blessing, Homer (son Geo.) farmer Risingsun Mon 73.

Blessing, Laura (dau Geo.) school girl Risingsun Mon 73.

Blessing, Thadious (Jessie) 1 ch laborer T H&L Risingsun Mon.

Blinn, Franklin (Blanch) farmer T H&L Front St Perrysburg Pbg B tel.

Blinn, Mary 3 ch ret O H&2a Freemont Road Perrysburg Pbg B tel.

Blodgett, C. O. (Liza Jane) 4 ch work furniture store O H&L Silver St Weston.

Blond, Frank Risingsun Per.

BLOOM, D. L. (Rosa) 4 ch farmer T 80a 1h 1c RI North Baltimore Hen 49.

Bloom, Emanuel (Hanna) laborer O H&L R2 Prairie Depot Por 114.

Bloom, Harvey (Hazel) 3 ch laborer 1h R2 Prairie Depot Por 114.

BLOOM, H. H. (Martha) 2 ch farmer O 80a 9h 7c R1 North Baltimore IIen 46.

Bloom, Isaac (Rose) 3 ch farmer T 100a 7h 2c R1 Rudolph Lib 76.

Bloom, Lydia A. RD North Baltimore Hen.

Bloomfield, Andrew farmer T 120a 3h Millbury Lake 46.

Bloomfield, Chas. Millbury Lake.

Bloomfield, Clarence (Myrtle) 1 ch farmer T 120a 2h 1c R1 Millbury Lake 46.

Bloomfield, Floyd Millbury Lake.

Bloomfield, Frank (Mary) 6 ch farmer O 80a 5h 7c Millbury Lake 46.

Bloomfield, Geo. farmer O 40a 1h 2c R1 Millbury Lake 46.

Bloomfield, Sarah ret O H&L 2d St Perrysburg Pbg B tel.

Blue, E. L. (Mary L.) printer O H&L Front St Perrysburg Pbg Ind tel.

Blue, Michael (Catherine) O Randolph St Bairdstown Blo.

Blyth, Bertha (dau Rebecca) housekeeper R1 Custar Jac 40.

Blyth, Della (dau Rebecca) housekeeper R1 Custar Jac 04.

Blyth, Henry (Ella) 2 ch farmer O 80a 4h 9c R1 Custar Jac 40.

BLYTH, JOSEPH R1 Custar Jac.

Blyth, Rebecca 4 ch ret O 127a 2h 7c R1 Custar Jac 40.

Boardman, H. H. RD North Baltimore Hen.

Two Crops—Wool and Mutton.

Boardman, W. H. RD N Baltimore Hen.

Boardner, Frank Corys St Portage Por.

Boatman, C. (Hattie) 3 ch farmer T 120a 6h 5c R1 Risingsun Per 97.

Bobcock, A. T. (Helen) 2 ch farmer T 40a 5h 2c R1 Prairie Depot Mon 39 B tel.

Bobcock, E. G. (Blanch) farmer T 60a 3h 1c R1 Prairie Depot Mon 45.

BOBEL, ADAM (Elizabeth) 5 ch farmer T 200a 6h 3c R1 Haskins Mid 49 B tel.

Bobel, Catherine housekeeper O H&L Tontogany Wash Ind tel.

Bobel, Chas. 2 ch carpenter T H&L Haskins Mid B tel.

Bobel, Christ RD Tontogany Wash.

Bobel, Freda (dau George) housekeeper R1 Tontogany Wash 38 Ind tel.

Bobel, George (Maggie) 3 ch farmer O 33a 8h 2c R1 Tontogany Wash 38 Ind tel.

Bobel, Mary (dau Catherine) milliner Tontogany Wash Ind tel.

Bockbrader, Anne R4 Bowling Green Cen 114.

BOCKBRADER, CARL laborer R1 Pemberville Fre 58.

Bockbrader, Mrs. Fred RD Luckey Tro.

Bockbrader, F. H. cattle RD Bowling Green Cen.

BOCKBRADER, GEO. F. (son Louisa) farm laborer R1 Luckey Tro 22 Ind tel.

Bockbrader, Henry (Amelia) 3 ch farmer T 120a 4h 5c R1 Walbridge Lake 16 B tel.

Bockbrader, H. H. (Mary) 4 ch farmer O 80a 3h 5c R3 Pemberville Fre 20 B tel.

Brockbrader, H. W. T H&L 1h R4 Bowling Green Cen 102.

Bockbrader, Ida (dau Louisa) housekeeper R1 Luckey Tro 22 Ind tel.

BOCKBRADER, J. H. (Dora) 4 ch farmer T 40a 2h 1c R1 Pemberville Cen 117.

Bockbrader, Mrs. Louisa 3 ch farmer 80a 3h 5c R1 Luckey Tro 22 Ind tel.

Bockbrader, Wm. (Minnie) 6 ch farmer O 80a 4h 3c R4 Bowling Green Cen 114.

Bockbroder, Albert R4 Bowling Green Cen 114.

Bockbroder, H. J. T H&L R4 Bowling Green Cen 102.

Bockenhauer, Christ RD Haskins Mid.

Bockenhauer, Louise RD Haskins Mid.

Bockover, Byrant farmer O 18a 6h 4c R1 Bradner Fre 86.

Bockover, J. Loy Bradner Fre.

Bockstete, Frank (Cora) 3 ch farmer O 40a 2h 4c R4 Bowling Green Cen 67.

Boehmer, Jacob (Ellen) carpenter O H&L Center St Wes B tel.

Boerne, August Rossford Ros.

Bogan, Harry (Imo) 1 ch laborer T H&L Rossford Ros.

BOGGS, CHAS. (Mertie) 5 ch farmer T 114a 10h 7c R3 Prairie Depot Mon 42 B tel.

Boggs, Elza (Clara) 2 ch farmer T 160a 4h 3c Rudolph Lib 79.

Boggs, Milton (Mary) farmer O 9a 1h E Toledo St East Toledo Lake Ind tel.

BOGGS, O. B. (Lily) 2 ch farmer T 40a 4h 1c R1 Prairie Depot Mon 45.

Bogle, Chas. W. RD North Baltimore Hen.

BOHN, H. H. (Hattie) 1 ch oil pumper T H&L R1 Bowling Green Pla 34 Ind tel.

Bohnlein, Chas. RD North Baltimore Hen.

Bohring, Charles (Zella A.) laborer T H&L Harrison St Bloomdale Blo.

Boice, Boyd (Audean) farmer T H&L 1h 1c R1 Risingsun Per 98.

Boice, Ella ret T H&L R1 Risingsun Per 98.

Boice, Harold (son Ella) laborer R1 Risingsun Per 98.

Boice, Sella (Bertha) farmer T 170a 2h 1c R1 Fostoria Per 127 Ind tel.

Boidik, Chas. (Agnes) 2 ch glass worker O H&L Box 402 Rossford Ros.

BOLKENHAUER, CHRIST (Louise) farmer O 123a 2h 4c R1 Haskins Mid 54 B tel.

Boland, Alonzo 1 ch farmer T 95a 4h R1 Hoytsville Jac 114 Ind tel.

Bolander, Geo. P. J. (Florence) 2 ch laborer T H&L Luckey Tro.

Bolander, John F. (son Phillip) engineer Luckey Tro.

BOLANDER, PHILLIP, SR., (Mary) 5 ch foreman & engineer O H&L Luckey Tro.

Bolander, Phillip H., Jr. (son Phillip) clerk Luckey Tro.

Bolander, Zoe (dau Phillip) milliner Luckey Tro.

BOLLARD, JOS. (Mary) 2 ch farmer T 60a 4h 2c R1 Tontogany Pla 19 Ind tel.

Bollenbacher, H. (Maud) 2 ch farmer T 80a 3h 4c R2 Weston Pla 17 Ind tel.

Bolles, Art 2 ch farmer T R2 Custar Mil 16.

BOLLINGER, ELIAS farmer O 40a 6h 5c R1 Portage Por 102.

36

BOLLINGER, JACOB farmer O 40a 6h 5c R1 Portage Por 102.

Bollinger, John (Clara) 1 ch farmer O 80a 6h 6c R3 Prairie Depot Por 96.

Bollinger, Lydia farmer O 80a R1 Portage Por 102.

Bollinger, Mrs. Wm. cattle RD Portage Por.

Bollini, Robt. Luckey Tro.

Bolton, F. W. (Mary) butcher T 14a 1h R1 Tontogany Wash 39 B & Ind tels.

Bolton, R. L. Bloomdale Blo.

Boltz, Clarence cattle RD Rudolph Por.

Bomer, Alice cattle RD Prairie Depot Por.

Bomer, Chas. (Rosa) 3 ch farmer O 36a 2h 2c R2 Pairie Depot Por 118.

Bomer, Fred (Mollie) farmer O 4a 1h 1c R2 Pairie Depot Por 118.

Bomlitz, Henry (Edith) farmer T 76a 2h 1c R4 Bowling Green Por 93 Ind tel.

Bomnitz, Wm. (Mary) farmer O 76a 2h 2c RD Bowling Green Por 95.

Bond, E. D. bakery Main St Bloomdale Blo B & Ind tels.

Bond, J. F. RD North Baltimore Hen.

Bond, W. E. RD North Baltimore Hen.

Boner, William A. (Ella) 1 ch well driller T H&L R2 Perrysburg Pbg 2.

Bonham, F. F. expressman bds J. D. Halsey Milton Center Mil.

BONNELL, V. R. R1 Risingsun.

BONNER, IRA (Alice) 6 ch concrete contractor O 20a 1h 2c R2 Pairie Depot Por 79 Ind tel.

Bonner, Wm. Walbridge Lake.

Bonsen, Charley O. (Verna) 2 ch oil pumper T 1h Bays Lib 106.

Book, George (Belle) 1 ch farmer 2h Harrison St Bloomdale Blo B & Ind tels.

Bookman, Mark (Ella) 2 ch farmer T 100a 3h 2c R4 Bowling Green Cen 20.

Boom, F. R. Freeport Mon.

Booorom, S. M. (Mary E.) 2 ch printer O H&L Grand Rapids Gr Rs Ind tel.

BOOYER, PETER B. (Mary J.) farmer O 40a 2h 2c R1 Jerry City Blo 67.

Borcherding, Emanuel laborer R1 Luckey Web 71 B tel.

Borcherding, F. W. Luckey Tro.

Borcherding, H. F. Luckey Web.

Bordman, E. N. (Harriett) 3 ch stock grain & general produce O 434a 13h 30c W Main St Weston Wes Ind tel.

BORDNER, A. L. R1 Prairie Depot.

Bordner, Frank (Martha) quarryman O H&L Findlay St Portage Por Ind tel.

Bordner, Geo. (Nellie) 3 ch farmer O 120a 4h 10c R1 Weston Lib 50 B tel.

Bordner, I. (Mary) farmer O 125a 4h 9c R1 Weston Lib 44 Ind tel.

Bordner, Jerry (Vina) 8 ch farmer O 74a R1 Weston Lib 50 B tel.

Bordner, Roy (Nellie) 1 ch farmer T 74a 5h 9c R1 Weston Lib 50 Ind tel.

Bordock, Bettie housekeeper R2 Prairie Depot Por 129 Ind tel.

Boren, Mrs. Erma laborer T Pemberville Fre 40.

BORN, REV. JOHN (Elizabeth) 1 ch minister Stony Ridge Tro Ind tel.

Born, Margaret (dau John) stenographer Stony Ridge Tro Ind tel.

BOROUGH, A. E. Weston Wes.

Borough, H. G. (May) 2 ch clerk T H&L Tontogany Wash Ind tel.

Borough, J. W. (Zella M.) 1 ch cashier T H&L RD North Baltimore Hen B & Ind tels.

BOROUG, W. I. R3 North Baltimore.

Borrel, Chas. (Ethel) 1 ch carpenter O H&L Rossford Ros.

Borsos, Mike (Mattie) 5 ch farmer T 60a 2h 2c R2 Curtice Ros 34.

Bortel, Amie Grand Rapids Gr Rs.

Bortel, A. W. (Stella) 2 ch carpenter T H&L Summer St Box 225 Weston Wes Ind tel.

Bortel, Dick (May) 2 ch laborer O H&P Grand Rapids Gr Rs Ind tel.

Bortel, F. L. (Rose) 1 ch grocery O H&L & store Mermill Por Ind tel.

BORTEL, IRA (Edna) 3 ch farmer T 55a 3h 1c R1 Grand Rapids Gr Rs 31.

Bortel, John (Nellie) 1 ch ret O H&L Grand Rapids Gr Rs Ind tel.

Bortel, Lewis (Jewel) mason T H&L Grand Rapids Gr Rs.

Bortel, Lewis (Susan J.) dry good store O H&L Grand Rapids Gr Rs.

Bortel, Mrs. M. B. 1 ch Center Weston.

Bortel, W. C. (Nancy M.) 1 ch tinner T H&L Grand Rapids Gr Rs.

Bortle, Clyde (Nancy) 1 ch laborer T H&L Grand Rapids Gr Rs.

Bortle, Henry C. (Elizabeth) 2 ch farmer O H&L 1h Grand Rapids Gr Gs.

BORTLE, J. H. 3 ch farmer O 88a 4h 4c R1 Grand Rapids Gr Rs 7 Ind tel.

Bortlett, C. E. tailor O H&L RD Bowling Green Por.

Borton, John (Martha) laborer O H&L Grand Rapids Gr Rs.

Bosler, A. D. R1 North Baltimore Hen.

Bosler, Augustus H. (Annie) farmer T 100a 6h 11c R3 North Baltimore Blo 36 B & Ind tels.

Bosler, Gus RD North Baltimore Blo.

Bossard, Jacob Perrysburg Pbg.

Bosse, Henry (Mary) 2 ch farmer T 111a 4h 5c R3 Pemberville Fre 25.

Bosse, H. Fred'k Pemberville Fre.

Bosse, John (Julia) 2 ch farmer O 50a 3h 6c R3 Pairie Depot Mon 9.

Bosse, Wm. (Mary) 3 ch farmer O 40a 2h 4c R1 Pemberville Fre 69.

Bossler, E. farmer O 170a 1h 1c R2 Pairie Depot Por 126 Ind tel.

Bossler, F. L. (Minnie B.) 3 ch school teacher & farmer T 100a 5h 6c R2 Prairie Depot Por 124 Ind tel.

Bossler, H. O. Pairie Depot Blo.

Bostdorff, Allen (Jennie) 1 ch teamster T H&L 2h Haskins Mid.

BOSTDORFF, EARL (Lucy) 2 ch mariner T 140a 6h 3c R2 Haskins Mid 21 B tel.

Bostdorff, John (Mary) 2 ch farmer O 15a 1h 1c R1 Haskins Mid 43.

Bostdorf, J. F. Haskins Mid.

Bostdorf, J. H. R2 Perrysburg Pbg.

Bostick, T. O. (Zona) 1 ch farmer T 120a 7h R1 Portage Por 56.

Bouback, Nick (Mary) 3 ch glass worker O H&L 287 Walnut St Rossford Ros.

Boudrie, J. L. (Merl) 2 ch meat market 1h 1c Cygnet Blo 6.

BOUGHTON, SEYMOUR (Minnie) 5 ch watchmaker O 8a 1h 2c R1 Millbury Lake 131.

Boulton, Fred (Maud) 1 ch operator H&L Grand Rapids Gr Rs.

Bourbina, J. E. (Rose) 5 ch foreman O H&L 120 Oak St Rossford Ros.

Bourchereing, F. W. (Emma) 3 ch farmer O 80a 5h 7c R1 Luckey Tro 20 Ind tel.

Bourchereing, John W. (son F. W.) R1 Luckey Tro 20 Ind tel.

Bourt, Frank (Jennie) 1 ch clerk O H&L Rossford Ros.

Bovie, Charles (Martha) 2 ch farmer T 80a 6h 2c R2 Bowling Green Pla 63.

Bovie, Jacob B. (Lydia A.) 2 ch ret O 60a 2h 3c R1 Pairie Depot Mon 13.

Bowe, Chas. H. Risingsun Mon.

BOWE, FRANK (Audora) 3 ch oil worker O H R1 Portage Lib 83 Ind tel.

Bowe, Harry laborer O H&L 1h Risingsun Mon.

Bowe, Mrs. Mary ret O H&L Risingsun Mont.

Bowe, Mike (Maud) 3 ch ret O H&L Risingsun Mon.

Bowe, Wm. F. (Margaret) pumper O H&L Stahl St Bradner Mon B tel.

Bowen, Floyd C. (Lula) laborer H 1h 1c R1 Rudolph Lib 67.

Bowen, Mrs. Tillie O 4a R1 Rudolph Lib 67.

Bower, A. F. (Ida) 1 ch farmer O 80a 4h 9c R1 Risingsun Mon 81 B tel.

Bower, A. J. West Millgrove Per.

Bower, Burhl (son William J.) school teacher bds R1 Weston Mil 55.

Bower, Carl (son William J.) student bds R1 Weston Mil 55.

Bower, Christopher Perrysburg Pbg.

Bower, Clarence Weston Mil.

Bower, Mrs. Cora 3 ch ret O H&L 1h 1c Haskins Mid B tel.

Bower, Ella Risingsun Mon.

BOWER, FRED (Jennie) 1 ch ret O 60a 4c R1 Risingsun Mon 84 B tel.

Bower, Grace RD North Baltimore Hen.

Bower, Harold (son A. F.) farmer R1 Risingsun Mon 81.

Bower, Ida Risingsun Mon.

Bower, I. S. (Elizabeth) 1 ch doctor O H&L Second St Perrysburg Pbg B tel.

Bower, Jno. C. Risingsun Mon.

Bower, J. P. (Manda) farmer O 90a 6h 6c R2 Prairie Depot Por 108 B tel.

Bower, J. W. (Pearl) farmer O 60a 2h 1c R1 Weston Mil 54 Ind tel.

Bower, Loniwa (dau F.) housekeeper 3h R1 Risingsun Mon 84 B tel.

Bower, Mary O. Weston Mil.

Bower, Paul (son A. F.) farmer 1h R1 Risingsun Mon 81.

Bower, Ruth E. Weston Mil.

Bower, Wm. (Ella) 1 ch driller T H&L 7th St Perrysburg Pbg.

BOWER, WALTER G. R1 Weston.

BOWER, WILLIAM J. (Elizabeth) O 60a 4h 1c R1 Weston Mil 55 Ind tel.

Bowerman, A. W. (Martha) 3 ch farmer T 100a 8h 3c R1 Rudolph Lib 66 Ind tel.

Bowers, Bert (Sadie) 2 ch sawmill T H&L 2h West Millgrove Per 68.

Bowers, Charlie (Maud) 3 ch laboring man O H&L Grand Rapids Gr Rs.

Bowers, Clarence (Ruth) T 98a 3h 5c R3 Weston Mil 89 Ind tel.

Bowers, Carl C. (Lucy) 1 ch farmer & engineer T 40a 1h 1c R2 Weston Wash 13 Ind tel.

Bowers, Daniel (Mattie) 1 ch carpenter T H&L West Millgrove Per 69.

Bowers, Ed. (Jane) ret O 5a 1h 1c R1 East Toledo Lake 132.

Bowers, Ella ret O H&L Risingsun Mon.

Bowers, Flora (Angeline) 1 ch janitor O H&L Risingsun Mon.

Bowers, F. E. (Lena) attorney O H&L Locust St Perrysburg Pbg B tel.

Bowers, Geo. (Ella) farmer O 40a 4h 2c R2 Weston Wash 14.

Bowers, I. S. Perrysburg Pbg.

Bowers, Mary O. RD North Baltimore Hen.

Bowers, Merlin (Louise) doctor O H&L Second St Perrysburg Pbg B tel.

Bowers, Walter C. (Oma) farmer O 80a 6h 8c R1 Weston Mil 55.

Bowersmith, Joseph (son Geo.) typesetter R2 Custar Mil.

Bowland, Geo. D. Walbridge Lake.

BOWLES, A. H. (Emma) farmer O 40a 2h 2c R3 Weston Mil 7 Ind tel.

Bowles, Charles (son W. M.) farm hand R3 Weston Mil 7.

Bowles, Geo. (son James) student Milton Center Mil.

BOWLES, JAMES (Sarah) ret O H&L Milton Center Mil.

Bowles, Jno. W. Weston Mil.

Bowles, W. M. (Emma) 6 ch farmer O 40a 3h 3c R3 Weston Mil 7 Ind tel.

Bowlus, Harry M. (Bertha) 4 ch proprietor of store O H&L Pemberville Fre 40 B tel.

BOWLUS, LLOYD G. Pemberville Fre.

Bowman, Chris Lime City Pbg.

BOWMAN, D. A. (Alila) 2 ch barber O H&L Verango St Cygnet Blo.

Bowman, Liza 5 ch housekeeper T H&L cor Summer & Oak Sts Weston Wes B tel.

BOWMAN, MILO L. R2 Box 71 North Baltimore.

Bowman, W. A. Millbury Lake.

Boxted, Frank cattle RD Bowling Green Cen.

BOYER, A. E. (Bertha) 5 ch farmer T 100a 4h 4c Bays Lib 99 Ind tel.

Boyer, Benj. F. (son D. H.) musician R1 Deshler Jac 25 Ind tel.

Boyer, Chas. H. (son D. H.) student R1 Deshler Jac 25 Ind tel.

Boyer, D. H. (Agnes) 8 ch farmer O 65a 7h 9c R1 Deshler Jac 25 Ind tel.

Boyer, E. O. RD Weston Lib.

Boyer, Harriet L. (dau D. H.) school teacher R1 Deshler Jac 25 Ind tel.

Boyer, Jos. (Frances) 1 ch farmer O 50a 2h 3c R3 Prairie Depot Por 111.

Boyer, J. A. RD Deshler Jac.

Boyer, J. L. (Ellen) 2 ch farmer O 80a 5h 2c R1 Weston Lib 14.

Boysen, Christ (Lydia) 3 ch farmer O 50a 1h 2c Latchie Lake 96 B tel.

Boysen, Sophia 1 ch ret O 20a 1c R1 Genoa Lake 45 B tel.

Bracey, Phillip (Martha) farmer O 2 H&L 1h 1c Sugar Ridge Mid 63.

Bradfield, Addie Tontogany Wash.

Bradfield, D. H. Pemberville Fre.

Bradley, Geo. W. farmer O 30a 1h 4c R2 Bowling Green Pla 92 B tel.

Bradley, L. O. (Floria) 1 ch laborer T 3a R1 Lime City Pbg 59.

Bradner, A. J. concrete contractor & farmer O 13 1-3a 1h Hatton Per 84 B & Ind tel.

BRADNER, G. A. (Daisy) 5 ch cement worker O H&L 1c E Sandusky St West Millgrove Per.

Bradshaw, Charles W. (Louisa E.) 4 ch contractor & builder O 5a 4c Oak St Weston Wes Ind tel.

BRADSHAW, C. B. Box 140 Weston Wes.

Bradshaw, C. H. (Bertha) 1 ch farmer O 40a 3h 3c R2 Prairie Depot Por 79 Ind tel.

Bradshaw, Florence Custar Milton.

Bradshaw, Gladys M. (dau Chas. W.) bookkeeper Oak St Weston Wes.

Bradshaw, G. W. (Florence) 4 ch farmer O 128a 4h 9c R2 Custar Mil 50 Ind tel.

Brakeman, A. Prairie Depot Mon.

Brand, A. J. Haskins Mid.

Brand, Mrs. Effie 1 ch farmer O 106a R2 Prairie Depot Por 122.

Brand, E. F. (Leila) 3 ch farmer T 134a 5h 5c R1 Haskins Mid 38 B tel.

Brand, F. J. (Louise) 1 ch ret O H&L Haskins Mid B tel.

Brand, F. W. (Minnie) 3 ch farmer T 120a 1c R1 Rudolph Lib 40.

BRANDEBERRY, A. E. (Garnett) hardware store T H&L Risingsun Mon.

BRANDEBERRY, CHARLES (Martha F.) 8 ch farmer O 230a 4h 25c R1 Bloomdale Blo 53 B & Ind tel.

BRANDEBERRY, CORA R2 Bloomdale.

Brandeberry, Clyde F. (son Chas.) R1 Bloomdale Blo 53 B & Ind tels.

BRANDEBERRY, C. W. (Comelia) auto O H&L 2h Sandusky St West Millgrove Per B tel.

Brandeberry, David (Lydia) ret minister O H&L S Main St Bloomdale Blo.

Brandeberry, Emma R. T H&L 1c R1 Bloomdale Blo 112.

BRANDEBERRY, FRANK (Annie L.) supt of infirmary R5 Bowling Green Cen 35 B & Ind tels.

Brandeberry, F. E. (Emma) 2 ch farmer O 145a 9h 12c R1 Fostoria Per 122 Ind tel.

Brandeberry, Geo. farmer O 160a R1 Fostoria Per 77 Ind tel.

Brandeberry, Guy (Lena) 1 ch farmer O 120a 3h 3c R1 Fostoria Per 77 Ind tel.

Brandeberry, Harry (May) 1 ch farmer O 80a 3h 5c RD Bloomdale Per 35.

Brandeberry, H. farmer O 39¼a 3h 1c R2 Bloomdale Blo 126.

Brandeberry, Ida (dau of W. N.) R1 Bloomdale Blo 51 B & Ind tel.

Brandeberry, Ira (Elizabeth) 1 ch laborer 1h 1c R2 Bloomdale Blo 133 B & Ind tel.

Brandeberry, I. E. (Manda) 2 ch farmer T 140a 2h 10c R1 Bloomdale Blo 127 B & Ind tel.

Brandeberry, Jos. F. Pemberville Fre.

Brandeberry, J. W. (Flora) 1 ch farmer O 330a 9h 30c R1 Fostoria Per 126 Ind tel.

Brandeberry, L. C. (Bertha) 2 ch farmer O 80a 3h 12c R1 Fostoria Per 74 Ind tel.

Brandeberry, Myron (son W. N.) R1 Bloomdale Blo 51 B & Ind tels.

Brandeberry, O. Bloomdale Blo.

Brandeberry, S. E. (Lucinda) 1 ch farmer O 100a 4h 4c R2 Bloomdale Per 59 B tel.

Brandeberry, Wm. (Cornelia) livery & feed stable H&L 2h West Millgrove Per 69 B tel.

Brandeberry, W. N. (Margaret A.) 1 ch farmer O 130a 4h 12c R1 Bloomdale Blo 51 B & Ind tels.

Branden, John (Tracy) ret O H&L 20a 1h Prairie Depot Mon B tel.

Brandhuber, Miss Celia Perrysburg Pbg.

Brandhuber, J. F. (Gertrude) 1 ch furniture business O H&L Front St Perrysburg Pbg B tel.

Brandon, H. P. Bradner Mon.

Brandon, J. C. oil worker S Main St Bradner Mon.

Brandon, J. H. Freeport Mon.

BRANDON, M. A. housekeeper T H&L Pemberville Fre.

Brandt, A. J. (Anna) 3 ch hardware O H&L 1h Haskins Mid 35 B tel.

Bratt, Mrs. A. O. 6 ch O H R1 Rudolph Lib 70 Ind tel.

Braun, August Pemberville Fre.

Braun, Chas. A. Perrysburg Pbg.

Brecht, Ora Jerry City Blo.

Breidt, Mrs. Mary ret T H&L Perrysburg Pbg.

Breisack, John (Mary) 5 ch farmer T 70a 2h 1c R2 Perrysburg Mid 2 B tel.

Brenamen, Martin E. (Alma) farmer O 80a 6h 1c Longley Per 99 Ind tel.

Breneman, Calvin (Victorine) ret O H&L West Millgrove Per 69.

Brengartner, C. (Anna) clothing store T H&L Prairie Depot Mon.

Brentlinger, Abraham Hoytsville Jac.

Brentlinger, S. B. (Levina) woodworker O H&L Hoytsville Jac.

Brentlinger, S. W. (Mina) laborer T H&L R1 Rudolph Lib 109.

Bresler, C. R. (Ellen) 3 ch farmer R2 Prairie Depot Per 7 B & Ind tels.

Bresler, J. T. (Laura) 2 ch farmer R2 Prairie Depot Per 6 B & Ind tels.

Bresler, Philip (Sarah Ann) ret O H&L 1h 1c Prairie Depot Mon B tel.

BRESSLER, G. F. (Leona) 4 ch farmer O 40a 3h 4c R1 Prairie Depot Mon 44.

Bressler, Mina Pemberville Fre.

Bressler, W. H. (Silva) 2 ch farmer O 40a 3h 3c R1 Prairie Depot Mon 44.

BREVER, CORA boarding house T H&L S Garfield St Bloomdale Blo B & Ind tels.

Brewer, Adney (Electa) 4 ch laborer O H&L Prairie Depot Mon.

BREWSTER, C. O. (Josephine) clerk O H&L Grand Rapids Gr Rs.

Brewster, Geo. (Edith) 1 ch railroader O H&L Walbridge Lake.

Brickel, H. E. oil worker O H&L Verango St Cygnet Blo.

BRICKEL, JAMES (Jane) 4 ch oil worker O H&L Cygnet Blo 6.

Bridges, Carrie A. housekeeper O joint deed City St Haskins Mid.

Bridges, F. W. oil contractor T H&L City St Haskins Mid.

Bridges, Jessie M. housekeeper Haskins Mid.

Briggs, Chas. H. (son James) laborer R1 Luckey Tro 20.

Briggs, Eva (dau James) housekeeper R1 Luckey Tro 20.

Briggs, Hattie H. (dau James) housekeeper R1 Luckey Tro 20.

BRIGGS, JAMES 7 ch farmer O 30a 2h 3c R1 Luckey Tro 20.

Briggs, Robert D. (son James) laborer R1 Luckey Tro 20.

Bright, J. E. (Emma) teamster T H&L Risingsun Mon.

Brillhart, Ben. (Etta) sexton O 10a 1h R1 Grand Rapids Wash 58 Ind tel.

Brillhart, Frank (Alice) 2 ch farmer O 64a 8h 4c R1 Grand Rapids Wash 68 Ind tel.

Brim, Geo. T. (Clara) farmer O 120a 6h 9c R3 Bowling Green Pla 84 Ind tel.

Brim, Harriet S. Millbury Lake.

BRIM, JAMES E. (Lena) 8 ch farmer O 80a 3h 9c R3 Bowling Green Pla 82 Ind tel.

Brim, Llyod (Emma) farmer T 116a 8h 24c Latchie Lake 95 B tel.

Brim, Logan (Ida) carpenter O H&L Walbridge Lake.

BRIM, OTTO R. (Selena) 3 ch coal dealer O H&L 1h Walbridge Lake. See adv.

Brim, W. W. (Harriett S.) 1 ch poultry raising O H&L 4h 1c Millbury Lake Ind tel.

Bringman, Alice (dau Hones) housekeeper R1 Lemoyne Tro 81 B tel.

Bringman, Bernhard (Ida) 2 ch farmer 20a 3c R1 Luckey Tro 27 Ind tel.

Bringman, Carrie (dau Hones) housekeeper R1 Lemoyne Tro 81 B tel.

Bringman, Henry (son of Hones) farm hand R1 Lemoyne Tro 81 B tel.

BRINGMAN, HONES (Anna) 10 ch farmer O 190a 6h 15c R1 Lemoyne Tro 81 B tel.

Bringman, Mrs. Ida Luckey Tro.

Bringman, Robert (son Bernhard) repairman R1 Luckey Tro 27.

BRINK, GEO. (Laura) 2 ch oil producer & hardware O 3a 5h R2 Custar Lib 34 B & Ind tels. See adv.

BRINK, LESTER E. R2 Custar.

Brinker, Fred (Anna) 6 ch farmer O 100a 4h 7c R1 Lime City Pbg 42 B tel.

Brinker, Henry farmer O 60a 2h 3c R1 Dunbridge Web 53 B tel.

Brinker, Jno. Dunbridge Web.

Brinker, Mrs. Julia 3 ch O H&L Luckey Tro Ind tel.

Brinker, Wm., Jr. (son Wm.) farmer R1 Lime City Pbg 38.

Brinker, Wm., Sr. (Mary) farmer O 140a 5h 3c R1 Lime City Pbg 38.

BRINKMEIER, O. L. (Anna) 3 ch farmer & stock raiser T 60a 3h 4c R1 Dunbridge Web 54 B tel. See adv.

BRISBIN, A. B. (Mary) 5 ch farmer T 120a 4h 5c R1 Rudolph Lib 79 Ind tel.

BRISBIN, C. H. (Minnie) 3 ch school superintendent O H&L Third St Jerry City Por Ind tel.

Brisbin, Lavina Rudolph Lib.

Briston, Oliver Millbury Lake.

BRITSCH, A. G. (Blanche G.) gardener O 10a & greenhouse 2h Wales Road East Toledo Ros 15 Ind tel.

Britten, Charles (Caroline) 1 ch farmer O 95a 5h 4c R1 Perrysburg Pbg 115 B tel.

Britton, Lester farmer 1h R1 Perrysburg Pbg 115 B tel.

BRITTON, MRS. RALPH R1 Perrysburg.

Brobst, Chas. RD North Baltimore Hen.

BROBST, HENRY (Mary) 3 ch farmer O 115a 7h 12c R1 North Baltimore Hen 49.

Brockbrader, Fred H. (Mary) 3 ch farmer T 40a 2h 3c R4 Bowling Green Cen 105 Ind tel.

Brockbrader, Henry (Mary) 1 ch farmer O 100a 4h 5c R3 Pemberville Fre 16 B tel.

Brocke, Wm. (Mary) 4 ch farmer O 80a 4h 6c R2 Dunbridge Mid 75.

Brodersen, Albert (Minnie) groceries T H&L Stony Ridge Tro Ind tel.

Broderson, Benjamin (Elizabeth) 3 ch farmer 38a 2h 1c R1 Stony Ridge Tro 10 Ind tel.

"Train Up a Child in the Way He Should Go."

Broderson, Emma (dau Benj.) house-keeper R1 Stony Ridge Tro 10 Ind tel.

Brohost, Wm. Luckey Tro.

Broka, Arson Perrysburg Pbg.

Broka, A. D. (Julia) 5 ch farmer T 265a 8h 3c R3 Bowling Green Web 13 B tel.

Broka, Harold (son A. D.) farmer R3 Bowling Green Web 13.

Broka, Henry (Clara) 1 ch ret O H&L Sixth St Perrysburg Pbg B tel.

Broka, Rutherford W. farmer R3 Bowling Green Web 13.

Bronson, C. D. grocery store O Bairdstown Blo 48 B & Ind tels.

Bronson, E. 3 ch concrete business O H&L Main St Jerry City Por.

Bronson, J. M. Bloomdale Blo.

Brook, Homer (Margaret) farmer T 140a 5h 1c R5 Bowling Green Cen 76 Ind tel.

Brooks, Clarence (Orla) 2 ch farmer T 90a 6h 7c Bloomdale Blo 116 B & Ind tels.

Brooks, Corena RD North Baltimore Hen.

Brooks, C. A. Haskins Mid.

Brooks, G. A. Bloomdale Per.

Brooks, Henry (Libbie) carpenter O H&L Haskins Wash 98 B tel.

Brooks, Herbert (Rosa) farmer O 80a 3h 7c R2 Bloomdale Per 21 B & Ind tels.

Brooks, H. R. ditcher & laborer R2 Custar Jac 97.

Brooks, Nierle (Bertha) oil man & teamster Railroad St Bairdstown Blo.

Brooks, T. L. (May) 3 ch painter 1c Main St Bairdstown Blo.

BROOKS, W. R. (Ida) 1 ch farmer & thresher O 10a 4h 4c R2 Custar Jac 97 B tel.

Brooster, Charlie (Josephine) dry goods clerk O H&L Grand Rapids Gr Rs.

Brossia, Conrad (Lillian) 2 ch teamster T 4a 2h 1c R3 Perrysburg Pbg 77.

Brossia, Edward (Ida) 1 ch farming T 20a 2h 1c R3 Perrysburg Pbg 129.

BROSSIA, GEORGE (Cora) 3 ch farmer T 120a 4h 3c R1 Millbury Lake 126.

Brossia, George (Clara) farmer O 40a 3h 2c R3 Perrysburg Pbg 129.

Brossia, Henry (Marjorie) 3 ch farmer T 40a 2h 1c R3 Perrysburg Pbg 129.

Brossia, Jno. RD Perrysburg Pbg.

Brossia, Phillip (Louise) 1 ch farmer O 80a 3h 3c R3 Perrysburg Pbg 84. ·

BROSSIA, WM. C. (Fredick) 5 ch farmer O 50a 3h 4c R3 Perrysburg Pbg 77 Ind tel.

Brossia, W. F. (Mary) 2 ch farmer O 74a 2h R3 Perrysburg Pbg 130.

Brotherly, Geo. (Sarah) ret O H&L Grand Rapids Gr Rs.

Brough, Ed. ret bds R1 LeMoyne Tro 42.

BROUGH, EDWARD (Mary) 4 ch farmer O 40a 4h 7c R1 Genoa Tro 38 B tel.

Brough, Ely (Caroline) 5 ch farmer O 34a R1 Genoa Tro 41.

Brough, Joseph farmer O 40a 4h 7c R1 Genoa Tro 38 B tel.

Brough, J. R. general store O stock Lemoyne Tro Ind tel.

Brough, Robert (son Ely) T 4h 2c R1 Genoa Tro 41.

BROUGH, SIMON (Anna) 7 ch farmer O 72a 7h 3c R1 Genoa Tro 38.

Brown, Alta (dau S.) dressmaker Pemberville Fre 40.

Brown, Archie (son Mrs. Geo. Young) farm hand R1 Deshler Jac 6 B tel.

BROWN, ARTHUR farmer O 63a 3h 4c R2 Bowling Green Cen 5 Ind tel.

Brown, August RD Dunbridge Mid.

Brown, A. J. (Sarah) 2 ch laborer O H&L Latchie Lake 83.

Brown, Baker pumper Evans St Bradner Mon.

Brown, Catherine Grand Rapids Gr Rs.

Brown, Chas. 1 ch office man T Box 82 Rossford Ros.

Brown, Chas. (Hattie) 4 ch pumper O H&L Risingsun Mon.

Brown, Charles (Mary) 3 ch plumber O H&L 6th St Perrysburg Pbg B tel.

Brown, Chas. E. Pemberville Fre.

Brown, Chas. N. (Myrtle) 4 ch clerk O H&L Third St Portage Por.

Brown, Clay (Emma) 3 ch farmer O 40a 4h 4c R1 Grand Rapids Gr Rs 31.

Brown, C. H. Risingsun Mon.

BROWN, C. M. (Elizabeth) farmer O 80a 1h 2c R1 Haskins Mid 54 B tel.

Brown, C. W. station agent Main St Bloomdale Blo B & Ind tels.

BROWN, D. C. (Hester Anne) 6 ch farmer O H&L 5h 5c R2 Deshler Jac 8/

BROWN, EARL (Lucy) 5 ch gen merchandise O H&L 5h Haskins Mid 35 B tel.

Brown, Edward (Carrie) 2 ch foreman O H&L Box 456 Rossford Ros Ind tel.

Brown, Edwin (Laura) 2 ch ret T H&L Front St Perrysburg Pbg B tel.

Brown, Elizabeth 8 ch O H&L Milton St Weston.

Brown, Elmer (Katie) 1 ch farmer O 20a 2h 4c R1 Weston Milton 77 Ind tel.

Brown, Emma 4 ch practical nurse O H&L Walnut St Weston Wes.

Brown, E. (Alice) 3 ch ret T H&L Front St Perrysburg Pbg B tel.

Brown, Mrs. E. J. ret O H&L Box 82 Rossford Ros.

Brown, Frank Bloomdale Blo.

Brown, Fred RD Dunbridge Mid.

BROWN, F. O. (Edith) 1 ch farmer T 5h 5c R1 Hoytsville Jac 47 B tel.

BROWN, F. S. Bloomdale Blo 121.

BROWN, GEO. (Nellie) 2 ch painter O H&2L R1 Haskins Mid 53 B tel.

Brown, George (son Lawrence) cooper Weston.

Brown, Geo. Marion (son Geo. W.) teacher Lemoyne Tro 36 B tel.

BROWN, GEO. W. (Mary) 6 ch farmer O 40a 3h 8c Lemoyne Tro 36 B tel.

Brown, Harriett Grand Rapids Wes.

BROWN, HOWARD (Allie) farmer 51a 3h 9c R1 Bowling Green Pla 74 Ind tel.

Brown, H. A. (Eliza) 5 ch farmer T 170a 6h 3c R1 Haskins Mid 86 B tel.

BROWN, H. C. (Maud) 1 ch laborer O H&L 1h R1 Haskins Mid 59.

Brown, John (Hannah) 2 ch O H&L Russ St Weston Ind tel.

Brown, John, Jr. RD Dunbridge Mid.

Brown, Jno. F. RD Dunbridge Mid.

BROWN, J. B. (Nancy Bell) 3 ch farmer & sawmill T 30a 3h R1 Jerry City Por 28.

Brown, J. E. oil well driller Walnut St Bloomdale Blo.

Brown, J. E. (Olive) 4 ch engineer T H&L East St Bradner Mon.

Brown, Kyle farmer R1 Grand Rapids Gr Rs 12.

Brown, Lawrence (Ida E.) 3 ch cooper O H&L Center St Weston Ind tel.

Brown, Lester (Ann) 2 ch farmer T 80a 3h 3c R2 Haskins Wash 37 Ind tel.

BROWN, MRS. LIBBIE Brown Elm Farm Haskins.

Brown, Mrs. Lucy 6 ch T H&L Jerry St Jerry City Blo.

Brown, Mabel L. (dau Geo. W.) teacher Lemoyne Tro 36 B tel.

Brown, M. N. (son D. C.) farm hand R2 Deshler Jac 8.

Brown, Ola (dau D. C.) housekeeper R2 Deshler Jac 8.

Brown, O. C. (Nellie) 1 ch farmer O 100a 9h R1 Grand Rapids Gr Rs 12 Ind tel.

Brown, Ray (Elsie) 2 ch farmer T 110a 5h 15c R1 Grand Rapids Gr Rs 33 Ind tel.

Brown, Robt. RD Bowling Green Pla.

Brown, R. A. Weston Mil.

Brown, Rubi I. (dau Geo. W.) teacher Lemoyne Tro 36 B tel.

Brown, Sibyl Cygnet Blo.

Brown, Sylvester (Mary) ret O H&L Pemberville Fre 80.

Brown, S. C. (Maud) 4 ch oil man T L 1h 2c R1 North Baltimore Hen 53 Ind tel.

Brown, Thomas (Margaret) laborer O H&L Box 146 Rossford Ros.

BROWN, TODD farmer 51a 3h 9c R1 Bowling Green Pla 74 Ind tel.

Brown, T. J. (Mattie J.) insurance business T 3a R1 East Toledo Lake 116 Ind tel.

Brown, T. S. (Gertrude)˙5 ch laborer O H&L 1h Bloomdale Blo 121 B & Ind tels.

Brown, Walter (Clara) 5 ch farmer O 5a 2h 1c R4 Bowling Green Por 3.

Brown, Walter W. (son Geo. W.) teacher Lemoyne Tro 36 B tel.

BROWN, WARREN (Almyra) 2 ch oil pumper T H&L 1h 1c R1 Rudolph Por 23 Ind tel.

Brown, Wm. Bloomdale Per.

Brown, Wm. D. (Susie) laborer Walnut St Bloomdale Blo B & Ind tel.

BROWN, W. M. (son J. F.) farmer 1h R1 Dunbridge Web 49 B tel.

BROWN, W. S. (Mabel) 5 ch farmer T 57a 2h 1c R2 Dunbridge Pbg 36.

Browne, Esther (dau O. B.) housekeeper R2 Haskins Mid 32.

Browne, Floyd (son O. B.) engineer R2 Haskins Mid 32 B tel.

Browne, O. B. (Bessie) 4 ch farmer T 80a 5h 5c R2 Haskins Mid 32 B tel.

Browneller, C. M. (Nellie M.) 3 ch farmer O 80a 3h 6c R2 Bloomdale Blo 119 B & Ind tels.

Browneller, Geo. (Ida M.) ret farmer O H&L Garfield St Bloomdale Blo.

Broyes, Louis (Anna) school teacher T H&L R1 Le Moyne Tro 31 Ind tel.

Brozsky, Sam junk buyer 1h Teaser St Bairdstown Blo 95 B & Ind tels.

Brubaker, C. B. (Lottie M.) farmer O 80a 7h 5c R1 Bloomdale Blo 95 B & Ind tels.

Brubaker, C. J. 2 ch farmer O 90a 6h Jerry City Blo 81 Ind tel.

Brubaker, G. M. (Stella) farmer O 80a 11h 5c R1 Fostoria Per 14 B & Ind tels.

Brubaker, Harry (son G. M.) R1 Fostoria Per 14 B & Ind tels.

BRUBAKER, JOHN W. (Ada M.) 2 ch farmer O 93a 7h 6c R1 Bloomdale Blo 100 B & Ind tels.

43

Brubaker, Thos. farmer T H&L R2 Prairie Depot Por 129 Ind tel.

Bruce, Emma 2 ch ret O H&L Fifth St Perrysburg Pbg.

Bruce, Jean 1 ch laborer T H&L Fifth St Perrysburg Pbg.

Bruce, Lewis (son M. E.) farmer R2 Dunbridge Mid. 79.

Bruce, M. E. (Lila) 5 ch farmer O 51a 6h 2c R2 Dunbridge Mid 79 Ind tel.

Brueggemeier, Casper (Mary) farmer O 188a 7h 9c R1 Dunbridge Web 59 B tel.

Brueggemeier, Fred Dunbridge Web.

Brueggemeier, Henry (Mame) 1 ch farmer T 4h 5c R1 Dunbridge Web 49 B tel.

Brueggemeier, John RD Luckey Troy.

Brueggemeier, Martin (Edith) farm laborer 3h R1 Dunbridge Web 59.

Brumagem, C. A. (Olga) poultry farm T H&L Washington St Cygnet Blo.

BRUMBAUGH, J. A. (Emma) 7 ch farmer T 160a 3h 7c R2 Custar Lib 19 Ind tel.

BRUNDAGE, MRS. M. 2 ch housekeeper O H&L Prairie Depot Mon.

Bruner, Ida housekeeper 98 Elm St Rossford Ros B tel.

Bruner, I. T. (Sarah) 3 ch farmer O 160a 4h R4 Bowling Green Cen 60 Ind tel.

BRUNHAM, J. E. M.D. physician Prairie Depot. See adv.

Bruning, Alfred (son August) farmer R2 Pemberville Fre 72.

BRUNING, AUGUST (Sophia) 3 ch farmer O 100a 5h 22c R2 Pemberville Fre 42.

Bruning, Chris (Dorelas) 1 ch farmer O 240a R1 Bradner Fre 79 B tel.

Bruning, Earl E. (Hazel) 3 ch farmer T R1 Bradner Fre 79.

Bruning, Fred (Anna) 3 ch r d mail carrier O H&L 1h Pemberville Fre 40 B tel.

Bruning, Henry (Caroline) 2 ch farmer O 245a 6h 2c Pemberville Fre 79 B tel.

Bruning, J. C. Bradner Fre.

Bruning, Otto (son August) college student R2 Pemberville Fre 42.

Brunner, Thomas farm hand bds Taylor St Weston.

BRUNS, G. C. (Edith) 2 ch farmer T 80a 4h 5c R1 Luckey Web 73 B tel.

Bruns, Henry ret O 80a R1 Luckey Web 73 B tel.

Bruns, Irene F. RD Perrysburg Pbg.

Bruns, Wm. (Irene) 1 ch dairy T 20a 3h 15c R3 Perrysburg Pbg 77.

BRUST, G. W. (Ida M.) 2 ch farmer O 84a 3h 5c R1 Pemberville Fre 56.

Bryan, F. A. (Nora) 4 ch mechanic O H&L East St Bradner Mon.

Bryan, George 1 ch ret O H&L East St Bradner Mon.

Bryan, J. C. 7 ch laborer T H&L S Main St Bradner Mon.

Bryan, J. H. Bloomdale Blo.

Bryan, Wm. 1 ch druggist O H&L Stahl St Bradner Mon.

Bryant, Colonel Ed. (Effie) asst adjt gen state of Ohio O H&L Main St Bloomdale Blo B & Ind tels.

Bryant, W. C. (Ella H.) laborer O H & L Harrison & Walnut Sts Bloomdale Blo B & Ind tels.

BUCHANAN, C. N. (Adia) 6 ch farmer O 78a 3h 3c R2 North Baltimore Hen 32 Ind tel.

Buchanan, Mrs. Mabel 6 ch ret O 80a R1 Deshler Jac 32 Ind tel.

BUCHER, AMBROSE (Hazel) 1 ch farmer T H&L 2h 2c R1 Grand Rapids Wash 66 Ind tel.

Buchmann, Martin cattle RD Bowling Green Cen.

Buchmann, Wm. cattle RD Bowling Green Cen.

Buck, A. H. (Julia) 4 ch blacksmith O H&L Luckey Tro.

Buck, A. R. (Estella) 3 ch ret O 80a H& 8Lots 1h 1c Main St Weston Ind tel.

Buck, Elsie 3 ch farmer O 106a 2c R2 Weston Wes 16 Ind tel.

BUCK, FRED (Margaretta) farmer O 25a 1h 2c R3 Perrysburg Pbg 23.

Buck, Hal. J. (Eldora) telephone manager 1h Weston Ind tel.

Buck, H. A. school teacher Luckey Tro.

Buckenberger, Jno. (Mary) 5 ch farmer T 71a 4h 3c R3 Perrysburg Pbg 137.

Buckingham, Charles O. (son J. W.) laborer 1h West Millgrove Per 10 B & Ind tels.

Buckingham, C. E. (Freda) 1 ch farmer T 80a 2h 2c RD Prairie Depot Per 6.

Buckingham, J. W. (Ida J.) farmer O 80a 4h 2c West Millgrove Per 10 B & Ind tels.

Buckingham, R. A. (Blanche) farmer T 39a 3h 2c West Millgrove Mon 90 B tel.

Buckler, D. A. (Eva) oil pumper T 80a 1h R1 North Baltimore Hen 110.

Budd, Chas. A. (Louise) farmer T 160a 6h R1 Portage Por 9.

Budd, David farmer 1h R1 Portage Por 9 Ind tel.

BUDD, WM. (Jane) 12 ch farmer O 24a H. 3h 3c Locust St Perrysburg Pbg B tel.

Buddemeyer, Elsie E. R3 Prairie Depot Mon 6.

Buddemeyer, Henry H. (Sofa A.) 1 ch farmer O 42a 2h 5c R3 Prairie Depot Mon 6.

Buehler, John J. (Lena) 4 ch farmer O 80a 4h 6c R1 Genoa Lake 44 B tel.

Buehning, Edith (dau Fred) housekeeper R2 Dunbridge Mid 66.

Buehning, Emma (dau Fred) housekeeper R2 Dunbridge Mid 66.

Buehning, Fred 2 ch farmer O 40a 3h 5c R2 Dunbridge Mid 66.

Buehning, Otto (son Fred) farmer R2 Dunbridge Mid 66.

Buehning, Philip RD Dunbridge Mid.

Buhler, Anna 4 ch ret O 80a R1 Deshler Jac 22 B tel.

BÜHLER, SAMUEL (Susie) 2 ch farmer T 80a 3h 3c R1 Deshler Jac 22 B tel.

BULLIS, F. H. (Clara) 2 ch farmer T 80a 2h 3c R1 Bowling Green Pla 32 Ind tel.

BULLIS, J. H. (Phoebe) 4 ch farmer O 112a 7h 4c R1 Bowling Green Pla 34 B tel.

Bullis, Merle (son J. H.) farmer R1 Bowling Green Pla 34.

Bumbarger, Leslie (Nettie) 2 ch drayman O H&L 2h Grand Rapids Gr Rs Ind tel.

Bunch, Mary 1 ch O H&L Milton St Weston.

Bunk, Anna (dau Geo.) housekeeper R1 Deshler Jac 37.

Bunk, Geo. 2 ch farmer T 60a 2h 1c R1 Deshler Jac 37.

Bunk, Maggie (dau Geo.) housekeeper R1 Deshler Jac 37.

Bunn, Amus (Mary) 2 ch farmer T 55a 2h 1c R2 Perrysburg Mid 5 B tel.

Bunn, B. F. (Mary) farmer O 8a 1h 2c R1 Bowling Green Pla 74 Ind tel.

Bunn, Noah Perrysburg Mid.

Bunting, S. R. Bairdstown Blo.

BURBAUGH, WALTER (Cora) 1 ch farmer O 59a 6h 5c R1 Bradner Mon 58.

Burch, W. O. Perrysburg Pbg.

Burdeker, August (Emma) 3 ch farmer T 118a 5h 5c R2 Pemberville Web 45 B tel.

Burdick, Mrs. Cornelia ret O H&L West Millgrove Per 69.

Burdick, F. C. (Dessa) 3 ch telegraph operator O H&L 4c West Millgrove Per 70.

Burdick, L. G. (Emma) 1 ch farmer T 57a 3h 3c West Millgrove Per 69 Ind tel.

Burditt, Arthur (Flora) 3 ch machinist T H&L Box 236 West Taylor St Weston.

Burditt, Charley (son J. S.) farmer R1 Tontogany Wash 75.

Burditt, Clarence (son J. S.) R1 Tontogany Wash 75.

BURDITT, CLAUD (son W. H.) farmer R2 Weston Wash 14 Ind tel.

Burditt, Donald (son J. S.) farmer R1 Tontogany Wash 75.

BURDITT, G. (Jennie) 4 ch farmer O 108a 2h 6c R2 Weston Wash 8.

Burditt, Josha (son J. S.) R1 Tontogany Wash 75.

Burditt, Jno. M. Tontogany Wash.

BURDITT, J. S. (Jennie) farmer T 140a 4h 6c R1 Tontogany Wash 75 Ind tel.

Burditt, Kate housekeeper O H&L RD Tontogany Wash.

Burditt, Retta RD Tontogany Wash.

Burditt, W. H. (Retta) farmer O 150a 4h 5c R2 Weston Wash 14 Ind tel.

Burditt, W. J. RD Tontogany Wash.

Burdo, F. R. (Jessie) 1 ch electrical T H&L Rossford Pbg 78.

Burdo, W. E. (Anna) 2 ch farming O 30a 2h 2c R3 Perrysburg Pbg 83.

Burdock, M. (Minnie) 5 ch oil worker - T 5a 1h RD Rudolph Lib 64 Ind tel.

Burdock, Tom (Rose) farmer T 84a 3h 3c R1 Hoytsville Jac 93 B tel.

Burdue, William (Bertha) 2 ch laborer O H&L Silver St Weston.

BURGER, REV. H. C. (Nellie) 2 ch minister parsonage Main St Prairie Depot Ind tel.

BURGESS, C. L. 1 ch farmer & stock raiser O 93a 3h 1c R2 Pemberville Web 64.

BURGESS, FRED (Eva C.) farmer O 93a 5h 4c R2 Pemberville Web 45.

Burgess, Luella (dau Fred) clerk R2 Pemberville Web 45.

Burgess, O. S. ret farmer R2 Pemberville Web 45.

Burgess, O. S., Jr. (son C. L.) laborer 1h R2 Pemberville Web 64.

Burgoon, Elias (Mary) 3 ch farmer O 40a 3h 3c Hoytsville Jac 71 Ind tel.

Burgoon, J. D. (Minnie) 1 ch farmer O H&L Hoytsville Jac.

Burgoon, W. E. Tontogany Wash.

Burk, C. V. RD Custar Lib.

Burke, Geo. (Lydia) farmer O 40a 3h 1c R1 Portage Por 8 Ind tel.

Burke, Verna (dau Geo.) student R1 Portage Por 8 Ind tel.

BURKEMYER, C. (Anna) 1 ch farmer T 72a 2h 4c R1 Pemberville Fre 35 B tel.

Burkemyer, Mrs. Florentine ret O 72a R1 Pemberville Fre 35.

Burket, Jesse 3 ch farming O H&L 1h Milton Center Mil.

Burkett, Sarah A. Grand Rapids Gr Rs.

Burkkart, Frank (Mary) 8 ch farmer T 80a 4h 3c R1 Perrysburg Pbg 25.

Burkholder, Miss Cora (dau John) housekeeper O Luckey Tro Ind tel.

Burkholder, Miss Elsie (dau John B.) housekeeper O Luckey Tro Ind tel.

Burkholder, Frank Luckey Tro.

Burkholder, Fred 4 ch farmer O 79a 3h 5c Luckey Tro 71.

Burkholder, Fred W. Dunbridge Web.

Burkholder, Gottlieb (Mary) 4 ch 165a 5h 15c R1 Luckey Tro 25 Ind tel.

Burkholder, John farmer T 103a H&L 1h 1c Luckey Tro Ind tel.

Burkholder, Mary Luckey Tro.

Burkholder, William (Bessie) 2 ch farmer O 20a 3h 2c R1 Luckey Tro 87 Ind tel.

Burkitt, Barney (Amelia) 2 ch farmer O 60a 4h 5c R2 Weston Wash 6.

Burnham, Fred Pemberville Fre.

BURNHAM, J. E. (Gertrude) physician O H&L 4h Pairie Depot Mon B tel. See adv.

Burning, Herman A. (Nellie) 2 ch barber O H&L Fifth St Perrysburg Pbg B tel.

Burns, Anne E. Prairie Depot Mon.

Burns, H. 2 ch farmer O 160a 2h 2c R1 Prairie Depot Mon 67.

Burns, J. A. farmer O 80a 3h 15c R1 Risingsun Mon 82.

Burns, Lydia 1 ch ret O H&L Milton Center Mil.

Burns, Mose (Maud) 1 ch garage T H&L Risingsun Mon.

Burns, Wm. RD Bowling Green Pla.

Burnisde, L. Bradner Mon.

Burr, Leonard M. blacksmith bds Weston.

Burrell, Sarah RD North Baltimore Hen.

BURRIS, C. A. (Josephine) 3 ch telegraph operator T H&L Union St Cygnet Blo 6.

Burris, C. E. (Elizabeth M.) 2 ch oil pumper O H&L 7c Bairdstown Blo 48.

Burris, Mat. (Mary) 5 ch farmer O 53a 4h 2c R3 Weston Mil 69.

Burrow, Robt. farmer 1h R2 Prairie Depot Mon 13 B tel.

Burrows, W. R. (Hattie M.) 1 ch pumper O H&L R2 Prairie Depot Mon 13 B tel.

Burseik, Aaron (son A. H.) farmer R1 Portage Por 91.

Burseik, A. H. (Anna) 2 ch farmer O 160a 5h 4c R1 Portage Por 91.

Burseik, Clarence (son A. H.) farmer R1 Portage Por 91.

Burseik, H. L. (Alice) farmer T 87a 5h 3c R1 Portage Por 100.

Burseik, Kate (dau A. H.) housekeeper R1 Portage Por 91.

Burseik, Wm. (son A. H.) farmer R1 Portage Por 91.

Burseik, F. H. Dunbridge Web.

BURSON, EMERY S. (Cora) 5 ch farmer O 40a 3h 5c R3 Weston Mil 1 Ind tel.

Burson, Leon (son Emery) laborer R3 Weston Mil 1.

Burton, I. M. RD North Baltimore Hen.

Burton, John (Cora) 4 ch farmer O 20a 4h 1c R2 Pairie Depot Mon 10 B tel.

Burton, Mary Prairie Depot Mon.

Burton, Mathew 2 ch ret R2 Prairie Depot Mon 10 B tel.

BURWELL, JAMES (Grace) 1 ch creamery agent O 80a H&L Grand Rapids Gr Rs Ind tel.

Burwell, Nancy J. Grand Rapids Gr Rs.

Busbeker, Gusta housekeeper Luckey Tro.

BUSCH, GEO. (Hattie) farmer O 40a 2h 2c R1 Millbury Lake 64.

Busdeker, August Pemberville Web.

Busdeker, Harmon Luckey Tro.

Bush, George farmer O 40a 2h 3c R1 Stony Ridge Lake 85.

Bush, Walter (Merty) 1 ch laborer T H&L 1c R2 Pembleville Web 26.

Bushdieker, Charles (Frances) 2 ch quarry worker O H&L Luckey Tro.

Bushee, Harry (Ida) blacksmith T H&L Latchie Lake 83.

Bushey, D. B. RD North Baltimore Hen.

Bushman, Alfred (son J. H.) oil pumper Pemberville Fre 40.

Bushman, Carl Pemberville Fre.

Bushman, Edith Pemberville Fre.

Bushman, Edw. Pemberville Fre.

Bushman, Eliza Pemberville Fre.

Bushman, Fred Pemberville Web.

Bushman, Geo. (Anna) oil pumper O H&L Pemberville Fre 40.

Bushman, Henry Pemberville Fre.

Bushman, H. J. Pemberivlle Web.

Bushman, John (Eliza) miller & oil man O H&L Pemberville Fre.

Bushman, J. August (Clara) oil pumper O H&L Pemberville Fre 40.

Bushman, J. E. (Clara) 1 ch oil pumper O H&L Pemberville Fre 40.

Bushman, J. H. (Rose) 1 ch miller O H&L Pemberville Fre 40.

Bushman, L. H. (Edith) farmer T 85a 3h 2c R2 Pemberville Web 35.

Bushman, Wm. (Mary) 4 ch oil worker O 4a 3h R3 Pemberville Fre 25 B tel.

Bushman, Wm. (Laura) 1 ch farmer T 120a 5h 4c R2 Bowling Green Cen 13 B tel.

Bushmell, T. (Criner) 2·ch farmer T 80a 4h 1c R1 Tontogany Pla 21.

Bushong, Guy (Martha) 3 ch farmer O 70a 3h 4c R3 4c R2 Weston Wes 25 Ind tel.

BUSINGER, A. (Alphena) 6 ch farmer O 127a 5h 15c R3 Weston Mil 85 Ind tel.

Businger, A. J. (son A.) R3 Weston Mil 85.

Busson, Frank (Anna) 7 ch farmer O 80a 4h 3c Station A East Toledo Ros 31.

BUSSON, HENRY J. (Grace) 2 ch farmer O 40a 2h 1c Station A East Toledo Ros 31.

BUSSON, JOSEPH E. (Gertrude) 2 ch farmer O 40a 3h 1c Station A East Toledo Ros 31.

Butcher, Joe (Icy) 3 ch section foreman O H&L 1c Milton Center Mil.

Buth, T. L. Custar Mil.

Butler, A. (son Rebecca) laborer Hoytsville Jac.

Butler, A. C. RD North Baltimore Hen.

Butler, Cyrus (Jane) 5 ch farmer T 15a 1217 Miami St East Toledo Ros 19.

BUTLER, DICK (Laura) 2 ch farmer T 166a 4h 1c Tontogany Wash 30.

Butler, E. F. RD North Baltimore Hen.

BUTLER, E. M. (Ada E.) 2 ch drug store Garfield St Bloomdale Blo B & Ind tels.

Butler, J. B. (Jennie) 4 ch general store O H&L Hoytsville Jac B tel.

BUTLER, MYRTLE Ashland Ave Perrysburg.

Butler, Rebecca 4 ch ret O H&L Hoytsville Jac.

Butler, Samuel ret O H&L Second St Perrysburg Pbg.

Butt, John W. (son T. L.)˙ Custar Mil 100.

Butt, T. L. (Sarah) 1 ch farmer O 140a 1h Custar Mil 100.

Buzzo, Steve RD North Baltimore Hen.

Byers, John 3 ch laborer T H&L Risingsun Mon.

Byington, H. L. (Emma) physician O H&L 1h Risingsun Mon B tel.

CABLE, H. (Elizabeth) 3 ch farmer T 50a 2h 2c R1 Walbridge Lake 12 Ind tel.

Cable, J. O. (Ellen) 1 ch carpenter O H&L 1h Caldwell St Bradner Mon B tel.

Cadaret, H. L. (Marie) farmer T R1 Walbridge Ros 24 Ind tel.

Cadaret, Joseph (Selina) farmer T 160a 3h 2c R1 Walbridge Ros 24 Ind tel.

Cadwallader, D. E. (Maud) 2 ch farmer T 138a 3h 3c R2 Dunbridge Mid 58 Ind tel.

Caldwell, B. W. (Wilhelmina) 4 ch real estate man O H&L 1c Front St Perrysburg Pbg B tel.

CALDWELL, CHAS. R1 Haskins Has· 50.

Caldwell, Frank (Helen) laborer T Main St Perrysburg Pbg.

CALDWELL, WM. R. (Helen) 1 ch farmer T 80a R1 Haskins Mid 53 B tel.

Caldwell, Williemina B. Perrysburg Pbg.

Caldwell, W. A. RD North Baltimore Hen.

Caldwell, W. N. 2 ch monument worker O H&L Weston Wes Ind tel.

Caldwell, W. W. Weston Wes.

Calkins, Harvey (Louisa) ret O H&L Grand Rapids Gr Rs.

The Best on the Tree.

CALKINS, J. W. Prairie Depot.

Calkins, Lucinda Freeport Mon.

Calkins, Wesley (Lucy) oil business O H&L 3c Prairie Depot Mon B tel.

Callan, K. C. hardware clerk Losee St Cygnet Blo.

Callan, Mrs. L. S. 3 ch washing O H&L Losee Cygnet Blo.

Callihan, C. R. cobbler & photographer H&L Prairie Depot Mon.

Camblin, R. G. (Ruby) 1 ch nitro-glycerin maker T H&L East St Bradner Mon B tel.

Cameron, J. K. RD North Baltimore Hen.

Camomile, W. M. (Mary) laborer O H&L R3 North Baltimore Blo.

Campbell, Cora M. RD North Baltimore Hen.

Campbell, C. C. 4 ch laborer T H&L Main St Cygnet Blo 6.

Campbell, C. E. RD North Baltimore Hen.

Campbell, C. R. (Nina P.) 1 ch banker O H&L Main St Bloomdale Blo B & Ind tels.

Campbell, E. Earl (son W. H.) student Milton Center Mil.

Campbell, F. B. (Cora M.) 1 ch farmer O 40a 3h 3c R1 North Baltimore Hen 99 Ind tel.

Campbell, Howard H. farmer RD Rudolph Lib 101 Ind tel.

Campbell, J. A. RD North Baltimore Hen.

CAMPBELL, J. J. (Melinda) 2 ch farmer T 160a 4h 5c R1 Rudolph Lib 101 Ind tel.

Campbell, J. O. RD North Baltimore Hen.

Campbell, Mary 3 ch ret O H&L Milton Center Mil.

Campbell, M. C. RD North Baltimore Hen.

CAMPBELL, O. F. banker O 10a Main St Bloomdale Blo B & Ind tels.

Campbell, T. G. Bloomdale Blo.

Campbell, T. J. (Emaline) banker Vine St Bloomdale Blo B & Ind tels.

Campbell, W. D. (Minnie) 3 ch carpenter & painter T H&L Lori St Cygnet Blo.

Campbell, W. H. (Bessie) 6 ch carpenter O H&L Milton Center Mil.

Campbell, W. S. RD North Baltimore Hen.

Candel, J. E. (Flora) 2 ch worker in garage T H&L Union St Cygnet Blo.

Canfield, Anson (Harriett) farmer & carpenter O 10a 2h 1c R2 Prairie Depot Por 78 Ind tel.

Canfield, A. A. (Fannie) farmer O R1 Pemberville Fre 57.

Canfield, A. L. cattle RD Prairie Depot Por.

Canfield, D. C. (Della) 5 ch doctor T H&L Second St Perrysburg Pbg B tel.

Canfield, D. R. Perrysburg Pbg.

Canfield, E. A. (Alice) 5 ch farmer T 50a 2h 2c R1 Pemberville Fre 57.

Canfield, E. F. (Maud) farmer O R1 Pemberville Fre 57.

Canfield, Harriet cattle RD Prairie Depot Por.

Canfield, Ruth (dau S. S.) housekeeper R1 Pemberville Fre 58.

Canfield, S. S. (Bida) 2 ch farmer O 118a 9h 4c R1 Pemberville Fre 57 Ind tel.

Cannon, J. L. (Menty) farmer O 81a 2h 1c R1 Pemberville Fre 71.

Canode, Mrs. Chas. 3 ch ret T H&L Fifth St Perrysburg Pbg.

Canterberry, A. J. (Cory) 4 ch farmer T 120a 5h 2c R1 Bowling Green Pla 80.

Canterberry, A. T. RD Bowling Green Pla.

Canterberry, W. M. (Ellen) 6 ch farmer T 90a 4h 3c R2 Bowling Green Cen 18.

CANTERBURY, A. F. (Lulu) farmer T 105a 10h 23c R2 Bowling Green Pla 86 B tel.

Capell, Fred (Violet) 2 ch farmer T 40a 2h R2 Custar Mil 33 B tel.

Capelle, L. J. (Mary) 4 ch farmer T 80a 3h 2c R1 Custar Mil 13 B tel.

Capelle, Wm. cattle RD Bowling Green Center.

Carbaugh, Adam (Ida) laborer O H&L Main St Bloomdale Blo.

Carbaugh, Nilna (dau Adam) telephone operator Main St Bloomdale Blo.

Cardlon, Leo. J. Perrysburg Pbg.

Cardozy, Edward (Stella) 3 ch laborer O H&L Millbury Lake.

Carey, Ben Pemberville Web.

CARIS, ADA Luckey.

CARIS, ADAM R1 Dunbridge Web.

Caris, Ella (dau Ely) housekeeper Luckey Tro.

Caris, Ely (Caroline) 3 ch ditcher O H&L Luckey Tro.

CARIS, FRANK C. (Elizabeth) 5 ch farmer O 102a 4h 10c R1 Luckey Tro 69 Ind tel.

Caris, Frank P. (son Ely) laborer Luckey Tro.

CARIS, FRED (Anna) 1 ch farmer T 120a 4h 11c R1 Luckey Tro 92 B tel.

48

Caris, Mrs. Sarah T H&L Main St Jerry City Blo 78.

Carl, May Weston Wes.

Carlson, J. M. (Bettie) 1 ch farm boss O L 1h 2c R1 North Baltimore Hen 70 Ind tel.

Carman, Mrs. H. Freeport Mon.

Carman, Jas. Pemberville Fre.

Carman, Manuel (Lillie) 1 ch oil man O H&L 2h Bairdstown Blo 44.

Carman, Thos. Bradner Mon.

Carmean, M. E. Bairdstown Blo.

Carner, Frank (Cora) 3 ch farmer O 48a 5h 3c R1 Hoytsville Jac 77.

Carnicom, Arthur E. (Pearl E.) 2 ch laborer T H&L Bairdstown Blo.

Carnicom, Earl (son T. E.) R1 Rudolph Lib 77 Ind tel.

Carnicom, Harry drives Ohio Oil Co truck Rudolph Lib 96 Ind tel.

CARNICOM, R. B. (Ida) 4 ch farmer O 33 1-3a 4h 5c Rudolph Lib 96 Ind tel.

Carnicom, J. W. (Nettie) 2 ch farmer T 160a 4h 3c R1 Bowling Green Pla 73 Ind tel.

Carnicom, Ray garage O Rudolph Lib 81 Ind tel.

CARNICOM, T. E. (Flora) 9 ch oil worker T H&L 2h 2c R1 Rudolph Lib 77 Ind tel.

Carnicom, Will (Freida) oil worker O H&L RD Rudolph Lib 96.

Carolan, Mrs. Thomas 2 ch ret O H&L 4h Pike St Perrysburg Pbg B tel.

CAROS, ELIE R1 Luckey.

Carpenter, Alf (Lillie) 5 ch farmer T 80a 2h 2c R1 Perrysburg Pbg 108.

Carpenter, Miss Anna teacher Rudolph Lib 81 Ind tel.

Carpenter, A. F. (Tina) 4 ch farmer O 80a 3h 13c R1 Prairie Depot Mon 84 B tel.

Carpenter, A. W. (Sarah) 5 ch farmer O 60a 5h 3c R1 Dunbridge Mid 69.

Carpenter, C. L. Tontogany Wash.

Carpenter, D. (Emma J.) farmer T 30a H&L R1 Prairie Depot Mon 84.

Carpenter, Frank (Anna) 7 ch farmer O 102a 5h 3c R1 Dunbridge Mid 69.

Carpenter, G. W. Portage Lib.

CARPENTER, JOHN (Martha) farmer O 40a 4h 2c R1 Bowling Green Pla 26 Ind tel.

Carpenter, J. (Mary) farmer O 80a 3h 1c R1 Perrysburg Pbg 108 B tel.

Carpenter, Lorania Milton Center Mil.

Carpenter, O. F. Weston Wes.

Carpenter, Phoebe 2 ch ret O 2H&6Lots Milton Center Mil.

Carpenter, P. B. (Katherine) 6 ch oil worker O 6a 1h 1c R1 Weston Lib 40 Ind tel.

CARPENTER, R. L. Bays.

CARPENTER, S. L. cattle RD Rudolph Por.

Carpenter, Wm. (Lora) 5 ch carpenter T H&5Lots Milton Center Mil.

Carpenter, W. H. Portage Lib.

CARPER, I. N. (Margaret) 1 ch farming T 46a 6h 2c R2 Weston Wes 45.

CARR, MRS. ANNA 6 ch O 40a R1 Rudolph Lib 70 Ind tel.

Carr, A. E. (Gladys) 2 ch farmer T 146a 3h 3c R1 Rudolph Hen 117.

Carr, Ed. (Goldie) 4 ch farmer T 80a 2h 1c R1 Bradner Mon 30.

CARR, E. T. (Hattie) 2 ch farmer T 75a 3h 5c R1 Bowling Green Pla 73 B & Ind tels. See adv.

Carr, Ida RD Rudolph Lib.

Carr, Joshua (Reba) 1 ch farmer T 100a 3h 6c R1 Haskins Mid 85.

Carr, J. A. (Bertha) 1 ch oil pumper O H&L 1h Prairie Depot Mon.

Carr, J. E. (Emma) farmer O 39a 2h 4c R1 Rudolph Hen 117.

Carr, Omar C. (Jennie) 1 ch oil pumper T H&L 2c Mermill Lib 95 Ind tel.

Carr, W. E. RD North Baltimore Hen.

Carrie, Rev. Don (Mabel) 1 ch minister T H&L Walbridge Lake.

Carrol, Carrie S. RD Tontogany Wash.

Carroll, Caroline O. O 160a 5h 2c R1 Tontogany Wash 17 Ind tel.

Carroll, C. R. (Essa) restaurant T H&L Pemberville Fre 40 B tel.

Carson, Chas. (Zella) farmer T H&L R1 Grand Rapids Gr Rs 22 Ind tel.

Carson, Edna cook Bradford St Cygnet Blo.

CARSON, F. M. Prairie Depot.

Carson, John (Sarah A.) 4 ch farmer O 97a 4h 11c R1 Bradner Mon 58.

Carson, Jno. E. Grand Rapids Gr Rs.

Carson, Luther (Lulu) farmer O 217a 7h 16c R1 Grand Rapids Gr Rs 13 Ind tel.

Carson, Mabel clerk Bradford St Cygnet Blo.

Carson, W. H. (Rachel) 7 ch tailor O H&L 1h Bradford Cygnet Blo.

Carter, Benett (Mary) 1 ch ret O H&L Second St Perrysburg Pbg B tel.

Carter, Earnest (son S. F.) farmer R1 Haskins Mid 90.

Carter, Edith (dau Geo. R.) housekeeper R1 Haskins Mid 16.

Carter, Ervin (Sadie) farmer O 160a 4h 4c R4 Bowling Green Cen 79 Ind tel.

4

Carter, E. E. (May) 2 ch farmer O 80a 5h 4c R3 Bowling Green Cen 83 Ind tel.

Carter, F. M. Perrysburg Pbg.

CARTER, GEO. (Myra) farmer T 80a 4h 3c R1 Portage Por 84.

CARTER, GEO. R. (Emma) farmer O 80a 6h 3c R1 Haskins Mid 16 B tel.

Carter, Miss Grace (dau S. F.) housekeeper R1 Haskins Mid 90.

Carter, Henry (Maude) farmer O 6a East St Toledo Lake 131.

Carter, Howard (son Geo. R.) farmer R1 Haskins Mid 16.

Carter, Irvin cattle RD Bowling Green Cen.

Carter, James ret O H&L Prairie Depot Mon B tel.

Carter, Jas. Perrysburg Pbg.

Carter, J. W. Freeport Mon.

CARTER, LAMBERT (Sarah) farmer O 43a 4h 7c R1 Haskins Mid 85 B tel.

CARTER, L. B. (Rosa M.) 4 ch farmer O 70a 5h 3c R1 Haskins Pbg 15 Ind tel.

Carter, Mrs. Mary ret O H&L Indiana Ave Perrysburg Pbg.

CARTER, M. R. (Mabel) farmer T 150a 7h 3c R1 Haskins Pbg 15 B tel.

Carter, Ray (Ester) 1 ch chauffeur O H&L Second St Perrysburg Pbg B tel.

Carter, R. E. Bradner Mon.

CARTER, S. F. farmer O 80a 4h 1c R1 Haskins Mid 90 B tel.

Carter, V. H. (Sarah) 1 ch veterinarian O H&L 1h Haskins Mid 35 B tel.

Cary, Ben farmer O 50a 3h R2 Pemberville Web 31.

Case, A. R. blacksmith 1h bds Weston Wes Ind tel.

Case, Seymore (Alice) 1 ch machinist T H&L R1 East Toledo Lake 112.

Casey, C. E. (Edith) delivery man T H &L R1 Walbridge Lake 26.

Casey, Harry farmer Cygnet Blo 2 Ind tel.

Casey, Jessie (Flora) 2 ch laborer O 1a H&L R1 Rudolph Lib 33 Ind tel.

Casey, M. J. (Anna) 6 ch farmer 72a 5h 7c Cygnet Blo 2 Ind tel.

Caskie, Alexander cattle RD Prairie Depot Por.

Caskie, Glenn (Alberta) 1 ch pumper T H&L 1h Prairie Depot Mon B tel.

Caskie, John (Ella) 2 ch tool dresser T H&L Prairie Depot Mon B tel.

Caskie, M. J. (Josephine) 2 ch pumper O H&L Prairie Depot Mon B tel.

Caskie, Orril cattle RD Portage Por.

Cass, L. L. (Florence) ret O 220a 9h 23c Taylor St Weston B & Ind tels.

Cassner, D. M. laborer O H&L Fraser St Bairdstown Blo.

Castel, John (Margaret) farmer O 82a 2h 5c R2 North Baltimore Hen 26 Ind tel.

Castle, Mrs. Robt. O H&L E Main St Portage Por.

Castner, J. J. (Lena) 2 ch farmer T 40a 2h 1c R2 Weston Wash 3 Ind tel.

Caswell, Floyd (son Mrs. Ida) laborer Milton Center Mil.

Caswell, Mrs. Ida 5 ch washing T H&L Milton Center Mil.

Caswell, J. C. Rossford Ros.

Caswell, Walter (Delilah) 2 ch farmer T 60a 2h R3 Weston Mil 7.

Catherman, Ralph Walbridge Lake.

Cathers, James (Harriett) 2 ch contractor T H&L RD North Baltimore Hen Ind tel.

CATRELL, E. L. (Jesse M.) laborer T H &L 1h 1c R3 North Baltimore Blo Ind tel.

Cavendish, O. F. hardware bds Weston.

Cavendish, T. A. (Florence) 1 ch hardware T H&L Weston Ind tel.

Cavett, C. S. RD North Baltimore Hen.

Caza, J. N. (Matilda) 1 ch bricklayer T H&L Box 24 Rossford Ros.

CEDOZ, CHAS. (Alma) 1 ch florist O H&L R1 E Toledo Ros 30.

Cedoz, Frank J. (son Joseph) farmer R1 East Toledo Ros 38 Ind tel.

Cedoz, George W. (son Joseph) farmer R1 Box 29 East Toledo Ros 38 Ind tel.

CEDOZ, JOSEPH (Mary) farmer O 120a 5h 3c R1 East Toledo Ros 38 Ind tel.

Cedoz, Mayme (dau Joseph) housekeeper R1 East Toledo Ros 38 Ind tel.

Cekauder, C. G. (Edith) 1 ch farmer T 80a 4h 2c R1 Hoytsville Hen 7.

Cessna, W. P. (Len) 4 ch laborer O H&L Prairie Depot Mon B tel.

CHALLEN, E. (Janett) farmer T 80a 4h 9c R3 Weston Mil 69 Ind tel.

Challen, Elmer (Pearl) 3 ch farmer T 120a 3h 6c R1 Weston Mil 71 Ind tel.

Challen, E. R. (Minnie) 3 ch farmer O 60a 5h 7c R1 Custar Jac 92 B tel.

Challen, James (Amelia) farmer O 9a 2h R1 Tontogany Wash 34 Ind tel.

Challen, John (Nettie) farmer O 40a 2h 2c R2 Weston Pla 16 Ind tel.

CHALLEN, L. A. (Elizabeth) 3 ch store-keeper O H&L Haskins Mid 35 B tel.

Challen, Thomas H. (Carrie) farmer O 33a 2h 4c R1 Tontogany Wash 26 Ind tel.

Challen, Wm. (Orpha) farmer O 40a 2h 2c R1 Weston Mil 60 Ind tel.

Chamberlain, B. W. (Anne) 1 ch farmer T 62a 2h 5c R4 Bowling Green Cen 114.

Chamberlain, Frank RD Rudolph Lib.

Chamberlain, Geo. RD Bowling Green Web.

Chamberlain, G. L. (Cynthia) 4 ch farmer T 40a 2h 2c R2 Dunbridge Web 1 B tel.

Chamberlain, Jennie cattle RD Bowling Green Cen.

Chamberlain, J. R. Freeport Mon.

CHAMBERLAIN, J. W. (Goldie) 2 ch farmer T 245a 6h 1c R3 Bowling Green Cen 84 Ind tel.

Chamberlain, J. W. cattle RD Bowling Green Cen.

Chamberlain, Kenneth (Laura) 4 ch farmer T H&L Haskins Mid.

Chamberlain, Leonard cattle RD Bowling Green Cen.

Chamberlain, Leo. mail carrier Rudolph Lib 94.

Chamberlain, Lewis (Emaline) 2 ch farming O 60a 4h 4c R5 Bowling Green Web 17 Ind tel.

Chamberlain, Lorin (Eva) 1 ch farmer T 2h 1c Waterville Mid 21 B tel.

Chamberlain, Luther (Ida) oil worker Rudolph Lib 81.

CHAMBERLAIN, L. F. (Alice M.) 2 ch janitor & sexton O H&L 1h 1c Rudolph Lib 94.

Chamberlain, Myron cattle RD Bowling Green Cen.

Chamberlain, Sherman RD Bowling Green Web.

CHAMBERLAIN, Z. R. (Flora) physician O H&L 1h Prairie Depot Mon B tel.

Chamberlin, L. B. (Lula) 3 ch farmer T 50a 2h 1c R4 Bowling Green Cen 107.

CHAMBERS, ARTHUR (Lucy) 6 ch farmer T 80a 11h 11c R1 Pemberville Fre 61 B tel.

Chambers, Eli (Jane) 1 ch farmer T 40a 2h 2c R3 Prairie Depot Por 129.

Chambers, Guy farmer RD Perrysburg Pbg 6.

CHAMBERS, JOHN W. (Jennie) 3 ch physician O H&L 1h 1c Bays Lib 75 Ind tel. See adv.

Chambers, J. F. (Grace) 5 ch farmer O 40a 4h 3c R2 Prairie Depot Por 129.

Chambers, Henry (Barbara) 1 ch laborer T H&L Millbury Lake 49.

Chambers, Lester (son J. F.) farmer R2 Prairie Depot Por 129.

Chambers, Mariah O 115a 3c R2 Prairie Depot Por 129.

CHAMBERS, WILLIAM (Rebecca) 7 ch farmer T 196a 8h 12c R2 Perrysburg Pbg 6.

CHAMBERS, WM. (Nellie) 1 ch farmer O 45a 5h 7c R2 Prairie Depot Por 117.

Chamblin, Chas. E. Pemberville Fre.

Chamblin, C. E. (Susan) farmer O H&L 1h Pemberville Fre.

Chamblin, Jas. R. Pemberville Fre.

Chamblin, Susan Pemberville Fre.

CHAMLON, JAMES R. 4 ch farmer 40a 2h 5c R3 Pemberville Fre 89.

Champion, Frank Tontogany Wash.

Champion, Maud E. (dau R. R.) telephone operator Tontogany Wash.

Champion, R. R. (Alma J.) farmer O 20a Tontogany Wash Ind tel.

Champoney, C. P. (Edith) druggist O H&L Front St Perrysburg Pbg Ind tel.

Chandler, Mary E. C. farmer O 12a 1h R3 Perrysburg Pbg 69 Ind tel.

Chantraine, Jno. Grand Rapids Gr Rs.

Chapin, Lauren H. (son W. J.) student Third St Portage Por Ind tel.

Chapin, Verna L. (dau W. J.) music teacher Third St Portage Por Ind tel.

CHAPIN, W. J. (Agnes M.) pumper O H&L Third St Portage Por Ind tel.

Chapman, A. E. (Fannie) 1 ch farm hand Weston Mil 72.

Chapman, A. E. (Ettie) 4 ch farmer T 1c R1 Custar Hen 41.

Chapman, A. M. (Viola) 4 ch coal dealer O H&L 2h 1c Center St Weston Ind tel.

Chapman, Clara C. Weston Lib.

Chapman, Eugena teacher O H&L Fourth St Perrysburg Pbg.

Chapman, E. B. (Jennie) farmer O 40a 2h 1c R2 Bowling Green Cen 14.

CHAPMAN, G. S. (Martha W.) farmer O 215a 7h 5c R2 Bowling Green Pla 63 Ind tel.

Chapman, Gertrude E. Perrysburg Pbg.

Chapman, L. L. (Gertrude) 2 ch doctor T H&L Fourth St Perrysburg Pbg B tel.

CHAPMAN, MRS. M. W. O R2 Box 91A Bowling Green Pla.

Chapman, Robert (Nellie) 2 ch oil man O H&L S Garfield St Bloomdale Blo.

CHAPMAN, S. E. (Libbie) 3 ch farmer T 80a 4h 2c R1 Weston Lib 5.

CHAPMAN, W. J. R1 Box 13 Walbridge.

51

Chapman, W. L. Prairie Depot Mon.

Chappell, Chester A. Perrysburg Pbg.

Charles, Albert A. (Hulda) farmer O 35a 2h 1c Waterville Mid 4 B tel.

Charles, A. E. RD Perrysburg Mid.

Charles, Francis 1 ch O H&1a 1c Pine & Seventh Sts Perrysburg Pbg B tel.

Charles, Harry (Pearl) 1 ch laborer T H&L Mulberry St Perrysburg Pbg B tel.

Charles, Leslie (Cora) laborer O H&L Seventh St Perrysburg Pbg.

Charles, Wm. (Jennette) laborer O H&L Sixth St Perrysburg Pbg B tel.

Charles, Wm, Jr. (Ethel) 2 ch insurance O H&L Mulberry St Perrysburg Pbg B tel.

Charlton, Frances farmer O 40a 2c R5 Bowling Green Cen 40 Ind tel.

CHARLTON, JOHN (Emma) 4 ch farmer T 107a 4h 3c R2 Bowling Green Pla 64.

Charlton, Mrs. Lorena farmer O 40a 1h R4 Bowling Green Cen 97 Ind tel.

Charlton, Nim (Millie) 3 ch farmer O 60a 4h 4c R3 Bowling Green Cen 19 Ind tel.

Charlton, Owen RD Bowling Green Pla.

Charlton, Sarah farmer O 40a 2c R5 Bowling Green Cen 40 Ind tel.

Charlton, Thomas (Mary) 1 ch farmer T 105a 5h 8c RD Bowling Green Pla 14.

Chase, Andrew farmer R1 Haskins Mid 57.

CHASE, A. F. (Mary M.) farmer O 40a 2h 2c R1 Haskins Mid 57 B tel.

Chase, Ella M. general store T H&L West Millgrove Per 70.

Chase, Geo. RD North Baltimore Hen.

Chase, John (Mertle) 3 ch pumper O H&L 1h Mermill Por 19 Ind tel.

Chase, T. J. (Ruth) 1 ch farmer T 120a 4h 4c RD North Baltimore Hen 56 B tel.

Cheatwood, Bert (Grace) 1 ch farmer T H&L R2 Haskins Mid 32.

CHEATWOOD, L. M. (Tressa) farmer O 81a 2h 5c R2 Haskins Mid 26 B tel.

Chilcote, A. M. (Ruth) physician O 360a 1h Main St Bloomdale Blo B & Ind tel.

Chilcote, Edwin J. (son A. M.) farmer O 80a 1h Main St Bloomdale Blo B & Ind tel.

Chilcote, Grada (dau A. M.) Main St Bloomdale Blo B & Ind tels.

Chilcote, Helen 1 ch ret O H&L West Millgrove Per 70.

CHILCOTE, H. M. (May M.) 2 ch farmer T 120a 4h 4c R2 Prairie Depot Blo 83.

CHILCOTE, LEE J. (Ettie) oil man O H&L 1h Main Bloomdale Per B & Ind tels.

CHILCOTE, M. A. oil man O ll&L Main St West Millgrove Per B & Ind tels·

Chilcote, Martha E. hotel O H&L West Millgrove Per 70.

CHILCOTE, MRS. S. H. O H&L Main St West Millgrove Per B & Ind tels.

Christ, Adler Custar Mil.

Christ, Joseph laborer Station A East Toledo Ros 31.

Christ, Otis Bloomdale Blo.

Christel, H. (Bertha) ret T H&L Main & Seventh Sts Perrysburg Pbg.

Christeller, J. H. (Eliza) farmer O 79a 3h 2c R3 Prairie Depot Por 96.

Christen Ameal Luckey Tro.

Christen, Charles (Anna) 2 ch farmer T 130a 5h 9c R1 Dunbridge Web 5 B tel.

Christen, E. (Mary) carpenter O H&L 1h Luckey Tro Ind tel.

Christen, E. R. telegraph operator & implement dealer O store building Lemoyne Tro Ind tel.

CHRISTEN, FRANK farmer T 40a 3h R2 Dunbridge Mid 75.

Christen, Geo. J. (Emma) 9 ch farmer 77a 3h 5c R1 Luckey Tro 26 Ind tel.

Christen, Godfrey Luckey Tro.

Christen, Jno. Luckey Tro.

CHRISTEN, MRS. J. F. 6 ch farmer O 60a 2h 4c R1 Luckey Tro 86.

Christen, Matilda (dau Mrs. J. F.) school teacher R1 Luckey Tro 86.

Christen, Mary Luckey Tro.

Christen, Mildred (dau Geo. J.) school teacher R1 Luckey Tro 26 Ind tel.

CHRISTEN, WM. (Mary) 1 ch farmer T 50a 4h 1c R1 Perrysburg Pbg 31 B tel.

Christian Chas. Dunbridge Web.

Christian, Louis laborer R1 Luckey Tro 52.

Christiansen, Christ (Ada) 3 ch farmer T 15a 1h 2c Latchie Lake 95.

Christiansen, Henry (Flora) 3 ch farmer T 40a 6h 1c Latchie Lake 95.

Christiansen, P. (Lizzie) 7 ch laborer T H&L Walbridge Lake.

Christicsan, Frank farmer O 15a R1 Walbridge Lake 102.

Christman, Celia (dau J. A.) Waterville Mid 20.

Christman, Gladys F. (dau J. A.) school teacher Waterville Mid 20.

52

Christman. John (son J. A.) student Waterville Mid 20.

Christman, J. A. (Fontaine) 1 ch auditor O 63a 2h 2c Waterville Mid 20 B tel.

CHRISTY, FRANK (Fanny) farmer T 125a 5h 4c R2 Bowling Green Pla 62 1nd tel.

CHRISTY, J. A. (Ella) 2 ch farmer T 80a 3h 2c R3 Bowling Green Pla 87 Ind tel.

Chronister, G. A. (Nellie) 1 ch engineer T H&L Bell St Bradner Mon B tel.

Chronister, Ira (Mollie) 1 ch mechanic O H&L Bradner Mon B tel.

Church, L. W. Prairie Depot Mon.

Claar, Clarence Bradner Mon 22.

Claar, Mrs. E. 4 ch farmer T 80a 5h 5c Bradner Mon 22.

CLAAR, W. M. (Eliza) farmer T 90a 5h 2c R1 Bowling Green Pla 76 B tel.

Clabaugh, Isaac Custar Jac.

Clabaugh, John (Pearl) laborer R2 Custar Lib 32.

Clabaugh, Joseph (Melissa) 2 ch O 1a H&L Silver St Weston.

Claggett, S. S. (Edith) 5 ch general store O H&L Custar Mil B tel.

Clair, Charles (Florence) painter T H&L Eighth & Hickery Sts Perrysburg Pbg.

Clantz, George (Emma) laborer O H&L Grand Rapids Gr Rs Ind tel.

Clapp, C. L. Custar Mil.

Clapp, Ed. (Myra) 6 ch ret O 120a 3h R1 Custar Mil 20 B tel.

Clapp, E. A. (Carrie) 2 ch farmer T 120a 3h 3c R1 Custar Mil 21.

Clapp, Theodore L. (Eva) 3 ch carpenter & paperhanger T H&L Locust St Box 154 Weston Wes B tel.

CLAPPER, C. C. (Rebecca) farmer O 30a 2h 3c R2 North Baltimore Hen. 31 Ind tel.

Clapper, Lou farm hand R1 Hoytsville Jac 64.

Clark, Bessie (dau Fred) R3 North Baltimore Blo Ind tel.

CLARK, CHAS. 25 Hannum Ave Rossford.

Clark, E. D. Weston Wes.

Clark, E. E. (Anna C.) 1 ch jeweler O H&L Perrysburg Pbg Ind tel.

CLARK, FRANK M. (Mabel) 8 ch oil worker O H&L Losee St Cygnet Blo Ind tel.

Clark, Fred O. (Laura) section foreman O ·H & 12L 1h 1c R3 North Baltimore Blo Ind tel.

How the Wood County pumpkin crop was damaged.

Clark, F. P. RD North Baltimore Hen.

Clark, Gertrude RD Rudolph Lib.

Clark, George student Losee St Cygnet Blo Ind tel.

Clark, Helen housekeeper Losee St Cygnet Blo Ind tel.

Clark, Jno. H. RD North Baltimore Hen.

Clark, J. E. Weston Wes.

CLARK, L. H. (Blanche) 1 ch agent O H&L Merrill Por 20 Ind tel.

Clark, Mary ret O 2a H Pine St Perrysburg Pbg.

Clark, Robert (Zelma) 2 ch teamster O H&L R1 Box 16 East Toledo Ros 26.

CLARK, WYCLIFFE (Ellen) 2 ch farmer O 115a 3h 10c R2 Bowling Green Pla 46.

CLARK, W. E. (Minnie E.) 2 ch farmer O 135a 4h 8c Bradner Mon 23 B tel.

Clark, W. E. (Elizabeth) 2 ch farmer O 90a 2h 4c R2 Bowling Green Cen 9 Ind tel.

CLARY, JNO. F. (Mabel) 4 ch farmer T 80a 3h 2c R3 Prairie Depot Cen 120.

Clasbaugh, Joseph (Mandy) 2 ch laborer O H&L ½a 1h R2 Custar Jac 97.

Claty, Arnold H. Weston Wes.

Claty, Leon J. (Annie) farmer O 80a 3h 3c Box 91 Milton Center Mil 92 Ind tel.

Claus, Frank H. ((Mamie) 3 ch shoe & harness store O H&L Luckey Tro.

Claus, G. F. (Julia) 1 ch shoe & harness store O H&L Luckey Tro.

CLAUS, W. J. (Anna) 4 ch farmer O 40a 9h 14c R24 McComb Jac 120 Ind tel.

Clauson, Julius (Anna) 7 ch farmer O 4a 2h 1c R1 Walbridge Lake 128 B tel.

Clay, E. L. (Ella A.) 2 ch president lumber company O H&L Perrysburg Pbg B tel.

Clay, Robt. W. (Elnora) 6 ch farmer & thresher T 80a 4h 3c R1 Deshler Jac 32 Ind tel.

Clegg, Edward J. (Agnes) 4 ch farmer O 80a 6h 2c R1 Lime City Pbg 55.

Clemens, Elizabeth Prairie Depot Mon.

Clemment, E. (Emily) 2 ch farmer T 80a 3h 1c Cygnet Hen 116.

Clement, Frank farmer T 65a 7h 21c R1 Grand Rapids Wash 66 Ind tel.

Clety, Geo. laborer O H&L 2h Milton Center Mil.

Clifton, John W. (Eva) 8 ch farmer T H&L 1c R1 Portage Por 56.

Cline, C. W. West Milgrove Per.

Cline, Ed. Walbridge Lake.

Cline, Elias (Mertie) 5 ch thresher 1h 1c R3 North Baltimore Blo B & Ind tels.

Cline, Geo. C. RD North Baltimore Hen.

Cline, J. W. (Sarah) 1 ch farming T 40a 1c R3 North Baltimore Blo Ind tel.

Cline, L. H. West Millgrove Per.

Cline, L. J. (Alice) 3 ch laborer O H&L 1h 1c Railroad St Bairdstown Blo.

CLINE, O. L. (Jennie) farmer T 98a 4h 3c R3 North Baltimore Blo 27 Ind tel.

Cline, Peter (Jennie) 1 ch laborer O H&L Walbridge Lake.

Cline, Mrs. Philip ret O H&L West Millgrove Per 70.

Clingo, Chas. Pemberville Web.

CLINTON, G. H. R2 Custar Hen 41.

Cloar, C. E. Perrysburg Pbg.

Close, Clayton L. (Fannie) teacher O H&L Findlay St Portage Por.

Close, Joseph S. (Samantha A.) carpenter O H&L Findlay St Portage Por.

Close, Wm. R. laborer Findlay St Portage Por.

CLOUGH, FRANK L. (Lena) 3 ch farmer O 26a 2h 3c R2 Bowling Green Pla 45 Ind tel.

Clousan, Chas. (Magdelena) farmer O 76a 2h 2c R1 Walbridge Lake 99 Ind tel.

Clousan, John W. (Elizabeth) 2 ch farmer O 50a 2h 1c R1 Stony Ridge Lake 100.

Clousan, Miss Mary R1 Walbridge Lake 99 Ind tel.

Clousan, Volley A. farmer R1 Walbridge Lake 99 Ind tel.

Clouse, Oliver (Nellie) oil worker O H&L 1h Union St Cygnet Blo Ind tel.

CLOUSER, G. A. (Jennie) 2 ch oil pumper O 40a 2h 1c R1 North Baltimore Hen 69 B & Ind tels.

Clouser, H. A. (Dela) 4 ch oil pumper O Lots R1 North Baltimore Hen 123 B tel.

Clover, A. L. (Anna) 1 ch laborer T H&L 124 Oak St Rossford Ros.

Clover, Lloyd barber bds with F. Klanchia 100 Elm St Rossford Ros.

Cluxton, G. H. 2 ch farmer O 40a 9h 4c R2 Custar Hen 41.

Cluxton, Nancy housekeeper R3 Weston Mil 67.

Cluxton, William farmer O 10a 2h R3 Weston Mil 67.

Coakley, John (Blanche) 4 ch farmer T 160a 1c Jerry City Por 34 Ind. tel.

Coats, Adam D. RD North Baltimore Hen.

Cobb, Geo. (Clara) 3 ch farmer T 160a 6h 1c R1 Weston Lib 8 Ind tel.

Cocanaur, Abraham L. (Anna) 3 ch draftsman O H&L Indiana Ave Perrysburg Pbg B tel.

Cochord, Mrs. Luella 2 ch farmer O 92a 4h 9c R1 Fostoria Per 124 Ind tel.

Cochran, H. W. (Sarah) 3 ch supt Ford Glass Co O H&L 191 Superior St Rossford Ros Ind tel.

Coe, Boston E. Weston Wes.

Coefman, H. E. RD Custar Lib.

Coen, U. E. (Daisy) 2 ch farmer O 40a 5h 4c R2 Bowling Green Pla 58 B tel.

Coger, Clarence farmer R1 Jerry City Por 35 Ind tel.

Coger, C. C. (Anna) 7 ch farmer T 180a 7h 2c R1 Jerry City Por 35 Ind tel.

COGER, WM. (Minnie) 2 ch farmer T H&L R1 Jerry City Por 36.

Cohrs, Henry (Emma) 3 ch farmer 128a R2 Deshler Jac 7 B tel.

Colborn, W. H. barber Milton Center Mil.

COLE, CHARLES (Ida) 3 ch farmer T 123a 4h 6c Box 77 Milton Cen Mil 102 Ind tel.

Cole, Elizabeth RD North Baltimore Hen.

COLE, ELMER (Ida) 1 ch farmer T 52a 1h 1c R1 Weston Pla 11 Ind tel.

Cole, Elmer L. (Gladys) 3 ch farmer T H&L 1h 1c R1 Haskins Mid 49 B tel.

Cole, Floyd (Maude) 4 ch T H&L 1c Milton Center Mil 94.

Cole, Jas. Custar Hen.

Cole, Jenett RD Weston Pla.

Cole, Jas. B. Bradner Mon.

COLE, J. W. Milton Center.

Cole, Lloyd (Maud) 4 ch laborer T H&L Milton Center Mil.

COLE, LESTER J. (Mabel) 3 ch farmer T 90a 3h 4c R2 Bowling Green Pla 52.

Cole, Lewis Risingsun Per.

COLE, L. L. (Lena) 5 ch farmer O 80a 5h 7c Bradner Mon 20.

Cole, W. R. (Mary K.) 1 ch farmer O 40a 1h 5c R1 Haskins Mid 44 B tel.

COLEMAN, MRS. D. K. RD North Baltimore Hen.

Coleman, Harry RD Bowling Green Pla.

Coleman, J. A. RD North Baltimore Hen.

Coleman, S. A. (Ada Z.) 3 ch farming 5h R1 Bowling Green Pla 38.

Colgan, Edward hired man R1 Walbridge Pbg 75.

Colgrove, F. R. operator bds with W. A. Hurrelbrink R1 Walbridge Ros 22.

Collier, W. A. (Louise) 7 ch farmer O 35a 3h 1c R2 Bowling Green Pla 90 Ind tel.

COLLIN, R. J. Tontogany.

Collins, Chas (Nancy) laborer T H&L Lincoln St Bloomdale Blo.

Collins, E .S. (Addie) 10 ch farmer O 200a 4h 3c R3 Bowling Green Cen 44.

Collins, E. V. Corp Portage Por.

Collins, Geo. RD Bowling Green Web.

Collins, Harry (son Chas.) laborer Lincoln St Bloomdale Blo.

Collins, Jas. RD Bowling Green Web.

Collins, J. E. (Lodema) 4 ch farmer O 40a 2h 1c R3 Prairie Depot Por 120.

Collins, James F. (Myrtle) 4 ch pumper T H&L R1 Rudolph Por 24½ Ind tel.

Collins, Ora (son Chas.) laborer Lincoln St Bloomdale Blo.

Collins, Thos. G. Millbury Lake.

Colvin, S. S. Pemberville Fre.

Colvin, Wm. Pemberville Fre.

Combs, R. L. (Mina) 1 ch laborer T H&L Walnut St Portage Por.

COMPTON, R. S. (Minnie) 2 ch real estate H&3a Walnut St Perrysburg Pbg.

Compton, S. W. (Hazel) 2 ch school teacher & drug clerk T H&L Summer Box 118 Weston Wes.

Comstock, Wm. (Mary) ret O H&L Front St Perrysburg Pbg B tel.

CONAL, MRS. WILL Prairie Depot.

Conard, A. S. RD North Baltimore Blo.

Conaway, C. E. Risingsun Mon.

Conditt, Cormelia R1 Tontogany Wash 11 Ind tel.

Conditt, Letty O 150a 1h 1c R1 Tontogany Wash 11.

Conell, Clem (Mary) 5 ch oil man O H&L Risingsun Mon.

Conkey, C. H. (Hattie) 6 ch farmer T 240a 10h 7c R1 Deshler Jac 9.

Conkey, King (son C. H.) farm hand R1 Deshler Jac 9.

CONKEY, W. G. (Nancy) 6 ch veterinary surgeon & dentist O 10a 2h R1 Rudolph Lib Ind tel. See adv.

Conklin, Charley (Phoebe) 3 ch carpenter O 3a H&L Center St Weston Ind tel.

Conklin, Fred RD Perrysburg Mid.

Conklin, G. R. laborer bds Cus Mil.

Conklin, Harris RD Weston Pla.

CONKLIN, H. S. (Carrie) 3 ch farmer O 3a 2h 1c R1 Hoytsville Jac 85.

CONKLIN, J. D. (Ella R.) insurance O₁ H&L Weston Wes B tel.

Conklin, Merlin (son W. H.) farmer R2 Weston Pla 5.

Conklin, W. H. (Electa) farmer O 123a 5h 9c R2 Weston Pla 5 Ind tel.

Conley, J. J. RD North Baltimore Hen.

CONLEY, J. W. (Elizabeth) 3 ch carpenter O H&L 1c cor Lightner & Stahl Bradner Mon.

Conley, P. H. T H&L Cygnet Blo 6.

Conn, A. C. Rossford Pbg.

Conn, A. L. (Grace) 2 ch lawyer O 5a Toledo Pbg 80 Ind tel.

CONN, G. H. (Ruth) 1 ch veterinarian T H&L 2h Prairie Depot Mon B tel. See adv.

Conn, S. L. (Della) 6 ch farmer T 70a 4h 3c R1 Rudolph Lib 33 Ind tel.

Connell, Jas. Risingsun Mon.

Connell, Martin (Ruby) 2 ch R R man T H&L Walbridge Lake..

CONNELL, M. B. (Florence) 1 ch farmer T 130a 6h 3c R1 Prairie Depot Mon 104 B tel.

Connell, William (Jennie) 1 ch ret O H&L Prairie Depot Mon B tel.

Connells, James (Orpha) farmer O 40a 3h 5c R1 Risingsun Mon 82.

Conner, D. H. (Elva) 4 ch farmer O 100a 5h 7c R1 Fostoria Per 122 Ind tel.

Conner, Edward (Lulu) 4 ch janitor O H&L Indiana Ave Perrysburg Pbg.

Conner, E. M. (son J. M.) laborer 98 Elm St Rossford Ros B tel. ·

Conner, J. M. (Jennie) foreman O H&L 98 Elm St Rossford Ros B tel.

Connolly, Jno. M. Weston Wes.

CONNOLLY, W. J. (Ella) 2 ch postmaster T H&L Grand Rapids Gr Rs.

Connor, J. A. RD North Baltimore Hen.

CONRAD, GEO. W. R1 Grand Rapids.

Conrad, Guy C. Grand Rapids Gr Rs.

CONRAD, HOWARD (Frances) 1 ch farmer T H&L 1h 1c R2 Weston Wes 15 Ind tel.

CONRAD, JOHN (Mary) 5 ch farmer O 53a 2h 3c R1 Grand Rapids Gr Rs 28 Ind tel.

Conrad, Jos. H. Weston Mil.

CONRAD, MARY ret O H&L Fifth & Main Sts Perrysburg Pbg.

CONRAD, MINNIE housekeeper R1 Grand Rapids Gr Rs 21.

CONRAD, SOL. (Delia) 7 ch farmer O 80a 5h 5c R1 Grand Rapids Gr Rs 20 Ind tel.

Conrad, T. (Belle) 1 ch farmer O 29a 4h 7c R1 Grand Rapids Gd Rs 21 Ind tel.

Conrad, Wm. O. (Bessie A.) 2 ch oil man T H&L 2c R3 North Baltimore Blo B & Ind tels.

Conraft, John oil worker T H&L Rudolph Lib 94.

Conway, John (Anna E.) farmer O 9a R1 East Toledo Lake 114.

Cook, Belle clerk O H&L Milton St Wes Ind tel.

Cook, Chas. (Elsie) 2 ch repairman T Walbridge St Walbridge Lake 3.

Cook, C. L. (Rose) farmer O 118a 4h 2m 5c R1 Tontogany Wash 28 Ind tel.

Cook, Dora (dau Fred) housekeeper R1 Genoa Tro 38 B tel.

Cook, Elizabeth H&L R1 Lemoyne Tro 42.

Cook, Fred (Tillie) 11 ch farmer O 100a 6h 13c R1 Genoa Tro 38 B tel.

Cook, F. M. RD Bowling Green Pla.

COOK, GLEN M. (Emma G.) 2 ch oil pumper T H&L Bays Lib 75 Ind tel.

COOK, HENRY photographer Front St Pemberville.

Cook, H. I. (Bertha) 1 ch farmer T 80a 3h 5c R1 Rudolph Lib 71.

Cook, James liveryman O barn &L 8h Perrysburg Pbg Ind tel.

Cook, Jno. Risingsun Mon.

Cook, J. H. RD Rudolph Lib.

Cook, J. M. C., M.D. (Dora M.) 4 ch physician O H&L Weston B & Ind tels.

Cook, Louise (dau Fred) housekeeper R1 Genoa Tro 38 B tel.

Cook, M. (Maude) 2 ch oil worker T H&L R1 Bowling Green Lib 87 Ind tel.

Cook, M. B. (Amelia C.) sawyer O H&L Main St Perrysburg Pbg.

COOK, O. L. (Emma) 1 ch laborer T 40a 1h 2c R1 Tontogany Wash 28 Ind tel.

Cook, Silas (Tina) 2 ch section hand H&L Risingsun Mon.

COOK, S. M. (Margaret A.) 5 ch farmer O 40a 2h 8c R1 Rudolph Lib 106 Ind tel.

Cook, Willard RD Bowling Green Lib.

COOK, W. F. (Mary) 8 ch farming T 175a 9h 8c R3 Weston Wes 55.

Cookson, Wm. Weston Lib.

Cooley, Charley laborer bds Perrysburg Pbg.

Coon, Chas. A. (son Chas. W.) farmer 1h R1 Box 23 East Toledo Ros 25.

Coon, Chas. W. (Lizzie) 4 ch farmer T 153a 6h 4c R1 Box 23 East Toledo Ros 25.

Coon, Louis Bradner Mon B tel.

Coon, M. O. (Mary) restaurant T Custar Mil.

Coonse, J. (Lucy) ditcher O H&L Second St Perrysburg Pbg.

Cooper, Frank (Mary) 6 ch farmer O 120a 6h R2 Custar Lib 14.

Cope, J. W. (Nora) 1 ch manager T H&L R2 North Baltimore Hen Ind tel.

Copeland, Ira J. (Sallie) 3 ch farmer T 68a 5h 4c R5 Bowling Green Cen 66 Ind tel.

Copp, C. H. RD North Baltimore Hen.

Coppeler, Chas. farmer R1 Portage Por 14 Ind tel.

Coppler, Albert (Della O.) 3 ch medicine wagon proprietor T H&L Bloomdale Blo.

Coppler, George (Matilda) 1 ch oil man T H&L R3 North Baltimore Blo 18 B & Ind tels.

Coppler, George P. (son Geo.) laborer R3 North Baltimore Blo 18 B & Ind tels.

Coppler, John (son Geo.) laborer R3 North Baltimore Blo 18 B & Ind tels.

Copus, George (Belle) farmer O 80a 2h 4c R2 North Baltimore Hen 21.

Copus, Wesley (Louisa) 1 ch H&L 2h Union St Cygnet Blo.

Copus, W. (Cora) farmer T 90a 5h 6c R2 North Baltimore Hen 21.

Copus, W. B. (Maggie) oil worker T H&L Portage Lib 90 Ind tel.

Copus, W. C. (Clara) 9 ch farmer T 80a 3h R3 North Baltimore Hen 102.

Corbett, John C. (Rhoda) 3 ch oil worker T 2c R1 Rudolph Lib 108 Ind tel.

Corbin, Chas. farmer R1 Portage Por 87 Ind tel.

Corbin, C. W. (Alvina) 5 ch farmer T 80a 2h 1c R1 Tontogany Wash 38.

Corbin, Earl (Nellie) 1 ch conductor T H&L Front St Perrysburg Pbg B tel.

Cordee, C. H. Prairie Depot Mon.

Cordrey, H. C. (Elma M.) farmer O H&L Prairie Depot Mon B tel.

Cordrey, Lottie housekeeper O 40a Dunbridge Mid 75.

Cordry, Renzel (Pauline) 3 ch laborer T H&L Fifth St Perrysburg Pbg.

Cordy, F. W. (Nellie) 6 ch farmer T H&L 1c R1 Haskins Mid 49.

Corey, W. E. 3 ch field boss T H&L Stony Ridge Tro B & Ind tels.

Corfman, D. W. (Pearl) 2 ch farmer O 80a 3h 3c R2 Custar Mil 39 B tel.

Corfman, H. E. (Clara) 3 ch farmer T 90a 3h 6c R2 Custar Lib 21 Ind tel.

Cormon, Tom O H&L N Main St Bradner Mon.

Cornelius, C. E. (Ena) 2 ch section hand T H&L Lime City Pbg 121.

Cornelius, Frank (Louise) 4 ch farmer T 60a 3h 1c R3 Perysburg Pbg 158.

Cornelius, L. S. (Flossie) 3 ch garage T H&L Pemberville Fre 40.

Cornelius, Peter (Barbara) 1 ch farmer O 40a 4h 3c R1 Lime City Pbg 122 B tel.

Cornell, Charlie (Mary) 2 ch laborer O H&L Grand Rapids Gr Rs.

Cornell, Vern (Dovie) 3 ch farmer T 80a 3h 5c R1 Custar Jac 41.

Cornell, Wm. 1 ch T H&L 1h R1 Rudolph Lib 101.

Cornwell, Lawrence (Celia) operator Hatton Per 85 Ind tel.

Cornwell, Levi (Margaret) 2 ch general store T H&L Main St Jerry City Blo 78 Ind tel.

Cotant, Anna (dau Geo. B.) R2 Bloomdale Blo 120 B & Ind tels.

Cotant, D. B. (Mary) O 40a 3h 2c R2 Bloomdale Blo 120 B & Ind tels.

Cotant, Edna (dau D. B.) R2 Bloomdale Blo 120 B & Ind tels.

Cotant, George B. (Helen) 4 ch farmer O 40a 2h 2c R2 Bloomdale Blo 120 B & Ind tels.

Cotant, Maude (dau Geo. B.) R2 Bloomdale Blo 120 B & Ind tels.

Cotterman, Raymond R. (Cora) 3 ch laborer T H&L RD Rudolph Lib 77.

Couplers, Ed. (Stella) teamster T H&L Union St Cygnet Blo 6.

Courtney, Richard Grand Rapids Wes.

Coutchure, Ed. (Louis M.) 1 ch farmer T H&L 1h 1c R1 Tontogany Wash 35.

Covach, Geo. (Anna) 4 ch glass worker O H&L Box 47X Rossford Ros.

Covel, Alonzo (Elizabeth) 4 ch farmer O 34a 4h 2c R2 Gibsonburg Fre 19.

Coveney, J. F. 7 ch telegrapher T H&L N Main St Bradner Mon.

Cover, C. B. (Lavina) 3 ch farmer T 80a 3h 1c R1 Box 46A East Toledo Ros 38.

Covey, W. E. Stony Ridge Tro.

Coward, W. W. Weston Wes.

Cowden, J. K. Pemberville Fre.

Cowles, Ellen ret O 104a R1 Walbridge Lake 10 Ind tel.

Cowles, Henry (Ella) 6 ch farmer O 55a 3h 9c R1 Walbridge Lake 118 Ind tel.

Cowles, Walter Walbridge Lake.

Cowley, Daniel (Kitty) farmer O 160a 10h 6c R2 Bloomdale Per 28 B tel.

Cox, August (Lucy A.) 1 ch farmer O 20a 3h 3c R1 Portage Por 55.

57

Cox, Blain cattle RD Rudolph Por.

Cox, Clyde (Leona) 3 ch O H&L Russ St Weston Ind tel.

Cox, C. M. (Grace) 1 ch farmer T 40a 1h R1 North Baltimore Hen 112.

Cox, Elizabeth T H&L R1 Portage Por 56.

Cox, E. (May) 2 ch farmer T 160a 9h 4c R1 Rudolph Lib 39 Ind tel.

Cox, JOHN H. (Naoma) 5 ch farmer O 80a 3h 6c R2 Bowling Green Pla 57 B tel.

Cox, JOSEPH farmer T H&L R1 Portage Por 14.

Cox, J. A. (Della) 2 ch oil man O H&L 3h Harrison St Bloomdale Blo B & Ind tel.

Cox, J. D. (Lorena) 1 ch farmer T 92a 3h 2c R2 Bowling Green Mid 44.

Cox, L. E. (Laura B.) 5 ch farmer T 120a 8h 5c R2 Dunbridge Mid 72.

Cox, Ralph RD Bowling Green Pla.

Coy, Aaron (son of Chas.) R1 Walbridge Ros 22 Ind tel.

Coy, Amos (Emma) farmer O 60a 2h E Broadway East Toledo Ros 20.

Coy, Arthur (Florence) 1 ch farmer T 90a 2h 2c Station A East Toledo Ros 20.

Coy, Chas. (Florence) 1 ch farmer O 164a 4h R1 Walbridge Ros 22 Ind tel.

Coy, Dewey (son of Chas.) R1 Walbridge Ros 22 Ind tel.

Coy, E. J. (Zuba) 3 ch ret O H&L Prairie Depot Mon B tel.

Coy, Fannie L. (dau of Chas.) R1 Walbridge Ros 22 Ind tel.

Coy, George A. (son of Amos Coy) 2h 14c E Broadway East Toledo Ros 20.

Coy, J. W. Prairie Depot.

Coy, Murr (Dora) 1 ch farmer O 1a H&L R1 Walbridge Ros 22.

Coy, Raymond (Mary) 1 ch farmer O 1a 2h 4c R1 Walbridge Ros 22.

Coy, William (Elizabeth) 2 ch farmer O 100a 5h 9c Station A East Toledo Ros 18 Ind tel.

Coykendall, Jno Cygnet Blo.

Craft, O. C. (Mary) 3 ch farmer O 110a 9h 11c Box No. 254 Weston Mil 64.

CRAGO, T. W. (Maggie) 2 ch farmer O 30a 3h 7c RD Walbridge Lake 94 B tel.

Crags, T. W. Walbridge Lake.

Craig, Mrs. Julia M. Perrysburg Pbg.

Craine, E. J. RD Perrysburg Pbg.

Cramer, Albert RD Rudolph Lib.

Cramer, J. R. (Florence) 3 ch Standard Oil agent T H&L Prairie Depot Mon B tel.

CRAMER, L. M. (Martha) 5 ch farmer O 47a 3h 5c R1 Deshler Jac 23.

Cramer, P. R. Prairie Depot Mon.

Cramer, W. H. (Ada) 1 ch stationary engineer O H&L 1h Maple St Bloomdale Bl.

Crandall, Bradley E. (Elma) 3 ch farmer T 50a 1h 3c R1 East Toledo Ros 28.

Crandall, Chester (Amelia) 6 ch farmer T 80a 2h 2c R1 Walbridge Lake 6 Ind tel.

CRANDALL, E. R. (Ila) 1 ch farmer O 20a 2h 3c R1 Walbridge Lake 6.

Crandall, Leon (Helen) 2 ch traveling T H&L Trout St Perrysburg Pbg B tel.

CRANDALL, S. O. (Angelia) ret O 20a 1h 2c R1 East Toledo Ros 28 Ind tel.

Crandall, T. B. (Alma) farmer T 47a 4h 4c R1 Walbridge Lake 10 Ind tel.

CRANDEL, PERRY A. (Gertrude M.) 2 ch farmer O 40a 3h 2c R1 Millbury Lake 119.

Crane, Henry L. R3 Perrysburg Pbg.

CRANE, WM. A. Box 185 Perrysburg.

Cranker, C. A. (son of John) farmer T 98a 4h 1c R3 Perrysburg Pbg 120 B tel.

Cranker, F. (Maria) ret O H&L Front St Perrysburg Pbg.

CRANKER, JOHN ret O 98a 1c R3 Lime City Perrysburg Pbg 120 B tel.

Cranker, Josephine ret O H&L Second St Perrysburg Pbg.

Cranson, Dr. B. S. doctor O H&L 1h Rudolph Lib 95 Ind tel.

Cranson, Clyde student Rudolph Lib 95 Ind tel.

Cranson, Mable (dau of B. S.) teacher Rudolph Lib 93 Ind tel.

Crawfoot, Ed Risingsun Mon.

Crawfoot, Jessie L. Prairie Depot Mon.

Crawfoot, J. A. (Alice) farmer O 51a 2h 3c R2 Prairie Depot Mon 109.

Crawfoot, J. A. Prairie Depot Mon.

CRAWFOOT, MRS. M. R1 Prairie Depot.

Crawford, Aletha L. (dau of D. G.) R1 Bloomdale Blo 90.

Crawford, Alton (Lula) 1 ch farmer T 40a 2h 3c R1 Portage Por 60.

CRAWFORD, CLARENCE (Elizabeth M.) 1 ch farmer O 40a 3h 1c R1 Jerry City Blo 64.

Crawford, Glen S. (Helen) 1 ch farmer O 5a 1h R1 Millbury Lake 131.

CRAWFORD, H. (Anna) 4 ch oil pumper O 46a 1h 3c R1 Pemberville Fre 68 B tel.

Crawford, James (Ollie) 3 ch farmer RD Rudolph Lib 37.

CRAWFORD, ORVILLE (Mary) 3 ch farmer T 100a 6h 3c R1 Jerry City Por 68.

Crawford, Otho T. (son of S. G.) R1 Bloomdale Blo 90.

Crawford, Rella (dau of S. G.) R1 Bloomdale Blo 90.

Crawford, Sam (Odie) 2 ch fireman O H&L Walnut St Weston Wes.

Crawford, S. G. 3 ch farmer O 40a 3h 3c R1 Bloomdale Bl 90.

Crawford, Thomas (Clara) 1 ch laborer O 1h R1 Millbury Lake 131.

Creager, L. G. (Elsie) 1·ch farmer T 80a 2h 2c R2 Weston Wes 16 Ind tel.

Credicott, W. J. R1 North Baltimore Hen.

Cregg, George (Julia) 1 ch motorman O H&L Second St Perrysburg Pbg B tel.

Crego, Chas. (Gertrude) 2 ch farmer T 160a 5h 5c R2 Dunbridge Mid 64.

Creighton, Harry (Sylvia) laborer O H&L Risingsun Mon.

Creps, A. C. (Mary) farmer O 40a 2h 4c R1 Grand Rapids Wash 68 Ind tel.

Creps, A. C., Jr. (son A. C., Sr.) farmer 3h R1 Grand Rapids Wash 68.

Creps, A. D. (Rosie E.) 2 ch farmer O 40a 3h 3c Rudolph Hen 64.

Creps, Chas. F. (son A. C., Jr.) farmer R1 Grand Rapids Wash 68.

Creps, Elizabeth W. Perryburg Pbg.

Creps, John (Mary) 4 ch farmer T 160a 5h 3c R1 Hoytville Jac 42.

Creps, John J. (Ruth) 1 ch farmer 2h 6c R1 Grand Rapids Wash 68.

Creps, J. L. RD Hoytsville Jackson.

Creps, Wm. (Clara) 1 ch farmer O 80a 4h 2c R3 Perrysburg Per 87.

Cretsinger, Lewis 4 ch ret O H&L Milton Center Mil.

Cribbs, H. F. (Jessie) 7 ch oil pumper T 5a 1c Bradner Mon 28.

Cribliver, Wesley 1 ch butcher T H&L Crocker St Bradner Mon.

Crist, Mrs. Marie 3 ch Prairie Depot Mon 65.

Crocker, Geo. (Louise) 7 ch farmer O 98a 1h 3c R2 Custar Lib 32 Ind tel.

Presbyterian Church, Bowling Green, Ohio.

CROCKER, JOHN (Jessie) 1 ch farmer T 98½a 3h 2c R2 Custar Lib 26.

Crocker, S. J. (Melissa) 3 ch ret farmer O 62a 4c R2 Custar Lib 34.

Crocker, T. V. (son William) farmer Taylor St Weston.

Crocker, William (Carrie) 1 ch farmer O 118a 4h 3c Taylor St Weston Ind tel.

Croll, Jacob C. Grand Rapids Gr Rs.

Croll, Jno. 2c Tontogany Wash.

CROM, C. W. 4 ch farmer O 140a 5h 3c R1 Bowling Green Pla 28 Ind tel.

Crom, J. A. (Grace) farmer O 59a 3h 4c R2 Bowling Green Cen 75 Ind tel.

Cronister, Amos (Mary K.) ret O H&L Bradner Mon.

Cronniger, Rush (Nellie) 3 ch elevator T H&L Grand Rapids Gr Rs.

Crook, O. F. (Emma) field foreman T H&L Woodside Fre 78 Ind tel.

Crosby, Jane R. ret O H&L Grand Rapids Gr Rs Ind tel.

CROSBY, LEWIS W. (Jane) ret O H&I R5 Grand Rapids Gr Rs.

Cross, Albert cattle RD Bowling Green Cen.

CROSS, EDWIN (Fanny) farmer T 80a 4h 3c R2 Dunbridge Mid 82 Ind tel.

Cross, Ernest cattle RD Bowling Green Cen.

Cross, Prudence E. RD North Baltimore Hen.

Cross, S. (Margretta) farmer T 80a 3h 3c R2 North Baltimore Hen 75.

Crosse, A. E. (Mary) 3 ch farmer O H&L 2h 4c R3 Bowling Cen 82.

CROSSE, THOMAS (Emily) 7 ch ret O 130a 4h 3c R3 Bowling Green Cen 82 Ind tel.

Crossett, H. A. Rossford Ros.

Crossman, Mrs. Adam ret O H&L Millbury Lake 54.

Crossman, Mrs. Mary ret O H&L Millbury Lake 54.

Crossaw, Chris, Jr. (Ethel) 1 ch oil worker O H&L R1 Rudolph Por 24½ Ind tel.

Crothener, Mac (Pearl) laborer T H&L Fifth St Perrysburg Pbg.

Crouch, L. D. (Gladys) laborer T H&L Hoytsville Jac.

Crowell, Leah ret O H&L Risingsun Mon.

Crowl, Ollie ret O H&L Risingsun Mon.

Culbertson, Ray farmer O 10a R1 Grand Rapids Gr Rs 14.

Culp, Jacob cattle R1 Mermill Por.

Culver, C. C. (Ella) 1 ch driller T H&L Factory St Jerry City Por.

Culver, Fred student Factory St Jerry City Por.

CUMING, HIRAM (Elizabeth) 1 ch farmer O 60a 3h 5c Haskins Mid 50 B tel.

CUMMING, CHAS. (Sarah) farmer O 10a 2c Bays Lib 100.

Cummings, C. O. (Hattie I.) 1 ch farmer O 48a 5h 3c Tontogany Wash 41 Ind tel.

Cummings, Edith nurse O 18a Tontogany Wash 41.

Cummings, James L. (Rosa) farmer T 55a 9h 6c R3 Prairie Depot Mon.

Cummings, O. C. RD Tontogany Wash.

Cummins, Charley (Hattie) 1 ch carpenter O H&L R2 Haskins Mid 37 B tel.

Cunningham, J. (Viola) 2 ch farmer T 60a 2h R2 Prairie Depot Per 5.

Cupp, A. M. (son U. S.) farmer 1h R2 Prairie Depot Por 77 B tel.

Cupp, Bert (Alma) 6 ch oil worker O H&L 1h RD Rudolph Mon.

Cupp, C. C. (Lydia A.) 1 ch grocery O B 1h Rudolph Lib 81 Ind tel.

Cupp, J. A. (Catharine) laborer O H&L R1 North Baltimore Hen 69.

CUPP, J. W. (May) 7 ch farmer T 78a 3h 3c R1 North Baltimore Hen 123.

Cupp, Lydia M. RD North Baltimore Blo.

CUPP, L. A. grocery store Rudolph Lib 81.

Cupp, N. S. cattle RD Prairie Depot Por.

Cupp, Pearnell (dau U. S.) housekeeper R2 Prairie Depot Por 77 B tel.

CUPP, SHERMAN (Lydia) 1 ch farmer O & T 57a 3h 2c R3 North Baltimore Blo 24 B & Ind tels.

Cupp, Willis (Dora) clerk O H&L Prairie Depot Mon.

Cupp, U. S. (Cora) 4 ch farmer T 80a 4h 3c R2 Prairie Depot Por 77 B tel.

CUPP, U. S., JR. (son U. S.) farmer R2 Prairie Depot Por 77 B tel.

Curlis, Thos. RD Weston Pla.

CURLIS, W. J. (Martha) 1 ch farmer O 16a 1h 1c R1 Rudolph Lib 98.

CURRENT, CHAS. (Grace) 4 ch farmer O 71a 3h 2c R1 Tontogany Wash 20 Ind tel.

Current, C. A. (Myrtle) 5 ch postmaster T H&L Dunbridge Mid 75.

Current, John (Caroline) store keeper O H&L 1h Dunbridge Mid 75 B tel.

Curry, Mrs. C. G. 2 ch gardening O 6a 1h Rossford Pbg 77.

Curry, Jesse (Fern) garage T H&L Bell St Bradner Mon.

Curry, S. H. (Dora) 1 ch oil contractor O H&L East St Bradner Mon B tel.

Curson, Chas. L. (Jennie) farmer O 28a 2h 3c Station A East Toledo Ros 23.

Curtin, J. S. (Anna) 3 ch construction forman O H&L Loci St Cygnet Blo.

Curtin, Rose trained nurse Loci St Cygnet Blo Ind tel.

Curtis, A. G. (Ida) 8 ch farmer T 160a 5h 6c R2 North Baltimore Jac 119.

Curtis, Dallas (Pauline) 1 ch farmer T 80a 3h 3c Hoytsville Jac 121.

Curtis, Dotty ret O H&L cor Third & Locust St Perrysburg Pbg B tel.

Curtis, Ellsworth (son A. G.) farm hand R2 North Baltimore Jac 119.

Curtis, Elver (Grace) laborer T H&L RD Sixth St Perrysburg Pbg.

Curtis, E. J. (Elizabeth carpenter O H&L Indiana Ave Perrysburg Pbg B tel.

Curtis, George (Ethel) 1 ch oil man T H&L R3 North Baltimore Blo.

Curtis, H. L. (Rose) oil worker T H&L Cygnet Blo 19 Ind tel.

Curtis, Irvin Perrysburg Pbg.

Curtis, Joe (Edith) 7 ch laborer O H&L 1h 1c Fifth St Perrysburg Pbg B tel.

Curtis L. W. (Mary E.) 3 ch farmer O 65a 2h 3c Cygnet Blo 19.

Curtis, Norton Perrysburg Pbg.

Cutcher, Joseph (Josephine) 1 ch hired man R3 Perrysburg Pbg 74.

Cuthbert, Mrs. Blanche 2 ch weaving O H&L Verango St Cygnet Blo.

Czelusta, F. J. Rossford Ros.

Czirr, Herman 4 ch farmer 83a 5h 3c R1 Pemberville Fre 65 B tel.

Dahms, Mrs. Agusta R1 Portage Por 107.

Dahms, Aimel (Pearl) farmer O 20a 3h 1c R1 Portage Por 107.

Dahms, Otto (Lena) farmer O 40a 7h 3c R1 Portage Por 107.

Dahms, Wm. (Dessie) 1 ch farmer T 80a 3h 1c R1 Jerry City Por 64.

Daily, Albert E. (Kate) 1 ch oil foreman T H&L Walnut St Portage Por Ind tel.

Daily, C. K. (Goldy) 3 ch farmer T 80a 3h 4c R2 Pemberville Web 24.

Daily, Ellen D. Prairie Depot Mon.

Daily, Geo. K. (Ellen) 9 ch ret farmer O 160a 1h 4c R3 Prairie Depot Mon 12 B tel.

Daily, J. L. Prairie Depot Mon.

Daily, Lew (Zula) 2 ch pumper O H&L R3 Prairie Depot Mon 12½.

Daily, Pearl music teacher R3 Prairie Depot Mon 12.

Daily, Roy G. RD Bowling Green Web.

Daily, T. B. (Gussie) 5 ch pumper O 5a S Main St Bradner Mon.

Daily, Wm. I. (Amanda) 2 ch pumper O 80a 1c R3 Prairie Depot Mon 12.

Dalden, A. C. (Clara) 2 ch farmer T 120a 5h 2c Weston Mil 60 Ind tel.

Daley, J. H. (Anna) gardener T H&L Seventh St Perrysburg Pbg.

Dalley, John S. 7 ch farmer O 160a 6h 10c R2 Bowling Green Pla 91 B tel.

Dalton, Emma C. Freeport Mon.

Dalton, W. E. Risingsun Mon.

Dalzell, A. I. Weston Mil.

Dalzell, Harrison RD Bowling Green Pla.

Damen, Henry Pemberville Web.

Dammon, F. W. (Sophie) farmer O 40a 2h 3c R1 Bradner Fre 93.

Danials, D. W. (Charlott) farmer O 40a 1c R1 Tontogany Wash 41.

Danials, J. A. farming T 5h R1 Tontogany Wash 41.

Daniell, Thomas ret O 45a 2c R1 Perrysburg Pbg 104.

Daniels, Allen F. (Bertha) 4 ch farmer T 82a 4h 4c R1 Tontogany Wash 84 Ind tel.

Daniels, Chas. (Dora) 3 ch laborer O H&L Bairdstown Blo.

Daniels, D. H. Tontogany.

Daniels, E. C. laborer R R St Bairdstown Blo.

Daniels, Henry (Emma C.) 2 ch ret O 100a 1h Main St Weston Wes B tel.

Daniels, J. C. laborer R R St Bairdstown Blo.

Dannenberger, L. A. (Violette) 3 ch carpenter O 40a 2h 1c R2 Bowling Green Cen 8 Ind tel.

Dannenberger, Merl oil pumper 1h R1 Bowling Green Pla 34.

Dannenberger, W. (Lavern) 3 ch farmer O 20a 2h 1c R3 Bowling Green Web 13 Ind tel.

Danner, Henry R3 Perrysburg Pbg.

Danner, John (Lena) farmer O 7a 1h 2c R3 Perrysburg Pbg 136.

Danz, Mrs. Rudolf 2 ch ret O H&L Second St Perrysburg Pbg.

Darrow, C. V. (Gertrude) garage Portage Lib 112.

Dart, Bert M. Millbury Lake.

Dart, Frank (Gertrude) 4 ch railroader T H&L Walbridge Lake.

Dart, Wm. Millbury Lake.

Dauer, Amelia school teacher R1 Haskins Mid 54 B tel.

Dauer, Albert F. (Cora) farmer joint owner 1a 6h 7c R1 Haskins Mid 54 B tel.

61

Dauer, Arnold F. (son F. J.) farmer R1 Haskins Mid 49.

Dauer, Carl (son C. A.) farmer R2 Haskins Wash 95 B tel.

Dauer, C. A. (Louisa) 2 ch farmer O 105a 4h 7c R2 Haskins Wash 95 B tel.

Dauer, C. F. (Hetta) rural mail carrier T H&L 2h Lime City Pbg 121.

Dauer, C. J. (Maggie) 4 ch farmer O 73a 3h 4c Haskins Mid 50 B tel.

DAUER, F. J. (Lizzie) 1 ch farmer O 80a 3h 7c R1 Haskins Mid 49 B tel.

Dauer, Geo. (Grace) 6 ch farmer O 120a 5h 4c R1 Perrysburg Pbg 16 B tel.

Dauer, J. F. (Anna B.) 1 ch farmer T 60a 5h 3c R1 Perrysburg Pbg 20.

Dauer, Lydia (dau C. A.) teacher R2 Haskins Wash 95 B tel.

Dauer, P. A. (Minnie) 3 ch farmer T 60a 5h 3c R2 Haskins Mid 37 B tel.

Dauer, Wm. RD Dunbridge Mid.

Daugherty, Henry Bloomdale Per.

Daul, Robert (Rose) 2 ch engineer O H&L Walbridge Lake.

Daum, J. A. (M. B.) farmer O 55a 2h 5c R2 Fostoria Per 117.

Daum, O. A. (son J. A.) farmer T 55a 2h 1c R2 Fostoria Per 117.

Daur, Henry oiler O H&L Lime City Pbg 121.

DAUTERMAN, CAROLINE M. O 60a 1h 1c R1 Portage Por 91.

Dauterman, Earl (Mina) 2 ch farmer O 80a 5h 2c R1 Portage Por Ind tel.

DAUTERMAN, MRS. F. J. R2 Weston Gr Rs.

DAUTERMAN, F. W. (Magdalene) 2 ch farmer O 100a 2h 2c Mermill Por 20 Ind tel.

Dauterman, Peter (Christiana) farmer O 40a 2h 2c R1 Portage Por 50.

Dauterman, Quincy (Ida) 3 ch farmer O 113a 6h 2c R1 Portage Por 91.

Davenport, Clesson (son E.) farmer 240 Maple St Rossford Ros.

Davenport, Edwin (Jennie) 3 ch carpenter O H&L 240 Maple St Rossford Ross.

David, Fred H. RD Prairie Depot Por.

David, Geo. farmer R2 Prairie Depot Por 103.

David, Henry farmer T 40a R2 Prairie Depot Por 103.

David, J. H. (Katie) farmer O 80a 4h 5c R3 Prairie Depot Por 106.

David, Mary farmer O 80a 2h 4c R2 Prairie Depot Por 103.

David, Wm. farmer T 40a 2h 3c R2 Prairie Depot Por 103.

Davidson, Alfred (Mary) ret O H&L West Millgrove Per 68.

Davidson, Arthur T. (son Alice) grocer Scotch Ridge Web 35 Ind tel.

Davidson, C. S. (Anna) farmer O 88a H&L 3h 2c Main St Portage Ind tel.

Davidson, Frank E. (son Alice) grocer Scotch Ridge Web 35 Ind tel.

Davidson, John (Cora) farmer O 70a 5h 5c R2 Prairie Depot Por 123.

Davidson, J. W. cattle RD Bowling Green Cen.

Davidson, Laura (dau Alice) housekeeper Scotch Ridge Web 35.

DAVIDSON, MARY housekeeper Scotch Ridge Web 30.

DAVIDSON, P. M. ice cream, coal & ice RD Bowling Green. See adv.

Davidson, R. F. Perrysburg Pbg.

Davidson, R. W. RD Bowling Green Fre.

Davidson, T. H. (Dosse) 8 ch farmer O 75a 7h 4c R4 Bowling Green Cen 112 Ind tel.

Davidson, Mrs. Wm. cattle RD Bowling Green Cen.

Davidson, W. H. (May) farmer O 140a 4h 7c R2 Prairie Depot Por 79.

Davidson, W. M. Pemberville Web.

DAVIDTER, EDWARD H. (son Herman) farmer 1h R1 Pemberville Fre 38.

Davidter, Herman (Eliza) ret O 53a 2h 3c R1 Pemberville Fre 38.

Davies, Chas. M. RD Hoytsville Jac.

Davis, Mrs. Anna ret O H&L Grand Rapids Gr Rs Ind tel.

Davis, Alice housekeeper O H&L Scotchridge Web 35.

Davis, B. F. (Edith) 3 ch farmer O 80a 3h 7c R1 Tontogany Wash 21 Ind tel.

Davis, Clarence (Glenna) 2 ch farmer & dairy T H&L 3h 6c Grand Rapids Gr Rs.

Davis, Clifford farmer T 65a 4h Portage Por 10 Ind tel.

DAVIS, CHAS. M. (Cordelia R.) 5 ch poultry buyer O 1a H 1h R1 Hoytsville Jac 115 Ind tel.

Davis, C. K. Grand Rapids Gr Rs.

Davis, Delmore (Millie) 4 ch farming T 105a 2h 2c Portage Por 10 Ind tel.

DAVIS, D. J. farmer T 120a 2h Jerry City Por 69 Ind tel.

Davis, Elmer (Minnie) farmer R1 Portage Por 38.

Davis, E. J. (Mary) 2 ch farmer O 34a 4h 6c Waterville Mid 3 B tel.

Davis, E. L. (Mary) 4 ch laborer 1c R1 Rudolph Lib 62½.

Davis, Frank RD Tontogany Wash.

Davis, Henry (Bertha) ret T 18a 1h 1c Rossford Pbg 79.

Davis, Mrs. H. E. housekeeper 4c Jerry City Por 69 Ind tel.

Davis, H. M. (Alice) laborer T H&L Sixth St Perrysburg Pbg.

Davis, H. N. Grand Rapids Gr Rs.

Davis, Jane RD Dunbridge Mid.

Davis, Julia A. Weston Gr Rs.

Davis, Josephine E. Perrysburg Pbg.

DAVIS, J. hardware O H&L Perrysburg Per Ind tel.

DAVIS, J. F. (Susan) farmer O 25a 2h 4c R1 Fostoria Per 111 Ind tel.

DAVIS, J. H. (Mary) farmer O 20a 2h 1c R2 Weston Wes 43.

Davis, J. T. (Mary E.) painter T H&L Railroad St Bradner Mon.

Davis, Kyle (Marie A.) laborer T H&L Rudolph Lib 96.

Davis, Marguerite (dau S. C.) student R1 North Baltimore Hen 95 Ind tel.

Davis, Mrs. Mary M. 3 ch housekeeper H&L Claron St Cygnet Blo 6 Ind tel.

Davis, O. T. (Bess) 5 ch hardware dealer O 2a H Main St Perrysburg Pbg B tel.

Davis, Mrs. Philip R3 Perrysburg Pbg.

Davis, Rudolph (son Mrs. Sam Deckrock) laborer Custar Mil B & Ind tels.

Davis, Ruth housekeeper Portage Por 10 Ind tel.

Davis, Sam (Agnes) 5 ch farmer O 40a 3h 2c R3 Perrysburg Pbg 157.

Davis, Sarah A. Tontogany Wash.

Davis, Solan 1 ch surveyor O H&L Center St Weston B tel.

Davis, Sar E. Perrysburg Pbg.

Davis, Susan M. Perrysburg Pbg.

DAVIS, S. C. (Anna) 1 ch farmer O 69a 3h 5c R1 North Baltimore Hen 95 Ind tel.

Davis, T. H. (Edna) 2 ch farmer O 80a 4h 1c R1 Weston Mil 55 Ind tel.

Davis, W. M. (Lucy) veterinary O 1h Jerry City Por.

Davison, Alice ret O H&L Millbury Lake.

Davison, W. A. (Alice) saloonkeeper Stony Ridge Tro.

Dawsey, F. C. (Carrie) 6 ch oil pumper T H&L Prairie Depot Mon.

Dawson, F. A. (Ester) 2 ch farmer T 147a 3h 5c R1 Fostoria Per 120.

DAWSON, GEO. Hoytville.

DAWSON, J. H. (Julia B.) 2 ch farmer T 62a 2h 6c R1 Haskins Mid 50 B tel.

Dawson, Robt. Haskins Wash.

Day, Chas. carpenter O H&L Risingsun Mon.

Day, Ezra (Ida) ret O H&L Risingsun Mon.

Deam, Lena ret O H&L Custar Mil.

Dean, A. L. Millbury Lake.

Dean, Caroline Custar Mil.

DEAN, EARL LE ROY (Millie) 1 ch farmer T 160a 7h 3c R1 Hoytville Jac 85 B tel.

DEAN, FLOYD (Hada) farmer T 40a 3h 2c R1 Hoytsville Jac 94.

Dean, Herman (Elizabeth) farmer O 100a 12h 4c R1 Hoytsville Jac 94 B tel.

Dean, John (Lila) 3 ch farmer T 196a 5h 4c R3 Bowling Green Cen 21 B tel.

Dean, Oliver ret O H&L R1 Genoa Lake 45.

Dean, Willard (Martha) farmer T H&L R2 Bowling Green Cen 7.

Dean, W. H. Pemberville Fre.

Dear, Martin 4 ch pool room Hoytsville Jac.

DEBOLT, GEO. (son T. H.) oil worker Rudolph Lib 94 Ind tel.

Debolt, Tom H. (Mary) 8 ch oil worker O H&L Rudolph Lib 94 Ind tel.

De Cant, A. (Nona) 4 ch laborer T H&L R1 Lime City Pbg 54.

Deck, Carl farmer T Portage Por 2.

Deckard, Ross laborer R1 Bloomdale Blo 123 Ind tel.

Decker, C. F. (Anna) 3 ch engineer O H&L Loci St Cygnet Blo Ind tel.

DECKER, D. F. (Addie) 2 ch farmer O 80a 4h 8c R1 Hoytsville Jac 64 Ind tel.

Decker, F. (Alice) 1 ch tailor T H&L Weston Wes.

Decker, R. C. (Verta) 1 ch farmer T 80a 5h 3c R1 Deshler Jac 13.

Decker, Walter L. (Goldie) 3 ch engineer & telegrapher O H&L Mermill Por 19 Ind tel.

Decker, Wm. 5 ch pumper O H&L 1h Mermill Por 19 Ind tel.

Decker, W. H. (Bessie) 2 ch restaurant T H&L Perrysburg Pbg.

Deckrosh, Mrs. Sam 3 ch ret O H&L Custar Mil B & Ind tels.

Deem, Mrs. Etta 3 ch housekeeper O H&L Lime City Pbg 121.

Deem, Sylvia (dau Mrs. Etta) housekeeper Lime City Pbg 121.

Dees, R. T. (Beulah) melter T H&L Box 176 Rossford Ros.

Degner, A. W. (Mary) 2 ch farmer O H&L Fourth St Perrysburg Pbg.

Degner, Clarence (Edna) 2 ch architect O H&L Sixth St Perrysburg Pbg B tel.

Deibert, Clarence Prairie Depot Mon.

63

Deibert, Frank (F.) shoemaker T H&L Evans Ave Bradner Mon.

Deimling, Charles (Louisa) 1 ch farmer O 27a 3h 5c Lime City Pbg 124.

Deimling, George (Ida K.) 1 ch farmer O 65a 4h 3c Lime City Pbg 121.

Deiter, A. P. Risingsun Mon.

Deiter, Jacob Prairie Depot Mon.

Deiter, Jess (Cora) 2 ch farmer T 87a 3h 5c R1 Bradner Mon 59.

Deiter, John Prairie Depot Mon.

Deiter, J. H. Prairie Depot Mon.

Deiter, Perry Prairie Depot Mon.

Delancy, Lewis S. (Cora B.) engineer O H&L R1 Jerry City Blo 62 B & Ind tels.

Delancy, Robert carpenter O H&L Cor Mulberry & Haison Sts Bloomdale Blo B & Ind tels.

Delancy, W. E. oil man T H&L R1 Jerry City Blo 60 B & Ind tels.

De Lander, Clate Pemberville Fre.

Delano, Jane Custar Mil.

Delcanys, G. R. (Anna) 2 ch painter Rudolph Lib 94 Ind tel.

Delette, C. M. Stony Ridge Tro.

Deloe, Mrs. Amuda C. 1 ch Maple St Bloomdale Blo.

Deloe, Isla (dau Amud C.) Maple St Bloomdale Blo.

Deloe, Robert (son Armuda) oil man roustabout Maple St Bloomdale Blo.

De Long, Lottie Weston Wes.

De Long, Thomas (Tressa) section hand T H&L High St Weston.

Delp, Chester (Sarah) 5 ch laborer O H&L 1h R1 Hoytsville Jac 116.

Delp, Morris T. (son Chester) laborer R1 Hoytsville Jac 116.

Delton, Wm. (Ada) 4 ch oil man O H&L 1h Risingsun Mon.

De Muth, R. S. Rossford Ros.

Denney, J. A. (Nellie) 5 ch farmer T 120a 5h 5c R1 Prairie Depot Mon 83 B tel.

Dennis, Alfred (Frances) 2 ch farmer O 37a H&L Lemoyne Tro Ind tel.

Dennis, Alta (dau W. H.) R1 Weston Lib 6 Ind tel.

Dennis, Amanda 11 ch ret O 18a Lemoyne Tro.

Dennis, A. C. (Georgia) 1 ch carpenter T H&L Dowling Mid 76.

Dennis, A. V. RD Dowling Mid.

Dennis, B. L. (May) 4 ch laborer O H&L Dowling Mid 76.

Dennis, Clifford (son W. H.) R1 Weston Lib 6 Ind tel.

Dennis, C. E. (Etta M.) 2 ch salesman T H&L Lincoln St Bloomdale Blo B & Ind tels.

Dennis, Eugene (Etta) 5 ch laborer T H&L Hoytsville Jac.

Dennis, E. M. RD Dunbridge Mid.

Dennis, Florence (dau of W. H.) R1 Weston Lib 6 Ind tel.

DENNIS, F. E. (Nara) 1 ch gas line manager T H&L 1h Main St Bloomdale Blo B & Ind tels.

Dennis, Glen (son Chas.) Lincoln St Bloomdale Blo B & Ind tels.

Dennis, Harley L. (Alice E.) 1 ch farmer O 31a T 48a 4h 4c R2 Bloomdale Blo 109 B & Ind tels.

Dennis, Jean Hoytsville Jac.

Dennis, Jno. L. Hoytsville Jac.

DENNIS, J. A. (Clara E.) 1 ch farmer O 102a 8h 6c R1 Jerry City Blo 62 Ind tel.

DENNIS, LAURA A. housekeeper R1 Bloomdale Blo 61 B & Ind tels.

Dennis, Manel S. farmer O 80a 6h 10c R1 Bloomdale Blo 61 B & Ind tels.

Dennis, Myrtie (dau W. H.) R11 Weston Lib 6 Ind tel.

Dennis, M. M. (Anna) oil man roustabout T H&L Mulberry St Bloomdale Blo B & Ind tels.

Dennis, Nettie (dau Amanda) housekeeper Lemoyne Tro.

DENNIS, OSCAR (Bertha) 3 ch farmer 116a 6h 15c Lemoyne Tro Ind tél.

Dennis, P. J. (Nettie) 3 ch salesman O H&L Hoytsville Jac B tel.

DENNIS, S. W. (Hattie) 1 ch farmer O 80a 6h 2c RD Bloomdale Blo B & Ind tels.

Dennis, Walter A. RD Hoytsville Jac.

Dennis, W. H. (Rosa) gas line Bloomdale O H&L 2h 1c S Main St Bloomdale Blo B & Ind tels.

DENNIS, W. H. (Anna) 9 ch farmer O 100a 8h 9c R1 Weston Lib 6 Ind tel.

Denny, J. A. (Nellie) 5 ch farmer T 120a 5h 5c R1 Prairie Depot Mon 83 B tel.

Denny, J. H. (Sarah E.) 1 ch insurance agent O H&L East St Bradner Mon.

Dent, I. D. (Martha) farmer O 81a 2h 6c R1 Dunbridge Web 49 B tel.

Depasse, Sylvester RD Perrysburg Pbg.

Dermer, A. B. (Della) 6 ch carpenter O H&L Hoytsville Jac.

DERMER, GEO. A. (Ivy L.) 2 ch lumber O H&L 1h 1c Hoytsville.

Dermer, Geo. N. (son A. B.) telegraph operator Hoytsville Jac.

Dermer, Guy P. Hoytsville Jac.

Dermer, John B. (Georgia) tile worker T H&L Hoytsville Jac.

Dern, Charles (Pearl) 4 ch paperhanger & painter T H&L Prairie Depot Mon.

De Rodes, Agnes RD North Baltimore Hen.

DeShetler, E. B. Rossford Ros.

DeSMICHT, ADOLPH (Pharaiode) 7 ch farmer T H&L R1 Bowling Green Pla 73.

Deter, Geo. P. RD North Baltimore Hen.

Deter, J. M. RD North Baltimore Hen.

Deter, J. W. RD North Baltimore Hen.

Deter, Mary E. RD North Baltimore Hen.

Deter, W. M. (Nellie) 3 ch farmer O 40a 4h 4c R2 North Baltimore Hen 24 Ind tel.

Dethloff, Amelia (dau F.) housekeeper R3 Perrysburg Pbg 77.

Dethloff, Frederick K. (Caroline) 1 ch farmer O 10a 1h 1c R3 Perrysburg Pbg 77.

DETRAY, C. I. (Rose) veterinarian T H&L 1h Pemberville Fre.

DeTray, Emery L. (Pearl) 1 ch insurance & real estate T H&L 1h Pemberville Fre B tel.

Detrick, Charles (Carrie) 2 ch sugar beet boss T H&L Prairie Depot Mon B tel.

Detwiler, J. W. Pemberville Fre.

DEUBLE, JOHN A. (Louise) 1 ch farmer O 50a 7h 13c R7 Luckey Tro 89 B tel.

Deuble, Mrs. J. J. 1 ch housekeeper O H&L Luckey Tro Ind tel.

DEUBLE, PAUL (Irene) carpenter O H&L R1 Luckey Tro Ind tel.

Deuble, Sarah M. Luckey Tro.

DEWALD, MRS. IDA L. housekeeper T H&L Millbury Lake 76.

Devault, J. W. (Mary) farmer T 160a 4h 4c R2 North Baltimore Hen Ind tel.

DeVerna, E. S. (Margarette) 4 ch farmer O 120a 6h 4c R1 Perrysburg Pbg 20 B tel.

DeVerna, Geo. (Grace) 3 ch farmer O 160a 5h 7c R1 Perrysburg Pbg 20.

DeVerna, H. A. (Dorthy) 1 ch farmer T 120a 1h R1 Perrysburg Pbg 20.

Devlin, Claude (son Mrs. J.) farmer bds 2h R2 Dunbridge Mid 46.

Devlin, Mrs. J. farmer O 80a 1c R2 Dunbridge Mid 46 Ind tel.

Devlin, Miranda RD Dunbridge Mid.

Devlin, Pansy (dau Mrs. J.) housekeeper R2 Dunbridge Mid 46.

DeWalt, J. W. RD North Baltimore Hen.

DEWALT, PAUL R2 North Baltimore Hen 81.

Dewalt, W. P. (Glidar) 2 ch farmer & thresher T 1½a 1c R2 North Baltimore Hen 81 Ind tel.

Dewees, Mary Jane 1 ch T H&L Center St Weston.

Dewese, A. R. (Annie) 4 ch farmer & stock dealer O 133a 5h 10c R2 Weston Wes 32 Ind tel.

Dewese, Burt (Jessie) 1 ch farming O 47a 4h 3c R2 Weston Wes 46.

Dewese, Burton S. (son W. A.) student bds R2 Weston Wes 32 Ind tel.

Dewese, Ernest (Edna) 3 ch farming O 40a 3h 3c R2 Weston Wes 30.

Dewese, Floyd M. (son W. A.) farmer bds R2 Weston Wes 32 Ind tel.

Dewese, W. A. (Elizabeth) 2 ch farmer O 160a 5h 9c R2 Weston Wes 32 Ind tel.

DeWitt, Frank (Bessie) 3 ch school teacher O 120a 8h 6c R1 Prairie Depot Mon 86.

DeWitt, Herbert (Myrtle E.) 1 ch farmer T 160a 5h 12c West Millgrove Per 65 Ind tel.

Before and After. The Old House and the New of One of Our Folks.

DEWITT, HERBERT (Vina) 2 ch farmer T 160a 4h 1c R2 Pemberville Web 44.

Dewitt, Lydia housekeeper O Water St Portage Por.

DEWITT, OTIS (Jane) farmer O 40a 3h 3c R1 Tontogany Wash 77 Ind tel.

Dewitt, S. W. Weston Wes.

Dewitt, Wallace laborer T H&L Water St Portage Por.

DeWitt, W. S. (Alma) ret 200a 2h 1c West Millgrove Per 69.

Dewland, Albert (Hazel) 1 ch real estate O H&L Front St Perrysburg Pbg B tel.

DEWYER, CLYDE (Vema) 2 ch banker T H&L Pemberville Fre 40 B tel.

DEWYER, MILO (Matilda) 4 ch farmer T 40a 5h 2c R2 Prairie Depot Mon 48.

DEWYER, ROSS (Ida) 4 ch ditcher T H&L Mermill Por 19 Ind tel.

Dewyer, Wm. Pemberville Fre.

Dey, Samuel (Sarah E.) 2 ch laborer O Bairdstown Blo.

DIBERT, ALFRED G. (Eva) 4 ch farmer T 40a 2h 2c R1 Perrysberg Pbg 103.

Dibert, Mrs. Mary ret O 40a 4c R1 Perrysburg Pbg 104.

DIBERT, MICHAEL (Lena) 3 ch farmer T H&L R1 Perrysburg Pbg 104.

Dibert, Mrs. W. M. farmer O 40a 1c R1 Perrysburg Pbg 103 B tel.

Dibling, Alphonse farmer T 20a 2h Custar Milton 97.

DIBLING, LEO (Mary) 12 ch farmer T 280a 9h 4c R2 Custar Mil 41 B tel.

Dibling, Louie (son Leo.) farm hand R2 Custar Mil 41 B tel.

Dibling, Louisa (dau Leo.) housekeeper R2 Custar Mil 41 B tel.

Dibling, Mary ret 20a 1c R1 Custar Mil 97.

Dibling, Wm. C. 4 ch laborer O H&L Third St Perrysburg Pbg.

Dicinger, Clel RD North Baltimore Hen.

Dick, Chas. (Edna) 1 ch tile worker T H&L Hoytsville Jac.

Dick, Earl E. (Edith M.) 1 ch oil man T H&L 1h 1c R3 North Baltimore Blo 15½ B & Ind tels.

Dick, Elmer (Mabel) 4 ch garage O H&L Hoytsville Jac B tel.

Dick, Frank (Alice) 2 ch oil pumper T 1h R1 North Baltimore Hen 71 B tel.

Dicken, Chas. (Mettie) 6 ch farmer O H&L Prairie Depot Mon B tel.

Dicken, Curtis painter O 2a R3 Prairie Depot Mon 108.

Dicken, J. (Minerva) fruit pruner & paper hanger O H&L Prairie Depot Mon.

Dicken, Wm. Prairie Depot Mon.

Dickens, Mrs. Sarah Harrison St Bloomdale Blo.

Dickinson, Mina R. 2 ch dressmaking T H&L cor Caldwell & East St Bradner Mon.

Diefenthaler, Antone (Caroline) ret O 120a R1 Millbury Lake 64 Ind tel.

Diefenthaler, Edward (Gustie) 2 ch tile yard O H&L Millbury Lake.

Diefenthaler, Henry (Martha) 3 ch farmer T 80a 6h 25c R1 Millbury Lake 64 Ind tel.

Diefenthaler, Philipp (Emma) 4 ch tile man O H&L Millbury Lake.

Diehl, Mrs. Eliza M. cattle RD Portage Por.

Dienst, Mrs. Elmer A. Portage Lib.

DIERKER, FRED (Anna) farmer O 70a 3h 9c R3 Pemberville Tro 56 B tel.

Dierker, Henry Luckey Web.

DIERKER, JOHN (Carrie) 4 ch farmer O 60a 2h 10c RD Luckey Tro 52 Ind tel.

Dierkier, H. F. (Bertha) 1 ch farmer O 80a 3h 5c Luckey Web 64 B tel.

Dierksheide, Chas. Bradner Fre.

Dierksheide, Gustave (Minnie) 5 ch farmer O 100a 6h 6c R3 Prairie Depot Fre 74 B tel.

DIERKSHEIDE, HENRY (Lueza) 5 ch farmer O 160a 5h 8c R3 Prairie Depot Fre 82 B tel.

Dierksheide, Wm. (Anna) 4 ch farmer O 123a 7h 10c R1 Bradner Fre 82 B tel.

Dieter, Chas. (Bertha) 6 ch hay baler H&L 1h Prairie Depot Mon.

Dieter, James (Cora) 2 ch farmer O 80a 4h 4c R1 Fostoria Per 98.

Dieter, John (Sarah) hay baler T H&L 1h Prairie Depot Mon.

Dieter, J. F. (Elizabeth) farmer O 80a 6h 6c R1 Prairie Depot Mon 119 B tel.

Dieter, J. H. (Gladys) 5 ch pumper & farmer O 80a 3h 7c R1 Prairie Depot Mon 113 B tel.

DIETER, J. R. R1 Prairie Depot.

Dieter, Perry (Daisy) 7 ch farmer O 80a 5h 4c R1 Prairie Depot Mon 114 B tel.

Dieter, Read (son J. F.) farmer R1 Prairie Depot Mon 119 B tel.

Dietrich, Carrie Portage Lib 90 Ind tel.

Dietrich, Charley (Hazel) 1 ch oil worker T H&L 1h R1 Portage Lib 87 Ind tel.

Dietrich, Lena R1 Portage Lib 90 Ind tel.

Dietrich, Philip oil worker 1h 2c R1 Portage Lib 90 Ind tel.

Dietrich, S. S. Bloomdale Blo.

Dietz, F. W. (Sophia) 4 ch minister T H&L Fifth St Perrysburg Pbg.

Dietz, Henry (Lena) 1 ch butcher & meat cutter O H&L Box 45A Rossford Ros.

DIEUST, E. A. (Orpha) 2 ch agent T H&L Portage Por.

DIGBY, BERT (Hope) 1 ch farmer T 150a 2h 4c R1 Grand Rapids Wash 54 Ind tel.

Digby, Elmer (Jennie) 2 ch farmer 2c R1 Grand Rapids Wash 54 B & Ind tels.

Digby, Frank (Florence) laborer O H&L Grand Rapids Gr Rs Ind tel.

Digby, Geo. RD Bowling Green Wash.

Digby, Martha RD Tontogany Wash.

Digby, Robert (Susan) 1 ch farmer O 150a 3h 3c R1 Grand Rapids Wash 54 Ind tel.

Dilbert, A. G. R1 Perrysburg Pbg.

Diley, Prof. J. M. (Cora) teacher T H&L Rudolph Lib 96 Ind tel.

Dill, Charles R2 Custar Lib 20 Ind tel.

Dill, Edward (Emma) 5 ch farmer O 160a 4h 5c R2 Custar Lib 20 Ind tel.

Dill, Floyd farmer 4h R2 Custar Lib 20 Ind tel.

Dill, Lester R2 Custar Lib 20 Ind tel.

Dill, Myron (Chloe) 2 ch farmer T 120a 4h 3c R2 Custar Mil 36 Ind tel.

Dilley, Mrs. Mary E. ret O H&L Pemberville Fre 40.

Dillinger, A. J. RD North Baltimore Hen.

Dillinger, C. L. (Blanche) 1 ch farmer T 225a 5h 5c Hoytsville Jac 121 B tel.

Dillinger, C. O. RD North Baltimore Hen.

Dillinger, H. H. (Bertha) 4 ch real estate & garage O Hoytsville Jac B tel.

Dimick, M. C. (Martha) 6 ch farmer O 129a 4h RD Bowling Green Cen 73 B tel.

Dimond, Ezra RD Rudolph Lib.

Dimson, James (Sophia) grocery O H&L Tontogany Wash.

Dindore, C. L. (Hattie) 1 ch farmer T 80a 4h 2c West Millgrove Per 76.

Dindore, James (Lovina) ret farmer 80a Sandusky St West Millgrove Per.

Dindore, W. E. West Millgrove Per.

Dings, W. H. (Almira) 1 ch farmer O 16a 1h 1c R1 Weston Mil 73 Ind tel.

Dirk, John (Marie) 1 ch elevator man O H&L Taylor St Wes B tel.

Dirk, J. B. RD North Baltimore Hen.

Dirk, M. E. RD North Baltimore Hen.

DIRK, W. M. R2 Custar Lib.

Dirkheide, Charles (Lena) 3 ch farmer O 80a 4h 4c Bradner St Bradner Fre 82 B tel.

Dirrin, Isaac C. Perrysburg Pbg.

Dishong, Elias (Emma) 2 ch farmer O 22a R1 Hoytsville Jac 47.

Dishong, Floris (son E.) farm hand R1 Hoytsville Jac 47.

Dishong, Floyd (son Elias) thresher 7h 3c R1 Hoytsville Jac 47.

Dishong, Geo. blacksmith T H&L R1 Hoytsville Jac 44.

DISHONG, H. B. (Dora) 3 ch farmer T 70a 6h 4c R1 Deshler Jac 33.

Dishong, John B., Sr. (Katherine) 4 ch farmer O 240a R1 Deshler Jac 32 Ind tel.

Dishong, John K. (Esther) 2 ch farmer T 80a 4h 5c R1 Deshler Jac 32 Ind tel.

Dishong, John M. 3 ch ret O 40a 1h 1c R1 Deshler Jac 45.

Dishong, J. M. (Marie) farmer 2h 5c R1 Deshler Jac 32 Ind tel.

Dishong, Lena (dau U.) school teacher Hoytsville Jac B tel.

Dishong, Lloyd (son U.) clerk Hoytsville Jac B tel.

DISHONG, U. (Ella) 8 ch general store O H&L Hoytsville Jac B tel.

Ditman, E. A. (son Fred) railroader bds Walbridge Lake.

Ditman, Fred (Eva) railroader O H&L Walbridge Lake.

Ditmire, E. laborer Pemberville Fre.

Dix, Wm. (Nellie) 1 ch farmer T 80a 5h 2c RD Portage Por 43 Ind tel.

DIXON, HARRY L. (Jennie D.) 1 ch oil man O H&L R3 North Baltimore Blo B & Ind tels.

DOEHRING, HENRY farmer T 240a 5h R1 Deshler Jac 58.

DOEHRING, W. C. (Julia) 1 ch farmer T 80a 5h 3c R1 Hoytsville Jac 58.

Doehring, William T. (Johanna) farmer O 240a 1h 4c R4 Deshler Jac 58.

Doering, Chas. M. (Maggie A.) 3 ch oil man O H&L Randolph St Bairdstown Blo.

Doering, Lloyd M. (son Chas. M.) laborer Randolph St Bairdstown Blo.

Doil, C. C. (Mary) 2 ch farmer T 200a 6h 3c R1 North Baltimore Hen 70.

Doman, I. H. (Verda) 3 ch farmer T 100a 5h 4c R1 Fostoria Per 91 Ind tel.

Donald, Wm. (Clara) 1 ch farmer O 80a 6h 5c R1 Deshler Jac 7 B tel.

DONALD, W. W. (Lizzie) 4 ch farmer & horse breeder O 80a 11h 5c R1 Grand Rapids Gr Rs 11 Ind tel.

Donaldson, Delmar (son James) farmer R1 Hoytsville Jac 70.

Donaldson, James (Mary) 7 ch farmer O 80a 6h 1c R1 Hoytsville Jac 70.

Donels, Wm. 3 ch hired man R1 Fostoria Per 109.

Donnan, M. L. (Sarah) ticket agent T L 1c R3 North Baltimore Hen 123 Ind tel.

Donzey, Flora RD Bowling Green Mid.

Doren, Maud (dau S.) clerk 183 Oak St Rossford Ros.

Doren, Orville (son Samuel) chauffeur 183 Oak St Rossford Ros.

Doren, Samuel (Martha) 1 ch engineer O H&L 183 Oak St Rossford Ros.

DORFMEYER, JOHN (Carrie) 2 ch farmer T 40a 3h 3c R1 Genoa Lake 40 B & Ind tels.

Dorko, Mary ret Lemoyne Tro 29.

Dotson, Geo. C. RD North Baltimore Hen.

Doty, Henry cattle RD Bowling Green Cen.

Douge, Henry (Jane) farmer O 10a 1h 1c R1 Portage Por 107.

Doughty, D. D. Walbridge Lake.

Doughty, J. B. (Katie) farmer O 40a 1h Milton Center Mil 53 Ind tel.

DOUGLAS, A. (Lurellia) 1 ch farmer O 44a 8h 7c RD Portage Lib 59 Ind tel.

DOUGLAS, E. (Edith) 3 ch teamster O H&L Rudolph Lib 81.

DOUSTER, FRED (Mary) 10 ch farmer T 15a 3h 2c R1 Tontogany Wash 39 Ind tel.

Dowd, W. F. concrete worker T H&L Sixth St Perrysburg Pbg.

Dower, Charles (Elizabeth) ret O H&L Sixth St Perrysburg Pbg.

Dower, Mrs. J. 4 ch housekeeper O H&L Haskins Mid.

Dowling, C. E. Prairie Depot Mon.

Dowling, Patrick (Yvonne) undertaker T H&L Second St Perrysburg Per B tel.

Dowling, W. E. (Ella) farmer O 130a 3h 4c R1 Prairie Depot Mon 104 B tel.

Down, Mrs. Catherine ret O H&L Haskins Mid.

Downham, Mary R. Hoytsville Jac.

Downing, Daniel D. (Ella A.) hotel O H&L 1c Millbury Lake 52.

Downing, Mary ret O H&L Fifth St Perrysburg Pbg.

Downing, Mary R. ret O H&L Hoytsville Jac.

DOWNING, W. H. (Katharine) farmer 71a 2c Jerry City Blo 1 Ind tel.

Doyle, C. C. RD North Baltimore Hen.

Doyle, John H. (Mary) 6 ch laborer T H&L Seventh St Perrysburg Pbg.

DOYLE, J. M. (Mary) 3 ch oil worker O H&L 1h Loci St Cygnet Blo Ind tel.

Drace, Isaac (Lyda) 1 ch farmer O 40a 2h 2c R2 Prairie Depot Por 109.

Drace, Jno. RD Rudolph Lib.

DRACE, JOSEPH (Mattie) 3 ch farmer O 51a 2h 2c R1 Rudolph Por 24½.

Drager, Wm. (Katherine) 2 ch farmer O 95a 4h 5c R1 Pemberville Cen 116 Ind tel.

Drain, Alfred (Electa) engineer O H&L Findlay St Portage Por.

Drain, Eldon (son Alfred) fireman Findlay St Portage Por.

Drake, A. A. (Rosa) 4 ch painter O H&L Pemberville Fre 40.

Drake, A. S. (Tillie) 2 ch oil pumper O R1 North Baltimore Hen 125 Ind tel.

Drake, Charles D. (Louisa) 6 ch tanner & road supervisor T 55a 3h 1c R1 Bloomdale Bl 112.

DRAKE, D. F. (Ida) 2 ch farmer T 120a 3h 6c R1 Bloomdale Blo 129 B & Ind tels.

Drake, E. B. RD North Baltimore Hen.

Drake, George (Velna A.) 2 ch farmer T 40a 4h 4c R1 Bloomdale Bl 100 B & Ind tels.

Drake, H. N. (Alice) ret T H&L Water St Portage Por.

DRAKE, JOSIAH (Margaret E.) farmer O 55a & 3Lots 1h 2c R1 Bloomdale Bl 112 B & Ind tels.

Drake, J. J. (Cora) 1 ch farmer T 100a R1 Bloomdale Bl 110.

Drake, Margaret C. Bloomdale Bl.

Drake, O. P. Bloomdale Bl.

Drake, O. W. (Mary) 3 ch physician & surgeon T H&L Grand Rapids Gr Rs Ind tel.

Drake, Perry (Mary) ret farmer 1h Maple St Bloomdale Blo B & Ind tels.

Draper, M. C. drugs Front St Cygnet Bl Ind tel.

Drayton, Hattie housekeeper Walbridge Lake.

Drayton, Wm. (Anna) 1 ch repair man O H&L Walbridge Lake.

Dreps, John 1 ch ret T H&L Second St Perrysburg Pbg.

Dreps, John farmer T 128a 2h R2 Perrysburg Mid 14.

DRESCHER, W. A. Grand Rapids.

Dresher, Dick (Pearl) 2 ch bridge builder T H&L Locust St Weston Ind tel.

Driftmyer, Edward (Edith) 4 ch farmer O 51a 2h 6c R2 Gibsonburg Fre 19.

Driscoll, Edward J. (Julia) 4 ch Feillanch Co T R1 Walbridge Ros 22.

Driscoll, J. W. (Mary) 6 ch laborer O H&L Losee St Cygnet Bl.

Drumheller, David farmer O H&L 1h R5 Bowling Green Cen Ind tel.

Drummer, Benjamin (son George) farmer R2 Custar Mil 38.

Drummer, George (Mary) 7 ch farmer O 120a 5h 4c R2 Custar Mil 38 Ind tel.

Drummer, Herman (son Joseph) electrician Custar Mil B & Ind tels.

Drummer, Joseph (Cunedundis) 5 ch hardware merchant O H&L Custar Mil B & Ind tels.

Drummer, Lawrence (son Joseph) hardware clerk Custar Mil B & Ind tels.

Drummer, Martin (son George) farmer T 40a R2 Custar Mil 38.

Drummond, Henry (Jane) 3 ch poultry & egg buyer O H&L Hoytsville Jac B tel.

Drummond, John. (Mary) 6 ch ret farmer O 5a 1h 1c R3 Weston Mil 86.

Drummond, S. E. Coop St Jerry City Por.

Dubbs, Amanda Milton Center Mil.

Dubbs, H. B. RD North Baltimore Hen.

Dubbs, Mrs. J. F. 1 ch ret O H&L Milton Center Mil.

Dubbs, Lewis 3c ret farmer O 40a H&L 228 Taylor St Weston Wes.

Ducat, Dan (Ada) 1 ch machinist T 1h R2 Custar Hen 1½.

Ducat, D. L. (Cora) auto livery T H&L Grand Rapids Gr Rs Ind tel.

Ducat, Earlman RD Rudolph Lib 66 Ind tel.

DUCAT, ELIZABETH R1 Rudolph Lib 66 Ind tel.

Ducat, Ernestine R1 Rudolph Lib 66 Ind tel.

DUCAT, EXEA R1 Rudolph Lib 66 Ind tel.

Ducat, E. L. (Maggie) 5 ch farmer T 150a 5h 6c R3 Bowling Green Cen 22 Ind tel.

DUCAT, MRS. JOSIE R5 Box 50 Bowling Green.

Ducat, J. H. Weston Wes.

Ducat, Leonard (Lilly) 1 ch farmer T 131a R1 Weston Pla 8 Ind tel.

Ducat, Le Roy farmer R3 Bowling Green Cen 22 Ind tel.

DUCAT, PETER E. (Josephine) farmer O 82a 3h 3c R5 Bowling Green Cen 105 Ind tel.

DUCAT, T. J. (Emma) 4 ch farmer O 40a 5h 3c R1 Rudolph Lib 66 Ind tel.

Dudderar, C. E. (Lulu) 3 ch painter T H&L Haskins Mid.

Duesler, Floyd (Sylvia) 1 ch oil pumper T R1 Rudolph Hen 63.

Duesler, H. C. (Venna) 2 ch farmer O 40a 4h 5c R1 Rudolph Lib 33.

Duesler, L. D. (Lillian) 1 ch oil pumper O L 1h R1 North Baltimore Hen 69 Ind tel.

Duesler, Miles (Minnie) 5 ch farmer T 57a 2h 3c R2 Custar Jac 97.

Duesler, Ottabein (son Miles) farm hand R2 Custar Jac 97.

Duford, John (Mary) 1 ch barber O H&L Second St Perrysburg Pbg.

Duhammel, Joe (Marian) laborer T H&L Fifth St Perrysburg Pbg.

Duhamel, Warren (Alma) garage T H&L Walbridge Lake.

DUKATT, DANIEL W. R2 Custar Hen 1½.

Dulaney, J. T. RD North Baltimore Hen.

Dulaney, Wm. H. (Ollie) 1 ch farmer T 251a 6h 2c R1 Portage Por 11.

Duleney, John (Bertha) 3 ch farmer T 160a 4h 2c R1 North Baltimore Hen 71.

Dull, D. L. (Alice) 3 ch ret O 138a H&L 1h Center St Weston B tel.

Dull, Gertrude (dau D. L.) music teacher Center Wes.

Dulliard, Mrs. ret O H&L Custar Mil.

Duncan, Frank (Eliza) 3 ch laborer O H&2Lots Haskins Mid 34.

Duncan, J. A. cattle RD Bowling Green Cen.

Dunipace, Harley 2 ch farmer 1h R2 Pemberville Web 41.

Dunipace, Jane housekeeper O R2 Pemberville Web 41.

Dunipace, Margaret housekeeper O 80a 5h 11c R2 Pemberville Web 41 Ind tel.

Dunipace, Robert (Lottie) 1 ch farmer O 320a 4h 8c R3 Bowling Green Web 15 Ind tel.

DUNIPACE, ROBT. L. (Grace) 5 ch cattle & swine breeder O 150a 6h 21c R2 Bowling Green Cen 6 Ind tel.

Dunlap, Wm. (Sarah) 1 ch laborer O H&L Risingsun Mon.

DUNN, GEO. F. (Ida M.) 5 ch farmer O 165a 9h 16c R1 Deshler Jac 24 Ind tel.

Dunn, Geo. F., Jr. (son Geo. F.) assistant cashier in bank R1 Deshler Jac 24 Ind tel.

Dunn, John (son T. M.) student Verango St Cygnet Blo Ind tel.

Dunn, Mary (dau T. M.) Verango St Cygnet Blo Ind tel.

Dunn, Mrs. Myrtle 4 ch farmer O 50a 1h 2c R1 Deshler Jac 15 Ind tel.

Dunn, Mildred L. (son Geo. F.) student R1 Deshler Jac 24 Ind tel.

Dunn, Margaret M. 2 ch farmer O 23½a R1 Deshler Jac 23 Ind tel.

Dunn, Reed B. (son Geo. F.) student R1 Deshler Jac 24 Ind tel.

Dunn, T. M. (Anna) 6 ch oil worker O H&2Lots Verango St Cygnet Blo Ind tel.

Dupey, Geo. (Barbara) 2 ch farmer O 60a 7h 4c R1 Deshler Jac 38 B tel.

Dupey, Vivian (dau Geo.) housekeeper R1 Deshler Jac 38 B tel.

Du Poy, B., Jr. (son B.) traveling salesman Milton Center Mil.

Duquette, Ion D. (Mabel) 2 ch farmer T 80a 3h 7c R1 Deshler Jac 37.

Durdel, Herman Weston Wes.

Durfee, Earl chemist T H&L Rossford Ros.

Durliat, Agnes (dau Jos. X.) housekeeper R2 Custar Mil 16 B tel.

Durliat, Edward Weston Mil.

Durliat, Frank Rossford Ros.

Durliat, Fred (son Joseph X.) farm hand R2 Custar Mil 16 B tel.

Durliat, Henry W. (Clara) 2 ch farmer O 90a T 90a 1h 2c Custar Mil 99.

Durliat, John M. (Rosa) 3 ch garage proprietor O H&L Custar Mil.

Durliat, Jos. X. (Emma) 11 children farmer O 165a 8h 7c R2 Custar Mil 16 B tel.

Durliat, J. B. (Marie) farmer O 80a 3h 3c R1 Custar Mil 20 B tel.

Durliat, Lawrence M. (Lena) livery T H&L Custar Mil B tel.

Durliat, Louis Custar Mil.

Durliat, Martin (son Jos. X.) farm hand R2 Custar Mil 16 B tel.

Durliat, Wm. Custar Mil.

Durliat, W. H. (Catherine) 2 ch farmer O 58a Rent 40a 3h 3c R1 Custar Mil 10.

DURLIAT, M. J. 2 ch farmer O 100a 5h 5c R1 Weston Mil 60 Ind tel.

Dusing, E. H. Pemberville Fre.

Dusing, F. H. Pemberville Fre.

Dusing, Henry Pemberville Fre.

Dusing, Louis Pemberville Fre.

Duty, Daniel (Amy) 1 ch farmer O 80a 3h 4c R1 Perrysburg Pbg 24.

Duty, Horley (son Daniel) farmer R1 Perrysburg Per 24.

Duty, Vindo (son Daniel) farmer R1 Perrysburg Pbg 24.

Dye, L. (Elizabeth) farmer O 100a 5h 13c R1 Millburg Lake 46 Ind tel.

DYER, G. R. (Maggie) 2 ch farmer T 80a 6h 4c R2 Prairie Depot Mon 40 B tel.

DYER, L. O. (Rebecca) 1 ch farmer T 140a 4h 5c West Millgrove Per 87.

Dyer, Sherman (Edith) 5 ch farmer T 8h 6c R1 Risingsun Mon 79.

Dyer, S. F. (Flora) 4 ch tile worker T 4a R1 Risingsun Mon 79.

DYKE, J. B. (Testa) 4 ch farmer O 160a 7h 6c R3 Weston Wes 53.

Dymond, E. (Mary) 2 ch oil worker T H&L Rudolph Lib 96.

Dysinger, Burley M. (Lulu D.) 1 ch thresher T H&L 1h Factory St Jerry City Por Ind tel.

Dysinger, Chas. (Emma) 3 ch farmer T 100a 3h 7c R1 Jerry City Blo 81½ Ind tel.

Dysinger, Clel (Pearl) 1 ch laborer R1 North Baltimore Hen 38.

Dysinger, Daniel bee business O H&L R1 Fostoria Per 78.

Dysinger, Howard farmer Jerry City Blo 81½ Ind tel.

Dysinger, John (Sarah J.) farmer O 80a 1h R1 Bloomdale Blo 101 B & Ind tels.

DYSINGER, ROYAL O. (Anna K.) 4 ch farmer T 80a 2h R1 Bloomdale Blo 101 Ind tel.

Eairlywine, E. W. RD North Baltimore Hen.

EAKEN, W. A. (Kathern) 7 ch farmer T 120a 4h 2c Portage Por 11.

Eaken, W. M. RD Portage Por.

Eames, Christiana housekeeper R3 Perrysburg Pbg 82.

Eames, Robt. R3 Perrysburg Pbg.

Earl, F. M. Risingsun Mon.

EARL, GEO. (Ethel) 2 ch farmer laborer 1h R1 Prairie Depot Mon 85 B tel.

Earl, Harry Risingsun Mon.

Earl, Ira (Elizabeth) farmer T 220a 5h 7c R1 Prairie Depot Mon 85 B tel.

EARL, SIMON Risingsun.

Earl, W. M. Risingsun Mon.

Earle, Charles (Annie) farmer farm hand 1h 1c R1 Weston Mil 60.

Earle, F. M. (Emma) farmer O 89a 1h 2c R1 Risingsun Mon 81.

Earlewine, G. W. (Eva) 3 ch oil O 1h 1c R1 North Baltimore Hen 70.

Easley, Claire (son J. L.) carpenter Mulberry & Cleveland Sts Bloomdale Blo B & Ind tels.

Easley, Edna Rose (dau Rosana) teacher Main & Vine Sts Bloomdale Blo B & Ind tels.

Easley, Floyd (son J.) carpenter Mulberry & Cleveland Sts Bloomdale Blo B & Ind tel.

Easley, George (son J. L.) carpenter Mulberry & Cleveland Sts Bloomdale Blo B & Ind tels.

EASLEY, J. L. (Alice) 1 ch carpenter & contractor O H&L Mulberry & Cleveland Sts Bloomdale Blo B & Ind tels.

Easley, Mark (son J. L.) carpenter Mulberry & Cleveland Sts Bloomdale Blo B & Ind tels.

Easley, Mrs. Rosanna O H&L Main & Vine Sts Bloomdale Blo B & Ind tels.

EASLEY, R. V. (Emma W.) 2 ch oil belt telephone exchange manager O H&L N Main St Bloomdale Blo B & Ind tels.

Easterwood, David (Elsie) 1 ch dairyman T 1716 Oak St E Toledo Ros 18.

Eberle, Catharine RD N Baltimore Hen.

Eberle, F. C. (Emma F.) shoe store O H&L Perrysburg Per B tel.

Eberly, J. C. farmer O 95a R1 Portage Por 7 Ind tel.

EBERSOL, G. W. (Vergie) 3 ch farmer O 80a 3h 6c R1 North Baltimore Hen 52 Ind tel.

Ebersole, D. O. (Mary) farmer T 58a 4h 3c R3 North Baltimore Hen 112 B tel.

Ebersole, J. A. RD North Baltimore Por.

Ebersole, Mary RD North Baltimore Hen.

Ebey, C. B. (Effie) 1 ch undertaker T H&L Rising Sun Mon B tel.

Ebilsizer, John (Bernice) 1 ch farmer O 17a 3h 2c RD Custar Lib 28 B tel.

Ebka, Amelia (dau Wm.) R1 Luckey Tro 75.

Ebka, Bertha (dau Wm.) housekeeper R1 Luckey Tro 75.

Ebka, Emmanuel (bro Wm.) farm hand R1 Luckey Tro 75.

Ebka, Wm. (Mary) 6 ch farmer O 80a 4h 9c R1 Luckey Tro 75.

Eccard, Fred RD Tontogany Wash.

Eccard, Frederick RD Tontogany Pla.

Echelbarger, Calvin (son C.) farmer R3 Prairie Depot Por 129.

ECHELBARGER, C. (Rebecca) farmer O 79a 4h 6c R3 Prairie Depot Por 129.

St. Louis Church, Custar, Ohio.

Echelbarger, Daisy (dau C.) R3 Prairie Depot Por 129.

Echelbarger, Daniel (Mina) 3 ch laborer O H&L Hatton Per 84.

Echelbarger, Dezza housekeeper Main St Jerry City Por.

Echelbarger, Edith (dau C.) housekeeper R3 Prairie Depot Por 129.

Echelbarger, Frank (Elizabeth M.) 1 ch farmer T 60a 5h 1c R1 Bloomdale Blo 95 B & Ind tels.

Echelbarger, Fred (Mabel) cashier in bank O H&L Prairie Depot Mon.

Echelbarger, Harley fireman Main St Jerry City Por.

Echelbarger, John farmer O 60a R1 Bloomdale Blo 95 B & Ind tels.

Echelbarger, Mrs. J. F. O H&L Main St Jerry City Por.

Echelbarger, M. (Amanda) 1 ch farmer O 1a 2h 2c Jerry City Por.

Eck, Wendal Perrysburg Pbg.

Eckel, Edward (Clara) farmer T 80a 4h 3c R1 Perrysburg Pbg 101.

ECKEL, FRED J. (Ida) 3 ch farmer O 55a 4h 6c R1 Perrysburg Pbg 105 B tel.

ECKEL, GEORGE (Sophia) 1 ch farmer O 166a 8h 6c R1 Perrysburg Pbg 118.

Eckel, George, Jr. farmer RD Perrysburg Pbg 118.

Eckel, Harley Dunbridge Web.

Eckel, Henry (Nellie) farmer T 60a 3h 1c R1 Dunbridge Web 54.

Eckel, Henry (Anna) 3 ch farmer O 160a 8h 8c R2 Dunbridge Mid 65.

Eckel, John F. (Effie) 2 ch farmer T 81a 4h 2c R1 Dunbridge Web 54.

Eckel, J. N. R3 Perrysburg Pbg.

Eckel, Leo (Ellen) 1 ch farmer T 122a 4h 8c R1 Lemoyne Tro 81 B tel.

Eckel, Leonard (Katharine) 3 ch farmer O 106a 2h 4c R2 Perrysburg Pbg 145 Ind tel.

Eckel, L. E. (Mary) 1 ch grocery T H&L Perrysburg Pbg B tel.

Eckel, Oscar (Katharine) farmer T 106a 2h 3c R2 Perrysburg Pbg 145.

Eckelberger, Andrew (Hattie) 2 ch laborer 1h R2 Prairie Depot Per 1.

Eckerman, Mrs. G. 2 ch farmer O 60a 4h 2c Station A East Toledo Ros 33.

Eckermann, Frank (Olive) 4 ch farmer O 41a 2h 5c R1 Millbury Lake 67.

Eckert, Bert (Zella) 1 ch farmer & hay baler T 70a 3h 2c R1 Portage Por 22 Ind tel.

Eckert, B. F. (Florence) 2 ch farmer O 40a 5h 3c R1 Jerry City Por 59.

Eckert, Clarence (Mae) farmer O 200a 10h 2c R1 Portage Por 88 Ind tel.

Eckert, Floyd (Alice) 1 ch farmer O 80a 4h 5c R1 Portage Por 60 Ind tel.

Eckert, Jacob (Ruth) 4 ch painter O H&L Bradner Mon.

Eckert, John (Edna) laborer O 1a 1h Main St Jerry City Por.

Eckert, Lennora farmer O 40a R1 Jerry City Por 59.

Eckert, M. (Lola) 5 ch drayman T 1h Prairie Depot Mon.

ECKERT, RALPH E. (Ada) 2 ch farmer O 80a 5h 3c R2 Prairie Depot Por 82.

Eckert, Rowland W. (Lillian) 2 ch farmer O 120a 6h 3c R1 Portage Por 39 Ind tel.

Eckert, Wm. (Ivah) 4 ch painter T H&L Evans St Bradner Mon.

Eckhart, Soloman (Mary) laborer O H&L 2c Second St Grand Rapids Gr Rs.

ECKLEY, W. W. (Joan) 1 ch mail carrier O H&L Custar Mil.

Eckman, C. farmer T 27a 2h R2 Custar Mil 43.

Eckman, Fred (Mary E.) oil man T H&L Garfield St Bloomdale Blo B & Ind tels.

Eckman, G. M. (Lillie M.) 1 ch oil man O H&L Randolph St Bairdstown Blo.

Eckman, H. B. (son Fred) oil man Garfield St Bloomdale Blo B & Ind tels.

Eckman, John C. farmer T 27a 2h R2 Custar Mil 43.

Eckman, Joseph D. farmer T 27a 2h R2 Custar Mil 43.

Eddmon, Phoebe Tontogany Wash.

Eddy, J. S. Perrysburg Pbg.

Edgar, Charles 2 ch teamster O H&L 6h Prairie Depot Mon B tel.

EDGAR, H. (Janette) electrical worker T 4a R2 Prairie Depot Mon 109.

Edgar, J. W. (Bell) 1 ch O 4L H&L N Main St Weston.

EDISON, ARTHUR M. (Lola) postmaster 1h Cygnet Blo B & Ind tels.

Edison, J. W. (Harriett) 2 ch hardware O H&L 1h cor Walbridge & Verango Sts Cygnet Blo Ind tel.

EDKA, WM. R1 Luckey.

Edmonds, D. (Dora) 3 ch farmer O 61a 1h 2c East St Bradner Mon.

Edmonds, W. P. (Lulu) 3 ch tinner O H&L Evans St Bradner Mon.

Edsall, Mrs. Frances milliner T H&L RD N Baltimore Hen Ind tel.

Edsall, Mrs. Ida 1 ch milliner T H&L RD N Baltimore Hen Ind tel.

EDSON, J. W. (Harriet) hardware store O 1h Front St Cygnet Blo B & Ind tels. See adv.

EDSON, J. W., JR. (Ruth) hardware store Front St Cygnet Blo B & Ind tels. See adv.

Edward, Vern (Mabel) laborer T H&L Custar Mil.

Edwards, E. E. (Elizabeth) 2 ch farmer T 50a 3h 1c R2 Custar Hen 2.

Edwards, Homer B. Rossford Ros.

Edwards, J. G. (Eva) carriage painter T H&L Grand Rapids Gr Rs.

Edwards, Ray (son Sina) farmer T 64a 3h R1 Custar Mil 40.

Edwards, Sina 6 ch housekeeper O 64a R1 Custar Mil 40 Ind tel.

Egbert, Claud (Grace) horse shoeing Bell St Bradner Mon.

Egbert, Mary A. Dowling Web.

EGBERT, W. C. (Clara) 2 ch school teacher T H&L Pemberville Fre 40.

Eggelson, Thos. (Lizzie) 1 ch carpenter O H&L 1h Second St Portage Por Ind tel.

EGGLESTON, C. T. (Alma) farmer O 58a 2h 6c R1 Walbridge Ros 21 Ind tel.

Eglar, Clark (Nellie) 3 ch operator O H&L Millburg Lake.

Ehlen, Emma (dau Mathias) housekeeper R2 Custar Mil 41 B tel.

Ehlen, Mathias (Katherine) 7 ch farmer O 60a 4h 5c R2 Custar Mil 41 B tel.

Eidson, A. M. Cygnet Blo.

EIDSON, J. W. hardware Cygnet. See adv.

Eiler, W. B. (Lola M.) farmer T 80a 3h 3c R1 Prairie Depot Mon 33.

Eilert, Ed. RD Dunbridge Mid.

Eilert, Fred 5 ch Luckey Tro Ind tel.

Eilert, Fred (son of Henry) farmer 1h R1 Dunbridge Web 6 B tel.

Eilert, Henry (Carrie) farmer O 80a 5h 6c R1 Dunbridge Web 6 B tel.

Eilert, Henry A. (son John) laborer R1 Dunbridge Web 5 B tel.

Eilert, Ida (dau of Henry) housekeeper R1 Dunbridge Web 6 B tel.

Eilert, John (Lizzie) 4 ch farmer O 80a 5h 6c R1 Dunbridge Web 5 B tel.

Eisenhauer, Ed Bradner Mon.

EISENHAUER, THEO. J. (Hazel) 2 ch laborer T H&L 1c East St Bradner Mon.

Eisenhour, Mrs. S. F. 1 ch O H&L East St Bradner Mon.

Eisenhut, Geo. Haskins Mid.

Eisenman, C. F. Woodside Fre.

Eisenminger, Christ cattle RD Prairie Depot Por.

Eishen, Charles (son John) R1 Rudolph Lib 97 Ind tel.

Eishen, John C. (Katherine) 5 ch farmer O 40a 4h 4c R1 Rudolph Lib 97 Ind tel.

Eishen, O. W. (Mae) 4 ch farmer T 73a 2h 1c Cygnet Por 28.

Eishen, Peter Cygnet Blo.

Eishen, P. M. (Theresa) 8 ch farming O 20a 3h 4c Jerry City Blo 75 Ind tel.

Eiting, Miss B. M. millinery T H&L RD North Baltimore Hen B tel.

Eiting, George (Barbara) farmer O 60a 2h 4c RD North Baltimore Hen 76 B tel.

ELARTON, F. D. (Lillie) 5 ch farmer O 40a 7h 6c R1 Risingsun Per 93 Ind tel.

ELARTON, T. J. (Ida) general store proprietor & postmaster O Store 1h Hatton Per 84 B & Ind tels.

Elder, C. C. (Fern F.) farmer T 80a 4h 2c R1 Bloomdale Blo 103 B & Ind tels.

Elder, H. A. (Viola E.) farmer O 97a 1h 4c R1 Prairie Depot Mon 104 B tel.

Elder, J. W. cattle RD Bowling Green Cen.

ELDER, WARD (Jessie) farmer T H&L 3h 3c R3 Bowling Green Cen 43 Ind tel.

Elder, Wm. H. (Gladys) farmer T 97a 2h 1c R1 Prairie Depot Mon 104 B tel.

Elder, William O 113a 2h R1 Stony Ridge Tro 31.

Eldrige, S. J. (Opal) 1 ch farmer T 77a 5h 4c R1 Hoytsville Hen 25.

Eli, Christ farmer R1 Wallbridge Lake 10.

Ellenwood, I. M. (Luella) foreman at Tile Mill O H&L Hoytsville Jac.

Ellerman, Edward (son of Mrs. Frank) farmer T 60a 2h R1 Lime City Pbg 120 B tel.

ELLERMAN, MRS. FRANK 2 ch farmer O 60a 1h 3c R1 Lime City Pbg 120 B tel.

Ellerman, Lewis (Vallie) 1 ch farmer T 57a 3h 2c R1 Lime City Pbg 120.

Ellerman, Mrs. R. R1 Lime City Pbg.

Elliot, Mrs. Frank RD North Baltimore Hen.

ELLIOTT, A. L. (Bessie B.) 2 ch elevator & grain buyer Stony Ridge Tro Ind tel. See adv.

Elliott, Clyde engineer on township roller Cygnet Blo 11 Ind tel.

Elliott, Geo. (Della) 3 ch oil worker H&L Risingsun Hen.

Elliott, M. H. (Josephine) 2 ch farmer T 79½a 5h 6c R3 North Baltimore Hen 88.

Elliott, Wm. (Lydia) 4 ch farmer 160a 5h 5c Cygnet Blo 11 Ind tel.

Ellis, Charles (Josephine) farmer O 6a 1h 1c R2 Weston Wes 43.

Ellis, C. W. RD North Baltimore Hen.

Ellis, D. J. (Laura) 18 ch farmer T H&L 1h R1 Weston Pla 10.

73

Ellis, Harriet (dau John) housekeeper R2 Custar Mil 41 Ind tel.

Ellis, John (Sylvia M.) 9 ch traveling moving picture show T H&L 3h R2 Custar Mil 41 Ind tel.

Ellis, Margaret ret O H&2Lots Third St Perrysburg Pbg.

Ellsworth, Eugene (Dorothy) 1 ch laborer T H&L R5 Bowling Green Cen 23.

ELLSWORTH, E. E. (Olive) farmer O 80a 4h 8c R2 Weston Gr Rs 36 Ind tel.

ELLSWORTH, GEO. B. (Alice) 2 ch farmer T H&L 2c R4 Bowling Green Cen 25 B tel.

Ellsworth, John (son Mrs. Lea) laborer R1 Custar Mil 16.

Ellsworth, Mrs. Lea 3 ch farmer O 40a 1c R1 Custar Mil 16.

Ellsworth, Nancy Weston Gr Rs.

Ellsworth, W. E. laborer T H&L R5 Bowling Green Cen 23.

ELSER, FRED (Ellen) 3 ch farmer O 80a 3h 8c R1 Lemoyne Tro 83 B tel.

EMCH, MRS. ADDIE 4 ch farmer O 131a 4h 5c R3 Perrysburg Pbg 89 B tel.

Emch, Anna ret O H&L Sixth St Perrysburg Pbg.

Emch, Charley Stony Ridge Tro.

Emch, C. H. (Minnie) 3 ch farmer T 81a 5h 16c R1 Lemoyne Tro 47 Ind tel.

EMCH, DELILAH Walbridge.

Emch, Ed Lime City Pbg.

Emch, Mrs. Emma R1 Lime City Pbg.

Emch, Frank (Sopha) 1 ch laborer T H&L R1 Lime City Pbg 91.

EMCH, MRS. FRED 4 ch farmer O 55a 2h 1c R1 Lime City Pbg 59 Ind tel.

Emch, Geo. RD Dowling Mid.

Emch, Geo. J. Rossford Ros.

Emch, Mrs. John R1 Lime City Pbg.

EMCH, J. J. (Catherine) 3 ch laborer O 9a 1h Millbury Lake 76.

Emch, Lewis (Julia) 1 ch farmer O 57a 3h 3c R1 Lime City Pbg 91.

Emch, Lina millinery T H&L Perrysburg Pbg.

Emch, Ralph (Freeda) farmer O 46a 5h 3c R1 Lime City Pbg 122.

Emch, Shelby (Luetta) motor builder T H&L Front St Perrysburg Pbg B tel.

Emch, Wm. (Maggie) farmer O H&L Sugar Ridge Mid 63.

Emch, W. H. (Ada) 1 ch farmer O 72a 4h 4c R1 Perrysburg Pbg 101.

Emel, Will laborer T H&L Evans St Bradner Mon.

Emerich, Gust. (Mattie) 3 ch farmer T 75a 3h 3c R4 Bowling Green Cen 32 Ind tel.

EMERSON, EARL W. auto salesman Main St West Millgrove Per.

Emerson, Mrs. E. P. Main St Bloomdale Blo.

EMERSON, H. W. (Cora F.) 3 ch farmer O 193a 5h 10c R1 Bloomdale Blo 114 B & Ind tels.

Emerson, Jennie (dau Wm.) Main St Bloomdale Blo.

Emerson, Mrs. Nick housekeeper T H&L West Millgrove Per 70.

EMERSON, RALPH W. novelty store & news stand 49 Main St Bloomdale Blo.

EMERSON, SCOTT S. (Victoria I.) 1 ch farmer O 90a 4h 2c R1 Bloomdale Blo 103 B & Ind tels.

Emerson, S. H. farmer T 35a 2h R1 Bloomdale Blo 103 B & Ind tel.

Emerson, Vic I. ret farmer O 40a H&L Main St West Millgrove Per.

Emerson, Wm. (Hester A.) 50 Main St Bloomdale Blo.

Emich, Michael 6 ch car repairer O H&L Rossford Ros.

Emison, G. H. (Bess) 1 ch truck driver T H&L Pemberville Fre 40.

Emmerick, Geo. C. Perrysburg Pbg.

Emmerick, Gust. cattle RD Bowling Green Cen.

Emmit, L. (Mabel) 3 ch carpenter O H&L 1h Luckey Tro.

Emmitt, Chas. (Alma) 4 ch farmer T 50a 2h 3c R1 Bowling Green Pla 76.

Emmitt, Isaac Dunbridge Web.

EMMITT, PERRY (Anna M.) 2 ch farmer O 120a 6h 3c R1 Dunbridge Web 57 B tel.

Empky, Henry (son Wm.) laborer R1 Dunbridge Web 49 B tel.

EMRICK, ERNEST (Goldie) 1 ch farmer T 80a 3h 4c R3 Weston Mil 5.

Emrick, George (Lavina) 6 ch farmer O 52a 4h 2c R3 Weston Mil 88 Ind tel.

Emrick, G. L. (Ethel) 2 ch school teacher T 5a 1h 1c R3 Weston Mil 88 Ind tel.

Emrick, Ida (dau George) school teacher R3 Weston Mil 88 Ind tel.

Emrick, L. L. Weston Mil.

Emsburger, J. E. RD North Baltimore Hen.

Ench, Geo. (Daisy) farmer T 60a 3h 5c Dowling Mid 76.

Enesi, Joe Walbridge Ros.

Engel, John laborer 1h R3 Prairie Depot Mon 6.

Engesser, F. J. Custar Mil.

Engesser, Joseph Custar Mil.

74

England, Geo. (Jenuie) 1 ch contractor O H&L Dowling Mid.

England, Jackson 1 ch laborer T H RD Waterville Mid 2.

England, J. C. (Hattie) farmer O 60a 2h 5c R1 Fostoria Per 57.

ENGLAND, W. (Estella) farmer T 60a 1h 1c R1 Fostoria Per 57.

Engle, Henry (Cora) 6 ch pumper T 1c Findlay St Portage Por 10.

Englehart, Philip Luckey Tro.

English, Frank RD North Baltimore Hen.

English, F. A. RD Bowling Green Pla.

English, H. E. (Jennie M.) 3 ch farmer O 130a 3h 1c R1 Bowling Green Pla 67 Ind tel.

Enis, Robt. L. Rossford Ros.

Enright, Thomas F. (Martha R.) 5 ch carpenter O H&L Haskins Mid B tel.

ENSBURGER, J. E. (Nettie) oil foreman T 80a 2h 5c R1 North Baltimore Hen 71 Ind tel.

ENSMINGER, A. A. ret farmer 870a 1 B R1 Grand Rapids Gr Rs 44.

Ensminger, Chas. E. Bairdstown Blo.

Ensminger, Emanuel (Lillian) 1 ch producer O H&L 1h Church St Bradner Mon 28.

ENSMINGER, F. G. (Frances) 1 ch general store & postmaster O 1c Bairdstown Blo B & Ind tels.

Ensminger, L. J. (Goldie M.) 1 ch producer T H&L 2h N East St Bradner Mon.

Entsminger, M. Bradner Mon.

Epke, Henry cattle RD Bowling Green Cen.

Erl, Wm. (Elda) 3 ch farmer O H&L 3h Risingsun Mon.

Erl, Willis (Myrtle) 6 ch teaming T H&L Risingsun Mon.

ERNSTHAUSEN, AUGUST J. (Martha) 3 ch farmer T 145a 6h 4c R3 Pemberville Fre 18 B tel.

Ernsthausen, Casper ret O 85a Pemberville Fre 18 B tel.

Ernsthausen, Mrs. Edward 1 ch O 80a R3 Pemberville Fre 18.

Ernsthausen, Ernest Pemberville Fre.

Ernsthausen, Fred C. (Edith) 1 ch farmer O 80a 4h 6c R4 Bowling Green Cen 117 B tel.

Ernsthausen, Fred J. (Minnie) 3 ch farmer O 80a 4h 3c R3 Pemberville Fre 21 B tel.

Ernsthausen, Geo. (Kate) 1 ch farmer T 85a 3h 4c R3 Pemberville Fre 18 B tel.

Ernsthausen, Henry J. (Alvina) farmer O 100a 4h 12c R1 Pemberville Fre 58.

Ernsthausen, H. C. (Anna) 2 ch carpenter O H&L 1h 1c R1 Pemberville Fre 66.

Ernsthausen, H. W. Pemberville Fre.

ERNSTHAUSEN, JOHN C. (Mary) 1 ch farmer O 74a 3h 6c R3 Pemberville Fre 18 B tel.

Ernsthausen, J. H. Pemberville Fre.

Ernsthauser, Wm. H. (Anna) 1 ch farmer O 98a 4h 4c R3 Pemberville Fre 25 B tel.

Errett, Ed. RD Tontogany Pla.

Errett, Frank Weston Mil.

Errett, Henry B. (Nettie) 2 ch farmer O 40a 4h 9c Bradner Mon B tel.

Errett, Jas. Weston Mil.

Errett, Nettie Bradner Mon.

Errett, W. J. Weston Lib.

Errings, Isador Latcha Lake.

Erven, J. L. Grand Rapids Wes.

Erven, Orrin W. (Jennie) 3 ch farmer O 106a 5h 7c R1 Grand Rapids Gd Rs 7 Ind tel.

Erwin, Wm. (Elizabeth) 2 ch laborer T H&L R2 Bloomdale Per 17.

Eschedor, A. G. (Annie M.) 2 ch carpenter T H&L 1h 2c R4 Bowling Green, Cen 105.

Eschedor, C. H. Pemberville Fre.

Eschedor, Fred (Grace) 5 ch farmer O 93a 3h 2c R3 Prairie Depot Mon 3 B tel.

Eschedor, H. W. (Mary) 1 ch farmer O 46a 2h 3c R3 Prairie Depot Mon 2 B tel.

Eschedoy, C. H. (Kate) farmer O 72a 4h 4c R1 Pemberville Fre 60 B tel.

ESCHEDOY, WM. (Emma) 1 ch farmer T R1 Pemberville Fre 60 B tel.

Essex, O. F. Risingsun Mon.

Essicks, Ora (Jennie) oil driller O H&L Risingsun Mon.

Esterly, W. A. (Leora) farmer O 80a 2h 6c R2 Prairie Depot Por 82.

Euler, David (Marie) 2 ch farmer O 137a 9h 3c R1 Tontogany Wash 39 Ind tel.

Euler, Frank (Maggie) 1 ch farmer O 80a 6h 7c R3 Bowling Green Cen 58.

EULER, GEO. (Edna) 1 ch farmer O 80a 7h 2c R4 Bowling Green Por 43 Ind tel.

Eurin, Wm. (Elizabeth) 2 ch laborer R2 Bloomdale Per 17.

Evans, C. O. (Lulu) 2 ch farmer O 3a 3h 3c R1 Prairie Depot Mon 89.

Evans, Eva Dunbridge Web.

Evans, Frank (Lillian) car repairer T H&L Walbridge Lake.

Evans, Howard (Gertrude) 2 ch hardware clerk O H&L Grand Rapids Gr Rs Ind tel.

Evans, J. B. Bradner Mon.

Evans, J. M. Bradner Mon.

Evans, J. P. (Rena) ret druggist O H&L cor Evans & Crocker Sts Bradner Mon B tel.

Evans, Martin 4 ch pumper O H&L 1h Lightner St Bradner Mon.

EVANS, W. J. (Emma) farmer T 60a 4h 1c R3 Bowling Green Web 15 Ind tel.

Evans, W. K. (Mary E.) hardware O H&L 1h Grand Rapids Gr Rs Ind tel.

Evens, Mack (Lizzie) 1 ch oil worker T H&L Portage Lib 90 Ind tel.

Everett, Edward (Sidney) 2 ch farmer T 40a 3h 4c R1 Tontogany Pla 19 Ind tel.

EVERETT, HARVEY G. (Ida) 1 ch farmer O 80a 5h 11c R2 Bowling Green Pla 57 B tel.

Everett, Henry (Nettie M.) saloon keeper O 40a T H&L 5h 28c Bradner Mon B tel.

Everett, James (Pearl) farmer T 90a 2h 4c R1 Weston Mil 57 Ind tel.

Everitt, H. J. RD North Baltimore Hen.

Evilsizer, John (Laura) 3 ch farmer T 53a 2h 2c R1 Bowling Green Pla 73 Ind tel.

Evinger, Guy RD Hoytsville Jac.

Evinger, Jno. Hoytsville Jac.

Ewegen, Gilbert (May) 2 ch farmer O 20a 3h 4c Dunbridge Mid 72.

Ewegen, J. E. (Mary) farmer O 145a 2h 2c R2 Dunbridge Mid 74.

EWING, A. G. (Nora) 1 ch farmer O 53a 4h 3c R1 Tontogany Wash 77 Ind tel.

Ewing, Elizabeth North Baltimore Hen.

Ewing, Jennie Weston Wes.

Ewing, J. L. (Harriet M.) 2 ch cashier O H&L Maple St Weston B tel.

Ewing, Loy E. RD North Baltimore Hen.

Ewing, R. RD Bowling Green Pla.

EWING, W. H. (Rhoda) 7 ch farmer O 160a 3h 5c R2 Bowling Green Pla 58 B tel.

Exline, A. RD North Baltimore Hen.

Exline, J. W. RD North Baltimore Hen.

FACER, WALTER L. (Ida) 3 ch farmer O 40a 6h 2c R1 Millbury Lake 46 Ind tel.

Fackelman, John (Josephine) 5 ch farmer T 100a 4h 2c R2 Perrysburg Mid 17 B tel.

Faeer, Walter Millbury Lake.

Fahl, Hellen mgr restaurant Front St Cygnet Blo Ind tel.

Fahl, O. H. (Hellen) oil worker T H Front St Cygnet Blo Ind tel.

Fable, August Luckey Tro.

Fable, Ed. Luckey Tro.

Fable, Elizabeth Luckey Tro.

Fable, Frank Dunbridge Web.

Fable, Fred (Sadie) 1 ch machinist T H&L Luckey Tro.

Fable, Fred (Augusta) 3 ch farmer O 120a 7h 3c R1 Luckey Tro 75 Ind tel.

Fable, Frieda (dau Wm.) housekeeper R1 Luckey Web 72 B tel.

Fable, Henry H. (Emma) 1 ch farmer T 72a 4h 6c R1 Pemberville Fre 35 B tel.

Fahle, Henry W. (Edith) 1 ch farmer T 120a 4h 7c R3 Pemberville Tro 64 Ind tel.

Fable, H. A. Dunbridge Web.

Fahle, H. F. (Emma) 2 ch farmer O 40a 3h 4c R1 Dunbridge Web 58 B tel.

Fable, John (Lizzie) 1 ch tile ditcher O H&L Luckey Tro.

Fable, Mary S. Luckey Tro.

Fahle, Will (Dora) 1 ch mason O H&L 1h Luckey Tro Ind tel.

Fable, Wm., Jr. (son Wm.) farm laborer R1 Luckey Web 72 B tel.

Fable, Wm. (Catherine) 1 ch farmer O 40a 3h 4c R1 Luckey Web 72 B tel.

Fahne, Ed. (Edna) 4 ch farmer T 37a 2h 3c R1 Luckey Tro 24 Ind tel.

Fahrer, Albert (Bessie) 2 ch farmer O 22a 3h 2c R1 Perrysburg Pbg 117.

Fahrer, Chas. E. (Ester) 3 ch farmer T 100a 3h 1c R1 Lime City Pbg 120.

Fabrer, C. O. (Verna B.) 2 ch mgr grain elevator T H&L Custar Mil B tel.

Fahrer, Fred R. R1 Perrysburg Pbg.

Fahrer, Mrs. Mary R1 Perrysburg Pbg.

Fahrer, Ralph (son Samuel) R1 Perrysburg Pbg 118.

FAHRER, ROY (Hazel) 1 ch farmer 1h R1 Perrysburg Pbg 118.

Fahrer, Mrs. Samuel farmer O 20a 1h 1c R1 Perrysburg Pbg 118.

Fair, Geo. (Helen) section hand T H&L Pemberville Fre.

Fairbank, Chas. L. Weston Wes.

Fairbanks, Frank (Lucinda) 9 ch farmer O 120a 4h 5c Bradner Mon 16.

Fairbanks, Grant (Myrtle) 4 ch pumper T 80a 1h 3c R1 Bradner Mon 28.

Fairbanks, J. F. (Lucy) 1 ch grocer O H&L N Main St Bradner Mon.

Fairbanks, M. (Sadie E.) 7 ch farmer 121a 7h 7c R2 Deshler Mil 15.

Faist, Christ 4 ch farmer O 16a 1h 1c Stony Ridge Tro 2 Ind tel.

Faist, Emma (dau Christ) housekeeper Stony Ridge Tro 2 Ind tel.

Faleoner, H. W. Perrysburg Pbg.

Faliere, Ella 9 ch ret O 160a R2 Custar Mil 29.

Faliere, Joe farmer T 160a 3h R2 Custar Mil 29.

Falise, C. Rossford Ros.

Fall, E. H. Port Clinton Fre.

Falls, M. Cygnet Blo.

Falor, Alvin (Eva) 7 ch laborer R1 Rudolph Lib 76.

Faneff, Mike (Mary) 4 ch R R man O H&L Walbridge Lake.

Faneuff, H. J. Walbridge Lake.

Faneuff, Jessie (Grace) 2 ch R R man O H&L Walbridge Lake.

Faneuff, Mary housekeeper O H&L Walbridge Lake.

Farley, Frank E. R2 Perrysburg Pbg.

Farley, Frank E. (Teresa) 3 ch farmer O 35a 2h 2c R2 Perrysburg Pbg 147.

FARMER, J. T. R1 Box 82 Millbury.

FARMER, J. T. (Nettie) 3 ch farmer O 30a 3h 8c R1 Millbury Lake 80.

Farmer, Sylvester (Matilda) 2 ch conductor T H&L Front St Perrysburg Pbg.

Farquharson, D. D. (Ethel) 2 ch farmer T 80a 2h 4c R1 Weston Mil 72 B tel.

Farwig, H. (Johanne) 1 ch farmer O 76a 5h 6c R1 Prairie Depot Mon 45.

Fasnaugh, W. F. (Jennie) 4 ch farmer T 55a 4h 3c R1 North Baltimore Hen 47.

Fast, Mrs. D. C. Bloomdale Blo.

Fast, R. B. Bloomdale Blo.

Fastnacht, Isadore Perrysburg Pbg.

Fauble, Levi E. (Lorenia) 2 ch farmer T 80a 3h 1c R3 Bowling Green Cen 19 Ind tel.

FAULKER, OTTO (Olive) 2 ch farmer T 4h 5c R1 Gibsonburg Fre 89 B tel.

Faulker, Wm. (Nellie) 2 ch salesman T H&L 1h Bridge St Pemberville Fre Ind tel.

FAUSNAUGH, E. L. (Gertrude) 1 ch farmer O 119a 4h 23c R1 Tontogany Pla 47 Ind tel.

Fausnaugh, Lawrence (Mabel) 2 ch farmer T 112a 6h 4c R2 Custar Mil 49 Ind tel.

Fausnaugh, M. A. (Wanda) 1 ch farmer T 40a 4h 6c R2 Prairie Depot Mon 35 B tel.

Fausnaugh, R. W. RD North Baltimore Hen.

Fausnaught, W. F. RD North Baltimore Hen.

Faws, Gertrude Milton Center Mil.

Faxon, C. W. (Lizzie A.) farmer T 50a 3h 3c R1 East Toledo Ros 36.

FAYLOR, C. A. (Elsie) farmer T 120a 3h 4c West Millgrove Mon 90.

Faylor, Wm. West Millgrove Per.

FEASEL, O. H. (Silva) 2 ch farming T 80a 4h 2c R3 North Baltimore Hen 113 Ind tel.

Feasel, Valdo (Elizabeth) farmer O 36a 6h 9c Jerry City Por Ind tel.

Feasel, V. S. Bloomdale Bl.

Feather, Geo. F. (Elizabeth) 5 ch farmer O 112a 8h 15c R1 Grand Rapids Gr Rs 44 Ind tel.

Fee, J. J. RD Rudolph Lib.

Feese, Sam'l F. RD North Baltimore Hen.

Fehr, C. A. (Anna) 2 ch druggist O H&L Pemberville Fre B tel.

Rectory of St. Louis Church, Custar, Ohio.

Feighner, Adam W. laborer Stony Ridge Tro.

Feighner, Lena O H&L Stony Ridge Tro.

Felkey, Al. laborer R1 Custar Lib 34.

Felkey, Mat. (Lizzie) 7 ch teamster T H 2h 1c R2 Custar Lib 34.

FELL, JOHN S. R3 Perrysburg Pbg 158.

Fellers, H. (Jennie) 1 ch farmer T 78a 3h 4c R1 Rudolph Lib 38 Ind tel.

Fellers, H. E. (Bertha) 1 ch farmer O 80a 3h 2c North Baltimore Hen 38.

Fellers, J. T. (Grace) 2 ch farmer O 80a 4h 5c R1 North Baltimore Hen 38.

Fellers, L. L. (Leona) ret O 120a Taylor St Weston Box 228 Wes B tel.

Fellers, Mary Hoytsville Jac.

Fellers, O. A. (Mabel) farmer O 2h 4c R1 North Baltimore Hen 8 Ind tel.

Fellers, Mrs. S. H. ret O H&L Hoytsville Jac.

Fellsey, Mat. RD Custar Lib.

Felsted, L. F. Tontogany Wash.

FELSTED, THOMAS Tontogany Wash.

FELTMAN, GEO. (Mary F.) bakery & restaurant O H&L Prairie Depot Mon B tel.

Feltman, Mary Freeport Mon.

Feltman, W. C. (Lorena) 1 ch drayman O H&L 5h Prairie Depot Mon B tel.

Pelzer, Henry Rossford Ros.

Fenton, Robert (Cordelia) 2 ch farmer O 13 5-100a 1h 2c R1 Dunbridge Web 49 B tel.

Ferguson, Allen S. (Alice) ret O H&L Hoytsville Jac.

Ferguson, Chas. (son Mandna) farm hand bds R1 Hoytsville Jac 77.

Ferguson, Deam RD Hoytsville Jac.

Ferguson, Demis (Reine) 5 ch farmer O 10a 3h 1c R1 Hoytsville Jac 70.

FERGUSON, DON C. R2 Bloomdale.

Ferguson, Flora (dau Jesse) waiter Hoytsville Jac.

Ferguson, F. R. (Jennie M.) farmer O 80a 9h 8c R2 Bloomdale Per 24 B tel.

Ferguson, James (Anna) 1 ch laborer T H&L R1 Hoytsville Jac 60.

Ferguson, Jesse 4 ch laborer T H&L Hoytsville Jac.

Ferguson, Joe RD Hoytsville Jac.

Ferguson, John A. (Elmer A.) 3 ch grocery store O 2h 1c R3 North Baltimore Bl B & Ind tels.

Ferguson, Lynn (son Jesse) bookkeeper Hoytsville Jac.

FERGUSON, MALCOLM (son Mandna) stallion groom bds R1 Hoytsville Jac 77.

Ferguson, Mandna farmer O 5a 3h R1 Hoytsville Jac 77.

Ferguson, Maude (dau A. S.) housekeeper Hoytsville Jac.

Ferguson, Samuel (Rachel) 3 ch farmer T 160a 9h 4c R1 Hoytsville Jac 79.

Ferguson, Vern RD Hoytsville Jac.

Ferguson, Winfield (Bertha E.) 3 ch farmer T 80a 3h 3c Cygnet Blo 60 B & Ind tels.

Fernside, Benj. (Maude) 3 ch farmer T 100a 6h 5c Bowling Green Lib 87 Ind tel.

Fernside, Henry (Anna) 4 ch ret O 151a 1h 1c R1 Bowling Green Lib 51 Ind tel.

Ferrell, Ernest assistant cashier bank Custar Mil B tel.

Ferrell, O. (Anna) 6 ch president of bank H&L Custar Mil B tel.

FERRELL, W. W. (Edith) 5 ch farmer O 80a 3h 7c R1 Hoytsville Jac 52 B tel.

Ferrenberg, A. W. (Josephine) 2 ch restaurant T H&L 1h Stahl St Bradner Mon.

Ferris, E. P. (Myrtle) auto salesman O 136a 6h R1 Haskins Mid 53 B tel.

Ferry, Anson (Cora) 2 ch painter O H&L Pemberville Fre 40.

Fetter, Henry Custar Mil.

Fetterman, Cyrus (Bessie) farmer O 12a Portage Por 10.

Fetterman, G. W. (Lottie) 2 ch farmer T 85a 3h 2c R2 Dunbridge Pbg 17 B tel.

Few, Edward (Mary) 6 ch laborer O H&L Risingsun Mon.

Fewneff, Henry (Mabel) 7 ch engineer T H&L Walbridge Lake.

Fife, J. B. (Susie) 2 ch farmer O 80a 3h 1c R3 Bowling Green Cen 84.

Fife, J. T. (Lina) 2 ch farmer O 160a 6h 4c R1 Hoytsville Jac 111.

Fife, Ray RD Hoytsville Jac.

Fifer, Theresa 3 ch ret T H&L Sixth & Pike Sts Perrysburg Pbg.

Fike, A. F. (Jerusha) ret O H&L Prairie Depot Mon B tel.

Fike, Charles (Verne) 1 ch driller T H&L Prairie Depot Mon B tel.

Fike, Frank H. (Lucy M.) dry goods & milliner O H&L Prairie Depot Mon B tel.

Fike, Mrs. Lois E. 1 ch stenographer Stony Ridge Tro Ind tel.

Fike, Lucy M. Prairie Depot Mon.

Fildes, Vincent (Sarah) 1 ch Justice of the Peace T H&L 193 Superior St Rossford Ros Ind tel.

Filiere, Alpha Milton Center Mil.

FILIERE, A. L. (Orrie) 7 ch farmer O 10a 4h 3c R2 Custar Mil 23 B tel.

Filiere, Claude L. (son A. L.) student R2 Custar Mil 23 B tel.

Filiere, Ely 1 ch butcher O H&L Milton Center Mil.

Filiere, Geo. (Lena) 1 ch pool room O H&L Milton Center Mil.

Filiere, Jos. W. Custar Mil.

Filiere, Leona (dau A. L.) housekeeper R2 Custar Mil 23 B tel.

Filiere, Orville farmer T 180a 4h 15c Rudolph Lib 93.

Filiere, William (son A. L.) student R2 Custar Mil 23 B tel.

Filmore, Alice 1 ch Center St Wes.

Filmore, Celia (dau Alice) telephone operator O H&L Center St Weston.

Filson Elmer RD North Baltimore Hen.

FINCH, FOREST (Minnie) 1 ch farmer T 80a 3h 3c R3 Prairie Depot Mon 108 B tel.

FINCH, F. C. (May) farmer O 7½a R3 Prairie Depot Mon 108 B tel.

Finch, Geo. Perrysburg Pbg.

Finch, Louis Perrysburg Pbg.

FINCH, M. V. Belmont Farm Perrysburg.

Findley, Harvey (Glenna) 1 ch farmer R1 Portage Por 48.

FINGER, AUGUST (Percy) 4 ch oil worker 1c R1 Portage Lib 83 Ind tel.

Finicle, Jno. RD North Baltimore Hen.

Fink, Fredericka Perrysburg Pbg.

Finkbeiner, W. A. Perrysburg Pbg.

FINKBINDER, C. Perrysburg.

Finkenbinder, Art (Minnie) 2 ch traveling man O H&L Second St Perrysburg Pbg B tel.

Finkenbinder, Geo. (Clara) 1 ch farmer O 43a 2h Grand Rapids Gr Rs 38.

Finkenbinder, Margaret 8 ch ret O H&L Grand Rapids Gr Rs.

Finkenbiner, T. S. Grand Rapids Gr Rs.

Finkhimer, C. (Martha A.) furniture store O H&L 305 N Front St Perrysburg Pbg B tel.

Finkler, Philip (Kathryn) 5 ch ret T H&L Prairie Depot Mon.

Finn, Chas. (son William, Sr.) laborer Luckey Tro.

Finn, Mary (dau William, Sr.) housework Luckey Tro.

Finn, William, Jr. (son William) laborer Luckey Tro.

Finn, William, Sr. (Carrie) 7 ch laborer T H&L Luckey Tro.

Finney, Bernard (son J. A.) farm hand R1 Deshler Jac 45.

Finney, Earnest (Tressie) farmer T 80a 1c R1 Portage Lib 86 Ind tel.

Finney, J. A. (Emma) 3 ch farmer O 200a 9h 6c R1 Deshler Jac 45.

FINNEY, MIKE (Martha) 4 ch farmer O 80a 9h 8c R1 Portage Lib 83 Ind tel.

Finney, Owd. farmer T 135a 7h 7c RD Weston Lib 48 B tel.

Finney, Parley RD Rudolph Lib.

Fish, Caroline Prairie Depot Fre.

Fish, C. F. (Lela) gasoline ditcher T H&L Prairie Depot Mon.

Fish, Ed. (Mary) 5 ch farming T H&L Second St Grand Rapids Gr Rs.

Fish, Henry (Marie) farmer O 40a 2h 8c R1 Pemberville Fre 58 B tel.

Fish, H. H. (son Henry) painter R1 Pemberville Fre 58 B tel.

Fish, Mrs. James O 42a R3 Prairie Depot Fre 74.B tel.

Fish, J. E. (Sarah M.) 1 ch treasurer O H&L Pemberville Fre.

Fish, J. W. (Martha) 2 ch farmer O 160a 2h 4c R5 Bowling Green Cen 61 B tel.

Fish, Nettie housekeeper O 35a Deshler Jac 32 Ind tel.

Fish, O. W. RD Bowling Green Fre.

Fish, Robert D. (son J. E.) laborer Pemberville Fre.

Fish, Roy (Bertha) 4 ch farmer O 40a 2h 4c R4 Bowling Green Cen 69 Ind tel.

Fisher, Dr. E. W. (Hattie L.) physician O H&L E Main St Portage Por 6 Ind tel.

Fisher, Florence 3 ch housekeeper R1 East Toledo Lake 116.

Fisher, G. Z. 1 ch station agent T H&L Lime City Pbg 91.

Fisher, H. E. RD North Baltimore Hen.

Fisher, Miss Kathryn milliner T H&L Pemberville Fre.

Fisher, Melchoir Pemberville Fre.

Fisher, Sammie (Winnifred) 2 ch farmer T 80a 4h 2c R1 Tontogany Wash 23 Ind tel.

Fisher, T. B. (Carrie) 4 ch hired man T H&L R1 Fostoria Per 126 Ind tel.

Fitch, F. J. (Nellie) huckster T H&L 2h Grand Rapids Gr Rs Ind tel.

Fitch, Frank Grand Rapids Gr Rs.

Fitch, Loren D. (Alice) 1 ch farmer T 50a 2h 3c R1 Grand Rapids Gr Rs 17.

Fitches, Fred (Nella) poultry merchant T H&L Grand Rapids Gr Rs Ind tel.

FITZGERALD, MRS. C. B. R1 Bradner.

Fitzgerald, Ed. (Lena) bookkeeper T H&L Second St Perrysburg Pbg.

Fitzgerald, J. S. (Mary) 4 ch oil worker O 3H & 3L 1c Union St Cygnet Blo 6 Ind tel.

Fitzgerald, S. S. (Minnie) 3 ch gauger O H&L Union St Cygnet Blo.

Fitzwater, Rev. F. E. (M. E. J.) 3 ch pastor T H&L Custar Mil.

Flaherty, P. J. Risingsun Mon.

Flahie, C. J. (Anna) 3 ch oil receiver O H&L Walbridge Ave. Cygnet Blo Ind tel.

Flaugher, J. L. clerk Main St Bloomdale Blo B & Ind tels.

Flausus, Mrs. ret T H&L Custar Mil.

Flechtner, C. A. (Amanda) farmer O 105a 6h 5c R1 Fostoria Per 123 Ind tel.

Fleckner, O. E. RD North Baltimore Hen.

Fledge, C. (Teenie) 6 ch laborer 60a R1 Lemoyne Tro 34.

Fleming, Ida RD Rudolph Lib.

Fleming, S. M. RD Rudolph Lib.

Flemming, Earnest 1 ch ret T H&L Eighth & Hickery Sts Perrysburg Pbg.

Flemming, J. M. (Sophia) ret T H&L 1h 1c Hickery & Eighth Sts Perrysburg Pbg.

Fletcher, Burt Weston Wes.

FLETCHER, DAVID (Bessie) 5 ch farmer T 173a 1h R3 Prairie Depot Mon 41.

FLETCHER, E. F. teamster O 1h R1 North Baltimore Hen 70 B tel.

Fletcher, Geo. (Amanda) 2 ch laborer T 1c R5 Bowling Green Web 17 Ind tel.

Fletcher, Wm. RD Tontogany Pla.

FLETCHER, W. H. (Bessie) 4 ch farmer T 160a 7h 3c R2 Bowling Green Cen 88 Ind tel.

Flory, Albert (Sarah) gardener O 10a West Millgrove Per 70.

FLORY, JOHN (Eliza) 1 ch farmer T 100a 3h 2c R1 Tontogany Wash 51 Ind tel.

Flory, S. H. Prairie Depot Mon.

Flouck, Delmar R. Estella) 2 ch painting H&L Mermill Por 20.

Flower, C. A. (Edna) conductor T H&L Front St Perrysburg Pbg B tel.

FLOYD, ARTHUR F. (Ida) 1 ch oil worker O¼a Bays Lib 100 Ind tel.

Floyd, J. E. (Julia A.) ret O H&L R1 Portage Por 3 Ind tel.

Flury, Alfred J. (Addie) farmer O 40a 2h 4c R1 Box 46A East Toledo Ros 3S.

Fogh, J. W. RD Weston Lib.

Fogh, P. A. RD Rudolph Lib.

Fogle, G. C. (Bertha) farmer T 140a 7h 4c R1 Tontogany Wash 31 Ind tel.

FOGLE, JAS. R1 Weston Lib 11 B tel.

Fogle, P. A. (Hazel) 3 ch oil worker T 1h 1c R1 Rudolph Lib 33.

Fogler, I. (Sophia) farmer O 90a 4h 5c R1 Tontogany Wash 21 Ind tel.

Foltz, A. RD North Baltimore Hen.

Foltz, Grover RD North Baltimore Hen.

Foltz, Harvey (Martha) 2 ch teamster T H&L 1h West Taylor Wes Ind tel.

FOLTZ, O. W. (Engle) 1 ch farmer O 80a 6h 3c R1 North Baltimore Hen 33.

Foor, J. C. (Toska) shoemaker Pemberville T H&L Pemberville Fre B tel.

Foos, Geo. Sr. (Lena) 9 ch farmer O 80a 6h 5c R3 Bowling Green Cen 13 Ind tel.

Foos, GEO. A. (Emma) farmer T 140a 5h 3c R3 Bowling Green Cen 13 Ind tel.

Foos, JOHN (Clarin) 5 ch farmer T 240a 7h 6c R1 Gibsonburg Sand 84.

Foos, J. A. Pemberville Fre.

Foote, A. D. Tontogany Wash.

Foote, Ella Tontogany Wash.

Forbush, F. J. (Edna) 3 ch clerk O H&L East St Bradner Mon B tel.

Force, E. A. (Bessie) 1 ch huckster O H&L 1h N Main St Bradner Mon.

Ford, Emma S. RD Custar Lib.

Ford, Geo. 2 ch oil worker O H&L 1h Rudolph Lib 81 Ind tel.

Ford, Geo. (Emma) 6 ch laborer T R2 Custar Lib 34.

FORD, JAMES H. (Jessie) bus driver T H&L Rudolph Lib Ind tel.

Ford, Walter (Frances) 5 ch laborer T H&L Second St Perrysburg Pbg.

Forrest, A. H. (Nellie) 2 ch farmer T 40a 3h 1c R2 Bowling Green Pla 64 Ind tel.

Forrest, Clare R1 Pemberville Cen 117 Ind tel.

Forrest, Mrs. Mary 3 ch farmer O 60a 3h 3c R1 Pemberville Cen 117 Ind tel.

Forrester, Mrs. Annie Pemberville Web.

Forrester, Chas. A. (Ida) 3 ch farmer T 80a 3h 8c R3 Bowling Green Web 13 B tel.

Forrester, H. R. (Helen) farmer T 120a 7h 3c R3 Bowling Green Cen 87 Ind tel.

Forrester, Jas. cattle RD Bowling Green Cen.

Forrester, R. D. Pemberville Web.

FORSH, G. (Elizabeth) 1 ch farmer O 57a 2h 3c R2 Haskins Mid 28 B tel.

PORTLANDER, J. F. (Flora) 4 ch oil worker T H&L Jerry St Jerry City Blo.

Portlander, Orville student Jerry St Jerry City Blo.

Fortlander, William F. (Louisa) 2 ch bartender O H&L Luckey St Tro.

80

Foryuharson, D. D. (Ethel) farmer T 80a 3h 3c R1 Weston Mil 64 B tel.

Foster, Mrs. Amanda Pemberville Fre.

Foster, Arthur (Iva) 4 ch farmer T 120a 3h 15c R1 Risingsun Mon 82.

Foster, Caroline H. Lemoyne Tro.

Foster, C. (Mollie) ret O H&L Front St Pemberville Fre 40.

Foster, C. E. Risingsun Mon.

Foster, D. D. farmer 40a R1 Lemoyne Tro 46 Ind tel.

Foster, Ed. Prairie Depot Mon.

FOSTER, E. A. (Marguerite) oil producer O H&L 1h Front St Cygnet Blo B & Ind tels.

Foster, E. M. (Catharine) blacksmith O H&L & shop Tontogany Wash Ind tel.

Foster, Frank (Rebecca) ret O 80a 1h 2c R1 Bradner Fre 92 B tel.

Foster, Harry (Iva) 2 ch farmer T H&L West Millgrove Per 69 B tel.

Foster, Joseph farming O 29a 2h R3 Perrysburg Pbg 137.

FOSTER, J. H. (Ella) 2 ch hotel O H&L Portage Lib 90 Ind tel.

FOSTER, J. H. hotel & waiting room Portage Lib 113 B & Ind tels.

Foster, J. W. (Zoe) blacksmith T H&L Wall St Tontogany Wash.

Foster, L. A. (Bertha Z.) 4 ch farmer O 28a 3h R3 North Baltimore Blo 36.

Foster, Maude (dau O. W.) housekeeper R1 Lemoyne Tro 46 Ind tel.

Foster, M. F. RD North Baltimore Hen.

Foster, Ovid (Jessie) farmer T 3h 3c R1 Bradner Fre 92.

Foster, O. W. (Caroline) 1 ch farmer O 40a 3h 4c R1 Lemoyne Tro 46 Ind tel.

FOSTER, S. F. (Minnie) 1 ch farmer O 80a 3h 11c R3 Pemberville Fre 94 B tel.

Foster, Vera Mae (dau L. A.) R3 North Baltimore Blo 36.

Foster, Wm. teamster & farmer O H&L West Millgrove Per 69.

Fought, D. H. (Clara) 4 ch farmer T 105a 4h 4c R1 Deshler Jac 6 B tel.

Foust, O. M. RD North Baltimore Hen.

FOWLER, MRS. C. T. ret O 60a R1 Bradner Mon 28 B tel.

FOWLER, FLOYD R1 Portage.

FOWLER, N. F. R2 Custar Hen 41.

Fowler, N. J. (Maggie) farmer & real estate dealer O 10a 2h 2c R2 Custar Hen 41.

Fowles, M. B. RD North Baltimore Hen.

Fox, A. farmer T 120a 8h 5c R2 Dunbridge Mid 72.

Fox, E. A. (E. V.) 2 ch farmer O 100a 5h 2c R1 Tontogany Pla 19 Ind tel.

Fox, E. H. (Mattie L.) ret O H&L Tontogany Wash Ind tel.

Fox, E. V. RD Tontogany Pla.

Fox, FRANK (Emma C.) 3 ch farmer O 59a 2h 4c RD Prairie Depot Mon 108.

Fox, F. E. (Nellie) 3 ch farmer T 124a 4h 10c R1 Perrysburg Pbg 14 B tel.

Fox, M. K. (Sarah E.) 1 ch farmer O 120a 6h 7c R1 Fostoria Per 58.

Fox, S. S. (Sarah E.) contractor Hoytsville Jac.

Fox, Warren 1 ch oil man O H&L Risingsun Mon.

Fox, Wm. A. Bradner Mon.

Fox, W. R. 3 ch oil man T H&2Ls Risingsun Mon B tel.

Fralic, Richard (Mary) fruit dealer O H&L 3h 1c Fifth St Perrysburg Pbg B tel.

Fralick, Alvin 1h R1 Bradner Mon 15 B tel.

Fralick, E. (Henriette) 3 ch farmer O 120a 4h 5c R1 Bradner Mon 15 B tel.

Fralie, Richard Perrysburg Pbg.

Frame, Mary housekeeper O H&L Walbridge Lake.

France, Edward (Nancy) 5 ch ret O 40a H&L Custar Mil.

France, Peter H. (Cora) 2 ch mail carrier O H&L 2h Custar Mil Ind tel.

France, R. B. (Clara) 4 ch farmer O 40a T 60a 3h 2c R1 Custar Mil 10 B tel.

Francis, James N. (Mary A.) 1 ch broom maker O 5a R4 Bowling Green Cen 68.

Francis, J. W. 1 ch farm hand R4 Bowling Green Cen 68.

FRANCISCO, B. S. life insurance RD North Baltimore. See adv.

Francisco, C. R. (Annelia) 3 ch oil pumper T 1h 1c R1 North Baltimore Hen 51.

FRANEY, T. M. cashier bank O H&L 1h Perrysburg Pbg Ind tel. See adv.

Frank, Ephrain RD North Baltimore Hen.

Frank, Homer J. (Elsie) 7 ch farmer T 94a 4h 3c R4 Bowling Green Cen 25 Ind tel.

FRANK, J. H. (May) 3 ch oil worker O & T H&L R1 Rudolph Lib 63 Ind tel.

Frankart, D. J. (Rose) 2 ch farmer T 140a 7h 5c R1 Fostoria Per 106 Ind tel.

6   81

Frankfather, C. A. (Nellie M.) 2 ch blacksmith O H&L Main St Jerry City Por.

FRANKFATHER, DAVID (Alice) 3 ch oil man O H&L R1 Jerry City Blo 60 B & Ind tels.

Frankfather, Gale (Marie) laborer T H&L Jerry City Por.

Frankfather, Lila Frankfather Ave Jerry City Por Ind tel.

Frankfather, O. B. 1 ch carpenter O 1h 1c cor Mulberry & Rose Sts Bloomdale Blo.

Frankfather, Wilson (Rhoda) laborer T H&L R1 Bloomdale Blo 61 B & Ind tels.

Frankfather, Wm. (Anna) 3 ch woodworker O 7a 1h 3c Jerry City Por.

Franklin, E. D. (Katherine) 6 ch farmer O 80a 1h 3c R1 Prairie Depot Mon 66.

Franklin, Wm. A. oil worker Rudolph Lib 81 Ind tel.

Franks, A. J. RD North Baltimore Hen.

Frantz, John (Susan) section hand O H&L Lime City Pbg 121.

Frantz, Mrs. O. 2 ch ret T H&L Fifth St Perrysburg Pbg B tel.

Frantz, Samuel H. (Amanda) 6 ch laborer O H&L 1h Lime City Pbg 121.

Franz, Herman F. (Edna) 3 ch farmer T 142a 3h 53c Stony Ridge Tro.

Franz, John (Cora) 1 ch farmer O 82a 5h 1c R1 Stony Ridge Lake 32 Ind tel.

Franz, Julius (Katherine) 4 ch farmer O 142a 1h 5c Stony Ridge Tro.

Frautschi, Arnold (Sophia) grocer T H&L 257 Superior St Rossford Ros.

Frautschi, Fred (Minnie) 2 ch grocer O H&L Rossford Ros.

Frautschi, Samuel (Lena) grocer & merchandise O H&L & store 189 Superior St Rossford Ros.

Frautschi, Samuel (Lena) 2 ch gen mdse O H&L Rossford Pbg 80.

Frautschi, Walter (Lillian) grocery O H&L Rossford Pbg 80 Ind tel.

Frazier, F. O. (Clara) 3 ch farmer T 116a 4h 11c R1 Lemoyne 42 B & Ind tels.

Frazier, W. T. (Rhea) 1 ch pumper T H&L R1 Rudolph Por 26 Ind tel.

FREDERICK, ANDY L. (Amy) 1 ch farmer T 80a 3h 2c R2 Fostoria Per 38 Ind tel.

FREDERICK, BYRON (Amanda) 2 ch farmer O 68a 2h 7c R1 Jerry City Blo 71 Ind tel.

Frederick, Charles section Jerry St Blo.

Frederick, Dan (Carrie) 5 ch section foreman T H&L Bradford St Cygnet Blo.

Frederick, Ernest (son C. E.) laborer Hoytsville Jac.

Frederick, E. M. (Etta M.) 3 ch farmer T 87a 4h 4c R3 North Baltimore Blo 40 Ind tel.

Frederick, G. T. (Anna) 2 ch farmer O 40a 2h 1c R1 Jerry City Por 75 Ind tel.

Frederick, H. A. (Anna) 1 ch farmer O 58a 2h 4c R3 Pemberville Fre 43.

Frederick, Johnus (Mary) 3 ch laborer O H&L Venango St Cygnet Blo.

FREDERICK, J. M. (Myranda) 4 ch carpet weaver O H&L Myers St Jerry City Blo.

Frederick, Maranda Jerry City Blo.

Frederick, Rev. M. L. (Mary) 7 ch minister T H&L Luckey Tro Ind tel.

Frederick, N. O. Bloomdale Blo.

Frederick, Samuel harness shop T shop Venango St Cygnet Blo.

Frederick, S. S. (Rebecca J.) farmer O 80a 3c R1 North Baltimore Hen 52.

Frederick, Mrs. W. M. 4 ch O H&L Jerry St Jerry City Blo.

Fredericks, C. E. (Lottie) 1 ch laborer O H&L 1h Hoytsville Jac.

FREDRICK, W. R. (Myrtle) 1 ch farmer T R1 North Baltimore Hen. 52.

Freece, Wallace (Grace) paperhanger & painter A H&L Grand Rapids Gr Rs.

Freed, Frank Tontogany Wash.

Freed, John (Susan) 2 ch ret O H&L 1h S Main St Bradner Mont.

Freed, Wm. (Cora) 1 ch farmer O 18a 2h 1c R1 Tontogany Wash 84 Ind tel.

Freeman, A. E. RD North Baltimore Hen.

Freeman, J. E. (Sadie) 3 ch farmer O 236a 12h 4c R1 Deshler Jac 24.

Freeman, Oliver (Mattie) 2 ch farmer O 85a 4h 5c R4 Deshler Jac 21 Ind tel.

FREER, N. A. (Flora) 2 ch grocer T H&L 5h R4 Bowling Green Por 95 Ind tel.

FREES, CLYDE C. (Genoa) 3 ch farmer O 60a 6h 13c R1 Bloomdale Blo 55 B & Ind tels.

Frees, Ira (M. C.) carpenter O H&L Bell Ave Bradner Mon Ind tel.

Frees, Merle Bell Ave Bradner Mon.

Frees, Norman A. cattle RD Bowling Green Por.

Fren, Mabelle 2 ch school teacher O H&L Prairie Depot Mon.

French, A. L. RD North Baltimore Hen.
French, J. F. (Kathryn) barber T H&L Weston Wes Ind tel.
French, Martha housekeeper O H&L Summer St Weston Wes B tel.
French, O. E. (Senora) 4 ch baker O H&L Center St Weston.
Fretter, E. A. (Sada) 2 ch garage worker O H&L 1c Palmer Ave Cygnet Blo 6.
FRETTER, FRANK R1 Hoytsville Jac.
Freyer, Mary Luckey Tro.
Freyman, Charley (May) oil worker O H&L Portage Lib 112.
Freyman, Earl (Essa) 1 ch clerk O H&L Water St Portage Por Ind tel.
Freyman, Henry RD North Baltimore Hen.
Freyman, Irvin I. (Ethel M.) 1 ch bank cashier O H&L Walnut St Portage Por Ind tel.
Freyman, Margaret RD North Baltimore Hen.
Freyman, P. E. (Alta) 2 ch farmer T 65a 3h 2c R1 Bowling Green Pla 81.
FREYMAN, MRS. WM. Box 132 Portage.
Frick, Abraham Rossford Ros.
Frick, Caroline Rossford Ros.
Fridley, J. B. real estate T H&L Second St Portage Por.
Friedly, John (Elizabeth) 7 ch O 1½a H&L R1 Luckey Tro 89.
Friend, E. E. RD Rudolph Lib.
Friends, Clyde H&L Rudolph Lib 94.
Frier, Annie (dau Frank) housekeeper R1 Luckey Web 74 B tel.
FRIER, FRANK (Louisa) 1 ch farmer O 80a 3h 4c R1 Luckey Web 74 B tel.
Fries, C. C. Bloomdale Blo.
Fries, Geo. (son Mary) laborer Custar Mil.
Fries, Louis (son Mary) laborer Custar Mil.

Fries, Mrs. Mary 4 ch ret O H&L Custar Mil.
Fries, Maude (dau Mrs. W. H.) seamstress Main St Bloomdale Blo B & Ind tels.
Friess, G. F. (Celia) 8 ch painter & paperhanger O 3a H&L Broadway St Box 275 Weston Wes.
Friess, Margarie (dau G. F.) tel operator Broadway St Weston Wes.
Fries, Robert (Marie) painter T H&L Walnut St Weston Wes.
Frisbie, E. E. (Della) 5 ch carpenter O H&L Prairie Depot Mon.
FRISBIE, H. C. (Anna) 2 ch farmer T 133a 2h 15c Rudolph Lib 82 Ind tel.
Frisbie, T. E. (Janet) general merchandise O H&L Prairie Depot Mon.
Fritts, Thomas (Lottie) farmer O 44a 2h 2c R1 Walbridge Ros 22.
Fritz, Chas. (May) 4 ch oil worker O H&L Bell St Bradner Mon.
Fritz, Jacob farming T 80a 3h R1 North Baltimore Hen 53.
Fritz, Joseph (Matilda) 4 ch pumper T 6a 1c R1 Bradner Mon. 23.
Fritz, W. M. RD North Baltimore Hen.
Frizzel, Henry 2 ch teamster T H&L Pemberville Fre.
Frobose, J. H. (Anna) 2 ch farmer O 80a 3h 2c R2 Pemberville Fre 53.
Frobose, Wm. Pemberville Web.
Frommer, John (Mary) 6 ch farmer O 80a 2h 10c R1 Hoytsville Jac 111.
Frommer, Leonard RD North Baltimore Hen.
FROST, MRS. JENNIE R5 Bowling Green.
Frost, W. E. (Jennie) 2 ch farmer T H&L 1h 1c R5 Bowling Green Cen.
Fruch, L. C. Perrysburg Pbg.
FRUSHER, C. D. (Lucy) 6 ch sugar business O 120a R1 Perrysburg Pbg 16 B tel.

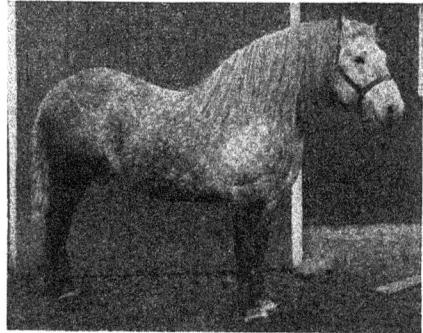

A Blue Ribbon Winner.

Frusher, Edward (Fannie) 8 ch farmer T 80a 3h 2c R1 Perrysburg Pbg B tel.

Frusher, Jas. Perrysburg Pbg.

Frusher, Mrs. Mary ret O 80a 1c R1 Perrysburg Pbg 16 B tel.

Frusher, Wm. 2 ch laborer bds R1 Perrysburg Pbg 16.

Fry, Clyde B. Prairie Depot Mon.

FRY, C. A. (Alice) 4 ch farmer O 120a 5h 7c R1 Jerry City Blo 63 Ind tel.

Fry, C. V. (Christina) 2 ch farmer O 80a 4h 13c R1 Prairie Depot Mon 54

Fry, Erastus (Ella) 1 ch farmer T 60a 2h 5c Hatton Per 85.

Fry, E. R. laborer Garfield St Bloomdale Blo.

Fry, F. B. Bloomdale Per.

Fry, Harry (Maude) 1 ch ditcher T H&L Evans St Bradner Mon.

Fry, Harry J. (son J. W.) farmer 2h 1c R2 Prairie Depot Por 131 Ind tel.

Fry, Isaac W. (Loretta J.) farmer & laborer O 3a 1h 1c R1 Bloomdale Blo 111 B & Ind tels.

Fry, J. B. RD North Baltimore Hen.

Fry, J. W. cattle RD Bowling Green Por.

Fry, Mrs. Mary J. O H&L Garfield St Bloomdale Blo.

Fry, Ross Bloomdale Per.

Fry, Thomas ret farmer O 2a R1 Rudolph Lib 104.

Fry, Wayne Bloomdale Per.

Fry, Wm. laborer 1h R1 Rudolph Lib 164.

FRY, W. H. (Anna) 3 ch poultry buyer O H&L Box 52 Milton Center Mil 93 Ind tel.

Frye, Geo. F. RD Rudolph Lib.

Fryman, Henry RD North Baltimore Jac.

Fuller, A. C. dry goods & shoes O H&L Perrysburg Pbg B tel.

Fuller, Chas. A. Rossford Ros.

Fuller, C. C. 6 ch O 60o 1h R2 Custar Lib 32 Ind tel.

Fuller, Elmer E. Haskins Mid.

Fuller, Frank (Bertha) 6 ch farmer T 120a 4h 5c R1 Jerry City Por 66 Ind tel.

Fuller, H. L. (Ruby) 3 ch garage T H&L Grand Rapids Gr Rs Ind tel.

FULLER, I. G. (Cora) 4 ch R1 Hoytsville Jac 89.

Fuller, J. S. (Mary A.) clerk O H&L Perrysburg Pbg Ind tel.

Fuller, T. J. (Ida A.) 5 ch farmer O 58½a 4h 3c R1 Dunbridge Mid 69 B tel.

FULTON, GEO. B. (Luella B.) 1 ch clerk O H&L RD North Baltimore Hen B & Ind tels.

FUNK, ABE (Alta) 1 ch farmer T 160a 8h 3c R1 North Baltimore Hen 38 Ind tel.

Funk, D. E. RD Hoytsville Jac.

Funk, Ephraim (Ada) 8 ch farmer T 160a 3h 4c R2 Custar Hen 42.

Funk, Frank (Lizzie) 3 ch farmer T 80a 4h 2c R1 Hoytsville Jac 102.

Funk, Henry RD North Baltimore Hen.

Funk, Mrs. Henry 8 ch farmer O 80a 1h 2c R1 Hoytsville Jac 104 B tel.

Funk, Israel (Lydia) 4 ch farmer 120a 10h 10c R1 Hoytsville Jac 86 B tel.

Funk, Jeremiah (Lydia) 3 ch farmer O 20a 3h 4c R1 Deshler Jac 46.

Furman, Chas. M. (Clara L.) ret O H&L Pemberville Fre.

Furrer, Mrs. Mary ret O 20a R3 Perrysburg Pbg 77.

Furry, Anson L. Pemberville Fre.

Furry, Bessie (dau J. W.) housekeeper R1 Stony Ridge Lake 87.

Furry, Edgar G. (Emma) farmer O 40a 2h 4c R1 Stony Ridge Lake 86 B tel.

Furry, Flossie (dau J. W.) housekeeper R1 Stony Ridge Lake 87.

Furry, Floyd Walbridge Lake.

Furry, F. A. (Ada) 1 ch farmer T 30a 2h 2c R1 Walbridge Lake 94 B tel.

Furry, Hattie 8 ch ret O 30a Stony Ridge Tro.

Furry, Henry (Dora) 1 ch clerk O H&L Stony Ridge Tro.

FURRY, J. W. (Deal) 2 ch farmer O 80a 4h 4c R1 Stony Ridge Lake 87 B tel.

Furry, Minnie dressmaking O H&L Pemberville Fre 40.

Furry, Ray R. (son Hattie) teacher Stony Ridge Tro.

Furste, Lucy E. Bradner Mon.

Gagen, John (Sarah) 2 ch contractor O H&L Custar Mil B tel.

Gagban, Jno. F. Custar Mil.

Gaines, Otto Prairie Depot Mon.

Galbraith, Roy (Lena) 2 ch laborer T H&L Prairie Depot Mon.

GALDEEN, HERMAN (Nora) 5 ch farmer T 85a 3h 2c R1 Weston Mil 61.

Galen, Geo. RD Hoytsville Jac.

Galey, J. B. (Elizabeth) ret O H&L Prairie Depot Mon.

Galispie, James (Ella) 1 ch barber O H&L Millbury Lake.

Gallager, Alex (Margaret) 1 ch glass finisher O H&L Box 14 Rossford Ros.

Gallagher, Frank (Addie) 4 ch farmer T 200a 6h 4c R2 McClure Gr Rs Ind tel.

84

Gallier, A. G. (Sarah) 3 ch farmer O 160a 4h 6c R5 Bowling Green Cen 59 Ind tel.

Gallier, H. A. cattle RD Bowling Green Cen.

GALLIER, J. G. (Pearl) 1 ch farmer T 80a 5h 4c R1 Portage Por 46 Ind tel.

· Gallier, Walter (Ethel) 1 ch farmer T 100a 4h 2c R3 Bowling Green Cen 59 Ind tel.

GALPIN, FRANK farmer O 80a 4h 14c R1 Haskins Mid 48 B tel.

Galpin, S. K. RD Haskins Mid.

Gamby, Bert (Sarah) 3 ch farmer T 90a 2h 2c R1 Bowling Green Pla 75 Ind tel.

Gamby, B. F. RD Bowling Green Pla.

Gammell, W. H. shoemaker O H&L Dowling Mid.

Gampher, Chas. (Myrtle) 1 ch cement block worker O H&L Box 35 Rossford Ros Ind tel.

Gampher, H. P. Rossford Ros.

GANDER, BENJ. (Katherine) 1 ch farmer T 160a 6h 6c R3 Bowling Green Cen 87 Ind tel.

Gander, Roy (Charity) farmer T 173a 4h 6c R1 Bowling Green Pla 73 Ind tel.

Gangwer, Jas. Risingsun Mon.

Gannon, P. E. (Louise C.) 1 ch molder T H&L R1 Custar Mil 99½.

GARBER, CONSTANCE L. 3 ch O 38a 1h 3c R1 Rudolph Lib 105.

GARBER, H. R. (Rosa M.) 6 ch farmer O 94a 4h 8c R1 Rudolph Lib 33 Ind tel.

Garber, James (Bertha) 4 ch tile burner T H&L Fifth & Locust Sts Perrysburg Pbg B tel.

GARBER, J. A. (Minnie) 3 ch laborer T H&L 1c R1 Bowling Green Lib 58 Ind tel.

Gardner, Lonette M. Grand Rapids Gr Rs.

Gardner, Wm. (Edith) 2 ch farmer T H&L R1 Prairie Depot Mon 87.

Gardner, W. E. (Clara) farmer O 60a 3h 5c R1 Millburg Lake 46 Ind tel.

Garey, S. P. (M. M.) 2 ch ticket agent T H&L East St Bradner Mon.

Garfield, Ora (Minnie) 2 ch stone worker T H&L Pemberville Fre 40.

GARLING, MRS. FRED 5 ch farmer O 54a 2h 2c R1 Luckey Tro 89 B tel.

Garner, Ella E. housekeeper R1 Walbridge Lake 99 Ind tel.

Garner, F. (Jessie) 3 ch farmer T 40a 4h 3c RD Portage Por 56 Ind tel.

Garner, George W. (Ide) 3 ch farmer O 37a 4h 3c R1 Walbridge Lake 99.

GARNER, URIAH (Emma) 3 ch farmer T 35a 1h 2c R1 Walbridge Lake 99 Ind tel.

Garno, L. (Laura) 8 ch farmer T 160a 7h 3c R2 Custar Hen 8 Ind tel.

Garrett, Bliss (son Elwood) Haskins Mid.

Garrett, Elwood (Grace) 5 ch meat market O H&L 1h Haskins Mid.

Garrett, F. J. (Mary) 1 ch farming City St Haskins Mid B tel.

Garrett, Gurdon 3 ch clerk bds Haskins Mid 35.

Garrett, John (Carrie) 2 ch cement contractor O H&L Haskins Mid B tel.

Garrett, Joseph ·(Charlotte) 1 ch farmer O 2a 1h 1c Haskins Mid B tel.

Garrett, Mrs. Katie ret O H&L Haskins Mid.

GARRETT, W. H. (Lodema) hotel O H&L Haskins Mid 35 B tel.

GARRISON, PAUL (Grace) elevator O H&L Milton Center Mil B & Ind tels.

Garrison, S. H. (Jessie) 4 ch farmer T 160a 10h 8c R1 Rudolph Hen 44.

Gary, Chas. (Mabel) 5 ch teamster T H&L Caldwell St Bradner Mon.

Gary, R. A. (Grace) 1 ch laborer T H&L N Main St Bradner Mon.

GAST, ARTHUR J. (Pearl) 3 ch fireman T 10a Walbridge St Walbridge Lake 119.

Gates, Eldo farmer R1 Dunbridge Web 52 B· tel.

Gaul, Chas. (son John) farmer T 84a 3h R1 Walbridge Lake 3.

Gaul, Geo. ret O 90a R1 Grand Rapids Gr Rs 21 Ind tel.

Gaul, John ret O 24a RD Walbridge Lake 3.

Gaul, Lena (dau John) housekeeper R1 Walbridge Lake 3.

Gaul, Robt. Walbridge Lake.

Gault, Elizabeth ret O 55a R1 Hoytsville Jac 61.

Gault, E. L. (Madie) 6 ch farmer O 60a 5h 2c R1 Hoytsville Jac 61.

GAULT, HOWARD R2 Bloomdale.

Geahlen, John (Emma) 4 ch farmer O 20a 1h 1c R5 Bowling Green Cen 23 Ind tel.

Geanol, J. A. (Ella) laborer O 5a 1h 1c R2 Weston Pla 6.

Gearey, Edward Bradner Mon.

Gearhart, Robt. RD North Baltimore Hen.

Geer, Chas. (Sadie) 3 ch farmer O H&L 2h Risingsun Mon.

Gehlen, John cattle RD Bowling Green Cen.

Geibel, John G. (Minnie) 1 ch oil man O H&L Risingsun Mon.

Geisbuhler, Fred (Ella) 2 ch laborer O H&L Luckey Tro.

Geisbuhler, Wm. Luckey Web.

Geldin, Charles (Minnie) 2 ch farmer O 80a 4h 8c R2 Dunbridge Web 2.

Geldin, Fred (Anna) farmer O 45a 2h 3c R2 Dunbridge Mid 74.

Geltz, W. A. (Mary) engineer O H&L 211 Maple St Rossford Ros B tel.

GEOGLINE, CHAS. (Iva) 2 ch farmer T 100a 4h 2c West Millgrove Mon 90.

George, A. R. RD Bowling Green Por.

George, B. B. (Anna) oil pumper T 1h R1 North Baltimore Hen 48 B tel .

George, David RD North Baltimore Hen.

George, Dennie (Ethel) farmer T H&L 2h 2c R5 Bowling Green Cen 62 Ind tel.

George, E. A. (Mollie) 2 ch farmer T 160a 4h 4c R5 Bowling Green Cen 67 Ind tel.

George, Galen (son Solomon) farm laborer R1 Hoytsville Jac 107.

George, O. M. (Lucinda) 2 ch farmer T 120a 5h 4c R5 Bowling Green Cen 62 Ind tel.

George Ralph farmer 2h R5 Bowling Green Cen 62 Ind tel.

George, Silas (Liza J.) ret O H&L Millbury Lake.

George, Solomon (Marilla) 9 ch farmer T 340a 9h 5c R1 Hoytsville Jac 107.

George, S. M. (Maggie) 5 ch farmer O 170a 6h 3c R5 Bowling Green Cen 62 Ind tel.

Gerdes, B. J. (Katherine) farmer O 71a 4h 3c R1 Lime City Web 53 B tel.

Gerdes, John 1 ch farmer O 78a 2h 7c R1 Perrysburg Pbg 31 B tel.

Gerdes, Kathryn (dau John) housekeeper R1 Perrysburg Pbg 31 B tel.

Gerding, Alice Pemberville Fre.

Gerding, Anna milliner T H&L Pemberville.

Gerding, Caroline milliner T H&L Pemberville.

Gerding, Chas. R. Pemberville Fre.

Gerding, Mrs. H. H. housekeeper T H&L Pemberville Fre 40.

Gerding, W. H. (son Mrs. H. H.) postmaster Pemberville Fre 40.

Gerdsen, Christ Latchie Lake.

Gerheart, Charley (son Sarah) painter Weston.

Gerheart, John (son Sarah) farm hand Western.

Gerheart, Sarah T H&L Weston.

Gerke, Fred H. Pemberville Fre.

Gerky, L. (Lily) conductor T H&L Second St Perrysburg Pbg B tel.

German, F. C. Prairie Depot Mon.

Gessner, John ret R1 Longway Per 99 Ind tel.

GEST, JOHN (Rena) farmer T H&L R2 Bowling Green Pla 63 Ind tel.

Getz, Mrs. Fred Perrysburg Pbg.

Getz, Geo. (Jennie) 5 ch farmer O 40a 2h 2c R2 Dunbridge Mid 78.

Getz, John (Mary) 3 ch farmer O 40a 2h 2c R2 Perrysburg Mid 11.

Getz, John (Winnifred) farmer T 60a 2h 1c R1 Tontogany Wash 74 Ind tel.

Getz, Mary ret O H&L Sixth St Perrysburg Pbg.

Geyer, Chas. F. Risingsun Mon.

Geyman, Joseph (Catherine) 2 ch ret O 10a 1h 2c R1 Custar Mil 17.

GIBBS, FRED J. (Lillian) ret O H&L Front St Perrysburg Pbg B tel.

Gibson, J. F. Prairie Depot Mon.

Gibson, V. (Hattie) 3 ch oil gauger T H&L East St Bradner Mon B tel.

Gibson, W. R. RD North Baltimore Hen.

GIBSON, W. W. Prairie Depot Mon.

Giebel, Jno. J. Risingsun Mon.

Gierke, A. C. Perrysburg Pbg.

GIERKE, CARL (Frieda) hotel T H&L Grand Rapids Gr Rs Ind tel.

GIERKE, PAUL (Teresa) 3 ch bakery O H&L Grand Rapids Gr Rs Ind tel. See adv.

Gifford, F. 1 ch housekeeper O H&L Prairie Depot Mon.

Giha, M. RD North Baltimore Hen.

Gilbert, Amelia 5 ch housekeeper O 7a R1 Walbridge Lake 101.

Gilbert, George (Polly) inspector O 1a Walbridge St Walbridge Lake 3.

Gilbert, Joseph (Anna) 2 ch R R man O H&L Walbridge Lake.

Gilbert, Joseph Walbridge Lake.

GILBERT, T. G. (Nellie) 3 ch gen mdse O H&L 2h Walbridge Lake. See adv.

GILDEA, JAS. (Ellen) 5 ch farmer T 50a 3h Bays Lib 75 Ind tel.

Gilham, Jno. Pemberville Fre.

Gill, C. E. (Carrie) 1 ch farmer T R2 Bowling Green Pla 63 Ind tel.

GILL, EARL H. (Nellie) 1 ch farmer T H 2h 1c R2 Weston Wash 5.

GILL, E. (Amelia May) farmer O 80a 4h 4c R2 Weston Wash 6 Ind tel.

Gill, E. G. (Mollie) 1 ch lumber, coal & gen merchandise O H&L & store 5h 2c RD Tontogany Wash Ind tel.

Gill, Frank 2 ch cement worker O H&L Grand Rapids Gr Rs Ind tel.

Gill, Fred (Minnie) 3 ch grocery T H&L Grand Rapids Gr Rs Ind tel.

Gill, Fred R. (Florence) 9 ch laborer T H&L Stony Ridge Tro.

Gill, George 1 ch farmer O 39a 3h 1c R2 Weston Pla 3.

Gill, Grace (dau Fred R.) housekeeper Stony Ridge Tro.

Gill, Henry (Nettie) 1 ch laborer T H&L Stony Ridge Tro.

Gill, H. E. Tontogany Wash.

Gill, H. P. farmer T 30a 3h 5c R2 Weston Wash 53 Ind tel.

Gill, John (Matilda) farmer O 35a 3h 3c R1 Stony Ridge Lake 28.

Gill, J. F. Grand Rapids Gr Rs.

Gill, Marie (dau Fred R.) housekeeper Stony Ridge Tro.

Gill, S. D. (Pearl) 4 ch farmer T 27a 2h Weston Wes 30.

GILLESPIE, BROUGH farmer T 40a 3h 3c R1 Tontogany Pla 1 Ind tel.

Gillespie, Elden (son Francis) Main St Weston.

Gillespie, Florence RD Bowling Green Pla.

GILLESPIE, FRANCIS (Sarah) 4 ch farm hand O H&L Main St Weston.

Gillespie, Horace RD Bowling Green Pla.

Gillespie, Rev. H. C. (Bird F.) 2 ch minister T H&L 1h Haskins Mid 35 B tel.

Gillespie, H. G. (Florence) 1 ch farmer T 80a 3h 5c R2 Bowling Green Pla 50 B tel.

Gillespie, Jas Millbury Lake.

GILLESPIE, J. H. (Louisa M.) 2 ch farmer O 50a 2h 14c R2 Weston Wash 6.

Gillion, C. A. RD Portage Lib.

Gilman, C. F. (Josephine) farmer T 180a 10h 3c R2 Custar Mil 30 Ind tel.

Gilmore, Henry (Elmira) 1 ch carpenter O 10a 1h 1c R2 Weston Wash 1 Ind tel.

Gilmore, Henry H. RD N Baltimore Hen.

Gilson, V. Bradner Mon.

Gilson, W. W. (Mary A.) 1 ch jeweler O 2a Prairie Depot Mon B tel.

Gilts, George (Cassie) 1 ch ret O H&L 168 Oak St Rossford Ros.

GINDER, D. O. (Ora M.) 1 ch foreman O H&L Weston.

GINDER, MRS. MARY millinery Weston. See adv.

Giner, Bernard Walbridge Lake.

Gingery, H. laborer Weston.

Gingery, Samuel 2 ch real estate & insurance bds Weston.

Gingrich, D. W. (Sarah) 6 ch farmer O 40a 3h 3c R3 Weston Mil 88 Ind tel.

Gingrich, Ethel Weston Mil.

Gingrich, Sherman (Mabel) 3 ch farmer O H&L Silver St Weston.

Gingrich, S. F. (Ellen) 2 ch farmer O 50a 2h 3c R3 Weston Mil 91.

Gingrich, W. H. (Orpha) 4 ch mason T H&L Weston Wes.

Gingrich, W. M. (Bessie) 2 ch farmer T 160a 5h 2c R1 Rudolph Hen 44.

GIRDHAM, T. G. (Olive) 2 ch farmer O 50a 3h 12c R1 Bowling Green Pla 70 Ind tel.

Girton, D. K. (Mary) 1 ch farmer O 119a 8h 14c R1 Fostoria Per 79 Ind tel.

Gladish, Mary Rossford Ros.

Glaser, C. J. (Lena) 3 ch farmer O 80a 7h 2c R1 Weston Lib 47.

Glaser, Philipp (Helen) 2 ch farmer O 67a 1h 2c R2 Perrysburg Pbg 4.

Glaser, Sophia O H&L Factory 4 Jerry City Por.

Glassburn, F. M. (Fannie) 1 ch farmer O 80a 4h 9c R1 Fostoria Per 127 Ind tel.

Glassford, Bessie housekeeper R1 Portage Por 20.

Glassford, J. M. (Rosie) 8 ch farmer T H&L R1 Portage Por 20.

Glassford, Robt farmer T H&L R5 Bowling Green Cen 37.

Glow, Wm. Pemberville Fre.

Glynn, M. laborer bds Perrysburg Pbg.

Gobel, Albert W. (Callie) 3 ch canvasser O 35a 1h Main St Jerry City Blo 78 Ind tel.

GOBEL, CHARLES A. (Hazel M.) 2 ch farmer T 40a 2h R1 Bloomdale Blo 61.

Gobel, D. C. Bloomdale Blo.

Gobel, Hallie (dau John) R1 Bloomdale Blo 61 B & Ind tels.

GOBEL, JOHN (Catharine) farmer & thresher O 40a 1h 1c R1 Box 49 Bloomdale Blo 61 B & Ind tels.

Gobel, Sol. (Doretta) 1 ch farmer O 40a 2h 1c R1 Jerry City Bl 72 Ind tel.

Goble, Doretta Jerry City Blo.

Goeckerman, C. F. (Dorothy) 1 ch bakery O H&L Pemberville Fre 40 B tel.

GOECKERMAN, FRED (Angeline) 7 ch farmer O 100a 6h 20c R1 Lemoyne Tro 35 Ind tel.

Goeckerman, F. W. (Eveline) 4 ch mason O H&L Pemberville Fre 40 B tel.

Goeckerman, J. H. (Emma) 2 ch section hand O H&L Pemberville Fre.

Goeckerman, W. M. (Caroline) mason O H&L Pemberville Fre.

GOEKE, FRED (Leo) ret O H&L 1h Perrysburg Pbg.

Goeke, H. W. (Mary) 2 ch farmer T 57a 2h 6c R3 Perrysburg Pbg 141 Ind tel.

GOEKE, JOHN F. (Lucy) 2 ch farmer T 94a 2h 5c R3 Perrysburg Pbg 141 Ind tel.

Goetz, E. (Josephine) 1 ch drugs O H&L Luckey Tro Ind tel.

Goetz, Morris (Hannah) driller O H&L Luckey Tro.

Goff, H. D. (Estella) farmer T H&L 1h 1c Longley Per 101.

Gogniat, Miss Henrietta housekeeper Station A East Toledo Ros 31.

GOKEY, JOHN (Neva) 2 ch teamster O H&L 1h Portage Lib 90.

Gokey, Mrs. Mary 1 ch O H&L Portage Lib 90.

Goldner, Frank RD North Baltimore Hen.

Gonyer, Daniel RD Bowling Green Mil.

Gonyer, William (Anna) 7 ch farmer T 120a 7h 6c R1 Rudolph Lib ·76 Ind tel.

Good, Carl M. (son L. R.) N Main St Bloomdale Blo B & Ind tels.

GOOD, L. R. (Edith M.) 4 ch grain elevator & coal O H&L 1c N Main St Bloomdale Blo B & Ind tels. See adv.

Good, Mabel A. (dau L. R.) N Main St Bloomdale Blo B & Ind tels.

Goodell, C. E. Luckey Tro.

Goodell, Helen A. Luckey Tro.

Goodell, Ira T. (Minnie) 1 ch barber O H&L Luckey Tro.

Goodell, Marion (Malinda) 5 ch ret O H&L Luckey Tro Ind tel.

Goodell, Myet D. Luckey Tro.

Goodell, Orrin (Celestia) 3 ch mail carrier O H&L ·1h Luckey Tro Ind tel.

Goodell, S. E. (Helen A.) hardware store O H&L Luckey Tro 95 Ind tel.

Goodell, T. J. hardware clerk Luckey Tro.

Goodenough, H. A. (Nellie) 2 ch farmer T 320a 14h 30c R1 Bowling Green Pla B tel.

Goodger, Harry (Rebecca) 4 ch farmer T 40a 2h 1c R1 Tontogany Wash 21 Ind tel.

Goodman, Chas. (Harriet) farmer O 40a 2h 3c R3 Perrysburg Pbg 89.

Goodman, Clarence (Lizzie) 1 ch farmer T 57a 3h 3c R1 Lime City Pbg 91.

Goodman, Earnest (son Chas.) farmer R3 Perrysburg Pbg 89.

Goodman, Elmer (Ada) 2 ch farmer O 84a 2h 4c R1 Millbury Lake 105.

Goodman, Fred laborer T R3 North Baltimore Blo 36.

Goodman, G. W. 1 ch ret O H&L Third St Perrysburg Pbg B tel.

Goodman, Roy (Elma) 2 ch farmer T 74a 2h 3c R1 Lime City Pbg.

Goodrich, Mrs. Fanny ret Prairie Depot Mon B tel.

GOODRICH, J. M. (Rebecca K.) furniture & undertaker O H&L 2h Prairie Depot Mon B tel. See adv.

Goodwin, Geo. P. furniture & undertaker O H&L Front St Cygnet Blo Ind tel.

Goodwin, Geo. R. Cygnet Blo.

GOODYEAR, A. B. (Grace G.) 4 ch blacksmith O H&L Garfield St Bloomdale Blo B & Ind tels.

Gordon, D. C. R1 Rudolph Por 24½.

Gordon, Earl (Edna) blacksmith T 6a 1h 1c R1 Prairie Depot Mon 104.

Gordon, H. N. (Susie) oil & gas contractor O H&L R1 Rudolph Por.

Gordon, J. A. Prairie Depot Mon.

Gordon, Mildred R1 Rudolph Por 24½.

Gordon, Roy (Nellie) 1 ch blacksmith T H&L Mermill Por 19 Ind tel.

GORDON, THOMAS C. (Emma C.) 8 ch blacksmith O 4L & shop Bays Lib 75 Ind tel. See adv.

Gornadson, Edward T R2 Custar Hen 8.

Gorrell, M. R. (Ida) 2 ch farmer O 160a 6h 3c R1 Bowling Green Pla 67 B tel.

GORSUCH, N. N. (Lucy) 1 ch garage T H&L Grand Rapids Gr Rs.

GORSUCH, ROBERT (Ethel) garage T H&L Grand Rapids Gr Rs Ind tel.

Gorton, J. W. cattle RD Jerry City Por.

Gorton, M. P. (Etha) motorman O H&L Fifth St Perrysburg Per B tel.

Goshe, Frank (son N. M.) farmer bds R1 Fostoria Per 116 Ind tel.

Goshe, Isabelle (dau N. M.) housekeeper R1 Fostoria Per 116 Ind tel.

Goshe, John (son N. M.) farmer bds 3h R1 Fostoria Per 116 Ind tel.

Goshe, Mary (dau N. M.) housekeeper R1 Fostoria Per 116 Ind tel.

Goshe, Michael (son of N. M.) farmer bds 4h·R1 Fostoria Per 116 Ind tel.

Goshe, N. M. 4 ch farmer T 320a 7h 35c R1 Fostoria Per 116 Ind tel.·

Gosnell, E. O. Prairie Depot Mon.

Gosnell, E. U. (Martha) 6 ch pumper & farmer O 54a 1h 3c R2 Prairie Depot Mon 103 B tel.

Gosnell, M. E. Prairie Depot Mon.

Gossett, M. (Catharine) ret O H&L Dowling Mid 76.

Gottemoller, F. H. (Catherine) 5 ch furniture dealer O H&L Custar Mil Ind tel.

Gottschalk, Edward farmer R2 Pemberville Web 34 B tel.

Gottschalk, John (Minnie) 2 ch farmer O 96a 4h 7c R1 Dunbridge Web 47 B tel.

Gottschalk, Lewis (Emma) 4 ch farmer T 160a 5h 5c R2 Pemberville Web 34 B tel.

Gottschalk, L. W. farmer R2 Pemberville Web 34 B tel.

Gould, Geo. laborer T H&L Prairie Depot Mon.

Gould, W. T. (Mary) 2 ch general merchandise T H&L 1h Weston Wes.

Gowdy, Mary 1 ch ret O H&L Risingsun Mon.

Grabenstetter, Berny Rossford Ros.

Grabenstetter, Thos. (Catharine) 3 ch farmer & carpenter O 18a 1h 1c R1 Lemoyne Tro 85 B tel.

GRABER, A. J. (Emma) farmer O 120a 4h 7c R1 Prairie Depot Mon 89 B tel.

Graber, Lulu (dau A. J.) R1 Prairie Depot Mon 89.

Graber, Mrs. Mary 2 ch ret H&L Risingsun Mon.

Graber, Park (Pearl) 2 ch farmer T 20a 3h 4c R1 Fostoria Per 122.

Graff, Loren E. (Gladys) farmer T 40a 3h 2c R2 Custar Mil 34 B tel.

Graham, A. W. (Nellie) 2 ch laborer O H&L 1c Main St West Millgrove Per.

Graham, B. W. (Sofia) 3 ch teamster O H&L 2h Bell St Bradner Mon B tel.

Graham, Chas. (Nettie) 1 ch horse dealer O 20a 5h 1c R3 Prairie Depot Por 119 Ind tel.

Graham, Chas. E. (Minnie) 2 ch farmer O 120a 4h R2 Dunbridge Mid 82 B tel.

Graham, Chas. H. (Ella) farmer T 60a 2h 1c R1 Portage Por 91.

Graham, C. R. cattle RD Prairie Depot Por.

Graham, C. W. (Anna) 1 ch farmer O 105a 4h 7c West Millgrove Per 73.

Graham, Harry (Carrie) thresher T R1 Haskins Mid 91.

GRAHAM, H. E. (Edna N.) manager T H&L Cygnet Blo Front St B & Ind tels.

Graham, Jess (Lottie) 3 ch laborer T H&L Prairie Depot Mon.

Graham, J. R. RD Haskins Mid.

A Filled Silo.

Graham, J. W. (Anna L.) 2 ch mail carrier O 40a H&L 1h Prairie Depot Mon.

Graham, Luella ret O H&L Second St Perrysburg Pbg.

Graham, Mrs. M. A. O 50a R2 Prairie Depot Por 112.

Graham, R. E. farmer Tontogany Wash 41.

GRAHAM, R. M. (Levina) 2 ch farmer O 80a 4h 3c Prairie Depot Mon 65 B tel.

Graham, Thos. A. 3 ch ret farmer O 60a 2h 1c Prairie Depot Mon 65.

Graham, W. A. (Nellie) 2 ch farmer O H&L West Millgrove Per 70.

Graham, W. J. (Lottie) 7 ch farmer O 90a 3h 6c R1 Portage Por 110.

Grames, Geo. (Mollie) farmer T 10a 1h 1c R1 Grand Rapids Wash 67 Ind tel.

Grames, Mary J. housekeeper O L 2h 3c R1 North Baltimore Hen 123 Ind tel.

Grange, James (Mary J.) ret O H&L Rudolph Lib 94.

Grant, C. G. RD North Baltimore Hen.

Grant, Geo. student Front St Cygnet Blo Ind tel.

Grant, Geo. E. (Mary) 2 ch general market O 233a Front St Cygnet Blo Ind tel.

Grant, Louis RD North Baltimore Hen.

Grant, Pearl housekeeper Front St Cygnet Blo.

Grau, Fred teacher Main St Jerry City Blo 78 Ind tel.

Gran, G. M. Jerry City Blo.

Gran, J. M. (Irene) 3 ch doctor O H&L 1h Main St Jerry City Blo 78 Ind tel.

Graves, Augusta M. Perrysburg Pbg.

Graves, H. H. (Margret O.) farming T 23a 2h 2c Maumee Pbg 4.

Graves, M. T. (Emma) gardener O 2a H 1h Main & Seventh St Perrysburg Pbg.

Graves, S. H. (Neva) 1 ch farmer T 80a 3h 3c R1 Fostoria Per 62 Ind tel.

Graves, Dr. W. S. (Gussie) dentist O 3a Perrysburg St Perrysburg Pbg 135 B tel.

Gray, James W. (Jessie M.) 1 ch laborer O H&L Fraser St Bairdstown Blo.

GRAY, LEVI (Lavina) farmer O 63a 2h 3c R1 Grand Rapids Wash 58 Ind tel.

Gray, Mrs. Phebe J. ret O 53a R3 Perrysburg Pbg 77.

GRAY, R. W. carriage & wagon builder bds Grand Rapids Gr Rs Ind tel. See adv.

Greeley, Sidney 1 ch ret farmer O 83a H&L Center St Weston B tel.

Green, A. E. (Eva) 3 ch farmer O 40a 2h 3c R2 Weston 45.

Green, F. R. (Grace) 3 ch farmer T 40a 2h 1c R1 North Baltimore Hen 95 Ind tel.

Green, H. (Mila) 3 ch farmer T 160a 4h 5c R2 Weston Pla 26 Ind tel.

Green, Mrs. H. farmer O 160a R2 Weston Pla 26.

Green, Mart (Lucy) laboring man T H&L Grand Rapids Gr Rs.

Green, R. C. RD North Baltimore Hen.

GREEN, R. H. (Maude) 3 ch farmer O 149a 5h 1c R1 Bowling Green Pla 26 Ind tel.

Green, Stanley (Laura) 3 ch farmer T 80a 4h 4c R2 Weston Pla 3 Ind tel.

Greenfield, Ethel (dau Lewis) telephone operator Taylor St Weston Wes.

Greenfield, Lewis (Nancy) 5 ch carpenter O H&L Taylor St Weston Wes B tel.

Greenhalgh, G. P. Perrysburg Pbg.

GREENLEE, E. L. (Sarah) 4 ch blacksmith & farmer O 36a 2h 3c R2 Prairie Depot Mon 109 B tel.

Greenough, Harvey O 180 RD Perrysburg Pbg 2 B tel.

Greer, Arthur Bloomdale Blo.

Gregg, Andrew RD Custar Lib.

GREGG, DR. C. E. Bradner.

Gregg, Jeff (Evaline) 2 ch laborer T H&L 2h R2 Custar Lib 26.

Gregg, John (Bertha) 2 ch laborer T H&L 1h 1c Woodside Fre 78.

Gregg, Rea Bell St Bradner Mon.

Gregg, Wm. (Kitty) 3 ch attorney O H&L Bell St Bradner Mon B tel.

Greiner, Dr. C. C. (Lorena) 3 ch physician O H&L Pemberville Fre 80 B tel.

Greiner, C. F. (Jessie A.) piano & sewing machines O H&L Luckey Tro Ind tel.

Greiner, C. W. Scotch Ridge Web.

Greiner, Edith (dau J. D.) housekeeper R1 Lime City Pbg 122.

Greiner, Jessie A. Luckey Tro.

Greiner, J. D. (Anna) farmer O 54a 1h 3c R1 Lime City Perrysburg 55 B tel.

Greiner, Lester (son J. D.) farmer 2h R1 Lime City Pbg 122.

Grenlich, Donald (son Paul) farm hand R1 Stony Ridge Tro 21.

GRENLICH, PAUL (Catherine) 1 ch farmer O 80a 4h 6c R1 Stony Ridge Tro 21 Ind tel.

Grey, N. C. (Bertha) 4 ch contractor O 1a & H Walnut St Perrysburg Pbg.

Gribben, C. K. (son J. P.) conductor Milton Center Mil.

Gribben, Goldie (dau J. M.) housekeeper R1 Custar Mil 13 B tel.

Gribben, Harry (son J. M.) farmer T 50a 3h R1 Custar Mil 13 B tel.

Gribben, Isaac laborer O H&L Milton Center Mil.

Gribben, J. M. (Lydia) 5 ch farmer O 40a 2h 4c R1 Custar Mil 13 B tel.

Gribben, J. P. (Emma) 5 ch farmer & hay baler O H&L Milton Center Mil.

Gribben, R. E. (son J. P.) conductor bds Milton Center Mil.

Gribben, Vadio (dau J. P.) student Milton Center Mil.

Gribben, Winifred (dau J. P.) housekeeper Milton Center Mil.

Grider, L. E. (Ellen) 3 ch farmer T H&L 3h 2c Caldwell St Bradner Mon.

Griene, Wm. (Clara) 5 ch farmer O 93a 3h 4c R1 Portage Por 46.

Griesinger, Ira (Lena) 2 ch gardener O H&L Sixth St Perrysburg Pbg B tel.

Griffin, Mrs. L. Tontogany Wash Ind tel.

Grigg, W. B. Bradner Mon.

Grimes, Charles (Ida) 4 ch janitor T H&L Fifth St Perrysburg Pbg.

Grimes, J. O. RD North Baltimore Hen.

Grimes, Richard (Edna) 2 ch steam fitter T H&L 211 Maple St Rossford Ros B tel.

Grimm, Chas. (son John) farmer 1h R1 Tontogany Ton 86 Ind tel.

Grimm, Esther (dau H. F.) housekeeper R2 Haskins Wash 37 B tel.

Grimm, Fred farmer R1 Tontogany Wash 86 Ind tel.

Grimm, F. L. (son J. F.) laborer R1 Haskins Wash 86 Ind tel.

Grimm, Geo. farmer R1 Tontogany Wash 86.

GRIMM, H. F. (Phoebe) O 60a 3h 2c R2 Haskins Wash 37 B tel.

GRIMM, JOHN (Minnie) 3 ch farmer O 80a 4h 6c R1 Tontogany Wash 86 Ind tel.

GRIMM, LEWIS H. (Bessie) farmer T 80a 3h 1c R1 Haskins Mid 50 B tel.

Grimm, W. J. (Mary) 1 ch farmer T 48a 3h 3c R2 Haskins Wash 91 B tel.

Griner, Mrs. Addie 1 ch housekeeper T H&L R1 Lime City Pbg 122.

GRINER, CLARENCE R. (Florence) framer O 60a 2h R1 Bowling Green Pla 72 Ind tel.

Griner, C. W. (Amelia) 1 ch blacksmith O H&L R2 Pemberville Web 30.

Griner, E. H. (son Mrs. Addie) farmer R1 Lime City Pbg 122.

Grise, L. C. (Laura) 1 ch tile carver T H&L Walnut St Bloomdale Bl.

Griss, Mrs. A. 1 ch ret O H&L Front St Perrysburg Pbg.

Griss, Charles (Emma) 1 ch plumber T H&L Second St Perrysburg Pbg.

Griss, Fred (Edith) 1 ch plumbing contractor T H&L Front St Perrysburg Pbg B tel.

Griswold, Orr 3 ch ret O H&L Stahl St Bradner Mon.

GROBMAN, LOUIS E. (Goldie) 4 ch veterinary surgeon T H&L 2h Garfield St Bloomdale Bl B & Ind tels. See adv.

Groff, George (Zella) 2 ch farmer O 200a 6h 12c R2 Custar Mil 32 B tel.

Groff, Loren Custar Mil.

Groff, Reid (son George) farmer Custar Mil 32.

GROH, I. G. (Amy C.) 1 ch farmer O 92a 3h 11c R1 Rudolph Lib 99 Ind tel.

Grolle, Carl (son W.) farmer R2 Dunbridge Pbg 23.

Grolle, Edward (son W.) farmer R2 Dunbridge Pbg 23.

Grolle, Henry (Elizabeth) farmer O 50a 2c R1 Perrysburg Pbg 31 B tel.

Grolle, Herman R2 Dunbridge Perrysburg.

Grolle, John (Mary) 1 ch farmer T 80a 2h 5c R1 Dunbridge Web 5 B tel.

Grolle, Louise (dau W.) housekeeper R2 Dunbridge Pbg 23.

GROLLE, W., SR. (Carrie) farmer O 60a 5h 4c R2 Dunbridge Pbg 23 B tel.

GROLLE, W. J., JR. (Lena) 3 ch farmer T 80a 2h 5c R2 Dunbridge Pbg 23 B tel.

Grose, E. A. hardware bds Weston B & Ind tels.

Grosjean, H. (May) 4 ch oil worker T H&L R1 Portage Por Ind tel.

Gross, Edna (dau Henry) housekeeper R1 Dunbridge Web 54 B tel.

Gross, Emanuel Walbridge Lake.

Gross, Estella (dau Henry) housekeeper R1 Dunbridge Web 54 B tel.

Gross, E. J. (Anna) 3 ch farmer O 166a 7h 23c Hoytsville Jac 121.

Gross, E. M. (Amelia) 8 ch farmer O 50a 4h 4c R1 Walbridge Lake 17 Ind tel.

Gross, Mrs. Hazel 2 ch housekeeper R2 Custar Mil 97 B tel.

Gross, Henry (Louisa) 3 ch farmer O 56a 5h 4c R1 Dunbridge Web 54 B tel.

GROSS, JACOB (Julia H.) 3 ch farmer O 80a 4h 4c Walbridge Lake 123.

Gross, P. E. (Florence) farming T 10a 3h 1c Weston Wes 41.

Gross, P. H. Weston Wes.

Gross, Wm. Weston Wes.

Gross, W. J. (Mary) 3 ch traveling salesman T H&L Locust St Weston Ind tel.

Grossman, J. E. oil man 1h R2 Bloomdale Blo 57 B & Ind tels.

Grover, Albert (Edna) 4 ch farmer T 82a 5h 2c R4 Bowling Green Cen 111.

Grover, C. M. RD Sugar Ridge Mid.

Grover, Ernest (Nora) 1 ch farmer T 90a 3h 1c Sugar Ridge Cen 52.

Grover, Miss Fern housekeeper R2 Pemberville Web 32.

Grover, Irvin cattle RD Bowling Green Cen.

GROVER, JOHN (Zora) 3 ch farmer O 40a 3h 4c R2 Pemberville Fre 52.

Grover, Nelson (son O. C.) machinist R2 Dunbridge Mid 59.

Grover, O. C. (Mary E.) farmer O 40a 1h 4c R2 Dunbridge Mid 59 Ind tel.

Grover, O. D. (Ellen) carpenter O H&L Sugar Ridge Mid 63.

Grover, O. M. RD Sugar Ridge Mid.

Grover, Wm. (Ella) farmer O 80a 2h 6c R2 Pemberville Web 32.

Groves, H. H. Perrysburg Pbg.

Grovey, Henry 6 ch farm hand R1 Luckey Tro 89 B tel.

Grow, Bertha RD North Baltimore Hen.

Grueshaber, Charles (Carrie) farmer O H&L 2h Indiana St Perrysburg Pbg B tel.

GRUESHABER, FRED C. (Clara) 2 ch farming T 70a 3h 3c R3 Perrysburg Pbg 137.

GRUNDEN, THOMAS O. (Mary) 2 ch laborer T H&L 1h 1c Woodside Fre 78.

GRUSHABER, FRED WM. farmer O 46a 2c R3 Perrysburg Pbg 138.

Grushaber, Mary housekeeper R3 Perrysburg Pbg 138.

Gschwind, Mrs. M. Risingsun Mon.

Guff, Herbert 1 ch carpenter T R1 East Toledo Lake 116.

Guin, C. T. (Edith) 2 ch drayman T H&L 5h Taylor St Weston Wes 130 B & Ind tels.

Gun, Lodema H&L Portage Lib 90 Ind tel.

Gunder, B. F. (Ella) farmer O 48a 2h 2c R2 Perrysburg Pbg 5 B tel.

Gunder, H. S. 1 ch contractor O 28a R2 Prairie Depot Por 116.

Gunder, John (Emily) ret O H&L Second St Perrysburg Pbg B tel.

Gunder, John (Alice) oil operator O 28a 1h 1c R2 Prairie Depot Por 116.

Gundy, D. V. ret R1 Tontogany Wash 39.

Gundy, J. M. (Nancy) farmer T 50a 4h 3c Tontogany Wash 30 Ind tel.

Gundy, L. A. 2 ch farmer O 55a 6h 2c R1 Tontogany Wash 39.

Gustin, B. F. (Mary) 2 ch farmer O 80a 4h 7c R2 Bowling Green Pla 64 Ind tel.

Guth, Daniel (Abbie) hired man R1 Perrysburg Pbg 12.

GUTHRIE, MRS. CARRIE Box 486 Perrysburg.

GUTHRIE, H. P. (Rose A.) 8 ch stone road contractor O 20a 1h 2c Cygnet Blo 15 Ind tel·

Guthrie, W. T. Cygnet Blo.

GUTZWEILER, GEO. E. (Della) 2 ch farmer O 60a 2h 2c R1 Lime City Pbg 42 B tel.

Guy, Joseph farmer O 102a 5h 2c R1 East Toledo Lake 116.

Guyer, Clemmay (dau Washington) housekeeper Maple St Weston.

GUYER, ED. (Mary) 2 ch farmer O 40a 3h 4c R3 Weston Wes 53 Ind tel.

Guyer, Emma 6 ch O H&L Center St Weston.

Guyer, Washington 3 ch ret T H&L Maple St Weston.

Gwinner, Matilda Bloomdale Per.

Haar, Carrie O Pemberville Tro.

Haar, Mrs. Clara 2 ch farmer 90a 3h 10c Lemoyne Tro Ind tel.

Haar, C. H. (Caroline) oil pumper 1h R1 East Toledo Ros 31.

Haar, Ed. Lemoyne Tro.

Haar, Fred (Carrie) farmer O 90a 4h 10c R3 Pemberville Tro 56 B tel.

Haar, Mrs. Fred 9 ch farmer 177a 3h 3c R1 Lemoyne Tro 84.

HAAR, GEO. H. F. farmer O 77a 5h 19c R1 Luckey Tro 52 Ind tel.

Haar, Ida (dau Mrs. Fred) housekeeper R1 Lemoyne Tro 84.

Haar, Irwin (son Clara) farm hand Lemoyne Tro Ind tel.

Haar, John H. (Pearl) 1 ch farmer T 120a 4h 8c RD Lemoyne Tro 85 B tel.

Haar, Julia (dau Clara) Lemoyne Tro Ind tel.

Haar, J. F., Jr. Pemberville Tro.

Haas, Alfred 1 ch farmer T 66a 2h 2c R1 Perrysburg Pbg 39 B tel.

Haas, A. F. (Pearl E.) 1 ch oil man O H&L RD Bairdstown Blo.

Haas, Anna M. Weston Mil.

Haas, Chas. (Leah) 2 ch farmer T 60a 4h 2c R2 Custar Mil 39 Ind tel.

Haas, Charley (son Joseph) farmer R1 Lime City Pbg 51.

Haas, D. P. (Hazel M.) 2 ch oil pumper 1c R1 Rudolph Lib 33 Ind tel.

Haas, Elmer (son Lewis A. H.) farm hand 1h R3 Weston Mil 5.

Haas, Frank (son John) farmer R1 Perrysburg Pbg 39.

Haas, Mrs. Frank ret O 66a R1 Perrysburg Pbg 39 B tel.

Haas, Fred (son Wygand) farmer R1 Perrysburg Pbg 97.

Haas, George 1 ch ret O H&L Mulberry St Perrysburg Pbg.

Haas, Haley (Matilda) 3 ch farmer T 50a 3h 6c R1 Stony Ridge Lake 32 Ind tel.

Haas, Harvey (son Lewis A. H.) farm hand 5h R3 Weston Mil 5.

Haas, Jacob (Anna M.) 8 ch ret O 40a 1h 2c Weston Mil 87 Ind tel.

Haas, John (Mary) 6 ch farmer O 100a 4h 5c R1 Perrysburg Pbg 39.

Haas, Joseph (Catharine) 8 ch farmer T 40a 2h 1c R1 Lime City Perrysburg 51 Ind tel.

Haas, Julius (Gertrude) 8 ch farmer T 200a 8h 4c R1 Custar Mil 8 Ind tel.

Haas, Leona (dau Joseph) housekeeper R1 Lime City Pbg 51.

Haas, Lewis A. H. (Sarah Jane) farmer O 155a 5h 7c R3 Weston Mil 5 Ind tel.

Haas, Vitus Perrysburg Pbg.

HAAS, WIGAND (Louisa) farmer O 80a 5h 2c R1 Perrysburg Pbg 97.

Haase, Fred (Augusta) 1 ch farmer T 60a 2h 2c R1 Luckey Tro 68.

Habler, Garrett (Mary) farmer O 28a 1h 2c R2 Pemberville Fre 1.

Hackenberg, J. H. Weston Wes.

Hacker, Chas. stock buyer T H&L 1h Pemberville Fre 41 B tel.

Hacker, Henry (Christina) 2 ch farmer O 80a 2h 7c R3 Pemberville Tro 64.

Hackett, J. M. (Mary) 12 ch mechanic T H&L West Taylor St Weston.

Hackman, Joe laborer Stony Ridge Tro.

Hadding, Chas. F. (Sarah) 6 ch engineer T 20a Walbridge St Walbridge Lake 119.

HADNETT, W. R. (Augusta) 2 ch seed merchant O 13a 1h R3 Perrysburg Pbg 81 Ind tel.

Haefner, Charles (Anna) 8 ch blacksmith O H&L Seventh St Perrysburg Pbg.

Haefner, William draying O 2a & H Walnut St Perrysburg Pbg.

Haeman, O. E. (Margaret) 2 ch farmer O 40a 3h 8c R1 Luckey Web 68 B tel.

Haemeyer, E. (Ethel) 2 ch farmer O 80a 3h 1c R4 Bowling Green Cen 104.

HAEN, GEORGE (Ada) farmer O 40a 4h 7c R3 North Baltimore Hen 107 Ind tel.

Haen, Lizzie ret O 80a R3 North Baltimore Hen 107.

Hafferman, James (Tedelia) section foreman O H&L 6th st Perrysburg Pbg.

Hafner, J. W. (Gladys) cashier Tontogany Bank O H&L & store Tontogany Wash Ind tel.

Hafner, Kasper Tontogany Wash.

Hagemeister, A. H. (Minnie) 3 ch farmer O 126a 6h 7c R3 Perrysburg Pbg 88.

Hagemeyer, Anna M. Pemberville Fre.

Hagemeyer, Bessie (dau J. F.) housekeeper R2 Pemberville Fre 2 B tel.

Hagemeyer, Emanuel cattle, RD Bowling Green Cen.

Hagemeyer, E. H. (Mary) 8 ch oil pumper O 56a 4h 4c R9 Pemberville Fre 46.

Hagemeyer, F. W. cattle RD Bowling Green Cen.

Hagemeyer, John W. (Sylvia) 7 ch laborer O H&L Luckey Troy.

Hagemeyer, J. F. (Mary) farmer O 80a 4h 5c R2 Pemberville Fre 2 B tel.

Hagemeyer, J. H. (Mary) 2 ch carpenter O H&L Pemberville Fre 40.

Hagemeyer, J. H. (Minnie) 2 ch farmer O 80a 3h 6c R4 Bowling Green Cen 102 Ind tel.

Hagemeyer, Nelson (son J. F.) farmer 2h R2 Pemberville Fre 2 B tel.

Hagemeyer, Wm. (Louise) 10 ch farmer O 80a 5h 4c R4 Bowling Green Cen 105.

Hagemeyer, Wm., Jr. (Mary) farmer T 100a 5h 5c R5 Bowling Green Cen 111.

Hagemeyer, W. H. Pemberville Fre.

Hagemyer, Fred. (Anna) farm laborer O H&L R1 Lime City Web 53 B tel.

Hagemeyer, W. H. (Anna) bartender T H&L Pemberville Fre 40.

Hager, Luther RD Hoytville Jac.

Hager, V. A. (Bernice) 1 ch laborer T H&L Hoytville Jac.

Hagerman, Nelson (Amelia) farmer T 52a 2h 3c R2 Perrysburg Pbg 148 B tel.

Hagerty, C. D. Pemberville Web.

Hagerty, Jerry Dunbridge Web.

Hagg, Arthur Haskins Mid.

Hagg, Grover (Loretta) T 60a Stony Ridge Tro 11 Ind tel.

Hagg, Harvey (son Henry) farmer T 60a 3h 3c Stony Ridge Tro Ind tel.

Hagg, Heiry (Helen) 4 ch farmer 150a 4h 3c Stony Ridge Tro Ind tel.

Haggard, M. E. (Sevilla) 5 ch laborer T H&L 2h 1c R2 Custar Jac 97.

HAHN, ALBERT (Yetta) 1 ch farmer T 58a 2h 4c R3 Perrysburg Pbg 128.

Hahn, August J. (Ella A.) lumber dealer O 1a Walbridge St Walbridge Lake 119.

HAHN, A. C. (Myrtle) 4 ch farmer O 96a 9h 3c R1 Lemoyne Tro 83 B tel.

Hahn, Christ R2 Perrysburg Phg.

Hahn, C. O. RD North Baltimore Hen.

Hahn, David J. R3 Perrysburg Pbg.

HAHN, MRS. EMMA (widow) 4 ch farmer O 120a 4h 40c R1 Lemoyne Tro 83 B tel.

Hahn, Fred. (Anna) farmer O 26a 2h 2c R3 Perrysburg Pbg 138.

Hahn, George (Gertrude) carpenter O H&6a 2h 1c East Boundary Perrysburg Pbg B tel.

HAHN, GEORGE R. (Anna M.) 4 ch farmer O 20a 3h 3c R3 Perrysburg Pbs 85.

Hahn, Henry G. (Catharine) 6 ch farming O 47a 2h 11c R3 Perrysburg Pbg 130.

Hahn, Herman R3 Perrysburg Pbg.

Hahn, H. D. (Mamie) lumber dealer O H&L Lemoyne Tro Ind tel.

Hahn, Jno. G. R3 Perrysburg Pbg.

Hahn, Nettie (dau Mrs. Emma) R1 Lemoyne Tro 83 B tel.

Hahn, O. F. farm hand R1 Lemoyne Tro 35 Ind tel.

Hahn, T. V. laborer Lemoyne Tro Ind tel.

Hahn, W. W. farm laborer R1 Lemoyne Tro 35 Ind tel.

Haight, A. A. (Susan) 3 ch farmer O H&L 3h 1c Grand Rapids Gr Rs.

Haight, Chas. F. (Mary) farmer O 10a 2h 1c R3 Bowling Green Pla 87 Ind tel.

Haight, C. E. Grand Rapids Gr Rs.

Haight, Fred. RD Jerry City Por.

Haight, Lee A. Grand Rapids Gr Rs.

Halbert, Ed. J. RD Perrysburg Mid.

Halbert, H. (Maria L.) ret O H&L Haskins Mid.

HALBERT, M. G. (May) 2 ch R F D mail-carrier O H&L 2h Haskins Mid B tel.

Halboth, Henry RD North Baltimore Hen.

Hale, A. G. RD Dunbridge Mid.

Hale, Burley (Sylvia) farmer T H&L R1 Grand Rapids Gd Rs 11.

Hale, J. J. Cygnet Blo.

Hale, R. B. (Hannah) 1 ch farmer O 37a 2h 4c R1 Prairie Depot Mon 45.

HALES, CHAS. (Julia) 2 ch farmer T 39a 2h 2c R1 Prairie Depot Mon 113.

HALES, VERGIL R1 Prairie Depot Mon 113.

Haley, W. M. Cygnet Blo.

Halford, Fred. D. Rossford Ros.

Hall, Bert (Olive) 3 ch oil man O H&L 1h 1c Risingsun Mon.

HALL, BYRON (Elsie) 3 ch farmer O 80a 4h 2c R1 Portage Por 48·

Hall, Clyde cattle RD Portage Por.

Hall, Daniel O 280a 7h 14c R2 Bloomdale Per 17.

Hall, Dow farmer O 280a 7h 14c R2 Bloomdale Per 17.

HALL, EDWARD D. (Dorthy M.) 2 ch gen mdse T H&L Lime City Pbg 91 B tel. See adv.

Hall, E. W. (Lena) 1 ch farmer T 40a 3h 2c R1 Fostoria Per 91.

Hall, Frank ret farmer 81a Sandusky St West Millgrove Per 67.

HALL, HARRY C. (Alice) farmer T 80a 2h 2c R1 Portage Por 50.

Hall, J. F. West Millgrove Per.

HALL, J. L. (Laura) 1 ch farmer O 20a 2h 1c R1 Weston Mil 60 Ind tel.

Hall, L. R. (Lemay) 4 ch ret O H&L Maple Wes Ind tel.

Hall, M. D. (May) 5 ch mechanic T H&L Milton Center Mil.

Hall, N. E. (Ida) farm laborer 1h R1 Rudolph Lib 37.

Hall, Owen farmer O 280a 7h 14c R2 Bloomdale Per 17.

Hall, Walter Walbridge Lake.

Hall, Wm. cattle RD Bowling Green Por.

Hall, W. P. (Annie M.) farmer O 80a 5h 4c R1 Fostoria Per 63 B tel.

Hallett, Wm. R1 Lime City Pbg.

Halley, L. M. RD Sugar Ridge Mid.

Hallman, H. H. (Sophia) tailor O H&L Pemberville Fre.

Hallowell, L. A. (Sara) 2 ch traveling salesman O H&L Front St Perrysburg Pbg B tel.

Halsey, J. D. (Blanche) ret O H&L Milton Center Mil.

HAME, JOSEPH (Emma) farmer T 55a 2h 1c R1 Millbury Ros 37.

Hamen, Margaret Luckey Web.

Hamen, Otto Luckey Web.

Hamilton, Fred. (Hattie) 2 ch farmer O 70a 3h 3c Risingsun Mon 73.

Hamilton, W. Fremont Mon.

Hampshire, Rufus (Rebecca) 1 ch laborer O H&L 1h Hatton Per 84.

Hamlin, E. H. Cygnet Blo.

Hamlin, Fred. Cygnet Blo.

Hamlin, J. W. (Ella) 1 ch farmer O 80a 4h 14c R2 North Baltimore Hen 26 Ind tel.

Hamman, Eulalia RD North Baltimore Hen.

HAMMAN, PERCY E. (Zira) 7 ch farmer T 40a 3h 2c R1 Jerry City Blo 65.

Hamman, P. W. Jerry City Blo.

Hammer, Nickolis (Philippena) 1 ch farmer O 40a 4h 5c R1 Fostoria Per 109 Ind tel.

HAMMERSMITH, JOSEPH (Emma) 6 ch farmer T 110a 5h 3c R3 Bowling Green Cen 49 Ind tel.

Hammes, Oswald (Catherine) farmer T 40a 3h 2c R1 Custar Mil 10.

Hammes, Tresea 2 ch ret O 40a 1h 1c R1 Custar Mil 10.

Hammon, Albert (Ethel S.) 1 ch oil man T H&L Cygnet Blo B & Ind tel.

Hammond, Edward D. (Eleanor) 'shoemaker T H&L Broad St Montgomery Wash.

Hammond, M. R. Risingsun Mon.

Hammond, Sam farmer O 40a R2 Prairie Depot Per 5.

Hampshire, C. C. Jerry City Blo.

Hampshire, C. W. (Ella) 2 ch farmer O 30a 2h 1c Jerry City Por 72.

Hampshire, Ellen Weston Wes.

Hampshire, Emma ret O 80a 4c R1 Fostoria Per 92 Ind tel.

Hampshire, E. H. Jerry City Blo.

Hampshire, Gene farm laborer O H&L Jerry City Blo.

Hampshire, Geo. (Minnie) 2 ch farmer O 80a 5h 4c R1 Fostoria Per 92 Ind tel.

Hampshire, J. H. (Ella) farming O 10a 1h R2 Weston Wes 30.

Hampshire, J. W. (Ida M.) farmer T 160a 1c R1 Jerry City Por 28 Ind tel.

Hampton, Cash (Sophia) clerk O H&L Second St Perrysburg Pbg B tel.

Hampton, Fia Z. Perrysburg Pbg.

Hampton, Mrs. S. A. O H&L Third St Portage Por.

Haney, A. J. RD North Baltimore Hen.

HANELY, ANDREW (Caroline) ret O 95a 3h 3c R1 Stony Ridge Lake 87 B tel.

Hanely, Bessie (dau. Andrew) R1 Stony Ridge Lake 87.

Hanely, Cora (dau of Samuel) R1 Stony Ridge Lake 88.

HANELY, EDWIN (Clara) farmer T 90a 3h 3c R1 Stony Ridge Lake 87.

Hanely, Harmon (son Samuel) farmer O 2h R1 Stony Ridge Lake 88.

Hanely, John (Sabine) 6 ch farmer O 40a 2h 3c R1 Stony Ridge Lake 88 Ind tel.

HANELY, SAMUEL farmer O 140a 2h 4c R1 Stony Ridge Lake 88 B tel.

Hanely, Mrs. Stella farmer T 80a 4h R1 Stony Ridge Lake 88 Ind tel.

Hanely, Walter farmer bds R1 Stony Ridge Lake 88 Ind tel.

HANELY, W. F. (Emma) 1 ch farmer-O 40a 2h 6c R1 Lemoyne Lake 86 B tel.

Hanks, Carl oil worker Caldwell St Bradner Mon.

Hanks, Chas. (India) 3 ch oil producer O H&L Caldwell St Bradner Mon.

Hanley, Clyde (Ruby) 1 ch laborer T H&L Stony Ridge Tro.

Hanley, Rebecca ret O H&L Front St Perrysburg Pbg B tel.

Hanline, David D. Bradner Fre.

Hanline, Minnie 3 ch farmer 80a 6h 10c R1 Bradner Fre 86 B tel.

Hanna Esther RD Rudolph Lib.

Hanna, E. J. (Florence M.) 1 ch farmer T 120a 5h 8c R1 Custar Jac 39 B tel.

Hanna Frank RD Rudolph Lib.

Hanna, Harry B. (Ada) farmer O 40a 9h 9c R1 Deshler Jac 13 B tel.

Hanna, John H. (Sarah) 3 ch farmer O 250a R1 Deshler Jac 13 B tel.

Peter Tumbledown's barn. This is situated in another county.

Hanna, Mable (dau W. H.) R1 Tontogany Wash 31 B & Ind tels.

Hanna, R. L. RD North Baltimore Hen.

Hanna, Sidney A. (Lulu A.) 4 ch laborer O H&L S Garfield St Bloomdale Blo.

Hanna, W. H. (Lucy B.) farmer O 111a 7h 4c R1 Tontogany Wash 31 B & Ind tels.

Hannah, Mrs. Carrie O H&L R1 Bloomdale Bl 114.

Hannah, Charles (Jennie) 12 ch gardener O 15a 2h 3c R1 Rudolph Lib 63 Ind tel.

Hannah, Mrs. Esther 6 ch O 50a Rudolph Lib ·82.

Hannah, M. L. (Mirna) 1 ch paper hanging O store 1h Rudolph Lib 81 Ind tel.

Hanneman, F. C. (Anna) section boss T H&L R1 Walbridge Lake 11.

Hanselman, C. R. Rossford Ros.

Hanselman, Martin Rossford Ros.

Hansen, Mrs. Alice 2 ch clerk T H&L Lime City Pbg 121.

HANSEN, CHARLEY (Mary) boarding house O H&L Pemberville Fre 40.

HANSEN, CHAS. H. (Emma) 6 ch farmer O 80a 4h 5c R1 Walbridge Lake 102 Ind tel.

Hansen, Edna (dau H. C.) R1 Genoa Tro 39 Ind tel.

Hansen, Ferdinand (Anna) 1 ch hired man T R1 Walbridge Lake 134.

Hansen, Frank son William student R1 Walbridge Lake 25.

Hansen, Frieda M. (dau Chas. H.) R1 Walbridge Lake 102 Ind tel.

Hansen, George ·(son William) farmer 1h R1 Walbridge Lake 25.

Hansen, Helen (dau William) R1 Walbridge Lake 25.

HANSEN, H. C. (Anna) 4 ch farmer T 115a 5h 26c R1 Genoa Tro 39 Ind tel.

Hansen, William C. (Katherine) 3 ch farmer O 85a 3h 3c R1 Walbridge Lake 25.

Hanson, Charles (Minnie) 1 ch glass maker O H 7th St Perrysburg Pbg B tel.

Hanson, Geo. cattle RD Bowling Green Cen.

HANSON, H. (Ella) 2 ch ret O H&L 1c Crocker St Bradner Mon.

HANSON, JACOB (Levellen) farmer O 40a 3h 3c R2 Custar Mil 39 B tel.

Hanson, Mary Pemberville Fre.

Hansen, Peter Woodville Tro.

Harbauer, Philip (Anna) 1 ch laborer O H&L 5th St Perrysburg Pbg B tel.

Harbough, J. E. (Stella) 2 ch mail carrier T H&L 2h Rudolph Lib 94 Ind tel.

Hardgrove, W. L. (Olive L.) 7 ch farmer O 1a R1 Rudolph Lib 105 Ind tel.

Harding, W. A. (Ella) elevator man O 2a R3 Bowling Green Pla 87.

Hardman, C. E. RD North Baltimore Hen.

Hardy, Albert J. (Clara) 2 ch farmer T 80a 3h 4c R1 Deshler Jac 35.

Hardy, Frank (Mary) 3 ch farmer T H&L 1h 1c R3 Prairie Depot Mon 16.

Hardy, J. W. Rossford Ros.

Harger, A. L. RD North Baltimore Hen.

Hariff, Frank (Vergie) 1 ch laborer T H&L Bell St Bradner Mon.

Harington, Daniel (Myrtle) 2 ch oil pumper T L 1h 1c R1 North Baltimore Hen 62.

Harker, Sara A. Rossford Ros.

Harkins, Charles W. (Ethel) 4 ch farmer O 66a 2h 1c R2 Perrysburg Mid 2 B tel.

Harkness, C. S. (Mary) farmer O 35a 2h 4c Jerry City Blo 71 Ind tel.

Harlan, T. R. RD North Baltimore Hen.

Harman, Alton (Jessie) 5 ch carpenter T 20a 1h 2c R3 Prairie Depot Por 122.

Harman, J. H. Prairie Depot Mon.

Harman, O. B. (Jennie) 1 ch farmer O 40a 5h 1c R3 Prairie Depot Por 119.

Harmeyer, Clara (dau J. H.) housekeeper R1 Luckey Tro 67.

Harmeyer, Edward (son J. W.) farmer R3 Pemberville Tro 60.

Harmeyer, Ellen (dau J. H.) housekeeper R1 Luckey Tro 67.

Harmeyer, Harmon Pemberville Fre.

Harmeyer, Julia Anna (dau J. W.) R3 Pemberville Tro 60.

Harmeyer, J. H. (May) 3 ch farmer O 80a 2h 67c R1 Luckey Tro 67.

Harmeyer, J. W. (Mary) 2 ch farmer O 80a 5h 5c R3 Pemberville Tro 60 B tel.

Harmeyer, Mary Pemberville Tro.

Harmeyer, Sophia Pemberville Fre.

HARMON, A. J. (Amanda J.) 3 ch farmer O 60a 2h 2c R3 Prairie Depot Mon 103.

Harmon, D. (Elizabeth) 1 ch minister O 10a 2h 3c R2 Prairie Depot Por 79.

Harmon, Fred painter R2 Prairie Depot Mon 103.

Harmon, F. P. (Martha) farmer O 10a 1h R3 Prairie Depot Por 111.

Harmon, J. H. (Elizabeth) 1 ch superintendent O H&L Prairie Depot Mon B tel..

HARMON, N. E. (Agnes) 4 ch farmer O 80a 4h 8c R3 Prairie Depot Mon 103 B tel.

HARMON, PAUL (son F. P.) farmer R3 Prairie Depot Por 111.

Harmon, Pearl June R3 Prairie Depot Mon 103.

Harmon, S. E. (Anna) 1 ch painter T H&L R3 Prairie Depot Mon 99.

HARNED, A. E. (Emma) 8 ch oil worker T 30a 1h 5c Cygnet Blo 8 Ind tel.

Harned, C. C. (Alice) 2 ch laborer O H&L Main St Jerry City Por.

Harned, Doyce H. teacher Main St Jerry City Por.

Harpel, F. A. (Minnie) 1 ch grocer & farmer T 47a 2h R1 Walbridge Lake 17 Ind tel.

HARPEL, GEORGE E.(Barbara) janitor O 22a 2h 2c R1 Walbridge Lake 17 Ind tel.

Harpel, George W. (Olive) 2 ch railroad engineer O 1a R1 Walbridge Lake 15 Ind tel.

Harper, Gertrude O H&L Center St Weston.

Harper, H. (Mary) machinist T H&L Perrysburg Pbg Ind tel.

Harper, Harvey (Jessie) 1 ch sexton Center St Weston.

Harper, W. A. (Cora B.) jeweler & diamond mounter O 3a R1 East Toledo Lake 116 Ind tel.

HARPER, ZENN (Mary) pool room T H&L Main St Perrysburg Pbg.

Harpster, Georgia East St Bradner Mon.

Harpster, Mrs. Jesse 2 ch O 15a 2h East St Bradner Mon.

Harpster, J. M. Bradner Mon.

Harpster, Mrs. Kate 5 ch O 20a H&L 2h 3c East St Bradner Mon.

Harringshaw, Joseph (Louisa) 3 ch farmer O 117a 11h 13c RD Custar Lib 21 B & Ind tels.

Harrington, Charles (Margaret) printer T H&L Fifth St Perrysburg Pbg.

Harris, Alfred A. Rossford Ros.

Harris, Arthur (Monie) 1 ch laborer R1 Rudolph Lib 63.

Harris, A. J. (Annie) laborer O 2a H&L R1 Rudolph Lib 63.

Harris, A. M. RD Rudolph Lib.

Harris, C. W. (Anna E.) meat cutter O H&L Rossford Ros.

Harris, David (Evelyn) 2 ch farmer 50a 3h 3c Milton Center Mil Ind tel.

HARRIS, FRANK B. (Lottie) 2 ch oil pumper O 40a 4c R1 Rudolph Lib 98.

Harris, G. A. (Tina) 2 ch farmer O 50a 3h 6c R1 Fostoria Per 57 Ind tel.

HARRIS, G. M. (Jennie) 4 ch farmer T 200a 4h 8c R2 North Baltimore Hen 57 B tel.

Harris, Harry E. Pemberville Frc.

Harris, J. W. (Eliza) 1 ch O H&L 2c Sycamore St Weston Wes Ind tel.

HARRIS, L. T. (Harriet) farming T R2 Perrysburg Pbg 2.

Harris, Nellie (dau David) school teacher Milton Center Mil Ind tel.

Harris, S. Lemoyne Tro.

Harris, W. C. (Elizabeth) ret O 33a 1c box 15 Rossford Ros.

Harrison, Mrs. Ella 1 ch housekeeper R1 Prairie Depot Mon 89 B tel.

Harrison, E. E. (Clara E.) farmer O 80a 7h 5c Longley Per 104 B tel.

Harrison, E. E. (Emma) 3 ch paperhanger & painter T H&L 91 Elm St Rossford Ros.

Harrison, Ivin L. (Ruby W.) farmer T 64a 1h 3c R1 Fostoria Per 77 Ind tel.

Harrison, R. W. (son Ella) farmer T 127a 3h R1 Prairie Depot Mon 89 B tel.

Harrison, Thomas (Almeta) 1 ch farmer O 80a 3h 1c R1 Portage Lib 60 Ind tel.

HARSH, CHAS. laborer T H&L 1h R2 Prairie Depot Por 78 Ind tel.

Hart, Bert M. (Fannie) signal man O H&L Millbury Lake 54.

Hart, C. O. (Alice) 4 ch farmer T 120a 4h 7c R1 Hoytsville Jac 65 Ind tel.

HARTER, CHARLES H. (Adda) 2 ch oil worker T H&L 1h Portage Lib 90 Ind tel.

Harter, Gladys (granddau L. M. Cramer) house keeper R1 Deshler Jac 23.

Harter, O. G. (Nellie M.) 2 ch oil pumper T H&L 1h 1c R2 Bowling Green Pla 64 Ind tel.

HARTER, O. W. (Arvilla) 3 ch farmer & stock dealer O 61a 3h 13c R1 Hoytsville Jac 77 B tel.

Hartgian, Margaret 6 ch O H&L Union St Cygnet Blo.

Hartgian, Patrick oil worker Union St Cygnet Blo.

Hartigan, Mary A. Cygnet Blo.

Hartigan, Will J. (Gertrude) 2 ch machinist T H&L Verango St Cygnet Blo Ind tel.

Hartley, Mrs. Nettie 2 ch boarding house T R2 Pemberville Fre 24.

Hartley, Ray (Leona) 2 ch hired man T H&L 1h 1c R4 Fostoria Per 108.

Hartley, S. P (Lora) 1 ch farmer O 86a 1h 3c R1 Fostoria Per 57 Ind tel.

Hartman, Albert (Matilda) 1 ch farmer hired man 1h 2c R2 Haskins Mid 89 B tel.

Hartman, Alfred farm hand R1 Deshler Jac 38 B tel.

Hartman, Alva (Inez) 2 ch stock buyer O 124a 1h 1c Center St Weston Ind tel.

Hartman, Anna 4 ch farmer O 91a R1 Luckey Tro 75 Ind tel.

Hartman, A. W. (Lena) 3 ch barber O H&L Cor Lightner & Evans Sts Bradner Mon.

Hartman, Bert (Claudia) 6 ch farmer T 120a 6h 4c R1 Fostoria Per 124.

HARTMAN, CHAS. Grand Rapids.

Hartman, Chas. F. (son Chas.) farmer R1 Hoytsville Jac 62.

Hartman, Christ (Ellen) 2 ch farmer O 80a 2h 2c R2 Haskins Mid 89 B tel.

Hartman, Con Cor Lightner & Evans Sts Bradner Mon.

Hartman, Ed. farmer T 91a 3h 6c R1 Luckey Tro 75 Ind tel.

Hartman, Mrs. Elizabeth 3 ch O H&L Evans Ave Bradner Mon.

Hartman, Etta M. (dau M.) housekeeper R1 Hoytsville Jac 61.

Hartman, Fred (son Jacob) farmer R2 Haskins Mid 89.

Hartman, George (Jane) blacksmith O H&L Grand Rapids Gr Rs.

Hartman, Miss Gertrude (dau C.) housekeeper R2 Haskins Mid 89 B tel.

Hartman, Gus (Nancie) 8 ch ret T Second St Grand Rapids Gr Rs.

Hartman, Jacob (Lizzie) farmer O 135a 4h 2c R2 Haskins Mid 89 B tel.

HARTMAN, J. F. (Mary A.) farmer O 240a 2h 9c R1 Deshler Jac 38 B tel.

Hartman, J. M. (Margaret M.) 1 ch oil man O H&L Main St Bairdstown Blo 48.

Hartman, Lewis Pemberville Fre.

Hartman, Marie (dau Alva) Center St Weston.

Hartman, Marion (Mary) 2 ch farmer O 80a 6h 2c R1 Hoytsville Jac 63 B tel.

Hartman, Mrs. Mary 5 ch O H&L Evans St Bradner Mon.

Hartman, Nancy 1 ch T H&L Grand Rapids Gr Rs.

Hartman, Mrs. Percilla T H&L Bairdstown Blo 48.

Hartman, S. F. (Mary A.) 1 ch farmer O 40a 5h 5c R1 Deshler Jac 50 B tel.

Hartman, Wm. laborer R1 Luckey Tro 75 Ind tel.

Hartranft, F. J. (Hazel) 2 ch drayman O H&L Main St Weston.

HARTSHORN, R. R. (Bess B.) cashier of bank O H&4L Perrysburg Pbg Ind tel. See adv.

Hartshorn, Stephen ret O H&L Indiana Ave Perrysburg Pbg.

Hartshorn, S. E. (Tilly) 3 ch railroad man O H&L Indiana Ave Perrysburg Pbg B tel.

Hartz, Harriet housekeeper 19a R1 Custar Mil 95.

Hartz, I. N. farmer O 19a R1 Custar Mil 95.

Hartz, Nellie housekeeper 19a R1 Custar Mil 95.

Hartzel, Chas. RD North Baltimore Hen.

Hartzel, N. S. RD North Baltimore Hen.

Hartzell, G. O. (Eva) 1 ch mason O H&L Rudolph Lib 94 Ind tel.

Hartzell, Howard (son G. O.) mason Rudolph Lib Ind tel.

Harvey, Frank (Grace) 2 ch farmer O 20a 2h 4c R3 Perrysburg Pbg 69 Ind tel.

Harvey, J. T. RD North Baltimore Hen.

Hasel, A. G. (Emma) 1 ch farmer 80a 3h 8c R1 Luckey Tro 28 Ind tel.

Hasel, Miss D. M. milliner & dressmaking O H&L Luckey Tro Ind tel.

Hasel, Ethel G. (dau Geo J.) R1 Stony Ridge Tro 9 Ind tel.

Hasel, Fred C. (Ada) 2 ch farmer O 60a 2h 6c R1 Dunbridge Web 49 B tel.

Hasel, Geo. G. (Amelia) 3 ch farmer O 42a 2h 6c R1 Stony Ridge Tro 9 Ind tel.

Hasel, Henry (Mary) 8 ch ret O 105a H&L Luckey Tro Ind tel.

Hasel, Henry F. (Anna) 3 ch farmer 40a 2h 3c R1 Luckey Tro 26 Ind tel.

Hasel, Henry L. (Edythe) 1 ch farmer T 105a 5h 16c R1 Luckey Tro 22 Ind tel.

Hasel, Lila M. (dau Geo. J.) housekeeper R1 Stony Ridge Tro 9 Ind tel.

Haskins, Chas. RD Perrysburg Mid.

Haskins, Frank (Emily) 3 ch farmer O 80a 3h 4c R2 Weston Pla 14 Ind tel.

Haskins, Raymond Grand Rapids Wes.

HASKINS, WALDO H. (Fanny E.) 2 ch farmer O20a T 61a 3h 3c R2 Bowling Green Pla 46 Ind tel.

Hassett, J. W. Weston Wes.

Hastings, Mrs. Ellen 11 ch O 80a 2h 3c R3 Prairie Depot Mon 7 B tel.

Hastings, Fanny RD North Baltimore Hen.

Hastings, Jack (Minnie) 1 ch ret O H&L Risingsun Mon.

Hastings, M. S. RD Bowling Green Mon.

Hastings, Perry contractor 1h R3 Prairie Depot Mon 7 B tel.

HASTINGS, ROBERT farmer R3 Prairie Depot Mon 7 B tel.

Hatcher, Mrs. Lena Perrysburg Pbg.

Hatcher, Martha (dau William) N Main St Weston.

Hatcher, Mary ret O H&L 5th St Perrysburg Pbg B tel.

Hatcher, William (Adaline) 8 ch ret O 197a H&L N Main St Weston Ind tel.

Hate, Fred (Mamie) 1 ch carpenter O H&L Main St Jerry City Por Ind tel.

Hatfield, Dr. Chas. B. (Ida F.) 1 ch physician O H&L 1h S Main St Bloomdale Blo B & Ind tels.

Hatfield, C. A. (Callie) 3 ch farmer O 20a 2h 4c R1 Fostoria Per 122 Ind tel.

Hatfield, Ella O 55a Vine St Bloomdale Blo B & Ind tels.

Hatfield, H. F. (Bell) 3 ch oil worker T H&L Portage Lib 90.

Hatfield, Ida Simon Bloomdale Blo.

Hatfield, J. J. (Lillian) stock dealer O H&L 1h West Millgrove Per 69 B tel.

Hatfield, Lela (dau Ella) Vine St Bloomdale Blo B & Ind tels.

Hatfield, Lloyd C. (son Dr. Chas. B.) 6c S Main St Bloomdale Blo B & Ind tels.

Hatfield, Neva V. (dau Dr. Chas. B.) S Main St Bloomdale Blo B & Ind tel.

Hatfield, R. D. Bloomdale Blo.

HÁTHAWAY,. CLIFF (Mame) 2 ch well driller O H&L 1h Stohl St Bradner Mon B tel.

Hathaway, G. D. 1 ch driller T H&L East St Bradner Mon B tel.

Hathaway, James (Georgia) 4 ch blacksmith O H&L Rudolph Lib 18 Ind tel.

Hathaway, John (Edith) 3 ch mgr Cass Elevator O H&L Milton Center Mil B tel.

Hathaway Jno. S. Luckey Tro.

Hathaway, J. B. (Flossie) farmer O 40a 2h 7c R1 Bradner Mon 22 B tel.

Hathaway, M. (Edyth) 2 ch laboring man O H&L Milton Center Mil.

Hatman, Mary ret O H&L Lemoyne Tro Ind tel.

HAUBACK, L. R. (Rena) farmer O 80a 6h 8c R1 Deshler Jac 6 B tel.

Haughawout, B. F. Bloomdale Blo.

Hauri, Sam watch maker Luckey Tro Ind tel.

Hauser, Elizabeth (wid M. U.) R3 Prairie Fre 75.

Hausman, Mrs. M. E. ret O H&L R1 Pemberville Fre 56.

Hawk, Ames P. (Minnie) 5 ch farmer T 80a 7h 4c R1 North Baltimore Hen 45.

Hawkins, Bert (Nellie) 2 ch farmer O 32a 5h 4c R1 Hoytsville Jac 52.

Hawkins, Edgar (son W. W.) crane man R1 Pemberville Fre 70.

Hawkins, L. (Bertha) garage & repair man O H&L Prairie Depot Mon B tel.

HAWKINS, PEARL R1 Weston Lib 49 B tel.

HAWKINS, W. W. (Maggie) 1 ch farmer O 98a 5h 8c R1 Pemberville Fre 70.

HAXWORTH, A. I. Bradner.

Hay, E. R. (Sarah L.) 7 ch carpenter T H&L Lincoln St Bloomdale Blo.

Hayes, Jack (Marie) 1 ch conductor O H&L Front St Perrysburg Pbg B tel.

HAYES, MARY R2 Perrysburg Pbg.

Hayes, Thomas (Mary) 2 ch clerk T H&L Indiana Ave Perrysburg Pbg.

Hayes, Tim (Lena) motorman O H&L 6th St Perrysburg Pbg B tel.

Haylett, Arthur (Edith) farmer O 40a 5h 6c R1 Portage Lib 91 Ind tel.

HAYLETT, EDWARD farmer O 104a 12h 6c R1 Rudolph Lib 62½ Ind tel.

HAYLETT, JNO. R1 Weston Lib.

Haylett, J. (Maggie) 1 ch farmer T 80a 3h 3c R1 Rudolph Lib 60.

Haylett, May R1 Rudolph Lib 62½ Ind tel.

Haylett, Robt. (Mattie) 1 ch farmer O 59a 6h 2c R3 Prairie Depot Mon 28.

Haymond, D. C. (Alice) janitor O H&L Pemberville Fre 40.

Hays, Mrs. Ella 4 ch Myers St Jerry City Blo.

Hays, Jno. Perrysburg Pbg.

Hays, Norman M. (Jane Y.) farmer O 120a 3h 6c R2 Bloomdale Por 59.

Hays, Thos. Perrysburg Pbg.

Hazard, C. A. (Esther) farmer O 62a 2h 3c R2 Deshler Jac 1 B tel.

Hazard, George (Frances) 1 ch elevator hand T H&L Weston box 215.

Hazel, F. C. Dunbridge Web.

Hazel, William (Jennie) 5 ch farmer O 24a 2c R1 Stony Ridge Lake 33.

Healey, Charles (Annie) farmer O H&L 2h Locust St Weston.

Healey, Florence Walbridge Lake.

Healey, Geo. (son Wm.) car repairer bds Walbridge Lake.

Healey, Irvin (son Wm.) switch tender bds Walbridge Lake.

HEALEY, JOHN J. (Mary E.) 2 ch oil man gauging O H&L 1h Main St Bairdstown Blo B & Ind tels.

Healey, Lloyd (son Wm.) laborer bds Walbridge Lake.

Healey, Sidney (Celia) R R conductor O H&L Walbridge Lake.

Healey, Wm. (Florence) switchman O H&L Walbridge Lake.

Healmaster, H. (Emily) wagon maker O H&L 5th St Perrysburg Pbg.

Heath, Clarence RD Portage Lib.

Heath, Mrs. Dora Grand Rapids Gr Rs.

Heath, James (Maggie) 1 ch ret farmer O 10a H 1h 2c R1 Rudolph Lib 64.

Heath, Maggie RD Rudolph Lib.

Heath, Sarah ret O H&L Prairie Depot Mon.
Heaton, C. C. Jerry City Blo.
Heban, Norbert Rossford Ros.
Hebeler, Mrs. L. (wid C.) housekeeper O H&L Bond St Pemberville Fre.
Hebler, Alma (dau John) dressmaker R1 Luckey Web 68 B tel.
Hebler, Edna (dau John) housekeeper R1 Luckey Web 68 B tel.
Hebler, Ernst (son John) farm laborer R1 Luckey Web 68 B tel.
Hebler, E. C. Dunbridge Web.
Hebler, Garrett Pemberville Fre.
Hebler, G. (Mary) 5 ch farmer O 30a 1h 2c R1 Luckey Fre.
HEBLER, JOHN (Carolina) 3 ch farmer O 120a 4h 8c R1 Luckey Web 68 B tel.
Heckart, Chas. (Mabel) 3 ch cement worker T H&L Luckey Tro.
Heckart, F. E. (May) 4 ch stationary engineer O H&L 1c Luckey Tro 90.
Heckart, Geo. 4 ch O H&L Evans St Bradner Mon.
Heckart, James (Bessie) 4 ch laborer T H&L Luckey Tro.
Heckart, S. 5 ch ret Luckey Tro.
Heckart, Wm. 2 ch manufacturer O 40a H&L N Main St Bradner Mon.
Hecker, Wm. 4 ch farmer T 80a 4h 1c R3 Pemberville Tro 57 Ind tel.
Heckerman, David Weston Wes.
Heckert, Fred Pemberville Fre.
Heckert, Wm. Bradner Mon.
Heckler, George (Sara) 2 ch laborer T H&L 4th St Perrysburg Pbg.
Heckler, John carpenter T H&L Second St Perrysburg Pbg.
Heckler, Mart clerk T H&L Second St Perrysburg Pbg.
Heckler, Phil (Roda) laborer O H&L Second St Perrysburg Pbg.
Heckley, Micheal (Margaret) 1 ch O H&L 1h Stony Ridge Tro.
Heckman, Amby (Sophia) cashier in bank H&L Pemberville Fre.
Heckman, Henry (Anna) 1 ch farmer O H&L 1h Pemberville Fre 40 B tel.
Heckman, H. W. (Anna) 2 ch farmer T 160a 5h 11c R2 Pemberville Web 64 B tel.
HECKMAN, JOHN (Mary) 2 ch farmer T 86a 4h 10c R1 Pemberville Fre 67 B tel.
Heckman, J. E. (Margaret) 4 ch barber T H&L Prairie Depot Mon.
Heckman, Tom 3 ch laborer T H&L Euclid St Bradner Mon B tel.
Heckman, Wm. (Eliza) 1 ch farmer O 85a 1h R1 Pemberville Fre 66 B tel.

Heckman, W. H. (Caroline) 2 ch farmer T 103a 4h 10c R1 Pemberville Fre 67 B tel.
HEDGE, C. B. (Barbara) 4 ch farmer O 120a 8h 17c R1 Prairie Depot Mon 45 B tel.
Hedge, F. T. (Martha) farmer O 39a 2h 2c R2 Prairie Depot Mon 43.
Hedge, Geo. (son F. T.) farmer R2 Prairie Depot Mon 43.
Hedge, G. W. (Caroline) ret O H&L Prairie Depot Mon B tel.
Hedge, J. (Bessie) 3 ch machinist T H&L Prairie Depot Mon.
HEDGES, CHAS. (Maude) 6 ch farmer T 40a 4h 2c R1 Tontogany Wash 16.
Heermeyer, Louise Pemberville Fre.
HEERS, HENRY (Wilkel Minnie) farmer O 120a R2 Custar Hen 1 B tel.
Heers, John (Stella) 1 ch farmer O 55a 4h 3c R2 Custar Mil 37 B tel.
Heeter, Fred (Etta) 1 ch grocer T H&L Grand Rapids Gr Rs Ind tel.
Heeter, P. W. (Mary) ret T H&L Grand Rapids Gr Rs.
Heffelfinger, E. L. (Lilly) 3 ch railroad man O 26⅔a 2h 2c R1 Walbridge Lake 4 Ind tel.
Hefferman, Jas. Perrysburg Pbg.
Hefferman, Wm. Perrysburg Pbg.
Heggerty, C. D. (Della) 1 ch farmer O 25a 9h 1c R2 Pemberville Web 47 B tel.
Hegly, E. C. (Mary E,) mechanic O 6a H 1h 1c Locust St Perrysburg Pbg B tel.
Heid, John cattle RD Bowling Green Cen.
Heide, Fred (Emma) 1 ch farmer T 35a 2h 2c R1 Stony Ridge Tro 9 Ind tel.
Heide, Louis Pemberville Fre.
Heider, Clarence (son P.) R1 E Toledo Ros 30 Ind tel.
Heider, Mary (dau P.) teacher R1 box 27 E Toledo Ros 30 Ind tel.
Heider, Myrtle (dau P.) R1 box 27 E Toledo Ros 30 Ind tel.
Heider, Peter (Amelia) 1 ch farmer & thresher O 129a 5h 3c R1 E Toledo Ros 30 Ind tel.
Height, Adelbert (Susan) 3 ch farmer O H&L 3h 1c Grand Rapids Gr Rs.
Heilman, Catherine Lime City Web.
HEILMAN, H. W. (Minnie) 2 ch farmer T 144a 2h 7c R1 Stony Ridge Tro 81 B tel.
Heilman, J. E. 4 ch farmer O 80a 6h 8c R2 Custar Jac 98.
Heilman, J. J. (Carrie) 3 ch farmer O 160a 6h 6c R1 Perrysburg Pbg 103 B tel.

.HEILMAN, J. W. (Ruth) farmer T 40a 2h 5c R1 Lime City Web 53 B tel.

Heilman, Mary O H&L Front St Perrysburg Pbg B tel.

Heilman, Peter R1 Perrysburg Pbg. .

HEILMAN, P. J. (Mary) 1 ch driller in oil field O 1a 1h R1 North Baltimore Hen 68 Ind tel.

Heiman, Alma (dau Wm. G.) housekeeper R2 Haskins Mid 19.

Heiman, August (Emma M.) 6 ch farmer T 220a 5h 6c R2 Bowling Green Mid 41.

HEIMAN, WM. G. (Minnie) 6 ch farmer T 240a 6h 6c R2 Haskins Mid 19 B tel.

Heinrichs, Gertrude (dau J.) dressmaker box 441 Rossford Ros B tel.

Heinrichs, Henry (Olga) 2 ch clerk T H&L 416 Oak St Rossford Ros.

Heinrichs, Jacob hotel keeper O hotel box 441 Rossford Ros B tel.

Heinsman, Henry (son B.) farm hand R1 Hoytsville Jac 105.

Heinsmen, I. B. (Eliza) 8 ch farmer T 160a 8h 3c R1 Hoytsville Jac 105.

Heinze, Chas. Custar Mil.

Heinze, Peter Custar Mil.

HEINZELMAN, OTTO A. (Hermine) minister T H&L R1 Pemberville Fre 56.

HELBERG, C. H. (Pearl) 2 ch farmer T 68a 5h 5c R1 Bowling Green Pla 75 Ind tel.

Held, Mrs. Anna 5 ch farmer O 66a 4h 6c R1 Genoa Lake 44 B tel.

HELLE, H. W. (Anna) 3 ch gen store O H&L 1h Woodside Fre 73 Ind tel. See adv.

Heller, Chas. F. Grand Rapids Gr Rs.

HELLFRISCH, P. M. (A. M.) news depot O H&L Perrysburg Pbg.

Helm, Hazel (dau Manroe) housekeeper R3 Prairie Depot Por 98.

Helm, Manuel (Etta) 3 ch farmer O 110a 8h 4c R1 Portage Por 49.

HELM, MARION (Nancy E.) farmer O 85a 5h 6c R1 Portage Por 49.

Helm, Monroe cattle RD Portage Por.

Helm, Ray B. (son Marion) farmer 1h R1 Portage Por 49.

Helmbrecht, Elizabeth (dau Wm.) R3 Perrysburg Pbg 79.

Helmbrecht, Wm. (Sarah) farmer O 40a R3 Perrysburg Pbg 79.

HELMROTH, H. E. (Louise) 3 ch farmer O 40a 4h 3c R1 Walbridge Lake 98 B tel.

Heltebrake, B. E. (Margarette) 2 ch carpenter T H Pemberville Fre 40.

Helvoight, August (Clara) 1 ch carpenter O H&L Center St Weston.

Helvoight, Chas. Weston Wes.

HELZER, FRED (Ada) 5 ch farmer T 51a 2h 2mules 10c R1 Grand Rapids Wash 65 Ind tel.

HELZER, GEO. 2 ch farmer T 80a 4h 3c R1 Tontogony Wash 20 Ind tel.

Helzer, Lewis (Kate) 1 ch contractor T H&L 2h Haskins Mid.

Helzer, Lydia (dau Lewis) housekeeper Haskins Mid.

Filling a Silo in the Modern Way.

Helzer, Mamie (dau Lewis) housekeeper Haskins Mid.

Hemelfpeck, E. J. laborer O H&L Tontogony Wash.

Heminger, A. J. (Hettie) 4 ch farmer O 74a 3h 4c R1 Prairie Depot Mon 111 B tel.

Heminger, Bert (Emma) 5 ch farmer O 27a 7h 7c Prairie Depot Mon 13.

HEMINGER, CHAS. A. (Sarah) 5 ch farmer 60a 3h 3c R3 Prairie Depot Mon 16 B tel.

HEMINGER, CHAS. F. (Fannie) 2 ch farmer T 100a 4h 4c R1 Bloomdale Blo 59 B & Ind tels.

Heminger, C. (Sopha) 1 ch farmer T 140a 3h 8c R2 North Baltimore Hen 53 Ind tel.

Heminger, Daniel (Josephine) 1 ch ditcher T H&L 1c Railroad St Bradnor Mon.

Heminger, Earl (Emma) laborer O H&L 1h Evans St Bradner Mon.

Heminger, Mrs. Elizabeth ret O H&L Prairie Depot Mon.

HEMINGER, EMANUEL farmer R1 Jerry City Por 75.

Heminger, F. W. (Martha) 4 ch farmer O 130a 5h 7c R3 Prairie Depot Mon 4 B tel.

Heminger, Harley R3 Prairie Depot Mon 16 B tel.

Heminger, Herbert R3 Prairie Depot Mon 16 B tel.

Heminger, Irvin RD North Baltimore Hen.

Heminger, Linton R3 Prairie Depot Mon 16 B tel.

Heminger, M. T. RD North Baltimore Hen.

Heminger, Marvin V. (Linda) farmer T R3 Prairie Depot Mon 7.

Heminger, O. Prairie Depot Mon.

Heminger, Robt. Prairie Depot Mon.

Heminger, Roy (Amos) 8 ch laborer T 5a 1c R1 Prairie Depot Mon 52.

Heminger, Samuel 2 ch farmer O 60a 2h 3c R3 Prairie Depot Mon 16 B tel.

Hemley, D. G. Perrysburg Pbg.

Hemminger, J. R. (Ida) 3 ch sec foreman T H&L Oak St Weston.

Henderson, Anna 209 Maple St Rossford Ro⁰.

Henderson, Clark RD Rudolph Lib.

Henderson, D. E. Prairie Depot Mon.

Henderson, George 1 ch carpenter T Grand Rapids Gr Rs.

Henderson, G. A. Rossford Ros.

Henderson, Jas. Prairie Depot Mon.

Henderson, J. K. (Anna) 2 ch agent for O E O H&L Oak St Weston Ind tel.

Henderson, R. D. Weston Wes.

HENDRICKS, C. E. (Helen A.) garage T H&L Prairie Depot Mon. See adv.

HENDRICKS, F. J. (Ada E.) 4 ch farmer O 225a 7h 17c R1 Bowling Green Pla 31 B tel.

HENDRICKS, JOHN (Mary) farmer O 80a 3h 1c R1 Bradner Fre 96.

Hendricks, L. (Cora) 1 ch farmer O 180a 9h 35c Weston Lib 46 B tel.

Hendricks, Roe R1 Weston Lib 46 B tel.

HENER, WM. (Anna Maria) cashier the Hoytville Bank O H&L 1c Hoytville Jac 116.

Henerman, Herman cattle RD Bowling Green Cen.

Henerman, Wm. Pemberville Fre.

Henery, A. (Ruby) farmer R1 Rudolph Lib 73 Ind tel.

Hengsteller, G. W. (Christinia) 1 ch farmer O 140a 7h 23c R1 Risingsun Mon 77 B tel.

Hengsteller, Samuel (Katy) carpenter O H&L Risingsun Mon.

Heninger, Albert W. Prairie Depot Mon.

Henlien, Geo. (Minnie) teaming T H&L 2h R2 Pemberville Fre 4.

Henline, Arthur Pemberville Fre.

Henline, Edw. (Marie) 2 ch farmer T 100a 3h 5c Bradner Mon 19.

Henline, G. M. (Eliza) farming T H&L Prairie Depot Mon.

Henline, Jacob (Nettie) 1 ch oil worker T H&L 1h Bradner Mon 20.

Henline, J. J. (Sallie) 2 ch oil man Garfield St Bloomdale Blo B & Ind tels.

Henline, Loy Pemberville Fre.

Henline, Minnie Bradner Fre.

Henline, O. S. (Della) 4 ch laborer O H&L Prairie Depot Mon.

Hennan, Floyd (Lillian) 3 ch carpenter O H&L 5th St Perrysburg Pbg.

Hennan, Lydia 5 ch laborer O H&L 3rd St Perrysburg Pbg.

Henning, A. (Mary) 2 ch farmer O 80a 4h 3c R3 Weston Mil 82 Ind tel.

Henning, Carmie Weston Mil.

Henning, C. E. (Gertrude) 7 ch auto shop T H&L Rudolph Lib 81.

Henning, David (Minnie) 1 ch farmer O 46a 3h 3c R1 North Baltimore Hen 110.

Henning, Fred (Arda) 1 ch carpenter & contractor O H&L Stony Ridge Tro Ind tel.

Henning, Geo. W. (Edythe) 2 ch carpenter O H&L Stony Ridge Tro Ind tel.

HENNING, G. W. (Ada) 2 ch carpenter & contractor O H&L Stony Ridge Tro Ind tel.

Henning, John (Caroline) farmer O 40a 2h 2c R1 Walbridge Lake 27 Ind tel.

Henning, J. W. (Laura) 1 ch farmer O 70a 4h 7c R1 Weston Mil 57 Ind tel.

Henning, J. W. (Lyza) 3 ch farmer O 40a 6h 3c R1 North Baltimore Hen 35.

Henning, R. E. (Maud) 5 ch tailor T H&L RD North Baltimore Hen.

Henning, W. B. RD North Baltimore Hen.

Henninger, George (Sofia) 3 ch farmer T 20a 2h 1c R2 Custar Ros 33.

Hennings, Bill (Fannie) 2 ch laboring man T H&L Grand Rapids Gr Rs.

Hennings, Fred (Minnie) 6 ch ret O 120a H&L Hoytville Jac.

Hennings, Walter (son Fred) farmer Hoytville Jac.

Hennings, Wm. (Sadie) 1 ch mason O H&L Milton Center Mil.

Henry, Dr. A. G. RD North Baltimore Hen.

Henry, B. (Lucydia) 1 ch farmer T 80a 6h 6c R2 Custar Hen 42.

Henry, Elmer farmer 1h R1 Perrysburg Pbg 115 B tel.

HENRY, F. A. (Sarah) 5 ch farmer O 103a 5h 4c R2 Weston Pla 2 Ind tel.

Henry, Fred E. (Alice) 3 ch farmer O 40a 7h 5c R1 Perrysburg Pbg 115 B tel.

Henry, Fred W. (Elizabeth) 1 ch farmer O 320a 11h 3c R1 Walbridge Lake 134 B tel.

Henry, Geo. (Emma) 3 ch farmer O 100a 6h 4c R1 Lime City Pbg 51 Ind tel.

HENRY, MRS. GEO. Risingsun.

Henry, Grace housekeeper RD Walbridge Lake 134.

Henry, Joseph A. (Anna) 1 ch laborer T H&L Hoytville Jac.

HENRY, J. F. farmer O 70a 4h 2c R1 Perrysburg Pbg 23 B tel.

Henry, J. G. (Jessie) 2 ch oil worker H&L Verango St Cygnet Blo.

Henry, J. W. Pemberville Fre.

Henry, O. W. (Bertha) automobile salesman O 40a T H&L 1c Garfield St Bloomdale Blo B & Ind tels.

Henry, P. C. (Sarah E.) livery O H&L 5h Risingsun Mon B tel.

Henry, T. J. (Alice) ret O 115½a 1h 2c West Millgrove Per 65.

Henry, Wm. (Clemmie) 2 ch laborer T H&L R5 Bowling Green Cen.

Henschen, Clara housekeeper R1 Dunbridge Web 3 B tel.

Henschen, Frank (Jennie) 6 ch farmer O 80a 4h 4c R2 Dunbridge Mid 68 B tel.

Henschen, Geo. (Annie) 1 ch farmer T 4h 9c R1 Dunbridge Web 11 Ind tel.

Henschen, Henry (Lena) 4 ch farmer O 100a 5h 3c R1 Dunbridge Web 3 B tel.

Henschen, H. M. (Lizzie) farmer T 80a 4h 3c R1 Portage Lib 83.

Henschen, William farmer 115a R1 Dunbridge Web 11 Ind tel.

Henschen, W. F. (Minnie) 2 ch farmer O 80a 5h 5c R1 Dunbridge Mid 67 B tel.

Hensiek, Clara (dau Fred) housekeeper R1 Luckey Tro 26 Ind tel.

Hensiek, Fred (Louise) 8 ch farmer 20a 1h 2c R1 Luckey Tro 26 Ind tel.

HENSIEK, JOHN R1 Box 150 Luckey.

Hentges, Catherine (dau Chas.) housekeeper Custar Mil.

HENTGES, CHAS. (Gertrude) 2 ch ret O 40a H&L Custar Mil.

HENTGES, JACOB (Martha) farmer RD Hoytville Jac 44.

Hentges, Joseph (Katherine) 12 ch farmer T 80a 2h 3c R5 Bowling Green Cen 37 Ind tel.

Herbert, Evan (Effie) 4 ch farmer T H&L 1c R4 Bowling Green Cen 91.

Herlmann, Catherine 9 ch housekeeper R2 Custar Jac 98.

Herman, Casper (son Mrs. H. C.) laborer Pemberville Fre.

Herman, Emery Latcha Lake.

Herman, Fred (Sophia) 2 ch farmer T 120a 2h 4c R3 Pemberville Fre 35 B tel.

Herman, G. J. (Alta) 1 ch farmer T 40a 3h R1 Stony Ridge Tro 10 Ind tel.

HERMAN, JOHN farmer O 120a 4h 7c R3 Pemberville Fre 35 B tel.

HERMAN, J. L. (Clara) 2 ch farmer O 130a 5h 20c R1 Stony Ridge Tro 31 Ind tel.

Herman, Lewis Lime City Pbg.

Herman, Matilda ret 40a R1 Stony Ridge Tro 10 Ind tel.

Herman, Samuel (Margaret) farmer O 60a 2h 2c R1 Walbridge Lake 17.

Hermer, Henry L. (Adele) timekeeper O H&L R5 Bowling Green Cen 23 Ind tel.

Herrel, Baxter RD Weston Lib.

Herriff, A. W. (Emma) 3 ch ret O H&L Prairie Depot Mon Bel tel.

Herriff, F. C. Bradner Mon.

Herriff, H. M. Freeport Mon.

Herringshaw, Bertha A. (dau Mrs. J. Y.) housekeeper 15a R1 Hoytsville Jac 103 B tel.

Herringshaw, Eliza (dau Louisa M.) Center St Weston.

HERRINGSHAW, E. S. (Anna) 4 ch farmer T 120a 6h 6c RD Weston Lib 41 B tel.

Herringshaw, Florence (dau Samuel) housekeeper & clerk Hoytsville Jac B tel.

HERRINSHAW, FRED R2 Custar Lib.

Herringshaw, Jos. RD Custar Lib.

Herringshaw, Mrs. J. Y. 8 ch farmer O 3a H&L 1h 1c R1 Hoytsville Jac 103 B tel.

Herringshaw, Louisa M. 6 ch O 120a H&L Center St Weston B tel.

Herringshaw, Samuel (Anna Eliza) 2 ch hardware O H&L Hoytsville Jac B tel.

Herringshaw, Samuel J. (Charlotte) 4 ch farmer & hay baler O 30a 3h 2c R1 Hoytsville Jac 103. ...

Herringshaw, Thos. RD Bowling Green Pla.

Herringshaw, Wm. Hoytsville Jac.

HERRINGSHAW, W. F. (Blanche) 1 ch farmer O 18a 5h 3c R2 Custar Lib 21 Ind tel.

Herrington, Sid (Martha) 4 ch laborer O H&L Walbridge Lake.

Herron, Wm. cattle RD Bowling Green Cen.

Hersh, Claude (son Geo. E.) student Grand Rapids Gr Rs.

Hersh, George E. (Elsie) 1 ch lumber dealer O H&L 1h Grand Rapids Gr Rs Ind tel.

Hersh, Ray (son Geo. E.) clerk Grand Rapids Gr Rs Ind tel.

Hespe, Henry farmer T 100a 4h 6c R3 Pemberville Fre 43.

Hespe, J. F. Pemberville Fre.

Hespe, Lewis H. (Mary) 2 ch farmer O 80a 4h 3c R3 Prairie Depot Mon 12.

Hess, B. R. (Matilda) farmer T 80a 4h R1 Jerry City Blo 60.

Hess, C. (Louisa) 3 ch farmer O 240a 8h 10c R1 North Baltimore Hen 34.

HESS, MRS. N. O. 2 ch swine breeder O 40a 2h 2c R1 Pemberville Fre 34. See adv.

Heverman, Wm. (Katie) 3 ch farmer O 3a 1h 1c R2 Pemberville Fre 40.

Hewitt, Henry (Emma) laborer O H&L Custar Mil.

Hewitt, Worthy (Jennie) 1 ch laborer T H&L Third St Perrysburg Pbg B tel.

Heyman, C. W. (Ethel) telegraph operator O H&L Tontogany Wash.

HEYMAN, MASTER DALE Box 87 Weston.

Heyman, Mrs. E. J. 4 ch farming O 90a 8h 12c R2 Weston Wes 20 Ind tel.

Heyman, E. O. Weston Gr Rs.

Heyman, E. W. telegraph operator O 2H&L Tontogany Wash.

HEYMAN, G. A. R3 Weston.

Heyman, J. S. (Nettie) attorney Pemberville Fre.

Heyman, L. W. (Estella) 3 ch farmer O 200a 2h 5c R1 Grand Rapids Gr Rs 12 Ind tel.

Heyman, P. W. J. Weston Wes.

Hickle, Edward (Horchye E.) 5 ch farmer O 100a 5h 3c R1 Tontogany Mid 39 Ind tel.

Hicks, Cylde J. (son Edward) farmer 1h 1c R1 Box 15 East Toledo Ros 26 Ind tel.

Hicks, Edward W. (Mary A.) farmer O 25a 5h 2c R1 Box 15 East Toledo Ros 26 Ind tel.

Hicks, June (dau Edward) R1 Box 15 East Toledo Ros 26 Ind tel.

HICKS, RAYMOND (Grace) 1 ch farmer T R1 East Toledo Ros 26.

Hicks, W. W. (Maria) ret O 85a 1c R1 box 15 East Toledo Ros 26.

Hidy, Fred (Mable) 1 ch fireman T H&L Box 549 Rossford Ros B tel.

Hienze, Charley (Maggie) 11 ch farmer O 80a 5h 5c R1 Custar Mil 12.

Hienze, Frank (son Charley) R1 Custar Mil 12.

Hienze, Fred (son Chas.) R1 Custar Mil 12.

Hienze, Mary (dau Chas.) R1 Custar Mil 12.

Hienze, Peter (Ida) 1 ch farmer T 80a R1 Custar Mil 8.

Hild, George (Sarah C.) 2 ch farmer O 3a 1h 1c R2 Bowling Green Pla 63 Ind tel.

Hilde, Casper laborer O H&L Pemberville Fre.

HILL, ADAM (Mary) 6 ch engineer O H&L 2h 1c Rising Sun Mon B tel.

HILL, CLAUD A. (Florence) 2 ch concrete worker T H&L Box 153 Pemberville Fre 40.

Hill, C. L. Grand Rapids Gr Rs.

Hill, Deck ret O H&L Milton Center Mil.

Hill, D. (Mary E.) farmer O 18a 2h 2c R1 Prairie Depot Mon 12.

Hill, D. E. (Jennie) 2 ch bakery O H&L Weston Wes Ind tel.

Hill, D. L. (Sarah D.) shoe cobbler O H&L 1c Findlay St Portage Por 2 Ind tel.

Hill, Elvira Weston Wes.

HILL, ERNEST A. (Alice) 4 ch station agent O H&L Custar Mil Ind tel.

Hill, E. Harold (son E. A.) office, clerk Custar Mil 99½ Ind tel.

Hill, F. M. (son R. E.) painter & paperhanger O Milton Center Mil.

Hill, Geo. (Percilla) farmer O 65a 2h 2c R2 North Baltimore Hen 84.

Hill, Harold (son Ernest A.) clerk Custar Mil B tel.

Hill, Henry 3 ch farmer O 83a 4h 4c R1 Prairie Depot Mon 45.

Hill, Howard (son Adam) laborer Risingsun Mon.

Hill, I. J. (Ellen) hotel T H&L Risingsun Mon B tel.

Hill, James (Stella) 4 ch laborer T H&L 87 Elm St Rossford Ros.

HILL, JENNIE 1 ch housekeeper T H&L West Mill Grove Per 69.

Hill, Mrs. J. B. 1 ch ret OH&L Custar Mil.

Hill, J. L. (Mary) 6 ch blacksmith T H&L Harrison St Bloomdale Blo.

Hill, L. F. (Alice) 2 ch farmer T 160a 7h 2c R3 Weston Mil 75 Ind tel.

Hill, Maude R. (son Adam) oil worker Risingsun Mon.

Hill, P. L. (Verna) 1 ch farmer T 90a 3h 2c R3 Weston Mil 75.

HILL, R. E. (Anna L.) 3 ch minister O H&L Milton Center Mil.

Hill, Sarah D. Corp St Portage Por.

Hillabrand, F. L. (Lena M.) 3 ch superintendent O H&L Rudolph Lib 81 Ind tel.

Hillard, C. (Millie) 1 ch blacksmith T H&L Haskins Mid.

Hillard, D. S. (Mary E.) farmer & dairyman T 74a 5h 6c RD North Baltimore Hen 87.

Hillard, F. A. (Alta) 3 ch farmer T 26a 2h 1c Jerry City Blo 72.

Hillard, George (Edith) 2 ch oil man pumping T H&L 1h R3 North Baltimore Blo 43 B & Ind tels.

Hille, Mrs. Clara 3 ch farmer O 80a 3h 4c R1 Pemberville Fre 35.

Hille, Elizabeth (dau Mary) farmer 80a R1 Woodville Tro 49.

Hille, Henry Millbury Lake.

Hille, H. H. Pemberville Fre.

Hille, John (son Mary) farmer O 80a 3h 7c R1 Woodville Tro 49.

Hille, Louise (dau Mary) farmer O 80a R1 Woodville Tro 49.

Hille, Mary 4 ch farmer O 80a R1 Woodville Tro 49 B tel.

Hille, Wm. C. (Annie) 3 ch farmer O 100a 4h 5c R2 Pemberville Fre 44 B tel.

Hiller, S. R. RD North Baltimore Hen.

Hillerbrand, Anderson (Lila) 1 ch laborer O H&L 6th St Perrysburg Pbg B tel.

Hillerbrand, Andrew (Anna) 2 ch laborer O H&L Second St Perrysburg Pbg.

Hillerbrand, Frank (Luella) 2 ch laborer O H&L 5th St Perrysburg Pbg B tel.

Hillerbrand, Frederick (Louise) 2 ch real estate O H&L Front St Perrysburg Pbg B tel.

Hillerbrand, Geo. (Mary) laborer O H&L 3rd St Perrysburg Pbg.

Hillerbrand, Lou (Josephine) 2 ch conductor O H&L 5th St Perrysburg Pbg B tel.

Hillerbrand, Robert (Edna) 1 ch traveling man T H&L Front St Perrysburg Pbg.

Hillery, J. O. Bloomdale Blo.

Hilliard, C. (Ida) laborer O H&L Prairie Depot Mon.

HILT, GEO. A. (Edna) 3 ch farmer T 120a 5h 10c R2 Prairie Depot Por 108.

Hilt, Paul (Leco) 8 ch farmer O 17a 4h Walbridge St Walbridge Lake 3.

Hilt, Wm. cattle RD Bowling Green Cen.

Hilyard, Arthur (Bessie) 1 ch farmer T R3 Perrysburg Ros 11.

HIMES, C. E. (Fannie) 3 ch field foreman H&L 2h 2c R1 Rudolph Lib 98 Ind tel.

Himmelmann, Cristina housekeeper T H&L R3 Perrysburg Pbg 139.

Himmler, Jno. RD North Baltimore Hen.

Hincher, H. O. (Mabel) 2 ch oil worker O H&L Virange St Cygnet Blo.

Hinckle, John (Mary) laborer O H&L Main & 2nd Sts Perrysburg Pbg.

Hindley, Stanley (Lulu) farmer T 110a 3h 1c R1 Bowling Green Pla 39.

Hinds, C. H. (Bertha) 1 ch farmer O 27a 3h 3c R1 Millbury Lake 73.

Hinds, Fred (Daisy) 2 ch painter T H&L 1h 1c Luckey Tro 94 Ind tel.

Hineline, T. J. farmer O 6a 1h R1 East Toledo Lake 131.

Hines, Miss Carrie O H&L Grand Rapids Gr Rs.

Hines, C. C. (Augusta) farmer O 49a 3h 3c Tontogany Wash 28 Ind tel.

Hines, E. farmer T 1h 1c R1 Tontogany Wash 71 Ind tel.

Hinesman, B. RD Hoytsville Jac.

HINESMAN, ERNEST (Cora) 1 ch farmer T 132a 5h 4c R3 Weston Mil 68 Ind tel.

Hinesman, John (Bertha) 1 ch farmer O H&L 2h Grand Rapids Gr Rs Ind tel.

Hinkel, John (Anna) laborer T H&L Perrysburg Pbg.

Hinkle, Margaret ret O H&L 5th St Perrysburg Pbg.

Hintsman, Harry RD Hoytsville Jac.

Hipp, Jacob (Minnie) 2 ch section foreman T H&L Walbridge Lake.

Hipsher, Mary 7 ch farmer O 40a 6h 2c R3 Bowling Green Cen 43 Ind tel.

Hirth, Andrew (Harriet) 2 ch blacksmith O H&L Silver St Weston B tel.

Hirth, Harry (Lela) manager Bell Tel Co T H&L Center Weston B tel.

HISER, A. A. (Mary) 3 ch gardener O 25a 2h 5c E Caldwell St Bradner Mon 23.

Hiser, Charles J. (Anna) 4 ch farmer O 40a 3h 4c R1 Pemberville Fre 93.

Hiser, Claude Caldwell St Bradner Mon.

Hiser, I. W. (Cora) 7 ch farmer T 105a 3h 3c R3 Pemberville Fre 34 B tel.

Hiser, Maude teacher Caldwell St Bradner Mon B tel.

Hiser, P. W. farmer O 40a 2h 2c R3 Pemberville Fre 29 B tel.

HISSONG, A. B. (Vina) 7 ch road engineer O H&L 1h 2c R1 Rudolph Lib 77.

Hissong, Bruce (son A. B.) R1 Rudolph Lib 77.

Hissong, Van (son A. B.) R1 Rudolph Lib 77.

Histe, C. W. (Anna) farmer O 75a 2h 1c R1 Portage Por 42.

Histe, Fannie O H&L E Main St Portage Por 6.

Histe, Geo. F. Corp St Portage Por.

Hitchcock, H. Bradner Mon.

Hitchcock, O. Bradner Mon.

Hite, Ella 1 ch housekeeper O H&L Grand Rapids Gr Rs.

Hite, Ezra (Ellen) farmer O 40a 1h 3c R1 Tontogany Wash 52 Ind tel.

Hite, Geo. W. (M.) machinist T H&L Grand Rapide Gr Rs.

Hite, G. M. (Caroline) clerk T H Dunbridge Mid 73.

Hite, John 1 ch farmer T 80a 2h 1c R3 Bowling Green Cen 50.

Hite, John (son Ezra) farmer 1h R1 Tontogany Wash 52.

Hite, J. A. (Mary J.) storekeeper O H&L 1h Dunbridge Mid 69 B tel.

Hite, Libbie Weston Wes.

Hite, M. (Maude) 3 ch oil pumper T L R1 North Baltimore Hen 122.

Hite, Nellie 3 ch O H&L Maple St Weston Ind tel.

Hite, S. A. (Edith) 3 ch barber T H&L Findley St Portage Por 10.

Hite, Wm. (Mary) 1 ch pumper O 45a 1h 1c R3 Prairie Depot Mon 12.

Hite, W. M. (Jessie W.) farmer T 80a 3h 5c R2 Dunbridge Pbg 21 B tel.

Hitt, E. C. blacksmith bds Custar Mil.

HITZKA, CHAS. (Alma) 2 ch laborer T H&L R2 Dunbridge Mid 74.

Hoag, F. J. (Maria) 6 ch ret O H&L Oak St Weston.

Hoagland, Geo. Haskins Mid.

HOAGLIN, N. W. (Amanda) 2 ch laborer T 7h 11c R2 Bloomdale Blo 106 B & Ind tels.

HOBART, C. S. Pemberviile Fre.

Hobart, Dora G. Pemberville Fre.

Hobart, E. M. (Lyda) 2 ch merchant O H&L Front St Pemberville Fre 40 Ind tel.

Hobart, Harry W. Pemberville Fre.

Hobart, Marcene (Catherine) 6 ch merchant O H&L Pemberville Fre 40 Ind tel.

HOBBS, W. M. (Amanda) farmer T hired man 1c R2 Dunbridge Mid 81.

HOBERT, C. S. (Marguerite) 3 ch proprietor of store O H&L Pemberville Fre B tel.

Hobert, H. W. (Anna) 2 ch gen store & agr implements O H&L Pemberville Fre 40 B tel.

HOCHANADEL, FRANK (Rose) 2 ch farmer O 76a 3h 1c R1 E Toledo Ros 30 Ind tel.

Hock, J. H. (Susie E.) 4 ch farmer & stock dealer O 240a 9h 8c R1 Hoytsville Jac 84 B tel.

Hockelmyer, Fred (Anna) laborer O H&L Luckey Tro.

Hodge, S. M. (Pearl) 2 ch farmer O 1½a Scotch Ridge Web 35.

HODGEMAN, F. A. 5 ch O 110a 4h R1 Weston Lib 49 B tel.

HODGES, H. L. publisher Prairie Depot. See adv.

HOEFFLIN, FRED C. (Louisa) farmer O 20a 2h 1c R1 E Toledo Ros 33.

Hoelle, Jno. Pemberville Web.

Hoelter, A. H. (Mary) 1 ch farmer O 60a 3h 7c R1 Luckey Tro 93 Ind tel.

Hoelter, Miss Carrie (dau Henry) nursing Luckey Tro Ind tel.

Hoelter, Mrs. Henry O H&L Luckey Tro Ind tel.

HOELTER, JOHN G. (Anna) 2 ch farmer T 80a 4h 6c R1 Luckey Tro 72 Ind tel.

Hoelter, Martha (dau W. L.) housekeeper Luckey Tro Ind tel.

Hoelter, W. L. (Emma) 5 ch general store O H&L Luckey Tro Ind tel.

Hofer, August Latchie Lake.

HOFFHIENS, O. W. (Emma) 3 ch jersey breeder & farmer O 46a 3h 6c R5 Bowling Green Cen 24 Ind tel.

Hoffman, Charles (Mayme) 7 ch saloon keeper O H&L Perrysburg Pbg B tel.

HOFFMAN, CHARLEY O. (Ethel) 2 ch bailer T 5a 2h 1c R1 Custar Mil 101.

Hoffman, Mrs. Chris. ret O H&L Second St Perrysburg Pbg B tel.

HOFFMAN, MRS. C. A. Second St Perrysburg.

Hoffman, Dennis RD Perrysburg Mid.

HOFFMAN, ELMER J. (Inez M.) 4 ch farmer O 84a 12h 10c R3 Perrysburg Pbg 141 Ind tel.

Hoffman, Ernest (Ida) farmer T 50a 2h Custar Mil 98.

HOFFMAN, FRANK C. (Lillian) farmer O 66a 1h 2c R1 Rudolph Lib 75 Ind tel.

Hoffman, Geo. A. (Catherine) 6 ch farmer T 110a 5h 3c R1 Haskins Mid 53 B tel.

Hoffman, G. F. (Lulu) 7 ch grocery O H&L Perrysburg Pbg B tel.

Hoffman, G. W. (Victoria) 1 ch cafe O H&L Front St Perrysburg Pbg B tel.

Hoffman, Henry (Mary) 2 ch farmer O 50a 6h 6c R1 Lime City Tro 21 Ind tel.

HOFFMAN, JACOB (Barbara) 5 ch farmer & thresher T 40a 1h 2c Custar Mil 12 B tel.

Hoffman, Mrs. John ret T H&L Grand Rapide Gr Rs Ind tel.

Hoffman, John 8 ch farmer O 40a 2h R2 Bowling Green Pla 95.

Hoffman, John oil worker O 1h 2c Bays Lib 75 Ind tel.

Hoffman, John A. (Margaret) ret R2 Perrysburg Mid 5 B tel.

Hoffman, J. L. (Alta M.) 1 ch druggist T H&L RD North Baltimore Hen Ind tel.

Hoffman, J. S. RD North Baltimore Blo.

Hoffman, Kate housekeeper R1 Stony Ridge Tro 31.

Hoffman, Mrs. Louise Perrysburg Web.

Hoffman, O. W. cattle RD Bowling Green Cen.

Hoffman, Raymond (son Henry) farm hand R1 Lime City Tro 21 Ind tel.

Hoffsis, Wm. RD North Baltimore Hen.

Hofner, Michael (Mary) 3 ch farmer O 40a 2h 2c R2 Haskins Mid 28 B tel.

Hoglen, Geo. (Susie) carpenter O H&L Haskins Mid.

Hoglin, J. E. (Carrie) 3 ch farmer T 160a 5h 2c RD North Baltimore Hen 12 Ind tel.

Hohls, Edith Pemberville Fre.

This Calf is Cleopatra and Every Inch a Queen.

Hohls, Herman Pemberville Fre.

Hohls, Mrs. Sophia ret O H&L R1 Pemberville Fre 56.

Hohn, Gilbert H. (son J. L.) farmer.R2 Custar Mil 31.

HOHN, J. L. (Mary) 6 ch farmer O 80a 5h 8c R2 Custar Mil 31 B tel.

HOILER, C. H. (Clara E.) garage O H&L garage Prairie Depot Mon B tel.

Hoiles, Clyde B. (Cora) 1 ch farmer T H&L 1h 1c R3 Prairie Depot Mon 28.

Hoiles, Harry (Maude I.) garage T H&L Prairie Depot Mon.

HOILES, MARY P. Prairie Depot.

Hoiles, P. C. (Matilda) farmer O 73a 5h 3c R3 Prairie Depot Mon 50.

Hoiles, P. H. 3 ch farmer O 80a 2h 5c R3 Prairie Depot Mon 50.

Holbrook, Grant (Clara) 1 ch supt of cemetery O ½a H&L 3rd St Perrysburg Pbg B tel.

Holcolm, Fred (Emma) 2 ch oil worker O 40a 2h 2c R3 Prairie Depot Mon 12½ B tel.

HOLCOMB, DAVID Bradner.

Holcomb, Levi ret O H&L Prairie Depot Mon.

Holden, Mrs. Cora E. 1 ch cor Maple & Walnut Sts Weston.

Holefka, Lawrence Rossford Ros.

Holewinski, F. W. (Agnes) 1 ch insurance man O H&L 265 Walnut St Rossford Ros Ind tel.

HOLLAND, P. A. Walbridge.

Hollenbeck, C. F. Perrysburg Pbg.

HOLLENBECK, D. K. (Frances) 2 ch lawyer O H&L Main St Perrysburg Pbg.

Hollenbeck, Mrs. Ed. ret O H&L 2nd St Perrysburg Pbg B tel.

Hollenbeck, Frank (Allie) painter & paper hanger O H&L Front St Perrysburg Pbg B tel.

Hollenbeck, Rosalie H. Perrysburg Pbg.

Hollinger, Conan J. (son J. W.) clerk in store Randolph St Bairdstown Blo B & Ind tels.

Hollinger; J. W. (Lizzie) 1 ch general store O Randolph St Bairdstown Blo B & Ind tels.

Hollman, H. H. (Sophia) 1 ch tailor O H&L Pemberville Fre 40.

Hollowpeter, Fred telephone 11a Bradford St Cygnet Blo Ind tel.

Hollowpeter, Lottie 3 ch T H&L Bradford St Cygnet Blo Ind tel.

Holmes, J. A. (Florence) 1 ch ret O H&L Maple St Weston B tel.

Holmes, Louise (dau J. A.) insurance office Maple St Weston.

Holtmeyer, Blanche (dau W. F.) housekeeper R1 Luckey Tro Ind tel.

Holtmeyer, Fred (son W. F.) student R1 Luckey Tro 51 Ind tel.

HOLTMEYER, WM. F. (Anna) 4 ch farmer O 100a 4h 10c R1 Luckey Tro 51 Ind tel.

Holtz, Lauritz Rossford Ros.

Holtz, Oscar Rossford Ros.

Holzhauer, Henry (Cora) 3 ch farmer O 120a 6h 15c R3 Weston Mil 81 Ind tel.

Homer, I. B. Weston Wes.

Hommes, George (Roda) laborer T H&L W Boundary St Perrysburg Pbg B tel.

Honer, Fred (Nettie) 3 ch farmer T 80a 2h 3c R1 North Baltimore Hen 70 B tel.

Honner, Henry Perrysburg Pbg.

Honner, John (Mary) 1 ch motorman T H&L Front St Perrysburg Pbg B tel.

Honnor, Wm. (Jenese) laborer 1 ch O H&L 6th St Perrysburg Pbg.

Hoodlebrink, Carl (Maria) 1 ch farmer O 70a 3h 6c R1 Pemberville Fre 49 B tel.

HOODLEBRINK, ED. (Mary) farmer O 117a 4h 4c R1 Pemberville Fre 38 B tel.

Hoodlebrink, Edward (son Geo.) farm hand R1 LeMoyne Tro 81.

Hoodlebrink, Ernest (Anna) 9 ch farmer T 160a 4h 6c R2 Pemberville Fre 49.

Hoodlebrink, Geo. (Louisa) 9 ch farmer O 435a 4h 42c R1 LeMoyne Tro 81.

Hoodlebrink, G. H. Pemberville Fre.

Hoodlebrink, Harmon H. Pemberville Fre.

Hoodlebrink, Henry 3 ch farmer O 77a 2h 5c Pemberville Fre 42.

HOODLEBRINK, JOHN W. (Julia) 2 ch farmer O 80a 3h 5c R3 County Line Road Pemberville Fre 32 B & Ind tels.

Hoodlebrink, J. F. A. (Anna) 2 ch farmer O 80a 3h 4c R1 Pemberville Fre 20 B tel.

Hoodlebrink, Mrs. Liza ret O H&L Pemberville Fre 40.

Hoodlebrink, Mary (dau Henry) housekeeper Pemberville Fre 42.

Hoodlebrink, Sophia (dau Geo.) housekeeper R1 LeMoyne Tro 81.

Hoodlebrink, William (son Geo.) farm hand R1 LeMoyne Tro 81.

Hoofer, Mrs. Ethel 5 ch housekeeper O H&L West Millgrove Per 68.

Hoofer, Sadie housekeeper R1. Deshler Jac 45.

Hoot, M. J. (Ella M.) farmer O 40a 3h 3c R4 Deshler Jac 15 B tel.

Hoover, Ethel (dau R. D.) R1 Risingsun Mon 21.

Hoover, H. M. (Mary) ret O H&L Perrysburg Pbg B tel.

Hoover, Kittie Tontogany Wash.

Hoover, R. D. (Hattie) 2 ch farmer O 80a 5h 5c R1 Risingsun Mon 81.

HOPKINS, C. R. (O..A.) 2 ch lumber dealer O H&L Custar Mil B & Ind tels.

Hopkins, Ella (dau C. R.) housekeeper Custar Mil B & Ind tels.

Hopkins, G. (Leona) 2 ch conductor T H&L 5th St Perrysburg Pbg B tel.

Horn, T. G. (Sarah L.) carpenter O H&L Garfield & Walnut Sts Bloomdale Blo B & Ind tels.

Hornbeck, G. G. (Helen) 1 ch farm laborer RD Rudolph Lib 66.

HORNBECK, Z. T. (Helene) 1 ch farm laborer R1 Rudolph Lib 66.

Horned, Sam Garfield St Bloomdale Blo.

Horner, Bert Bloomdale Per.

Horner, Clarence barber Bell St Bradner Mon.

Horner, Mrs. Elizabeth 7 ch ret O H&L Custar Mil.

Horner, J. F. Bloomdale Per.

Horner, J. L. (Minerva) 3 ch oil worker O H&L Bell St Bradner Mon.

Horner, L. L. (Daisy) 4 ch shoe repairer O H&L Custar Mil.

Hornmeyer, Herman farmer O 73a 2h 4c R3 Pemberville Fre 9.

Hosey, Jno. Bradner Mon.

HOSKINSON, JACOB (Lulu) 4 ch farmer T 160a 6h 4c R1 Rudolph Lib 68.

HOSKINSON, LEVI (Bertha) farmer T 240a 8h 6c R1 Bowling Green Lib 57.

HOSLER, J. A. (Bertha) 5 ch teamster T 2h R1 Randolph Lib 107 Ind tel.

Hotchkiss, Fred mail carrier bds Milbury Lake.

HOUGH, E. G. R1 Walbridge.

Hough, H. W. bakery bds RD North Baltimore Hen Ind tel.

Hough, W. L. RD North Baltimore Hen.

Houghwarst, B. F. (Mabel) 4 ch farmer T 95a 3h 2c R1 Bloomdale Blo 129 B & Ind tels.

Houpt, L. H. (Lectia) school teacher T H&L Maple St Weston.

House, E. (Frances) 4 ch farmer T 40a 2h 1c R1 Prairie Depot Mon 38.

House, G. O. RD North Baltimore Hen.

House, J. G. (Ledalia) 3 ch farmer T 80a 3h 3c R1 Bradnor Mon 15.

Householder, Elmer RD Bowling Green Pla.

HOUSEKEEPER, G. C. (Cemelia) 4 ch farmer O 40a 3h 9c R5 Bowling Green Cen 93 Ind tel.

Housely, Mary P. Grand Rapids Gr Rs.

Housely, R. A. Grand Rapids Gr Rs.

Houser, Addie housekeeper 1h R1 Walbridge Ros 22 Ind tel.

HOUSER, CARL (Nellie) 3 ch farmer T 120a 4h 4c R3 Prairie Depot Fre 75.

Houser, Emma housekeeper R1 Walbridge Ros 22 Ind tel.

Houser, Miss Fannie teacher R1 Walbridge Ros 22 Ind tel.

Houser, Frank RD Bowling Green Pla.

Houser, Mrs. Ida 'Mamie 2 ch optical Weston.

Housholder, E. E. (Lettie) 9 ch farmer O 177a 6h 31c R2 Bowling Green Pla 98 B tel.

Housholder, L. A. (Verna) 2 ch painter T 5a 1c R5 Bowling Green 20.

Housholder, S. E. (Harriet) farmer O 19a 2h 1c R2 Bowling Green Pla 90 Ind tel.

Housley, Dick (Mollie) ret O 300a H&L Grand Rapids Gr Rs Ind tel.

HOUSLEY, R. A. (Mary) auto agt & farmer O H&L farm Grand Rapids Gr Rs Ind tel.

Housmer, Frauk (Cora) 6 ch farmer O 40a 6h 6c R1 Deshler Jac 45.

Housmer, Wayne (son Frank) farm laborer R1 Deshler Jac 45.

Houston, C. B. (Ida) 2 ch field foreman T H&L R1 Rudolph Lib 65 Ind tel.

Houston, C. E. (Cora B.) 2 ch farmer T 40a 3h 1c R1 Pemberville Fre 62.

HOUSTON, C. S. (Martha A.) 3 ch farmer O 155a 5h 9c R1 Hoytsville Jac 102.

HOUSTON, EARL (son C. E.) farmer R1 Pemberville Fre 62.

Houston, Emma ret O H&L Front St Perrysburg Pbg.

Houston, Glen (Julia) farm hand 1c R1 Rudolph Lib 62½.

Houston, King (Lillian) 1 ch field foreman O 40a 3h 4c R1 Rudolph Lib 70 Ind tel.

Horra, Caleb 5 ch pumper O H&L 1h Prairie Depot Mon.

Howard, Anne (dau Mrs. A. B. Young) 1166 Oak St E Toledo Ros 19.

Howard, Royce (son Mrs. A. B. Young) 1166 Oak St E Toledo Ros 19.

Howard, W. H. RD North Baltimore Hen.

Howe, D. N. (Clara) 15 ch farmer O 80a 7h 8c R1 Custar Jac 43.

Howe, J. Ruskin (son D. N.) school teacher R1 Custar Jac 43.
Howe, L. Merrill (son D. N.) school teacher R1 Custar Jac 43.
Howe, Raymond R. (Mable) insurance agt T H&L Washington St Cygnet Blo 15. See adv.
Howey, Ben. (Glennie) 4 ch oil worker T H&L Risingsun Mon.
Hoxworth, A. 1 ch butcher & grocer O H&L Caldwell St Bradner Mon B tel.
Hoxworth, A. I. (Zana) clerk T H&L Caldwell St Bradner Mon.
Hoxworth, F. L. Bradner Mon.
Hoylett, John (Maggie) 1 ch farmer T 120a 5h 2c R1 Weston Lib 41 Ind tel.
Hoylett, Robert (Mattie) 1 ch farmer O 59a 5h 2c R3 Prairie Depot Mon 28.
Hoyman, J. S. Pemberville Fre.
Hoyt, Walter (Lottie) farmer T 120a 5h 2c R1 Tontogany Wash 47 Ind tel.
Hubbell, C. L. Corp St Portage Por.
Hubbell, F. S. RD North Baltimore Hen.
Hubbell, Rodrick (Cella) 5 ch farmer T R3 Perrysburg Ros 12.
Hubbs, Dean Dunbridge Web.
Huber, Jos., Jr. Lime City Pbg.
Huber, Sam (Mary) 4 ch farmer O 68a 3h 3c R3 Prairie Depot Mon 4 B tel.
Hubscher, J. A. (Lena) 3 ch watchmaker O 4a R1 Millbury Lake 131.
Hubscher, J. E. Millbury Lake.
Huddle, Stella RD North Baltimore Hen.
Hudson, C. E. 1 ch farmer O 55a 3h 3c R1 Deshler Jac 23 B tel.
Hudson, Mrs. E. S. 3 ch ret O H&L Milton Center Mil.
Hudson, H. P. Cygnet Blo.
Hudson, T. A. 1 ch livery & feed barn 3h Portage Lib 112 Ind tel.
Huebner, H. W. (May) 3 ch carpenter O 40a 3c R1 Grand Rapids Wash 68 Ind tel.
Huebner, John F. R1 Grand Rapids.
Huecker, Saml. Pemberville Fre.
Huff, Albert F. (Maude) 6 ch farmer O 84a 9h 1c R1 Rising Sun Mon 71 B tel.
Huff, Charley (son Albert J.) oil worker R1 Rising Sun Mon 71.
Huff, Emma (Alice) 3 ch farmer T 110a 5h 2c R1 Walbridge Lake 2 Ind tel.
Huff, E. B. (Della) farmer O 52a 2h 2c R2 Haskins Wash 90 & 89 Ind tel.
Huff, E. G. Walbridge Lake.
Huff, Mrs. Isabell 1 ch ret T H&L 7th St Perrysburg Pbg.

Huffaker, Lilla A. 1 ch nurse T H&L Walnut St Portage Por.
Huffman, Arthur (Lulu) 2 ch draying O H&L 2h Grand Rapids Gr Rs Ind tel.
Huffman, Clyde (Margurete) 1 ch farmer T 160a 4h 16c R1 Grand Rapids Wash 56 Ind tel.
Huffman, C. F. (Nevada) 2 ch farmer O 90a 2h 10c R1 Grand Rapids Gr Rs Ind tel.
Huffman, Dan (Dora) ret O 80a H&L 1h 1c Grand Rapids Gr Rs B & Ind tels.
Huffman, Dora Grand Rapids Gr Rs.
Huffman, D. B. (Carrie) 2 ch gen store & post master O H&L Longley Per 103 B & Ind tels.
Huffman, Emma Grand Rapids Gr Rs.
Huffman, Edd (Blanch) 5 ch grocer O H&L 2h Grand Rapids Gr Rs Ind tel.
Huffman, Floyd (Ina I.) 5 ch laborer O H&L Grand Rapids Gr Rs.
Huffman, Mrs. Hattie 1 ch O H&L Bell Ave Bradner Mon.
Huffman, H. D. (Grace) farmer T 80a 6h 3c R1 Grand Rapids Wash 54 Ind tel.
Huffman, Jacob (Elizabeth) farmer O 285a 1h 2c R1 Grand Rapids Wash 41 Ind tel.
Huffman, Joseph (Dorcas) farming T 119a 4h 7c R1 Grand Rapids Wash 57 Ind tel.
Huffman, J. E. (Elsie) ret O H&L Grand Rapids Gr Rs Ind tel.
Huffman, J. F. Bell St Bradner Mon.
Huffman, J. W. (Mary D.) 1 ch farmer O 40a 5h 6c R1 Pemberville Fre 71.
Huffman, O. P. 6 ch O H&L N Main St Bradner Mon.
Huffman, P. B. (son J. W.) teacher R1 Pemberville Fre 71.
Huffman, W. J. (Mary) 2 ch clerk O H&L Grand Rapids Gr Rs.
Hufford, Bert R1 Perrysburg Pbg.
Hufford, Catherine R3 Perrysburg Pbg 137.
Hufford, Charles (Margaret) 3 ch farmer T 62a 3h 3c R1 Perrysburg Pbg 117.
Hufford, Emmaline ret O H&L 4th St Perrysburg Pbg B tel.
Hufford, Frank G. (Ellen) 3 ch carpenter O 2a 1h 1c R3 Perrysburg Pbg 137 Ind tel.
Hufford, George 4 ch laborer T H&L 4th Perrysburg Pbg.
Hufford, Harvey (son Isaac) 1h R1 Stony Ridge Lake 90.

Hufford, Henry 2 ch farming O 76a 4h 4c R3 Perrysburg Pbg 137.

Hufford, Isaac (Adeline) farmer O 60a 3h 3c R1 Stony Ridge Lake 90.

Hufford, Joe (Julia) 2 ch farmer O 1a 3h 1c R3 Perrysburg Pbg 136.

Hufford, John (Mary) ret O H&L Plank Road Perrysburg Pbg.

Hufford, J. H. (Amaretta) 1 ch florist O H 4a 2h 1c 6th St Perrysburg Pbg B tel.

Hufford, Robt. Perrysburg Pbg.

Hufford, Wm. (Victoria) 2 ch laborer T H&L Perrysburg Pbg.

Huffs, Samuel (Lulu) 3 ch laborer T H&L Rising Sun Mon.

Hughes, Burt RD Bowling Green Cen.

Hughes, C. J. RD North Baltimore Hen.

Hughes, Frank (Myrian) 2 ch farmer O 60a 2h 5c R1 Bowling Green Pla 38 Ind tel.

Hughes, Homer H. (Loretta A.) retail meat market prop O Main St Bloomdale Blo B & Ind tels.

Hughes, J. M. RD North Baltimore Hen.

Hughes, J. W. RD North Baltimore Hen.

Hughes, Orlanda (Louise) 4 ch farmer O 120a 5h 8c R3 Bowling Green Cen 17 Ind tel.

Hughes, R. A. Cygnet Blo.

Hull, A. L. Weston Wes.

Hull, C. (Blanche) 3 ch farmer T 273a 8h 23c R3 Prairie Depot Mon 9.

Hull, Judith (dau L. F.) school teacher R3 Weston Wes 75.

HULL, L. F. (Alice) 2 ch farmer T 160a 7h 3c R3 Weston Mil 75 Ind tel.

Hull, L. V. Portage Lib.

Hull, P. L. Weston Mil.

Hull, S. F. (Kate) 3 ch farmer O 60a 2h 1c R1 Weston Lib 45.

Hull, Walter (Abby) 2 ch railroadman O H&L Walbridge Lake.

Hulse, E. G. RD North Baltimore Hen.

Hum, Alva (Emily) 2 ch ret O 2H& 2 Lots 6th St Perrysburg Pbg B tel.

Hum, Earl (Cora) 1 ch laborer T H&L Plank Road Perrysburg Pbg.

Hum, W. C. (Elma) farmer O 72a 2h 4c R2 Perrysburg Pbg 12 B tel.

Humes, Grant (Rebecca) farmer O 40a 3h 3c R1 Grand Rapids Gr Rs 9 Ind tel.

Humes, Quay R1 Rudolph Lib 98 Ind tel.

Hummel, Alice (dau D.) housekeeper R1 Pemberville Fre 73 B tel.

Hummel, Clinton (Sarah) 1 ch farmer T 10a 4h 2c R1 Grand Rapids Wes 14 Ind tel.

Hummel, D., Jr. farmer O 121a 4h 14c R1 Pemberville Fre 73 B tel.

Hummel, Ervin (son D.) farmer R1 Pemberville Fre 73 B tel.

Hummel, Frank (Jennie) 2 ch farmer T 40a 3h 2c Jerry City Blo 69.

HUMMEL, GEO. H. (Margaret) farmer & teacher O 5a 1h R2 Prairie Depot Por 127.

HUMMEL, H. C. (Louise) 3 ch blacksmith O 11a 1h 1c R1 Pemberville Fre 59 B tel.

Hummel, J. F. (Martha Jane) farmer O 60a 2h 4c R2 Prairie Depot Por 127 Ind tel.

Hummel, M. E. (Carrie) 4 ch farmer O 80a 4h 6c R1 Grand Rapids Gr Rs 9.

Hummel, Reuben (Alice) 1 ch farmer T 73a 3h 2c R1 Pemberville Fre 66 B tel.

Humphrey, J. E. (Maude) steam fitter O H&L Rossford Pbg 81.

Humphry, S. E. Rossford Ros.

Hund, Eliza E. Rossford Ros.

Hund, Wm P. R3 Perrysburg Pbg.

Hundley, Esther (dau J. P.) Taylor St Weston Wes.

Hundley, J. P. (Katie) 9 ch farmer O 27a 5h 4c Taylor St Weston Wes Ind tel.

Hunger, Chas. Bloomdale Blo.

Hunger, Flora housekeeper R1 Dunbridge Web 3.

Hunger, Fred carpenter R1 Dunbridge Web 3.

Hunger, Henry farmer O 55a 2h 6c R1 Dunbridge Web 3.

Hunger, John farm laborer R1 Dunbridge Web 3.

Hunger, Wm. stove crusher R1 Dunbridge Web 3.

Hunlock, Jacob (son P. M.) student Hoytsville Jac.

Hunlock, P. M. (Diantha) 4 ch blacksmith O H&L Hoytsville Jac.

Hunlock, W. L. 3 ch butcher O H&L 6h Main St Bloomdale Blo B & Ind tels.

Hunt, Ada 3 ch canvasser O H&L Prairie Depot Mon.

Hunt, Albert E. (son J. E.) farmer R3 North Baltimore Blo 27.

Hunt, Clyde E. (son J. E.) farmer R3 North Baltimore Blo 27.

Hunt, Jacob (Almeda) 5 ch laborer O H&L Hatton Per 84.

Hunt, John (Sarah) 1 ch farmer O 12a 4h 2c R1 Prairie Depot Mon 13.

Hunt, J. E. (Linie) 4 ch oil pumper T H&L 2h 2c R3 North Baltimore Blo 27.

Hunt, Nelson (May) 1 ch section foreman T H&L Bell St Bradner Mon.

111

Hunt, Wilson Bradner Mon.

Hunt, W. H. (Hattie) 2 ch farmer T 80a 2h 5c R3 North Baltimore Hen 113 Ind tel.

Hunter, Lorin (Ida M.) 7 ch farmer O 336a R1 Hoytsville Jac 96.

Hunter, Steven W. (Susan) 1 ch ret O H&L Custar Mil.

HUNTER, WM. D. (Fern) 3 ch farmer T 80a WOS 4h 1c R1 Grand Rapids Gr Rs 4 Ind tel.

HUNTER, W. D. poultry breeder R1 Grand Rapids 4.

HUNTER, W. W. (S. B.) 3 ch farmer O 60a 5h 3c R2 Weston Wes 4.

Huntsman, Herman (Hattie) 4 ch farmer O 35a 2h 3c R2 Perrysburg Mid 1 B tel.

Hurd, Z. T. (Elizabeth) farmer T 80a 4h 2c R1 Deshler Jac 22.

Hurrel, Clifford T. (son W. A.) printer Harrison St Bloomdale Blo.

HURREL, W. A. (Della) 2 ch editor & publisher O paper H&L Harrison St Bloomdale Blo.

Hurrelbrink, Edward (E m m a) 1 ch farmer T 105a 3h 9c R1 Woodville Tro 43 B tel.

Hurrelbrink, John (Carrie) 3 ch farmer T 94a 2h 2c R1 Walbridge Lake 102 Ind tel.

Hurrelbrink, W. A. (Martha) maintainer O 7½a 1h R1 Walbridge Ros 22.

Hurst, Chas. (Allie) farmer O 10a 1h 1c R5 Bowling Green Cen 23 Ind tel.

Hussey, Jno. (Agnes) 6 ch oil gauger O H&L 1h R1 Bays Lib Ind tel.

Hussey, W. J. RD Bays Lib.

Husted, Clarence (Clara) 3 ch poultry business T H&L Oak St Weston Wes.

Husted, Mrs. Emma 5 ch O H&L Silver St Weston B tel.

Husted, Josie (dau Mrs. Emma) school teacher Silver St Weston.

Husted, L. M. blacksmith Hoytsville Jac.

Husted, R. T. (Mary) 2 ch carpenter T H&L Weston Wes.

Huston, Earl (Mary) 1 ch pumper T H&L 1h 1c R1 Rudolph Lib 69 Ind tel.

Huston, J. I. Tontogany Wash.

Hutchinson, Archie (son J. L.) farmer R1 North Baltimore Hen 99.

Hutchinson, Cornelia Milton Center Mil.

Hutchinson, Cash (Mary C.) 1 ch auto liveryman T H&L Grand Rapids Gr Rs Ind tel.

Hutchinson, H. W. Grand Rapids Gr Rs.

Hutchinson, Jacob 5 ch ret O H&L cor East & Caldwell Sts Bradner Mon.

Hutchison, J. C. (Eulalia) 3 ch farmer O 97a 2h 7c Deshler Jac 5 B tel.

Hutchinson, J. L. (Etta) 6 ch farmer T 160a 8h 3c R1 North Baltimore Hen 99.

Hutchinson, J. N. (Lucy) 2 ch wagon maker O H&L N Main St Bradner Mon.

Hutchinson, May (dau J. L.) housekeeper R1 North Baltimore Hen 99.

HUTCHINSON, P. (Cornelia) 5 ch ret farmer O H&L Milton Center Mil.

Hutchison, Ray D. (Alta) 1 ch farmer O 80a 9h 5c R4 Deshler Jac 18 B tel.

HUTCHINSON, R. (Mary) 2 ch glass worker O HL 1h 1c R1 North Baltimore Hen 109.

Hutchison, Wm. glove & mitten fac cor Caldwell & East Sts Bradner Mon.

Hutton, Claude R1 Bradner Mon 15 B tel.

Hutton, James (Emma) 6 ch farmer T 165a 5h 5c R1 Bradner Mon 15 B tel.

Hutton, John (Phila) 2 ch laborer O H&L 1h 1c Prairie Depot Mon.

HUTTON, ROBT. (Minnie) 3 ch farmer O 210a 7h 25c R1 Bradner Mon 59.

Hyde, Jennie housekeeper O H&L Prairie Depot Mon.

Hyte, S. A. Portage Lib.

Hyter, S. C. Bradner Mon.

Ice, W. E. (Katie) 2 ch minister Garfield St Bloomdale Blo B & Ind tels.

ICKES, ALBERT (Linda) 2 ch farmer O 120a 10h 9c R1 Bloomdale Blo 55 B & Ind tels.

Ickes, Levi (Phoebe) farmer O 80a 1h 2c R2 Pemberville Web 25.

Ickes, Louise M. (dau Albert) R1 Bloomdale Blo 55 B & Ind tels.

Ickes, L. C. (Laura) 1 ch farmer T 122a 4h 7c R2 Pemberville Web 25 Ind tel.

Ickes, Mildred E. (dau Albert) R1 Bloomdale Blo 55 B & Ind tels.

Ickes, Parker A. (son Albert) R1 Bloomdale Blo 55 B & Ind tels.

Ickes, Wm. (Ada) 4 ch real estate O H&L cor Caldwell & Stahl Sts Bradner Mon B tel.

Ickles, W. A. farmer O 96a 3h 6c R1 Bowling Green Pla 12 Ind tel.

Iler, J. A. (Leona) 4 ch general store T H&L R2 Prairie Depot Por 114 Ind tel.

Iles, Jay C. Walbridge Ros.

IMBROCK, REV. H. (Emmilie) 2 ch minister T H&L 1h R4 Bowling Green Cen 105.

Imerson, H. H. (Kate) 1 ch fisherman O H&L Grand Rapids Gr Rs.

IMMEL, JOHN I. R1 Bradner.

Indlkofer, B. (Catherine) 3 ch manager elevator O H&L W Main St Weston Ind tel.

Ingerson, Henry (Mary) carpenter 4 ch O 60a 6c Latchie Lake 95 B tel.

INGRAHAM, O. B. (Sarah) 6 ch oil worker T H&L Cygnet Blo 6.

Ingraham, Plate (Florence) farmer Portage Por 3.

Ink, Samuel 5 ch day laborer O H&L Custar Mil.

Inman, Sarah A. RD North Baltimore Hen.

Inman, Theodore (Kathryn) 2 ch sailor O H&L 5th St Perrysburg Pbg B tel.

INSTONE, WM. (Rose) 4 ch oil worker guager O 17a 1h R1 Portage Lib 59 Ind tel.

Irean, Etta 2 ch O H&L 1c Second St Portage Por.

Irelan, John (Effie) 1 ch T Cygnet Hen 115.

Irelan, Mrs. Rose R2 Custar Lib 22.

Ireland, A. Blanch Custar Mil.

Ireland, Eman Risingsun Mon.

Ireland, J. M. (Emma) barber O H&L 3c Risingsun Mon.

Ireland, Mrs. Sarah 5h 3c R1 Rudolph Lib 109 Ind tel.

Irick, Frank (Emma) 3 ch laborer T H&L Bradner Mon.

Irwin, Harriet P. Tontogany Wash.

Irwin, S. L. (Hattie) hardware. O H&L Tontogany Wash Ind tel.

Irwin, William (Debbie) 5 ch farmer O 3a 2h 1c Weston Wes 42.

Isabell, H. (Nettie) 5 ch farmer O 20a 2h 1c R1 Luckey Tro 27.

Isabell, John (Clara) plumber O H&L Vine St Pemberville Fre.

Isabell, Lester (Nancy) 3 ch railroader O H&L Walbridge Lake.

Isabelle, Roscoe (Ada) 2 ch railroadman T H&L Walbridge Lake.

Isbell, Hiram Luckey Tro.

Isch, Edwin (Lorinda) 2 ch farmer O 40a 4h 6c R1 Walbridge Lake 11 B tel.

Isch, Frank L. (Hattie) 3 ch farmer O 113a 3h 8c R1 Walbridge Lake 13 Ind tel.

Isch, F. J. (Laura) 3 ch farmer O 40a 3h 3c R1 Walbridge Lake 9 Ind tel.

Isch, John (Rosetta) commissioner O 80a 1h R1 Walbridge Lake 11 Ind tel.

Ishell, Roscoe Walbridge Lake.

Jackson, D. E. (Nancy) ret O H&L 1h 1c Prairie Depot Mon.

Jackson, Harry J. (Ethel) 1 ch farmer T 102a 3h 1c R2 Deshler Jac 2.

Jackson, John (Effie) painter O H&L Millbury Lake.

Jackson, William (Lydia) 5 ch farmer T 172a 8h 7c R2 Deshler Jac 4 B tel.

Jacobs, Carrie R1 Perrysburg Pbg.

Jacobs, Elsie (dau Fred) housekeeper R1 Luckey Tro 53.

Jacobs, Fred laborer lives with Julia H. Milton Center Mil.

Jacobs, Fred (Mary) 12 ch farmer T 149a 8h 6c R1 Luckey Tro 53 B tel.

Jacobs, Frederick (son Fred) laborer R1 Luckey Tro 53 B tel.

JACOBS, GEO. F. (Mary) 4 ch farmer T 20a 2h 1c R1 Luckey Tro 67.

JACOBS, HERMAN (Ada) thresher T H&L Luckey Tro Ind tel.

Jacobs, John (Emma) contractor O 3a 1h R3 Perrysburg Pbg 82.

Jacobs, John (Mary) 4 ch farmer & thresher O 60a 6h 5c R1 Luckey Tro 89 B tel.

Jacobs, Julia H. 2 ch ret O H&L Milton Center Mil.

Jacobs, Norman (son John) laborer R1 Luckey Tro 89 B tel.

Jacobs, Sam (son John) R1 Luckey Tro 89 B tel.

James, Agnes Rudolph Lib 94.

James, A. E. (Ida M.) farmer O 53a 2h 2c R3 Perrysburg Pbg 74 Ind tel.

Secrets.

James, Byron E. Bradner Mon.
James, C. D. (Hattie) 3 ch postmaster O H&L N Main St Bradner Mon.
James, Detruva Millbury Lake.
James, Henry (Emma) 3 ch Overland worker O H&L Rudolph Lib 94.
James, H. K. (Maude) 1 ch farm mgr R1 Custar Jac 88.
James, J. O. poultryman & gardener O 12a 1h Bairdstown Blo 40 Ind tel.
James, Mrs. Philena East St Bradner Mon B tel.
James, Thomas painter O H&L W Caldwell St Bradner Mon.
Jameson, Edith (dau Milan) housekeeper Dowling Web 1 B tel.
Jameson, Julius (son Milan) farmer Dowling Web 1 B tel.
Jameson, Merritt (son Milan) farmer Dowling Web 1 B tel.
Jameson, Milan (Althea) 2 ch farmer T 120a 3h 2c Dowling Web 1 B tel.
Jannas, Simon (Anna) 2 ch laborer T H&L R1 Haskins Mid 38.
Janney, Wm. P. implement dealer bds Prairie Mon B tel.
Jansen, Jno. B. Dunbridge Mid.
Jansen, M. G. farmer O 60a 2h 4c R2 Dunbridge Pbg 21.
Jaques, J. S. (Sarah) 4 ch section foreman T H&L Pemberville Fre 40.
Jarrett, I. H. (Frances) 5 ch shoemaker T H&L Lime City Pbg 121.
Jarvis, Edw. machinist O H&L Caldwell St Bradner Mon.
JEFFERS, ALBERT Grand Rapids.
Jeffers, Howard engineer O H&L Tontogany Wash.
Jeffrey, George farmer O 19½a R1 Walbridge Lake 13.
Jeffrey, James farmer O 52a 2h 3c R1 Walbridge Lake 13 Ind tel.
Jeffrey, James (Bessie) 4 ch laborer O H&L Weston.
Jeffrey, Jasper 9 ch Clark St .Weston.
Jeffrey, Wesley (Anna) farmer O 40a R1 Walbridge Lake 13.
Jemison, E. H. (Edna) oil pumper T R1 North Baltimore Hen 46.
Jenings, Geo. 1 ch farmer O H&L 4h 2c Grand Rapids Gr Rs.
Jenkins, Mrs. 6 ch housekeeper T H&L Pemberville Fre.
Jennings, Cary Grand Rapids Gr Rs.
JENNINGS, GEO. W. Grand Rapids Gr Rs.
Jennings, Jos. (Annie) 2 ch ret carpenter T H&L 1h Caldwell St Bradner Mon B tel.
Jenny, W. P. Prairie Depot Mon.
Jenos, Geo. Haskins Mid.
Jenos, Simon Haskins Mid.

Jenson, Jennie housekeeper O H&L Haskins Mid B tel.
Jenssen, J. C. Perrysburg Pbg.
Jerrett, M. U. (Nellie) telephone manager O H&L Main St Perrysburg Pbg B tel.
Jewel, C. E. Weston Wes.
Jewel, Grant cattle RD Mermill Por.
Jewel, Samuel RD Bowling Green Pla.
Jewel, T. A. Weston Wes.
JEWELL, JOHN (Julia) 3 ch farmer T 94a 5h 4c R4 Bowling Green Por 5 Ind tel.
Jewell, Melinda 3 ch Center St Weston.
Jewell, S. D. (Minnie) 1 ch contractor O H&L Center St Weston Ind tel.
Jezzard, Fred (Sarah) grocery O H&L Perrysburg Pbg B tel.
Jezzard, Gilbert RD Haskins Mid.
Jimerson, Lloyd Hoytsville Jac.
Jimison, Allen R4 Bowling Green B tel.
Jimison, A. H. (Clarinda) farmer O 40a 1h 3c R1 North Baltimore Hen 43 B & Ind tels.
Jimison, B. R. (Clara) 1 ch traveling salesman T H&L Hickory St Pemberville Fre Ind tel.
Jimison, Carl (Susie) 4 ch carpenter O H&L Hoytsville Jac.
Jimison, Clark (Dortha) 2 ch farmer T 139a 6h 8c R1 Pemberville Fre 69 B tel.
Jimison, Cora 2 ch O 23a 3h 1c R1 Portage Por 51.
Jimison, D. (Rachel) 1 ch farmer T 80a R3 Bowling Green Pla 87.
Jimison, J. J. (Elnora) 4 ch farmer O 50a 8h 6c R2 North Baltimore Jac 119 Ind tel.
Jimison, L. H. (Lilly) 1 ch decorator T H&L Hoytsville Jac.
Jimison, P. H. RD North Baltimore Hen.
Jimison, Wesley (Cora) 8 ch farmer 125a 6h 4c R1 Pemberville Cen 114 B tel.
JIMISON, WILLIAM (Emma) farmer O 80a 4h 6c R1 Tontogany Wash 86 Ind tel.
Jinks, Geo (Lulu) 1 ch farmer T H&L R1 Fostoria Per 122.
Jizzard, J. E. (Emma) farmer O 51a 2h 2c R1 Haskins Mid 91 B tel.
Joehlin, George Jacob (Ernstine) farmer O 60a 4h 3c R2 Curtice Ros 34.
Joehlin, Lena (dau G. J.) R2 Curtice Ros 34.
Joehlin, Mary (dau G. J.) R2 Curtice Ros 34.
Joehlin, William (son G. J.) R2 Curtice Ros 34.
Johann, Charles (Lorett) 2 ch farmer T 100a 5h 2c R2 Custar Mil 33 B tel.

JOHANN, JOSEPH (Emma) 7 ch farmer O 75a 3h 4c Custar Mil 91.

Johann, M. (Catherine) 3 ch farmer O 85a 7h 7c R1 Custar Mil 19 B tel.

Jobaun, Netta Custar Mil.

Johann, Peter (Lizzie) 6 ch farmer O 120a 4h 13c R2 Custar Mil 45 B tel.

Johann, Philip (son M.) fireman R1 Custar Mil 19.

Johanssen, Rev. J. A. (Eliza) 3 ch preacher 1h R3 Pemberville Tro 54 Ind tel.

Johanssen, J. M. Pemberville Tro.

Johanssen, Marth (dau J. A.) housekeeper R3 Pemberville Tro 54 Ind tel.

Johanssen, Paula (dau J. A.) housekeeper R3 Pemberville Tro 54 Ind tel.

Johanssen, Winifred (dau J. A.) housekeeper R3 Pemberville Tro 54 Ind tel.

Johns, George 5 ch teamster O H&L 2h 1c Caldwell St Bradner Mon.

Johnson, Mrs. A. B. ret O H&L Millbury Lake 76.

Johnson, A. D. (Rebecca) farmer T 5h 7c Bairdstown Blo 40 Ind tel.

Johnson, Albert L. Prairie Depot Mon.

Johnson, A. M. (Belna) 1 ch section hand O H&2Lots R3 Prairie Depot Mon 50.

Johnson, A. P. Bairdstown Blo.

Johnson, Belle Prairie Depot Mon.

JOHNSON, MRS. B. A. Box 104 Bradner.

Johnson, B. F. Walbridge Lake.

Johnson, Charles (Mary) 5 ch farming O 60a 3h 5c R3 Perrysburg Pbg 126.

Johnson, Clarence laborer O 12a R3 Perrysburg Pbg 77.

Johnson, Clifford (Hazel) 1 ch section hand T H&L Taylor St Weston Wes.

Johnson, Cyrus (Angeline) farmer O 43a 2h 1c R2 Bowling Green Mid 44 B tel.

Johnson, C. E. (Lizzie) 2 ch junk buyer O H&L Sycamore St Weston Wes.

Johnson, C. G. RD North Baltimore Hen.

Johnson, C. M. (Elizabeth) 1 ch switchman O H&L Walbridge Lake B tel.

Johnson, D. J. R1 Bowling Green Lib 55 Ind tel.

Johnson, Earl RD Rudolph Lib.

Johnson, Edna (dau W. J.) Rudolph Lib 81 Ind tel.

Johnson, Edna R. R3 Perrysburg Pbg 77.

Johnson, Elizabeth RD North Baltimore Hen.

Johnson, Emery (Laura) 3 ch farmer O 40a 3h 2c R1 Walbridge Lake 20 B tel.

Johnson, Ferdinand 3 ch ret O H&2Lots Main St Perrysburg Pbg.

Johnson, Frank (Maggie) 2 ch farmer O 20a 2h R1 Walbridge Lake 26 Ind tel.

Johnson, Frank A. (Nora) 2 ch blacksmith O H&L 1h Weston Wes.

JOHNSON, GEORGE (Ella) poultry O H& 9Lots Main St Jerry City Blo 79 Ind tel.

Johnson, Henry Hoytsville Jac.

Johnson, Henry E. (Grace) 2 ch carpenter O H&L Hoytsville Jac.

Johnson, Hubert (son Clarence) laborer R3 Perrysburg Pbg 77.

Johnson, Ira (Clara) 3 ch contractor O 44a 1h 2c R1 Walbridge Lake 100 Ind tel.

Johnson, John 5 ch oil worker O H&L Portage Lib 90 Ind tel.

Johnson, J. H. (Julia) 2 ch laborer O H&L Dowling Mid.

Johnson, John T. (Angeline) 6 ch farming O 150a 2h 4c R2 Dunbridge Pbg 37.

JOHNSON, JOHN W. (Belle) farmer O 50a 1h 2c R1 Prairie Depot Mon 101.

Johnson, Miss Laura E. R3 Perrysburg Pbg 77.

Johnson, Levi (Lucy) farmer O 14a 1h 1c R5 Bowling Green Cen 23.

Johnson, Lew (Nora) 1 ch farmer O 80a 2h 7c R3 Bowling Green Web 8 Ind tel.

Johnson, Loy (Della) 3 ch farmer T 35a 2h 2c R1 Walbridge Lake 27 Ind tel.

Johnson, L. M. (Daisy) 1 ch farmer T 43a 1h R2 Bowling Green Mid 44.

Johnson, Metta 3 ch farming O 40a 2h 3c R1 Custar Mil 19.

Johnson, N. (Barbara N.) 1 ch ret O H&L Caldwell St Bradner Mon.

Johnson, Otto (son W. J.) Rudolph Lib 81 Ind tel.

Johnson, O. C. (Maude) packer T H&L R3 Perrysburg Pbg 77.

Johnson, Ralph Perrysburg Pbg.

Johnson, Roy Walbridge Lake.

Johnson, R. W. Tontogany Wash.

Johnson, Willard (Dorothy) clerk in RR office T H&L Walbridge Lake.

Johnson, W. F. RD Dunbridge Pbg.

Johnson, W. R. (Sarah) gardener O 15a 2h R2 Weston Pla 6 Ind tel.

JOHNSTON, ALVIN R1 Custar.

Johnston, A. W. (Rosa) farmer O 80a 3h 5c R3 Weston Wes 53.

JOHNSTON, B. (Cora E.) 2 ch farmer T 120a 4h 23c R1 Fostoria Per 121 Ind tel.

Johnston, Charles (Myrtle) 1 ch conductor T 6th St Perrysburg Pbg.

Johnston, C. F. (Jessie) 3 ch farmer T 120a 1h R2 Prairie Depot Por 89.

Johnston, Dora Weston Mil.

Johnston, Emma ret O 120a R1 Fostoria Per 121 Ind tel.

Johnston, Floyd (Daisy) 1 ch mail carrier O H&L 1c Russ St Weston Ind tel.

Johnston, Geo. W. (son Mattie B.) farmer R1 Custar Mil 23 B & Ind tels.

Johnston, Grant (Sadie) farmer O 40a ·2h 4c R1 Portage Por 51.

Johnston, Henrietta Haskins Mid.

Johnston, Henry (Sadie E.) oil man pumper T H&L 1h R3 North Baltimore Blo 16.

Johnston, H. J. Tontogany Wash.

Johnston, John, Jr. RD Bowling Green Por.

Johnston, Mattie B. 2 ch farmer O 80a R1 Custar Mil 23 B & Ind tels.

JOHNSTON, RAY A. (son Mattie B.) farmer 7h 4c R1 Custar Mil 23 B & Ind tels.

JOHNSTON, S. A. (Rosemond) 2 ch farmer T 200a 8h 2c R1 Weston Mil 57 Ind tel.

Johnston, S. W. (Cynthia) 6 ch farmer T 80a 4h 6c R2 Bowling Green Pla 56 Ind tel.

Johnston, Wm. (Ella) 2 ch farmer O 80a 3h 1c R4 Bowling Green Cen 102 Ind tel.

Johnston, Wm. A. Weston Wes.

JOHNSTON, W. J. (Elizabeth) 2 ch supt Ohio Oil Co O 240a Rudolph Lib 87 Ind tel.

JOLLEY, B. A. (Iona) 3 ch farmer T 160a 8h 2c R1 Weston Mil 61 Ind tel.

Jones, Albert (May) 3 ch farmer T 80a 3h 3c R1 Rudolph Lib 33 Ind tel.

Jones, Alvia Pemberville Fre.

Jones, Allen H. farm laborer T H&L 40a 2h R3 North Baltimore Blo 21.

Jones, A. K. (Vida) 2 ch minister Garfield St Bloomdale Blo.

Jones, Ballard W. (Genna) 5 ch farmer T 240a 8h 35c R3 North Baltimore Blo 21 B & Ind tels.

Jones, Blanch Evans Bradner Mon.

Jones, Chas. RD North Baltimore Hen.

Jones, Cornelius (Ella) 4 ch farmer O 5a T 75a 2h 6c Rudolph Lib 81.

Jones, Coy D. (Nettie) 3 ch pumper O 60a 1h 3c R2 Bradner Mon 15 B tel.

Jones, C. H. 1 ch farmer T 70a 4h R1 Jerry City Por 68.

Jones, C. L. (Emma) wagon maker T H&L Haskins Mid.

Jones, C. V. Bradner Mon.

Jones, Daisy dressmaker R1 North Baltimore Hen 99.

Jones, Dan (Almina) 1 ch farmer T 80a 4h 2c R1 North Baltimore Hen 99.

JONES, ELMER D. (Violet) 3 ch music teacher O 18a 1c R1 Prairie Depot Mon 101.

Jones, E. J. Weston Wes.

Jones, E. L. Haskins Mid.

Jones, F. E. (Nanie B.) 3 ch general store & postmaster H&L Main st Jerry City Por Ind tel.

Jones, Mrs. Fred M. druggist O store & goods Rudolph Lib 81 Ind tel.

Jones, Geo. (Mae) 5 ch laborer O H&L Frasen St Bairdstown Blo.

Jones, G. F. (Cora) 1 ch ret 70a 1h 2c R1 Custar Mil 98.

Jones, Henry cattle RD Jerry City Por.

Jones, Hobart (son Ora H.) barber & student Custar Mil.

Jones, H. H. (Bertha) 1 ch assistant cashier O H&L Taylor St Weston B tel.

Jones, H. M. RD Haskins Mid.

Jones, John 4 ch ret farmer O H&L Evans St Bradner Mon.

Jones, J. E. (Emma) 4 ch garage O H&L Weston Wes Ind tel.

Jones, Leona (dau J. E.) Center St Weston.

Jones, L. D. RD North Baltimore Hen.

Jones, Myra O H&L Taylor Weston Ind tel.

Jones, M. (Blanche) 3 ch farmer T 80a 4h 2c R2 Bowling Green Wash 24 Ind tel.

Jones, Omer J. (Emma) farmer O 110a N Main St Weston.

Jones, Ora H. (Minnie A.) 7 ch barber O H&L Custar Mil.

Jones, Robert (Mary) 1 ch laborer O H&L Rossford Ros.

Jones, Ruth (dau Ora H.) housekeeper Custar Mil.

JONES, S. E. Jerry City Por B & Ind tels.

Jones, S. K. (Sarah) 1 ch farmer T 40a 3h 3c R1 Bradner Mon 30.

Jones, Wm. A. (Barbara E.) 1 ch farmer O 165a 6h 11c Randolph St Bairdstown Blo Ind tel.

Jones, W. H. (Creath) 3 ch farmer T 75a 3h 4c R1 Bowling Green Pla 42.

Jordan, S. E. (Ora) 1 ch farmer R1 Bowling Green Pla 67.

Jorden, E. P. (Julia) 3 ch laborer T H&L Haskins Mid.

JORDON, O. C. Rossford Ros.

Joseph, Alfred L. (Clara) 3 ch farmer O 40a 4h 4c R4 Bowling Green Cen 111.

Joseph, Charles (Belle) 1 ch farmer T 3h 3c R5 Bowling Green Cen 61 B tel.

Joseph, Frank (Mary) 4 ch farmer O 160a 5h 14c R1 Luckey Tro 79 Ind tel.

Joseph, F. J. (Margaret) 1 ch farmer T H&L Millbury Lake.

Joseph, G. F. (Lydia) 2 ch station agt implement dealer O H&L LeMoyne Tro Ind tel.

Joseph, Lewis (Frances V.) 7 ch farmer O 120a 4h 6c R5 Bowling Green Cen 110 B tel.

Joseph, Mary Luckey Tro.

Josett, Frank RD North Baltimore Hen.

Joster, Mrs. Ed. Prairie Depot.

Jourdon, M. C. Prairie Depot Mon.

Joyce, H. S. laborer bds Dowling Mid 76.

Judd, B. W. (Alice) 3 ch farmer O 160a 6h 16c R1 North Baltimore Hen 40 Ind tel.

Judson, A. D. (Harriett) carpenter O 50a 1h 2c R1 Grand Rapids Gr Rs 14 Ind tel.

Judson, H. G. (Elizabeth) laborer O H&L Grand Rapids Gr Rs Ind tel.

Judson, Joe (Anna) 1 ch farmer O 70a 4h 11c Grand Rapids Gr Rs 21 Ind tel.

Judson, J. (Ella) 1 ch farmer T 240a 2h 1c R1 Hoytsville Jac 106 B tel.

Judson, J. R. (Elizabeth A.) 4 ch ret farmer O 53a 1h R1 Bowling Green Lib 51 B tel.

Judson, L. D. Grand Rapids Gr Rs.

Judson, W. C. (Anna) 3 ch farmer T 53a 5h 5c R1 Bowling Green Pla 78 B tel.

Juergens, Bertha (dau Chas. A.) housekeeper R1 Luckey Tro 86 B tel.

Juergens, Chas. A. (Anna) 6 ch farmer T 90a 5h 8c R1 Luckey Tro 86 B tel.

Juergens, Elsie (dau Chas. A.) housekeeper R1 Luckey Tro 86 B tel.

Juergens, Mabel (dau Chas. A.) housekeeper R1 Luckey Tro 86 B tel.

Juhos, C. G. Rossford Ros.

Julien, E. S. RD North Baltimore Hen.

Juliet, Chas. (Mary) motorman O H&L 5th St Perrysburg Pbg.

June, I. F. Cygnet Blo.

June, James (Clara) 5 ch oil gauger T H&L 1h Main St Jerry City Por Ind tel.

June, W. E. (Pearl) 2 ch oil worker T H&L Walbridge St Cygnet Blo Ind tel.

Junk, John (Mary) 4 ch farmer O 42½a 4h 3c R1 Custar Mil 18.

Junk, Katherin (dau John) housekeeper R1 Custar Mil 18.

Junkins, C. L. (Inex) 2 ch farmer O 95a 3h 11c R3 Weston Mil 84.

Junkins, Ernest (son E. W.) farm hand R3 Weston Mil 87.

Junkins, E. W. (Anna) 6 ch farmer O 200a 18h 8c R3 Weston Mil 87 Ind tel.

Junkins, P. C. (Sarah) 3 ch farmer O 160a 5h 17c R2 Weston Wes 17 Ind tel.

Junkins, R. S. Weston Wes.

Junkins, T. P. (Catherine) 2 ch farmer O 60a 3h 1c R3 Weston Mil Ind tel.

Junkins, Zardie (Gladys) farm hand R3 Weston Mil 87.

Jurgens, Chas. Luckey Tro.

Kacheley, M. (Anna) 3 ch ret O H&L 1c Grand Rapids Gr Rs.

Kaeding, Geo. RD Bowling Green Pla.

Kaemming, Harmon J. Luckey Tro.

Kaemming, Henry (Anna) farmer T 80a 1h 1c R1 Luckey Tro 67.

Kaetzel, Ed. cattle RD Mermill Por.

Kagy, Henry (Rena) 2 ch farmer T 95a 4h 2c R4 Bowling Green Por 43 Ind tel.

Kahlonberg, Henry H., Jr. (Carrie) 3 ch farmer T 62a 2h 6c R3 Pemberville Fre 15.

Kahnbach, O. M. Millbury Lake.

Kahrer, Joseph (Maud) engineer T H&L Walbridge Lake.

Kaiser, Oscar (Augusta) 1 ch O H&L 1h Stony Ridge Tro.

Kaiser, Peter 4 ch farmer T 40a 2h 4c Bradner Mon 20 B tel.

Kale, James carpenter O H&L Union St Cygnet Blo 6.

Kale, J. M. (Liberta) 5 ch farmer O 123a 6h 6c RD Custar Lib 32 Ind tel.

Kale, Martin R2 Custar Lib 32 Ind tel.

Kalinbrink, Henry 1 ch farmer O 80a 2h 3c R1 Perrysburg Pbg 24.

Kalmbach, Fred (Pauline) 1 ch grain & coal O H&L 2h RD North Baltimore Hen Ind tel.

Kalmbach, Kate ret O H&L Millbury Lake.

Kalmbach, Oscar (Hazel) 2 ch electrician O H&L Millbury Lake.

Kander, C. G. C. Hoytsville Hen.

Kander, Harry RD North Baltimore Hen.

Kapp, Chas. (Katharine) farmer O 40a 3h 6c R1 E Toledo Lake 68.

Kapp, Fred C. (son Chas. farmer R1 Millbury Lake 68 Ind tel.

Kapp, John (Amelia) 6 ch farmer O 40a 4h 4c R1 E Toledo Lake 68.

Karnes, J. H. (Angeline) 4 ch farmer O 20a 2h 1c R3 Pemberville Fre 27 B tel.

Karns, Henry (Cora) 2 ch farmer O 48a 4h 3c R1 Hoytsville Jac 77 B tel.

Karns, Jess farm laborer R1 Custar Mil 26 Ind tel.

Karns, Menzo 1 ch farmer O 25a 2h Prairie Depot Mon 50.

Karns, Raymond (son Henry) farmer RD Hoytsville Jac 77.

KARRICK, C. E. (Lola) 1 ch farmer T H&L 1c R2 Bloomdale Per 31.

KASEMAN, HENRY (Theresa) 1 ch farmer T H&L 1h 1c R3 Prairie Depot Mon 12.

Katon, Clyde (Gertrude) 2 ch farmer O H&L 30a farm 3h 3c Grand Rapids Gr Rs Ind tel.

Kauffman, Frank 3 ch laborer O H&L Hoytsville Jac.

Kauke, Edward (son Henry) farmer R1 Portage Por 38 Ind tel.

KAUKE, HENRY (Dean) 2 ch farmer T 120a 5h 2c R1 Portage Por 38 Ind tel.

Kavanagh, Mrs. Mary T H&L Walbridge Ave Cygnet Blo Ind tel.

Kavanagh, Mike oil worker T H&L Walbridge Ave Cygnet Blo Ind tel.

Kazmaier, Albert (Jane) 4 ch farmer T 80a 3h 5c R1 Perrysburg Pbg 14 B tel.

KAZMAIER, ANDREW (Mary) 1 ch farmer O 40a 3h 2c R2 Perrysburg Mid 15 B tel.

Kazmaier, Charles (Alice) 4 ch farmer O 80a 5h 6c R2 Bowling Green Pla 98 B tel.

KAZMAIER, F. C. (Emma) 3 ch farmer O 57a 3h 6c Lime City Pbg 92 B tel.

Kazmaier, F. H. (Anna) 3 ch farming O 133a 7h 5c R2 Perrysburg Pbg 6 B tel.

Kazmaier, George (Christina) 2 ch farmer O H&L 2h Main St Perrysburg Pbg.

Kazmaier, Geo. J. (Emma) 2 ch farmer O 42a 5h 3c R1 Perrysburg Pbg 14.

Kazmaier, Harvey (Minnie) traveling man O H&L 2nd St Perrysburg Pbg B tel.

Kazmaier, H. A. (Katie) meat market O H&L 1h Perrysburg Pbg B tel.

Kazmaier, John (Mary) ret O H&L Front St Perrysburg Pbg B tel.

Kazmaier, John W. (Mazie) 3 ch farmer T 54 3h 3c R7 Perrysburg Pbg 14 B tel.

KAZMAIER, MERLIN farmer R2 Perrysburg Pbg 14.

Kazmaier, Russel (Julia) 3 ch laborer O H Main St Perrysburg Pbg B tel.

Kazmaier, R. F. (Lulu) 1 ch grocery T H&L Perrysburg Pbg B tel.

Kazmaier, Wm. (Minnie) painter O H&L 6th & Main Sts Perrysburg Pbg.

Kazmaier, Wm. (Sara) farmer O H&L Indiana Ave Perrysburg Pbg.

Kazmaier, W. A. (May) 2 ch farmer O 80a 4h 12c R1 Perrysburg Pbg 147 Ind tel.

Kearn, Ray 7 ch laborer Losee St Cygnet Blo.

Kechele, E. C. Pemberville Web.

Kechele, Edw. C. Pemberville Fre.

Keckley, Lewis (Florence) 1 ch dry goods clerk O H&L Grand Rapids Gr Rs Ind tel.

Kecheley, M. Grand Rapids Gr Rs.

KEELER, C. M. (Anna) ret O H&L 1h Haskins Mid B tel.

Keeler, Gurdon Haskins Mid.

KEELER, HENRY (Rosie) 3 ch farmer T 104a 4h 2c R1 Tontogany Wash 76 Ind tel.

Keeler, Martin (Mary) saloonkeeper O H&L Milton Center Mil.

Keeler, R. O. laborer T H&L Milton Center Mil.

KEENER, MRS. JENNIE milling O mill Weston B & Ind tels. See adv.

Keer, William (Ella) merchant O H&L 40a farm Grand Rapids Gr Rs Ind tel.

Keeran, Mrs. S. E. RD Hoytsville Jac.

Keeton, W. (Emma) 1 ch T H&L Longley Per 103.

Kefler, Wm. F. (Pearl) 6 ch farmer O 100a 5h 4c R1 Lime City Perrysburg 45 Ind tel.

Kehlnbrink, Henry R1 Perrysburg Pbg.

KEHRER, CHRIST farmer T 60a 3h 4c R1 Lime City Lake 23.

Kehrer, Joe Walbridge Lake.

Keiffer, Frances E. (dau John R.) milliner Milton Center Mil 93.

Keiffer, Harry (Bertha) 2 ch cement worker T H&L 3rd St Perrysburg Pbg B tel.

Keiffer, John R. (Martha E.) 2 ch farmer O 46a 2h 3c Milton Center Mil 93.

Keil, Edward (Julia) hardware O H&L Pemberville Fre B tel.

Keil, H. H. Weston Wes.

Keil, Rhea (dau Edward) Pemberville Fre.

Keil, Ruth (dau Edward) Pemberville Fre.

Keiser, D. L. (M. E.) pumper O H&L Caldwell St Bradner Mon B tel.

Keiser, Peter Bradner Mon.

Keith, Thelma (dau W. D.) R1 Walbridge Ros 22.

Keith, W. D. (Laura) 1 ch boilermaker O H&L R1 Walbridge Ros 22.

Keldo, Maggie (ret) O H&L 6th St Perrysburg Pbg.

Keldon, Robert ret O H&L 6th St Perrysburg Pbg.

Kellar, Louis (Lena) 5 ch farmer R1 LeMoyne Lake 34.

Kellar, Willie farm hand R1 LeMoyne Tro 34 B tel.

Kellberger, F. (Barbara) 4 ch farmer O 50a 2h 2c R2 Perrysburg Mid 14.

Keller, Miss Anna housekeeper R1 Walbridge Lake 26.

Keller, August (son Lewis) R1 Tontogany Wash 73.

Keller, A. D. (son F. B.) farmer T 2h 1c R1 Stony Ridge Lake 89 Ind tel.

Keller, C. F. (Emma) farmer O 40a 1h 2c R1 Lime City Pbg 51.

Keller, Frank (Katie) 9 ch farmer O 70a 5h 3c R1 Walbridge Lake 18.

Keller, F. B. (Cora) 2 ch farmer O 122a 3h 16c R1 Walbridge Lake 20 Ind tel.

Keller, Harry Risingsun Mon.

Keller, Henry (son Lewis) farmer R1 Tontogany Wash 73.

Keller, Lewis (Lena) 4 ch farmer O 80a 7h R1 Tontogany Wash 73.

Keller, Mrs. Martin Milton Center Mil.

Keller, O. S. RD Bowling Green Web.

Keller, Rose ret O H&4Ls Locust St Perrysburg Pbg.

Kellermeier, Christina RD Perrysburg Mid.

Kellermier, Miss Clara (dau Mrs. M. C.) housekeeper R2 Dunbridge Mid 65.

Kellermier, Frank (son Mrs. Mary) farmer T 80a 3h 3c R2 Perrysburg Mid 4 B tel.

Kellermier, Joe (Catherine) 4 ch farmer O 40a 3h 3c R2 Perrysburg Mid 10 B tel.

Kellermier, John (Barbara) 2 ch farmer O 40a 4c R2 Perrysburg Mid 11.

KELLERMIER, J. A. (Lucy) 1 ch farmer T 120a 5h 4c R3 Bowling Green Pla 85 Ind tel.

KELLERMIER, J. W. (Clara) 1 ch farmer T 50a 2h 1c Sugar Ridge Mid 63.

Kellermier, Mrs. Mary farmer O 180a R2 Perrysburg Mid 4 B tel.

Kellermier, Max (Anna) 3 ch farmer T 70a 2h 2c R2 Perrysburg Mid 2 B tel.

KELLERMIER, MRS. M. C. 1 ch farmer O 39a 1h 3c R2 Dunbridge Mid 65.

Kellermier, Peter (Frances) farmer T 64a 2h 2c R2 Perrysburg Mid 13.

Kelley, Alba M. (dau Flora) student R2 Perrysburg Mid 2.

Kelley, C. E. (Rockey) 1 ch farmer T 160a 4h 5c R3 North Baltimore Blo 22 Ind tel.

KELLEY, D. C. (Julietta) farmer O 25a 2h 1c R2 Perrysburg Mid 2 B tel.

The Same Row of Apple Trees in Blossom and Fruit.

Kelley, E. E. housekeeper Pemberville Fre Ind tel.

Kelley, Mrs. Flora farmer O 24a 1h 1c R2 Perrysburg Mid 2.

Kelley, Gladys (dau H. R.) Garfield St Bloomdale Blo B & Ind tels.

Kelley, H. R. (Martha) medicine wagon T H&L 2h Garfield St Bloomdale Blo B & Ind tels.

Kelley, H. R. Risingsun Mon.

Kelley, John (Bertha) 1 ch canvasser O H&L West Millgrove Per 69.

Kelley, Lewis (Gertrude) 3 ch laborer O 1a 1h R1 Fostoria Per 112 B tel.

KELLY, JOHN farmer O H&L 1h R2 Bowling Green Pla 86.

Kelly, Ralph (Nora) 2 ch farmer O 40a farms 70a 4h 10c West Millgrove Per 68.

Kelly, Resin ret 400a West Millgrove Per 68.

Kelly, W. S. (Rella M.) 2 ch mail carrier O 20a 1h 4c R1 Bradner Mon 59.

Kelsey, Wade (Aura) 3 ch grocery clerk O 6a 1h R3 Weston Mil 80.

Kemmerling, Emma farming O 12a 1c R2 Weston Wes 25.

Kemner, August Pemberville Fre.

Kemner, Henry (Minnie) 3 ch farmer O 65a 3h 7c R1 Pemberville Fre 63 B tel.

KEMNER, WM. H. (Carrie) 1 ch farmer O 80a 3h 8c R1 Pemberville Fre 58 B tel.

Kempf, Michel Custar Mil.

Kempher, E. P. Prairie Depot Mon.

Kempher, George ret O H&L cor Summer & Oak Sts Weston Wes.

Kempher, K. A. (Delia) farmer T 1h R2 North Baltimore Hen 18.

Kemps, Leo (son Michael) farmer Custar Mil 100.

Kemps, Louise (dau Michael) housekeeper Custar Mil 100.

Kemps, Michael (Magdaline) 8 ch farmer O 60a 3h 4c Custar Mil 100.

Kendall, J. E. Cygnet Blo.

Kenemuth, J. A. RD Rudolph Lib.

KENISTON, A. B. (Anna) farmer T 148a 10h 4c R1 Luckey Tro 80 Ind tel.

Kenner, August (Minnie) farmer T 34a 4h 6c R2 Pemberville Fre 48 B tel.

Kent, J. F. (Eva) ret O H&L Factory St Jerry City Por.

Kepp, Henry (Olme) 3 ch laborer E Walnut St Bloomdale Blo.

Kepp, John laborer O H&L Second St Perrysburg Pbg.

Kepperley, I. T. Perrysburg Pbg.

Keppler, Fred J. Luckey Tro.

Keppler, Wm. R1 Lime City Pbg.

Kern, Clara Luckey Tro.

Kern, G. A. (Trenna) 2 ch pumper O H&L Cadwell St Bradner Mon.

KERN, JAMES N., JR. laborer O ¼a H &L R1 Pemberville Fre.

Kern, Ray Cygnet Blo.

Kerns, H. RD North Baltimore Hen.

Kerr, Miss Allie Rudolph Lib 63 Ind tel.

Kerr, Mrs. Ann ret O H&L Grand Rapids Gr Rs Ind tel.

Kerr, Bert (Dora) 7 ch farmer T 100a 4h 2c R1 Jerry City Por 35 Ind tel.

Kerr, Ed. cattle RD Mermill Por.

KERR, EMERY (Louise) 5 ch farmer T 140a 5h 4c R1 Jerry City Por 28 Ind tel.

KERR, EMMET (Mary) 3 ch farmer T 160a 6h 2c R1 Jerry City Por 30 Ind tel.

Kerr, Florence housekeeper R1 Portage Por 15.

Kerr, Hettie O 20a 3c R1 Rudolph Lib 63 Ind tel.

Kerr, Irvin farmer R1 Portage Por 15.

Kerr, J. B. (Ella) 2 ch farmer T 116a 2h R1 Portage Por 12 Ind tel.

Kerr, J. H. Grand Rapids Gr Rs.

Kerr, T. M. (Marinda) 4 ch farmer T 130a 5h 3c R1 Portage Por 15.

Kerr, W. B. (Elizabeth Jane) O 80a 3h 5c Jerry City Por 70 Ind tel.

Kerr, W. E. Grand Rapids Gr Rs.

Kersey, Emry E. laborer Claron St Cygnet Blo 6.

Kersey, John (Emmy E.) 5 ch teamster O H&L 1h 1c Claron St Cygnet Blo 6.

Kershner, E. D. (Myrtle) 1 ch barber O H&L Haskins Mid 35.

Kessen, Lizzie housekeeper O R2 Pemberville Fre 39.

Kessen, Robert farmer O 78a 5h 1c R2 Pemberville Fre 39.

Kessen, Wm. farmer O R2 Pemberville Fre 39.

Kestler, Mary E. O H&L Main St Bairdstown Blo.

Kestler, Wm. D. (son Mary E.) Bairdstown Blo.

Ketcham, Gertrude M. housekeeper O H &L West Millgrove Per 70.

Ketcham, Mrs. Rosa ret O H&L West Millgrove Per 70.

Ketcham, Richard B. (Olive B.) 3 ch farmer O 103a 5h 5c West Millgrove Per 75 B & Ind tels.

Ketcham, Carl Millbury Lake.

Ketzeline, Floyd farmer 1h R1 Portage Por 14 Ind tel.

Ketzenbarger, Earl W. (Goldie) 2 ch farmer O 95a 7h 2c R3 Bowling Green Cen 21 B tel.

KETZENBARGER, E. L. R4 Bowling Green.

KETZER, FRANK (Tillie) 1 ch machinist T 5a 1h 1c Rossford Pbg 80 Ind tel.

Keys, D. W. (Katherine) farmer O 69a 2h 2c R1 Grand Rapids Gr Rs 9 Ind tel.

Keys, Emory (son G. W.) farmer 4h R2 Prairie Depot Por 77.

Keys, G. W. (Mary E.) 1 ch farmer T 60a 2h 3c R2 Prairie Depot Por 77.

Keys, Viola (dau G. W.) R2 Prairie Depot Por 77.

Kibel, John priest T H&L Front St Perrysburg Pbg B tel.

Kibler, Artie R1 Bowling Green Lib 54 Ind tel.

Kibler, Bernice (dau T. W.) R1 Bowling Green Lib 54 Ind tel.

KIBLER, T. W. (Mary) 3 ch farmer T 105a 3h 6c R1 Bowling Green Lib 54 Ind tel.

Kidd, Donald (Alice) 1 ch laborer O H&L Frankfather Ave Jerry City Por.

Kidd, John S. RD Bowling Green Pla.

KIDD, KENNETH, A. confectionery & ice cream O store Rudolph Lib 81 Ind tel.

KIDD, LAWRENCE A. (Agatha) 1 ch pool room & lunch counter Third St Jerry City Por.

Kidd, John S. (Lillian) 2 ch oil pumper T 40a R2 Bowling Green Pla 55 Ind tel.

Kidd, Ralph (Mable) farm laborer RD Weston Lib 4.

Kidd, Samuel (Myrtle) 4 ch farmer O 40a 2h 6c R1 Bowling Green Pla 8.

Kidney, Ralph Z. Perrysburg Pbg.

Kidwell, C. N. (Mary) 2 ch machinist O 1a Weston Mil 80.

Kiefer, John (Anna) 3 ch farmer O 66a 7h 4c R2 Haskins Mid 89 B tel.

Kiefer, Jos. Haskins Mid.

Kiefer, R. O. farm hand R1 Custar Mil 25 B tel.

Kieffer, Arnold (son D. F.) farm laborer Milton Center Mil.

Kieffer, Candace (dau D. J.) music teacher R2 Custar Mil 34 B tel.

Kieffer, Charles (son Dave) blacksmith helper Milton Center Mil.

Kieffer, D. J. (Elsie) 3 ch farmer O 40a 1h 3c R2 Custar Mil 34 B tel.

Kieffer, D. T. (Bertha) 4 ch ditcher T H&L Milton Center Mil.

KIEFFER, F. M. 4 ch engineer bds Milton Center Mil Ind tel.

Kieffer, Jacob (Sarah) ret O H&L Milton Center Mil.

Kieffer, Melvin (son D. F.) ditcher Milton Center Mil.

Kieffer, Mike (son Mrs. Ula) ret Milton Center Mil.

Kieffer, R. H. (Nellie M.) 3 ch farmer O 60a 3h 2c R1 Weston Mil 54 Ind tel.

Kieffer, S. E. (Cora) farmer T H&L 2h 1c R1 Deshler Jac 9.

Kieffer, Mrs. Ula 2 ch ret O H&L Milton Center Mil.

Kiel, Anna (dau Herman) bookkeeper Walnut St Weston.

Kiel, Frank (son Herman) farmer Walnut St Weston.

Kiel, Harriet (dau Herman) Walnut St Weston.

Kiel, Herman (Wilmoth) 3 ch farming O 70a H&L 4h 1c Walnut St Weston B tel.

Kiel, Wilhelmina Weston Wes.

Kiger, A. P. Hoytsville Jac.

Kiger, Bert (Katie) 1 ch farmer O 53a 2h 1c Cygnet Blo 19 Ind tel.

Kiger, Geo. A. (Nellie Pearl) 1 ch barber O H&L Hoytsville Jac.

KIGER, H. A. (Ida) 1 ch oil worker T Bays 15 Ind tel.

KIGER, MRS. H. S. R1 Weston.

Kiger, L. G. Cygnet Blo.

Kiger, Orpha 2 ch ret T H&L Hoytsville Jac.

Kiger, T. A. (Gussie) 5 ch farmer T H&L Cygnet Blo 14.

Kilgore, S. R. (Mary) 2 ch mail carrier T H&L 1h Portage Lib 113.

Kille, R. V. (Hattie) 3 ch teamster O H&L 2h Stahl St Bradner Mon B tel.

Killian, H. C. (Cal) 6 ch farmer O 80a 3h 5c Portage Lib 112.

Killy, Levie (Ellen) ret 39a 1c R1 Bradner Fre 84 B tel.

Killyen, Geo. 2 ch farmer O 40a 2h 1c R1 Grand Rapids Gr Rs 41 Ind tel.

Killyen, J. D. RD Bowling Green Pla.

Kilmer, Charley (Lydia) farmer R1 Haskins Mid 84.

KILMER, JOHN (Sarah) 1 ch farmer T 63a 3h 5c R1 Haskins Mid 83.

KILMER, JOHN H., JR. (Marion) 1 ch farmer T 40a 2h 1c R2 Bowling Green Pla 88 B tel.

Kimberlin, Roy J. (Florence) 1 ch farmer T 75a 3h 4c R1 Lime City Pbg 122.

Kimble, C. P. Prairie Depot Mon.

KIMBLE, FRANCISE Main St Prairie Depot.

121

Kimble, Joel ret T 180a R1 Gibsonburg Fre 84 Ind tel.

Kimble, M. 5 ch laborer T H&L N Main St Bradner Mon B tel.

Kimmel, Wm. (Hannah) laborer O H&L Main St Pemberville Fre Ind tel.

Kindell, O. D. (Blanche S.) 3 ch oilman pumping T H&L R3 North Baltimore Blo 21 B & Ind tels.

KINDERBATER, FRED R. (Lora) farming O 31a 3h 3c R3 Perrysburg Pbg 129.

KINDERWATER, FRED R3 box 31 Perrysburg Pbg.

Kinderwater, Henry R3 Perrysburg Pbg.

Kinderwater, Mrs. Herman R3 Perrysburg Pbg.

KINDLE, PETER (Anna) 1 ch farmer T 160a 4h 2c R1 Portage Lib 92.

KING, MRS. ALICE R1 Millbury.

KING, ALMA Pemberille.

KING, A. H. (Bell) ret O H&L 160a LeMoyne Tro Ind tel.

KING, CHAS. (May) farmer O 150a 9h 18c R2 Custar Hen 41 Ind tel.

King, D. B. R1 Perrysburg Pbg.

King, Ella E. farming O 80a R2 Haskins Mid 32.

King, Emma O 30a 1c R2 Custar Hen 41.

King, Erva C. farming O 80a R2 Haskins Mid 32 B tel.

KING, E. H. (Alice M.) farmer O 43a 2h 2c R2 Haskins Mid 32 B tel.

King, F. E. Cygnet Blo.

King, F. P. (Lucy) liveryman O H&L 5h Prairie Depot Mon B tel.

King, John (Maude) blacksmith O H&L 1h Main St West Millgrove Per.

KING, JOHN A. (Mary E.) 1 ch farmer O 10a 2h 2c R2 Weston Wes Ind tel.

King, Joseph (Anna) farmer 40a 3h R1 Custar Jac 3.

King, J. E. (Nellie) 1 ch poultryman O 10½a R2 Haskins Mid 21 B tel.

King, O. E. (Alma) carpenter T H&L Pemberville Fre 40.

King, W. A. (Marie) 2 ch glass cutter T H&L 121 Oak St Rossford Ros.

Kingsley, N. S. (Edith) oil worker O H&L Caldwell St Bradner Mon.

Kingsley, S. C. (Emma) 2 ch salesman O H&L E Main St Portage Por.

Kinker, Bertha Luckey Tro.

Kinker, Will (Bertha) 3 ch lime plant O H&L Luckey Tro Ind tel.

Kinney, Clyde L. RD Portage Lib.

KINNEY, E. B. (Lottie M.) 5 ch farmer O 63a 3h 6c R1 Prairie Depot Mon 62.

Kinney, E. E. (Blanch) 2 ch oil worker T H&L 1h Cygnet Blo 19 Ind tel.

Kinney, Eugene G. (Jessie) 1 ch oil pumper T H&L 1h 1c R3 North Baltimore Blo 27 Ind tel.

KINNEY, G. A. (Clara) 3 ch farmer T 120a 4h 5c Finley Pike Mermill Lib 111 Ind tel.

KINNEY, MACK R. (Susie) 1 ch grain dealer O H&L Second St Portage Por Ind tel.

Kinney, Quincy RD Rudolph Lib.

Kinney, Ray (Edna R.) oilman pumping O H&L Randolph St Bairdstown Blo.

Kinsely, Chas. (Fern) 1 ch farmer T 85a 3h 12c R1 Prairie Depot Mon 55.

Kinsely, Daniel (Josephine) 1 ch farmer O 180a 4h 5c R1 Prairie Depot Mon 55.

Kinsely, Floyd (Mabel) 2 ch farmer T 23a H&L 3h 6c Stahl Road Prairie Depot Mon 62.

Kinsey, A. (Ida) 3 ch oil pumper O 6a 1h 2c R3 Prairie Depot Mon 108.

Kinsey, Harvey (Daisy) 4 ch pumper O H&L 1h 1c Prairie Depot Mon.

KINSLEY, BERT (Martha) dentist O H&L Front St Perrysburg Pbg.

Kirchhoff, H. (Mary) 3 ch farmer O 40a 3h 3c R3 Perrysburg Pbg 77 Ind tel.

Kirian, E. H. (Amy) 4 ch farmer T 100a 3h 5c R1 North Baltimore Hen 52.

KIRIAN, WM. C. (Ellen) 3 ch oil worker O H&L R1 Rudolph Lib 77 Ind tel.

Kirk, Edw. (Annie) 1 ch harnessmaker O H&L Caldwell St Bradner Mon B & Ind tels.

Kirk, Ollie (son Wm.) farm laborer Luckey Web 72.

Kirk, Wm. (Alice) 1 ch farmer O 40a 2h 2c Luckey Web 72.

Kirtland, Victor Pemberville Fre.

Kis, Paul (Anna) laborer O H&L box 450 Rossford Ros.

Kiser, Joseph (Maud) laborer T H&L Risingsun Mon.

KISOR, MRS. MARY E. ret O 10a 1h Station A East Toledo Ros 31.

Kisor, Miss Mary S. (dau Mary) farmer Station A East Toledo Ros 31.

Kissack, Wm. Walbridge Lake.

Kistler, F. L. R3 Perrysburg Pbg.

Kistler, Mary A. Bairdstown Blo.

Kistler, M. F. farmer O 18a 2h 2c Rossford Pbg 79.

Kistner, John J. (Lena) 2 ch groceries & restaurant O H&L Custar Mil B & Ind tels.

Kitchen, Charles (Lily) 1 ch farmer O 80a R1 Tontogany Pla 18 Ind tel.

Kitchen, Geo. (Anna) 1 ch ret O 80a H&L Custar Mil Ind tel.

Klanchia, Fred (Gertrude) painter T H&L 100 Elm St Rossford Ros.

Klaus, Ernest Pemberville Fre.

Kleckner, James C. (Fairy Fern) 3 ch oil man T H&L R1 Jerry City Blo 20 B & Ind tels.

Kleeberger, Frank RD Perrysburg Mid.

Kleeberger, H. B. (Ethel Grace) 1 ch clerk T H&L Lime City Pbg 91.

Kline, A. T. Perrysburg Pbg.

Kline, Elijah (Minnie) 4 ch farmer O 160a 6h 8c R1 Hoytsville Jac 63 Ind tel.

Kline, Geo. (Jennie) 8 ch farmer T 40a 3h 3c R4 Deshler Jac 28.

Kline, Lee N. (son Geo.) farm hand R4 Deshler Jac 28.

Kline, Arvill RD North Baltimore Blo.

Kline, Dr. Theodore (Katharine) dentist O H&L Front St Perrysburg Pbg B tel.

Klingensmith, J. C. (Anna) 2 ch fireman O H&L 1h Front St Cygnet Blo Ind tel.

Klingensmith, Paul student Front St Cygnet Blo Ind tel.

Klingensmith, Wm. tank builder Front St Cygnet Blo Ind tel.

Klingman, Mabel Bell St Bradner Mon.

Klingman, W. A. 6 ch carpenter O H&L Bell St Bradner Mon.

Klink, Bruce W. (Pearl) 6 ch laborer O H&L Stony Ridge Tro.

Klink, Nelson (Mary) 2 ch carpenter O H&L Stony Ridge Tro.

Klink, Roy (son Nelson) carpenter Stony Ridge Tro.

Klippel, J. P. (Frances) 8 ch carpenter T H&L 1h 1c Custar Mil 45.

Klippel, Peter (son J. P.) carpenter R2 Custar Mil 45.

KLOFFENSTEIN, GEO. (Jennie) 4 ch farmer O 67a 5h 10c R4 Bowling Green Cen 36 Ind tel.

Kloffenstein, Julia 4 ch O 5a R5 Bowling Green Cen 23 Ind tel.

Kloffenstein, Lee RD Bowling Green Cen.

Kloffenstein, M. G. farmer R4 Bowling Green Center 36 Ind tel.

Kloffenstein, W. E. (Mary) 2 ch mail carrier T 30a 1h 4c R5 Bowling Green Cen 23 Ind tel.

Klotz, C. A. (Elsie) 2 ch fruit farmer O 20a 3h 3c R5 Bowling Green Cen 23 B & Ind tels.

Knaggs, A. W. Portage Lib.

Knaggs, G. C. Corp St Portage Por.

Knaggs, J. W. Portage Lib.

Knapp, Albert (Nora) 1 ch laborer O H &L Grand Rapids Gr Rs.

Knapp, Mrs. Edna V. 3 ch general store T H&L Custar Mil.

Knapp, J. Walbridge Lake.

Knapp, Mrs. J. Grand Rapids Gr Rs.

Knapp, Mrs. Lillie E. ret Custar Mil.

Knarr, C. (Myria) ret O H&L Sixth St Perrysburg Pbg B tel.

Knauss, Adolph RD Sugar Ridge Mid.

Knauss, A. J. (Mary B.) farmer O 40a 2h 2c R2 Dunbridge Mid 60 Ind tel.

Knauss, Chas. RD Bowling Green Pla.

Knauss, Christo (Gwendoline) 1 ch farmer O 110a 6h 5c R2 Bowling Green Pla 86 B tel.

Knauss, C. R. (Villa) 2 ch principal of schools T H&L Hoytsville Jac.

Knauss, Ed RD Haskins Mid.

Knauss, Gilbert RD Haskins Mid.

Knauss, G. F. (Bertha) 1 ch butcher O 173a H&L 2h 30c Ash St Weston B & Ind tels.

KNAUSS, H. A. (Rena) farmer O 80a 3h 5c Cygnet Blo 12 Ind tel.

Knauss, Jay (Lucy) 1 ch farmer T 84a 4h 1c R3 Bowling Green Cen 21 Ind tel.

Knauss, John, Jr. (Hattie) 2 ch farmer O 100a 4h R2 Dunbridge Mid 81 Ind tel.

Knauss, John farmer O 40a 2h 3c R1 Haskins Mid 60.

Knawgs, Forest (son J. W.) Portage Lib 90.

KNAWGS, J. W. 4 ch farmer O 64a 2h 1c Portage Lib 90.

KNAWSS, FRANK Weston.

Knepper, Alfred (Fannie) farmer O 80a 3h 6c R1 Bradner Fre 90 B tel.

Knepper, Mary 5 ch O H&L Water St Portage Por.

KNEPPER, W. I. stock raiser Tifflin. See adv.

Knerr, George (Pearl) 2 ch janitor O H&L Rossford Ros.

Knettle, Harvey (Nettie) 3 ch farmer T 60a 4h 6c R1 Dunbridge Web 57 B tel.

KNETTLE, JOHN farmer T 140a 7h 4c Portage Por 2.

Knicely, Floyd Prairie Depot Mon.

Knicely, Roscoe Prairie Depot Mon.

Kniefer, Frank (Mary) laborer O H&L Second St Perrysburg Pbg B tel.

Knight, Deyo R. (Laura) farmer O 80a 7h 10c R2 Weston Pla 17 Ind tel.

KNIGHT, HOWARD M. Portage.

Knight, Dr. Thomas W. (Maud) 5 ch physician O 40a 3h 7c Portage Lib 112 Ind tel.

Knisel, Olive Prairie Depot Mon.

KNISELY, CHAS. H. R1 Prairie Depot.

Knisely, Daniel Prairie Depot Mon.

Knisely, J. RD North Baltimore Hen.

Knitz, Lewis J. (Mamie) 5 ch laborer bds 1c Luckey Tro 90.

Knobbs, T. E. (Irma) 2 ch laborer O 1½a H R1 Portage Lib 57 Ind tel.

Knodle, Wm. (Eva) 3 ch oil man R1 Bloomdale Blo.

Knopp, Jud (Hannah) 1 ch farmer T 100a 8h 3c R1 Walbridge Lake 2 Ind tel.

Knost, Gerhart (Mary) farmer O 40a 3h 4c RD Walbridge Lake 128 B tel.

Knudson, Casey (M.) 1 ch farmer & dairyman T 140a 6h 25c R1 Walbridge Ros 23.

KNUDSON, FRED (Pearl) 3 ch farmer O R1 Millbury Lake 125 Ind tel.

KNUDSON, HENRY (Minnie) 4 ch farmer O R1 Millbury Lake 105 Ind tel.

KNUDSON, LOUIE (Florence) 2 ch farmer O R1 Millbury Lake 125 Ind tel.

KNUDSON, MARTIN (Louise) farmer O R1 Millbury Lake 125 Ind tel.

Knull, Erril (Mary) ret O HL Third St Perrysburg Pbg.

Knull, Ira (Allmira) ret O H&L Third St Perrysburg Pbg.

Koch, Mrs. Bell Weston Wes.

KOCH, CHAS. (Mary) 3 ch farmer O 40a 3h 3c R1 Weston Mil 79 Ind tel..

Koch, Frank (Clara) 4 ch railroad man T H&L Walbridge Lake.

Koch, Henry F. (Anna) carpenter T H&L 1h R1 Pemberville Fre 66 B tel.

Koch, John M. (Clara) 2 ch farmer O 140a 6h 10c R3 Weston Mil 84 Ind tel.

Koch, Leo (son Chas.) farmer R1 Weston Mil 64.

KOEDING, GEO. F. R2 Box 4 Bowling Green.

Koehler, L. (Amelia) 3 ch bartender T 10a 2c Cygnet Blo 6.

Koenig, John (Louise) 3 ch farmer O 100a R1 East Toledo Ros 28.

Koenig, L. (Louise) 2 ch farmer 3h 2c Station A East Toledo Ros 31.

Koerber, Jno. Perrysburg Pbg.

Koester, Mary Bradner Mon.

KOESTER, WILLIAM (Bertha) 4 ch farmer & furrier T 20a 2h 1c R1 East Toledo Ros 28.

Kohl, C. (Lucinda) farmer O 80a 1h R1 Perrysburg Pbg 105 Ind tel.

KOHL, WILSON R1 Perrysburg Pbg.

Kohler, Inez (dau John) school teacher Le Moyne Tro Ind tel.

Kohler, John (Eliza) 4 ch carpenter & farmer O 30a H&L 1h 1c Le Moyne Tro Ind tel.

Kohring, A. H. (Lanada) 5 ch farmer T 140a 4h 4c R1 Pemberville Fre 56 B tel.

Kohring, Christina (dau H. F.) housekeeper Front St Pemberville Fre 40.

Kohring, Clarence (son John) carpenter 1h R3 Pemberville Tro 66.

Kohring, F. H. (Kate) 3 ch carpenter O H&L Pemberville Fre 40.

Kohring, F. L. (Mary) 3 ch farmer O 71a 2h 2c R2 Pemberville Web 31 B tel.

Kohring, Geo. (Kate) 2 ch farmer O 50a 2h 3c R3 Pemberville Fre 4 B tel.

Kohring, Henry ret O H&L Front St Pemberville Fre 40.

Kohring, Henry (Ida) 1 ch farmer T 130a 4h 10c R3 Pemberville Tro 60 B tel.

KOHRING, MRS. IDA R3 Pemberville.

KOHRING, JOHN (Anna) 1 ch farmer T 60a 2h 8c R3 Pemberville Tro 66 B tel.

KOHRING, LEWIS G. (Maltida K.) 2 ch farmer O 80a 4h 5c R1 Luckey Tro 69.

KOHRN, AUGUST (Elizabeth) 5 ch farmer T 100a 4h 3c R1 Tontogany Wash 75 Ind tel.

KONALD, R. V. (Zila) farmer T 100a 4h 1c West Millgrove Per 65 B & Ind tels.

Konkey, Henry cattle RD Jerry City Por.

Konrad, Eugene ((Mary) 4 ch carpenter O H&L Milton Center Mil.

KONRAD, JOS. (Catherine) 6 ch farmer O 40a 3h 5c R3 Weston Mil 75 Ind tel.

Konrad, Mike farmer O 40a Weston Mil 75.

Koons, Alfred (Ora) 2 ch laborer O H&L 1h 1c R1 Postoria Per 90.

Koons, Clyde (Ella) 2 ch farmer T 80a 3h 3c R4 Bowling Green Cen 107 Ind tel.

Koons, Frank (Nellie) 5 ch farmer O 50a 4h 3c R1 Portage Por.

Koons, Geo. (Susan) oil man O H&L Railroad St Bairdstown Blo.

Koons, Isaac (Annie) 6 ch laborer O 6a 1h 2c R1 Prairie Depot Mon 111..

Koons, Jacob (Ella) farmer O 3a 1h R1 Fostoria Per 128.

Koons, O. C. Hatton Per.

Koontz, Clyde cattle RD Bowling Green Cen.

Kopp, Albert (Florence) 2 ch farmer O 112a 3h 32c R1 Luckey Tro 25 Ind tel.

Kopp, Fred R2 Perrysburg Pbg.

Kopp, George (Anna) 6 ch laborer O H&L Sixth St Perrysburg Pbg.

Kopp, Henry R3 Perrysburg Pbg.

Kordee, C. H. (Myrtle) 3 ch farmer T 2a 2h 1c R1 Prairie Depot Mon 101 B tel.

Kordee, F. H. (Eliza) farmer O 120a 6h 7c R3 Prairie Depot Mon 109 B tel.

KORDEE, H. H. (Bertha) farmer O 170a 16h 21c R1 Prairie Depot Mon 104 B tel.

. KORDEE, REBECCA Prairie Depot Mon.

KORN, ANDREW (Anna) 2 ch farmer O 30a 2h 2c R1 Walbridge Lake 129 B tel.

Korn, Clare (Alta) railroad man T H&L Walbridge Lake.

Korn, Frank (Mina) 3 ch car repairer O H&L R1 Walbridge Lake 15 Ind tel.

Korn, John (Nettie) 3 ch railroader T H&L Walbridge Lake.

Korn, Joseph (Minnie) 4 ch farmer O 15a 2h 1c Stony Ridge Lake 95 B tel.

Korn, Nettie Walbridge Lake.

Kornasienwòcz, Jos. Rossford Ros.

Korta, Chas. F. (Geneva) 5 ch hotel keeper O business prop Custar Mil B tel.

Kortier, C. H. (Ella) 2 ch grain & coal dealer O H&L 1h cor Crocker & Bell Sts Bradner Mon B tel.

Kortier, H. R. (May) 3 ch merchant O H&L 1h S Main St Bradner Mon B tel.

Kost, Helene (stepdau W. H.) student Findlay St Portage Por.

Kostik, Henry Rossford Ros.

Kotowitz, Paul Rossford Ros.

Kotowski, Steve Rossford Ros.

Koxtka, Andy Rossford Ros.

Krabill, Rev. J. P. (Melissa) 1 ch O 18a 2h 1c R3 Prairie Depot Por 111.

Kraft, John (Maggie) 3 ch carpenter T H&L Pemberville Fre.

Krakow, Frank 2 ch pot maker T H&L 195 Superior St Rossford Ros.

Kramer, L. H. (Irene) 1 ch farmer O 33a 4h 3c Portage Por 2.

Kramer, Margaret RD Bowling Green Pla.

Kramer, Russell (son· L. H.) farmer Portage Por 2.

Kramp, Clarence (Minnie) farmer T 7h 10c R2 Bowling Green Pla 46.

KRAMP, HENRY P. (Ida) 6 ch farmer T 80a 2h 3c R2 Bowling Green Pla 50.

Kramp, John (Cora) 2 ch farmer T 160a 5h 5c R2 Bowling Green Pla 65 Ind tel.

Kramp, Peter, Jr. (Vallie) 3 ch farmer T 7h 4c Mermill Por 20 Ind tel.

Kramp, Ralph (Nellie) 3 ch farmer T 7h 10c R2 Bowling Green Pla 46.

Kramp, Wallace RD Bowling Green Pla.

Krassow, Chris (Lydia) laborer O H&L R1 Rudolph Por 24½.

KRATZER, I. E. (Lucy) ret O H&L Main St Pemberville Fre.

Kratzer, I. E., Jr. (son I. E. Sr.) clerk Main St Pemberville Fre Ind tel.

KRATZER, WM. (Florence) 1 ch farmer T 40a 2h 1c Pemberville Fre B tel.

Twin Colts.

Krause, Fred (Alice) 2 ch farmer O 79a 8h 11c R2 Custar Lib 19 Ind tel.
Krebs, Henry (Carrie) 9 ch farmer O 120a 7h 5c R3 Weston Mil 7 Ind tel.
Krebs, Leo (son Henry) farm hand R3 Weston Mil 7.
Kreger, H. M. (Eliza) oilman tool dresser O H&L Harrison St Bloomdale Blo.
Kreinkamp, Herman (Marie) 2 ch farmer O 80a 2h 5c R3 Prairie Depot Mon 8.
Kreinkamp, Wm. (Carrie) 1 ch farmer O 80a 5h 15c R1 Bradner Fre 82 B tel.
Kremer, Peter farm hand R2 Deshler Jac 1.
KRING, M. painter T H&L R1 Portage Por 14.
Kroeger, John ret farmer O 19a Custar Mil 18.
Kroetz, Florence (dau Tony) Luckey Tro Ind tel.
Kroetz, Stella (dau Tony) Luckey Tro Ind tel.
Kroetz, Tony (Hannah) 4 ch bartender O H&L Luckey Tro Ind tel.
Kroftschick, Mrs. Henrietta housekeeper O 48a R2 Haskins Wash 91 B tel.
Krohn, Ad. (Mary) 1 ch elevator prop O H&L Custar Mil B & Ind tels.
Kroleck, John (Mary) foreman O H&L 178 Oak St Rossford Ros.
Kromberg, John (Jessie) 5 ch farmer T 40a 5h 3c box 85 Milton Center Mil 92 Ind tel.
Kronberg, Jno. Milton Center Mil.
Krontz, Delbert (Cora) 6 ch oil pumper T 1h 1c R1 Rudolph Hen 64.
Krontz, Ora (Chloie) 2 ch laborer O H&L Hatton Per 84.
Krontz, V. K. laborer R1 Rudolph Hen 64.
Krotzer, H. N. (Maude) laboring man O H&L Luckey Tro.
Krotzer, John (Lucy) 1 ch farmer O 130a 6h 6c R1 Bradner Fre 91.
Krotzer, Joseph Franklin (Mary E.) 4 ch laborer O H&L Luckey Tro.
Krotzer, M. (Anna) 1 ch oil worker O H&L Rudolph Lib 94.
Krotzer, Nute Luckey Tro.
Krotzer, Wm. Pemberville Fre.
Krouse, J. C. (Jennie) 4 ch farmer O 73a 5h 5c R3 North Baltimore Blo 29.
Krout, F. B. (Blanch) 2 ch farming O 80a 4h 2c R3 Weston Wes 47.
Krover, I. K. (Florence) 3 ch farmer O 28a 2h 2c R2 Bowling Green Cen 4 Ind tel.
Krueger, Wm. (Anna) 1 ch inspector T H&L Walbridge Lake.

Kruger, Elsie Perrysburg Pbg.
KRUNEMEYER, ARNOLD (son Ernest) farmer R1 Pemberville Fre 58 B tel.
Krukemeyer, Ernest (Anna) 3 ch farmer O 123a 5h 6c R1 Pemberville Fre 58 B tel.
Krukemyer, Emma R4 Bowling Green Cen 124.
Krukemyer, Fred (Eliza) 4 ch farmer O 80a 3h 7c R4 Bowling Green Cen 124 B tel.
KRUMMEL, MRS. JANE housekeeper O 80a 1h 6c R1 Genoa Lake 42 B tel.
Krummell, C. (Hattie) 1 ch farmer O 74a H&L 4h 5c R1 Genoa Lake 45 Ind tel.
Kummer, W. A. (Carrie) 2 ch glass worker O H&L 253 Superior St Rossford Ros.
KRUFF, GEO. (Inez) 2 ch farmer T H&L 4h 6c R1 Fostoria Per 99 Ind tel.
Krupp, John farmer O 100a 3h 5c R1 Fostoria Per 99 B tel.
Kruff, Lyle (dau John) housekeeper R1 Fostoria Per 99 B·tel.
Kruse, Charles C. (Bessie E.) 1 ch section hand T H&L Bairdstown Blo 48.
Kruse, Wm. (Anna) 2 ch section foreman T H&L Bairdstown Blo.
Krutsch, Libbie RD North Baltimore Hen.
Kuder, Augusta Tontogany Wash.
KUDER, C. C. (Della) 2 ch farmer O 100a 6h 4c R1 Tontogany Wash 71 Ind tel.
KUDER, G. S. (Cora A.) ret O 120a 1h Box 127 Tontogany Wash Ind tel.
Kuerton, John (Mary) 1 ch farmer T H&L R1 Tontogany Wash 39.
Kuhlman, C. F. 1 ch farmer O 50a 2h 4c R2 Pemberville Fre 2.
Kuhlman, Fred (Florence)1 ch farmer T 80a 1h 2c R2 Pemberville Web 32.
Kuhlman, F. A. (Ollie) 4 ch farmer T 60a 4h 4c R3 Prairie Depot Mon 112 B tel.
Kuhlman, Geo. F. (Gertrude) farmer O 130a 5h 17c R3 North Baltimore Blo 42.
Kuhlman, J. H. (Anna) 2 ch farmer O 48a 4h 2c R3 Prairie Depot Por 96.
Kuhlman, Oliver (Edna) 2 ch buggy trimmer O H&L 1h R1 Fostoria Per 112 B tel.
Kuhlman, Ross (son Geo. F.) farmer R3 North Baltimore Blo 42.
Kuhman, W. F. farmer T 160a 6h 10c R1 North Baltimore Hen 69.
Kuhn, G. F. (Marie) 2 ch farm hand R3 Weston Mil 68.
Kuhn, I. N. (Maggie) 2 ch farmer T 80a 4h 2c R3 Prairie Depot Por 99.

Kuhn, John W. (Katie) 1 ch farmer O 10a 1c R1 Stony Ridge Tro 8 Ind tel.

Kummer, Wm. Rossford Ros.

Kunkle, Elizabeth Grand Rapids Gr Rs.

Kunkle, Mary O H&L Grand Rapids Gr Rs.

Kunkle, Wad Jerry City Blo 81 Ind tel.

Kunkler, Christina Corp St Jerry City Por.

KUNKLER, E. C. (Lora) 5 ch farmer O 90a 6h 7c R1 Jerry City Blo 81 Ind tel.

Kunkler, Shirley RD Jerry City Blo 81 Ind tel.

KURFESS, J. F. farmer O 80a 5h 7c R1 Lime City Pbg 43 Ind tel.

KURFESS, W. L. (Anna) 2 ch farmer O 140a 6h 6c R1 Lime City Pbg 44 B tel.

Kurfis, Frank farmer R1 Stony Ridge Lake 31.

Kurfis, Geo. F. R3 Perrysburg Pbg.

Kurfis, J. M. (Loie) 3 ch body builder O H&L Stony Ridge Tro Ind tel.

Kurfis, Walter L. (Aldah) 1 ch rural carrier O 21a 2h 1c R1 Stony Ridge Lake 28 Ind tel.

Kurtz, J. H. (Ida) 1 ch engineer & operator O H&L Pemberville Fre B tel.

Kusian, A. E. Walbridge Lake.

Kusner, Jack Rossford Ros.

Kusner, Mike (Agnes) 3 ch glass worker O H&L box 430 Rossford Ros.

Kyder, Lawrence (Addie) 1 ch farmer T 63a 3h 2c R7 Perrysburg Pbg 16 B tel.

LACK, GEO. F. 3 ch harness maker O 1a H&L R4 Bowling Green Por 97 Ind tel.

Ladd, A. M. ret O H&L Front St Perrysburg Pbg.

Ladd, George (Jennie) 2 ch ret O 150a H&L 4h Taylor St Weston Ind tel.

Ladd, George M. (son George) Taylor St Weston.

Ladd, G. B. (May) 1 ch contractor O H&L Cor Taylor & Maple Sts Weston Ind tel.

Ladd, Mrs. Mae Weston Wes.

La Farce, Jno. Perrysburg Pbg.

Lafarree, George (Mary) ret O H&L Commercial St Perrysburg Pbg.

La Farree, Harry (Lucille) 1 ch painter T H&L 2d St Perrysburg Pbg B tel.

La Farree, Lein (Kitty) 1 ch painter O H&L 5th St Perrysburg Pbg B tel.

Lafarree, Max (Josephine) 1 ch carpenter T H&L Commercial St Perrysburg Pbg B tel.

LA FLUER, ALBERT (Anna) 2 ch laborer T H&L 2h Millbury Lake 76.

Lahey, David farmer O 185a 4h 2c Dowling Web 52 B tel.

Lahey, David (Mary) 5 ch farmer T 70a 2h 4c Dowling Pbg 35.

Lahey, Tom (son David) farmer Dowling Web 52 B tel.

Lahey, Wm. E. (Grace A.) 3 ch oil pumper T H&L Bays Lib 75 Ind tel.

Lahman, Clarence farmer T 40a 1h R1 Dunbridge Mid 67 B tel.

LAHMAN, C. E. (Gertrude) 3 ch farmer T 85a 6h 6c R1 Haskins Mid 38. See adv.

Lahman, David Dunbridge Web.

Lahman, Harry Dunbridge Web.

LAHMAN, MRS. SUSAN farmer O 40a 2h 3c R1 Dunbridge Mid 67 B tel.

Lahman, Viola (dau Susan) housekeeper R1 Dunbridge Mid 67 B tel.

Lahman, William (Millie) 5 ch farmer T 160a 4h 3c R1 Tontogany Pla 18.

Lahman, Wilson W. RD Rudolph Lib.

Lahrer, Martin (Cora) 4 ch foreman O H&L Main St Perrysburg Pbg.

LAING, S. J. A. (Emma) 2 ch plant grower O 6a R3 Perrysburg Pbg 137.

Lake, Katherine farmer O 49a 1h 3c R1 Tontogany Wash 32.

Lake, J. C. Tontogany Wash.

Lake, V. R. (Leota) 3 ch farmer T 80a 4h 6c R1 Grand Rapids Wash 66 Ind tel.

Lally, Mary 1 ch ret O H&L 5th St Perrysburg Pbg B tel.

Lamb, L. M. (Edna) 3 ch farmer T 120a 3h 3c R1 Portage Por 50.

Lamb, O. (Elizabeth J.) 3 ch farmer O 40a 1h 3c R2 Custar Mil 41 B tel.

Lamb, Pearl B. (dau O.) housekeeper R2 Custar Mil 41 B tel.

Lambert, Rev. H. minister bds Custar Mil B tel.

LAMBERT, HARLEY (June) 1 ch farmer T 81a 3h 1c R5 Bowling Green Cen 81 Ind tel.

LAMBERT, H. J. (Lucy) 2 ch farmer O 80a 3h 2c R5 Bowling Green Cen 65 Ind tel.

LAMBRIGHT, J. F. (Annie) ret O 82a 1h 3c West Mill Grove Mon 90 B tel.

Lambright, J. M. (Bertha) meat market emp O H&L Cemeland St Bloomdale Blo.

Lamen, Lena ret O H&L Main St Perrysburg Pbg.

Lamfrom, Moses RD North Baltimore Hen.

127

Lamfrom, M. (Stella) 2 ch clothing store O H&L RD North Baltimore Hen Ind tel.

Lamfrom, R. L. RD North Baltimore Hen.

Lampbert, D. A. (Ester) livery T H&L 4h RD North Baltimore B & Ind tels.

Lampson, Robert J. (Marie) 1 ch merchant O H&L Indiana Ave Perrysburg Pbg.

Lamson, Robt. J. Perrysburg Pbg.

LANCASHIRE, W. W. motor cars Toledo. See adv.

Lance, Albert (Emma) 11 ch farmer O 40a 2h 3c R3 Weston Mil 90.

Lance, David (Katie) carpenter O 20a Milton Center Mil 102.

Lance, Emily 9 ch ret O 80a H&L Milton Center Mil Ind tel.

LANCE, GEO. W. (Luvern) 3 ch farm laborer T 5a H&L 3h 1c R1 Custar Jac 39.

Lance, John E. (Blanche) 5 ch farmer O 5½a 2h 1c R1 Custar Mil 18.

Lance, Mrs. J. C. Milton Center Mil.

Lance, J. F. (Grace) 1 ch furniture & undertaker T H&L Weston B & Ind tels.

Lance, Lloyd R. (son Albert) school teacher R3 Weston Mil 90.

Lauce, Mrs. Mary A. 2 ch ret O 40a H &L Milton Center Mil.

Lance, Orlo RD Hoytsville Jac.

Lance, Sara J. Bloomdale Blo.

LANDERS, ALVA (Ruth) farmer T 80a 2h 2c Tontogany Wash 29.

Landers, Chas. (Martha) 2 ch laborer T H&L 1c Dowling Mid 76.

Landers, S. L. RD Bowling Green Pla.

Landis, A. N. (Myrtle) 5 ch farming T 120a 5h 5c R1 Prairie Depot Mon 112 B tel.

Landis, Ed. W Millgrove Mon.

Landis, E. D. (R.) 2 ch farmer T 100a 3h 6c R3 Prairie Depot Mon 105 B tel.

Landis, Hannah RD Dunbridge Mid.

Landis, W. M. farmer O 40a 1h 5c R2 Prairie Depot Por 77.

Landwehr, Carrie (dau Henry) housekeeper Luckey Tro Ind tel.

Landwehr, Frank (son Henry) farm hand Luckey Tro Ind tel.

LANDWEHR, FRED W. (Dora) 1 ch farmer O 53a 3h 6c R1 Luckey Tro 91 B tel.

Landwehr, G. F. (L. L.) 1 ch farmer O 60a 3h 4c R1 Luckey Web 72 B tel.

Landwehr, Henry (Louise) 7 ch farmer 110a 3h 11c Luckey Tro Ind tel.

Landwehr, Jno. Dunbridge Web.

Landwehr, Will (Stella) O H&L Luckey Tro Ind tel.

Lane, Joe RD Bowling Green Pla.

Lane, Moses, Jr. farmer 1h R1 Bowling Green Pla 31 B tel.

Lanel, A. H. (Myrtle J.) 2 ch farmer O 106a 7h 2c R1 Weston Mil 60 Ind tel.

Laney, Chas. (Adaline) 3 ch farmer T H&L R2 Prairie Depot Mon 43.

Laney, J. W. RD North Baltimore Hen.

LANEY, PETER (Pearl B.) 6 ch laborer T 3h 1c R1 Rudolph Lib 100.

Laney, T. C. RD North Baltimore Hen.

Laney, William (Emma) glassworker O H&L 174 Oak St Rossford Ros.

Lang, Arnold (son Wm.) farmer 4h 2c bds R1 Fostoria Per 121.

Lang, A. D. (Martellia) 1 ch oil worker T H&L 1h R1 Bowling Green Lib 49 Ind tel.

Lang, F. J. (son J.) farmer 2h R1 Dunbridge Mid 75.

Lang, Herman RD Dunbridge Mid.

Lang, J. (Susan) farmer O 56a 1h 2c R2 Dunbridge Mid 75.

Lang, L. C. clerk Mermill Por 20 Ind tel.

Lang, Michael Dunbridge Web.

Lang, M. (Laura) 4 ch auctioneer T H&L Milton St Weston.

Lang, Wm. H. (Anna) 5 ch farmer O 80a 1h 1c R1 Fostoria Per 121.

Lange, Henry (Mary) 1 ch farmer O 80a 3h 3c R2 Dunbridge Mid 72.

Langell, B. B. (Minnie) 2 ch farmer O H&L 1c Maple St Bradner Mon.

Langmade, L. D. RD North Baltimore Por.

LANIER, W. C. (Mabel) 3 ch veterinarian O H&L 2h 1c cor Cherry St Weston B & Ind tels.

Lanis, Dora (Tillie) 8 ch machinist T H&L 2h Bradner Mon 20 B tel.

Lanker, Emma 1 ch ret O H&L Grand Rapids Gr Rs.

Lantz, Alvin (Nealy) 8 ch farmer O H&L 3h 2c R3 Prairie Depot Mon 12½.

Lantz, Clate (Pearl) 1 ch farmer O 50a 2h 2c R3 Prairie Depot Mon 16 B tel.

Lantz, Hattie housekeeper T H&L Prairie Depot Mon B tel.

Lantz, S. L. (Sarah J.) clerk O H&L Main St Bloomdale Blo B & Ind tels.

Lapish, Geo. 1 ch section foreman O H&L Millbury Lake.

Lapish, Geo. (Maud) 1 ch farmer O 40a 3h 5c Latchie Lake 45 Ind tel.

Lapish, Jno. Millbury Lake.

LAPISH, MARY housekeeper Latchie Lake 45 Ind tel.

Lapish, Wm. (Ella) 2 ch section hand T H&L 2h Millbury Lake.

LAPLANT, A. O. (Lucy) 5 ch farmer O 80a 5h 2c R1 North Baltimore Hen 125.

Laplant, J. H. (Anna) 1 ch oil pumper T L 1h R1 North Baltimore Hen 68 Ind tel.

Laplante, Giddeon (Melvina) 3 ch farmer O 40a 4h 3c R1 Genoa Lake 43 B tel.

Larcom, Pearl (Dollie J.) farm laborer 1h R1 Bloomdale Blo 102.

Laremore, Oliver Corp St Portage Por.

Laremore, O. O. (Addie) 3 ch machine shop & garage O H&L Walnut St Portage Por Ind tel.

LARROWE, JOHN Rossford.

LARZIN, EMILE (Jennie) 1 ch farmer O 109a 3h 1c station A East Toledo Ros 31.

Lashaway, F. J. (son Henry) farmer R3 Weston Mil 88.

Lashaway, Hamilton (son Jennie) painter Main St Weston.

Lashaway, Henry (Augusta) 4 ch farmer O 80a 6h 4c R3 Weston Mil 86.

Lashaway, James (Mary) 7 ch laborer T H&L W Taylor St Weston.

Lashaway, Jennie 5 ch T H&L Main St Weston.

Lashaway, Lloyd (son Henry) R3 Weston Mil 86.

LASHAWAY, ROLLO G. C. (Ethel) 3 ch T H&L Main St Weston.

LASHAWAY, VERN (Leah) 2 ch plasterer O H&L R2 Weston Ind tel.

Lashley, Alice C. Prairie Depot Mon.

Lashley, D. E. Weston Wes.

Lashley, G. C. (Agnes S.) 3 ch minister T H&L Jerry St Jerry City Blo.

Lashley, Pearl (dau T. C.) school teacher R2 Custar Mil 51.

Lashley, Ruby (dau T. C.) clerk Custar Mil 99½.

Lashley, T. C. (Pauline) 2 ch farmer O 25a 4h 2c R2 Custar Mil 51 Ind tel.

Lashway, Avery (Annie) carpenter T H&L Broadway Box 120 Weston Wes.

Lashway, A. E. (C. E.) 2 ch ret O 260a 2h 1c Rudolph Lib 81 Ind tel.

Lashway, A. M. (Louella) 2 ch farmer O 120a 10h 15c Rudolph Lib 94 Ind tel.

LASHWAY, D. L. (Alma) 6 ch laborer T H&L Broadway cor Oak St Weston Wes.

Lashway, L. A. (Edna) 4 ch farmer O 93a 10h 4c R3 Weston Mil 65 B tel.

Lashway, Stanley (Pearl) farmer T 120a 5h 15c R1 Weston Lib 43 Ind tel.

Laskey, C. L. Grand Rapids Gr Rs.

Laskey, Geo. Custar Mil.

LASKEY, G. S. (Carrie) farmer O 160a 6h 20c R1 Custar Mil 26 B tel.

LASPEY, C. L. (Anna) asst cashier in bank O H&L Grand Rapids Gr Rs B tel.

Latham, S. E. (Katy) 3 ch farmer T 50a 2h 1c R2 North Baltimore Hen 82 Ind tel.

LATHROP, GEO. (Dora) farmer T 80a 3h 6c R1 Weston Lib 10 Ind tel.

Lathrop, G. L. RD North Baltimore Hen.

LATHROP, W. C. (Maria) 6 ch farmer O 40a 2h R1 Weston Mil 38.

Langheed, Geo. (Sarah) laborer T H&L R1 Genoa Lake 45.

Laumall, Anna (dau G.) station A East Toledo Ros 31.

Laumall, G. (Elise) 2 ch farmer O 40a 2h 4c station A East Toledo Ros 31.

Laumall, Sophia (dau G.) station A East Toledo Ros 31.

Lauman, Edward (Helen) 5 ch machinist O 1a H 7th St Perrysburg Pbg B tel.

Laverner, Fred (Julia) 2 ch farmer T 120a 3h 1c R1 Weston Lib 46.

Lavernier, Jacob (Mina) farmer T 141a 5h 3c Portage Lib 90 Ind tel.

Lawrence, Nellie G. RD North Baltimore Hen.

LAWRENCE, S. R. (Eva) farmer O 40a 2h 1c R1 North Baltimore Hen 43.

LAWRENZ, O. R. (Martha) 1 ch furniture & undertaker T H&L Grand Rapids Gr Rs Ind tel. See adv.

LAYLOR, H. B. (Lottie L.) 3 ch farmer O 400a 25h 6c R1 Rudolph Lib 62½ Ind tel.

Layman, Anna B. Lemoyne Tro.

Layman, Edward (son John) farmer & stock raiser R1 Luckey Web 69 B tel.

Layman, Frank (son John) farmer & stock raiser R1 Luckey Web 69 B tel.

Layman, Gotlip (son John) farmer Luckey Web 64 B tel.

Layman, Henry (son John) farmer Luckey Web 64 B tel.

Layman, John Portage Lib 112.

Layman, John, Jr. (Carrie) 6 ch farmer T 160a 8h 7c Luckey Web 64 B tel.

Layman, Lewis Dunbridge Web.

Layman, Minnie (dau John) housekeeper Luckey Web 64 B tel.

Layman, Peter (Chole) O 180a 1h 1c Luckey Web Ind tel.

LAYPORT, ALICE GUNDY housekeeper O 40a H&L Tontogany Wash Ind tel.

Laytart, Chas. C. (Martha A.) 5 ch farmer T 42a 3h 1c R1 Bowling Green Pla 34.

Laytart, L. T. (Le Ella) 5 ch farm laborer 2h 1c RD Custar Lib 38.

Lea, W. M. (Clara) 2 ch oil man producer contractor O HL 2c West Millgrove Per 67.

Leach, B. L. (Josephine) 1 ch farmer T 109a 4h 9c Portage Lib 88.

Leaf, Clement (Barbara) ret O H&L Second St Perrysburg Pbg.

Leaf, H. C. (Lillian) 3 ch farmer O 80a 2h 3c R1 Hoytville Jac 116 Ind tel.

Leaker, W. H. 2 ch clerk O H&L Locust St Webster.

Leaming, Pearl (dau W. M.) milliner Milton Center Mil.

Leaming, W. M. (Jane Z.) 2 ch druggist O H&L Milton Center Mil B tel.

Leatherman, J. M. RD North Baltimore Hen.

LEATHERMAN, SHERMAN (Ida) 6 ch farmer & miller O 25a 1h 5c Hoytsville Jac B tel.

Leathers, Bessie E. (dau B. W.) millnery R1 Bloomdale Blo 116 B & Ind tels.

LEATHERS, B. J. (Henrietta) farmer O 52a 2h 5c R1 North Baltimore Hen 124.

LEATHERS, B. W. (Olive L.) 7 ch farmer O 40a 12h 13c R1 Bloomdale Blo 116 B & Ind tels.

LEATHERS, ED. S. (Stella P.) 1 ch farmer T 160a 7h 13c R1 Bloomdale Blo 51 B & Ind tels.

Leathers, E. O. (Martha S.) 3 ch undertaker O H&L Main St Bloomdale Blo B & Ind tels.

LEATHERS, E. W. (Cora) 2 ch farmer O 10a 4h 11c R1 North Baltimore Hen 123 Ind tel.

Leathers, G. B. RD North Baltimore Hen.

Leathers, J. C. RD North Baltimore Hen.

Leathers, J. J. (Maude) 3 ch farmer T 160a 12h Bairdstown Blo 47 B & Ind tels.

Leathers, M. C. RD North Baltimore Hen.

Leathers, M. F. (Mary) 1 ch farmer O 280a 7h 30c R1 North Baltimore Hen 119.

LEATHERS, NAOMI R1 Bloomdale.

Leathers, Park E. (son B. W.) laborer R1 Bloomdale Blo 116 B & Ind tels.

Leathers, Seba (son J. J.) Bairdstown Blo 47 B & Ind tels.

LEATHERS, WESLEY E., JR. (Caroline J.) farmer T 40a 3h 1c R1 Bloomdale Blo 103 B & Ind tels.

LEBEAU, MRS. Bradner.

Le Comte, E. J. (Edna) 6 ch oil worker T 40a 1h 1c R1 Prairie Depot Mon 64 B tel.

Le Comte, Harold (son E. J.) farmer R1 Prairie Depot Mon 66 B tel.

Le Comte, Pearl (dau E. J.) school girl R1 Prairie Depot Mon 66 B tel.

LEE, CHARLES T. (Eva) 2 ch farmer T 215a 8h 12c R1 Weston Pla 14 Ind tel.

Lee, Chas. W. (Ella) 1 ch manager of Nat Supply O H&L Bell St Bradner Mon B tel.

Lee, C. C. (Helene) 4 ch restaurant & confectionery H&5L Main St Jerry City Blo 78.

LEE, DERASTUS (Mary E.) farmer O 160a 2h 1c R1 Jerry City Blo B tel.

Lee, Emma C. Bloomdale Blo.

Lee, E. C. ret O H&L Front & Locust St Perrysburg Pbg B tel.

Lee, Harry H. (Elsie) 1 ch oil man roustabout O H&L 1h R3 North Baltimore Blo 22.

Lee, Helen W. music teacher Bell St Bradner Mon B tel.

LEE, JOHN (Fidelia) laborer O H&2L R1 Haskins Mid 53.

Lee, John (Mary) 2 ch farmer T 88a 4h 2c R3 North Baltimore Blo 22 Ind tel.

LEE, JOHN (Minerva) farmer T 80a 3h 6c R1 Bloomdale Blo 94.

Lee, John W. (Lucy) 3 ch oil worker O H&L Second St Portage Por Ind tel.

Lee, Joseph 8 ch farmer T 165a 2h 1c R5 Bowling Green Cen 40 Ind tel.

Lee, J. S. (Maude) 6 ch fireman T H&L Milton Center Mil.

Lee, Maelee R5 Bowling Green Cen 40 Ind tel.

Lee, Mary E. Jerry City Blo.

Lee, Nita R2 Prairie Depot Blo 85 Ind tel.

Lee, Orma (dau John) R1 Bloomdale Blo 94.

LEE, P. M. (Maggie) 4 ch farmer T 120a 5h 6c R2 Prairie Depot Blo 85 Ind tel.

Lee, Roy (son John) laborer R3 North Baltimore Blo 22.

LEE, THOMAS (Dora) 3 ch farmer T 140a 17h 3c R1 Bowling Green Lib 55 Ind tel.

LEE, T. H. (Mary) 2 ch oil worker O H&L Main St Jerry City Blo 78.

LEE, WILSON (Emma C.) farmer T 80a 5h 5c R1 Bloomdale Blo 102 B & Ind tels.

Lee, W. M. West Millgrove Per.

Lee, Z. P. (Elina) farming O 43a 1h 2c Weston Wes 5 Ind tel.

LEFFINGWELL, L. (Maggie) ret O 30a 7c R1 Risingsun Mon 61.

Leffler, Harvey (Estella) 4 ch farmer O 25a 4h 7c R4 Bowling Green Por 94 Ind tel.

Leflar, L. J. (Mattie) 2 ch farmer O 67a 1h 6c Jerry & Bronson Sts Jerry City Blo Ind tel.

Lefler, C. J. Jerry City Blo.

Lefler, Geo. farmer & oil operator O 175a 2h R1 Jerry City Blo 60 B & Ind tels.

Lefler, G. C. Bloomdale Blo.

Lefler, Mattie A. Jerry City Blo.

LE GALLEY, CHARLEY (Emma) 2 ch farmer O 135a 7h 10c R2 Bowling Green Pla 60 B tel.

LE GALLEY, HARRY B. (Florence) 4 ch farmer T 40a 5h 1c R2 Bowling Green Pla 89 B tel.

LE GALLEY, J. W. (Eva G.) 2 ch farmer O 142a 1c R2 Bowling Green Pla 60 B tel.

LE GALLEY, RAY W. (Blanche) 1 ch farmer T 40a 4h 4c R2 Bowling Green Pla 88 B tel.

Le Galley, Silia RD Bowling Green Pla.

Le Galley, Wm. T. (Celia) 1 ch farmer O 32a 2h 2c R2 Bowling Green Pla 60 Ind tel.

Legett, Harvey (Bessie) 3 ch laborer T H&L 3d St Perrysburg Pbg.

Leggett, A. E. (Chloe) pumper O H&L Mermill Por 19.

Leggett, D. E. (Effie) 4 ch jeweler & optician O H&L East St Bradner Mon B tel.

LEGGETT, D. E. (Mabel) blacksmith T H&L 1h R3 Prairie Depot Cen 120.

Leggett, Elijah (Sarah) 7 ch ditcher O 3a 1h R4 Bowling Green Cen 75.

Leggett, W. E. Prairie Depot Mon.

Lehman, Mrs. Barbara ret O 1a H&L Lemoyne Troy 29.

Lehman, Grover Pemberville Fre.

Lehman, Henry (Ida) 2 ch farmer O 87a 3h 4c R1 Walbridge Lake 134 B tel.

LEHMAN, JACOB (Melissa) 2 ch farmer O 80a 3h 15c R1 Lime City Troy 18 Ind tel.

Lehman, Joe painter O ½a H&L Custar Mil.

Lehman, John carpenter O ½a H&L Custar Mil.

Lehman, J. A. (Mary) 3 ch butcher O H&L Custar Mil.

Lehman, Lena Perrysburg Pbg.

Lehmann, L. (Anna) 7 ch farmer O 80a 5h 7c R1 Dunbridge Web 5 B tel.

Lehmann, Thomas (son L.) farmer R1 Dunbridge Web 5 B tel.

Lehnert, Clarence (son of Wm.) farmer R1 Tontogany Wash 12.

Lehnert, Florence (dau Wm.) school teacher R1 Tontogany Wash 12.

LEHNERT, WM. (Jennie) 4 ch farmer O 52a 5h 2c R1 Tontogany Wash 12 Ind tel.

Lehr, Mrs. Carrie R3 Perrysburg Pbg.

Lehr, Mrs. Clara 3 ch T H&L Evans Bradner Mon.

Lehr, Mrs. H. W. 3 ch farming O 6a R3 Perrysburg Per 158.

Leigh, Harrison (Allie) 1 ch hostler O H&L Walbridge Lake.

LEIMGRUBER, J. B. (Ellen) 1 ch farmer T 160a 5h 1c R1 Rudolph Hen 64.

LEIMGRUBER, ROBERT (Grace) 2 ch farmer T 80a 3h 1c R1 Bowling Green Pla 32 Ind tel.

Lein, Mrs. Addie RD Portage Por.

Demonstration of Spraying by State Department of Agriculture.

131

LEIN, ALLEN (Ellen) 2 ch farmer O 40a 3h 5c R4 Bowling Green Cen 107 Ind tel.

Lein, H. A. cattle RD Portage Por.

LEIN, JOHN (Addie I.) farmer O 88a 3h 1c R1 Portage Por 90 Ind tel.

Leindecker, Nicholas 8 ch ret O H&L Custar Mil.

Leindecker, Wm. (Ida) 3 ch draying O H&L 1h Custar Milton.

Leiter, A. (Emma) coal and ice O H&L Custar Mil B tel.

Leiter, Brittanua (dau Dill) student Milton Center Mil.

Leiter, Dill (Emma) 7 ch village marshall O H&L Milton Center Mil.

LEITER, H. (Fay) 2 ch garage T H&L RD North Baltimore Hen B & Ind tels.

Leiter, Seneca S. (Salemma) 4 ch farmer O 91a 3h 4c R3 Bowling Green Cen 22 Ind tel.

LeKing, Fred (Sophia) 4 ch farmer O 80a 3h 6c R1 Luckey Tro 51.

LeKing, Henry (Julia) 3 ch farmer O 46a 2h 8c R1 Lemoyne Tro 85 B tel.

LeKing, Henry, Jr. (Anna) 2 ch farmer T 55a 2h 6c R1 Stony Ridge Tro 44 Ind tel.

Leking, H. L. (Louisa C.) 3 ch farmer O 80a 2h 2c R3 Pemberville Tro 56 B tel.

Leking, L. H. Pemberville Tro.

LEINBRICH, ELMER E. farmer O 44a 3h Portage Por 12.

Lembrich, Fred (Gustin) carpenter O H&L Portage Lib 112 Ind tel.

LEMBRICH, F. W. (Alice) 1 ch farming O 59a 2h 2c R3 Weston Wes 55.

Lembrich, Verma milliner E Main St Portage Por.

LEMBRICK, MRS. ALICE R1 Weston.

Lemmer, Henry (Katherine) farmer O 6a 1h 1c R1 Dunbridge Web 47.

Lemmerbrock, Carl farmer R4 Bowling Green Cen 93.

Lemmerbrock, Chas. (Rickie) 3 ch farmer O 140a 6h 3c R4 Bowling Green Cen 104.

Lemmerbrock, Fred 1h R4 Bowling Green Cen 93.

Lemmerbrock, Herman R4 Bowling Green Cen 93.

Lemmerbrock, Louise 7 ch farmer O 343a 10h 26c R5 Bowling Green Cen 93.

Lemmerbrock, Wm. R4 Bowling Green Cen 93.

LEMON, BEN (Susan) 2 ch farmer & pumper O 10a R1 Bradner Fre 79.

Lemon, Lee (Nettie) field boss T H&L Stahl St Bradner Mon.

Len, Russel laborer Tontogany Wash.

Lenz, Alma Lemoyne Tro.

Leonard, George F. (Mary) farmer O 58a 3h 5c R1 Gibsonburg Fre 79.

Leonard, H. I. (Katherine) 6 ch farmer T 80a 6h 16c R1 Rudolph Lib 76 Ind tel.

Leonard, James RD Rudolph Lib 76 Ind tel.

Leonard, Lawrence Rudolph Lib 76.

Leonard, Veldon Rudolph Lib 76 Ind tel.

Lepper, A. C. (Ella) 5 ch carpenter O. 10a 1h 1c R1 Perrysburg Pbg 100.

Lergier, Amelia (dau Fred) R3 Weston Mil 81.

Lergier, Fred (Katie) 4 ch farmer O 40a 1h 3c R3 Weston Mil 81 Ind tel.

Lergier, G. A. (Dora) 3 ch poultry & country produce O H&L Weston Wes Ind tel.

LERGIER, HERMAN F. (Dorthea) farmer T 130a 4h 3c R1 Weston Lib 62 Ind tel.

Leroy, Louise 4 ch housekeeper R1 Lime City Lake 23.

LESHER, A. K. (Caroline) farmer O H&L Prairie Depot Mon B tel.

Lesley, C. E. (Etta) farmer T 160a 4h 5c R1 Jerry City Blo 19 Ind tel.

Leslie, Chas. RD Bloomdale Per.

Leslie, C. E. Jerry City Blo.

Leslie, D. L. (Celester A.) farmer O 40a 3h 2c R2 Bloomdale Blo 115 B & Ind tels.

Leslie, Frank B. (Irene) farmer O 37a 3h 3c R1 Bloomdale Per 21.

Leslie, Fred R1 Perrysburg Pbg.

Leslie, Katherine R1 Perrysburg Pbg.

Lester, Chas. Perrysburg Pbg.

Lester, S. C. Perrysburg Pbg.

LETHERER, HARDY R1 Perrysburg.

Lethers, George (Thresa) 3 ch laborer O H&L 5th St Perrysburg Pbg B tel.

Letsis, Harry (Elbina) 2 ch motorman T H&L Front St Perrysburg Pbg B tel.

Leveck, Albert (son George) farm hand R2 Deshler Jac 3 B tel.

Leveck, Geo. 7 ch farmer T 80a 5h 4c R2 Deshler Jac 3 B tel.

Leveck, James (Melinda) 8 ch ret Rudolph Lib 80.

LEVECK, JESSIE (Anna) 1 ch T 124a 3h 11c R3 North Baltimore Hen 112.

Leveck, Lewis farmer T 32a 1h Rudolph Lib 80.

Leveck, Myrtle (dau Geo.) housekeeper R2 Deshler Jac 3 B tel.

Levers, D. W. RD Weston Lib.

Leverton, Frank (Sylvenia) 1 ch farmer O 60a 3h 4c R1 Bowling Green Pla 77 Ind tel.

Leverton, Frank (Edith) 1 ch farmer T 80a 3h 5c R1 Dunbridge Web 3 B tel.

Leverton, Samuel E. farmer O 80a 3h 3c R2 Dunbridge Pbg 22 B tel.

Levleit, S. J. (Jennie) 2 ch oil worker H&L RD Rudolph Lib 77 Ind tel.

Lewis, A. W. Hoytsville Jac.

Lewis, Chas. C. (Dorothy) bookkeeper Hoytsville Jac B tel.

Lewis, C. H. RD North Baltimore Hen.

Lewis, Ed. RD North Baltimore Hen.

Lewis, Frank (Lizzie) 1 ch laborer T H&L Cora St Cygnet Blo 6.

Lewis, Frank (Emma) 2 ch oil worker T H&L 1h RD Portage Lib 57. Ind tel.

Lewis, Fred (Emily) 1 ch carpenter T H&L Rossford Ros.

Lewis, G. R. (Nellie) 6 ch oil worker O H&L 2h 2c Prairie Depot Mon.

Lewis, Omer V. RD North Baltimore Hen.

Lewis, Shan (Cora) drayman T H&L Cora St Cygnet Blo 6.

Lewis, W. G. R2 Perrysburg Pbg.

LEWIS, W. W. (Laura) 1 ch tile and bldg blk mfg O H&L factory Hoytsville Jac B tel.

Leydorf, Anna M. R2 Perrysburg Pbg 16.

Leydorf, A. E. 2 ch agent O 82a 3h 1c R2 Perrysburg Pbg 12 B tel.

Leydorf, C. C. (Nellie) meat market T H&L Perrysburg Pbg B tel.

LEYDORF, FRED G. (Estella) 2 ch farmer T 52a 4h 2c R1 Perrysburg Pbg 14 B tel.

Leydorf, Henry C. (Jane) 1 ch laborer O H&L Main and 6th Sts Perrysburg Pbg B tel.

LEYDORF, H. J. (Wellstead) farmer T 1c R2 Perrysburg Pbg 12.

Leydorf, Louisa A. R2 Perrysburg Pbg 16.

Leyon, J. J. Weston Mil.

Lhot, August (Mary) glass worker O H&L Rossford Ross.

Lhot, Mrs. Josephine housekeeper O H&L Box 74 Rossford Ross B tel.

Lhot, Victoria (dau Mrs. J.) bookkeeper Box 74 Rossford Ross B tel.

Libbe, John (Louise) 3 ch farmer O 120a 6h 4c R1 Stony Ridge Lake 89 Ind tel.

Liebhair, Henry (Clara) 4 ch switchman T H&L 1h 1c Cherry St Perrysburg Pbg B tel.

LIEBHERR, B. (Hannah) 6 ch farmer O 80a 8h 6c R1 Haskins Mid 51 B tel.

LIEBHERR, CHARLEY R1 Haskins Has 43.

Liebherr, Chas. (Nora) farmer T 80a 3h 2c R1 Haskins Mid 43 B tel.

Liedizk, August (Martha) 2 ch glass worker T H&L 95 Elm St Rossford Ros.

Liffert, Ada (dau Wm.) housekeeper R1 Fostoria Per 126.

Liffert, Wm. 2 ch farmer T 200a 6h 6c R1 Fostoria Per 126.

LILJE, REV. J. OTTO (Horetta) 7 ch minister T H&L 1h Latchie Lake 95 B tel.

Limmer, Anthony (May) carpenter O H&2Lots Indiana Ave Perrysburg Pbg B tel.

Limmer, A. J. Perrysburg Pbg.

Limmer, Mrs. Barbara ret O 20a R1 Perrysburg Pbg 97.

LIMMER, EDGAR (Julia) 2 ch farmer T 36a 1c R1 Haskins Mid 38 B tel.

Limmer, Geo. R3 Perrysburg Pbg.

LIMMER, GEO. F. (Mildred) 2 ch farmer O 20a 4h R1 Perrysburg Pbg 31 B tel.

Limmer, Henry C. R3 Perrysburg Pbg.

Limmer, Henry F. (Sophia) 1 ch farmer O 50a 3h 4c R3 Perrysburg Pbg 88 B tel.

Limmer, H. W. R3 Perrysburg Pbg.

Limmer, Jno., Jr. R3 Perrysburg Pbg.

Limmer, L. H. (Dora) 3 ch farmer T 55a 3h 2c R1 Lime City Pbg 120 B tel.

Limmer, L. J. (Helen) 1 ch farmer O H&L 2h R3 Perrysburg Pbg 77.

Limmer, W. A. Perrysburg Pbg.

Linch, Mrs. A. ret O H&L 6th & Pike Sts Perrysburg Pbg.

Linch, George (Mary) 6 ch carpenter O H&3Lots 5th & Pike Sts Perrysburg Pbg B tel.

Linch, Ira (Sada) 6 ch laborer T H&L 6th St Perrysburg Pbg.

Linch, Lou (Nellie) 5 ch laborer O H&L 6th St Perrysburg Pbg B tel.

Linch, Louis (Edith) 5 ch laborer O H&3Lots Perrysburg Pbg B tel.

Linch, Percy (Frances) painter T H&L Main St Perrysburg Pbg B tel.

Lindell, Geo. (Ruby) 3 ch railroader T H&L Walbridge Lake.

Lindermier, August (Matilda) 2 ch farmer O 40a 5h 4c R1 Perrysburg Pbg 24 B tel.

Lindermier, Henry (Lizzie) ret O 50a R1 Perrysburg Pbg 24 B tel.

Lindhurst, Geo. (Rosa) 1 ch laborer T H&L 1h Luckey Tro.

Lindley, Chas. (son James) farmer O 52a 3h 4c R1 Prairie Depot Mon 86.

Lindley, James (Cinderella) farmer O 52a R1 Prairie Depot Mon 86.

Lindower, John (Ida) 1 ch farmer O 80a 3h 1c R1 Risingsun Per 99 Ind tel.

Lindquist, Clark E. (Oma) 2 ch farmer T 60a 4h 3c R1 Hoytsville Jac 94.

Lindquist, Floyd (Laura) 2 ch laborer T H&L 1c R1 Hoytsville Jac 103.

Lindquist, John (M.) 1 ch farmer O 60a 10h 3c R1 Hoytsville Jac 99 B tel.

Lindsay, Carey (Della) 1 ch carpenter O ½a H Walnut St Perrysburg Pbg B tel.

Lindsay, Joseph (Sophia) 1 ch carpenter O ½a H Main St Perrysburg Pbg B tel.

Lindsley, Burt telegraph operator Milton Center Mil.

Lindsley, Ira S. Weston Wes.

LINES, MRS. S. 6 ch O 11a 1c Portage Por Ind tel.

Linge, John (Lucy) 3 ch merchant T H&L 1h 1c Sumner St Weston Wes Ind tel.

Lingo, Edward (Mable) 2 ch car repairer O H&L 281 Walnut St Rossford Ros.

Lingo, Harry (Mildred) 1 ch barber O H&L Milton St Weston.

Lingo, J. W. (Lucy) grocery O H&L 1h 1c Weston Wes Ind tel.

Lingo, Samuel (Eliza) ret O H&L 282 Walnut St Rossford Ros.

Linhart, Mrs. Belle 1 ch O H&L 1h Vine St Bloomdale Blo B & Ind tels.

LINHART, C. J. (Marguerite) 2 ch secretary of Building & Loan Co T H&L Harrison St Bloomdale Blo B & Ind tels.

Linhart, Mrs. J. B. Main St Bloomdale Blo.

Linhart, J. H. ret Harrison St Bloomdale Blo.

Linhart, Marguerite Bloomdale Blo.

LINHART, S. A. (Laura C.) saw planing mill O 2h Main St Bloomdale Blo B & Ind tels. See adv.

Linhart, Wm. Cassius (Margaret A.) lumber O H&L Vine St Bloomdale Blo B & Ind tels.

Linke, Anna Luckey Tro.

Linke, Henry Luckey Tro.

Linke, Herman Woodville Tro.

Lintner, Alfred (son J. A.) farmer 2h R1 Lime City Pbg 40.

Lintner, Esther (dau J. A.) housekeeper R1 Lime City Pbg 70.

Lintner, F. E. (Edna) 3 ch general merchandise T H&L Lime City Pbg 91 B tel.

LINTNER, GEO., JR. (Christina) 2 ch farmer O 20a 4h 5c R1 Lime City Pbg 93 B tel.

Lintner, Geo. (Anna) ret O 80a 1c R1 Lime City Pbg 93.

Lintner, Geo. (son John F.) huckster 1h R1 Lime City Pbg 119 B tel.

Lintner, J. A. (Lena) farmer O 130a 2h 2c R1 Lime City Pbg 40 B tel.

LINTNER, JOHN F. (Elizabeth) farmer O 45a 2h 3c R1 Lime City Pbg 119 B tel.

Lintner, Mrs. Louis R3 Perrysburg Pbg.

Linville, Mary A. housekeeper R1 Fostoria Per 112 B tel.

Linweber, Harvey M. (Jennie) 1 ch fruit grower T 12a 1h 1c Rossford Ros.

Lisemer, L. J. (Mary) publisher T H&L Grand Rapids Gr Rs Ind tel.

Lisher, A. Prairie Depot Mon.

LITKEMEIER, F. H. 19 Front St Pemberville.

Littek, Fred (Alice) 1 ch laborer T H&L 122 Oak St Rossford Ros.

Littleton, E. N. Risingsun Mon.

Litzenberg, Sherman (Lizzie) 2 ch farmer T 120a 5h 3c R1 Deshler Jac 27 Ind tel.

Lloyd, A. M. RD North Baltimore Heu.

LLOYD, H. E. confectionery store Front St Cygnet Blo Ind tel.

Loan, Lewis Weston Wes.

LOBER, CHAS. R1 Perrysburg.

LOBER, FRED C. R3 Perrysburg.

Lober, George (Lena) 3 ch farmer O H&L 1h Main St Perrysburg Pbg B tel.

Lober, Merlin R1 Perrysburg Pbg.

Lochmiller, Gust (Carrie) 1 ch works in store T H&L 1h 1c R1 Pemberville Fre 56.

Lochmiller, John 1 ch farmer T 120a 3h 1c R2 Prairie Depot Por 109.

Lochmiller, Lyda R2 Prairie Depot Por 109.

Lock, Margaret Vine St Bloomdale Blo B & Ind tels.

Lockhart, Mrs. J. B. Prairie Depot Mon.

Lockhart, R. E. (Susan) ret O H&L East St Bradner Mon.

Lockmiller, Clara (dau Henry) housekeeper R3 Pemberville Fre 43.

Lockmiller, Henry (Mary) 4 ch farmer T 135a 9h 3c R3 Pemberville Fre 43.

Lockmiller, Louis (Mary) 3 ch farmer O 40a 4h 1c R1 Pemberville Mon 61.

Loe, A. L. (Laura) farmer O 11a 5h 2c Jerry City Por 32 Ind tel.

Loe, Cecil farmer 1h Jerry City Por 32 Ind tel.

Loe, Clarence teamster 6h Jerry City Por 32 Ind tel.

Loe, Forest teamster Jerry City Por 32 Ind tel.

Loe, I. N. Bloomdale Blo.

Loe, Reva housekeeper Jerry City Por 32 Ind tel.

Loe, Virgil F. RD North Baltimore Hen.

Loeffler, John (Edna) 1 ch laborer O H&L Indiana Ave Perrysburg Pbg B tel.

LOEHMAN, HENRY C. farmer O 30 2h R1 Millbury Lake 117.

Logal, F. H. Jerry City Blo.

Logal, J. P. Jerry City Blo.

Logan, Wm. painter T H&L Haskins Mid.

Logle, Jam (Alice) 1 ch oil worker O H&L Jerry St Jerry City Blo Ind tel.

Logue, Mrs. Fannie 5ch O H&L N Main St Bradner Mon.

LOHFINK, JOHN (son Margarite) farmer T 80a 4h 4c R1 Walbridge Pbg 75.

Lohfink, Mrs. Margarite housekeeper R1 Walbridge Pbg 75.

Loman, Martin (Mary) farmer T 50a 2h 2c R1 Fostoria Per 76 B & Ind tels.

Lombard, C. S. meat market 1h bds Prairie Depot Mon B tel.

Lombard, Ira (Catherine) 6 ch farmer T 120a 3h 3c R1 Prairie Depot Mon 64.

Lombard, Jacob (Nettie) 1 ch clerk O H&L Prairie Depot Mon.

Lombard, Roy (Josie) 1 ch school teacher T H&L Prairie Depot Mon.

LONGE, MRS. ABRAM Milton Center.

Long, Adam (Laura) 2 ch foreman T H&L 1c Pemberville Fre B tel.

Long, Addie (dau John) Grand Rapids Gr Rs Ind tel.

LONG, ALBERT 1 ch farmer O 40a 3h 3c R1 Grand Rapids Gr Rs 38 Ind tel.

Long, Alex cattle RD Portage Por.

Long, Alice 1 ch O H&L Lincoln St Bloomdale Blo.

Long, A. J. (Mabel) 1 ch farmer O 70a 2h 4c R4 Bowling Green Cen 68 Ind tel.

LONG, A. R. (Ella) farmer T 170a 7h 6c Grand Rapids Gr Rs 46 B & Ind tels.

Long, A. W. RD North Baltimore Hen.

Long, B. E. (Nellie) 4 ch farmer T 160a 6h 3c R1 Weston Mil 60 Ind tel.

Long, B. J. Grand Rapids Gr Rs.

Long, Carrie housekeeper Jerry City Blo.

Long, Cora (dau George) Weston.

Long, C. E. (Eva) 2 ch farmer T 80a 3h 4c R2 Haskins Mid 18 B tel.

Long, D. F. (Kate) farmer O 150a 8h 9c R1 Bloomdale Blo 102 B & Ind tels.

Long, D. W. (Isabelle) farmer O 160a 3h R1 Bairdstown Blo 50 B & Ind tels.

Long, Earl Pemberville Fre.

Long, Elmer (Lafrana) 4 ch farmer O 6h R4 Bowling Green Por 94 Ind tel.

Long, Ernest (Tressie) 4 ch farmer T 160a 6h 3c R1 Portage Por 22 Ind tel.

LONG, E. C. cattle R1 Portage Por.

LONG, E. J. (Ella) 1 ch farmer O 80a 5h 4c R2 Weston Wash 7 Ind tel.

LONG, E. M. (Nellie) 2 ch section hand T H&L Pemberville Fre.

Long, George (Hannah) 6 ch ret O H&L Weston.

Long, Henry (Sarah) farmer T 60a R2 Pemberville Web 33.

Long, Howard (Pearl) 1 ch farmer T 90a 3h 7c R1 Grand Rapids Gr Rs 27 Ind tel. .

Long, Jas. cattle RD Portage Por.

Long, John (Catharine) ret O H&L Grand Rapids Gr Rs Ind tel.

Long, John (son Osborn) carpenter R2 Weston.

Long, J. B. (Nell) 5 ch farmer O 74a 6h 4c Bowling Green Cen 72 Ind tel.

Long, J. E. (Amelia) 2 ch blacksmith T H&L Grand Rapids Gr Rs.

Long, Lawrence (Maletha) 2 ch laborer T H&L Weston.

Long, Mrs. Lenna 3 ch T H&L 1h 1c R1 Jerry City Por 76.

Long, L. R. (Elizabeth) 4 ch carpenter T H&L Bradner Mon 19.

Long, Murl (Clara) 4 ch farmer T 129a 4h 2c R2 Weston Pla 5.

Long, Mrs. M. farming O 21a 1c Weston Wes 30 Ind tel.

Long, Osborn (Alice) 3 ch O H&L R2 Weston.

Long, Pete (Jane) laborer O H&L Grand Rapids Gr Rs.

Long, S. S. (Lottie) farmer & clerk O H&L Prairie Depot Mon.

Long, Watson (Jennie) 1 ch farmer O H&L Risingsun Mon.

Long, W. H. (Martha) 7 ch farmer T 80a 4h 6c Jerry City Blo 78 Ind tel.

Longacre, Fannie O 100a R2 Prairie Depot Por 128.

Longacre, Geo. farmer T 100a 5h 6c R2 Prairie Depot Por 128 Ind tel.

LONGACRE, R. W. 3 ch oil pumper T H&L Bays Lib 75 Ind tel.

LONGBRAKE, A. N. (Lydia A.) farmer O 100a 1c R1 Weston Mil 54 Ind tel.

LONGBRAKE, W. A. (Archie) garage O H&L Milton Center Mil 93 Ind tel. See adv.

Longsdorf, A. J. B. (Bessie N.) supt Cygnet High School O H&L Cygnet Blo B & Ind tels.

Lougsdorf, Lydia E. (mother A. J. B.) Cygnet.

Longshore, Emma A. housekeeper Luckey Tro.

Longstreet, Ezzra (Orfa) 3 ch farmer O 15a 1h R2 Bowling Green Cen 9.

Longway, J. F. (Anna L.) 4 ch farmer O 82a 3h 10c West Millgrove Per 75.

Looman, Upton Rudolph Lib.

Loomis, Caroline housekeeper R2 Pemberville Web 31 B tel.

Loomis, Charles C. (Fai) 3 ch farmer O 180a 5h 10c R2 Pemberville Web 29 B tel.

Loomis, C. A. (Maud) 3 ch farmer T 5h 2c R5 Bowling Green Cen 61 B tel.

Loomis, David Pemberville Web.

LOOMIS, D. H. Scotch Ridge.

Loomis, Emmet (Stella) farmer T 80a 3h 3c R2 Pemberville Web 26.

Loomis, E. E. (Iva) 2 ch farmer O 60a 2h 8c R5 Bowling Green Web 17 B tel.

LOOMIS, E. L. (Jennie) 7 ch farmer O 80a 7h 14c R2 Bowling Green Pla 91 B tel.

Loomis, Fai Pemberville Web.

Loomis, Frank (May) 1 ch garage O H&L Perrysburg Pbg B tel.

Loomis, F. S. Perryseburg Pbg.

Loomis, Henry (Bertha) 1 ch farmer O 80a 4h 4c R2 Dunbridge Mid 72 B & Ind tels.

Loomis, Martha Pemberville Web.

Loomis, Put Pemberville Web.

Loomis, Ruth Bowling Green Web.

Loomis, R. P. (Martha A.) farmer O 50a 3h 7c R2 Pemberville Web 31 B tel.

Loomis, S. D. (Anna) farmer O 60a R5 Bowling Green Web 20 Ind tel.

Loop, C. A. (Nettie) 3 ch railroader O H&L Walbridge Lake.

Loop, C. J. (Matilda) gardener O H&L Walbridge Lake.

Loop, Geo. N. (Katherine) ret O H&L 1c Walbridge Lake.

Loop, Matilda C. Walbridge Lake.

Loop, S. B. (Carrie) switchman T H&L Walbridge Lake.

Lord, Mrs. Mary 1 ch ret O H&L Maple St Perrysburg Pbg B tel.

LORENZEN, MINEHART (Fadilia) 4 ch farmer T 120a 4h 3c R3 Bowling Green Cen 49.

LOTT, F. W. farmer O 40a 2h 1c R1 Custar Mil 40.

Lotzenhiser, E. B. RD North Baltimore Hen.

Loucks, A. G. (Ama) 5 ch laborer O H&L Cleveland St Bloomdale Blo.

LOUCKS, ROY (son A. G.) laborer Cleveland St Bloomdale Blo.

Loucks, Samuel Bloomdale Per.

Loung, Henry (Julia) 3 ch carpenter O H&L 7th St Perrysburg Pbg.

Louse, Frank (Mary) 6 ch farmer O 80a 6h 12c R1 Custar Mil 42.

Louys, Genevieve (dau Mrs. John) housekeeper Custar Mil.

Louys, Mrs. John 11 ch rooming house O H&L Custar Mil.

Louys, Mrs. Lizzie 3 ch ret O H&L Custar Mil.

Lovelace, Arthur (Ida) 3 ch inspector T H&L Walbridge Lake.

Lovelace, T. T. 2 ch laborer T H&L Prairie Depot Mon.

Lovell, Mrs. Estella Custar Jac.

Lovell, Mrs. Frances 3 ch ret Milton Center Mil.

Lovell, Nellie housekeeper Milton Center Mil.

Lovell, Samuel (son Mrs. S. L.) farmer R2 Custar Jac 97.

Lovell, Mrs. S. L. 4 ch farmer O 40a 2h 3c R2 Custar Jac 97.

Lovell, Vivian (dau Mrs. S. L.) housekeeper R2 Custar Jac 97.

Lovenlauch, Margaret ret O H&L Commercial St Perrysburg Pbg.

Lovett, C. farmer O 160a 7h 1c R2 Custar Lib 18 B tel.

LOVETT, MRS. D. W. RD Custar.

Lovett, Jno. Custar Hen.

Lovett, Mrs. Nellie O ½a H&L bds Milton Mil.

Lovey, John (Ida) tool maker T H&L Indiana Ave Perrysburg Pbg.

Lowe, Edward (Carrie) 5 ch farmer O 2a 1h R2 Bowling Green Pla 42.

Lowe, Lincoln (Ena) 3 ch farmer T 57a 4h 2c R1 Bowling Green Pla 74 B tel.

LOWELL, L. A. (Sylva) farmer T 150a R1 Rudolph Lib 75 Ind tel.

Lowmaster, Willis Grand Rapids Gr Rs.

Lownsbury, G. B. Perrysburg Pbg.

Lowry, W. J. RD North Baltimore Hen.

Loy, Oscar (Grace) 4 ch clerk T H&L Main St Weston.

Loy, U. E. (Eva) 3 ch farmer O 11a 1h R2 Bowling Green Pla 93.

Lucas, Ben R1 Perrysburg Pbg.

Lucas, Condy (Hortanse) 2 ch traveling man O H&L 2d St Perrysburg Pbg B tel.

Lucas, G. F. (Mary) 6 ch farmer O 43a '4h 3c R3 Perrysburg Pbg 77 Ind tel.

Lucas, John (Emma) 2 ch farmer O 73a 3h 8c R1 Le Moyne Tro 85 B tel.

LUCAS, J. E. (Hariet) blacksmith T H&L 2h East St Bradner Mon B tel.

Lucas, L. M. Perrysburg Pbg.

LUCE, ABE (Ethel L.) 1 ch farmer T H&L 2c R5 Bowling Green Cen 74.

Luce, Abraham farmer O H&L 1h Mermill Por 20.

Luce, Elmer J. (Amelia) 1 ch carpenter O H&L Second St Portage Por.

Luckow, John (Jessie) ret T 2a R2 Haskins Wash 80.

Lucus, J. E. Bradner Mon.

Lucy, Wm. (Atha) farmer O 20a 2h 4c R1 Fostoria Per 122 Ind tel.

Ludwig, H. (Ida) 3 ch farmer O 26¼a 3h 4c Jerry City Blo 19 Ind tel.

LUGABIHL, PETER (Susan) 9 ch farmer T 200a 7h 6c R1 Bowling Green Pla 28 Ind tel.

Lugabihl, Samuel (Nellie) 5 ch farmer T 52a 2h 1c R1 Weston Mil 64.

Luis, W. G. farming O 120a 9h 8c R2 Perrysburg Pbg 2 B tel.

Luman, Clarance A. (Mable) farmer T 150a 1h R1 Fostoria Per 49 Ind tel.

Luman, J. B. (Mary A.) farmer O 150a 7h 9c R1 Fostoria Per 49 Ind tel.

Luman, O. W. Bradner Mon.

Luman, Samuel (Edith) 2 ch farmer T 150a 2c R1 Fostoria Per 49.

Luman, Uptom (Evelyne) 3 ch farmer 2h R1 Rudolph Lib 67.

Lumer, O. C. 1 ch thresher T 10a R3 Prairie Depot Mon 50.

Lumsden, George (Linda) carpenter T H&L Mermill Lib 20.

Lundy, Fred RD Bowling Green Pla.

LUNDY, J. F. (Mary) 2 ch farmer O 15a 2h 1c R2 Bowling Green Pla 86 B tel.

Luwick, John farm hand Luckey Tro 71.

Lurton, Dick (Annie) field foreman O H 2h R1 Rudolph Lib 70 Ind tel.

Lusher, B. F. (Margurett) farmer O 120a 1h 2c R1 Millbury Lake 126 Ind tel.

Lusher, C. S. Walbridge Lake.

Lusher, Mrs. Delilah O 64a R1 Walbridge Lake 22.

Lusher, Ellery F. (son F. D.) farmer 1h 2c R3 Perrysburg Pbg 62 Ind tel.

Lusher, Elmer H. (son F. D.) carpenter R3 Perrysburg Pbg 62.

Lusher, Miss Emeline R1 Walbridge Lake 22.

Lusher, Ezra farmer O 90a 3h 3c R1 Walbridge Lake 22.

Lusher, F. D. (Emma C.) 2 ch farmer O 100a 5h 4c R3 Perrysburg Pbg 62 Ind tel.

Lusher, Freeman D. (Son F. D.) farmer 1h 1c R3 Perrysburg Pbg 62.

Lusher, Lester A. (son F. D.) farmer 1c R3 Perrysburg Pbg 62.

Lusher, Margaret Millbury Lake.

Harvesting Wood County Wheat.

137

Lusk, Mrs. D. 3 ch housekeeper O H&L Prairie Depot Mon.

Lusk, J. H. (Ophelia A.) ret O H&L Prairie Depot Mon.

Lusk, Nettie Prairie Depot Mon.

Lusk, Ophelia A. Prairie Depot Mon.

LUTHER, MARY C. T H&L Box 104 Portage Por.

Luther, Orvil (son Mary C.) section hand Second St Portage Por.

Lutman, Geo. (Louise) 3 ch laborer O H&L Millbury Lake.

Lutman, John (Emma) 1 ch laborer O H&L Millbury Lake.

Lutz, Alvin (son A. S.) school teacher R1 Deshler Jac 33 B tel.

Lutz, A. S. (Eleanor) 6 ch farmer O 80a 4h 5c R1 Deshler Jac 33 B tel.

Lutz, Zulu (dau A. S.) housekeeper R1 Deshler Jac 33 B tel.

Lybarger, M. M. RD Weston Wash.

LYDEY, J. D. RD Tiffin.

LYLE, E. (Alice) 3 ch farmer O 80a 4h 7c R1 Deshler Jac 22 B tel.

Lyle, W. R. (Sarah) 2 ch farmer T H&L 2c R1 Deshler Jac 22.

Lyndemyer, Henry cattle RD Portage Por.

Lynn, Melvin RD Bowling Green Pla.

Lyon, A. B. (Alice) 2 ch farmer O 6h 12c North Baltimore Hen 84½ Ind tel.

Lyon, F. L. (Martha) 3 ch farmer O 3a 2h 3c R2 Perrysburg Mid 2.

Lyon, F. W. (Jennie L.) farmer O 30a 2h 3c R2 Perrysburg Mid 2.

LYON, MRS. HENRY L. RD North Baltimore.

Lyon, Jessie (dau O.) school teacher R2 Perrysburg Mid 2 B tel.

Lyon, J. L. RD North Baltimore Hen.

Lyon, J. M. (Nanna D.) 2 ch farmer O 53a 5h 8c RD North Baltimore Hen 106 Ind tel.

Lyon, L. S. RD North Baltimore Hen.

Lyon, Maggie O. RD North Baltimore Hen.

Lyon, O. farmer O 75a 2h 3c R2 Perrysburg Mid 2 B tel.

Lyons, Miss Emma dressmaker O H&L East St Bradner Mon.

Lyons, Harry Hoytsville Jac.

Lyons, John (Amanda) 1 ch farmer T 40a 1h 1c R1 Weston Mil 55 Ind tel.

Lyons, J. W. Perrysburg Pbg.

Lyons, Sam (Pearl) 2 ch reed worker T H&L Second St Perrysburg Pbg B tel.

Lytle, Bert (son Wm.) farmer 2h R2 Perrysburg Mid 1.

Lytle, Harvey (son Wm.) farmer 1h R2 Perrysburg Mid 1 B tel.

Lytle, Irvin (Helen) farmer T 2h 2c R2 Perrysburg Mid 1 B tel.

Lytle, Ross (son Wm.) farmer R2 Perrysburg Mid 1 B tel.

LYTLE, WM. (Mary) farmer O 80a 1h 8c R2 Perrysburg Mid 1 B tel.

MacLachlan, R. B. (Nina) 1 ch post office inspector T H&L Front St Perrysburg Pbg B tel.

McAdams, Ella housekeeper O H&L Risingsun Mon.

McAdams, J. W. Risingsun Mon.

McAllister, Cynthia ret O H&L 5th St Perrysburg Pbg B tel.

McAllister, N. A. (Manda) ret O H&L Walbridge Lake Ind tel.

McALPINE, G. A. (Lottie) 9 ch farmer O 1a T 100a 3h 4c R3 Prairie Depot Mon 12.

McATEE, DORAL E. (Mary E.) farmer T 100a 4h 4c R2 Custar Lib 20 Ind tel.

McCain, Jim farmer R1 Bowling Green Lib 114.

McCaine, Angeline ret O H&L Grand Rapids Gr Rs Ind tel.

McCallister, James (Sadie) ret O H&L Bronson St Jerry City Por.

McCaney, Pete (Alta) 2 ch oil worker O H&L Jerry St Jerry City Blo Ind tel.

McCann, Bert (Lily) laborer O H&L Rudolph Lib 81 Ind tel.

McCARLY, MARY E. chiropodist RD Bowling Green.

McCartney, Guy laborer Randolph St Bairdstown Blo Ind tel.

McChesney, J. R. (Flaria) 2 ch farmer T 55a 3h 5c R2 North Baltimore Hen 28 Ind tel.

McClain, Arthur A. (Corilla) 2 ch glass worker T 267 Walnut St Rossford Ros.

McClain, Harry A. (Emma) 3 ch oil pumper O H&2Lots 1h Pemberville Fre.

McClellan, Harry (Alta) 2 ch picture show T H&L Front St Perrysburg Pbg B tel.

McClellund, Mrs. H. H. 2 ch O H&L Myers St Jerry City Blo.

McCLUNG, CARL (Grace) 5 ch farmer T 80a WOS 2h 4c R1 Grand Rapids Gr Rs 42.

McClung, John G. (Josephine) farmer O 70a 3h 3c R1 Portage Por 59.

McClure, Frank (Lena) 3 ch oil foreman T 80a 2h 1c R1 Portage Por 16 Ind tel.

McClure, Gladys housekeeper R1 Portage Por 16 Ind tel.

McClure, Guy (Pearl) 2 ch farmer T 120a 7h 3c R3 Weston Mil 3 Ind tel.

138

McClure, G. C. (Alta) farmer T 110a 5h 1c R1 Jerry City Por 61.

McColley, C. W. Tontogany Wash.

McColley, Margaret E. Tontogany Wash.

McComb, S. W. (Cora) 1 ch farmer O 55a 4h 3c R1 Bradner Mon 28.

McCombs, W. H. (Anna) 5 ch farmer O 80a 5h 5c Tontogany Wash 46 Ind tel.

McConaha, Mrs. Emma 1 ch ret O H& 2Lots Indiana Ave Perrysburg Pbg B tel.

McCone, Burley (Emma) 3 ch farmer O 55a 4h 2c R1 Jerry City Por 57 Ind tel.

McCone, Thos. (Laura) 3 ch farmer O 160a 3h 3c R1 Portage Por 48.

McConnel, Geo. (Clara) 2 ch farmer T 120a 3h 2c R2 Custar Lib 32.

McCormic, I. J. (Ida) 3 ch laborer O H&L Hoytsville Jac B tel.

McCormic, Mrs. Mary J. 1 ch ret O H&L Hoytsville Jac.

McCormick, Chas. Bradner Mon.

McCormick, C. A. Hoytsville Jac.

McCormick, George (Hazel) 1 ch laborer T H&L Prairie Depot Mon.

McCormick, H. A. RD Bowling Green Lib.

McCormick, James O. (Ethel) 2 ch laborer O H&L Main St Jerry City Blo 78.

McCormick, J. chemist T H&L Rossford Ros.

McCormick, Martha ret O H&L West Millgrove Per 68.

McCormick, W. B. (Ella) 5 ch electrician O H&L 1c Lightner Ave Bradner Mon B tel.

McCoy, Clyde (Winifred) farmer T 93a 3h 2c R4 Bowling Green Por 45 Ind tel.

McCoy, C. E. (Florence) 2 ch oil pumper T H&L 1c Haskins Mid 38.

McCoy, C. S. RD North Baltimore Hen.

McCoy, Mrs. Frank Cygnet Blo.

McCoy, G. W. (Minerva) farmer T 90a 3h 2c R1 Portage Por 3.

McCoy, J. F. (Elizabeth) 2 ch farmer T 120a 4h 1c R1 Portage Lib 56 Ind tel.

McCoy, Ray farmer 1h R3 Prairie Depot Por 119.

McCray, Brink pumper T H&L R1 Rudolph Por 25.

McCray, Dorr (Ursa) 3 ch pumper T H&L R1 Rudolph Por 25.

McCray, G. S. (Addie) oil producer T H&L R1 Rudolph Por 25.

McCready, J. W. (Henrietta) 2 ch gardener T H&L Perrysburg Pbg.

McCreary, Mary housekeeper T H&L Scotch Ridge Web 30.

McCreary, Ray (Mabel) 2 ch machinist T 3a R2 Pemberville Web 31.

McCrory, E. L. (Cora) 2 ch tile business T H&L 1h Hatton Per 84.

McCrory, Frank 6 ch laborer O 3a Rudolph Lib 99.

McCrory, H. A. (Cora) 2 ch farmer O 160a 2h 4c R2 Custar Mil 39 Ind tel.

McCrory, John (Lydia) farmer T 40a 2h 1c R2 Dunbridge Mid.

McCrory, Mrs. Julia A. 2 ch O 220a R1 Rudolph Blo 106 Ind tel.

McCrory, Ollie B. Dickson St Jerry City Por.

McCrory, Sarah ret H&L Rising Sun Mon.

McCrory, S. E. RD North Baltimore Hen.

McCullich, Mrs. A. ret H&L Risingsun Mon.

McCullogh, Chas. Perrysburg Pbg.

McCutchen, Chas. H. shoemaker Stony Ridge Tro.

McCutchen, Wilbur R. (Emma) farmer O 40a 3h 4c Stony Ridge Tro 2.

McCutcheon, S. A. Stony Ridge Tro.

McDaniel, Foster RD Bowling Green Lib.

McDaniel, F. (Nellie) farmer T 60a 3h 2c R1 Bowling Green Lib 55.

McDole, Geo. (Laura) 4 ch farmer T 95a 3h 4c R3 North Baltimore Blo 26 B & Ind tels.

McDonald, A. C. RD Bowling Green Pla.

McDonald, J. R. RD North Baltimore Hen.

McDonald, Thos. Dunbridge Web.

McDonnell, Thomas (Amelia) farmer & laborer O 5a 1h 1c R1 Dunbridge Web 49.

McDougal, A. Millbury Lake.

McDowell, J. B. (Rebecca) 2 ch farmer T 96a 4h 9c R1 Bowling Green Lib 115 Ind tel.

McDowell, L. (Ollie) 3 ch gauger O H&L Prairie Depot Mon B tel.

McDoyle, J. RD North Baltimore Blo.

McEvoy, Mr. RD North Baltimore Hen.

McEwen, B. W. teacher & farmer R1 Jerry City Por 69 Ind tel.

McEwen, D. T. (Maude) 5 ch farmer T 80a 4h 3c R1 Jerry City Por 76.

McEwen, Howard 2 ch laborer T H&L R2 Prairie Depot Por 114.

McEwen, Matthew Risingsun Mon.

McEwen, Myrtle 1 ch farmer O 40a 2c Longley Per 104.

McEwen, M. D. (Mary) farmer O 120a 3h 2c Longley Per 104 Ind tel.

McFall, Earl (Stella) 3 ch laborer T H&L 5th St Perrysburg Pbg.

McFerren, Roxie dressmaker Weston.

McGann, Mrs. C. F. RD North Baltimore Hen.

McGARVEY, B. L. (Loma) 1 ch oil worker O 107a 2h 3c R3 North Baltimore Blo 42 Ind tel.

McGARVEY, W. J. (Minnie B.) 2 ch oil man farm foreman O H&L 1h Main St Bairdstown Blo B & Ind tels.

McGee, G. E. (Emma) 1 ch contractor O H&L Front St Perrysburg Pbg B tel.

McGee, L. C. (S. J.) farmer O H&L R5 Bowling Green Cen 23 Ind tel.

McGiffin, Alva (Ethel) 2 ch farmer 100a 4h 2c R1 Jerry City Por 67.

McGIFFIN, W. A. (Bell) 3 ch farmer T 145a 5h 1c R1 Rudolph Lib 106 Ind tel.

McGill, Geo. A. (Jessie) 6 ch farmer O 1¼a T 190a 12h 5c Bays Lib 75 Ind tel.

McGill, J. W. RD Bowling Green Pla.

McGlothling, D. H. (Isabel) oil pumper O 6a 1h R1 North Baltimore Hen 69 B tel.

McGlothling, D. H. school teacher R1 North Baltimore Hen 69.

McGriffin, Alvia cattle RD Jerry City Por.

McGuire, A. A. RD North Baltimore Hen.

McGuire, C. W. (Grace) 2 ch machinist T H&L 1h R1 Bowling Green Pla 75 Ind tel.

McGuire, Jas. J. Bays Lib.

McHenry, E. O. (Della) 3 ch farmer T 55a 5h 1c R1 Hoytsville Jac 78.

McIlhenney, Edwin (son J. J.) laborer R1 Millbury Lake 131 Ind tel.

McIlhenney, J. J. (Ida) 1 ch laborer O 15a 1h 1c R1 Millbury Lake 131 Ind tel.

McIntire, F. E. RD Rudolph Lib.

McIntosh, J. (Laura) 1 ch laborer O H&2Lots Main St Perrysburg Pbg.

McIntyre, W. D. (Nellie) fireman T 1120 Miami St East Toledo Ros 15.

McKean, A. J. (Rebecca) 1 ch shoe cobbler & laborer O H&L Hoytsville Jac.

McKean, B. S. (Anna) gauger T H&L Prairie Depot Mon B tel.

McKean, Mrs. J. A. Scotch Ridge Web.

McKee, E. W. RD North Baltimore Hen.

McKee, Flora M. Weston Gr Rs.

McKee, John (Mary) T H&L Garfield & Walnut Sts Bloomdale Blo B & Ind tels.

McKee, J. F. Weston Gr Rs.

McKEE, MRS. JOHN W. R2 Weston.

McKee, Loy RD North Baltimore Hen.

McKee, W. H. (Dora) 6 ch engineer & operator O H&L Haskins Mid.

McKelney, Geo. E. (Anna) 2 ch oil man pumping O H&L Bairdstown Blo 44.

McKenzie, C. W. (Bessie) 2 ch farmer T 40a 2h 3c R2 Bowling Green Pla 65 B tel.

McKEO, BERTHA R2 Custar.

McKeo, Priscilla RD Custar Lib.

McKinney, C. B. (Anna) oil man O H&L Pemberville Fre 40 B tel.

McKinnis, R. E. (Louise) 3 ch oil worker T H&L Rudolph Lib 81.

McKnight, Calvin ret O H&L 2d St Perrysburg Pbg B tel.

McKnight, Lina ret O H&L 2d St Perrysburg Pbg B tel.

McKormic, Chas. (Maggie) 1 ch farmer O 20a 2h 4c Crocker St Bradner Mon B tel.

McKown, Mary R. Grand Rapids Gr Rs.

McLain, Angeline Grand Rapids Gr Rs.

McLargin, James (Mary) 1 ch laborer O H&L Millbury Lake.

McLargin, Mary Millbury Lake.

McLaughlin, D. H. RD North Baltimore Hen.

McLAUGHLIN, DAVID P. (Mamie) 5 ch field foreman T H&L 2h 1c R1 Portage Lib 59 Ind tel.

McLaughlin, F. R. (Mabel) 2 ch teacher R1 Rudolph Lib 62½ Ind tel.

McLaughlin, James 4 ch ret T H&L Bell Ave Bradner Mon.

McLaughlin, J. D. (Clise) farmer O 5a 2h R1 Weston Mil 61 Ind tel.

McLaughlin, Mary RD North Baltimore Hen.

McLochen, Florence (dau Stella) teacher Lincoln St Bloomdale Blo.

McLochen, Nina (dau Stella) student Lincoln St Bloomdale Blo.

McLochen, Mrs. Stella nurse T H&L Lincoln St Bloomdale Blo.

McMahan, C. J. (Mable) T H&L Myers St Jerry City Blo.

McMahan, Frank RD North Baltimore Hen.

McMahan, H. (Pearl) 9 ch oil worker T H&L 2h 1c Bradford St Cygnet Blo.

McMahan, Jno. RD North Baltimore Hen.

McMAN, W. R. (Minnie) 2 ch farmer O 40a 2h 2c R1 Bowling Green Pla 41 Ind tel.

McMaster, F. A. (Catherine) 2 ch farmer T 140a 5h 4c R1 Hoytsville Jac 44 B tel.

McMaster, Walter (son F. A.) farm hand R1 Hoytsville Jac 44 B tel.

McMelia, P. J. (Nora) 8 ch oil worker O H&L 1h 1c Union St Cygnet Blo Ind tel.

McMurray, J. H. (Daisy E.) 2 ch farmer T 160a 4h 7c Bairdstown Blo 45 B & Ind tels.

McNally, J. C. farmer O 49a 2h 1c R1 Perrysburg Pbg 106.

McNally, James J. farmer O 49a 2h 1c R1 Perrysburg Pbg 106.

McNally, Mary M. housekeeper O 49a R1 Perrysburg Pbg 106.

McNelly, Wm. (Clara) farmer T H&L 1h R2 Weston Wes Ind tel.

McNerney, Mrs. Magdalene 1 ch dressmaker O H&L Custar Mil.

McNicoll, John (Grace) 2 ch foreman in sugar beet factory T H&L R1 Walbridge Lake 17 Ind tel.

McNulty, Frank bricklayer Crocker St Bradner Mon.

McNulty, Mike (Maggie) 4 ch farmer O H&L 1h Crocker St Bradner Mon.

McNulty, W. F. laborer T H&L East St Bradner Mon.

McNulty, Wm. Bradner Mon.

McPherson, A. L. Garfield St Bloomdale Blo B & Ind tels.

McPherson, W. R. (Velma) 1 ch manager Bloomdale Tile & Brick Co O H&L Main St Bloomdale Blo B & Ind tels.

McQuillen, David (son Susian) farmer T 40a 3h R3 Perrysburg Pbg 69 Ind tel.

McQuillen, Susian housekeeper O 40a 1h 1c R3 Perrysburg Pbg 69 Ind tel.

McStay, James (Elizabeth K.) insurance agent T H&L Front St Cygnet Blo Ind tel. See adv.

McStay, Leo E. student Front St Cygnet Blo.

McTurk, Mrs. 1 ch housekeeper O R1 North Baltimore Hen 69.

McUrie, S. E. (Nellie) 2 ch farmer T 80a 3h 2c R1 North Baltimore Hen 52.

McVelia, Harold oil worker Union St Cygnet Blo Ind tel.

McVelia, Marie clerk Union St Cygnet Blo Ind tel.

McVelia, P. J. Cygnet Blo.

McWilliams, J. F. Weston Gr Rs.

Maas, Frank (Christina) farmer T 80a 3h 1c R2 Custar Mil 45.

Maas, Jacob (son Nick) farm hand R2 Custar Milton 45 B tel.

Maas, Mary O 20a 1c Milton Center Mil 52.

Maas, Matilda (dau Nick) housekeeper R2 Custar Mil 45 B tel.

Maas, Matt (Zalla) 2 ch farmer T 80a 4h 3c R1 Deshler Jac 36 B tel.

Maas, Nick (Mary) 11 ch farmer O 108a 4h 5c R2 Custar Mil 45 B tel.

Maas, Peter J. (Annie) 6 ch farmer 20a 3h 3c Custar Mil 45.

Macey, Wm. RD Dunbridge Mid.

Mack, T. E. (Lydia) farming O 4a 1h R3 Perrysburg Pbg 136.

Mackey, John F. (Josephine) grocery store H&L O Front St Bloomdale Blo B & Ind tels.

Mackey, May Box 62 West Millgrove Per 64.

Madden, Alonzo (son Thomas) fireman R1 East Toledo Lake 131 Ind tel.

Madden, E. S. (son Thomas) gauger RD East Toledo Lake 131 Ind tel.

Madden, James R. (son Thomas) laborer R1 East Toledo Lake 131.

Madden, Thomas (Catharine) farmer O 8a 1h 1c R1 East Toledo Lake Ind tel.

Madden, W. H. RD North Baltimore Hen.

Maddy, C. L. Perrysburg Pbg.

Maenter, H. F. (Emma) 2 ch clerk O 3a H&L Pemberville Fre.

Mahaffey, Jno. cattle RD Prairie Depot Por.

Mahl, Chas. (Alice) farmer O 40a 1h 2c R2 Weston Gr Rs 30 Ind tel.

Mahl, S. D. Grand Rapids Gr Rs.

Mahler, Mrs. E. milliner T H&L Grand Rapids Gr Rs.

Mahler, Everett (Bertha) 1 ch laborer T H&L 6th St Perrysburg Pbg.

Mahler, Fred (Lena) 5 ch painter O H&L 1c Seventh St Perrysburg Pbg B tel.

Mahler, George laborer Custar Mil 87.

Mahler, Lou 1 ch laborer O H&L Pine St Perrysburg Pbg.

Mahlman, Margaret Perrysburg Pbg.

Mahnen, Anthony (son C. F.) clerk Custar Mil.

Mahnen, C. F. (Maggie) 6 ch grocery & meats O H&L Custar Mil.

Mahnen, Rose Custar Mil.

Mahr, Fred L. furniture O store & L Perrysburg Pbg Ind tel. See adv.

Maidlow, Harry RD Weston Lib.

Maidment, George Eli (Mary) 7 ch farmer T 80a 3h 5c R1 Bowling Green Lib 54 Ind tel.

Main, Albert Perrysburg Pbg.

Main, Charley 3 ch farmer T 78a 4h 3c R3 Weston Mil 7 Ind tel.

Main, Clay RD Bowling Green Pla.

Main, C. A. (Blanche) 5 ch farmer T 2h Bays Lib 100.
Main, C. W. RD Bowling Green Wash.
MAIN, DAVID (Lucy) ret O H&L Front & Maple Sts Perrysburg Pbg B tel.
MAIN, E. C. (Elizabeth) 6 ch laborer T 2h Bays Lib 98.
MAIN, E. C. (Olive) 6 ch farmer T 120a 4h 4c R2 Bowling Green Pla 50 B tel.
Main, Fred (Altha) 2 ch farmer T 60a 2h 5c R2 Bowling Green Wash 25 Ind tel.
MAIN, GEO. W. R1 Dunbridge Web.
Main, Marie (dau Charley) college student R3 Weston Mil 7 Ind tel.
Main, Nancy J. Weston Mil.
Maire, Augustine (Marie) 1 ch laborer T H&L R1 Millbury Lake 73.
MAIRE, EDWARD (son Julia) farmer bds R1 Millbury Lake 73.
Maire, Elenore (dau of Hippolyte) R1 Box 17 East Toledo Ros 26.
Maire, Evelyn (dau H.) cashier R1 Box 17 East Toledo Ros 26.
Maire, Hippolyte (Sophia) 3 ch farmer T 73a 4h 4c R1 Box 17 East Toledo Ros 26.
Maire, Joseph (Katharine) 2 ch section hand T H&L R1 Millbury Lake 73.
Maire, Mrs. Julia 2 ch farmer O 20a 2h R1 Millbury Lake 73.
Maire, Marie (dau H.) clerk R1 Box 17 East Toledo Ros 26.
Majeski, John (Sadie) 4 ch glass worker O 5a 1h 1c R3 Perrysburg Pbg 77 Ind tel.
MAJOR, ALEXANDER (Louisa) 1 ch oil pumper O H&L 1h R1 Rudolph Lib 36 Ind tel.
Malkebber, J. C. farmer O 30a 2h R1 East Toledo Ros 30.
Mallon, James (Nellie) laborer O H&L Fifth St Perrysburg Pbg B tel.
Mallon, J. I. (Eliza) 4 ch engineer O H&L Union St Cygnet Blo Ind tel.
Mandell, Ernest R3 Perrysburg Pbg.
Mandell, H. Elbert (Della S.) 3 ch farmer O 21a 4h 3c R3 Perrysburg Pbg 65 Ind tel.
Mandell, Ray (Lily) 2 ch mail carrier O H&L 2h Indiana Ave Perrysburg Pbg B tel.
MANDELL, W. A. (Ella) 1 ch farmer O 100a 3h 7c R3 Perrysburg Pbg 86 Ind tel.
MANECKE, Ross (Lelia) 4 ch farmer T 158a 8h 16c West Mill Grove Per 72.
MANER, C. R1 Grand Rapids.

Manley, D. V. R. (Virginia M.) 3 ch manager National Cement & Rubber Mfg Co T H&L Front St Perrysburg Pbg B tel.
Mann, C. K. (Katie L.) farmer T 109a 3h 8c R2 Bowling Green Pla 45.
Mann, C. W. (Mary E.) farmer O 80a 1h 3c R2 Bowling Green Wash 25 Ind tel.
Mann, D. F. (Violet) 1 ch farmer O 160a 6h 15c R1 Lemoyne Lake 34 Ind tel.
Mann, F. L. (Mame) 1 ch farmer T 78a 2h R2 Bowling Green Wash 22 Ind tel.
Mann, Geo. D. (son D. F.) farmer R1 Lemoyne Lake 34.
Mann, Grace L. 1 ch housekeeper R1 Tontogany Pla 18 Ind tel.
Mann, Harry stationary engineer T H&L Milton Center Mil.
MANN, J. K. farmer O 109a R2 Bowling Green Pla 45.
Mann, Nelson (Rosie) 1 ch laborer O H&L Milton Center Mil.
MANN, W. H. (Lulu B.) 3 ch farmer T 146a 4h 11c Risingsun Mon 73 B tel.
Mannell, Samuel, Jr. (Margaret) 2 ch foreman T H&L 255 Superior St Rossford Ros.
Mannell, Samuel, Sr. (Ellen) ret O H&L 255 Superior St Rossford Ross.
Mannhardt, Mrs. Louisa 3 ch ret O H&L Custar Mil B & Ind tels.
Mannhardt, Mabel (dau Louisa) school teacher Custar Mil B & Ind tels.
MANNHARDT, DR. W. W. (Lottie) 1 ch doctor O H&L Custar Mil B & Ind tels.
Mannhart, Mrs. H. Custar Mil.
Manor, J. B. (Etta) 8 ch contractor O H&L 1h Second St Grand Rapids Gr Rs Ind tel.
Manore, Wm. (Ida) 1 ch section foreman O H&L Walbridge Lake.
Mansfield, Avanelli (dau W. V.) R1 Rudolph Lib 77 Ind tel.
Mansfield, B. R. (son W. V.) clerk R1 Rudolph Lib 77 Ind tel.
MANSFIELD, W. V. (Elizabeth) 9 ch grocery O ¾a H 1h R1 Rudolph Lib 77 Ind tel.
Mantel, A. B. cattle RD Mermill Por.
Mantel, Horace (Hattie) 2 ch farmer O 80a 6h 4c R1 Weston Lib 47 Ind tel.
Mantel, Ora V. (Vita) farmer T 27a 4h Cygnet Blo 6.
Manville, Mrs. Alice RD Bowling Green Cen.

Manville, Alice J. RD Bowling Green Jac.

Manville, Alice L. RD Bowling Green Por.

Mapes, Arthur (Grace) 2 ch oil pumper O H&L Prairie Depot Mon.

Mapes, Chas. (son Martha J.) farmer T 115a 3h R1 Hoytsville Jac 74 Ind tel.

Mapes, David Hoytsville Jac.

Mapes, J. F. laborer O H&L R1 Deshler Jac 31.

Mapes, Martha J. 2 ch farmer O 115a 2c R1 Hoytsville Jac 74 Ind tel.

Maple, E. E. (Minnie) 1 ch farmer R1 Portage Por 11.

MARBLE, LEE W. (Pearl) 1 ch farmer T .55a 2h 4c R1 Bowling Green Pla 72 Ind tel.

MARCH, ALVIN (Mary L.) 5 ch field supt O H&L 1h E Main St Portage Por Ind tel.

March, Clarence (son Alvin) student E Main St Portage Por Ind tel.

March, Eunice (dau Alvin) teacher E Main St Portage Por Ind tel.

March, John (Mary) 2 ch ret O H&L 1h 1c Stony Ridge Tro.

Market, Chas. (Sarah) 2 ch farmer T R1 East Toledo Ros 37.

Markin, Frances 1 ch T H&L Second St Portage Por.

Markle, E. C. (Lida B.) 4 ch laborer O Cleveland St Bloomdale Blo.

Markle, Mrs. Kate O H&L Cherry St Bloomdale Blo.

Markle, Mrs. Leo 1 ch T H&L Bloomdale Blo.

Markle, W. T. Bloomdale Blo.

Markley, T. (Amenda) fireman O H&L Bradford St Cygnet Blo.

Marks, Fred (Anna) 2 ch laborer O H&L R1 East Toledo Ros 26.

Marks, John (Anna) 3 ch farm laborer 1c R1 Weston Lib 56 Ind tel.

Marks, LeRoy drayman 1h bds Milton Center Mil.

Marks, Robert R1 Weston Lib 56 Ind tel.

Marks, W. C. Milton Center Mil.

Markwood, C. E. (Ella) telegraph operator O H&L R3 North Baltimore Blo.

MARKWOOD, JACOB O. (Elsie) 2 ch carpenter O 8a 2h R1 Millbury Lake 126.

Markwood, Jess (Maude) wood worker O 4a R1 Millbury Lake 132 Ind tel.

Markwood, Omer (Nina) 2 ch wood worker T 3a 1h R1 East Toledo Ros 23.

MARLEAU, DAVID paints & agricultural implements West Toledo. See adv.

Maroney, Mrs. Delia RD North Baltimore Hen.

Marriott, Jas. Perrysburg Pbg.

Marsell, J. D. Pemberville Fre.

Blooded Holstein Cattle in the lower part of the County.

143

Marsh, Mrs. A. E. Pemberville Fre.

Marsh, Clara M. RD Bowling Green Per.

Marsh, C. E. Jerry City Blo.

Marsh, Jacob H. Walbridge Lake.

Marsh, James A. (Aggie) farmer O 40a 7h 3c R1 Bloomdale Blo 101 B & Ind tels.

Marsh, John (Mary) farmer O 75a 1h 1c R1 Pemberville Fre 54.

Marsh, L. O. Perrysburg Pbg.

Marsh, Perry (Edith) farmer O 80a 4h 6c R1 Stony Ridge Lake 34 Ind tel.

MARSH, SIDNEY (Ida) ret O 4a H 2h 1c Mulberry St Perrysburg Pbg B tel.

Marsh, Thos. E. Latchie Lake.

Marshall, Fred Millbury Lake.

Marten, Geo. Lemoyne Tro.

MARTEN, H. E. (Mary) 4 ch thresher T H&L Pemberville Fre 24 B tel.

Marten, J. F. (Minnie) 6 ch farmer O 100a 5h 5c R2 Pemberville Web 38 B tel.

Marti, James (Ada) conductor T H&L Fifth St Perrysburg Pbg.

Martin, B. O. RD North Baltimore Hcn.

Martin, C. C. (Mae) Luckey Elevator Co O H&L Luckey Tro.

Martin, Chas. E. Prairie Depot Mon.

Martin, C. F. (Theresa) 1 ch RD mail carrier O H&L 1h Millbury Lake 54.

Martin, C. H. (Flora) 5 ch farmer T 80a FOS 5c Prairie Depot Mon 112.

MARTIN, MRS. C. M. 2 ch hotel mgr O hotel Front St Cygnet Blo Ind tel.

MARTIN, ED. farmer T 80a R3 Pemberville Tro 58.

Martin, Ernest Pemberville Web.

MARTIN, E. H. (Hattie) farmer O 20a 1h 1c Box 155 Rossford Pbg 77.

Martin, F. H. (Carrie) 5 ch farmer O 30a 2h 4c Pemberville Fre 9 B tel.

MARTIN, GLENN J. R2 Weston Wes.

Martin, Harold (Dena) farmer T H&L Front St Pemberville Fre 40.

Martin, H. E. (Mary) 6 ch thresher T H&L Pemberville Fre 24 B tel.

Martin, Henry H. (Louise) 4 ch farmer O 103a 4h 5c R3 Pemberville Fre 18 B tel.

Martin, H. W. (Elsie) 1 ch laborer 1c Prairie Depot Mon 112.

Martin, Isabelle F. RD North Baltimore Hen.

Martin, Jacob (Eva) carpenter O H&L N Main St Bloomdale Blo B & Ind tels.

Martin, John N. (Julia) 2 ch farmer O ·80a 5h 6c cor Gibsonburg & County Line Road Gibsonburg 89 B tel.

Martin, J. W. Pemberville Web.

Martin, Kate 1 ch farmer 80a 2h 3c R3 Pemberville Tro 58.

MARTIN, LEONARD (Clemence) 4 ch farmer T 40a 2h 1c R1 East Toledo Ros 38.

Martin, Lester Prairie Depot Mon 112.

Martin, Luretia Weston Wes.

MARTIN, L. H. (Margarette) 4 ch farmer O 60a 5h 6c R1 Pemberville Fre 68 B tel.

Martin, Milo W. (Lena) farmer 2h Prairie Depot Mon 112.

MARTIN, PETER (Sadie) 3 ch general merchandise O H&L Millbury Lake 54 Ind tel. See adv.

Martin, Ronold (son Leonard) R1 Box 27 East Toledo Ros 38.

Martin, S. V. Prairie Depot Mon.

Martin, Thomas (Bertha) 3 ch station agt O H&L Rising Sun Mon.

Martin, Wm. (Anna) 4 ch carpenter O H&L Pemberville Fre 40 B tel.

Martin, W. R. (Laura) physician & surgeon O 3H&L Grand Rapids Gr Rs Ind tel.

Martins, Henry (Anna) 5 ch farmer O 20a T 20a 3h 4c R1 Custar Mil 101.

Marton, Glen (Elzey) farmer O 150a 4h 5c R2 Weston Wes 16.

Masamer, S. O. (Margarite) 1 ch farmer O 60a 5h 5c R1 Fostoria Per 129 Ind tel. .

Mason, Mrs. Alice nurse T H&L Locust St Weston Ind tel.

Mason, Clarence (son J. W.) R1 Bowling Green Lib 54 Ind tel.

Mason, Enid teacher Evans St Bradner Mon B tel.

Mason, Mrs. E. A. Hoytsville Jac.

Mason, E. L. (Welley) 1 ch farmer O 81a 4h 7c County Line Road Gibsonburg 82 B tel.

Mason, H. C. Weston Wes.

MASON, H. I. (Alta) 1 ch farmer T H&L 1h R2 Haskins Mid 19.

Mason, H. W. (Mollie) 2 ch contractor O H&L Hoytsville Jac.

Mason, James (Dora) 2 ch pumper O H&L 1h Evans St Bradner Mon B tel.

Mason, Jno. A. RD Tontogany Wash.

Mason, J. W. (Lydia E.) 4 ch farmer T 160a 4h 4c Bowling Green Lib 54 Ind tel.

Mason, Lewis Westley (Elizabeth) 3 ch ret O H&L Hoytsville Jac.

Mason, Oscar E. Walbridge Lake.

MASON, O. V. (Della) 2 ch farmer T 206a 3h 2c R1 Portage Lib 58 Ind tel.

Master, Chas. (Ora A.) 2 ch farmer O 80a 4h 7c Longley Per 105 Ind tel.

Master, Geo. W. Grand Rapids Gr Rs.

Master, Wash (Katherine) laborer T H&L Grand Rapids Gr Rs Ind tel.

Matheny, Clarence (Stella) farmer T 150a 4h 2c R2 Custar Mil 34 B tel.

MATHENY, EARL (Eva) 1 ch farmer T 80a 3h 3c R3 Weston Mil 4 Ind tel.

Matheny, John (Hattie) 5 ch farmer T 190a 11h 5c R3 Weston Mil 4 Ind tel.

Matheny, J. M. RD Hoytsville Jac.

Matheny, Murel (son John) farm hand R3 Weston Mil 4.

Matheny, Jno. (M. J.) farming O 40a 2h 2c R2 Weston Wes 41.

Mather, Emil (Amelia) 6 ch farmer O 160a 7h 14c R2 North Baltimore Hen 30 Ind tel.

Mathews, A. R. RD North Baltimore Hen.

MATHEWS, J. H. (Julia) clerk T H&L Walbridge Lake.

Mathews, J. M. (Safronil ret O 7a 1h 1c R1 Fostoria Per 111.

Mathews, W. B. Bloomdale Blo.

Mathias, Jacob (Minnie) 5 ch oil worker T H&L 3h R1 Rudolph Por 24.

Mathias, John (May) 4 ch pumper T H&L 1h R1 Rudolph Por 26.

Mathias, M. G. (Dorthea) 1 ch laborer O H&L 1h R1 Fostoria Per 112.

Mathile, C. B. RD North Baltimore Hen.

MATHILE, LEWIS (Alli) 4 ch farmer T 70a 4h 2c R1 Portage Por 22.

Matthes, Emil North Baltimore Hen.

MATTHEWS, A. R. (Mary E.) 3 ch farmer O 37a 4h 7c R1 Genoa Lake 40 Ind tel.

Matthews, Fred (Lena) 1 ch farmer & laborer O 2a H&L 1h R1 Deshler Jac 38.

Matthews, T. S. (Katie) 1 ch laborer T 3a 1c R1 Millbury Lake 119.

Matthews, Wm. B. (Alice E.) farmer T 120a 9h 5c R1 Bloomdale Blo 57 B & Ind tels.

Matz, Ezra (Maggie) 2 ch oil worker O H&L Rudolph Lib 96.

Matzinger, Amelia Perrysburg Pbg.

Maurer, Chas. A. (Cora A.) 4 ch farmer T 160a 2h R2 Bowling Green Pla 91.

Maurer, Elan (Arvilla) 1 ch publisher T H&L Bradner Mon B tel.

Maurer, E. A. RD Bowling Green Pla.

Mawer, A. RD Bowling Green Wash.

Mawer, Currey (Lulu) 2 ch farmer T 80a 3h 5c R1 Grand Rapids Wash 55 Ind tel.

Mawer, E. C. RD Weston Wash.

Mawer, Hattie V. Weston Wash.

Mawer, Helen J. Weston Wash.

Mawer, J. V. (Hattie) 3 ch farmer T 80a 3h 3c R2 Weston Wash 3.

Mawer, Robert (Adella) 1 ch ret O H&L Perrysburg Pbg.

Mawer, Septimus RD Grand Rapids Wash.

MAWER, SIDNEY R1 Grand Rapids.

Mawer, W. W. (Annie) 1 ch farmer O 70a 1h 2 mules 4c R1 Grand Rapids Wash 53 Ind tel.

Maxwell, Edward (Mollie) oil worker O H&L Walbridge Ave Cygnet Blo Ind tel.

Maxwell, Geo. RD Bowling Green Pla.

Maxwell, Mary (dau Printiss J.) teacher Findlay & Walnut Sts Portage Por.

Maxwell, Printiss J. (Cora F.) 1 ch teamster T H&L 2h Findlay & Walnut Sts Portage Por.

Maxwell, Sam Corp St Portage Por.

MAXWELL, WM. (Edna) 3 ch teamster T 12a 3h 1c R1 Bowling Green Pla 74 Ind tel.

May, Carl (Madge) 3 ch painter & paperhanger T H&L Locust St Weston.

May, Joseph, Latchie Lake.

May, Wesley Millbury Lake.

May, W. W. (Anna) 1 ch section foreman O H&L Latchie Lake 23.

Mays, Grant RD North Baltimore Hen.

Mead, O. J. (Eva) farmer O 10a 2h Jerry City Por.

Meade, A. O. (Icie) 4 ch farmer & painter O 17a 3h 2c RD Fostoria Per 90.

Meagley, A. D. (Estella) 4 ch farmer T 80a 3h 2c R1 Haskins Mid 49 B tel.

Mearing, Mary E. RD Bowling Green Pla.

Mears, Anna O H&L Findlay St Portage Por.

Mears, Daniel (Mary) 1 ch farmer O 160a 6h 3c R1 Portage Por 58 Ind tel.

Mears, Earl (Agnes) farmer O 20a 5h 5c R1 Portage Por 58 Ind tel.

Mears, Elizabeth housekeeper O H&L Prairie Depot Mon.

Mears, Mrs. Olga housekeeper T H&L West Millgrove Per 69.

Measell, J. D. (Mary) 6 ch teacher T H&L Hickory St Pemberville Fre.

MEEK, BEN Bradner.

MEEK, CHAS. E. 4 ch farmer O 5h R1 Grand Rapids Wash 54 Ind tel.

Meek, C. O. (Naoma) farmer T 100a 3h R5 Bowling Green Cen 61.

Meek, Elmer E. (Luna) 7 ch engineer T H&L Findlay St Portage Por.

Meek, James (Alice) 4 ch farmer T 240a 8h 6c R1 Pemberville Fre 70.

Meeker, Alton C. (Fay) 6 ch carpenter O 1a H&L R5 Bowling Green Cen 74.

Meeker, Catherine Perrysburg Pbg.
Meeker, Mrs. Daniel ret O H&L Sixth St Perrysburg Pbg B tel.
Meeker, Edward (Lina) 7 ch laborer O H&L 2h Third St Jerry City Por.
Meeker, F. M. RD Haskins Mid.
Meeker, Hazel housekeeper Third St Jerry City Por.
Meeker, I. E. (Louisa) 1 ch oil man & teamster O H&L 2h 1c Main St Bloomdale Blo B & Ind tels.
Meeker, John cattle RD Bowling Green Cen.
Meeker, J. F. (Marcia) 6 ch farmer O 83a 1h R3 Bowling Green Cen 21 B tel.
Meeker, Leslie (Susie) stock man O 2a 4h Custar Mil 44 B tel.
Meeker, Mrs. L. A. 3 ch housekeeper O H&L Haskins Mid B tel.
MEEKER, MARCIA R3 Bowling Green.
Meeker, P. T. (Marilla) ditcher T H&L Portage Lib 90.
MEEKER, W. T. (Mary) 1 ch farmer O 20a 6h 8c R1 Rudolph Por 26 Ind tel.
Meeks, Chas. E. RD Grand Rapids Wash.
Meeks, Mrs. Rosa 1 ch R1 Rudolph Lib 63 Ind tel.
Megginson, William (Alice) ret O H&L Grand Rapids Gr Rs Ind tel.
Meggison, Elizabeth Tontogany Wash.
Megill, J. F. (Myrtle) 2 ch farmer T 80a 5h 4c R1 Grand Rapids Gr Rs 11 Ind tel.
Mehaffey, Chas. (son John) school teacher R2 Prairie Depot Por 82 B tel.
MEHAFFEY, JOHN (Anna) 2 ch farmer O 80a 3h 4c R2 Prairie Depot Por 82 B tel.
MEHLING, RICHARD Walbridge.
Meikle, Jno. RD Bowling Green Gr Rs.
Meinert, Geo. farmer O 80a 5h 8c R3 Pemberville Fre 5.
Meinert, Mary Pemberville Fre.
Meinert, Sophia Pemberville Fre.
Meister, M. (Elizabeth) laborer O 5a 1h 1c R3 Bowling Green Web 13 B tel.
Melcher, Annie (dau Wm.) housekeeper R1 Dunbridge Web 6 B tel.
Melcher, Herman (Anna) 4 ch farmer O 106a 4h 4c R1 Walbridge Lake 128 B tel.
Melcher, Lena (dau Wm.) housekeeper R1 Dunbridge Web 6 B tel.
Melcher, Wm. (Mary) 1 ch farmer O 50a 4h 6c R1 Dunbridge Web 6 B tel.
Mellinger, W. H. Grand Rapids Gr Rs.
Mellott, John (Belle) hired man T H&L 1c R2 Fostoria Per 37.
Menke, Geo. H. (Cora) 2 ch farmer O 135a 5h 4c R1 Weston Pla 10 Ind tel.

Menke, John (Louise) 4 ch blacksmith O H&4Lots 1c Hickory St Perrysburg Pbg.
Menke, Louise Perrysburg Pbg.
Menter, Carl (Carrie) 1 ch farmer O 80a 6h 9c Luckey Tro 70 Ind tel.
Menter, Wm. (Mary) ret O 4a 1h 1c Pemberville Fre.
Menter, Wm., Jr. (Edith) 1 ch farmer O 37a 5h 4c R3 Pemberville Tro 60 B tel.
Mercer, Alanus (Emma C.) 4 ch farmer O 140a 12h 19c RD Rudolph Lib 65 Ind tel.
Mercer, Alice E. 2 ch farmer O 120a 5h 4c R2 Custar Mil 34 B tel.
Mercer, Ann E. RD Rudolph Lib.
Mercer, A. A. (Eliza A.) 1 ch farmer O 6a 2c R1 Rudolph Lib 64 Ind tel.
Mercer, A. U. (Millie) 4 ch manager O Lumber Co Rudolph Lib 94 Ind tel.
Mercer, Ben RD Bowling Green Wash.
Mercer, Bert (Emma) 3 ch farmer T 100a 5h R1 Weston Lib 9 Ind tel.
MERCER, CLEM (Ellie) 3 ch farmer O 40a 3h 4c Rudolph Lib 94 Ind tel.
Mercer, Charles A. (Anna) 4 ch farmer O 34a 2c R1 Rudolph Lib 64 Ind tel.
MERCER, CLARENCE A. (Zelba) 7 ch farmer T 120a 5h 3c R3 Weston Mil 76 Ind tel.
Mercer, C. F. (Fallie) farmer O 80a 4h 4c R1 Perrysburg Pbg 12 Ind tel.
Mercer, Devillis RD Rudolph Lib.
MERCER, D. O. (Rosa) farmer O 53a 2h 1c R1 Tontogany Wash 76 Ind tel.
Mercer, Ester E. RD Rudolph Lib.
Mercer, Eugene (Jerusha) 3 ch farmer O 80a 3h 5c R1 Rudolph Lib 66 Ind tel.
Mercer, E. H. Grand Rapids Gr Rs.
Mercer, Frank (Lena) 2 ch clerk O H&L Rudolph Lib 87.
Mercer, Frank (Roda) 6 ch oil pumper O 3Lots 1h R2 North Baltimore Hen 59 B tel.
Mercer, F. M. RD Bowling Green Lib.
Mercer, Geo. RD Bowling Green Fre.
MERCER, HARRY (Bertha) 1 ch farmer T 80a 3h 1c R1 Weston Mil 56 Ind tel.
Mercer, H. C. Freeport Mon.
Mercer, H. F. Rudolph Lib.
MERCER, IRA (son Alice E.) farm hand R2 Custar Mil 34.
Mercer, James 2 ch ret O H&L Prairie Depot Mon.
Mercer, Jerusha RD Rudolph Lib.
Mercer, J. D. RD Bowling Green Mid.
Mercer, Lashuay Weston Wash.
Mercer, Leon RD Rudolph Lib.

Mercer, Lizzie (dau Mary E.) R1 Rudolph Lib 65 Ind tel.

Mercer, Lloyd farmer 2h R1 Rudolph Lib 64 Ind tel.

Mercer, L. S. (Caroline) 5 ch farmer O 64a 2h 5c Waterville Mid 20 B tel.

Mercer, Mary E. 5 ch O 40a 2c R1 Rudolph Lib 65 Ind tel.

Mercer, Owen (son Alice E.) farm hand R2 Custar Mil 34.

Mercer, O. 2 ch oil worker O H&L Rudolph Lib 81.

Mercer, Porterfield Weston Lib.

Mercer, P. F. (Ida) 7 ch ret O 240a H&L 1h N Main St Weston Ind tel.

Mercer, R. M. (Minnie) 3 ch laborer T 1c Bays Lib 98.

MERCER, S. A. R1 Weston Lib.

Mercer, Wm. (Susan) 3 ch farmer O 40a 1h 3c Rudolph Lib 82.

Mercer, W. S. farmer R1 Tontogany Wash 76.

Mergler, Rev. J. C. (Laura) 2 ch minister H&L Locust St Weston Ind tel.

Mericle, Geo. F. Perrysburg Pbg.

Merkley, Blanche Tontogany Wash.

Merricle, John (Elsie) 1 ch mail carrier T H&L Sixth St Perrysburg Pbg.

Merricle, Lou (Mary) 1 ch laborer T H&L Sixth St Perrysburg Pbg.

MERRIFIELD, ALMA farmer R1 Haskins Mid 53.

Merrill, Glenn M. Cygnet Blo.

Merrill, J. M. (Margaret) 3 ch oil worker O H&L Walbridge Ave Cygnet Blo Ind tel.

Merriot, Jim (Lucy) laborer O H&L Fifth St Perrysburg Pbg.

Merritt, Arlton D. (son G. W.) farm hand R4 Deshler Jac 28.

Merritt, D. C. (Samantha) 4 ch blacksmith T H&L Hoytsville Jac.

MERRITT, G. W. (Susan A.) 6 ch farmer T 80a 6h 3c R4 Deshler Jac 28.

Merritt, Jessie housekeeper R4 Deshler Jac 28.

Merritt, Raymond P. (Cora) 1 ch farmer O 75a 4h 1c RD Rudolph Lib 102.

Merschman, Joe Rossford Pbg.

Mertz, Fred (Zella) 3 ch oil man driller O H&L Garfield St Bloomdale Blo.

Mervin, Miss Liza ret O H&L Rising Sun Mon.

Messer, F. B. RD North Baltimore Hen.

Messer, Grace Walbridge Lake.

Messer, H. L. (Elna) 5 ch druggist O H&L Prairie Depot Mon B tel.

Messer, S. M. (Anna E.) farmer O 40a 2h 3c R1 Walbridge Lake 98 B tel.

Messinger, R. E. Perrysburg Pbg.

Messner, C. W. Bairdstown Blo.

METTER, A. (Cora) 1 ch driller T H&L Jerry St Jerry City Blo.

Metter, Gladys school teacher R3 Prairie Depot Por 119.

Metz, J. A. (Madia) 5 ch farmer T 247a 10h 11c R1 Hoytsville Hen 7.

METZ, Jos. S. R1 Hoytsville Hen.

METZGER, A. R. (Anna) 3 ch farmer O 50a 8h 37c R1 Luckey Tro 20 Ind tel.

Metzger, Bertha (dau Jacob) housekeeper Stony Ridge Tro.

Metzger, Chas. (Vivian) 2 ch farmer T Walbridge St Walbridge Lake 3.

Metzger, E. F. (Adelia) 4 ch surveyor & farmer O 6a 1c Stony Ridge Tro Ind tel.

Metzger, Ferdinand (Sarah) 2 ch farmer O 90a 3h 11c R5 Bowling Green Cen 23 Ind tel.

METZGER, FRANK B. farmer R5 Bowling Green Cen 23 Ind tel.

Metzger, George (son M. B.) farm hand R3 Weston Mil 84.

Metzger, Jacob 3 ch ret O H&L 80a 1h Stony Ridge Tro.

METZGER, M. B. (Mary) 4 ch farmer O 106a 7h 7c R3 Weston Mil 84 Ind tel.

Metzger, O. E. Luckey Web.

Metzger, Raymond (son M. B.) farm hand R3 Weston Mil 84.

Meurer, Agnes T. (dau Henry) school teacher Custar Mil.

Meurer, Gertrude (dau Henry) housekeeper Custar Mil.

Meurer, Henry (Catherine) 9 ch harness maker O H&L Custar Mil.

Meurer, Lawrence P. (son Henry) clerk Custar Mil.

Meurer, Phillip (Josephine) farmer and thresher T H&L 2h Custar Mil.

Meurer, P. J. (Mary) farmer T 80a 3h 5c R2 Deshler Jac 4.

Meyer, Ada housekeeper Luckey Tro 70 Ind tel.

Meyer, Henry P. (Clara) farmer O 80a 3h 5c R1 North Baltimore Hen 45.

MEYER, IVAN E. R2 Custar Hen 41.

Meyer, Mrs. Jessie 1 ch canvasser T H&L Stony Ridge Tro.

MEYER, M. blacksmith O Luckey.

Meyers, F. E. (Pearl) 1 ch farmer O 80a 4h 3c R1 North Baltimore Hen 8.

Meyers, Geo. Custar Mil.

Meyers, Harry (Anna) 2 ch farmer T 40a 2h 1c R1 Tontogany Wash 31 Ind tel.

Meyers, Henry Luckey Web.

Meyers, John (Maggie) carpenter O 2Lots Luckey Tro Ind tel.

Meyers, O. E. (Jessie) 2 ch farmer O 80a 3h 5c R2 Custar Hen 41 Ind tel.

MEYERS, O. J. (Effie) 2 ch farmer O 80a 3h 3c R1 Weston Lib 41 Ind tel.

Meyers, Philip (Anna) laborer O H&L Indiana Ave Perrysburg Pbg.

MIASELL, J. D. Pemberville.

Michaelis, Sophia (wid William) 4 ch farming O 56a 6h 5c R2 Haskins Wash 98 Ind tel.

Michaelis, Walter RD Haskins Wash.

Michaelis, Wm., Jr. (Noradell) farmer O 20a 3h R1 Tontogany Wash 41.

Micheal, F. W. (Ella) farmer R1 Luckey Tro 20 Ind tel.

Michel, Adam (Carrie) 1 ch section O H&L Pemberville Fre 40.

Michel, Alex. (Rena) farmer O 70a 3h 4c R3 North Baltimore Hen 92 B & Ind tels.

Michel, Bertha (dau Adam) P O clerk Pemberville Fre 40.

Michel, E. H. Pemberville· Fre.

Michel, Fred H. Luckey Tro.

Michel, Henry (Annie) 1 ch farmer O 80a 3h 6c R1 Dunbridge Web 62 B tel.

Michelsen, Garhard farmer R3 Perrysburg Pbg 137.

Michelson, Hans C. Latchie Lake.

Michelsen, Mrs. Helene 1 ch farmer O 41a 3h 3c R3 Perrysburg Pbg 137.

Michelsen, Henry (Carrie) 3 ch farmer O 80a 5h 9c R1 Le Moyne Tro 36 B tel.

Mickens, Harry farmer Station A East Toledo Ros 23.

Mike, T. C. gen store & confectionery Front St Cygnet Blo Ind tel.

Milbourn, H. M. Cygnet Blo.

MILBOURN, RILEY (Elva F.) 1 ch farmer O 40a 3h 4c R1 Jerry City Blo 65.

MILBOURN, RUTH E. (dau Riley) R1 Jerry City Blo 65.

Milbourn, Willis Jerry City Blo.

Miles, Chas. (Amanda) 3 ch steam engineer O H&L R3 Prairie Depot Mon 99.

Miles, M. F. (Margaret) ret O H&L Prairie Depot Mon B tel.

Miley, Isaiah (Arosie) 3 ch farmer T 80a 4h 6c R3 Weston Mil 5 Ind tel.

Miller, Alfred (Clara) 2· ch farmer T 80a 3h 5c R1 Luckey Web 73 B tel.

Miller, Allen 13 ch laborer T H Weston.

MILLER, ARTHUR C. (Madge) farmer O 80a 5h 3c R1 Tontogany Wash 83 Ind tel.

MILLER, MRS. B. E. 1 ch housekeeper R1 Haskins Mid 55 B tel.

Miller, Carl Dunbridge Web.

Miller, Carrie (dau John) housekeeper Luckey Tro 87 Ind tel.

Miller, Chas. (Mary) 5 ch farmer O 72a 3h 5c R1 Pemberville Fre 63.

MILLER, CHARLES J. (Lizzie) 4 ch farmer O 80a 3h 5c R1 Luckey Tro 23 Ind tel.

Miller, Clifford (Edith) laborer T H&L Main St Weston.

Miller, C. A. (Pearl) 1 ch oil worker O H&L Portage Lib 90.

MILLER, D. L. (Mabel B.) 2 ch machinist plumbing O H&L Harrison St Bloomdale Bld B & Ind tels.

Miller, D. W. cattle RD Prairie Depot Por.

MILLER, EDWARD (Myrtle) 3 ch farmer O 20a 2h 1c R1 Walbridge Lake 24 Ind tel.

Miller, Edith Lime City Pbg.

Miller, Edwin C. Bloomdale Per.

Miller, Elias (Ida) farmer O-82a.5h 2c R1 Fostoria Per 91 Ind tel.

Miller, Ernest (son Lucian) farm hand R1 Luckey Tro 88 Ind tel.

Miller, E.· 8 ch farming O 20a 2h 2c R3 Weston Wes 55.

Miller, E. F. RD North Baltimore Hen.

MILLER, E. W. (Ada) 4 ch farmer T 80a 3h 3c R2 Bowling Green Pla 50 B tel.

Miller, Frank farmer T 160a 5h 7c R1 Portage Lib 84 Ind tel.

MILLER, FRANK Dunbridge.

MILLER, FRED (Eliza) 3 ch farmer 193a 4h 10c R1 Dunbridge Web 59 B tel.

Miller, Fred J. farmer O 36a 2h Haskins Mid B tel.

Miller, Frieda (dau George) housekeeper O Luckey Tro Ind tel.

Miller, George (Louise) farmer O 2Lots 1h 1c Luckey Tro Ind tel.

Miller, George (Rose) 5 ch coal dealer O H&L 1h Grand Rapids Gr Rs Ind tel.

Miller, George (Mary) 1 ch farmer O 51a 2h 2c R1 Lime City Pbg 54.

Miller, Mrs. Grace 10 ch ret Stony Ridge Tro.

MILLER, GEO. F. (Mae) 1 ch gen mdse O·H&L 4h Walbridge Lake B & Ind tels. See adv.

Miller, Geo. W. (Sarah E.) farmer O 53a 1h R1 Lime City Pbg 53.

Miller, Mrs. Henry housekeeper O 58a 4h 5c R1 Dunbridge Web 59 B tel.

Miller, Hermon (Annie) 3 ch farmer O 80a 4h 6c Luckey Web 64 B tel.

Miller, H. D. Bloomdale Blo.

Miller, H. V. (May) 2 ch farmer O 40a 3h 3c R2 Bloomdale Per 19.

Miller, Irvin (Ida) 1 ch farmer T 81a 2h R1 Dunbridge Web 49 B tel.

Miller, John (Maggie) 4 ch farmer O H&L 2h 2c Risingsun Mon.

MILLER, JOHN (Carolyn) 1 ch laborer O 5a H E Boundary St Perrysburg Pbg B tel.

MILLER, JOHN (Ollie) 1 ch farmer T 150a 3h 8c R5 Bowling Green Cen 37 Ind tel.

Miller, John (Katie) 4 ch farmer O 187a 6h 8c Luckey Tro 87 Ind tel.

Miller, Jerry A. (Urie) 4 ch farmer T 53a 2h 4c R1 Lime City Pbg 53.

Miller, John F. (Bessie) 3 ch bailing T H&L 2h 1c Oak St Weston Ind tel.

Miller, J. B. (Minnie) blacksmith O H&L & blacksmith shop 1h Le Moyne Tro Ind tel.

Miller, J. G. (Lila) 2 ch railroad man O 10a R1 Walbridge Lake 7.

Miller, J. J. (Erva) farmer O 40a 2h 2c R1 Walbridge Lake 7 Ind tel.

Miller, J. L. (Elva) 2 ch farmer T 160a 2c R1 Prairie Depot Mon 63.

Miller, J. W. (Eusebia) hardware store prop O H&L Main St West Millgrove Per B & Ind tels.

Miller, Lane (Cloe) 3 ch farmer T 2h R1 North Baltimore Hen 39 Ind tel.

Miller, Louis N. (Jennie) 1 ch farmer T 112a 4h 3c R1 Walbridge Lake 10 Ind tel.

MILLER, LUCIAN (Julia) 7 ch farmer 5h 21c R1 Luckey Tro 88 Ind tel.

Miller, Lulu housekeeper Haskins Mid B tel.

Miller, L. A. (Bertha) 1 ch thresher T H&L R2 Prairie Depot Por 118.

Miller, Maria ret Hoytsville Jac.

Miller, Melissa R2 Prairie Depot Por 108.

Miller, Mirick (Alice) 4 ch railroader T H&L Walbridge Lake.

Miller, Mrs. Nettie 1 ch ret O H&L Risingsun Mon.

Miller, Nix 2c R2 Perrysburg Pbg.

Miller, N. A. RD North Baltimore Hen.

Miller, Perry (Jessie) 3 ch farmer O 80a 4h 4c R1 Hoytsville Jac 70.

MILLER, PHILLIP R1 Walbridge.

MILLER, ROYAL J. (Bertha) 2 ch farmer T 80a 4h 4c Rudolph Lib 75 Ind tel.

Miller, Samuel (Feneuer) farmer O 60a 2h 1c R2 North Baltimore Hen 81.

Miller, T. C. 5 ch ret O H&L Milton Weston B tel.

Good, Sound Stock Is Always an Asset.

Miller, V. A. (Eda C.) 1 ch railroad man section foreman T H&L Garfield St Bloomdale Blo B & Ind tels.

Miller, Virgil C. (Pearl) 2 ch farmer T 80a 3h 3c R2 Bloomdale Per 18.

MILLER, WILLIAM (son John) farm hand Luckey Tro 87 Ind tel.

Miller, Wm. farming R1 Pemberville Fre 67.

Miller, Wilson Bloomdale Blo.

Miller, W. C. (Helen) oil worker O H&L R1 Jerry City Por 32 Ind tel.

Miller, W. H. carpenter O H&L W Crocker St Bradner Mon.

Miller, Wm. J. R3 Perrysburg Pbg.

Millford, Mrs. Bonnie 3 ch dressmaker T H&L Waterville Mid 21 B tel.

Millford, M. H. (son Mrs. Bonnie) driller Waterville Mid 21 B tel.

Milligan, B. B. (Maxine) farmer T 80a 2h 4c R1 Risingsun Per 94 B tel.

Milligan, Chas. (Jula) farmer T 46a 3h 6c R1 Risingsun Mon 79.

Milligan, J. B. farmer O 80a 3h 15c R1 Risingsun Mon 76.

Milligan, Katherine R1 Prairie Depot Mon 111.

MILLIGAN, LLOYD (Phoebe) 1 ch farmer O 2a 1h R1 Hoytsville Jac 47 B tel.

MILLIGAN, S. J. (Alta) 1 ch farmer O 80a 6h 2c R1 Hoytsville Jac 47 B tel.

Millirom, D. S. (Sarah) 7 ch farmer T 126a 5h 6c Cygnet Blo 14.

MILLIRON, D. A. Cygnet Blo 14.

Milliron, D. S. Cygnet Blo.

Milliron, Harvey (Clara) 3 ch farm laborer R1 Weston Lib 43.

Milliron, J. D. Rudolph Hen.

Milliron, Mrs. Wm. 4 ch farmer O 20a 1h R1 Deshler Jac 46.

Milliron, W. B. (Ida) 3 ch farmer T 80a 6h 3c R1 Hoytsville Jac 94.'.

Mills, C. W. (Sarah) 6 ch stationary engineer O H&L Rudolph Lib 95 Ind tel.

Mills, J. C., Jr. (Eva) 1 ch farmer T 208a 5h 17c R1 Fostoria Per 77 Ind tel.

MILLS, J. T. (Sarah) farmer T 80a 5h 3c R1 Bloomdale Blo 57.

Mills, Ruth (dau C. W.) Rudolph Lib 95 Ind tel.

Mills, Wm. (Grace) 1 ch drayman O H&L Second St Perrysburg Pbg B tel.

MILNER, MRS. EVA R2 Prairie Depot.

Milner, Geo. Prairie Depot Blo.

Milse, T. C. Cygnet Blo.

Mincks, Andrew O. (Lorena) farmer & thresher O 90a 2h 5c R1 Bloomdale Blo 123 B & Ind tels.

Mincks, Cloyce RD Weston Pla.

Mincks, C. E. cattle RD Bowling Green Cen.

Mincks, C. J. (son C. J.) farmer T 2h R2 Weston Pla 2.

Mincks, Henry cattle RD Bowling Green Cen.

Mincks, Hoadly (Lucy) 2 ch thresher O H&L Randolph St Bairdstown Blo.

Mincks, Jacob (Lizzie) farmer O 80a 3h 8c R2 Weston Pla 2 Ind tel.

Mincks, J. B. (Lucy E.) 1 ch thresher 2h 1c Bairdstown Blo 45 & 47 B & Ind tels.

MINER, H. V. Tontogany.

Miner, Simon RD North Baltimore Hen.

Minium, C. pumper T H&L Prairie Depot Mon.

Minium, Linna housekeeper T Prairie Depot Mon.

Minium, Lucy C. Freeport Mon.

Minium, Wm. Freeport Mon.

Minks, C. E. (Ethel) 2 ch farmer T 85a 3h 3c R4 Bowling Green Cen 70 Ind tel.

Minks, H. P. Bairdstown Blo.

Minks, John (Frances) 3 ch wagon maker T H&L Bradford St Cygnet Blo.

Minks, J. B. Bairdstown Blo.

Minner, Simon (Lea) laborer O L 1c R1 North Baltimore Hen 68.

Minnick, Albert Grand Rapids Gr Rs.

Minnick, Earl (Josephine) 1 ch ret T H&L Grand Rapids Gr Rs Ind tel.

Minnick, Elias Risingsun Mon.

Minnick, J. A. Risingsun Mon.

Minning, Jno. Luckey Tro.

Minning, W. F. Luckey Tro.

Minton, F. B. (Letitia) physician O H&L Millbury Lake 54 Ind tel.

Mintz, Chas. carpenter R1 Luckey Tro 19 Ind tel.

Mintz, John farmer 40a 2h R1 Luckey Tro 28.

Misamore, E. W. Cygnet Blo.

Miser, Ray (Hazel) 2 ch farmer T H&L 2h R1 Weston Pla 10.

Missler, Anton RD Perrysburg Mid.

Missler, Anthony Perrysburg Pbg.

Missler, Mrs. John ret O 20a 1h R2 Perrysburg Mid 5 B tel.

Missler, Joseph L. (Ona) 2 ch farmer T 60a 4h 1c R2 Haskins Mid 89 B tel.

Missler, Julia A. RD Perrysburg Mid.

Missler, T. J. (Marie) 1 ch farmer T 60a 3h 2c R2 Haskins Mid 89 B tel.

Mitchel, E. D. (Bertha) 8 ch farm laborer Jerry City Blo 71 Ind tel.

Mitchel, Jos. cattle RD Bowling Green Cen.

Mitchell, Alex RD North Baltimore Hen.

Mitchell, E. 6 ch grain dealer T H&L 2c Prairie Depot Mon.

Mitchell, Mrs. Francelia ret O H&L Milton Center Mil.

Mitchell, George 1 ch lather O H&L Broadway Weston Wes 120.

Mitchell, John (Anna) 3 ch laborer T H&L Stony Ridge Tro.

Mitchell, O. J. (Samantha) 1 ch mason O H&L Church St Bradner Mon B tel.

Mix, Emma Haskins Mid.

Mizer, C. S. (Julia) 7 ch farmer T 160a 6h 3c R2 Custar Lib 19 B tel.

Mizer, E. J. (Florence) 1 ch farmer T 100a 5h 2c R1 Weston Lib 6 Ind tel.

Mizer, Ray RD Weston Pla.

Mlademus, Milton Perrysburg Pbg.

Mocherman, Mrs. Alice housekeeper R1 Portage Por 102.

Mocherman, Z. Jerry City Blo.

MODERWELL, H. H. Hill Top St Perrysburg Pbg.

Moe, Fred (Elizabeth) 2 ch laborer T H&L 1h R1 Deshler Jac 46.

Moenter, Carl Luckey Tro.

Moenter, Henry F. Pemberville Fre.

Moenter, H. W. (Anna K.) 4 ch farmer O 149a 6h 14c R1 Pemberville Fre B tel.

. Moenter, Julia Pemberville Fre. 41.

MOENTER, J. T. (Clara S.) garage O H&L Pemberville Fre 40 Ind tel.

Moenter, Mrs. J. H. ret O H&L Pemberville Fre 41.

MOENTER, L. H. (Mollie) 5 ch clerk O H&L Front St Pemberville Fre 40.

Moenter, Mary Pemberville Fre 41.

Moenter, Wm.. Sr. Pemberville Fre.

Moenter, W. H. F. Pemberville Tro.

Moenter, W. J. (Lena) 3 ch farmer T 3h 6c R1 Luckey Tro 88.

Moffett, M. W. West Millgrove Per.

Moffett, W. J. painter & paperhanger O H&L Main St West Millgrove Per.

Mogle, D. W. (Matilda) 2 ch grocer & butcher O H&L Box 549 Rossford Ros B tel.

Mogle, John (Christina) 7 ch farmer T 80a 7h 5c R1 Lime City Pbg 93 B tel.

Mogle, Russell (son John) farmer R1 Lime City Pbg 93 B tel.

Mogle, Ruth (dau John) housekeeper R1 Lime City Pbg 93 B tel.

MOHLER, FRED farmer T 55a 2h Sugar Ridge Mid 63.

Mohler, George (Louise) farmer T 145a 5h 6c R1 Grand Rapids Gr Rs 13 Ind tel.

Mohler, Mattie (dau Geo.) housekeeper R1 Grand Rapids Gr Rs 13.

Mohr, Mrs. W. H. T H&L Main St Bloomdale Blo B tel.

Mollenberg, Fred RD Portage Por.

Mollenberg, Fred J. (Rosa) farmer O H&L 1c R1 Portage Por 11.

Mollenberg, Karl (son Fred J.) teacher R1 Portage Por 11.

Molnor, Steve (Sulpha) farm laborer Cygnet Blo 1.

Molter, John (Myrtle) 5 ch farmer T 40a 2h 2c R1 Bradner Mon 30.

Molter, Myrel (Louise) laborer T H&L Bradner Mon 28.

Monaghan, James F. (Alice) laborer T H&L 2c Rudolph Lib 96.

MONAGHAN, J. F. (Lyla) 2 ch farmer T 120a 3h 6c R1 Portage Lib 92 Ind tel.

Monasmith, Erney (son J. H.) R3 North Baltimore Blo 21 B & Ind tels.

MONASMITH, ESTHER B. R3 North Baltimore Blo 21 B & Ind tels.

Monasmith, F. W. (Nancy J.) 1 ch farmer O 240a 8 h 12c R3 North Baltimore Blo 21 B&Ind tels.

MONASMITH, J. H. (Ella) 3 ch farmer O 230a 7h 16c R3 North Baltimore Blo 21 B & Ind tels.

Monasmith, Pearl (dau J. H.) R3 North Baltimore Blo 21 B & Ind tels.

Monasmith, W. E. RD North Baltimore Hen.

Mong, Berton O. RD North Baltimore Hen.

Moninec, Tony (Flora) 1 ch laborer T H&L Haskins Mid.

Monrose, Mrs. E. B. ret OH&L Pemberville Fre.

Montgomery, H. A. (Drusilla) 5 ch driller T H&L Prairie Depot Mon.

Montgomery, J. C. RD North Baltimore Hen.

Monthaven, Allan RD North Baltimore Hen.

MOODY, L. A. (Evelyn) oil man T H&L R2 Bowling Green Pla 44 Ind tel.

Moon, Albert (Susanna) farmer T H&L 1h R3 North Baltimore Hen 102 Ind tel.

Moon, N. V. (Dencey) 2 ch farmer T 45a 2h R1 Rudolph Lib 78.

Mooney, John (Glenn) 2 ch laborer T H&L Maple St Bradner Mon.

Moore, Al laborer T H R1 Deshler Jac 22.

MOORE, A. A. (Alice) farmer O L 6h 1c R1 North Baltimore Hen 70.

Moore, Charles (Imo) 1 ch oil pumper T L R3 North Baltimore Hen 111.

MOORE, REV. CHAS. D. N. (Mary E.) 4 ch pastor T H&L Findlay St Portage Por Ind tel.

Moore, C. A. plumbing O store room 1h RD North Baltimore Hen Ind tel.

Moore, Clyde W. RD North Baltimore Hen. •

Moore, C. H. (Anna) 1 ch teamster T H&L Hoytsville Jac.

Moore, Daniel (Oline B.) 1 ch farmer T 280a 7h 5c R1 Bloomdale Blo 46 B & Ind tels.

Moore, David (Emma D.) 3 ch farm laborer R1 Bloomdale Blo 46 B & Ind tels.

Moore, E. A. 2 ch ret T H&L Center St Weston.

Moore, George (Sarah) laborer O H&L 1h 2c Sugar Ridge Mid 63.

MOORE, GEO. L. (Edith) 1 ch oil pumper T L 1h R1 North Baltimore Hen 69.

Moore, Harrison (son Daniel) R1 Bloomdale Blo 46 B & Ind tels.

Moore, Herbert (Bertha) 7 ch farm hand 2c R1 Weston Mil 54.

Moore, John farmer T 80a 2h 2c R1 Perrysburg Pbg 20 B tel.

Moore, J. C. (Rena) 2 ch ret O H&L cor Maple & Walnut Sts. Weston.

Moore, J. F. (Sarah) 2 ch telegraph operator T H&L R1 Walbridge Ros 22.

Moore, J. H. (Anna) 4 ch manager O H&L 1c Rudolph Lib 94 Ind tel.

Moore, J. M. (Mary) 4 ch farmer T 80a 2h 2c R1 Perrysburg Pbg 20.

Moore, Rev. Lewis Risingsun Mon.

Moore, Walter (Hazel) 4 ch farmer T 90a 3h 1c R1 Tontogany Wash 81 Ind tel.

MOORE, W. F. (Jessie) 5 ch hardware dealer O H&L Haskins Mid 35 B tel.

Moore, Z. S. (Lydia A.) ret O H&L Bell St Bradner Mon.

Moorhead, Fred RD North Baltimore Hen.

MOORHEAD, M. M. (Ella) 6 ch farmer O H&L T 80a 7h 2c Taylor St Weston.

Moorhead, Thomas (Alice) 1 ch paperhanger T H&L R1 North Baltimore Hen Ind tel.

MOOSMAN, SAM (Helen) farmer T 197a 6h 2c R2 Perrysburg Mid 2 B tel.

Moran, Frank (Mary A.) 7 ch farmer O 10a 1h Bays Lib 100.

Morehouse, A. (Hulda) farmer O 40a 2h 2c R1 Custar Mil 16.

Morhouse, E. W. (son Sam) blacksmith helper bds Milton Center Mil Ind tel.

Morehouse, Hazel (dau Samuel) R3 Weston Mil 88.

Morehouse, Leonard L. (son Samuel) farm hand R3 Weston Mil 88.

Morehouse, Leonard S. farmer O 105a 3h 5c R3 Weston Mil 88.

Morehouse, Samuel (Anna) 7 ch farmer O 115a 3h 5c R3 Weston Mil 88 Ind tel.

MORELOCK, H. F. (Minnie) 3 ch farmer O 52a 3h 3c R2 Dunbridge Web 4.

Morelock, L. J. (Ada) 4 ch farmer & stock raiser O 52a 3h 6c R2 Dunbridge Web 4.

Morgan, Abner (Lucina) 1 ch farmer O 47a 2h 2c R1 Risingsun Mon 81.

Morgan, Adella Prairie Depot Mon.

Morgan, Anne seamstress Crocker St Bradner Mon.

Morgan, Carlton (son J. J.) clerk R2 Weston.

Morgan, Chas. (Nellie) 3 ch farmer T 60a 6h 4c R1 Risingsun Mon 81.

Morgan, Mrs. Hester A. 4 ch O 239a 2h 6c R2 Prairie Depot Mon 9 B tel.

Morgan, J. J. (Stella) 1 ch truck farming O 11a 1h 1c R2 Weston.

Morgan, Mabel (dau S. C.) milliner R1 Prairie Depot Mon 101 B tel.

Morgan, Rose Crocker St Bradner Mon.

Morgan, S. G. (Ida) farmer O 80a 4h 7c R1 Prairie Depot Mon 101 B tel.

Morgan, Thomas (Mary) 7 ch farmer O 6a 1h 2c Crocker St Bradner Mon. •

MORGORT, S. B. (Minnie) 4 ch farmer O 80a 3h 9c R1 Fostoria Per 54.

Moritz, Frank (Eva) 3 ch farmer T 40a 3h 1c R1 Rudolph Lib 33 B tel.

Morlock, Henry Dunbridge Web.

Morlock, Mrs. Ida K. ret O 20a R1 Perrysburg Pbg 66.

Morlock, J. W. R1 Perrysburg Pbg.

Morlock, Louise ret O H&L Seventh St Perrysburg Pbg.

Morlock, L. J. Dunbridge Web.

MORLOCK, TONY G. (Ethel) 3 ch farmer O 40a 2h 1c R1 Perrysburg Pbg 96.

Morlock, Wm. (Ada) farmer O 40a 2h R1 Perrysburg Pbg 30.

MORLOCK, W. O. (Martha) 2 ch oil pumper T H&L City St Haskins Mid B tel.

Morris, Chas. 2 ch laborer bds Milton Center Mil.

Morris, D. M. (Bridget) ret O H&L Front St Perrysburg Pbg B tel.

Morris, Geo. (Rosa) 6 ch farmer T 31a 3h 1c R1 Bowling Green Pla 76 Ind tel.

Morris, G. G. (Belle) oil worker O H&L Rudolph Lib 94.

Morris, Jessie school teacher R1 Hoytsville Mil 42.

Morris, S. D. (Matilda) farmer T 95a
6h 3c R1 Bowling Green Cen 26 Ind
tel.
Morris, Wm. RD Bowling Green Cen.
Morris, W. H. (Elsie) 3 ch farmer O
H&L Euclid St Bradner Mon.
Morrison, A. G. (Lucy) 1 ch garage
T H&L Grand Rapids Gr Rs Ind tel.
Morrison, D. K. Risingsun Mon.
Morrison, Etta East St Bradner Mon.
Morrison, George (Elmina) 4 ch team-
ing T H&L Silver St Weston Ind tel.
Morrison, Mrs. Jennie M. dressmaker
R2 Dunbridge Mid 68.
Morrison, Leanor Bradner Mon.
Morrison, M. C. (Nettie) 2 ch oil pro-
ducer O H&L Evans 'Ave Bradner
Mon Ind tel.
Morrison, W. E. (Zadie) 3 ch farmer
T 40a 4h 6c R1 Fostoria Per 106 Ind
tel.
Morrow, Elsie (Harriett) farmer T Lot.
1c R2 North Baltimore Hen.
Morrow, H. A. Cygnet Blo.
Morrow, T. A. (Mary) machinist O
H&L Venango St Cygnet Blo Ind tel.
Morse, D. M. Perrysburg Pbg.
Morse, James (son Nathan) farmer 3h
R3 Prairie Depot Por 98.
Morse, Jos. cattle RD Prairie Depot
Por.
Morse, Lottie RD Prairie Depot Por.
Morse, Nathan (Eliza) farmer O 80a
3c R3 Prairie Depot Por 98.
Morse, S. B. (Mary) 3 ch laborer O
H&L Pemberville Fre 40.
Morton, Geo. M. (Phylisa) 1 ch ret O
4a H&L 2c Lemoyne Tro Ind tel.
Mortz, Fred Dunbridge Web.
Moser, Mrs. Barbara Perrysburg Pbg.
MOSER, E. W. (Bertha) file mfr T 190a
4h 2c R2 Perrysburg Pbg 6 B tel.
Moser, Geo. V. Perrysburg Pbg.
Moser, Harvey (Jeanette) 4 ch farmer
T 100a 4h 2c R1 Deshler Jac 13 B tel.
MOSER, HERMAN (Helena) farmer T 39a.
2h 1c R2 Haskins Wash 37 B tel.
Moser, Jno. R1 Perrysburg Pbg.
Moser, J. E. (Martha Ellen) 2 ch
farmer O 80a 4h 7c Deshler Jac 34 B
tel.
Moser, William H. (Pearl) 2 ch farmer
T 190a 5h 6c R2 Perrysburg Pbg 6
B tel.
Moss, John 1 ch farmer O 10a R1 Jerry
City Por 33.
MOSS, MRS. SUSAN Box 74 Jerry City
Por.
Mossbarger, Lark (May) 5 ch farmer T
40a 2h 1c R2 Prairie Depot Por 108.

Mossbarger, R. L. cattle RD Prairie
Depot Por.
Motter, W. W. RD North Baltimore
Hen.
Moulton, Mary E. (wid J. H.) ret O
H&L Front St Perrysburg Pbg B tel.
Mourdock, C. E. (Gertrude) laborer T
H&L Haskins Mid 35.
Mourdock, David RD Haskins Mid.
Mourdock, R. (Enna) 3 ch oil worker
O H&2Lots 2h Haskins Mid B tel.
Mowan, Len. (Jennie) 3 ch laborer O
H&L Grand Rapids Gr Rs Ind tel.
Mowen, Allen J. (Maggie) 1 ch barber
O H&L Grand Rapids Gr Rs.
Mowen, Martin (Julia) ret O H&L Ris-
ing Sun Mon.
Moyer, Geo. (Amanda) farming O 40a
1h 3c Grand Rapids Gr Rs 45 Ind tel.
Moyer, J. A. Jerry City Blo.
MOYER, J. E. (Eva) 7 ch oil pumping T
H&L R1 Pemberville Fre 69 B tel.
Mozena, E. F. ret T H&L Tontogany
Wash.
MUELLER, FRANK (Margaret) 1 ch
laborer O 2a H Mulberry St Perrys-
burg Pbg.
MUHEY, THOS. R2 Bowling Green.
Muir, A. P. Pemberville Web.
Muir, Charles (Kathryn) 6 ch conductor
T H&L Sixth St Perrysburg Pbg.
Muir, Clayton (Rose) 5 ch farmer T
202a 5h 2c Rudolph Lib 81 Ind tel.
MUIR, C. C. farmer T 120a 4h 2c R2
Pemberville Web 21.
Muir, Henery (Sofia) laborer O H&L
Fifth St Perrysburg Pbg.
Muir, James G. farmer 2h 5c R2 Pem-
berville Web 41.
Muir, Jas. H. Pemberville Fre.
Muir, Jane R2 Pemberville Web 41.
MUIR, JOHN, JR. (Jane) 5 ch farmer O
3a 1h R2 Pemberville Web 31.
Muir, Margret housekeeper R2 Pember-
ville Web 41.
Muir, P. C. (son C. C.) farmer R2 Pem-
berville Web 21.
Muir, Ray W. (Mary) 1 ch farmer T
100a 5h 5c R4 Bowling Green Cen 70
Ind tel.
Muir, Will (Rachel) 3 ch driller O H&L
1h 4c Evans St Bradner Mon.
Muir, W. A. Pemberville Web.
Muir, W. M. (Isabelle) farmer O 88a
10h 16c R2 Pemberville Web 31 B tel.
Muir, W. S. Pemberville Web.
Mullholand, C. E. RD North Baltimore
Hen.
MULLINS, W. N. (Lucy) 2 ch farmer O
73a 2h 2c R1 Bowling Green Pla 42
Ind tel.

153

Mullins, W. W. RD Bowling Green .Pla.

MULNEY, A. J. farmer T 40a 3h 3c R2 Bowling Green Pla 15 B tel.

Mulvey, Catherine 6 ch farmer O 50a 3h 3c R2 Bowling Green Cen 14 B tel.

Munch, Jno. Millbury Lake.

Mund, Joseph (Marguret) 6 ch farmer O 38a 3h 4c Custar Mil 44.

Mund, P. J. Custar Mil.

Mundwiler, Arthur (Josephine) 3 ch farmer T 76½a 5h 7c R1 Hoytsville Jac 125.

Mundwiler, Helen (dau W. J.) music teacher R2 Custar Mil 31.

Mundwiler, H. G. (Cora) 2 ch farmer 100a 8h 5c R1 Hoytsville Jac 89 B tel.

Mundwiler, Olen (Lena) farmer R2 Custar Mil 31.

Mundwiler, W. J. (Miranda) 3 ch farmer T 100a 5h R2 Custar Mil 31 B tel.

Mundwiter, Harry RD Hoytsville Jac.

MUNDWYLER, MRS. G. R. Hoytsville.

Munger, Ada ret O H&L Second St Perrysburg Pbg.

Munger, Charles (Carrie) 3 ch butcher O H&L Indiana Ave Perrysburg Pbg.

Munger, C. F. (Amanda) farmer O 100a 3h 9c R1 Fostoria Per 110 Ind tel.

Munger, Elizabeth Perrysburg Pbg.

Munger, George (Elizabeth) 3 ch butcher O H&L Second St Perrysburg Pbg B tel.

Munger, George (Minnie) 3 ch butcher & insurance O H&L Second St Perrysburg Pbg B tel.

Munger, Henry Perrysburg Pbg.

Munger, R. F. (Rhoda) 2 ch farmer O 40a 6h 18c RD Fostoria Per 122 Ind tel.

Munn, Clarissa RD Bowling Green Pla.

Munn, G. C. (Altha) 3 ch banker & farmer O 600a Main St Portage Por Ind tel.

Munn, Mrs. G. F. O 40a Portage Lib 90 Ind tel.

Munn, Lavina Portage Lib.

Munn, Leota Main St Portage Por Ind tel.

Munn, M. R. (Inez) 1 ch farmer O 50a 2h 4c R1 Bowling Green Pla 75 Ind tel.

MUNN, ROBT. F. teacher Findlay St Portage Por.

MUNSEL, A. (Maggie) 1 ch farmer T 160a R3 Prairie Depot Mon 13.

MUNSEL, M. S. (Emma) farmer T 134a 4h 8c R3 Bowling Green Cen 13 B tel.

Munsell, Penlop ret O 18a R1 Bradner . Fre 84.

Munsell, S. D. (Singal) pumper oil field 2c R1 Bradner Fre 84.

Munshower, G. W. RD Bowling Green Lib.

Murbach, Esther R3 Perrysburg Pbg 158.

MURBACH, J. J. A. (Elizabeth) farmer O 6a 2h 2c R3 Perrysburg Pbg 158.

Murdock, Agnes (dau J. W.) housekeeper Third St Portage Por Ind tel.

Murdock, David (Ada) 1 ch farmer T 140a 4h 3c R2 Haskins Mid 21 B tel.

Murdock, J. W. (Annabelle) driller O H&L Third St Portage Por Ind tel.

Murdock, Sarah 5 ch farmer O 40a 1h 2c R3 Bowling Green Cen 46 Ind tel.

MURPHEY, B. (M.) 10 ch oil worker O H&L Verango St Cygnet Blo Ind tel.

Murphey, Claude oil worker Verango St Cygnet Blo.

Murphey, Edward student Verango St Cygnet Blo.

Murphey, E. J. (Bridget) 4 ch oil worker O H&L Verango St Cygnet Blo.

Murphey, John oil worker Verango St Cygnet Blo.

Murphey, Miss Lizzie dressmaker Taylor St Weston.

Murphey, Maurice J. (Florence) gauger H&L Union St Cygnet Blo 6 Ind tel.

Murphey, Morris 2 ch oil worker O 2H&2Lots 1h Verango St Cygnet Blo.

Murphy, Geo. R. Pemberville Fre.

Murphy, James (Emma) liveryman O H&L 11b Weston Wes B & Ind tels.

Murphy, Joseph (Sarah) 3 ch farmer T 40a 5h 4c R1 Weston Mil 61 Ind tel.

Murphy, K. W. (Edith) farmer T 118a 3h 2c R1 Bradner Mon 21.

Murphy, S. A. (Hannah) 2 ch farmer O 40a 4h 5c R1 Weston Mil 64 Ind tel.

MURRAY, CHAS. P. (Emma) 3 ch farmer T 160a 5h 3c R3 Bowling Green Cen 46 Ind tel.

Muschler, Albert (Ida) farming T 40a 2h R2 Perrysburg Mid 9.

Musser, Abbie O 20a R3 Prairie Depot Por 119.

Musser, B. F. (Nellie) 8 ch farmer O 100a 3h 4c Portage Lib 57 Ind tel.

Musser, Chas. (Maggie) 4 ch laborer O H&L R3 Prairie Depot Por 130.

Musser, Clayton (Almeda) 2 ch farmer O 80a 4h R2 Prairie Depot Per 4.

Musser, Dennis (Caroline) farmer O 20a R3 Prairie Depot Por 119.

Musser, D. W. 3 ch carpenter T 20a 1h 2c R3 Prairie Depot Por 119.

Musser, John (Catharine) farmer O 40a 1h 2c R2 Custar Hen 42.

Musser, Lewis (Georgia) 2 ch. driller T 5a 2h 1c R3 Prairie Depot Por 119.

Musser, Oda farmer R3 Prairie Depot Por 115.

MUSSER, ORAL Risingsun Mon.

Musser, Reuben Pemberville Fre..

Musser, S. A. (Eliza) 3 ch farmer O 120a 5h 10c R1 Portage Lib 57 Ind tel.

Musser, Wm. Custar Hen.

Mutchler, Dorthy farming O 80a R2 Perrysburg Mid 10 B tel.

Mutchler, Ervin (son Dorthy) farmer T 80a 2h R2 Perrysburg Mid 10.

Mutchler, Fred (Elizabeth) 6 ch farmer O 33a 2h 2c R1 Perrysburg Pbg 30.

Mutschler, Albert RD Perrysburg Mid.

Mutschler, Carl RD Perrysburg Mid.

MUTSCHLER, CHAS. (Mary) 6 ch farmer T 75a 3h 2c R2 Perrysburg Mid 14.

Mutschler, Mrs. D. E. farmer O 80a 1c R2 Perrysburg Mid 13 B tel.

MUTSCHLER, IRVIN (son Mrs. D. E.) farmer T 40a 3h 1c R2 Perrysburg Mid 13 B tel.

Myberry, Mrs. Anna 1 ch housekeeper R2 Deshler Jac 4 B tel.

Myerholt, G. F. Freeport Mon.

Myerholtz, John C. (son Rosina) farmer O 6a H&L Luckey Tro.

Myerholtz, Rosina 3 ch ret O H&L Luckey Tro.

Myers, A. F. (Myrtle) 2 ch salesman T H&L Pemberville Fre 40 B tel.

Myers, A. H. (Blanche) 1 ch farmer T 78a 2h 5c Vine St Bloomdale Blo 121 B & Ind tels.

Myers, C. (Elizabeth) 1 ch farmer & veterinarian O H&L Prairie Depot Mon.

Myers, C. E. (Rosetta) 1 ch O H&L Pemberville Fre 40 B tel.

MYERS, C. L. (Berdie) farmer O 76a 4h 4c Cygnet Por 25.

Myers, D. S. (Angeline) farmer T 70a 3h 4c R1 Jerry City Por 76.

Myers, Edward (Ettie) 1 ch barber T H&L Main St Jerry City Por.

Myers, Elizabeth Tontogany Wash.

Myers, Eunice (dau John F.) school teacher R1 Luckey Tro 23 Ind tel.

MYERS, ESTELLA O H&L R1 Jerry City Por 68.

Myers, Eva housekeeper H&L Le Moyne Tro Ind tel.

Myers, Fred J. (son John F.) farm laborer R1 Luckey Tro 23 Ind tel.

Myers, F. E. (Sarah) 1 ch farmer T H&L 1c R1 Prairie Depot Mon 104.

Myers, F. H. (Ruby) 3 ch clerk in hardware store O H&L Luckey Tro.

Myers, F. W. (Ida) 2 ch dry goods & general store O H&L Luckey Tro Ind tel.

Myers, Geo. (Edna) 1 ch foreman road contracts O H&L Custar Mil B tel.

Myers, Grant D. (Minnie) 5 ch laborer R1 Bloomdale Blo 114.

Myers, Gus (Cora) saw mill O H&L Risingsun Mon.

Myers, Henry gardener T 40a 2h R1 East Toledo Ros 28.

Myers, Henry.(Annie) farmer & painter O 20a R1 Luckey Web 73 B tel.

Myers, Henry W. (Elizabeth) 5 ch works on elevator T H&L Luckey Tro.

Myers, H. W. (Phoebe) 1 ch dry goods & general store O H&L Luckey Tro Ind tel.

Myers, Jacob M. 4 ch farmer T 100a 5h 10c R1 North Baltimore Hen 77 B tel.

MYERS, JASPER (Viola) 2 ch farmer O 20a 2h R1 Jerry City Por 68.

Myers, John farmer O 28a 2h 2c Le Moyne Tro Ind tel.

Myers, John R1 Rudolph Lib 70.

Myers, John F. (Elmira) 4 ch farmer & laborer T 1h Hoytsville Jac 114.

Myers, John F. (Christina) 3 ch farmer O 37a 2h 3c R1 Luckey Tro 23 Ind tel.

Myers, Joseph (Mary) bridge worker O 1a R1 East Toledo Ros 23.

Myers, Josiah farmer O 80a 3h 3c R1 Bloomdale Blo 101 B & Ind tels.

"Pigs is Pigs."

155

MYERS, J. C. (Eliza I.) farmer O 36a 5h
15c-R1 Risingsun Per 100 Ind tel.
MYERS, J. F. (Fannie) sexton O H&L
1h Pemberville Fre Ind tel.
Myers, J. W. Hoytsville Jac.
Myers, Maggie Luckey Tro.
Myers, Mary ret O H&L Risingsun Mon.
Myers, Michael farmer O 10a 2h R1 Jerry
City Por 68.
Myers, O. J. RD Weston Lib.
MYERS, O. W. (Alma) 3 ch oil worker T
1h R1 Rudolph Lib 70 Ind tel.
Myers, P. D. RD North Baltimore Hen.
MYERS, P. E. Hoytsville.
MYERS, S. M. (Laura) dry goods store
Front St Cygnet Blo B & Ind tels.
Myers, Viola M. RD Jerry City Por.
Myers, Wm. Cygnet Blo.
Myers, William F. (Mary) 2 ch teamster
O H&L 2h 1c Le Moyne Tro Ind tel.
Myreholt, G. F. (Emma) 5 ch laborer O
H&L Prairie Depot Mon B tel.
Myres, J. C. RD Risingsun Per.
Myrose, F. H. (Kate) 5 ch farmer O
104a 5h 8c R1 Le Moyne Tro 85 B tel.
Myrose, H. L. (Sarah) 1 ch farmer O
56a 2h 4c R1 Le Moyne Tro 85 B tel.
Myrose, W. H. Le Moyne Tro.
Naegele, Fred (Dora) farmer O 114a 2h
4c R1 Haskins Mid 83.
NAEGELE, M. D. (Minnie) 3 ch farmer T
65a 2h 1c R1 Haskins Mid 83.
Nafus, Aaron (Kathryn) farmer O H&L
1h Grand Rapids Gr Rs.
Nafus, A. W. (Kathryn) ret O H&L
Grand Rapids Gr Rs Ind tel.
Nafus, Howard (Anna) 1 ch electrician
O H&L Grand Rapids Gr Rs Ind tel.
Nagel, John (Anna) 2 ch farmer O 40a
2h 3c R1 Custar Mil 95.
Nagel, John, Jr. (son John) machine
shop & shoe repairer R1 Custar Mil 95.
Nagel, John P. (son John, Sr.) shoe
store & repair shop Custar Mil.
NANLINE, ALBERT farmer R1 Bradner
Fre 92 B tel.
Neale, A. M. Scotch Ridge Web.
Neale, E. W. (May) 1 ch farmer T 40a
3h 3c R5 Bowling Green Web 20.
Neale, Mabel M. Scotch Ridge Web.
NEANHISER, ERNEST (Annie) farmer O
80a 2h 7c R1 Pemberville Fre 63 B
tel.
Needham, A. B. 10 ch ret R1 Custar Mil
13 B tel.
Needham, Burt E. (Elnora) 1 ch farmer
80a 4h 2c R1 Custar Mil 13 B tel.
Needles, F. W. (Laura) farmer O 126a
2h 1c Hoytsville Hen 9.
Needles, Jno. H. Hoytsville Jac.

NEEDLES, JOHN W. (Nellie A.) 2 ch
farmer 120a 11h 9c Hoytsville Jac 114
Ind tel.
Needles, Ora (Maude) 5 ch laborer O 3a
&H R1 Hoytsville Jac 115.
Needles, Vern (son Ora) laborer R1
Hoytsville Jac 115.
Neiderhous, Fred C. Perrysburg Pbg.
Neiderhouse, Alfred (Lillian) 3 ch
butcher O H&L Sixth St Perrysburg
Pbg.
Neiderhouse, Edward R1 Perrysburg
Pbg.
Neiderhouse, Frank R1 Perrysburg Pbg.
Neiderhouse, Wm. (Ida) ret O 3a&H
Main St Perrysburg Pbg.
Neier, D. J. (Etta) 1 ch laborer O 53a
2c R1 North Baltimore Hen 66.
Neier, Lewis A. RD North Baltimore
Hen.
Neier, Louise 1 ch farmer O 160a 4h 6c
R1 North Baltimore Hen 52 B tel.
Neifer, Adam 4 ch ret Milton Center
Mil 92.
NEIFER, A. M. 3 ch farmer O 140a 3h 6c
R3 Weston Mil 80 Ind tel.
Neifer, C. A. (Ocea) 4 ch coal yard O
H&L Locust St Weston.
Neifer, Mrs. Ella M. 5 ch gardening O
9a 1h 1c Center Weston.
Neifer, Goldy May (dau John N.) house-
keeper R2 Weston Wash 10 Ind tel.
NEIFER, JAMES O. R2 Weston.
NEIFER, JOHN N. (Gertrude) 6 ch farmer
T 50a 4h 2c R2 Weston Wash 10 Ind
tel.
Neil, J. RD North Baltimore Hen.
Neiswender, Chas. M. (Florence) 2 ch
farmer O 40a 3h 2c R1 Deshler Jac 26
Ind tel.
Neiswander, Peter Grand Rapids Wes.
Nellis, Kathryn housekeeper H&L Main
St Perrysburg Pbg.
Nelson, E. E. (Della) 3 ch farmer O
120a 6h 4c R3 Bowling Green Cen 87
Ind tel.
Nelson, John (Myrtle) 5 ch farmer O
100a 4h 1c R4 Bowling Green Cen 33
Ind tel.
Nelson, Oscar (Grace) 2 ch oil worker O
H&L Portage Lib 113.
NESMITH, REV. DR. L. M. (Sarah Ellen)
3 ch chiropractor Custar Mil B & Ind
tels. See adv.
Nesmith, Sarah Milton Center Mil.
Nestlerod, A. 1 ch O H&L Main St Jerry
City Blo 78.
NEUBAUER, JOE (Catherine) 1 ch farmer
T 45a 2h 2c R2 Perrysburg Pbg 10.

NEVILLS, ISAAC C. (Mary A.) 9 ch oil worker O 80a 5h 2c Rudolph Lib 94 Ind tel.

Nevills, M. laborer T H&L 1h R1 Rudolph Lib 94.

Newbauer, Joe R1 Perrysburg Pbg.

Newcomer, Lewis ret Prairie Depot Mon.

Newell, Edward N. ret farmer O H&L Le Moyne Tro.

NEWLOVE, FRANCIS (Catharine) 1 ch farmer T 80a 5h 3c R2 North Baltimore Hen 28 Ind tel.

Newlove, John (Mattie) 2 ch farmer T 55a 3h 1c R2 North Baltimore Hen 28 Ind tel.

Newlove, J. R. (Rosa) 4 ch farmer T 120a 5h 2c R2 North Baltimore Hen 59 Ind tel.

Newlove, W. F. RD North Baltimore Hen.

Newsome, R. O. (Emma) 3 ch oil worker O H&L Rudolph Lib 81.

Newton, Chas. (Mary) 4 ch beet man T 20a R1 Stony Ridge Lake 28.

Newton, C. B. (Elizabeth) farmer T 160a 1c R3 Bowling Green Cen 17 B tel.

Newton, Jess (Ollie) 4 ch laborer T H&L Sixth St Perrysburg Pbg.

Ney, Eddie R. bds cor Oak & Maple Sts Weston.

NICELEY, F. J. (Mary) 1 ch farmer T 120a 3h 6c R1 Grand Rapids Gr Rs 41 Ind tel.

Nichelsen, H. C. (Sike) 2 ch ret O 50a 2h 8c R1 Stony Ridge Lake 95 B tel.

Nicholas, F. C. (Leonora) 2 ch machinist T H&L Rudolph Lib 96.

Nicholas, S. (Jane) 7 ch farmer O 50a 4h 3c R5 Bowling Green Cen 110 Ind tel.

Nichols, D. R. (Mae) 1 ch farmer T 80a 3h 8c R1 Custar Mil 16.

Nichols, F. H. (son J.) farm hand R1 Hoytsville Jac 105.

Nichols, Guy (son James) laborer Custar Mil.

Nichols, James (Eunice) 3 ch laborer O H&L Custar Mil.

Nichols, John (Pearl) 3 ch farmer T 80a Hoytsville Jac 121.

Nichols, J. (Annie B.) 4 ch farmer T 140a R1 Hoytsville Jac 105 Ind tel.

Nichols, W. M. (Lena) 5 ch shoe repairer T H&L Custar Mil.

Nicodemus, Ernest (Mary) farmer T 20a 1h R1 Stony Ridge Lake 89 Ind tel.

Nicodemus, Oscar (Maggie) 2 ch farmer T 93a 5h 3c R1 Le Moyne Lake 89 Ind tel.

NIEDERHOUSE, C. H. R1 Perrysburg.

NIEMAN, E. HENRY (Mary) 2 ch farmer O 103a 4h 10c R3 Pemberville Tro 60 B tel.

Nieman. H. (Lizzie) 4 ch furniture store O H&L & store Pemberville Fre 40 B tel.

Nieman, John (Mary) farmer O 90a 3h 7c R2 Pemberville Web 34.

Nieman, Myron L. (Clarinda) farmer T 20½a 5h R1 Stony Ridge Tro 31 Ind tel.

Nietz, Edward E. Freeport Mon.

Nietz, Fred (Nora) 5 ch farmer O 32a 2h 3c R1 Walbridge Lake 5 Ind tel.

Nietz, George (Pearl) 3 ch farmer O 32a 2h 4c R1 Walbridge Lake 5 Ind tel.

NIETZ, ROBERT E. (Bertha) 4 ch farmer O 32a 2h 4c R3 Perrysburg Pbg 49 Ind tel.

NIGH, C. G. RD North Baltimore Hen.

Nigh, Mary A. RD North Baltimore Hen.

Nigh, S. R. RD North Baltimore Hen.

Nims, H. J. (Grace) 1 ch laborer T H&L Front St Pemberville Fre 40.

Nims, Mrs. Lydia RD Bowling Green Cen.

Nims, Z. B. (Lyda) farmer O 87a 2h 3c R3 Bowling Green Cen 13 B tel.

Ninke, Robt. Pemberville Fre.

NINKE, WM. (Minnie) 1 ch farmer T 80a 3h 11c R3 Pemberville Fre 34 B tel.

Nisen, John (Cristina) 5 ch farmer T 5a 3h 3c Lime City Pbg 121.

Nissen, Andrew farmer O 25a 2h 2c R1 Lime City Pbg 59.

Nissen, Freeda (dau Martin) R3 Perrysburg Pbg 99.

NISSEN, H. C. farmer O 25a 2h 2c R1 Lime City Pbg 59.

Nissen, Martin (Etta) 1 ch farmer T 60a 3h 2c R3 Perrysburg Pbg 69.

Nixon, A. O. Pemberville Web.

Nixon, Harry (Alice) 9 ch farmer T 160a 8h 11c RD Pemberville Fre 48 B tel.

Nixon, John (Sarah A.) farmer T 87a 3h 11c RD Pemberville Fre 50 B tel.

Nixon, John, Jr. (Minnie) 4 ch farmer T 120a 5h 4c R2 Pemberville Web 28 Ind tel.

Nixon, M. housekeeper Tontogany Wash.

Nixon, Robert (Arminda) 2 ch farmer T 80a 5h 2c R2 Pemberville Web 41 Ind tel.

Nixson, William (Dessie) 2 ch laborer T H&L Scotch Ridge Web 35.

Nobbs, Irma A. RD Portage Lib.

Nobis, Fred (Minnie) 5 ch carpenter O H&L Pemberville Fre.
Nobis, Fred, Jr. (Hannah) photographer T H&L Pemberville Fre.
Noble, Frank (Addie) 2 ch carpenter O H&L 1h 1c Fifth St Perrysburg Pbg.
Noble, Forrest E. Perrysburg Pbg.
Noble, F. H. RD North Baltimore Hen.
NOBLE, DR. J. F. (Anna) 1 ch physician O H&L Custar Mil B & Ind tels.
Noellert, Jno. F. Walbridge Lake.
Noland, Henry Lime City Pbg.
Nollenberger, Alta (dau E. C.) housekeeper R1 Stony Ridge Tro 31 Ind tel.
Nollenberger, A. (Hattie) 3 ch farmer O 52a 5h 4c R1 Stony Ridge Tro 2 Ind tel.
Nollenberger, E. C. (Mary) 9 ch farmer 40a 3h 5c R1 Stony Ridge Tro 31 Ind tel.
Nollenberger, Ed. E. Stony Ridge Tro.
Nollenberger, F. J. (Emma) 2 ch farmer O 76a 4h 5c R1 Stony Ridge Tro 7 Ind tel.
Nollenberg, Harold farm hand & sub mail carrier R1 Stony Ridge Tro 7 Ind tel.
Nollert, Henry laborer O H&L 1h Lime City Pbg 121.
Nonnemaker, Frank (Daisy) 2 ch driller T H&L Prairie Depot Mon.
NONNEMAKER, G. M. (Celia) 2 ch farmer O 77a 3h 9c Prairie Depot Mon B tel.
Norcross, E. A. (Emma) 4 ch publisher O H&L Custar Mil 44 Ind tel.
Norcross, G. J. (son E. A.) laborer Custar Mil 44.
Norcross, T. D. (son E. A.) manager print shop Custar Mil 44.
North, Frank (Sophia) 1 ch jeweler O H&L Haskins Mid.
North, Harry oil pumper O H&L Haskins Mid.
North, O. E. 1 ch barber O H&L Haskins Mid 35.
North, W. H. (Libey) watchman O H&L Haskins Mid.
Northrup, Chas. RD North Baltimore Hen.
Northrup, M. J. Rudolph Lib.
Northrup, William (Ida) 2 ch farmer T 77a 3h 2c R2 North Baltimore Hen 30.
NORTON, JAMES A. farmer T 64a 3h 1c R2 Dunbridge Cen 1.
Norton, J. E. (Betty) 2 ch farmer T 160a 6h 3c R2 Dunbridge Mid 70 Ind tel.
NORTON, M. L. 4 ch farmer & poultry raiser O 2a H Milton Center Mil.

NORTON, MRS. N. J. farmer O 80a 3h 4c R2 Dunbridge Mid 68 B tel.
Norton, Ralph (son Mrs. M. L.) station agt O E Milton Center Mil.
Norton, W. L. (Mary) 1 ch farmer O 80a 4h 5c R1 Haskins Mid 57 Ind tel.
Norway, Elmer E. (Naomi) 2 ch tool dresser T H&L Mermill Por 19 Ind tel.
Notestine, Henry Risingsun Mon.
Notestine, Jno. H. Risingsun Mon.
Notestine, Sylvanus laborer R1 Tontogany Wash 83.
Nowlin, I. W. Bairdstown Blo.
Noyes, Lizzie Milton Center Mil.
NOYES, W. R. (Lizzie) 5 ch cashier Custar State Bank O H&L Milton Center Mil B tel.
NUNGESTER, CHAS. E. (Hattie) 7 ch laborer 1h R3 North Baltimore Blo 27.
Nusbaum, Finley O H&L Bairdstown Blo 48.
Nutter, Floyd L. (son Geo. T.) school teacher R2 Custar Mil 43.
Nutter, Geo. T. (Mellie) 2 ch farmer T 90a 3h 2c R2 Custar Mil 43.
Nutter, Gertrude (dau Geo. T.) housekeeper R2 Custar Mil 43.
Nutter, Sarah 6 ch ret O H&L Custar Mil.
Nye, E. D. (Erma) livery T H&L 6h Grand Rapids Gr Rs Ind tel.
Nyswander, Edw. (Lora) jeweler O H&L Grand Rapids Gr Rs.
Nyswander, Leura Grand Rapids Gr Rs.
Nyswander, Peter (Susan) 6 ch farming T H&L 1h 1c Second St Grand Rapids Gr Rs.
Oates, Geo. (Tena) 2 ch farmer O 120a 5h 6c R4 Bowling Green Por 1 Ind tel.
Oates, John farmer T 40a 3h 1c R1 Tontogany Pla 19 Ind tel.
Oates, Mary farmer O 40a 1c R1 Tontogany Pla 19.
Oates, Ralph (son Geo.) farmer R4 Bowling Green Por 1 Ind tel.
Oats, Riley (Carrie) 1 ch blacksmith H&L shop Cygnet Blo 6.
Obblinger, John 2 ch laborer O H&L Walbridge Lake.
Ober, John B. (Carrie) 1 ch teacher T H&L Dickson St Jerry City Blo.
Oberdick, Anna (dau Henry) housekeeper R1 Dunbridge Web 6 B tel.
Oberdick, August (son Henry) farmer 1h R1 Dunbridge Web 6 B tel.

158

Oberdick, Ernest (Clara) 7 ch farmer O 60a 8h 5c R1 Dunbridge Mid 67 B tel.

Oberdick, E. H. (son H. W.) laborer 1c R1 Dunbridge Web 5 B tel.

Oberdick, Henry, Sr. (Katie) farmer O 160a 6h 5c R1 Dunbridge Web 6 B tel.

Oberdick, Henry, Jr. (son Henry, Sr.) laborer R1 Dunbridge Web 6 B tel.

Oberhause, A. F. (Minnie) 4 ch laborer O H&L Pemberville Fre 40.

Oberle, E. N. Grand Rapids Gr Rs.

Oberle, Edd. (Blanche) contractor O H&L Grand Rapids Gr Rs Ind tel.

Oberle, Mrs. Mary 3 ch ret T H&L Grand Rapids Gr Rs.

Oberley, W. A. (Maude) 3 ch farmer T 137a 3h 3c R1 Weston Pla 7 Ind tel.

Obermeyer, Dora (dau John) housekeeper R1 Woodville Tro 44 B tel.

Obermeyer, Edna (dau Henry) R1 Stony Ridge Tro 47 Ind tel.

Obermeyer, Fred, Sr. (Anna) 6 ch farmer O 165a 6h 8c R1 Genoa Tro 41 Ind tel.

Obermeyer, Fred, Jr. (son Fred) farm hand R1 Genoa Tro 41 Ind tel.

Obermeyer, Henry (Carrie) 6 ch farmer O 100a 1h 4c R1 Stony Ridge Tro 47 Ind tel.

OBERMEYER, JOHN (Mary) 5 ch farmer O 160a 2h 19c R1 Woodville Tro 44 B tel.

Obermeyer, Mabel (dau John) housekeeper R1 Woodville Tro 44 B tel.

Obermyer, Chas. (Luella) 1 ch hardware & pump fitting O H&L Luckey Tro Ind tel.

Obermyer, J. J. Prairie Depot Mon.

Oblinger, Elisa 1 ch ret O H&L Fourth St Perrysburg Pbg B tel.

OBLINGER, L. I. Perrysburg.

O'Brein, John (Katherine) 6 ch oil worker O H&L Rudolph Lib 96 Ind tel.

O'BRIEN, MAURICE (Theresa) 3 ch farmer O 13a 2h R1 Millbury Lake 131 Ind tel.

O'Brien, Moses (Lura) 4 ch farmer O 61½a 4h 4c Scotch Ridge Web 31 & 34 Ind tel.

O'Brien, Steven (Dot) 2 ch garage O H&L & garage East St Bradner Mon B tel.

Obrock, Henry (Rickey) 4 ch farmer O 40a H&L Luckey Tro Ind tel.

Obrock, Henry H. (Leona) 1 ch farmer T 40a 3h 10c R1 Stony Ridge Lake 34 Ind tel.

Odell, B. (F. C.) ret O H&L Main St Jerry City Por.

O'Donald, Ed. R3 Perrysburg Pbg.

Oehmke, Henry Dunbridge Web.

Oestreich, C. H. Pemberville Fre.

Oestreich, Henry (Sophia) 5 ch farmer O 71a 4h 4c R3 Prairie Depot Por 101 B tel.

Offerman, Alice Pemberville Fre.

Offerman, Henry Pemberville Fre.

Offerman, J. H. harness shop O H&L Pemberville Fre 40 B tel.

Offerman, Kate Pemberville Fre.

Ohler, Edward L. (son H. E.) farmer Prairie Depot Mon 51.

Ohler, H. E. (Anna) farmer O 40a 2h 2c Prairie Depot Mon 51.

Ohler, Mary A. Risingsun Per.

Ohler, Philipp (Mary) farmer O 63a 2c R1 Risingsun Per 95 B tel.

Ohler, Rolla J. (son H. E.) farmer Prairie Depot Mon 51.

Ohler, R. S. (May) 1 ch farmer T 142a 6h 20c R1 Fostoria Per 88 B tel.

Ohlrich, Christ 4 ch ret O 50a 3c Custar Mil 98.

Ohlrich, John (Mary) 4 ch farmer T 40a 3h 1c Custar Mil 98.

Ohls, R. C. (Ada) 6 ch piano teacher O H&2½a Main St Perrysburg Pbg B tel.

Ohm, Wm. (Edith) 1 ch farmer T 60a 3h 4c Pemberville Fre 18.

Ohr, Wm. RD Tontogany Wash.

Ohlrich, Christ Custar Mil.

Ohlrich, Jno. Custar Mil.

Oker, H. W. cattle RD Mermill Por.

OLDER, CHAS. E. (Rosa) 7 ch farmer & fruit grower O 3a 1h 1c R1 Grand Rapids Gr Rs 4 Ind tel.

Older, J. O. painter O H&L Grand Rapids Gr Rs Ind tel.

Older, J. W. Grand Rapids Gr Rs.

OLDER, M. B. (Eva) 5 ch farmer T 80a 2h 2c R2 Custar Lib 19 Ind tel.

O'Leary, Ellen housekeeper O 40a R1 Walbridge Lake 27.

O'Leary, Johanna housekeeper O 40a R1 Walbridge Lake 27.

O'Leary, John farmer O 40a 4h 6c R1 Walbridge Lake 27.

O'Leary, Mary housekeeper O 40a R1 Walbridge Lake 27.

O'Leary, Thomas A. farmer R1 Walbridge Lake 27.

Ollendorf, Wm. Haskins Mid.

Ollige, John (Elizabeth) 1 ch farmer O 50a 3h 1c R2 Haskins Wash 92 B tel.

O'Neal, Burley (son Harry) Silver St Weston.

159

O'Neal, Harrison (son Harry) laborer Silver St Weston.

O'Neal, Harry (Josephine). 7 ch section hand O H&L Silver Weston.

O'Neal, John (Annie) 3 ch laborer O H&L Main St Weston.

Oneal, Lyman laborer O H Main St Weston.

Oneal, W. M. (Sara) farmer O 3a 2h 1c R2 Weston Wes 51.

Onsel, Chas. E. oil producer O H&L Risingsun Mon B tel.

Onsel, E. J. oil producer O H&L Risingsun Mon.

Ousel, John ret Risingsun Mon.

Osmer, Chas. (Marie) farmer O 40a 4h 7c R1 Hoytsville Jac 86 B tel.

Osmun, David (Alice) farming & laboring O 2a H&L Luckey Tro 91.

Osmun, Phidelia 1a bds Luckey Tro 91.

OPPERMAN, ANNA housekeeper R2 Bowling Green Mid 45.

Opperman, Elizabeth housekeeper O H&L Tontogany Wash.

Opperman, F. Antone RD Tontogany Wash.

Opperman, F. W. RD Tontogany Wash.

Opperman, Mrs. Helen farmer O 80a R2 R2 Bowling Green Mid 45.

Opperman, John G. farmer T 80a 3h 3c R2 Bowling Green Mid 45.

Opperman, Orrie RD Tontogany Wash.

Opperman, Paul farmer R2 Bowling Green Mid 45.

Opperman, S. W. (Emma) 3 ch farming O 40a 5h 8c RD Tontogany Wash 47 Ind tel.

Ora, Garfield (Minnie) 2 ch farm laborer T H&L R1 Stony Ridge Tro 31 Ind tel.

Ordway, B. T. (Millie) 1 ch farmer T 160a 6h 5c R1 North Baltimore Hen 54.

O'Reilly, Bernard Perrysburg Pbg.

Orman, Georia ret O H&L Locust St Perrysburg Pbg B tel.

Ormond, Mary Perrysburg Pbg.

Orr, A. Bloomdale Blo.

Orr, Leslie (Ida) 1 ch farmer T 40a 3h R4 Bowling Green Por 94 Ind tel.

Orr, Peter (Mary) painting T H&L Tontogany Wash.

Orr, W. A. (Nellie) farmer T 120a 5h 6c R1 Jerry City Blo 66.

ORR, W. W. (Mary E.) 1 ch farmer O 40a 3h 2c R1 Portage Por 54.

Orwig, J. L. (Clara) 4 ch moulder O H&L 1h R5 Bowling Green Cen 23 Ind tel.

Ory, G. F. (Matilda) meat market T H&L 1h Prairie Depot Mon.

Osborn, David Luckey Tro.

Osborn, Mrs. Frances 8 ch O H&L Rudolph Lib 100 Ind tel.

Osborn, G. G. RD North Baltimore Hen.

Osborne, H. (Kate) 3 ch boiler maker O H&L 2h Rudolph Lib 94 Ind tel.

Osborn, H. B. (Sadie) 1 ch farmer T 75a 2h R1 Rudolph Lib. 101 Ind tel.

Osborn, John R. (Bell) 1 ch farmer R1 Bowling Green Lib 52 Ind tel.

Osborn, Mrs. Kate Rudolph Lib.

Osborn, Matilda J. RD North Baltimore Hen.

Osborne, S. M. (Belle) pumper O H&L Prairie Depot Mon B tel.

Osmer, Chas. RD Hoytsville Jac.

Osten, Anna L. M. Luckey Tro.

OSTEN, MRS. ELIZA 1 ch ret O 6a H Luckey Tro 90.

Oster, Geo. (Anna) 9 ch farmer O 60a 5h 4c R1 Custar Mil 42 B tel.

Oster, Urian J. (son Geo.) farm hand R2 Custar Mil 42 B tel.

Osterhout, Chas. (Pearl) 6 ch oil pumper O 60a 1c R1 Haskins Mid 53 B tel.

Ostrander, Edward (son W.) farmer R1 Prairie Depot Mon 101.

Ostrander, Erwin (son W.) farmer R1 Prairie Depot Mon 101.

Ostrander, S. (Carrie) 5 ch pumper T H&L Caldwell St Bradner Mon.

OSTRANDER, W. (Eliza) farmer O 77a 13h 6c R1 Prairie Depot Mon 101.

Ostrander, W. G. (Susie) laborer T 80a 4h 4c R2 Prairie Depot Mon 48 B tel.

Oswald, J. M. (Sarah) 1 ch lumber & coal merchant O 2H&L Maple St Weston B tel.

Oswald, L. T. (Allene) salesman T H&L Maple St Weston.

Oswald, S. C. (Jennie B.) lumber & coal dealer O H&L Maple St Weston B tel.

Otte, Geo. Dowling Pbg.

Otterbach, G. (Hulda) 3 ch ret farmer O 72a Bays Lib 75.

Otterbach, Hulda Bays Lib.

OTTERBACH, S. J. (Kate) 3 ch teamster T 3h 2c Bays Lib 75 Ind tel.

Otto, E. Park (Grace) grocery T H&L Hoytsville Jac.

Otto, Mrs. E. T. 5 ch ret O 80a H&L Hoytsville Jac.

Otto, Geo. 1 ch farmer O 33a 2h 3c R2 Dunbridge Pbg 21.

Otto, Rev. R. G. (Anna) minister T H&L 1h Dowling Pbg 35.

Otto, R. S. (Elsie) 1 ch farmer T 90a 3h 6c R1. Deshler Jac 32 B tel.

OVERHOLT, CLARENCE L. farmer T 300a 6h 7c R3 North Baltimore Blo 26 B & Ind tels.

Overholt, Clem (Sadie) 2 ch farmer T 300a 3h 2c R3 North Baltimore Blo 26.

OVERHOLT, J. S. Bloomdale.

Overholt, L. J. RD North Baltimore Blo.

Overly, R. laborer O H&L 1h Grand Rapids Gr Rs.

Overmyer, Ida R1 Prairie Depot Mon 37.

OVERMYER, J. J. 3 ch farmer T 40a 1h 2c R1 Pairie Depot Mon 37.

Overmyer, Martha Perrysburg Pbg.

Overmyer, Wm. G. 1h R1 Prairie Depot Mon 37.

OVERY, FRANK (Alta) 4 ch farmer T 40a 2h R3 Weston Mil 75 Ind tel.

Ovitt, J. W. (Gertrude) 1 ch farmer R2 Haskins Mid 89 B tel.

Ovitt, Sophia RD Haskins Mid.

Owens, C. B. (Stella) 2 ch clerk Rudolph Lib 94.

Owens, I. (Martha) 1 ch laborer T H&L Walbridge Lake.

Owens, Lewis (Stella) 1 ch clerk O H&L Grand Rapids Gr Rs.

Page, Claude clerk Main St Jerry City Blo.

PAGE, C. E. Walbridge.

Page, Edward (Luella) 3 ch railroader T H&L Walbridge Lake.

Page, Leo C. teacher Main St Jerry City Blo.

Page, T. O. 6 ch harness maker O H&L Main St Jerry City Blo.

Pahl, A. D. (Veronica) 5 ch farmer O 45a 5h 7c R2 Fostoria Per 110.

Painter, Peter S. Bloomdale Blo.

PALMER, F. C. (Laura) 3 ch farmer T 80a 3h 3c R1 Bowling Green Pla 78.

Palmer, Isadore L. Weston Wes.

Palmerton, Albert RD North Baltimore Hen.

Palmerton, Andrew (son W. M.) laborer R1 Portage Por 12.

Palmerton, Henry (son W. M.) farmer R1 Portage Por 12.

Palmerton, James (son W. M.) laborer R1 Portage Por 12.

Palmerton, Jerry Jerry City Blo.

Palmerton, P. F. (Carrie J.) 4 ch ret O H&L Main St Jerry City Blo 78.

Palmerton, W. M. (Jane) 1 ch farmer T 25a 2h 1c R1 Portage Por 12.

Paltz, Emma G. O H&L cor Oak & Maple Sts Weston Ind tel.

Pantenburg, Adam (Catherine) 4 ch farmer O 60a 5h 3c Custar Mil 98.

Pantenburg, Peter (Anna Mary) 3 ch farmer O 60a 3h 3c Custar Mil 91.

Pape, Arthur Millbury Lake.

Parche, Pierce (Lula) 3 ch farmer T 80a R1 North Baltimore Hen 4.

Parcher, J. W. (Emma) 3 ch oil pumper T 10a 1h R1 North Baltimore Hen 66.

Pargellis, Alex. C. Perrysburg Pbg.

PARGELLIS, H. C. farmer T 80a 2h R1 Haskins Mid 87 B tel.

Pargellis, Robt. Perrysburg Pbg.

Paris, M. Pemberville Fre.

PARK, ALLEN J. (Katie) 2 ch farmer T H&L 2h 4c R1 Grand Rapids Wash 65 Ind tel.

PARK, JAMES C. (Sarah E.) farmer O 119a 3h 3c R1 Grand Rapids Wash 65 Ind tel.

PARKER, ABNER (Mary) 6 ch laborer T H&L R2 Perrysburg Mid 15.

Parker, Charlie (Pearl) 1 ch farmer T 40a Luckey Web 71 B tel.

Parker, Cyntha Dowling Pbg.

Parker, C. C. (Cora) auto salesman & barber O H&L Stony Ridge Tro.

Parker, C. R. RD Haskins Mid.

Parker, Fred (Mary) 1 ch pumper O H&L Mermill Por 18 Ind tel.

Parker, Geo. RD North Baltimore Hen.

Parker, Geo. Haskins Mid.

Parker, Julia clerk Mermill Por 19 Ind tel.

Chores.

Parker, W. laborer T H&L 1h East St Bradner Mon B tel.

Parker, W. M. huckster O H&L 2h East St Bradner Mon.

PARKIN, GILES A. (Bertha) 2 ch timekeeper O 2a 1h care American Bridge Co East Toledo Ros 20.

PARKINS, W. J. (Maryetta) 4 ch farmer T 109a 5h 5c R4 Bowling Green Cen 115 Ind tel.

Parmalee, H. A. RD North Baltimore Hen.

Parr, W. M. (Suzanna) 3 ch farmer O 3a H 1h 1c Cygnet Blo 6.

Parrish, E. E. Dunbridge Mid.

Parson, David RD North Baltimore Hen.

Parsons, A. R. RD North Baltimore Hen.

Parsons, Henry (Theresa) laborer T H&L Second St Portage Por.

Parsons, Lottie (dau Henry) housekeeper Second St Portage Por.

Parsons, Rufus RD North Baltimore Hen.

Parsons, Scott (son Henry) farmer Second St Portage Por.

PAS, HENDRICK W. (Gotthuffe) 6 ch farmer O 117a 7h 6c R1 Deshler Jac 58 B tel.

Paton, H. RD North Baltimore Hen.

Patten, Edw. (Lena G.) 2 ch farmer O 80a 3h 8c R1 Jerry City Por 64 Ind tel.

Patten, Jasper (Elizabeth) farmer O 10a 1h 1c R1 Jerry City Por 63.

Patten, Stanley (Ida) 1 ch farmer T 10a 1h 1c R1 Jerry City Por 63.

Patter, Clarence RD Rudolph Lib.

Patter, Dudley (Cora) 2 ch farmer O 80a 2h 11c R1 Tontogany Wash 26 Ind tel.

Patter, Logan RD Rudolph Lib.

Patterson, A. RD Rudolph Lib.

Patterson, Charles (Lucy) 2 ch engineer T 2a 2c R3 Weston Mil 80 Ind tel.

Patterson, Chas. E. (Florence) 1 ch carpenter & teamster O H&L 2h R1 Rudolph Por 24½.

Patterson, D. S. (Sylvia) druggist O H&L 1h Weston Wes Ind tel.

Patterson, Esther Custar Hen.

Patterson, E. E. (Esther) 1 ch farmer T 80a 11h 3c R1 North Baltimore Hen 49.

Patterson, Jno. cattle RD Rudolph Por.

Patterson, M. J. (Agnes) 1 ch laborer T H&L Hoytsville Jac.

Patterson, N. D. (Ella) 4 ch ret O H&L Center St Weston Ind tel.

Patterson, Orrin W. (Gertrude) 2 ch farmer O 80a 3h 3c R1 Portage Por 58.

Patterson, R. (Lida) 6 ch farmer T 220a 6h R1 Rudolph Lib 37.

Patterson, Mrs. Wilson 3 ch O H&L Ash & Ohio Sts Weston Ind tel.

Patton, Clark Grand Rapids Gr Rs.

Patton, C. F. (Jennie) 1 ch contractor T H&L Grand Rapids Gr Rs Ind tel.

PATTON, HARRY (Grace) 3 ch farmer T 80a 2h 2c R1 Rudolph Lib 98 Ind tel.

Patton, J. W. (Bertha) pumper T H&L 1h Prairie Depot Mon.

PATTON, W. H. (Daisy) 7 ch drilling & farmer O 80a 5h 5c R1 Rising Sun Mon 75.

Pauff, Andrew (son P. J.) laborer Sycamore & Orange Sts Weston.

Pauff, Eugene Tontogany Wash.

Pauff, Frank (son P. J.) carpenter Sycamore & Orange Sts Weston.

Pauff, Jno. F. Tontogany Wash.

Pauff, Mary M. (dau P. J.) Sycamore & Orange Sts Weston.

Pauff, P. J. (Catherine) 5 ch laborer O 2H&L Sycamore & Orange Sts Weston B tel.

Peabody, Dr. G. F. (Kate H.) physician & surgeon O H&L Pemberville Fre 40 B tel.

Peach, Albert (Wilhelmina) laborer O H&L Risingsun Mon.

Pearce, C. C. (Mable) 2 ch farmer T H&L R5 Bowling Green Cen 74.

Pearsol, Lewis (Merrel) plumbing T H&L Millbury Lake.

Peebles, Arthur (son James) farmer T 106a 3h 5c R2 Bloomdale Per 29 B tel.

Peebles, James farmer O 106a 1h R2 Bloomdale Per 29 B tel.

Peebles, J. W. (Almeda) farmer O 90a 5h 5c R2 Bloomdale Per 19 Ind tel.

Peinert, Agnes (dau E. O.) Russ St Weston.

Peinert, Amelia 5 ch O H&L Russ St Weston.

Peinert, Charlotte (dau Amelia) Russ St Weston.

PEINERT, E. O. (Ida M.) 1 ch meat cutter O H&L Weston Wes Ind tel.

Peinert, Floyd RD Haskins Mid.

Peinert, Francis Rudolph Lib.

Peinert, Mrs. Fred Bowling Green Wash.

Peinert, F. H. RD Haskins Wash.

Peinert, Ida M. Weston Wes.

PEINERT, O. C. (Biddie E.) farmer 3h 10c R1 Tontogany Wash 72 Ind tel.

PEINERT, RAY (Grace) farmer T 150a 2h 1c R1 Tontogany Wash 72 Ind tel.

Peinert, W. F. (Harriet) clerk O H&L Locust St Weston.

Pelmerton, Jerry (Clara) section man T H&L cor Brown & Jerry Sts Jerry City Blo 77.

Pelton, Arthur oil worker Main St Cygnet Blo 6.

Pelton, A. J. (son R. C.) farmer R2 Bloomdale Per 24.

Pelton, Benjamin printer Main St Cygnet Blo 6.

Pelton, Burr (Elizabeth) 1 ch carrier O 40a 2h 2c County Line Road Bloomdale Blo B & Ind tels.

Pelton, Cassie Bloomdale Blo.

Pelton, Clyde M. farmer T 80a 3h R1 Bloomdale Blo 114 B & Ind tels.

Pelton, Ed (son R. C.) farmer R2 Bloomdale Per 24.

Pelton, E. T. (Lola E.) 3 ch farmer O 80a 8h 3c R1 Bloomdale Blo 103 B & Ind tels.

Pelton, F. E. Prairie Depot Blo.

Pelton, George (Eleanor) 3 ch oil worker O H&L Main St Cygnet Blo 6.

Pelton, G. A. (Ruth) 1 ch farmer T 80a 3h 2c R1 Fostoria Per 60.

Pelton, G. W. (Grace) 1 ch farmer T H&L 1h Lime City Pbg.

Pelton, Harry S. music teacher R2 Bloomdale Blo 20 B & Ind tels.

PELTON, HOWARD S. (Hazel) 1 ch meat market Cygnet Blo B & Ind tels.

Pelton, H. D. (Eliza) 1 ch farmer O 42a 4h 2c R1 Fostoria Per 60.

Pelton, Ina A. (dau T. V.) R1 Bloomdale Blo 114 B & Ind tels.

Pelton, P. F. cattle RD Bowling Green Cen.

PELTON, R. C. (Eliza V.) 2 ch farmer O 60a 2h 2c R2 Bloomdale Per 24 B tel.

Pelton, Samuel laborer O H&L R2 Prairie Depot Por 114.

Pelton, Sara A. Bloomdale Blo.

PELTON, S. S. (Glenn D.) 4 ch farmer & life insurance T 120a 4h 3c R2 Bloomdale Per 20 B & Ind tels. See adv.

PELTON, T. V. farmer O 80a 4h 3c R1 Bloomdale Blo 114 B & Ind tels.

Pember, D. H. farmer O 20a H&L 2h 5c W Crocker St Bradner Mon 28.

Pember, Ira Bradner Mon.

Pember, M. E. Bradner Mon.

Penalton, Orlando farmer O 12a 1h R2 Fostoria Per 110.

Pence, Fred (Lillian) engineer T H&L 182 Oak St Rossport Ros.

Pence, L. O. (Isabelle) postmaster O 5a H&L Hoytsville Jac.

Pence, W. W. (Rebecca) 3 ch farmer T 40a 2h R1 Prairie Depot Mon 113.

PENDLETON, D. L. (Myrth) 2 ch farmer T 240a 1c R1 Jerry City Por 31 Ind tel.

Pennock, Ed Weston Wes.

Pennock, Geo. W. Weston Wes.

Penny, Frank (Harriet) ret O H&L Prairie Depot Mon.

Penrod, Wm. laborer R1 Le Moyne Tro 85.

Pentenberg, Adam Custar Mil.

Pentenberg, Peter (Sarah) 2 ch farmer 40a H&L Milton Center Mil Ind tel.

Pentenburg, C. (Lydia) 4 ch farmer O 55a 4h 4c R3 Weston Mil 91 Ind tel.

Pentenburg, Ruby (dau C.) R3 Weston Mil 91.

Penwell, Ray (Freda) 2 ch craneman T H&L Findlay St Portage Por.

Peoples, D. O. (Ida) 5 ch farmer T 70a 3h 3c R2 Prairie Depot Por 63.

PEOPLES, E. R. (Louise) 3 ch oil pumper O H&L Pemberville Fre 41 B tel.

Peoples, Mrs. Jennie 3 ch housekeeper O H&L Vine St Pemberville Fre.

Peoples, Milton 10 ch gardener O H&L Mermill Por 95.

Peoples, R. J. Pemberville Fre.

Peoples, Sam (Sarah) 4 ch farmer O 40a 4h 5c R2 Pemberville Fre 19 B tel.

Peoples, W. D. (Grace) 2 ch salesman O H&L Pemberville Fre B tel.

PEPPER, JOHN Rossford.

Pepper, Matt ret T H&L Rossford Ros.

Perkins, A. G. (Hattie) 2 ch farmer O 53a 3h 2c R2 Dunbridge Mid 71.

Perkins, Fred (son Joseph) farmer R3 Perrysburg Pbg 88.

Perkins, Geo. M. (Minnie) farmer T 90a R3 Perrysburg Pbg 88.

PERKINS, JOSEPH 2 ch farmer O 90a 4h 4c R3 Perrysburg Pbg 88.

Perkins, J. E. (Matilda O.) 4 ch farmer O 80a 5h 2c R2 Dunbridge Mid 70 Ind tel.

Perkins, Wm. pumper bds Prairie Depot Mon.

Perrin, W. C. R2 Perrysburg Pbg.

Perrine, Chas. (Alice) 3 ch farmer T 40a 3h 4c R2 Bloomdale Per 28.

Perrine, J. A. (Della) 1 ch ret O H&L Main St Bloomdale Blo B & Ind tels.

Perry, Earl A. (Leona) 1 ch oil worker T H&L Rudolph Lib 81.

Perry, E. H. (Maud) confectionery T H&L Pemberville Fre B tel.

Perry, Glaby farmer Rudolph Por 25 Ind tel.

Perry, G. (Adelia) 3 ch farmer O 40a 7h 8c R1 Rudolph Por 25 Ind tel.

Perry, G. E. (Rose) 3 ch farmer O 20a 3h 2c R1 Bradner Mon 31 B tel.

Perry, L. F. (Elizabeth) 2 ch traveling salesman T H&L Pemberville Fre 40 B tel.

Perry, M. H. RD North Baltimore Hen.

Perry, Ray farmer R1 Rudolph Por 25 Ind tel.

Perry, Walter (Gertrude) 1 ch conductor T H&L Front St Perrysburg Pbg B tel.

Pertner, Anna (dau Mrs. Henry) R1 Luckey Tro 19 Ind tel.

Pertner, Clara (dau Mrs. Henry) R1 Luckey Tro 19 Ind tel.

Pertner, Mrs. Henry 9 ch farmer 99a 6h 8c R1 Luckey Tro 19 Ind tel.

Pertner, John (son Mrs. Henry) farm hand R1 Luckey Tro 19 Ind tel.

PERVINE, CHAS. 1 ch mechanic Hoytsville Jac.

Pervis, Charley (Cora) 2 ch motorman O H&L Indiana Ave. Perrysburg Pbg.

Peter, J. W. (Safronier) grocery T H&L RD North Baltimore Hen.

Peter, Wm. 2 ch farmer O 120a 3h 4c R4 Bowling Green Cen 119.

Peters, August (Louisa) 6 ch farmer T 40a R1 Bowling Green Pla 80.

Peters, B. H. RD North Baltimore Hen.

PETERS, DICK (son John) farmer O 30a 2h 2c R2 Custar Milton 50.

Peters, D. W. RD North Baltimore Hen.

Peters. E. A. (Daisy) 4 ch blacksmith T H&L Grand Rapids Gr Rs.

Peters, Fred Hoytsville Jac.

Peters, Harry RD North Baltimore Hen.

Peters, Henry (Jerusha) laborer O H&L Grand Rapids Gr Rs.

PETERS, HENRY, JR. (Edith) farmer T 60a 2h 3c R3 Prairie Depot Mon 9 B tel.

Peters, John (Anna) 8 ch ret R2 Custar Mil 50.

Peters, J. F. farmer O 20a 2h R1 North Baltimore Hen 47 Ind tel.

Peters, J. F. (Birdie) 5 ch laborer T H&L 2c R1 Hoytsville Jac 115.

Peters, J. S. (Florence) 6 ch farmer O 80a 5h 4c R1 North Baltimore Hen 71 B tel.

Peters, M. C. RD North Baltimore Hen.

Peters, O. V. (son Mrs. Sarah) laborer Grand Rapids Gr Rs.

Peters, Mrs. Sarah ret O H&L Grand Rapids Gr Rs.

Peters, Theodore (Mary) 2 ch laborer T H&L Rossford Ros.

Peters, Wm. cattle RD Bowling Green Cen.

Petersen, Joe (Louise) 3 ch butcher O 2½a R1 Walbridge Lake 15 Ind tel.

PETERSEN, ROBT. (Celia) 2 ch farmer O 40a 4h 3c R1 Genoa Lake 37 Ind tel.

Peterson, Chas. (Dora) 2 ch farmer T H&L 1c R1 Lime City Pbg 91.

Peterson, Chas. (Edna) 4 ch pumper operator O 10a 2c R1 Bradner Mon 27.

Peterson, Cora Bradner Mon.

Peterson, Mrs. Elsie 2 ch dressmaker O H&L N Main St Bradner Mon.

PETERSON, EMMANUEL (Freda) 3 ch butcher O 15a 2h 1c R1 Stony Ridge Tro 4 Ind tel.

Peterson, E. E. (Phebe) 1 ch farmer T 80a 2h 4c R1 Custar Jac 39.

Peterson, E. H. (Ella) farmer T 2h R2 Prairie Depot Por 128 Ind tel.

Peterson, G. W. (Anna) ret O H&L 1h Prairie Depot Mon.

Peterson, M. C. (Edna) 6 ch telegraph operator O H&L Bradner Mon 27 B tel.

Peterson, Silas (Emma) farmer T 1h 1c Bradner Mon 28 B tel.

PETERSON, S. F. (Ella) 6 ch oil man pumping T H&L R1 Bloomdale Blo 129 B & Ind tels.

Peterson, V. L. Bradner Mon.

Peterson, Mrs. William 4 ch T H&L Walnut St Weston.

Petrie, Lislie (Helen) 1 ch laborer T Flat Front St Perrysburg Pbg.

Petteys, C. A. (son D. J.) school teacher R1 Grand Rapids Gr Rs 40.

Petteys, David N. Weston Wes.

PETTEYS, D. J. (Nettie M.) swine breeder O 80a 3h 3c R1 Grand Rapids Gr Rs 40 B & Ind tels. See adv.

PETTEYS, H. L. (Jessie) 1 ch farmer T 140a 5h 4c R2 Weston Wes 28 Ind tel.

PETTEYS. L. A. (Sarah E.) farming O 116a 4h 4c R2 Weston Wes 28 Ind tel. See adv.

Pettys, A. N. Tontogany Wash.

Pettys, Newton (Mattie) 4 ch farmer O 40a 3h 2c R1 Tontogany Wash 26.

Pew, R. C. (Nellie) 5 ch supt to Standard Oil Co O 4a H 2h 1c Front St Perrysburg Pbg B tel.

Pfeifer, William farmer bds with Frank Hochanadel farmer R1 Box 25 East Toledo Ros 30 Ind tel.

Pfeiffer, John (Mary) 3 ch farmer O 50a 5h 3c R4 Bowling Green Cen 69 Ind tel.

Pfeiffer, Joseph (Teresa) 3 ch farmer O 105a 4h 4c R2 Bowling Green Cen 4.

PFISTER, MRS. LEWIS R3 Box 114 Perrysburg.

Pfisterer, Conrad M. (Anna C.) farmer T 40a 2h 1c R3 Perrysburg Pbg 125.

Pheils, Fredrick (Effie) 6 ch farmer O 40a 3h 4c R1 Walbridge Lake 13 Ind tel.

Pheley, Wm. H. (Amelia) 3 ch minister O H&L Front St Perrysburg Pbg B tel.

Phelps, Nettie RD North Baltimore Hen.

Phelps, Chas. E. (Jennie) 6 ch manager krout factory T H&L Box 37 Weston Ind tel.

Phifister, Geo. (Mary) laborer O H&L Sixth St Perrysburg Pbg B tel.

Philbin, Phillip Perrysburg Pbg.

Philipps, S. T. (May) 2 ch cigar store O H&L Perrysburg Pbg.

Philipps, Wm. (Ella) 2 ch farmer O H&L Risingsun Mon.

PHILIPS, ALVIN Y. farmer O 116a 6h 2c R1 Perrysburg Pbg 100.

Philips, Austin (Pearl) 2 ch carpenter & farmer O 22a 2h 1c R1 Perrysburg Pbg 100.

Philips, Chas. (Jessie) 6 ch farmer T 80a 4h 15c R1 Risingsun Mon 72.

Philips, Charles (son Alvin) farmer R1 Perrysburg Pbg 100.

Philips, D. C. (Elizabeth) 2 ch farmer O 10a 1h 1c R1 Rudolph Lib 97.

PHILIPS, D. E. (Pearl) 7 ch teamster T 1c Bays Lib 75.

Philips, Frank (Lily) machinist O H&L Bradford St Cygnet Blo.

Philips, J. S. (Icie) 1 ch printing office O H&L Front St Cygnet Blo Ind tel.

Philips, Wm. (Kathryn) 3 ch carpenter O H&L Sixth St Perrysburg Pbg.

Philipson, A. R. (Caroline) farming O 2a 3h R2 Pemberville Web 28.

PHILLIPS, CHAUNCEY R2 Pemberville.

Phillips, Eliza Tontogany Wash.

Phillips, Mrs. Elnora 9 ch 2Lots Myers St Jerry City Blo.

Phillips, E. E. Risingsun Mon.

Phillips, E. W. (Laura) 3 ch farmer T H&L 8h 11c R1 Grand Rapids Gr Rs 44 Ind tel.

Phillips, Fred (Mary) 4 ch farming T 20a 2c R2 Weston Wes 33.

Phillips, F. W. Risingsun Mon.

Phillips, Geo. H. Risingsun Mon.

Phillips, G. B. (Sarah) telephone manager O H&3Lots 1h Tontogany Wash Ind tel.

Phillips, Hal (Zephia) 2 ch elevator helper T H&L Factory St Jerry City Por.

Phillips, Hannah 3 ch farming O 22a 2h 2c R1 Perrysburg Pbg 109.

PHILLIPS, JAY (Ica) 2 ch telephone manager O H&L Washington St Tontogany Wash Ind tel.

Phillips, John (Mary J.) 2 ch farmer O 32a 2h 3c R1 Grand Rapids Gr Rs 9 Ind tel.

Phillips, J. J. Dunbridge Web.

PHILLIPS, J. S. (Icie M.) 1 ch printer pub Cygnet Review O H&L Cygnet Blo B & Ind tels. See adv.

PHILLIPS, J. S. (Harriett W.) 3 ch farmer & elevator O 62a 6h 6c Tontogany Wash 47 Ind tel.

Phillips, J. T. Cygnet Blo.

Phillips, J. W. Pemberville Web.

Phillips, L. (Emma) 2 ch carpenter T H&L 1h 1c Dowling Mid.

Phillips, Mrs. Mary 2 ch O H&L Luckey Tro.

Phillips, Mrs. Pearl R1 Perrysburg Pbg.

Phillips, Seth (Nora) 2 ch ret O 80a 1h 1c R5 Bowling Green Cen 34 Ind tel.

Phillips, Shan (Barbara) 2 ch T H&L' S Main St Bradner Mon.

Phillips, Thos. Weston Wes.

Phillips, Walter Pemberville Web.

PHILLIPS, W. R. (Mary) 3 ch farmer O 150a 6h 7c R5 Bowling Green Cen 39 Ind tel.

Phillipson, A. R. Pemberville Web.

Philo, Clifford farm laborer R1 Dunbridge Web 3 B tel.

PHILO, C. F. (Sadie) 2 ch farmer T 120a 5h 6c R1 Dunbridge Web 57 B tel.

PHILO, MRS. E. J. 4 ch farm O 2a 1h R2 Pemberville Web 47 B tel.

PHILO, FITCH farmer O 20a 2h R1 Dunbridge Mid 67.

PHILO, GEORGE (Mary) 2 ch farmer O 40a 4h 6c R1 Dunbridge Web 57 B tel.

PHILO, J. D. (Maria) farmer 146a 6c R1 Dunbridge Web 57 B tel.

PHILO, L. E. (Minnie) 2 ch farmer T 50a 2h 3c R1 Dunbridge Web 47 B tel.

Philo, Mary O H&L Second St Portage Por.

Philo, Ralph 1 ch teamster O H&L 2h Second St Portage Por.

PHILO, W. A. (Clara) 2 ch farmer O 40a 3h 4c R1 Dunbridge Web 57 B tel.

Phipps, Anderson (son Wm. H.) farm hand Hoytsville Jac 114 Ind tel.

Phipps, William H. (Eliza E.) 1 ch farmer O 80a 3h 1c Hoytsville Jac 114 Ind tel.

Phister, Chas. (Jessie) driller T H&L Risingsun Mon.

Phister, Conrad (Minnie) railroad man O H&L Sixth St Perrysburg Pbg B tel.

Phister, Jacob (Rosa) ret O H&L Risingsun Mon.

FHISTER, J. C. (Myrtle) 1 ch hardware T H&L 2h Bell St Bradner Mon B tel.

Phister, Mary 2 ch O H&L Crocker St Bradner Mon B tel.

Phole, Bertha housekeeper Custar Mil.

Phole, Mrs. Mary 5 ch farmer O 40a Custar Mil.

Pickens, II. O. Grand Rapids Gr Rs.

PICKERING, GEO. W. (Altie) 2 ch farmer T 34a 2h 5c R2 Dunbridge Mid 82.

Piddock, Clarence (son Wm.) R1 Weston Lib 43 Ind tel.

Piddock, Harry J. (Ida) 6 ch farmer T 140a 6h 3c R2 Perrysburg Pbg 6.

Piddock, Ida R2 Perrysburg Pbg.

PIDDOCK, WM. (Sarah) 6 ch farmer T 160a 5h 9c R1 Weston Lib 43 Ind tel.

Pieper, Mrs. Carrie 1 ch T R3 Perrysburg Ros 16.

Pieper, William (son Carrie) 64a R3 Perrysburg Ros 16.

Pierce, C. H. Prairie Depot Mon.

Pierce, E. farmer T 100a R1 Prairie Depot Mon 110.

Pierce, E. M. Freeport Mon.

Pierce, II. F. (Addie) 6 ch farmer O 67½a 5h 6c R3 Prairie Depot Mon 94.

Pierce, Sarah S. Perrysburg Pbg.

Pierce, Wm. (Martha) 1 ch T 112a 8h 5c R3 North Baltimore Blo 26 B & Ind tels.

PIFE, ADD R1 Luckey.

PIFER, J. W. (Ruth) 7 ch farmer O 80a 4h 10c R1 Fostoria Per 122.

Pike, Mrs. A. housekeeper O H&L Sugar Ridge Mid 63.

Pike, A. L. RD Dunbridge Mid.

Pike, L. W. (Emma) 9 ch farmer T 120a 3h 2c R3 Bowling Green Cen 50 Ind tel.

Pilloid, August 1 ch miller O H&L Grand Rapids Gr Rs Ind tel.

Pinegar, J. W. Weston Mon.

Pinegar, W. H. (Regina) 1 ch ret O 79a H&L Silver St Weston B tel.

Pinniger, James (Sabina) justice of peace O H&L Millbury Lake 54.

Pinniger, J. H. (Myrtle) 2 ch farmer O 40a 4h 4c R1 Millbury Lake 80 Ind tel.

Piper, J. E. Haskins Mid.

Pisel, Geo. Bloomdale Blo.

Pisel, Joseph L. (Caroline) farmer O 40a 1h 2c R1 Bloomdale Blo 90 B & Ind tels.

Pisel, M. M. Prairie Depot Blo.

Pisel, W. E. (Edna F.) auto salesman Garfield & Walnut Sts Bloomdale Blo.

Pisor, Geo. H. RD North Baltimore Hen.

Pitcher, Chas. carpenter Haskins Mid.

Pitcher, Electa 1 ch housekeeper O H&L Haskins Mid B tel.

Piter, James E. (Lucy) paperhanger T H&L Haskins Mid.

Pitman, May RD Bowling Green Mid.

Pittenger, H. C. (Rose) farmer O H&L 1h Prairie Depot Mon B tel.

Place, Chas. RD Dunbridge Mid.

Place, John (Clara) farmer T H&L 3h Dunbridge Mid 69.

Plantz, Anna C. ret O H&L Rising Sun Mon.

Plantz, A. F. Prairie Depot Mon.

Plantz, Floyd 1 ch farmer T 40a 4h 3c R3 Prairie Depot Mon 98.

Plantz, Geo. (Linda) 5 ch farmer O 30a 3h 1c Bradner Mon 23 B tel.

PLANTZ, I. F. (Magdelene) 3 ch ret O H&L 1h 1c Evans St Bradner Mon B tel.

Plantz, Peter ret O H&L East St Bradner Mon.

Plantz, Will farmer O 20a 6c cor Evans & Lightner Sts Bradner Mon B tel.

Plantz, W. H. 6 ch ret O H&L Bell St Bradner Mon.

Pletcher, Edw. Pemberville Fre.

Pletcher, S. A. RD North Baltimore Blo.

Plocker, Jacob (Mary) 4 ch oil pumper O 40a 1h 4c RD North Baltimore Hen 77 B tel.

Plotner, J. D. (Cloy) 4 ch farm laborer R1 Jerry City Blo 71 Ind tel.

Plotts, A. J. (Lille) 2 ch farmer & thresher T 70a 3h 3c R4 Deshler Jac 30 Ind tel.

Plouck, D. R. RD Mermill Por.

Plouck, H. L. (Margaret) pumper O H&L Mermill Por 19.

Plouck, Sherman (Asenath)) pumper O H&L 1h 1c Mermill Portage 19 Ind tel.

PLOWRIGHT, CURTIS (Nora) 6 ch farmer O 150a 8h 10c R1 Bowling Green Pla 40 Ind tel.

Plowright, Harold RD Bowling Green Pla.

Plumey, Alphonse farmer O 20a 2h R1 East Toledo Ros 32.

Plummer, E. A. (Ella) 4 ch insurance T H&L Risingsun Mon.

Poates, Jno. Milton Center Mil.

Poe, Chas. E. (Maggie) 4 ch farmer O 80a 7h 7c R2 Pemberville Web 28.

Poggemur, Henry (Carrie) 3 ch farmer O 80a 3h 5c R1 Bradner Fre 82.

166

Pogue, W. (May) 2 ch manager telephone co T H&L Prairie Depot Mon B tel.

Pohle, E. Custar Mil.

Poland, Clarence (son Amanda) school teacher bds R1 Weston Mil 55.

Poland, Donovan (son Amanda) student bds R1 Weston Mil 55.

POLAND, JOE (Bertha) farmer T 160a 5h 2c R1 Weston Mil 58 Ind tel.

Poland, John (son Amanda) school teacher bds R1 Weston Mil 55.

Poland, Pearl (dau Amanda) housekeeper R1 Weston Mil 55.

Pollard, A. L. (Anna) 3 ch farmer & thresher O 103a 5h 4c R2 Prairie Depot Por 113.

Pollard, Chas. T. (Anna M.) 3 ch farmer O 56a 4h 2c R2 Prairie Depot Por 118.

Pollard, Mrs. Fred Bloomdale Blo.

Pollock, C. J. West Millgrove Per.

Pollock, Ed. RD North Baltimore Hen.

Pollock, Elizabeth Grand Rapids Gr Rs.

Pollock, Tom (Emma) 5 ch ret O H&L 1c Grand Rapids Gr Rs.

Polster, Andrew farmer O 20a 1h R1 East Toledo Ros 32.

Polster, Joseph (Mary) 4 ch farmer O 20a 1h 1c R1 East Toledo Ros 32.

Pomeroy, Walter (Mary) railroad man O H&L Second St Perrysburg Pbg B tel.

Pope, Amelia bds with John R1 Luckey Tro 75.

Pope, Arthur (Emma) 1 ch barber O H&L Millbury Lake.

POPE, A. A. (Pearl) 1 ch farmer T 60a 4h 1c R1 Haskins Mid 53.

Pope, C. E. Pemberville Web.

POPE, FRED A. farmer T 80a 5h 15c R1 Haskins Mid 50 B tel.

POPE, JOHN (Anna) 1 ch farmer O 118a 7h 9c R1 Luckey Tro 75 Ind tel.

POPE, JOHN (Edith) 4 ch farmer O 100a 5h 2c R1 Perrysburg Pbg 111.

Pope, N. E. (Rose E.) fireman O H&L R1 Bloomdale Blo 112.

Porter, Arthur teacher Cygnet Blo 1.

Porter, A. M. (Sada) 6 ch oil worker O H T L 1c Cygnet Blo 1.

PORTER, A. W. (Anna) 2 ch farmer O 80a 5h 6c R3 Weston Mil 84 Ind tel.

Porter, Charity M. Cygnet Blo.

Porter, Charles (Hester) 2 ch farming O 20a 2h 1c R2 Weston Wes 45 Ind tel.

Porter, C. D. (Ruth) farmer T 100a 2h 2c R3 Weston Mil 83 Ind tel.

Porter, Floyd (Jennie) railroad man T H&L Walbridge Lake.

Porter, Kenneth (son A. W.) farm hand R3 Weston Mil 84.

Porter, Laura (dau N. S.) school teacher R1 Weston Mil 38.

The Holt Caterpillar Tractor. Removes the stump as well as the tree.

Porter, Leonard J. (Elinor) 2 ch laborer O 6a H 1h 2c Main St Perrysburg Pbg B tel.

Porter, Mable dressmaker Cygnet Blo 1.

Porter, M. A. RD Bowling Green Pla.

Porter, N. S. (Sarah) 4 ch farmer O 80a 5h 14c R1 Weston Mil 38 B tel.

Poss, Anthony (son Peter) school teacher R1 Custar Mil 22 B tel.

Poss, Edward Fred (son Peter) farm hand R1 Custar Mil 22 B tel.

Poss, Elizabeth (dau Peter) housekeeper R1 Custar Mil 22 B tel.

POSS, PETER (Margaret) 5 ch farmer O 80a 7h 14c R1 Custar Mil 22 B tel.

Potes, John farmer T 10a 2h Milton Center Mil 91.

POTLER, LOGAN horse breeder R1 Rudolph Lib.

Potter, A. L. (Lucinda J.) farmer O 2a 2h R1 Grand Rapids Gr Rs 9 Ind tel.

POTTER, CHAS. H. Rossford.

POTTER CLARENCE (Luella) 2 ch farmer O 3500a 40h 3c R1 Rudolph Lib 37 Ind tel. See adv.

Potter, Dudley RD Tontogany Wash.

Potter, Edna Weston Wes.

Potter, Frank (Hazel) 3 ch O H&L Clark St Weston.

Potter, G. W. (Hattie) 2 ch farmer O 80a 3h 4c R3 Weston Wes Ind tel.

Potter, L. C. (Minerva A.) farmer O 80a 3h 3c R1 Grand Rapids Wash 61 Ind tel.

Potter, M. H. laborer ½ interest H&L R1 Grand Rapids Gr Rs 9 Ind tel.

Potter, Ruth (dau Clarence) R1 Rudolph Lib 37 Ind tel.

POTTERS, D. J. R1 Grand Rapids.

Potts, John teaming T 10a 2h Milton Center Mil 101.

Poulson, C. A. RD North Baltimore Hen.

Powel, J. P. (Anna) 5 ch ret O H&L Luckley Tro.

Powel, Mikey stone cutter Luckey Tro.

Powell, Anna Marie (dau F. E.) housekeeper R4 Deshler Jac 30 Ind tel.

Powell, Charles (Nellie) 3 ch farmer T 55a 3h 2c R3 Deshler Jac 62 Ind tel.

Powell, Chauncey RD Bowling Green Pla.

Powell, Mrs. C. L. ret O H&L Weston Ind tel.

Powell, Daniel P. Grand Rapids Gr Rs.

Powell, E. A. RD North Baltimore Hen.

Powell, F. E. (Ida May) 10 ch farmer O 40a 3h 5c R4 Deshler Jac 30 Ind tel.

Powell, Dr. Geo. V. (Anna W.) physician O 96a H 1h 8c Portage Lib 112 Ind tel.

Powell, Harry Tontogany Wash.

Powell, Iva L. (dau F. E.) housekeeper R4 Deshler Jac 30 Ind tel.

Powell, Joseph (Amanda) section hand O H&L Sycamore St Weston Wes.

Powell, Sam (Lillie) ret O H&L Grand Rapids Gr Rs Ind tel.

Powell, Wm. (Mae) 1 ch traveling man O H&L Front St Perrysburg Pbg B tel.

Powell, William M. barber T Bays Lib 75.

Powell, William Roscoe (son F. E.) laborer R4 Deshler Jac 30 Ind tel.

POWERS, CLAUDE H. (Emma) 2 ch farmer O 20a 3h 1c R2 Bowling Green Pla 94.

Powers, Jessie E. farmer T 80a R2 Dunbridge Mid 68.

Powers, John laborer T H&L R1 Custar Jac 44.

Powers, Martin (Alida) ret O H&L Locust St Perrysburg Pbg.

Powers, Maude M. housekeeper R2 Dunbridge Mid 68.

Powers, P. A. (Jennie) 1 ch farmer T 80a 4h 1c R1 Hoytsville Jac 42.

Powers, Mrs. Sarah T H&L Tontogany Wash Ind tel.

Powers, Wm. (Pearl) 1 ch farmer O 5a 1h R2 Bowling Green Pla 90.

Powless, R. E. (clara) telegraph operator T H&L R1 Walbridge Ros 22.

Powley, R. S. (Mamie) 1 ch cashier T H&L Risingsun Mon B tel.

Pratt, C. T. farmer O 50a 1h R2 Perrysburg Pbg 4 B tel.

Pratt, Guy (Elizabeth) 2 ch farmer O 56a 3h 2c R2 Perrysburg Pbg 4.

Pratt, J. J. RD North Baltimore Hen.

Pratt, Miss May farming O 47a R2 Perrysburg Pbg 4 B tel.

PRATT, THOMAS (Cora) 2 ch farmer T 40a 2h Jerry City Blo 77 Ind tel.

Praute, Fred Pemberville Fre.

Preisendorfer, A. J. (Anna) 1 ch druggist O H&L Custar Mil.

Preslar, S. (Amy) farmer T R2 Dunbridge Mid 72.

Presler, Mrs. Hattie RD North Baltimore Hen.

Preston, L. D. Pemberville Fre.

PRICE, ALBERT A. (Nellie) 1 ch farmer T H&L Sugar Ridge Mid 63.

Price, Georgia (dau Dr. W. H.) student Stony Ridge Tro.

Price, Herman RD Dunbridge Mid.

Price, H. A. (Ethel) laborer T H&L Sugar Ridge Mid 63.

Price, H. H. (Marella) teamster R1 Bloomdale Blo 130.

PRICE, JOHN (Sofa) 8 ch farmer T 160a
5h 3c Sugar Ridge Cen 52.
PRICE, J. C. 1 ch cream, egg & poultry
buyer O H&L Custar Mil B tel.
PRICE, LEWIS (Grace) thrasherman T
H&L 2h Sugar Ridge Mid 63 Ind tel.
Price, Dr. Wm. H. (Florence) 4 ch physi-
cian O H&L Stony Ridge Tro B & Ind
tels.
Priddy, L. B. (Mary) 3 ch meat market
O H&L Main St Jerry City Por Ind
tel.
Priebe, H. D. RD North Baltimore Hen.
Priest, Chas. (Martha) 2 ch laborer O
H&L Hoytsville Jac.
Priest, C. W. (Alice E.) 8 ch laborer O
H&L Main St Cygnet Blo 6.
PRIEST, EDWARD (son John) laborer R1
Luckey Web 59.
Priest, E. D. (Jennie) laborer O H&L
Front St Perrysburg Pbg B tel.
Priest, F. H. Luckey Tro.
Priest, John (Martha) 1 ch ret O 40a 2h
2c R1 Luckey Web 74.
Priest, Nettie Main St Cygnet Blo 6.
PRIEST, N. A. (Jessie) farmer T 140a 4h
2c R2 Custar Mil 36 Ind tel.
Priest, Robt. H. RD Dunbridge Mid.
Pringle, Calvin (Minnie) 5 ch well drill-
ing O H&L Lime City Pbg 91.
Pringle, Jacob Perrysburg Pbg.
Pringle, Minnie Lime City Pbg.
Pringle, Sant (Grace) 5 ch mechanic T
4a 1h R3 Perrysburg Pbg 137.
Probert, Curtis A. Bloomdale Blo.
Probert, M. A. Bloomdale Blo.
Proctor, Mrs. G. H. RD North Baltimore
Hen.
Prosser, Omille J. (Ethel M.) 1 ch farmer
T 80a 5h 2c R3 North Baltimore Blo
B & Ind tels.
Prosser, Mrs. Wm. 1 ch T 80a R3 North
Baltimore Blo B & Ind tels.
PROVENS, W. C. (Myrtle) 4 ch school
teacher T 3a 1c R2 Bowling Green Pla
86.
Pugh, Clarence W. (May) 5 ch oil
pumper T H&L 1h R1 Bowling Green
Pla 33 Ind tel.
Pugh, Mrs. Dan 3 ch O 36a 1h R1
Portage Lib 59 Ind tel.
Pugh, Jay (Sadie) 4 ch farmer O 80a
5h 7c R3 Weston Mil 1 Ind tel.
Pugh, T. J. (Maude M.) 2 ch garage
salesroom O H&L Weston Wes Ind tel.
Pugh, Wm. H. Weston Wes.
Puls, Wm. (Barbara) 4 ch farmer T 40a
4h 3c R1 Weston Mil 60 Ind tel.
Pultz, David (Viola) 1 ch farmer T 160a
3h 3c Mermill Lib 94.

Pultz, George (son Perry) farmer R1
Bowling Green Pla 42.
Pultz, Newton (Rebecca) farmer O 20a
2h 3c R1 Portage Por 9.
Pultz, Perry G. (Myrtle) 6 ch farmer
O 20a 4h 4c R1 Bowling Green Pla 42
Ind tel.
Purcell, Mrs. Maria housekeeper O H&L
Pemberville Fre.
Purdue, A. J. RD North Baltimore Hen.
Purdy, A. H. (Hattie A.) 1 ch teacher
T 2a 2h R3 Perrysburg Pbg 62.
PURDY, HIRAM (Helen) 1 ch farmer O
5a 1c R1 Millbury Lake 131 Ind tel.
Purdy, Wm. (Mabel) 3 ch drayman O
H&L 3h Risingsun Mon.
Purkey, J. A. (Anna) ret O H&L Mul-
berry St Bloomdale Blo B & Ind tels.
Pursell, G. A. (Floy E.) 6 ch farmer O
227a 8h 2c R2 Fostoria Per 37.
PURTEE, S. F. (Adeline) 2 ch laborer
T H&L 1c R1 Bowling Green Cen 29
Ind tel.
Purtee, Tom (Rebecca) 7 ch laborer
O H&L Portage Lib 90.
Puse, Carl Lime City Pbg.
Puse, Chas. (Augusta) 7 ch farmer O
120a 4h 5c R1 Walbridge Lake 98 B
tel.
Puse, Fred farmer R1 Lime City Lake
23 B tel.
Puse, G. J. (Christina) ret O 157a R1
Lime City Per 56 Ind tel.
Puse, John farmer O 50a 4h 2c R1 Lime
City Lake 23 B tel.
Puse, L. G. (son S. J.) farmer T 157a
3h 4c R1 Lime City Perrysburg 56
Ind tel.
Putman, Geo. F. (Elizabeth S.) high
school principal T H&L Haskins Mid.
Quaintance, Elmer (Ida) 3 ch farmer
80a R3 Pemberville Fre 89.
Quinn, S. E. 3 ch ret T H&L Front St
Perrysburg Pbg.
Rabb, Gust. (Anna) gen store O H&L
Luckey Tro.
Rade, Henry (Lizzie) 1 ch farmer O
40a 3h 2c R2 Dunbridge Mid 65 B tel.
Rade, Louise housekeeper R2 Dunbridge
Mid 65.
Radebaugh, Jay RD North Baltimore
Hen.
Radeloff, Andrew F. C. Luckey Tro.
Radeloff, Lewis G. Luckey Tro.
Radeloff, Lizzie Luckey Tro.
Rader, E. W. (Mary) 2 ch farmer T
122a 5h 3c R2 Weston Pla 15.
RADER, F. H. (Eliza) 2 ch farmer T 40a
3h 5c RD North Baltimore Hen 100
Ind tel.

RADER, JESSE (Girdy) 2 ch farmer T 11a 3h 1c R2 North Baltimore Hen 81 Ind tel.

Rader, T. E. (Lillie) 4 ch farmer T 160a 4h 3c R1 North Baltimore Hen 14.

Rader, Wm. (Lavina) 3 ch farmer T 103a 3h R1 Hoytsville Jac 111.

Radloff, L. G. (Mamie) 1 ch farmer O 80a 4h 8c R1 Luckey Tro 50 Ind tel.

Raedloff, Mrs. Andrew Luckey Tro Ind tel.

Ragan, Mike (Mary) 2 ch motorman T H&L Second St Perrysburg Pbg.

RAGER, ALF. (Nellie) 4 ch hotel O 3c Main St Bloomdale Blo B & Ind tels. See adv.

Rahe, August Pemberville Fre.

Rahe, Edward (son Fred) farmer R3 Pemberville Fre 3.

Rabe, Fred (Anna) 4 ch farmer O 70a 7h 1c R3 Pemberville Fre 3 B tel.

Rahe, Fred (son Fred) farmer R3 Pemberville Fre 3.

Rahe, Henry (Annie) 7 ch farmer O 94a 5h 9c R1 Pemberville Fre 69 B tel.

Rahn, Edward (Lizzie) 4 ch farmer T 40a 2h 1c R1 Deshler Jac 36.

RALPH, AMOS R2 Weston Wes 16.

Ralston, Sarah W. 4 ch farmer O 80a 4h 5c R4 Bowling Green Cen 30 Ind tel.

Ralston, Thomas (Gertrude) 3 ch hardware & house furnishings O H&L RD North Baltimore Hen Ind tel.

Raney, C. A. (Della) 4 ch hotel prop O & T bldg Rudolph Lib 81 Ind tel.

Raney, D. J. Pemberville Web.

Raney, Elizabeth RD Weston Pla.

Raney, John Rudolph Lib 81 Ind tel.

Raney, O. S. (Anna) farmer T 105a 4h 5c R1 Bradner Mon 57.

RANEY, RAY (Coral) 1 ch farmer T 3h 2c R2 Weston Pla 15 Ind tel.

Ranger, Mrs. Mary Jane T H&L Weston.

Rangler, Jno. Hoytsville Jac.

Ranker, Gus (Louise) 2 ch laborer O H&L Fifth St Perrysburg Pbg.

Ranker, John (Margaret) ret O H&L Sixth St Perrysburg Pbg.

Rankin, Howard W. farm laborer R1 Deshler Jac 6 B tel.

Rassel, J. W. (Roselie) 1 ch farmer O 96a 2h 1c R1 Lime City Pbg 122 B tel.

Rathbun, Henry (Helen) 1 ch teamster T 10a 2h 2c R1 Haskins Mid 53 B tel.

Rathbun, S. T. farmer T 160a 5h 40c Cygnet Blo 12 Ind tel.

Rathburn, Clarance farmer T H&L Cygnet Blo.

Ratty, Alice housekeeper R1 Millbury Lake 131.

Ratty, William (Marian) 3 ch carpenter O 16a 4h 1c R1 Millbury Lake 131.

Raub, H. M. (Kate) laborer T H&L R1 Walbridge Lake 15.

Raub, R. G. 1 ch cement Main St Jerry City Por.

Raubenolt, L. L. (Fern) furniture & undertaking O H&L Russ St Weston Ind tel.

Rauch, Verne (Lucy) general work T H&L Center St Weston.

Raumacker, Jos. J. Weston Wes.

Ray, Florence I. housekeeper R1 Hoytsville Jac 86 B tel.

RAY, GEO. E. (Wilda) 4 ch oil producer O 8a 1h 1c R1 Rudolph Lib 71 Ind tel.

RAY, J. H. (Lillie) 4 ch farmer T 80a 6h 1c Rudolph Lib 81 Ind tel.

Ray, Wm. H. farmer O 40a 3h R1 Hoytsville Jac 87.

Raymond, John (Theresa) laborer T H&L Latchie Lake 83.

Rayner, Ed. (Nellie) 3 ch laborer O H&L Claron St Cygnet Blo 6.

Readin, D. W. RD North Baltimore Hen.

Reagle, Henry Haskins Mid.

Reahing, H. (Barbara) 2 ch motorman T H&L Fifth & Main Sts Perrysburg Pbg B tel.

Reaker, Jacob Weston Gr Rs.

Ream, Charles H. (Anna M.) 2 ch farmer T 115a 2h 2c West Millgrove Per 65.

Ream, Harriett ret T H&L Walbridge Lake.

Ream, J. W. pool room Custar Mil.

Ream, W. J. (Orpha) 3 ch carpenter O H&L 1c Bronson St Jerry City Por.

Reams, Abram (Susan) 3 ch ret farmer O H&L Center St Weston Ind tel.

Reams, Clara R2 Weston.

Reams, James (Irene) 2 ch laborer T H&L Risingsun Mon.

REAMS, J. W. (Libbie) 3 ch farmer O 40a 4h 3c R1 Tontogany Wash 17 Ind tel.

Reamsnyder, Ed. Luckey Tro.

Reape, Joe (Eva) conductor O H&L Indiana Ave Perrysburg Pbg B tel.

Reardon, Ella (dau Hannah) dressmaker Taylor St Weston.

Reardon, Hannah 2 ch dressmaker O H&L Taylor St Wes.

Rearick, J. F. (Eliza D.) general store O H&L Main St Bloomdale Blo B & Ind tels.

Rearick, Kate M. housekeeper Factory St Jerry City Por Ind tel.

Rearick, Merle (Violet) insurance S Main St Bloomdale Blo B & Ind tels.

Rearick, S. C. laborer O H&L Factory St Jerry City Por Ind tel.

Reasoner, Elizabeth RD North Baltimore Hen.

Rebbe, Mrs. C. A. housekeeper O 67a 2c Tontogany Wash 44 Ind tel.

Rebbe, Edith Tontogany Wash.

Rebbe, Jno. RD Tontogany Wash.

Rebbey, Mary housekeeper Tontogany Wash 44.

Rebensal, Frank (Kathryn) 2 ch laborer O H&L Main St Perrysburg Pbg.

Reber, Julius (Nellie) 2 ch farmer T 80a 4h 12c R4 Bowling Green Cen 37 Ind tel.

Recker, C. W. (Lynda) 6 ch farmer O 102a 4h 23c R1 Genoa Tro 38 Ind tel.

RECKER, FRED H. (Anna) farmer T 98a 5h 14c R1 Genoa Tro 40 B tel.

Recker, Hope (dau J. C.) housekeeper R1 Lemoyne Tro 83 B tel.

RECKER, J. C. (Lena) 6 ch farmer O 276a 4h 15c R1 Lemoyne Tro 83 B tel.

RECKER, J. F. (Mabel) 3 ch farmer T 176a 4h 20c R1 Lemoyne Tro 35 B tel.

Recker, Lizzie (dau Mrs. Christ Bahnsen) R1 Genoa Lake 45 B tel.

Recker, Otto (son Mrs. Christ Bahnsen) farmer R1 Genoa Lake 45 B tel.

Recker, William J. R. farm laborer R1 Genoa Tro 40 B tel.

Reekerd, Henry (Mary) 9 ch farmer T 40a 2h R1 Hoytsville Jac 99.

Rectenwald, Frank (Lulu) 3 ch farmer T 120a 4h 1c R2 Perrysburg Pbg 147.

Rectenwald, Henry R2 Perrysburg Pbg.

RED, LEWIS (Mary) 2 ch farmer O 60a 6h 1c R1 Deshler Jac 9 B tel.

REDDIN, DR. D. W. RD North Baltimore.

REDDING, DAVID E. (Bessie) 1 ch farmer T 12a 1h 1c R1 Tontogany Wash 16 Ind tel.

Redfern, E. T. (Jeannette) ret O 80a H&L 1h W Mulberry St Bloomdale Blo B & Ind tels.

Redfern, J. R. (Jennie) ret O H&L Main St Bloomdale Blo.

Redman, A. (Evelyn) farmer T H&L R3 Perrysburg Lake 1.

REDMAN, CARL D. R1 Box 88 Bowling Green.

Redman, Mrs. Emma 2 ch farmer O 50a 2h 4c R1 Bowling Green Pla 74.

Redman, Floyd (Maud) operator T H&L Sixth St Perrysburg Pbg.

Redman, Lucy A. 3 ch Stahl St Bradner Mon.

Redman, Neva Myers St Jerry City Blo.

REDMAN, WM. V. (Edith) 1 ch farmer T 80a 1h 3c Bays Lib 75 Ind tel.

Reece, Inman (Maud) 1 ch painter O H&L 1h Risingsun Mon.

Reece, John (Grace) 1 ch blacksmith O H&L Risingsun Mon.

Reed, Estella Weston Wes.

Reed, E. W. (Lillian) 1 ch delivery T H&L 3h Fifth St Perrysburg Pbg B tel.

Reed, John (Edna) lineman T H&L Grand Rapids Gr Rs Ind tel.

Reed, John (Anna) 3 ch pumper O H&L Mermill Por 19 Ind tel.

Reed, J. H. (Lulu) 2 ch storekeeper H&L store Sugar Ridge Mid 69 B & Ind tels.

Reed, Rev. R. E. (Carra) 1 ch minister T H&L 1h East St Bradner Mon B tel.

Reed, R. G. Hoytsville Jac.

Reed, W. C. Weston Wes.

Reef, Fred (Emma) 2 ch section hand O H&L Pemberville Fre 24.

Rees, A. D. Pemberville Fre.

REES, A. W. carpenter O H&L Bradner Mon B tel.

Rees, Chester B. Luckey Tro.

Rees, Florence Cygnet Blo 6 Ind tel.

Rees, J. A. Risingsun Mon.

REES, J. H. (Lucy) 8 ch oil worker O H&4Lots Claron St Cygnet Blo 6 Ind tel.

Rees, Morris (Mary) 3 ch ret O H&L Pemberville Fre.

Rees, Verna housekeeper R3 Prairie Depot Por 100 B tel.

Reese, C. L. Prairie Depot Mon.

Reese, Floyd (Olive) 3 ch farmer & pumper T 20a 2h 5c R1 Bradner Mon 27.

Reese, I. C. Risingsun Mon.

Reese, R. T. (Nellie) 2 ch farm laborer RD Rudolph Lib 37.

Reese, Simon (Anna) 9 ch laborer O H&L Milton Center Mil.

Reese, Thomas (Clara) farmer O 3a 1h R1 Portage Por 16.

Reese, W. T. (Anna) 1 ch oil pumper T H&L R1 Portage Por.

Reetz, A. (Nettie) 1 ch farmer O 97a 3h 2c R1 Perrysburg Pbg 15 Ind tel.

REGAL, GLENN (Wilda) 1 ch cigar maker T H&L Custar Mil.

Regal, Roy (Gertrude) 2 ch bakery store Rudolph Lib 81 Ind tel.

Rehner, Albert bds with Max glass worker 118 Oak St Rossford Ros.

Rehner, Max (Rosie) engineer oiler O H&L 118 Oak St Rossford Ros.

Rehner, Omar H. (Emma) 1 ch glass worker O H&L Box 2 Rossford Ros.

Reiber, John (Ida) farmer O 60a 4h 2c R2 Haskins Mid 32 B tel.

Reichert, F. (Florénce) 2 ch blacksmith O H&L Rudolph Lib 96.

Reichert, J. H. (Mary) farmer T 40a 6h 2c R1 Weston Mil 60 Ind tel.

Reid, R. E. Bradner Mon.

Reider, M. B. RD Bowling Green Por.

Reif, Emma Pemberville Fre.

Reif, Herman Le Moyne Tro.

Reife, A. J. Luckey Web.

Reifert, Henry (Caroline) 4 ch ret Stony Ridge Tro.

Reigle, F. P. RD Bowling Green Hen.

Reigle, Frank P. RD Bowling Green Jac.

Reigle, J. H. (Ora E.) 1 ch bakery T H&L Main St Bloomdale Blo B & Ind tels.

Reiling, H. Perrysburg Pbg.

Reis, Frank (Zulah) 1 ch bookkeeper O H&L Sixth St Perrysburg Pbg B tel.

Reither, Wm. (Mildred) 2 ch engineer O H&L Sixth St Perrysburg Pbg.

Reitz, A. H. (Adella) 1 ch farmer T 90a 5h 13c R3 Perrysburg Pbg 62 Ind tel.

Reitz, Edward R3 Perrysburg Pbg.

Reitz, G. P. (Mary) ret O 90a R3 Perrysburg Pbg 62 Ind tel.

Reitz, W. G. (Sadie) 2 ch farmer O 20a 2h 3c R1 Lime City Pbg 56.

Reitzel, Albert (Julia) 1 ch farmer O 150a 4h 7c R1 Lime City Pbg 40 B tel.

Reitzel, Anna (dau Albert) housekeeper R1 Lime City Pbg 40 B tel.

Reitzel, Carl (Ella) 1 ch farmer T 40a 2h 1c R1 Lime City Pbg 47 Ind tel.

Reitzel, Carrie (dau Albert) housekeeper R1 Lime City Pbg 40 B tel.

Reitzel, Chester (son Lewis) butcher R1 Lime City Pbg 55 B tel.

Reitzel, Emil (son Albert) farmer R1 Lime City Pbg 40 B tel.

Reitzel, Erwin Dunbridge Web.

Reitzel, Ferdinand (son Albert) farmer R1 Lime City Pbg 70 B tel.

Reitzel, George (Katy) 1 ch farmer T 40a 2h 3c R2 Dunbridge Pbg 36.

Reitzel, Harold (son R. H.) farmer R1 Lime City Pbg 96.

REITZEL, HENRY (Laura) 4 ch farmer O 40a 2h R1 Lime City Pbg 54.

Reitzel, Lewis farmer O 12a 1h R1 Lime City Pbg 55 B tel.

Reitzel, R. H. (Mary) 4 ch farmer O 100a 5h 6c R1 Lime City Pbg 96.

REITZEL, WM. (Emma) 1 ch farmer T 40a 2h 2c R1 Perrysburg Pbg 97 B tel.

REMSSELL, LOIS R1 Millbury.

Rensch, Mrs. May RD North Baltimore Hen.

Resh, John (Minnie) 6 ch fireman O H&L Hoytsville Jac.

Ressler, C. S. (Etta) 1 ch postal telegraph worker T H&L R1 Fostoria Per 110 Ind tel.

Ressler, J. H. (Sadie) farmer O 1a R1 Fostoria Per 116 Ind tel.

RESTEMYER, AUGUST (Sophia) 2 ch farmer O 202a 4h 7c R3 Pemberville Fre 90 B tel.

RESTEMYER, FRED (Caroline) 2 ch farmer O 80a 3h 10c R3 Pemberville Fre 92.

Restle, John (Maggie) 2 ch O 40a 2h 2c R1 Perrysburg Pbg 108.

Restle, William (Josephine) farmer O 40a 2h 2c R1 Perrysburg Pbg 108.

Reuthinger, J. Fred R3 Perrysburg Pbg.

Revard, Mrs. Anna 5 ch farmer T 2a 1h Perrysburg Pbg 141.

Rex, Henry J. (Allis) 1 ch farmer O 80a 3h 2c R3 Pemberville Tro 59 B & Ind tels.

Reynolds, Blanch (dau H.) student R2 Prairie Depot Por 112.

Reynolds, Clyde (Ella) 1 ch farmer R2 Prairie Depot Por 112.

Reynolds, C. N. (son Margaret) farmer O R2 Prairie Depot Mon 43 B tel.

Reynolds, Ella Corp St Prairie Depot Por.

REYNOLDS, GEO. (Mary) 5 ch laboring man T H&L Milton Center Mil.

Reynolds, Hattie A. RD Bowling Green Pla.

REYNOLDS, HUGH (Etta) farmer O 40a 6h 5c R2 Prairie Depot Por 112.

Reynolds, H. E. Hoytsville Jac.

Reynolds, H. H. (Bertha) 2 ch farmer O 142a 6h 6c R3 Prairie Depot Mon 100 B tel.

REYNOLDS, H. P. (Clenie) 3 ch farmer T 160a R1 Grand Rapids Gr Rs 6.

Reynolds, John (Carrie) 5 ch farmer O 118a 7h 5c R3 Prairie Depot Mon 42 B tel.

Reynolds, Margaret Prairie Depot Mon.

Reynolds, Martin G. salesman bds Perrysburg Pbg.

Reynolds, Robert (Hazel) 1 ch farmer T 180a 4h 4c R2 Prairie Depot Por 131 Ind tel.

REYNOLDS, WM. H. (Vivian) 1 ch farmer T 40a 1h 1c R1 Prairie Depot Por 110.

Reynolds, Wm. J. (son Margaret) farmer O R2 Prairie Depot Mon 43 B tel.

Reynolds, W. W. (Hattie) 2 ch farmer T 40a 1h 2c R1 Bowling Green Pla 80.

Rheinfrank, J. H. (Sophia) doctor O H&L Front St Perrysburg Pbg B tel.

Rheinfrank, J. W. Perrysburg Pbg.

Rheinfrank, William (Virginia) 1 ch doctor O H&L Walnut St Perrysburg Pbg B tel.

Rhine, C. M. (Maude) 1 ch farmer O 62a 2h 5c R1 Bloomdale Blo 51 B & Ind tels.

Rhoad, C. W. (son L.) Bairdstown Blo 40.

Rhoad, E. C. (Glenn) 2 ch O H&L Main St Bairdstown Blo.

Rhoad, J. L. Bairdstown Blo.

Rhoad, Lela (dau L.) Bairdtsown Blo 40 B & Ind tels.

Rhoad, L. (Emma) farmer O 160a 6h 6c Bairdstown Blo 40 B & Ind tels.

Rhoad, V. H. (Flossie) 2 ch laborer T H&L Hoytsville Jac.

Rhoades, J. M. Risingsun Mon.

Rhoads, Rev. D. Earl (Blanche) minister T H&L East St Bradner Mon B tel.

Rhoads, D. E. Bradner Mon.

Rhoda, Chas. F. Pemberville Fre.

Rhoda, Ernest Pemberville Fre.

Rhoda, F. W. (Martha) 2 ch farmer O 40a 2h 5c Custar Mil 44.

Rhoda, Mrs. Margaret 4 ch ret O H&L Fifth St Perrysburg Pbg B tel.

Rhodes, C. W. (Marie H.) 2 ch confectionery O H&L Walbridge Lake.

Rhodes, Mrs. Harriet 2 ch T H&L Weston.

Rhodes, J. A. (Jennie) 8 ch farmer O 80a 5h 2c R3 Prairie Depot Mon 7 B tel.

Ricard, Edward E. (Mary) 3 ch farmer O 75a 3h R3 Prairie Depot Por 99.

Rice, C. F. (Elma) farmer T 100a 5h 5c R2 Weston Wes 50.

Rice, C. W. (Estella) automobile salesman O H&L Front St Pemberville Fre 40 Ind tel.

Rice, Fred oil worker O H&4Lots Main St Bloom 6.

Rice, Mrs. Rosa farmer T Portage Por 2 Ind tel.

Rice, Roy oil worker Main St Cygnet Blo 6.

Rice, Russell (Katy) 5 ch O H&L Main St Cygnet Blo 6.

RICE, W. H. (Edna) contractor O H&L 2h 1c Tontogany Wash 29.

Richard, Bert (Minnie) 2 ch laborer O H&L Prairie Depot Mon.

Richard, Cora (dau Mrs. W. S.) bookkeeper Vine & Maple Sts Bloomdale Blo B & Ind tels.

RICHARD, C. O. (Denmies) 2 ch farmer T 80a 4h 4c R1 Bloomdale Blo 58 B & Ind tels.

Richard, Delbert cattle RD Portage Por.

Richard, Delilah O H&L Vine St Bloomdale Blo B & Ind tels.

Richard, Florentine (Sadie) 5 ch farmer T 50a 4h 2c R2 Bowling Green Pla 64 Ind tel.

The way we used to do it.

173

RICHARD, FRED L. (Lulu) 2 ch farmer T 140a 3h 3c R4 Deshler Jac 28 Ind tel.
Richard, Geo. Bloomdale Blo.
Richard, Helen M. Cygnet Blo.
Richard, Ira W. (Ethyl) carpenter T H&L Harrison St Bloomdale Blo.
Richard, Lenora housekeeper R4 Deshler Jac 28 B tel.
Richard, Melneir (Alice) farmer O 40a 2h 3c R2 Bloomdale Per 26 B & Ind tels.
Richard, Nelson (Ola) 9 ch farmer T R1 Bloomdale Blo 111.
Richard, Phoebe Bloomdale Blo.
Richard, R. J. (Ella) 3 ch farmer O 140a 1h 8c R4 Deshler Jac 28 B tel.
RICHARD, STANLY RD Hoytsville.
RICHARD, W. M. R2 Bloomdale.
RICHARD, W. S. (Gale) 3 ch farmer T 60a 2h 3c R1 Deshler Jac 24 Ind tel.
RICHARD, MRS. W. S. O H&L Vine & Maple Sts Bloomdale Blo B & Ind tel.
Richards, A. B. Prairie Depot Mon.
Richards, Bert farmer T 20a 2h Prairie Depot Mon 52.
Richards, F. RD Bowling Green Pla.
Richards, Geo. L. Corp St Jerry City Por.
Richards, J. Chas. Rudolph Lib.
Richards, Mary housekeeper O H&L Prairie Depot Mon B tel.
RICHARDS, S. J. (Susie) 2 ch farmer O 60a 3h 2c R1 Hoytsville Jac 70 Ind tel.
Richards, W. E. Freeport Mon.
Richardson, Benjamin (Ella) 3 ch janitor O H&L Custar Mil.
Richardson, Chas. (Harriet) 2 ch elevator T H&L Custar Mil.
Richardson, E. J. (Jessie) farmer T 60a 3h 1c R3 Weston Mil 5 Ind tel.
Richardson, Hazel (dau Benj.) stenographer & bookkeeper Custar Mil.
RICHARDSON, HENRY A. (Ada) 2 ch oil man T H&L 1c R1 Jerry City Blo 60 B & Ind tels.
Richardson, Howard T H Custar Mil.
Richardson, Hugh (Bertha E.) 1 ch oil worker O H&L Rudolph Lib 95 Ind tel.
RICHARDSON, MARIEL R3 Weston.
Richardson, S. G. (Addie) 3 ch farmer O 55a 1h 5c R4 Bowling Green Cen 37 Ind tel.
RICHMAN, HENRY RD3 Grand Rapids.
Richmond, B. A. Freeport Mon.
Richmond, Charles G. (Florence) 3 ch oil worker O H T Land Portage Lib 88.
Richmond, F. H. RD North Baltimore Hen.

Richmond, James (Viola) 2 ch laborer T H&L Hoytsville Jac.
Richter, Herman (Kate) 4 ch farmer O 56a 2h 2c R4 Bowling Green Por 45.
RICKARD, DELBERT L. (Lucinda) 3 ch farmer T 80a 1h 1c R1 Portage Por 41.
RICKARD, I. E. (Geneva) 1 ch blacksmith T H&L & shop Tontogany Wash. See adv.
Rickard, J. F. Prairie Depot Mon.
Rickard, Perry laborer Tontogany Wash.
RICKELS, HENRY (Elizabeth) 7 ch farmer O 110a 4h 4c RD Lime City Pbg 42 Ind tel.
Rickels, Wm. (son Henry) farmer R1 Lime City Pbg 42.
Rickerd, J. F. (Mary) 4 ch farmer O 40a 6h 2c R1 Prairie Depot Mon 118.
Rickerd, Lucinda 5 ch ret 120a H&L 1h Hoytsville Jac.
Rickerd Pearl (dau Lucinda) housekeeper Hoytsville Jac.
Rickerd, Tom (son Lucinda) laborer Hoytsville Jac.
Ricket, A. J. (Lucy) laborer O H&L Rudolph Lib 94 Ind tel.
Ricket, Frank (Nellie) 2 ch farmer O 48a 3h 2c R4 Bowling Green Cen 107.
RICKET, JOHN D. oil worker Mermill Por 19.
RICKET, MATILDA O H&L Mermill Por 19.
Rickly, E. L. (Gertrude) 4 ch farmer T 100a 4h 5c R1 Weston Mil 54 Ind tel.
RICKLY, JOHN (Almeda) farmer O 60a 1h 1c R3 Weston Mil 74 Ind tel.
Rideout, Bertha (dau H.) Station A Box 123 East Toledo Ros 31.
Rideout, Chas I. (Lucy) 2 ch farmer O 39a 2h 1c E Broadway St East Toledo Ros 20.
RIDEOUT, DARWIN (Carrie) 3 ch wholesale butcher O 35a 2h 2c Sta A East Toledo Ros 20 Ind tel.
Rideout, Dale E. (son Rose) oil gauger R1 East Toledo Ros 26 Ind tel.
Rideout, Edwin (Ira) farmer O 40a 3h R1 Box 27-A East Toledo Ros 38 Ind tel.
Rideout, Emma (dau H.) Station A Box 123 East Toledo Ros 31.
Rideout, George (son H.) Station A Box 123 East Toledo Ros 31.
Rideout, Harold (son Thomas) R1 Box 15 East Toldeo Ros 26 Ind tel.
Rideout, Harvey (son H.) Station A Box 123 East Toledo Ros 31.
RIDEOUT, HENRY H. (Alice) farmer & gardener O 53a 4h 4c Station A Box 123 East Toledo Ros 31.

Rideout, Irvin (son Darwin) Station A East Toledo Ros 20 Ind tel.

Rideout, James (Reldia) 2 ch farmer T Station A Box 123 East Toledo Ros 31.

Rideout, Martha (dau Thos.) housekeeper R1 Box 15 East Toledo Ros 26 Ind tel.

Rideout, Ray (son H.) Station A Box 123 East Toledo Ros 31.

Rideout, Mrs. Rose 1 ch O 11a 2h R1 East Toledo Ros 26 Ind tel.

Rideout, Roy (son H.) Station A Box 123 East Toledo Ros 31.

Rideout, Thomas (Olive) farmer O 78a 2h 2c R1 Box 15 East Toledo Ros 26 Ind tel.

Rideout, Will (Bert) 4 ch farmer O 55a 4h 6c R1 Walbridge Lake 2 Ind tel.

Rider, C. F. hardware O 98a 5h 6c Lime City Pbg 120 B tel.

Rider, Frank RD Haskins Mid.

Rider, Harold (Linda) laborer T H&L Main St Perrysburg Pbg.

RIDER, JAMES F. (Margaret) 2 ch farmer T 1c R1 Tontogany Wash 17 Ind tel.

Rider, Jos. RD Haskins Mid.

Rider, Ray (Evelyn) laborer T H&L Fourth St Perrysburg Pbg.

Rider, Thos. Pemberville Fre.

Rider, W. F. (Lovina) laborer O H&L Main St Bloomdale Blo.

Ridey, George (Mabel) 1 ch runs steam ditcher T R1 Custar Mil 101.

Ridey, Henry 5 ch ret R1 Custar Mil 99½.

Ridgley, Geo. M. 3 ch barber O H&L Main St Jerry City Blo 78.

Riegler, Joseph RD Helena.

RIEHM, GEO. P. (Pearl) 3 ch farmer O 100a 6h 5c R3 Perrysburg Pbg 62.

Ries, Geo. (Dora) 5 ch laborer T H&L Main St Jerry City Por.

RIES, MRS. J. C. 4 ch farmer O 40a 1c R4 Bowling Green Cen 98.

RIES, OTIS L. (Bertha) 5 ch farmer T 80a 3h 2c R3 Bowling Green Gen 51.

Rife, A. J. (Minnie) 3 ch farmer T 40a 2h 5c R1 Luckey Web 68 B tel.

Rife LeRoy Pemberville Fre.

Rife, Louis (Julia) 3 ch laborer O H&L Luckey Tro.

Rife, Mrs. Racheal 4 ch housekeeper O H&L Pemberville Fre 40.

Rife, Samuel 2 ch farm laborer Luckey Tro.

Riffer, F. A. (Julia) auto livery O H&L Luckey Tro Ind tel.

Riffer, Julia Luckey Tro.

Riffl, L. T. (Nora) 3 ch oil worker T H&L Rudolph Lib 94.

Riffle, Samuel 4 ch laborer T H&L Mermill Por 19.

Riger, W. H. (Emma) 6 ch ret O H&L Hoytsville Jac.

Rigg, Chas. (Fannie) 2 ch farmer O 62a 2h 4c R1 Grand Rapids Gr Rs 53 Ind tel.

Rigg, Frank J. (Ethel) carpenter Tontogany Wash Ind tel.

RIGG, HARRY E. R2 Weston.

RIGHT, R. W. (Margaret) 4 ch farm laborer R1 Custar Lib 14.

Rights, Jim oil worker O H&L Bradford St Cygnet Blo.

Riker, P. (Anna) 2 ch farmer T 196a R1 Bradner Mon 25.

Riley, A. D. 3 ch pumper O H&L W Caldwell St Bradner Mon.

Riley, Chas. ret O H&L Risingsun Mon.

Riley, Chas. L. (Sophia) grocer T H&L N Main St Bradner Mon B tel.

Riley, G. H. (Alice J.) laborer O H&L 2h 1c R2 Prairie Depot Mon 109.

Riley, Mrs. Hannah 1 ch ret O H&L Risingsun Mon.

Riley, Henry Prairie Depot Mon.

Riley, Joseph (Willametta) farmer O 76a 3h 2c R1 Risingsun Per 96 Ind tel.

Riley, Martha Risingsun Mon.

Riley, Wm. (Dora) 5 ch oil worker T H&L East St Bradner Mon.

Riley, Willametta Risingsun Per.

Rine, Dr. A. H. (Lydia M.) 1 ch physician O H&L Walbridge Lake Ind tel.

Rinebolt, Chas. B. (son N.) farmer R1 Prairie Depot Mon 84 B tel.

RINEBOLT, N. (Mary H.) farmer O 79a 3h 2c R1 Prairie Depot Mon 84 B tel.

Rinker, C. F. (Mary) 2 ch farmer O 40a 3h 4c R3 Perrysburg Pbg 77 Ind tel.

Rinker, Henry (Flora) 5 ch fruit grower O 33a 2h 1c Rossford Pbg 80 Ind tel.

Risser, Chas. E. (Jessie I.) 4 ch postmaster at West Millgrove T H&L 1c Main St West Millgrove Per.

RISSER, MRS. LETTIE R2 Prairie Depot.

Risser, Lewis (Hattie) ret H&L West Millgrove Per 70.

Risser, T. C. (Celestie O.) 3 ch farmer O 80a 5h 5c R2 Prairie Depot Mon 92.

Ritchey, Vere (Bessie) farmer T 80a 1h R2 Bloomdale Blo 106 B & Ind tels.

Ritchey, W. E. Jerry City Blo.

Ritter, Chas. L. (Mary) 2 ch monument worker T H&L RD North Baltimore Hen.

175

Ritz, Delbert D. (Estella) farmer T 40a 4h 8c R3 Prairie Depot Mon 12½ B tel.

Rive, Dr. A. H. Walbridge Lake.

Roab, Gust. Luckey Tro.

ROACH, CHAS. F. (Mary) 3 ch glass worker T H&L Lime City Pbg 91.

Roach, Michael RD North Baltimore Hen.

ROACH, MRS. SARAH A. R2 Grand Rapids.

Roadanel, M. C. (Eliza) 3 ch farmer O H&L 4h 5c Haskins Mid B tel.

Roadarmel, H. C. Haskins Mid.

Roadarmel, J. W. (Clara) farmer O H&L 3h Haskins Mid 35 B tel.

Roather, Jacob 3 ch laborer O 18a 1h 1c R1 Perrysburg Pbg 100.

ROBBINS, L. V..(Susan) barber shop T H&L Main St Bloomdale Blo B & Ind tels.

Roberson, O. S. (Ida) 5 ch oil worker T R1 North Baltimore Hen 74.

ROBERTS, ALBERT A. (Delia) 4 ch farmer O 160a 1h 2c R1 Rudolph Lib 106 Ind tel.

Roberts, A. A. (Emma) 4 ch grocery T H&L 1h Perrysburg Pbg B tel.

Roberts, Carry M. (son J. M.) barber Grand Rapids Gr Rs Ind tel.

Roberts, C. W. (Nellie) 2 ch laborer T H&L Seventh St. Perrysburg Pbg.

Roberts, Delia M. RD Rudolph Lib.

Roberts, Ed. (Maud) 2 ch machinist T H&L Indiana Ave Perrysburg Pbg.

Roberts, Edward (Eva) laborer O H&L Sixth St Perrysburg Pbg.

Roberts, Eliza carpet weaver O H&L Custar Mil.

Roberts, Gertrude (dau J. H.) employee Third St Portage Por Ind tel.

Roberts, Glenn (Hazel) farmer R1 Portage Por 12.

Roberts, George H. (Kathryn) laborer T H&L Indiana Ave Perrysburg Pbg.

Roberts, Harry (Hazel) T H&L Fourth St Perrysburg Pbg.

Roberts, Henry (Elizabeth) 2 ch traveling salesman O 2a H 1h 1c Walnut St Perrysburg Pbg.

Roberts, J. H. (Lillie) farmer O H&L Third St Portage Por Ind tel.

Roberts, J. K. (Jenny) farmer O 20a 2h 2c R2 Weston Wes 25.

Roberts, J. M. (Lorena) 1 ch barber O H&L Grand Rapids Gr Rs Ind tel.

Roberts, Theodore Perrysburg Pbg.

Roberts, Ula (dau J. H.) employee Third St Portage Por Ind tel.

ROBERTS, W. J. (Mary) 1 ch pumper O H&L Findlay St Portage Por.

Robertson, A. F. (Margaret E.) ret O H&L Prairie Depot Mon.

Robertson, C. C. RD Rudolph Lib.

Robertson, Elizabeth Haskins Mid.

Robertson, F. R. (Ida May) 1 ch farmer & garage man O 80a 2c Tontogany Wash 28 B & Ind tels.

Robertson, H. P. (Edith) 1 ch buyer & manager T H&L Indiana Ave Perrysburg Pbg B tel.

Robertson, L. F. RD Haskins Mid.

Robertson, Mrs. Mary E. ret O H&L Haskins Mid B tel.

Robinette, C. (Helen) 1 ch farmer O 10a 2h 1c R1 Fostoria Per 112 B tel.

Robins, Aaran (Lizzie) glass worker T H&L 93 Elm St Rossford Ros.

Robinson, Earl (son E. F.) farmer R2 Weston Pla 6.

Robinson, Miss Erma (dau E. F.) nurse R2 Weston Pla 6.

Robinson, E. F. (Rachel) 1 ch farmer T 155a 6h 4c R2 Weston Pla 6 Ind tel.

ROBINSON, GEO. Bradner.

Robinson, G. W. (Bertha) blacksmith O H&L Bell St Bradner Mon B tel.

Robinson, Mrs. Hanuah 5 ch O 20a Bays Lib 99.

Robinson, Isabell Grand Rapids Gr Rs.

ROBINSON, JAMES W. (Maude) 8 ch driller O L 1h 1c Bays Lib 75 Ind tel.

ROBINSON, LYMAN (Winafred) 1 ch laborer O H&2Lots R1 Haskins Mid 53.

Robinson, Nathan (Lizzie) 4 ch laborer O H&L Stony Ridge Tro.

Robinson, O. S. RD North Baltimore Hen.

Robinson, Phil (Lillian) 3 ch carpenter T H&L Main St Perrysburg Pbg.

Robinson, Ross Tontogany Wash.

Robinson, Samuel (Mary) 1 ch section foreman T H&L Walbridge Lake.

Robinson, Steven (Isabell) ret O H&L Grand Rapids Gr Rs.

Robinson, T. A. RD North Baltimore Hen.

Robinson, W. D. (Stella) 2 ch oil pumper O 30a 1h 3c R1 Rudolph Lib 33 Ind tel.

ROBINSON, W. L. (Grace) 1 ch restaurant T H&L Weston Wes Ind tel.

ROBISON, B. E. (Henrietta) farmer 120a 4h 2c R1 Rudolph Por 25.

ROBISON, H. W. proprietor Interstate Stock Yards O Central Station Box 312 Toledo Ros 22.

ROBISON, O. S. R1 North Baltimore Hen 83.

Robison, S. T. Walbridge Lake.

Robson, Florence Weston Wes.

Robson, Goldie school teacher Maple St Weston.

Rockwell, C. J. RD North Baltimore Hen.

Rockwell, C. K. RD North Baltimore Hen.

Rockwell, Fred RD North Baltimore Hen.

Rockwell, G. G. RD North Baltimore Hen.

Rockwell, Hannah J. RD North Baltimore Hen.

Rockwell, Mrs. Q. R. RD North Baltimore Hen.

Rockwood, E. C. RD Bowling Green Pla.

Roderick, Chas. (Pearl) 2 ch inspector O 3a 1h Walbridge Lake.

Roderick, J. W. (Myrtle) 3 ch oil worker O H&L Rudolph Lib 94.

Roderick, Vera (dau J. W.) Rudolph Lib 94.

Roderick, Will (Myrtle) 4 ch oil worker O H&L 1h Corry St Cygnet Blo 6 Ind tel.

Roe, Anna housekeeper R2 Weston Wash 3 Ind tel.

Roe, Bernice (dau Caleb E.) housekeeper R1 Hoytsville Jac 42 B tel.

Roe, Caleb E. (Myrtle) 2 ch farmer O 160a 5h 3c R1 Hoytsville Jac 42 B tel.

ROE, CHAS. (Jane) 1 ch farmer O 40a 1h 3c R1 Perrysburg Pbg 103 B tel.

ROE, CHAS. (Blanche) garage T H&L Weston.

Roe, Elmer RD Weston Lib.

Roe, Emily (dau Robert) school teacher Locust & Maple Sts Weston.

Roe, Emma (dau Frank) housekeeper R1 Haskins Mid 38.

ROE, FRANK (Anna) 5 ch gauger O 25a 2h 1c R1 Haskins Mid 38 B tel.

Roe, Geo. (Eliza) farmer O 80a 2h 4c R1 Hoytsville Jac 42.

ROE, H. P. (Myrtilla) 4 ch farmer T 40a 2h 3c R1 Rudolph Lib 73 Ind tel.

Roe, L. D. (Cora) 6 ch farmer O 50a 3h 3c R3 Weston Mil 67 Ind tel.

Roe, Mrs. Marguerite RD Bowling Green Pla.

Roe, Robert (Ada) 4 ch ret O 130a H&L cor Locust & Maple Sts Weston Ind tel.

Roe, Tom (Annie) 7 ch farmer O 2a 1h Tontogany Wash 21½ Ind tel.

Roe, Wm. 6 ch farmer O 80a Weston Lib 2 Ind tel.

Roecker, J. C. Le Moyne Tro.

Roecker, Mrs. J. C. Le Moyne Tro.

Roecker, J. F. Le Moyne Tro.

Roether, A. G. Perrysburg Pbg.

Roether, Henry (Laura) 1 ch doctor O H&L Front St Perrysburg Pbg B tel.

Roether, Julia ret O H&L Sixth St Perrysburg Pbg B tel.

Roether, Laura RD Perrysburg Mid.

Roetker, Edith (dau W.) clerk 1606 Oak St East Toledo Ros 17.

Roetker, William (Emma) ret O 10a 1h 1c 1606 Oak St East Toledo Ros 17.

Roger, Alf. Bloomdale Blo.

ROGERS, ANNA PEARL Prairie Depot.

Rogers, Mrs. E. B. ret O H&L Latchie Lake 95.

Rogers, H. (Martha) 2 ch tank builder O H&L 1h Venango St Cygnet Blo Ind tel.

Rogers, James (Frances) telephone manager O H&L Pemberville Fre B tel.

Rogers, John B. (Emma) 1 ch farmer O 39½a 1h 1c R1 Bloomdale Blo 105 B & Ind tels.

Rogers, L. S. cattle RD Bowling Green Cen.

Rogers, Nancy R. RD North Baltimore Hen.

Rogers, Roy (Ida) 1 ch section hand T H&L Latchie Lake 83.

Rogers, R. B. (Anna) farmer O 80a 3h 4c R1 Bloomdale Blo 102 B & Ind tels.

ROGERS, R. E. R5 Bowling Green.

Rogers, T. A. (Eva J.) 2 ch general merchandise O H&L Prairie Depot Mon.

Rogers, W. H., Jr. Latchie Lake.

ROGERS, W. P. RD North Baltimore.

Rogers, W. S. RD North Baltimore Hen.

Rolf, Carrie (dau Harmon) housekeeper R2 Woodville Tro 55 Ind tel.

Rolf, Clarence (son Harmon) farmer R2 Woodville Tro 55 Ind tel.

ROLF, E. J. (Dora) 3 ch saloon T H&L Pemberville Fre 40 B tel.

ROLF, FRANK J. (Jessie E.) 2 ch farmer O 60a 3h 4c R2 Pemberville Fre 45 B tel.

ROLF, FRED P. (Amelia) 7 ch farmer O 53a 3h 7c R1 Luckey Tro 77 Ind tel.

Rolf, Freda (dau Harmon) housekeeper R2 Woodville Tro 55 Ind tel.

ROLF, F. W. (Daisy) saloon T H&L Pemberville Fre 40 B tel.

Rolf, Harmon (Flora) 6 ch farmer O 120a 4h 12c R2 Woodville Tro 55 Ind tel.

Rolf, H. H. (Mary) ret O 52a 4h 3c Pemberville Fre.

Rolf, Mrs. Mary ret O H&L Pemberville Fre 40.

Rolf, Wm. H. (Carrie) 2 ch farmer T 80a 3h 5c R3 Pemberville Fre 18 B tel.

Rolfes, Clarence trucking Luckey Tro Ind tel.

Rolfes, Geo. L. (Carrie) 4 ch carpenter O H&L Luckey Tro Ind tel.

Rolfes, Henry (Mary) 2 ch drayman O H&L 1h Luckey Tro Ind tel.

Rolfes, Mrs. Louis O H&L Luckey Tro Ind tel.

ROLFES, L. H. (Kate) 7 ch farmer O 120a 4h 15c R3 Pemberville Tro 56 Ind tel.

Rolfes, Nora (dau Geo. L.) housekeeper O' H Luckey Tro Ind tel.

Rolfes, Will pumper O H&L Luckey Tro Ind tel.

Roller, Bertha L. Dowling Mid.

Roller, Martha Dowling Mid.

Roller, Michael (Gertrude) 4 ch farmer T 80a 4h 4c R2 Dunbridge Web 2.

Roller, Wm. (Martha) farmer O 96a 2h 1c Dowling Mid 76 Ind tel.

Roller, Wm., Jr. (Bertha) 4 ch farmer T 80a 5h 6c R2 Dunbridge Mid 74.

Romaker, Frank (Margaret) 11 ch farmer O 50a 4h 3c R2 Custar Mil 51 Ind tel.

ROMAKER, FRANK B. (Rose M.) 1 ch farmer T 100a 2h 2c R3 Weston Mil 82 Ind tel.

Romaker, George (Maggie) 6 ch farmer O 40a 2h 3c R1 Custar Mil 46 B tel.

Romaker, Joseph (Adell) 1 ch farmer T 80a 2h 2c R3 Weston Mil 90 Ind tel.

Romaker, Lawrence (son Frank) farm hand R2 Custar Mil 51.

Romaker, Mike (son George) farm hand R1 Custar Mil 46.

Romey, Ed. RD North Baltimore Hen.

Romey, Ray RD North Baltimore Hen.

Ronan, Anna 1 ch ret O H&L Indiana Ave Perrysburg Pbg.

Roose, W. H. Perrysburg Pbg.

Root, Arthur Le Moyne Tro.

Root, A. C. (Cora) 1 ch telephone mgr O H&L Le Moyne Tro.

ROOT, M. O. (Elizabeth) minister O 3H&L 1h Frankfather Ave Jerry City Por.

Rope, John H. (Bertha J.) 3 ch farmer O 80a 4h 9c R2 Custar Lib 32 Ind tel.

ROPER, ALLEN B. (Gertrude) 1 ch truck farmer O 2a R2 Pemberville Web 34½.

Roper, Charles ret 60a R1 Dunbridge Web 49 B tel.

Roper, Hubert (Mary) 3 ch farmer T 108a 5h 3c R1 Pemberville Fre 57.

Roper, P. G. (Mary) farmer O 124a 6h 10c R1 Dunbridge Web 49 B tel.

Roper, Thos. Scotch Ridge Fre.

Roper, W. Hugh Pemberville Fre.

Rosbach, Mrs. Fred 3 ch ret T Fifth & Maple Sts Perrysburg Pbg.

Rosbach, Fred (Mary) poolroom T H&L Second St Perrysburg Pbg B tel.

Rosbach, Joseph 5 ch musician O H&L Main St Perrysburg Pbg B tel.

Rosco, Jonas W. Walbridge Lake.

Roscoe, Geo. railroader O H&L Walbridge Lake.

Rose, F. H. RD North Baltimore Hen.

Rose, Herschel C. (son Wm. S.) R1 Bloomdale Blo 102.

Rose, John (Alta) tool dresser T L R1 North Baltimore Hen 69 Ind tel.

Rose, J. E. (Blanche) laborer T R2 Custar Lib 32 Ind tel.

Rose, L. S. (Hannah) 3 ch farmer T 80a 3h 1c R1 Bowling Green Pla 74 Ind tel.

Rose, Mabel L. (dau Wm. S.) R1 Bloomdale Blo 102.

Rose, Wm. (May) 3 ch farmer T 200a 6h 5c R1 Fostoria Per 87 Ind tel.

Rose, Wm. S. (Laura B.) 4 ch farmer T 80a 3h 2c R1 Bloomdale Blo 102.

ROSENBERGER, A. (Laura) 1 ch stationary engineer O H&L Milton Center Mil.

ROSENBERGER, MRS. C. L. Milton Center.

Rosenberger, James (Martha) 3 ch laborer O H&L Grand Rapids Gr Rs.

Rosencrantz, J. (Ollie) painter & paperhanger O 2H&L 1h Silver St Weston B tel.

Rosendale, Arthur (Edith) 4 ch farmer O H&L 4h 8c West Milgrove Per 68.

Rosendale Alice M. Bloomdale Blo.

Rosendale Mrs. A. O. ret O 80a R1 Bloomdale Per 14 B & Ind tels.

Rosendale, Ben H. (Edna B.) 1 ch garage Mulberry St Bloomdale Blo B & Ind tels.

Rosendale, Chester Bloomdale Blo.

Rosendale, Charles J. (Luella M.) 4 ch farmer O 80a 3h 2c R1 Bloomdale Blo 103 B & Ind tels.

Rosendale, C. A. (Ethel) 1 ch farmer O 4h 4c R1 Bloomdale Blo 106 B & Ind tels.

Rosendale, C. R. West Millgrove Per.

Rosendale, E. B. (Adda) 2 ch farmer O 160a 4h 6c R2 Bloomdale Blo 104 B & Ind tels.

Rosendale, Edna H. Bloomdale Per.

Rosendale, Fannie (dau W. A.) R1 Bloomdale Blo 130 B & Ind tels.

Rosendale, Guy M. (Stella) 2 ch farmer O 80a 4h 7c R1 Bloomdale Per 14 B & Ind tels.

Rosendale, H. O. (Mary M.) 4 ch farmer O 80a 4h 6c R1 Bloomdale Blo 116 B tel.

Rosendale, Mae (dau W. A.) R1 Bloomdale Blo 130 B & Ind tels.

Rosendale, Raymond J. (son C. J.) R1 Bloomdale Blo 103 B & Ind tels.

Rosendale, R. R. (Maude) farmer O 80a 6h 4c R1 Bloomdale Blo 114 B & Ind tels.

Rosendale, Stanley (son C. J.) R1 Bloomdale Blo 103 B & Ind tels.

Rosendale, Scott E. farmer O 80a 3h R1 Bloomdale Blo 102 B & Ind tels.

Rosendale, Thos. A. (Adda B.) 1 ch . farmer O 80a 4h 3c R2 Bloomdale Blo 112.

ROSENDALE, W. A. (Clara C.) 4 ch farmer O 80a 7h 5c R1 Bloomdale Blo 130 B & Ind tels.

Rosendale, W. W. (Irene) 2 ch ret 260a Main St West Millgrove Per.

Ross, E. E. (Catharine) 3 ch farmer T 65a 11h 2c Cygnet Hen 116.

Ross, Floyd (Hazel) 4 ch farmer T 120a 3h 2c R1 Jerry City Por 29 Ind tel.

Ross, Grant (Mollie) 8 ch farmer T 160a 7h 5c R2 North Baltimore Hen 72.

Ross, J. D. (Emma) 1 ch carpenter O 33a 1h 2c R2 Bowling Green Pla 59 B tel.

Ross, Mrs. Margaret ret O H&L Prairie Depot Mon.

Ross, Wm. A. (Lena) 1 ch oil driller O H&L Rising Sun Mon B tel.

Ross, W. L. (Louesa) 6 ch ret O H&L N Main St Weston Ind tel.

Rossbach, Fred P. Perrysburg Pbg.

Rossbach, Jas. Perrysburg Pbg.

ROSSITER, J. W. veterinarian Fostoria. See adv.

Rossler, Peter (Louise) 3 ch glass worker O H&L 263 Walnut St Rossford Ros.

Rossow, A. C. (Hattie) 1 ch farmer T 80a 3h 2c R1 Custar Mil 101 B tel.

Rossow, Bertha (dau Sophia) dry goods clerk bds Custar Mil.

Rossow, Mrs. Jos. Custar Mil.

Rossow, Lewis (son Sophia) fireman in grain elevator bds Custar Mil.

Rossow, Sophia 5 ch ret O H&L Custar Mil.

Roth, Chas. (Cora) 1 ch farmer T 13a 3h 2c R1 Tontogany Wash 17 Ind tel.

Roth, Geo. RD Grand Rapids Wash.

Rothenbeler, Wilbur farm hand R1 Luckey Tro 20 Ind tel.

Rothenbuehler, Henry (Sophia H.) farmer O 160a 5h 5c R1 Luckey Web 69 B tel.

Rothenbuhler, Albert (son J. F.) laborer Luckey Web 70 B tel.

ROTHENBUHLER, FRANK (Anna(farm laborer R1 Luckey Tro 26 Ind tel.

Rothenbuhler, Fred 3 ch farmer O 97a 4h 7c R1 Luckey Tro 26 Ind tel.

Rothenbuhler, Gottlieb (Rose) 6 ch farmer 60a 3h 5c R1 Luckey Tro 19 Ind tel.

Rothenbuhler, Herbert (son J. F.) farm laborer Luckey Web 70 B tel.

ROTHENBUHLER, J. F. (Mary) 5 ch farmer O 40a 5h 6c Luckey Web 70 B tel.

Rothenbuhler, Laura (dau Gottlieb) housekeeper R1 Luckey Tro 19 Ind tel.

Rothenbuhler, Wilbert Luckey Tro.

Rothrock, H. A. Grand Rapids Gr Rs.

Rothrock, R. A. (Esther) preacher T H&L 1h Grand Rapids Gr Rs Ind tel.

"Peep! Peep!"

Rouf, H. H. (Mary) saloonkeeper O H&L & saloon 4h Pemberville Fre 40 B & Ind tels.

Rounds, Mrs. Frances O H&L Luckey Tro.

Rouse, Lee RD Bowling Green Lib.

Roush, George (Jane) 5 ch farmer O 80a 3h 6c R2 Custar Lib 29 B tel.

Roush, Howard R2 Custar Lib 29.

Routson, Curt farmer 1h R1 Bowling Green Lib 53.

Routson, E. E. 2 ch farmer O 50a 1h 3c R1 Bowling Green Lib 53.

Routson, J. W. (Exariffa) 1 ch ret O H&L Hoytsville Jac.

Routson, Olive RD Bowling Green Lib.

Roux, F. R. (Lettee) 1 ch barber Garfield St Bloomdale Blo.

Rowe, Fred (son Isaac) student R1 Fostoria Per 127.

Rowe, Golda (dau Isaac) college student R1 Fostoria Per 127.

Rowe, Iris school teacher Caldwell St Bradner Mon B tel.

Rowe, Isaac (Lizzie) 3 ch farmer T 117a 8h 20c R1 Fostoria Per 127.

Rowe, John (son Isaac) farmer 1h R1 Fostoria Per 127.

Rowe, W. E. (Lizzie) 2 ch gauger O H&L 1c Caldwell St Bradner Mon B tel.

Rowell, L. J. (Nettie) 2 ch hotel & restaurant O bldg Hoytsville Jac B tel.

Rowland, Addie M. Grand Rapids Gr Rs.

Rowland, J. A. (Gertrude) 2 ch gen store O HS&L 1h Mermill Por 20 Ind tel.

Rowland, J. W. (Ida May) pumper O 3a H&L Main St Jerry City Por Ind tel.

Roy, C. G. RD North Baltimore Hen.

Rozelle, Mrs. Anna 3 ch O 30a 1h 1c Caldwell St Bradner Mon B tel.

Rozelle, Bert (Ethel) 3 ch pumper & farmer O H&L 1h 2c Caldwell St Bradner Mon B tel.

Rubel, Cora (dau W. H.) housekeeper R2 Prairie Depot Por 112.

Rubel, Walter (son W. H.) threshing R2 Prairie Depot Por 112.

Rubel, Wm. (Esther) 2 ch oil worker O H&L Cor Crocker & Evans Sts. Bradner Mon.

Rubel, W. M. (Eliza) 2 ch farmer O 40a 2h 3c R2 Prairie Depot Por 112.

Ruble, Frank (Nora) ret O H&L Prairie Depot Mon.

Ruble, F. S. (Emma) 2 ch O H&L Prairie Depot Mon.

Ruch, A. Luckey Tro.

Ruckereigel, Mary ret O H&L Fifth St Perrysburg Pbg.

Rudd, C. R. Tontogany Wash.

Ruder, Wm. C. (Grace) 5 ch hardware O H&L Hoytsville Jac.

RUDOLPH, MRS. CHAS. ret 2c R1 Walbridge Lake 101.

Rudolph, E. C. (Mary) 4 ch farmer O 38a 6h 8c R1 Walbridge Lake 101.

Rudolph, Gus (Carrie) 1 ch farmer O 57a 3h 3c R2 Haskins Wash 98 Ind tel.

Rudolph, John 5 ch farmer O 40a 1h 5c R2 Custer Mil 45 B tel.

RUEDY, AL. (son Louise) farmer T 37a Station A East Toledo Ros 23.

Ruedy, John (son Louise) blacksmith Station A East Toledo Ros 23.

Ruedy, Mrs. Louise ret 2h 1c Station A East Toledo Ros 23.

Ruedy, Oliva (dau Louise) Station A East Toledo Ros 23.

Ruelle, Mary RD North Baltimore Hen.

Ruffner, Jas. P. RD North Baltimore Hen.

Ruggley, Robert (Nancy E.) 5 ch section foreman T H&L Haskins Mid.

RUGH, E. E. (Mame) 1 ch farmer O 160a 3h 4c R2 Weston Pla 26 Ind tel.

Rumbaugh, J. H. (Ella) carpenter O 13a 1h Hatton Per 85.

Rumler, B. F. (Alvissa) 3 ch ret O H&L Taylor St Wes Ind tel.

Rumler, Jessie (Barbara) farmer O 53a 2h 8c R3 Prairie Depot Mon 108.

Rumler, Wm. (Susan) 4 ch farmer O 53a 2h 5c R3 Prairie Depot Mon 108.

Rummel, I. E. (Nettie) 1 ch cement contr O H&L Milton Center Mil Ind tel.

Rundlett, Warren M. (Cora) 3 ch driller O H&L 1h Mermill Por 19 Ind tel.

RUPP, DAVID (Susie G.) store keeper O H&L Haskins Mid 35 B tel.

Rupp, J. C. (Mary) 1 ch railroader T H&L Front St Pemberville Fre 40.

RUSH, C. L. (Cora) 7 ch farmer T 100a 4h 6c R1 Deshler Jac 6 B tel.

Rust, Lucy C. 1 ch ret O 100a R1 Deshler Jac 6 B tel.

Russel, Frank (Lee) ret O 160a 2h 1c R5 Bowling Green Cen 92 B tel.

Russel, May R5 Bowling Green Cen 92 Ind tel.

Russel, Robert (Martha) farmer O 40a 1h R3 Weston Wes 53 Ind tel.

Russell, Mrs. Allie W. (wid R. B.) 1 ch housekeeper O H&L Front St Pemberville Fre 40.

Russell, Blanch (dau C. A.) R1 Weston Lib 11 Ind tel.

RUSSELL, C. A. (Pearl) 5 ch farmer T 80a 5h 6c R1 Weston Lib 11 Ind tel.

Russell, C. H. (Myrta B.) 3 ch farmer T 4h 2c R5 Bowling Green Cen 61.

Russell, C. W. (son Fanny) barber bds Prairie Depot Mon.

Russell, Emma C. O 125a 1h 1c R1 Millbury Lake 124 Ind tel.

Russell, Erven I. (Bertha) farmer T 64a 3h 9c R1 Walbridge Pbg 64.

Russell, E. L. (Alta) 1 ch meat cutter O H&L Evans St Bradner Mon.

Russell, Mrs. Fanny 1 ch housekeeper T H&L Prairie Depot Mon.

Russell, Fred J. (son Mrs. Allien) farmer Pemberville Fre.

RUSSELL, GEO. (Bertha) farmer T 80a 4h 3c R3 Bowling Green Cen 42 Ind tel.

RUSSELL, GEO. O. (Millie) 2 ch farmer T 60a 3h 2c R5 Bowling Green Cen 108 Ind tel.

RUSSELL, MRS. HOMER R2 Bloomdale.

Russell, Irene Bloomdale Blo.

Russell, Janett (dau A. W.) housekeeper Front St Pemberville Fre 40.

Russell, John O H&L Cor of Mulbury & Garfield Sts Bloomdale Blo.

Russell, Mrs. Joseph farmer R5 Bowling Green Cen 92 Ind tel.

Russell, J. A. (Clara) 1 ch farmer T 143a 5h 7c R2 Dunbridge Mid 48 Ind tel.

Russell, J. L. (Catherine) 2 ch farmer T 80a 3h 1c R4 Bowling Green Cen 60 Ind tel.

RUSSELL, LOUIS R1 Millbury.

Russell, L. E. (Edith) farmer O 75a 5h Bowling Green Cen 74 Ind tel.

Russell, Mary (dau A. W.) school teacher Front St Pemberville Fre 40.

Russell, Mary E. 3 ch O H&L Toledo Ave Bradner Mon.

Russell, Oliver (son C. A.) R1 Weston Lib 11 Ind tel.

RUSSELL, RAYMOND (Lulu) 1 ch farmer T 40a 4h 8c R1 Millbury Lake 80.

Russell, William 5 ch farming O 40a 3h 1c R3 Weston Wes 53.

Russell, Wm. A. (Susan) ret O H&L Dickson St Jerry City Por.

Rust, C. F. (Louisa) 3 ch ret O 80a 2h 7c R1 Genoa Lake 41 B tel.

Rust, Fred (Elma) farmer O 80a 3h 5c R1 Genoa Lake 40.

RUSWINKLE, WM. (Mary) 4 ch farmer O 102a 3h 9c R1 Luckey Tro 53 Ind tel.

Ruth, Adam E. (Louisa) 8 ch farmer O 35a H&L 5h 8c Luckey Tro Ind tel.

Ruthinger, Fred (Minnie) 2 ch farmer O 160a 6h 3c R3 Perrysburg Pbg 74 Ind tel.

Rutledge, C. C. (Grace O.) 1 ch sanitarium T H&L Cor Maple & Perry Sts Pemberville Fre B tel.

Ryan, Alexander (Anna) 1 ch ret O H&L Seventh St Perrysburg Pbg.

RYAN, GRACE Perrysburg Pbg.

Ryan, Grant (Catherine) laborer T H&L Perrysburg Pbg.

Ryder, F. E. 1 ch farmer T 80a 3h 3c R1 Haskins Mid 55 B tel.

Ryder, Geo. F. (Selma) 4 ch pumper O H&L 1h 1c Stahl Ave Bradner Mon B tel.

Ryder, Harry H. (son T. J.) farmer R1 Haskins Mid 91.

Ryder, Helen Stahl Ave Bradner Mon B tel.

RYDER, JOSEPH (Harriett) farmer O 80a 4h 6c R1 Haskins Mid 53 B tel.

Ryder, Lawrence R1 Perrysburg Pbg.

Ryder, Leroy (son Joseph) farmer R1 Haskins Mid 53 B tel.

RYDER, THOS. J. (Jeanettie) farmer O 40a 5h 2c R1 Haskins Mid 94 B tel.

SABISCH, MISS RUTH (dau Paul Wm.) housekeeper Luckey B tel.

Sable, Louis (Lizzie) 7 ch glass worker O H&L Rossford Ros.

Sader, L. A. Haskins Mid.

Sadler, W. E. (Charlotte) hotel Main St Bloomdale Blo.

Safford, Mrs. M. RD North Baltimore Hen.

Sage, Al Freeport Mon.

SAGE, CHAS. S. (Jessie B.) general store H&L 1h Prairie Depot Mon B tel.

Sage, E. R. Prairie Depot Mon.

Sage, H. A. (Maude) 1 ch undertaker T H&L Prairie Depot Mon.

Sage, John (Lelah) 4 ch painter O H&L 2c Prairie Depot Mon.

Sage, Naomi (dau O. O.) student Prairie Depot Mon.

Sage, O. O. (Anna) furniture & undertaking O H&L 2h Prairie Depot Mon B tel.

Sage, Robert E. M. (son Chas. S.) school teacher Prairie Depot Mon.

Sage, W. E. pipe line bds Prairie Depot Mon.

Sager, Clara Rudolph Lib 94.

Sahr, Albert Millbury Lake.

SAILOR, ALLEN M. (Harriet) 1 ch track foreman O H&L Myers St Jerry City Blo Ind tel.

Sailor, Floyd Myers St Jerry City Blo.

181

Sailor, W. M. (Nora) 4 ch laborer T H&L 2h 1c Brown St Jerry City Blo.
Salisbury, J. W. Hoytsville Jac.
Salters, Pearl (Anna) laborer O H&L S Garfield St Bloomdale Blo.
Sampson, G. T. (Lillie) 1 ch farmer T 145a 5h 4c West Millgrove Per 82.
SAMPSON, I. H. (Hila) farmer T H&L 1h 1c West Millgrove Per 81.
Samson, E. F. (Dora) clerk O H&L Luckey Tro.
Samson, Fred (Eliza) 4 ch general store O H&L Luckey Tro Ind tel.
SAMSON, HENRY (Lizzie) 5 ch farmer O 145a 6h 14c R3 Pemberville Tro β3.
Samson, Herman farmer T 40a 2h 1c R1 Luckey Tro 78 B tel.
SAMSON, WILLIAM F. (Mabel) farmer T 40a 2h 1c R1 Luckey Tro 78 B tel.
Sander, Ernest H. Pemberville Fre.
Sander, Henry (Minnie K.) carpenter O H&L Pemberville Fre 40.
Sander, J. H. (Sophia) 1 ch farmer O 40a 4h 12c R3 Pemberville Tro 64 Ind tel.
Sander, William (son J. F.) farmer R2 Pemberville Web 39 Ind tel.
Sanders, Alice (dau Levi) Pemberville Fre 6.
Sanders, August Luckey Tro.
Sanders, Carl (son Frank) farmer R1 Pemberville Fre 38.
Sanders, Chas. H. (Clara) 3 ch farmer O 45a 2h 5c R1 Millbury Lake 126 Ind tel.
Sanders, Clarence (son Levi) farmer Pemberville Fre 6.
SANDERS, ED (Leila) 1 ch saloonkeeper T Perry St Pemberville Fre.
Sanders, Elwena (dau Lewis) housekeeper R3 Pemberville Tro 59 Ind tel.
Sanders, Florence (dau Frank) housekeeper R1 Pemberville Fre 38.
Sanders, Frank (Anna) farmer O 90a 4h 7c R1 Pemberville Fre 38.
Sanders, Fred (Edith) 1 ch farmer T 80a 4h 6c R3 Pemberville Fre 5.
SANDERS, FRED. JR. (son Fred) farmer R1 Genoa Lake 45 B tel.
SANDERS, FRED, SR. (Carrie) 2 ch farmer O 80a 4h 9c R1 Genoa Lake 45 B tel.
Sanders, George (Mabel) 2 ch farmer T 3h 4c R3 Pemberville Fre 91.
Sanders, Gus (Anna) 1 ch farmer T 80a 4h 6c R1 Luckey Tro 88 Ind tel.
Sanders, Harry (son Lewis) farmer R3 Pemberville Tro 59 Ind tel.
Sanders, John (son Frank) farmer R1 Pemberville Fre 38.
Sanders, John F. (Annie) 3 ch farmer O 100a 7h 10c R2 Pemberville Web 39.

Sanders, John H. (Anna) 3 ch farmer O 57a 3h 8c R1 Dunbridge Web 62 B tel.
Sanders, Levi (Anna) farmer O 70a 2h 2c Pemberville Fre 6 B tel.
SANDERS, LEWIS (Mary) 8 ch farmer O 120a 5h 11c R3 Pemberville Tro 59 Ind tel.
Sanders, Lewis E. (Clara) farmer T 80a 2h 2c R2 Pemberville Web 35.
Sanders, Marie (dau Fred) housekeeper R1 Genoa Lake 40 B tel.
Sanders, Martin (son Lewis) farmer R3 Pemberville Tro 59 Ind tel.
Sanders, Orla L. Weston Wes.
Sanders, Rube (Lulu) 1 ch carriage trimmer T H&L Grand Rapids Gr Rs.
Sanders, S. I. (Eva) 1 ch farmer O 40a 2h 2c R1 Bowling Green Pla 36 Ind tel.
Sanders, Wilbur Millbury Lake.
SANDERS, WM. (Ella) 2 ch farming, R1 Tontogany Wash 71.
Sanders, Wm. F. (Mary) 4 ch farmer O 60a 2h 4c R3 Pemberville Tro 57 Ind tel.
Sanderson, Ernest Prairie Depot Mon.
Sanderson, Wm. Prairie Depot Mon.
Sandow, John laborer T H&L Third St Jerry City Por.
Sandwisch, Chas. (Martha) 7 ch farmer O 70a 5h 13c R1 Stony Ridge Tro 33 Ind tel.
Sandwisch, Ed (Anna) farmer T 60a 2h 6c R2 Pemberville Fre 40.
Sandwisch, Lewis (son Chas.) farm hand R1 Stony Ridge Tro 33 Ind tel.
Sanglier, Adeline RD Bowling Green Pla.
Sankey, C. H. Rising Sun Mon.
Santmire, Parker (Chloe) 1 ch laborer O H&L Bairdstown Blo 48.
SANTMIRES, MARTHA A. 1 ch O H&L 1c Bairdstown Blo 48.
Santmyer, Orville (Iva) 3 ch farmer T 115a 2h 5c R1 Rudolph Lib 75.
Santmyer, R. C. (Anna C.) 2 ch farmer O 268a 9h 11c R1 Rudolph Lib 75 Ind tel.
Santschi, Wm. G. (Ellen M.) 1 ch laborer O 3a H 1c Hickory St Perrysburg Pbg.
SARGENT, AARON (Mary) 3 ch farmer O 80a 4h 3c R2 Dunbridge Pbg 17 B tel.
Sargent, Anna R2 Dunbridge Pbg 17.
Sargent, A. C. (Essie) 4 ch grocery O H&L 1h Portage Lib 113 Ind tel.
Sargent, Eugene Custar Mil.
Sargent, Georgia (dau O. C.) Portage Lib 113 Ind tel.
Sargent, H. H. (Anna) 1 ch manufacturer O H&L Front St Perrysburg Pbg B tel.

Sargent, Jacie (dau A. C.) Portage Lib 113 Ind tel.

Sargent, Joseph farmer R2 Dunbridge Pbg 17 B tel.

Sarver, Earl (Bernice) expressman O H&L Front St Perrysburg Pbg B tel.

Sarver, Grant (Beulah) 2 ch glass cutter T H&L Second St Perrysburg Pbg B tel.

Sarver, Jess (May) 6 ch laborer T H&L Front St Perrysburg Pbg B tel.

SASS, H. C. grocery & bakery O H&L 1h Risingsun Mon B tel. See adv.

Sattler, Aloysius (son Frank) farmer 1h R1 Lime City Pbg 51.

Sattler, C. (Clara) 3 ch farmer O 34a 6h 4c R1 Lime City Pbg 50 Ind tel.

SATTLER, FRANK (son Frank) farmer R1 Lime City Pbg 51.

SATTLER, FRANK (Barbara) 10 ch farmer O 100a 6h 4c R1 Lime City Pbg 51 B tel.

Sattler, John ret R1 Stony Ridge Tro 7 Ind tel.

SATTLER, JOSEPH (Anna) 6 ch farmer T 143a 5h 4c R1 Lime City Pbg 55.

Sattler, J. A. (Mary Hazel) farmer O 53a 2h 12c R1 Stony Ridge Tro 7 Ind tel.

Sattler, J. B. (Louise) 3 ch farmer O 66a 3h 10c R1 Lime City Pbg 45 Ind tel.

Sattler, Phillip (Anna) farmer O H&L Lime City Pbg 121.

Sattler, P. J. (Mary) 4 ch farmer O 71a 5h 6c R1 Lime City Pbg 50 Ind tel.

Sanderson, Wm. (Rachel) 2 ch farmer O 30a 3h 6c R1 Prairie Depot Mon 64.

Sautter, Andrew Tontogany Wash.

Sautter, Carl RD Bowling Green Pla.

Sautter, E. G. (Eugene) 2 ch farmer T 160a 5h 10c R2 Weston Pla 17 Ind tel.

Sautter, Henry F. (Elizabeth) farmer O 13a 1h 3c R1 Bowling Green Pla 42 Ind tel.

Sautter, H. (Elizabeth) 8 ch farmer O 14a 4h 2c R1 Bowling Green Pla 42 Ind tel.

Sautter, Hugh F. (son Henry F.) farmer 3h R1 Bowling Green Pla 42 Ind tel.

Sautter, Jacob (Caroline) ret O 160a 1h R2 Weston Pla 17.

Sautter, Jacob, Jr. (son Jacob, Sr.) carpenter R1 Bowling Green Pla 42.

Savage, Charles (Grace) 2 ch laborer O H&L Grand Rapids Gr Rs.

Savage, Chas. W. (Helen G.) 2 ch painter O H&L Grand Rapids Gr Rs.

SAVAGE, W. M. (Cora) 2 ch farmer T 25a 2h R1 Box 45 A East Toledo Ros 37.

SAVIAL, HARRY (Anna B.) farmer T 96a 6h 12c R2 Bloomdale Blo 124 B & Ind tels.

Savidge, G. A. RD North Baltimore Hen.

Savils, Jno. Bloomdale Blo.

Savoy, Thomas carpenter Walbridge St Lake 119.

Sawyer, Alice (dau Thomas) housekeeper West Millgrove Per 81.

Sawyer, Chas. L. (Bernice) general store O H&L Hoytsville Jac B tel.

Sawyer, Clarence R1 Perrysburg Pbg.

Sawyer, C. E. (Edith) 2 ch farmer T 60a 2h 2c R1 Perrysburg Pbg 101.

Sawyer, Curt Weston Wes.

Sawyer, Ethan R1 Perrysburg Pbg.

Sawyer, Mrs. F. F. 2 ch O 1a H R1 Portage Lib 57.

Sawyer, F. G. (Anna J.) 3 ch general store O H&L Hoytsville Jac B tel.

Sawyer, Herbert Perrysburg Pbg.

Sawyer, Oliver (Ella) engineering O 4½a Custar Mil 99.

Sawyer, Thomas (Floy) 9 ch farmer & stock dealer O 80a 5h 10c West Millgrove Per 81 B tel.

Saxby, Chas. B. (Nettie) 2 ch grocery business O H&L Weston Ind tel.

Saxby, Mrs. Effa B. Weston Wes.

Saxby, Helen K. (dau C. B.) Weston.

Saxby, Martha 1 ch Weston.

Sayler, Wm. Jerry City Blo.

Saylor, Bernice (dau H. B.) R1 Rudolph Lib 62 Ind tel.

Saylor, Elizabeth (dau W. H.) clerk Portage Por.

Saylor, H. B. cattle RD Rudolph Por.

Saylor, W. H. (Alice) hardware store O H&L Findlay St Portage Por Ind tel.

Sayre, N. W. (May) 1 ch farmer O 80a 2h 2c R3 North Baltimore Hen 113 Ind tel.

Scaller, Albert (Edith) 1 ch farmer T 80a 3h 2c R2 Perrysburg Mid 14 B tel.

SCANLON, ED. farm hand R2 Deshler Jac 16 Ind tel.

SCARR, MRS. A. A. Box 55 Bloomdale.

Schaberg, D. T. (Tiny) 1 ch farmer O 90a 4h 8c R3 Prairie Depot Fre 74.

Schaberg, Etta (dau D. F.) housekeeper R3 Prairie Depot Fre 74.

Schaberg, Harmon (Hazel) laborer T H&L Bradner Mon.

Schaberg, Vada (dau D. T.) housekeeper R3 Prairie Depot Fre 74.

Schaeffer, C. W. (Mary) 2 ch farmer T 145a 4h 9c R2 Fostoria Per 117.

SCHAFER, GOTLOB J. R1 Luckey.

Schaffer, Adelia (dau John) R1 Hoytsville Jac 74.

183

Schaffer, John B. (Mandy) 5 ch farmer T 160a 9h 3c R1 Hoytsville Jac 74.

Schaffer, Ray (Martha) 2 ch farmer T 120a 7h 3c Hoytsville Jac 122.

Schaller, Albert RD Perrysburg Mid.

Schaller, Andrew (son Steven) farmer R2 Perrysburg Mid 10.

Schaller, August ret O 226a 4c Waterville Mid 3 B tel.

Schaller, Charles (Helen) ret O H&4Lots Main & Seventh Sts Perrysburg Pbg.

Schaller, Christy Perrysburg Pbg.

Schaller, Cora (dau Steven) housekeeper R2 Perrysburg Mid 10.

Schaller, Earnest (son Steven) farmer R2 Perrysburg Mid 10.

SCHALLER, EDWARD (Lyla) farmer T 80a 3h R1 Line City Pbg 59 Ind tel.

Schaller, Elizabeth RD Perrysburg Mid.

Schaller, Elmer (son Steven) farmer R2 Perrysburg Mid 10.

Schaller, Frank (Rose) 2 ch ditcher O H&2Lots 1h Sixth St Perrysburg Pbg B tel.

Schaller, Frederick Perrysburg Pbg.

SCHALLER, FRED. J. (Ella) 1 ch farmer T 40a 3h 3c R3 Perrysburg Pbg 64.

Schaller, Henry R2 Perrysburg Pbg.

Schaller, Herman (Minnie) 1 ch farmer O 60a 2h 2c R3 Perrysburg Pbg 99.

Schaller, Jacob R3 Perrysburg Pbg.

SCHALLER, J. H. (Irma) 1 ch auctioneer T 69a 2h 2c R1 Tontogany Wash 26 B & Ind tels. See adv.

SCHALLER, J. W. (Mary) 3 ch farmer O 60a 2h 2c R3 Perrysburg Pbg 62.

Schaller, L. B. (Mary) 1 ch farmer O 140a 4h 2c R2 Perrysburg Mid 14 B tel.

Schaller, Samuel RD Haskins Mid.

Schaller, Steven (Sarah) farmer O 80a 4h 2c R2 Perrysburg Mid 10.

Schanery, Edward (Anna) 2 ch farmer T 60a 2h 8c R3 Pemberville Fre 9 B tel.

SCHANKS, HARVEY D. Scotch Ridge.

Schauweker, Andrew F. (Mary) farmer O 40a R1 Portage Por 39.

Schauweker, Frank (farmer) O 40a 4h 1c R1 Portage Por 39.

SCHAUWEKER, W. N. (Florence) 2 ch farmer O 120a 6h 2c R1 Portage Por 38 Ind tel.

SCHAUWEKER, W. W. R1 Bowling Green.

Scharf, Jos. 3 ch farmer T 200a 9h 28c Portage Por 3.

Schauffer, Samuel RD Bowling Green Pla.

Schaufelberger, C. W. Hatton Per.

Schaumloeffel, Gus (Kathryn) 3 ch laborer O H&L Main St Perrysburg Pbg B tel.

Scheechemier, G. Portage Lib.

SCHEER, FRANK (Myrtle) 2 ch painter O H&L Hoytsville Jac.

Scheer, Roy (Rose) 2 ch mail carrier O H&L Hoytsville Jac.

Scheeren, T. O. (Mary) 4 ch grocery clerk O H&L Custar Mil.

SCHEERER, H. F. (Mary) 4 ch ret grocery keeper O H&L Hoytsville Jac.

Scheffler, Chas. 2 ch RD mail carrier O H&L Risingsun Mon.

Scheid, Daniel RD Haskins Mid.

Scheider, Fred J. Perrysburg Pbg.

Schell, G. A. (Idella) 8 ch laborer O H&L East St Bradner Mon.

Schell, R. H. (Edna) 2 ch oil worker O H&L Caldwell St Bradner Mon B tel.

Scheller, Alexander (Elizabeth) ret O H&L Indiana Ave Perrysburg Pbg.

Scher, Clarence farmer R1 Tontogany Wash 77.

Scher, Fred farming O 30a R1 Tontogany Wash 77 Ind tel.

Scher, John farming O 30a 4h 2c R1 Tontogany Wash 77 Ind tel.

Scherff, Carl Milton Center Mil.

Scherman, Catherine housekeeper O H&L Pemberville Fre.

Scherping, Chas. R1 Rudolph Lib 70.

Schieder, Fred (Carrie) laborer O H&L Sixth St Perrysburg Pbg B tel.

Schieder, John (Maggie) 2 ch carpenter O H&L Indiana Ave Perrysburg Pbg.

Schiermeyer, Fred H. Pemberville Fre.

Schiermeyer, F. C. Pemberville Fre.

Schiermyer, Ada (dau J. H.) school teacher Pemberville Fre 24.

Schiermyer, Henry Dunbridge Web.

Schiermyer, J. H. (Julia) 1 ch farmer O 70a 3h 12c Pemberville Fre 24 B tel.

SCHIFFERD, CHAS. (Atta) 2 ch saloonkeeper T H&L Luckey Tro Ind tel.

Schiffgens, J. (Minïs) 5 ch glass worker O H&L 259 Superior St Rossford Ros.

Schillinger, Carrie ret O H&L Fourth St Perrysburg Pbg.

Schillinger, Dan ret O H&L Fourth St Perrysburg Pbg.

SCHILLINGER, FREDERICK (Mary) ret O 5a 1h 1c Box 513 Rossford Pbg 80 Ind tel.

Schings, Peter, Jr. (son Peter) 172 Oak St Rossford Ros.

Schings, Peter, Sr. (Margaret) 10 ch glass worker O H&L 172 Oak St Rossford Ros.

Schlea, Edw. Pemberville Fre.

Schlea, Geo. Pemberville Web.

Schlea, John (Millie) 3 ch teamster O 10a 2h 1c Pemberville Fre 24.

Schlea, Lewis (Verna) section hand T Pemberville Fre 40.

SCHLECT, WM. (Mary) 2 ch implement. dealer O H&L 1h Perrysburg Pbg Ind tel.

Schlick, Oscar Walbridge Lake.

Schlie, Lewie (Ricky) farmer O H&L 1c R2 Pemberville Web 35.

Schlotter, Rev. A. (Josephine) 1 ch preacher T H&L Grand Rapids Gr Rs Ind tel.

Schlotter, F. G. Grand Rapids Gr Rs.

Schlyer, Albert laborer bds Milton Center Mil.

Schlyer, C. H. (Laura) thresher O H&L Milton Center Mil.

Schlyer, Edwin F. (Bessie) 2 ch laborer T H&L Milton Center Mil.

SCHMASSMAN, H. Box 22 Rossford.

Schmaus, George ret O 8a H Walnut St Perrysburg Pbg.

Schmeltz, Arnold (Minnie) 5 ch farmer & laborer O 10a 1h 1c R1 Luckey Tro 86 B tel.

Schmeltz, Harmon (Caroline) 4 ch farmer O 20a 2h 1c R1 Luckey Tro 25 Ind tel.

Schmeltz, Willie (son Harmon) soldier R1 Luckey Tro 25 Ind tel.

Schmidt, A. P. RD North Baltimore Hen.

Schmidt, Ed. barber Custar Mil.

Schmidt, F. B. (Katherine) 4 ch farmer O 120a 4h 6c R3 Bowling Green Cen 82 Ind tel.

Schmidt, Henry Pemberville Fre.

Schmidt, Herman II. (Louise) 3 ch farmer O 101a 4h 5c R5 Bowling Green Cen 34 Ind tel.

Schmidt, Jno. H. Tontogany Wash.

SCHMITZ, REV. G. M. pastor St Louis Church Custar Mil.

Schmitz, Michael (Mary) 1 ch farmer O 50a 3h 3c Portage Por 10.

Schmitz, P. J. (Anna) mgr grocery & meat market O Custar Mil.

SCHMYR, JOHN Milton Center.

Schmyr, John (Addie) 1 ch general store O H&L Milton Center Mil.

SCHMYR, R. N. (Katharine) 1 ch farmer T 40a 3c R1 Haskins Mid 50.

Schneider, Adolph (son Samuel) farmer R1 Lime City Lake 23 B tel.

Schneider, Alf. (Ada) farmer T H&L R1 Perrysburg Pbg 105 B tel.

Schneider, Charles (son Samuel) farmer 1h R1 Lime City Lake 23 B tel.

Schneider, Chas. H. (Anna) 3 ch farmer O 108a 6h 10c R1 Pemberville Fre 38.

Schneider, C. J. Perrysburg Pbg.

Schneider, Ella (dau Samuel) housekeeper R1 Lime City Lake 23 B tel.

A Popular Watering Place.

Schneider, Harry R1 Perrysburg Pbg.

Schneider, Jno. Perrysburg Pbg.

Schneider, Jno. Custar Mil.

Schneider, Mary (dau Matt) housekeeper R1 Custar Mil 95 Ind tel.

Schneider, Mathia Custar Mil.

Schneider, Matt (Gertrude) 4 ch farmer O 150a 4h 5c RD Custar Mil 95 Ind tel.

SCHNEIDER, M. A. R1 Perrysburg Pbg 107.

Schneider, M. G. (son Matt) farm hand R1 Custar Mil 95 Ind tel.

Schneider, Nicholas (Katie) ret O 40a 1h R1 Custar Mil 10.

Schneider, Pete (son Matt) farm hand R1 Custar Mil 95 Ind tel.

Schneider, Samuel (Elizabeth) farmer O 90a 7h 4 R1 Lime City Lake 23 B tel.

Schnell, Edward (Tillie) 3 ch milk man T 569 Oak St Toledo Lake 1 B tel.

SCHNELL, MRS. ELIZABETH ret O 10a 7h 41c 569 Oak St Toledo Lake 1 B tel.

Schnell, Fred (Dora) farmer T 569 Oak St Toledo Lake 1 B tel.

Schnelle, Adam H. ret O 80a 1h 3c R1 Millbury Lake 110.

SCHNIDER, CLARENCE E. (Ella) 2 ch farmer O 55a 3h 3c R1 Perrysburg Pbg 118.

Schnider, Frank (Amela) 5 ch farmer O 50a 4h 2c R2 Dunbridge Pbg 37.

Schnider, F. A. (Ida) 1 ch farming & threshing T 6h 2c R1 Perrysburg Pbg 117 B tel.

Schnitker, Henry farmer O 20a 4h 1c R3 Pemberville Fre 35.

Schober, J. L. Walbridge Lake.

Schoenberger, A. C. (Edith) 2 ch post master T H&L Risingsun Mon.

Schoenberger, Edith Risingsun Mon.

Scholl, Carl Grand Rapids Gr Rs.

SCHOLL, FRANK (Katie) 2 ch farmer T 78a 2h 1c R1 Lime City Pbg 94.

Scholl, Jacob (Matilda) ret O 78a 1c R1 Lime City Pbg 94.

Scholler, Christ (Mable) 2 ch tiler O 2a R3 Perrysburg Pbg 82.

Schon, Jasper Custar Mil.

Schon, Margaret 9 ch ret O 40a 4c R1 Custar Mil 95.

Schon, Nicholas (Mary) 5 ch farmer O 40a 3h 3c R1 Custar Mil 18.

SCHON, PETER (Agnes) 3 ch farmer O 30a 3h 2c R1 Custar Mil 95.

Schon, Peter S. 7 ch farmer 5a 3h 2c Custar Mil 97.

Schon, Varona (dau Peter S.) housekeeper Custar Mil 97.

Schondelmyer, F. S. RD Rudoplh Lib.

SCHONDELMYER, M. (Salina) 3 ch ret O 260a Rudolph Lib 81 Ind tel.

Schonmyer, George A. (son M.) Rudolph Lib 81 Ind tel.

Schooner, Grant Woodside Mon.

Schorfheide, Frank (Mary) 1 ch farmer O 49a 2h 5c R1 Pemberville Fre 38.

SCHOVER, J. Walbridge.

Schrader, Stanley Main St Pemberville Fre Ind tel.

Schrage, H. W. North Baltimore Hen.

Schrall, H. D. RD North Baltimore Hen.

Schramm, Esther (dau Mary) housekeeper R3 Perrysburg Pbg 140.

Schramm, Jacob (Carrie) 5 ch farmer O 60a 4h 3c R3 Perrysburg Pbg 137 B tel.

Schramm, John H. (Clara A.) 2 ch farmer O 40a 3h 2c R3 Perrysburg Pbg 123.

Schramm, Louis (Nellie) 1 ch farmer T 100a 4h 3c R1 Lime City Pbg 116.

Schramm, Mrs. Mary farmer O 45a 2h 3c R3 Perrysburg Pbg 140 B tel.

Schramm, Oscar (Lelah) farmer T 40a 2h 1c R3 Perrysburg Pbg 69.

SCHRAMM, W. J. (Bessie) 3 ch farmer T 40a 4h 2c R3 Perrysburg Pbg 140.

Scheffler, Nancy O 21a R1 Bradner Mon 19.

Scheffler, Thos. (Augustus) 1 ch bartender O H&L 1h Toledo Ave Bradner Mon.

SCHRENK, CHARLES (Mary E.) 6 ch farm mgr T 146a 6h 1c R2 Bowling Green Cen 18 B tel.

Schriber, F. J. Walbridge Lake.

Schrier, J. A. (Ida H.) 2 ch fruit grower T 22a 2h Rossford Pbg 80.

Schrier, M. H. (Lora M.). 1 ch fruit grower T H&L Rossford Pbg 80 Ind tel.

Schrister, Anton Perrysburg Pbg.

Schroder, Miss Agnes milliner T H&L Pemberville Fre.

Schroder, Edward H. (son J. H.) shoe store O H&L Pemberville Fre B tel.

SCHRODER, ELMER (son F. H.) Pemberville Fre Ind tel.

SCHRODER, E. H. (Nellie) 3 ch farmer T 80a 1h 1c R3 Bowling Green Web 19.

Schroder, J. H. ret Pemberville Fre.

Schroder, R. H. (Mable) 2 ch decorator T H&L Station A East Toledo Ros 23.

Schroeder, Chas. H. Pemberville Fre.

Schroeder, C. F. (Anna) 2 ch farmer T 60a 4h 1c R1 Portage Por 54.

Schroeder, Dale T. (grandson E. H.) Pemberville Fre.

Schroeder, Edith (dau Mrs. L.) house-
keeper R1 Dunbridge Tro 16 Ind tel.
Schroeder, E. H. (Gladys) 3 ch farmer
T 194a 3h 2c Dowling Pbg 34.
Schroeder, Fred (Louise) 7 ch farmer
O 82a 4h 11c R1 Le Moyne Tro 85 B
tel.
Schroeder, Fred, Jr. (son Fred) laborer
R1 Le Moyne Tro 85 B tel.
SCHROEDER, F. H. (Anna M.) 4 ch rail-
road agt O 10a H&L 2c Pemberville
Fre B tel.
Schroeder, Geo. P. Dowling Pbg.
Schroeder, Henry A. (Carrie) farmer O
118a 1h 1c Dowling Mid 76.
Schroeder, John F. farmer O 136a 4h
2c R1 Perrysburg Pbg 27.
Schroeder, J. F. (Mary) 8 ch farmer O
50a 3h 3c R4 Bowling Green Cen 104
Ind tel.
Schroeder, Mrs. L. 4 ch farmer O 84a
1h 3c R1 Dunbridge Tro 16 Ind tel.
Schroeder, Mary 2 ch ret O H&L Sixth
St Perrysburg Pbg B tel.
Schroeder, Sophia R1 Perrysburg Pbg.
SCHROEDER, W. C. (Grace M.) manager
Cygnet Grain & Hay Elevator Co T
H&L Cygnet Blo B & Ind tels. See
adv.
Schroeder, William H. (Mary) 5 ch
farmer O 87a 2h 15c Luckey Tro 90.
Schroyer, Burley Jerry City Por.
Schroyer, D. N. (Dorothy) T H&L N
Main St Bradner Mon.
Schroyer, Jas. Risingsun Mon.
Schroyer, Jennie 3 ch O 16a Caldwell
St Bradner Mon.
Schroyer, N. C. Bradner Mon.
Schuamberger, G. F. (Hazel) 3 ch
farmer T 116a 6h 9c R1 Millbury
Lake 105.
Schudel, Fred (son Geo.) laborer R1
Luckey Troy 89 Ind tel.
SCHUDEL, GEO. (Mary) 10 ch farmer O
40a 3h 12c R1 Luckey Tro 89 B &
Ind tels.
Schudlick, H. H. (Anna) 2 ch salesman
O H&L Perry St Pemberville Fre Ind
tel.
SCHUEREN, T. Box 53 Custar Mil.
Schueres, Theodore (Mary) 4 ch clerk
O 2a Custar Mil 44.
Schuerman, August Pemberville Fre.
Schuerman, Christ (Ella) 2 ch farmer
O 80a 3h 10c R2 Pemberville Fre 45
B tel.
Schuerman, H. A. (Katie) 2 ch farmer
O 80a 3h 7c R3 Pemberville Fre 21
B tel.

Schuerman, H. F. (Anna) 4 ch farmer
O 80a 3h 10c R3 Pemberville Fre 25
B tel.
Schuff, Chas. C. (Cora) farmer O 50a
3h 7c R1 Fostoria Per 122.
Schuicheimer, G. Corp St Portage Por.
Schulte, Fred (Sophia) 7 ch farmer O
145a 8h 10c R1 Genoa Lake 84 B tel.
Schulte, Henry (Minnie) 5 ch farmer O
115a 6h 6c R1 Genoa Lake 42 B tel.
Schulte, Wm. (Ilah) farmer T 80a 2h
2c R1 Genoa Lake 42 B tel.
Schultz, Maude M. RD North Baltimore
Hen.
Schum, A. farmer 60a 2h 5c R3 Bowl-
ing Green Web 12 B tel.
Schum, J. A. (Dora) farmer T 160a 7h
2c R3 Bowling Green Web 12.
SCHUMACHER, MRS. CHAS. 1 ch farmer
O 40a 2h 5c R3 Bowling Green Cen
55 Ind tel.
Schumaker, J. (Catharine) shoe store
O H&L Perrysburg Pbg Ind tel.
Schumaker, Wm. RD Dunbridge Mid.
Schuster, Peter (Gertrude) 5 ch farmer
O 5a 2h 2c Custar Mil 51.
Schutzberg, H. C. Haskins Mid.
Schutzberg, Jno. RD Haskins Mid.
Schutzberg, Pauline RD Haskins Mid.
Schutzberg, P. E. RD Haskins Mid.
Schutzberg, Verna Haskins Mid.
Schutzberg, Wm. RD Haskins Mid.
SCHWAB, FRANK (Marie) 2 ch farmer T
93a 4h 4c R2 Deshler Jac 4.
Schwab, L. J. RD North Baltimore Hen.
Schwab, Rose RD North Baltimore Hen.
Schwamberger, Grover Millbury Lake.
Schwan, Mrs. F. housekeeper O H&L
Luckey Tro.
Schwan, Mrs. Will housekeeper Luckey
Tro Ind tel.
Schwane, Frank W. Pemberville Fre.
Schwane, Fred J. (Mary) 2 ch farmer
T 75a 5h 5c R2 Pemberville Fre 50 B
tel.
Schwane, John (Louisa) 3 ch farmer
O 80a 3h 5c R1 Luckey Web 70 B tel.
Schwane, Louise Luckey Web.
Schwane, Willis (Emma) farmer T 95a
4h 3c R2 Pemberville Web 34 B tel.
Schwarte, Mrs. Herman Pemberville
Fre.
Schwarte, John (Eliza) 1 ch farmer T
90a 3h 7c R1 Pemberville Fre 72.
Schwartzwalder, Fred Millbury Lake.
Schwartzwalder, Jno. Millbury Lake.
Schwecheimer, Frank (son Geo.) stu-
dent First St Portage Por Ind tel.
Schwecheimer, G. (Amelia) meat
market O H&L First St Portage Por
Ind tel.

Schwecheimer, Mildred (dau G.) housekeeper First St Portage Por Ind tel.

Schwecheimer, Robt. (son Geo.) clerk First St Por Por Ind tel.

Schweihart, Mike (Maude) 3 ch farmer O 355a 17h 4c R1 Hoytsville Jac 44 B tel.

Schwenk, Henry (Sadie) farmer O 92a 3h 3c R2 Perrysburg Mid 14 B tel.

SCHWENK, MARTIN (son Henry) farmer R2 Perrysburg Mid 14.

Schwind, Edward traveling salesman bds R2 Perrysburg Mid·10.

Schwind, Geo. RD Perrysburg Mid.

SCHWIND, J. E. (Gertrude) restaurant & waiting room T H&L Perrysburg Pbg Ind tel.

Schwind, Mrs. Mary ret O H&L Rising Sun Mon.

Schwind, Valentine (Margaret) ret O H&L Locust St Perrysburg Pbg.

Schwind, Valentine, Jr. (Caroline) 18 ch farmer T 80a 3h 2c R2 Perrysburg Mid 10 B tel.

SCOTT, A. D. (Emma) farmer O 40a 1h 1c R1 Tontogany Wash 48 Ind tel.

Scott, C. E. (Elizabeth) 1 ch engineering T H&L Walbridge St Cygnet Blo.

SCOTT, ELERY M. (Edith) 3 ch hotel O H&L Walbridge Lake 121 B tel.

Scott, Francis (Bertha) farmer T H 1c R2 Tontogany Wash 71 Ind tel.

Scott, Geo. F. RD North Baltimore Hen.

Scott, G. W. (Jane) 1 ch farmer O 390a 9h 14c R1 Grand Rapids Wash 58 Ind tel.

Scott, Howard (Inez) farmer T 80a 3h 1c R1 Grand Rapids Gr Rs 40 Ind tel.

Scott, H. R. (Alice) 1 ch farmer O 37a R1 Walbridge Ros 24 Ind tel.

Scott, James (Lillian) laborer T H&L Front St Perrysburg Pbg.

Scott, John (Anna) 1 ch farmer O 40a 2h 2c R1 Walbridge Lake 10 Ind tel.

Scott, Lena J. (dau H. R.) student R1 Walbridge Ros 24 Ind tel.

Scott, Matilda M. Cygnet Blo.

Scott, M. E. Cygnet Blo.

Scott, Selby (Alice) 4 ch farmer O H&L Hatton Per 89.

Scott, William (Mary) mail carrier O H&L Sixth St Perrysburg Pbg.

SCOTT, WM. A. hotel O H&3Lots Walbridge Lake 121 B tel.

Scott, W. B. Freeport Mon.

SEARLE, FRED (Rose) farmer O 19a 1h 1c 1701 Tracy St East Toledo Ros 19.

Sears, Mrs. Barbara 2 ch O H&L Custar Mil.

Sears, Cora Weston Wes.

Sears, C. (Sarah) 2 ch farmer O 80a 5h 4c R1 Tontogany Wash 60 Ind tel.

Sears, Don Tontogany Wash.

Sears, O. E. RD Tontogany Wash.

Sebastian, John (Rose) log cutter O H&L Pemberville Fre Ind tel.

Sebebrecht, Barney (Lizzie) 5 ch switchman T H&L Walbridge Lake.

See, Margaret ret T Main St Perrysburg Pbg.

Seeger, Adam Stony Ridge Troy.

SEEL, FREDERICK (Mary) 4 ch farmer O 20a 2h 4c R2 Haskins Wash 98.

SEELAND, CRIST ret farmer R2 Haskins Wash 98.

Seeland, Edith housekeeper R2 Haskins Wash 98.

SEELAND, FRED O 40a 2h 9c R2 Haskins Wash 98.

Seely, E. B. (Hattie) 4 ch pumper T H&L Bell St Bradner Mon B tel.

Seely, Jeanette Bell St Bradner Mon B tel.

Seem, Ed (Lonn) 9 ch laborer T R1 Bradner Fre 79 Ind tel.

SEEM, JOHN (Anna) 2 ch farmer 39a 2h 2c R1 Bradner Mon 15.

Seem, Samuel (Minnie) 11 ch laborer T R1 Bradner Fre 79 B tel.

Seeman, Caroline (dau Wm.) housekeeper Custar Mil 18.

Seemann, Chas. Milton Center Mil.

Seemann, Wm., Jr. (son Wm.) laborer Custar Mil 18.

Seemann, William 5 ch farmer O 18a 2c Custar Mil 18.

SEEMS, HENRY (Mary) carpenter O H&L Second St Portage Por.

Seibert, F. W. (Pearl G.) 3 ch general merchandise O Tontogany Wash Ind tel.

Seibert, Robt. M. (Clotelda H.) 2 ch laborer 1h R1 Bloomdale Blo 114.

Seickles, Floyd (Blanche) 2 ch electric engineer T H&L Sycamore St Weston Wes B tel.

Seifert, Anthony Dunbridge Web.

Seik, F. W. Pemberville Web.

Seiler, J. C. (Lulu) painter & paperhanger O 5a 1h 1c Pemberville Fre 6 B tel.

Seiling, Christ (Delia) 7 ch farmer O 15a 5h 7c R3 Perrysburg Pbg 141.

Seiling, Conrad (Mary) ret O 7a 1h 2c R3 Perrysburg Pbg 141 Ind tel.

Seiling, Fred (Bertha) 1 ch farmer T 50a 2h 5c R3 Perrysburg Pbg 141 Ind tel.

Seiling, Mabel (dau C.) housekeeper R3 Perrysburg Pbg 141.

Seiling, Merlon (son Christ) farmer R3 Perrysburg Pbg 141.

Seiple, Frank A. (Hazel) 2 ch farmer T 115a 4h 1c R1 Portage Por 7 Ind tel.

Seiple, F. J. 4 ch farmer T 60a 3h 7c R4 Bowling Green Cen 111.

Seiple, Lester (son O. D.) farmer Portage Por 3 Ind tel.

Seiple, M. L. RD Bowling Green Por.

SEIPLE, O. D. (Maggie) farmer T 120a 7h 2c Portage Por 3 Ind tel.

SEITZ, C. S. (Celia) farmer O 103a 11h 14c R1 Weston Lib 4 Ind tel.

SELF, ARTHUR R2 Bowling Green.

Self, Frank farmer O 187a 3h 20c R2 Bowling Green Pla 92.

Selfe, Jno. Millbury Lake.

Selfe, V. M. Millbury Tro.

Sell, Albert (Emma) farmer O 10a 1h 1c R3 Weston Mil 69.

Sell, J. N. carpenter bds Milton Center Mil.

Semler, Elwood (E.) 6 ch machinist O H&L R5 Bowling Green Cen 23 Ind tel.

SERGEN, JOHN A. (Mary A.) 3 ch laborer H&3Lots 1h Le Moyne Tro Ind tel.

Sergen, Lawrence (son Wm.) farm hand R1 Lime City Tro 18 Ind tel.

SERGEN, WM. (Elizabeth) 3 ch farmer O 50a 2h 9c R1 Lime City Tro 18 Ind tel.

Servell, Herbert RD North Baltimore Hen.

Sevenish, Mary housekeeper 416 Oak St Rossford Ros.

Severcool, Mills J. stock raising O 140a 6h 20c R1 Bradner Mon 25.

Sewell, H. C. (Tella) 5 ch oil pumper T 30a 1c R3 North Baltimore Hen 90.

Sewell, N. G. (Dora C.) 2 ch oil man O H&L Randolph Ave Bairdstown Blo.

Sewell, Sam (Laura) 1 ch R3 North Baltimore Blo B & Ind tels.

Seymour, S. RD North Baltimore Hen.

Shabnow, Parker (Kitty) 1 ch laborer O H&L Rossford Ros.

Shade. Alden (son W. E.) farm hand R3 Weston Mil 1.

Shade, Geo. Walbridge Lake.

Shade, W. E. (Mary) 2 ch farmer O 60a 4h 2c R3 Weston Mil 1 Ind tel.

Shafer, C. E. Hoytsville Hen.

Shafer, Ell. Weston Wes.

Shafer, Mrs. Elsie Hoytsville Jac.

Shafer, H. T. (Sadie) 3 ch grocery O H&L Taylor St Weston Wes Ind tel.

Shafer, L. (Mary) O H&L N Main St Weston.

Shafer, Ray Hoytsville Jac.

Shafer, Sarah O 110a 1h 4c R1 Hoytsville Hen 10.

Shaffer, Bert (Bertha) 1 ch laborer T H&L Taylor St Weston Wes.

Shaffer, D. B. RD North Baltimore Hen.

Shaffer, Ed (Ida) 4 ch farmer O 90a 4h 3c Jerry City Por 76.

Shaffer, Elzie (son Ed) student R1 Jerry City Por 76.

SHAFFER, FRANK (Alle) 1 ch mail carrier O H&L Pemberville Fre Ind tel.

Shaffer, George (Mary) 2 ch ret O H&L N Main St Weston Ind tel.

Shaffer, G. M. (Lottie) 2 ch oil pumper H&L 1h 2c R1 Rudolph Lib 39 Ind tel.

Shaffer, Henry (Harriett) 1 ch farmer O 2a 2h 1c R1 Jerry City Por 73.

Shaffer, Ida RD Jerry City Por.

Shaffer, John farmer T 80a 1h 2c Portage Por 13.

Shaffer, Jno. B. RD Hoytsville Jac.

Shaffer, L. W. (Elizabeth) farmer O 10a 2h 1c R2 Prairie Depot Por 66.

Shaffer, Ora (Edna) school teacher & farmer T 10a 2h 1c R1 Jerry City Por 76.

Shaffer, Pearl (dau Ed) student R1 Jerry City Por 76.

Shaffer, Roy (Grace) farmer T 258a 10h 16c R4 Deshler Jac 16 Ind tel.

SHAFFER, R. D. (Naoma) 1 ch grocery O store 1h R1 Rudolph Lib 107 Ind tel.

Shaffer, S. B. (Susan) 6 ch oil producer O 7a R1 Rudolph Lib.

Shaffer, S. C. (Hazel) 3 ch oil worker T H&L Rudolph Lib 81.

Shaffer, Wm. 1 ch farmer O 40a 12h 10c Hoytsville Jac 123 Ind tel.

Shaffstall, Florence housekeeper Deshler Jac 32 Ind tel.

Shaffstall, Frank S. 3 ch farmer O 41a 2h 3c Deshler Jac 32 Ind tel.

Shafner, Elgar (Carrie) 1 ch merchant O H&L Grand Rapids Gr Rs Ind tel.

Shall, Roll (Alta) 1 ch carpenter O H&L Grand Rapids Gr Rs Ind tel.

SHAMP, BLAINE (Florence) 1 ch farmer O 5a 3h 1c R1 Dunbridge Web 47 B tel.

Shane. Geo. 5 ch teamster T H&L Lincoln St Bloomdale Blo.

SHANE, J. L. (Cora A.) 5 ch laborer T H&L R3 North Baltimore Blo B & Ind tels.

Shaner, A. C. (Rachel) 2 ch plasterer T H&L 1h Dunbridge Mid 72.

Shaner, Ed RD Dunbridge Mid.

SHANER. H. H. (Mary) 5 ch oil worker O H&L Rudolph Lib 96 Ind tel.

SHANER, LENA (dau H. H.) Rudolph Lib 96 Ind tel.

SHANER, M. W. (Rosannoh) painter & decorator T H&L Rudolph Lib 81.

Shank, Hala nursing O L R1 North Baltimore Hen 69.

Shank, Lewis Pemberville Web.

Shank, Robert Pemberville Web.

Shanks, D. B. Pemberville Web.

Shanks, D. V. (Grace) 1 ch farmer T 120a 3h 10c R2 Pemberville Web 28.

Shanks, D. W. (Ida May) 3 ch farmer T 20a 2h 2c R5 Bowling Green Cen 39 Ind tel.

Shanks, H. D. Pemberville Web.

Shanks, Linda Pemberville Web.

Shanks, S. L. (Sophia) general store proprietor O 1h Main St West Millgrove Per B & Ind tels.

Shanks, Thos. Scotch Ridge Web.

Shanks, Wm. cattle RD Bowling Green Cen.

SHANKS, W. H. D. Scotch Ridge Web 30.

Shannon, E. A. (Abbie) 2 ch farming T 140a 5h 10c R3 Weston 52.

SHANOWER, A. B. (Lucy A.) farmer O 140a 5h 10c R1 Tantogany Wash 86 Ind tel.

Shanower, G. G. farmer R1 Tontogany Wash 86.

Sharnas, Geo. (R.) 3 ch confectionery T H&L Prairie Depot Mon.

Sharp, Christopher C. (Alice J.) stock buyer O H&L 1h 3c South Main St Bradner Mon B tel.

Sharp, Della RD North Baltimore Hen.

Sharp, Earl H. farmer 2h Cygnet Blo 19 Ind tel.

Sharp, Laurel E. farmer Jerry City Blo 19 Ind tel.

SHARP, WM. W. (Addie) 5 ch farmer O 30a 2c R1 Jerry City Blo 19 Ind tel.

Shartzer, C. M. (Alice) 2 ch laborer T H&L Hoytsville Jac.

Shatzer, E. J. (Daisy) farmer T 93a 3h 5c R1 Luckey Tro 72.

Shatzer, J. (Elizabeth) 7 ch farmer O 4a 3h 7c R2 Pemberville Web 30.

Shaw, Byron Pemberville Fre.

Shaw, Chas. 3 ch farmer T 5a 3h 3c R1 Risingsun Mon 70.

Shaw, Dell (Anna) 3 ch block maker O H&L Pemberville Fre.

Shaw, I. L. (Effie B.) 2 ch elevator prop at Hatton West Jackson St Fostoria Per.

Shaw, Mrs. Jane Tontogany Wash.

Shaw, S. S. elevator O H&L Risingsun Mon B tel.

Shearer, Scott Freeport Mon.

Shears, Mrs. Chas. ret O H&L Walbridge Lake.

Shears, Wm. (son Mrs. Chas.) janitor Walbridge Lake.

Sheats, Bertha P. Prairie Depot Mon.

Sheats, F. L. (Nettie) 5 ch farming O H&L 2h 2c Third St Grand Rapids Gr Rs 713 Ind tel.

Sheats, Nettie C. Grand Rapids Gr Rs.

Sheats, O. J. (Abbie) 1 ch farmer O 79a 2h 4c R2 Bloomdale Blo 121.

Shedenhelm, M. E. Bradner Mon.

Shedron, Albert (Laura) 3 ch laborer T H&L Weston Box 238 Wes.

Shedron, B. L. RD Tontogany Wash.

Sheely, Levi ret O H&L Grand Rapids Gr Rs Ind tel.

Sheely, L. H. Grand Rapids Gr Rs.

Sheets, Chas. (Carrie) farmer O 20a 4h 2c R2 Prairie Depot Por 77.

Sheets, Curtis (Bertha Pearl) 3 ch farmer O 40a 3h 2c R1 Prairie Depot Mon 66.

Sheets, Geo. Millbury Lake.

Sheets, J. E. farmer O 60a 3h 3c R2 Prairie Depot Por 77.

Sheets, Lash cattle RD Prairie Depot Por.

Sheets, Lloyd (son Chas.) farmer 1h R2 Prairie Depot Por 77.

SHEETS, MICHAEL C. (Anna) 3 ch farmer O 60a 3h 10c R1 Luckey Tro 68 Ind tel.

Sheets, Oscar J. (son Wm.) farmer R2 Prairie Depot Por 77.

Sheets, Pearl teacher R3 Prairie Depot Mon 99.

Sheets, Percy (son Michael C.) farmer R1 Luckey Tro 68 Ind tel.

Sheets, Plen farmer 1h R3 Prairie Depot Mon 99.

Sheets, Thos (Sarah) 4 ch farmer O 70a 3h 2c R3 Prairie Depot Mon 99.

Sheets, Wm. (Cornelia) 1 ch farmer O 110a 7h 5c R2 Prairie Depot Por 77.

Sheffer, Frank P. Pemberville Fre.

Sheffer, John J. (Rue Ella) barber T H&L Pemberville Fre.

Sheffer, Win (Julia) 2 ch farmer T 60a 6h 5c R1 Pemberville Cen 114.

Sheffer, W. N. cattle RD Bowling Green Cen.

Sheffler, Conrad (Kate) ret O H&L Risingsun Mon.

Sheffler, E. S. Risingsun Mon.

Sheffler, G. C. Risingsun Mon.

Sheffler, Hattie M. Risingsun Mon.

Sheffler, Sue E. Freeport Mon.

Shefler, Jas. Bradner Mon.

Sheldon, Dr. E. (Lula) 4 ch physician O H&L office on Main St Bloomdale Blo B & Ind tels.

Sheldrick, Harry (Sadie) 2 ch farmer T 150a 5h 4c R1 Lime City Pbg 120 B tel.

Sheldrick, J. W. (Ella) 3 ch farmer O 100a 7h 8c R1 Lime City Pbg 44 B tel.

Sheldrick, Thomas H. (Mary) 3 ch farmer O 54a 2h 3c R1 Lime City Pbg 122.

Shelhouse, F. W. (Edna) 1 ch farmer T 164a 4h 8c R1 Bloomdale Per 10.

Sheline, Isaac RD Portage Lib.

Shell, G. A. Bradner Mon.

Shelley, Charley (Katy) oil worker T H&L R1 Portage Lib 83.

Shelly, Wm. (Anna) oil man teamster T H&L Randolph St Bairdstown Blo.

Shelton, Clay Pemberville Web.

SHEPARD, EDWARD (Jennie) 1 ch farmer T 86a 3h 3c R2 Haskins Mid 89 B tel.

Shepard, Frank Grand Rapids Gr Rs.

Shepard, M. A. (Myrtle) 2 ch Dist Supt Schools T H&L Custer Mil Ind tel.

Shepard, Wm. O H&L Haskins Mid.

Sheperd, S. L. (Effie) confectionery & ice cream T H&L Perrysburg Pbg Ind tel.

Shepherd, Frank (Tillie) farmer T 80a 6h 6c R2 McClure Gr Rs 6 Ind tel.

SHEPERD, W. P. (Amanda) 7 ch farmer O 64a 4h 6c R1 Grand Rapids Wash 66 Ind tel.

Shepherst, Mrs. A. C. 1 ch O 8a 1c R1 East Toledo Lake 131 Ind tel.

Shepherst, Helen (dau Mrs. A. C.) teacher R1 East Toledo Lake Ind tel.

SHEPLER, BARNEY (Edna) 3 ch fruit tree agent T H&L Crocker St Bradner Mon.

SHEPLER, C. B. Bradner.

Shepler, George W. (Singel) farmer O 55a 2h 10c R1 Bradner Fre 86.

Sheper, G. W. (Maud) 4 ch farmer T 95a 4h 3c R2 Perrysburg Pbg 147.

Sheppard, M. A. Custar Mil.

Sherbrook, Grant (Margaret A.) 2 ch oil man roustabout T H&L Bairdstown Blo 48.

Sherdian, Phil (Theresa) painter T H&L Elm St Perrysburg Pbg.

Sherer, Harvey H. Tontogany Wash.

Sheriff, Henry (Katherine) 2 ch ret O H&L Milton Center Mil.

Sherman, Alma (dau L. F.) teacher R1 Stony Ridge Lake 89 Ind tel.

Sherman, Chester Lime City Pbg.

Sherman, C. H. (Christina) farmer O 24a 2h Pemberville Fre 40.

Sherman, C. L. (Emma) 5 ch oil pumper T H&L R1 Portage Lib 36 Ind tel.

Sherman, C. W. (Mable) 1 ch farmer T 265a 6h 21c R1 Fostoria Per 62 Ind tel.

Sherman, F. H. (Nora) 1 ch drayman O H&L 2h Main St Pemberville Fre Ind tel.

Sherman, Henry (Carrie) 5 ch farmer O 100a 7h 5c Lime City Pbg 120 B tel.

Sherman, Mrs. H. C. housekeeper T H&L Pemberville Fre.

Sherman, I. S. (Gladys) 1 ch farmer T H&L R1 Grand Rapids Gr Rs 36.

Sherman, John (Minnie) 1 ch farmer O 120a 3h 6c R121 Woodville Tro 48 B tel.

Sherman, John F. (Catherine) traveling man O H&L Main St Pemberville Fre.

Sherman, Kate Pemberville Fre.

"Ducks are Dollars."

191

Sherman, L. F. (Mary) 2 ch farmer O 160a 6h 6c R1 Stony Ridge Lake 89 Ind tel.

Sherringshaw, Joseph (Mary Ann) farmer O 50a 1h 3c Hoytsville Jac 116 Ind tel.

Sherrod, Bessie (dau J. H.) telephone operator R3 North Baltimore Hen 109 Ind tel.

SHERROD, J. H. (Mary) farmer O 40a 1h 1c R3 North Baltimore Hen 109 Ind tel.

Sherwood, Mrs. J. F. 2 ch T H&L Grand Rapids Gr Rs Ind tel.

SHERWOOD, R. E. (Cora) 1 ch carriage & wagon builder T H&L Grand Rapids Gr Rs Ind tel. See adv.

Sheseley, J. D. (Ella) 3 ch pumper O H&L Risingsun Mon.

Shetley, Frank 3 ch teamster O 1a 2h 1c R1 Fostoria Per 112.

Shetzer, Eva May housekeeper Portage Por 7 Ind tel.

Shetzer, Jas. H. (Mary) 2 ch contractor T 13a 1h 1c Portage Por 7 Ind tel.

Shetzer, Lawrence carpenter Portage Por 7 Ind tel.

Shetzer, Ralph student Portage Por 7 Ind tel.

Shider, George (Anne) farmer O 140a 4h 3c R1 Perrysburg Pbg 117 B tel.

Shiermyer, J. F. (Mary) ret O H&L 1h Main St Pemberville Fre.

Shiermyer, J. H. (May L.) 1 ch drayman O H&L 2h Bond St Pemberville Fre Ind tel.

Shiery, Oren Lime City Pbg.

Shiffert, Allen (Eva) 3 ch section foreman O H&L Walbridge Lake.

Shilling, James O. (Ida F.) 4 ch oil man operator 1h N Randolph St Bairdstown Blo B & Ind tels.

Shimer, Andy Weston Wes.

Shimer, L. S. farming O 16½a 2h 1c R2 Weston Wes 25.

Shimer, N. G. (Emma) farmer T 80a 3h 4c R1 Deshler Jac 46 B tel.

Shimmins, S. R. (Mary) ret O H&L Front St Perrysburg Pbg B tel.

Shine, Mike ret O 40a R1 Millbury Lake 123.

SHINE, THOMAS (Sophie) 5 ch farmer T 40a 3h 1c R1 Millbury Lake 124.

Shinew, Chas. (Mae) 1 ch engineer T H&L R1 Portage Por 8.

Shinew, Dennis (Bessie) farmer T 100a 5h 1c R5 Bowling Green Cen 92.

Shinew, Frank (Esther) 1 ch farmer O 120a 5h 3c R1 Portage Por 50 Ind tel.

Shinew, Garold (son L. N.) farmer R1 Portage Por 8 Ind tel.

Shinew, Goldie (dau Jacob) housekeeper Second St Portage Por Ind tel.

SHINEW, G. R. (Georgia) farmer T R2 Custar Hen 61.

Shinew, Harold (son L. N.) farmer R1 Portage Por 8 Ind tel.

SHINEW, HOMER R2 Custar Hen 41.

Shinew, Isaac Weston Wes.

Shinew, Jacob (Jennie) 2 ch ret O H&L Second St Portage Por Ind tel.

Shinew, James (Helen) 2 ch farmer T 120a 3h 2c R1 Portage Por Ind tel.

Shinew, Lester (son Thos.) farmer O 60a 1h R1 Portage Por 8 Ind tel.

SHINEW, L. N. (Margaret) farmer O 40a 2h 1c R1 Portage Por 8 Ind tel.

Shinew, Thos. (Evalena) 1 ch farmer O 80a 6h 9c R1 Portage Por 8 Ind tel.

Shinew, Verne (dau Thos.) housekeeper R1 Portage Por 8 Ind tel.

Shinew, W. B. (Frankie) 2 ch farmer O 173a 5h 9c R2 Custar Lib 24 Ind tel.

Shipel, Bertha (dau John) housekeeper R2 Perrysburg Mid 5.

Shiple, Bernard (son John) farmer R2 Perrysburg Mid 5.

Shiple, Chas. G. (son Joseph) farmer R2 Perrysburg Mid 13.

Shiple, F. J. (Myrtle) 1 ch farmer T H&L 1c R2 Perrysburg Pbg 9.

Shiple, Genevieve M. (dau Joseph) housekeeper R2 Perrysburg Mid 13.

SHIPLE, JOHN, SR. farmer O 20a 4h 1c R2 Perrysburg Mid 5.

Shiple, John S. (son Joseph) farmer 1h R2 Perrysburg Mid 13.

Shiple, Joseph (Louisa G.) 1 ch farmer O 110a 5h 6c R2 Perrysburg Mid 13 B tel.

Shiple, May (dau John) housekeeper R2 Perrysburg Mid 5.

Shipler, James (Carrie) 2 ch farmer O 140a 8h 20c Bradner Mon 20.

SHIPLEY, W. J. (Isola) caretaker of State property T 2h 3c R2 Perrysburg Pbg 148 B tel.

Shipman, Charley (Alice) 2 ch butcher O 10a 1c Cherry St Weston Ind tel.

Shipman, C. L. (Mary A.) 1 ch meat market O H&L Weston Ind tel.

Shipman, Ida O 1a H&L Weston.

Shipman, Louis (Della) 1 ch ret O H&L Fourth St Perrysburg Pbg B tel.

SHIPTON, J. F. (Sadie) 2 ch farmer T 280a 12h 6c R1 Custar Mil 26 Ind tel.

Shirk, Jake (Alma) painter O H&L East St Bradner Mon B tel.

Shirk, W. S. harness shop O H&L Risingsun Mon.

Shirley, R. E. 6 ch oil man pumping T H&L R3 North Baltimore Blo 16.

Shively, C. H. (Amilda J.) 4 ch farmer O 89a 3h 5c R4 Deshler Jac 19 Ind tel.

Shively, Mrs. Emma ret O H&L Rising-sun Mon.

Shively, P. J. (Mae) 3 ch farmer O 60a 4h 7c R4 Deshler Jac 19.

Shively, Ralph (Altha) 2 ch farmer T H&L 1c R1 Pemberville Fre 70.

Shockey, Ben (Missouri) 1 ch farmer T 80a 4h 3c R1 Weston Mil 57.

Shockey, Herman (son Wm.) R1 Rudolph Lib 77.

Shockey, H. S. (Millie) 3 ch laborer T H&L R2 Custar Lib 29.

Shockey, Wm. (Jane) 7 ch farmer T 70a 4h 1c R1 Rudolph Lib 77.

Shoe, Wm. (Susie) 1 ch laborer O H&L Third St Perrysburg Pbg.

Shoemaker, E. F. RD Rudolph Lib.

Shoemaker, F. B. Perrysburg Pbg.

Shoemaker, H. B. (Effie) farmer O 80a 4h 5c R2 Dunbridge Mid 74.

Shoemaker, Jno. Perrysbnrg Pbg.

Shoemaker, Reuben (Mary A. E.) 1 ch farmer O 78a 1h R3 North Baltimore Blo 16.

Shoemaker, W. W. (Emma) farmer T 7a 1h R1 Haskins Mid 38.

Shondelmyer, Fred (Nora) 2 ch grocer T H&L Rudolph Lib 11.

Shook, Amos (Frances) 4 ch hotel keeper & farmer O 20a hotel Stony Ridge Tro Ind tel.

Shook, Chas. (Minnie) farmer 55a 2h 6c Stony Ridge Tro Ind tel.

Shook, Donna (dau Pearl) Rudolph Lib 94.

Shook, Ira (Louise) 3 ch general store & postmaster Stony Ridge Tro Ind tel.

SHOOK, JOHN E. (Nettie) 1 ch farmer & thresher O 75a 4h 6c R1 Stony Ridge Lake 31 Ind tel.

Shook, Lee (Ruby) 3 ch painter & paperhanger O H&L Stony Ridge Tro.

Shook, Mrs. Pearl 1 ch O H&L Rudolph Lib 94.

Shook, Rolla (Ethel) farmer T 1h R1 Stony Ridge Lake 31.

Shouk, Otto (Daisy) 1 ch farmer T 80a 6h 3c R1 Weston Pla 12 B & Ind tels.

SHOUP, A. L. (Carrie W.) farmer O 160a 4h 6c Bloomdale Blo 50 B & Ind tels.

Shoup, Bert (Bertha) 5 ch farmer 6h 4c R3 Prairie Depot Por 100.

Shoup, Harry J. (Grace M.) farmer T 160a 1h Bloomdale Blo 50 B & Ind tels.

13

Shoup, James Garfield St Bloomdale Blo.

Shoup, John (Martha) farmer O 160a 2h 3c R3 Prairie Depot Por 100 B tel.

Showalter, S. L. (Marie) section worker T H&L Main St Prairie Depot Mon 52.

Showalter, Wm. Portage Lib.

Showers, E. W. (Bertha) farmer T H&L Haskins Mid.

Shrader, W. C. (Grace) mgr elevator T H&L Bradford St Cygnet Blo Ind tel.

Shreffler, Clayton Bell St Bradner Mon.

Shreffler, Fred (Florence) 2 ch pumper O H&L Bell St Bradner Mon.

Shreffler, Fred, Sr. (Mary) 5 ch carpenter T H&L Rudolph Lib 96.

Shreffler, Fred, Jr. (son Fred, Sr.) Rudolph Lib 96.

Shreffler, Thos. Bradner Mon.

Shrider, Frank (Belle) 2 ch assistant yardmaster O H&L Walbridge Lake.

Shroll, Earl (son Wm.) livery man bds RD North Baltimore.

SHROLL, WM. (Elmira M.) 1 ch livery O H&L 4h RD North Baltimore B & Ind tels. See adv.

Shroyer, Alva (Mary) 2 ch farmer O 80a 4h 5c R3 Prairie Depot Por 99.

SHROYER, MRS. AUGUSTA Jerry City.

Shroyer, A. G. (Della) grain T H&L Second St Portage Por.

Shroyer, Burley (Augusta) farmer O 20a 3h 2c Jerry City 70.

SHROYER, G. L. (Lula) 1 ch farmer T 164a 9h 5c R2 Deshler Jac 7.

Shroyer, Henry (M. C.) ret farmer O 102a 3h 7c R3 Prairie Depot Cen 120 Ind tel.

SHROYER, O. J. (Nellie) 4 ch farmer T 147a 7h 4c R1 Weston Pla 10 Ind tel.

SHROYER, JOE (Elizabeth) farmer O H&L 1h 2c R1 Portage Por 49.

Shroyer, John (Mae) grain business T H&L E Main St Portage Por.

Shroyer, Milton (Susan) 2 ch painter O H&L Caldwell St Bradner Mon.

Shroyer, N. C. (Ella) pumper O H&L Caldwell Bradner Mon.

Shroyer, O. J. RD Weston Pla.

Shroyer, Samuel (Catherine) 11 ch ret O 16a H&L 1c Center St Weston Ind tel.

Shroyer, W. N. (Mary) 3 ch painter O H&L Caldwell St Bradner Mon.

Shryer, W. R. (Tilla) 4 ch farmer T H&L 2h R2 Bowling Green Pla 63.

Shuler, Anna Portage Lib.

Shuler, Florence Rudolph Lib 87.

Shuler, Hazel Rudolph Lib 87.

Shuler, P. P. RD North Baltimore Hen.

SHULER, W. H. store Portage Lib 113 Ind tel.
Shuler, W. I. Rudolph Lib.
Shull, Carl (Allie) 1 ch laborer T H&L Grand Rapids Gr Rs Ind tel.
Shull, C. RD Bowling Green Cen.
Shull, Joe (Katherine) carpenter O H&L Grand Rapids Gr Rs.
Shull, R. J. Grand Rapids Gr Rs.
Shultz, August (Edith) 3 ch laborer T H&L Seventh St Perrysburg Pbg.
Shumacher, Mrs. W. 5 ch farmer O 60a 3h 4c R2 Dunbridge Mid 74 B tel.
Shumaker, Chas. cattle RD Bowling Green Cen.
Shumaker, E. P. (Stella) 3 ch farmer O 97a 3h 24c R1 Fostoria Per 113 B tel.
Shupe, Bert (Nellie) farmer O 40a 6h 3c R1 North Baltimore Hen 109 Ind tel.
Shupe, H. W. RD North Baltimore Hen.
Shupe, Ralph G. (Vallie) farmer T 40a R1 North Baltimore Hen 109 Ind tel.
Shure, Arthur G. (son R. H.) farmer O 24a 2h 5c R1 Stony Ridge Lake 28 Ind tel.
Shure, A. H. (Caroline) carpenter O 21a R1 Stony Ridge Lake 28 Ind tel.
Shutz, William (Clara) 3 ch laborer T H&L Second St Perysburg Pbg B tel.
Sibbersen, Chris (Myrtle) 6 ch car inspector T Walbridge Lake 119.
SIBBERSEN, LUDOLF (Velma) 4 ch farmer O 20a 2h 1c R1 Genoa Lake 45.
Sibbersen, Minnie (dau S. M.) housekeeper Latchie Lake 85.
Sibbersen, P. L. (Dora) 3 ch farmer T H&L 3h 1c Latchie Lake.
Sibbersen, S. M. (Hannah) ret O 70a 1h 4c Latchie Lake 95.
Sibert, Chas. Weston Mil.
SIBERT, F. M. G. (Jennie R.) real estate broker O H&L Taylor St Weston B & Ind tels. See adv.
Sibert, John (Catherine) 3 ch farmer O 10a 1h 2c Box 103 Weston Mil 77 Ind tel.
SIBERT, ROLLAND M. (son F. M. G.) student Weston B & Ind tels.
Sidle, Anda (Lillie) laborer T R2 North Baltimore Hen 73.
Sidle, Ed (Agnes) 1 ch laborer T H&L Hoytsville Jac.
Sieber, H. A. (Susie) farmer O 110a 5h 11c R1 North Baltimore Hen 40 Ind tel.
Siebrasse, August (Helena) 3 ch farmer T 60a 3h 2c R1 Prairie Depot Mon 83.
Sick, August J. (Susie) 3 ch farmer T 2h 4c R1 Bradner Fre 94.
Siek, Fred (Gustia) 1 ch farmer O 60a 2h 3c R2 Pemberville Web 32 B tel.

Siek, Henry (Kate) ret farmer O 40a 1h R1 Bradner Fre 94 B tel.
Siek, H. (Minnie) 7 ch farmer T 45a 4h 4c R2 Pemberville Fre 44.
SIEK, W. H. (Anna) blacksmith O H&L Pemberville Fre.
Sielschott, J. H. Freeport Mon.
Sielschott, W. H. (Clara) 1 ch pumper T H&L Prairie Depot Mon.
Sielschowt, Louis (Ida) 5 ch farmer T 96a 4h 6c R1 Luckey Tro 72.
SIELSCOTT, JOHN (Anna) 1 ch farmer O 84a 3h 16c R1 Le Moyne Tro 47.
Sieving, Carl (Louise) 1 ch farmer T 80a 3h 6c R1 Pemberville Fre 38.
Sieving, Edwin (son Mrs. E.) farmer R1 Pemberville Fre 68 B tel.
Sieving, Mrs. E. farmer O 65a 6h 5c R1 Pemberville Fre 68 B tel.
Sieving, Fred (son Mrs. E.) farmer R1 Pemberville Fre 68 B tel.
Sieving, Henry Pemberville Fre.
Sieving, John C. (son Mrs. E.) farmer R1 Pemberville Fre 68.
Sieving, J. H. (Eliza) farmer O 72a 3h 5c R1 Pemberville Fre 68.
Sigler, Chas. (Eliza) 1 ch foreman T H&L Walbridge Lake.
Sigler, Earl (Erma) garage T H&L Walbridge Lake.
Sigler, Frank (Lulu) 1 ch railroader O H&L Walbridge Lake.
Sigler, Frank (Loretta) 1 ch railroad man O H&L Walbridge Lake.
Sigler, Lydia ret O H&L Walbridge Lake.
Sigler, Thomas (Jane) 2 ch farmer T 15a 1h R1 Walbridge Ros 23.
Sigler, W. F. Walbridge Lake.
Sigus, Mrs. Amy C. 1 ch Bairdstown Blo.
Silverwood, Chas. (Myrtle) 3 ch laborer T H&L W Caldwell St Bradner Mon.
SILVERWOOD, F. A. (Mary) 2 ch coal dealer & oil producer O H&L East St Bradner Mon B tel.
Silverwood, Mrs. Mary Bradner Mon.
Simmer, George (Barbara) 3 ch farmer O 97a R3 Perrysburg Pbg 125.
Simmer, William (Anna) 3 ch carpenter O H&L Fifth St Perrysburg Pbg B tel.
Simmons, A. A. (Julia) ret O H&L Prairie Depot Mon B tel.
Simmons, Mrs. Chas. O H&L Center St Weston.
Simmons, D. (Adelia) 2 ch farmer O 50a 3h 2c R1 Perrysburg Pbg 109 B tel.
Simmons, Del (Mary) 2 ch farmer T 140a 7h 2c R3 Perrysburg Pbg 139 Ind tel.
Simmons, Earl (Julia) 5 ch laborer O H&L Fifth St Perrysburg Pbg B tel.

Simmons, E. H. (Minnie) 1 ch ret O 40a 2h 1c R3 Perrysburg Pbg 141.

Simmons, Frank A. (Mae) 3 ch oil worker T H&L Venango St Cygnet Blo Ind tel.

Simmons, Fred 2 ch laborer O H&L Main St Jerry City Blo 78.

SIMMONS, GEORGE (Jane) 5 ch farmer T 65a 2h 2c R3 Perrysburg Pbg 158.

Simmons, Geo. 4 ch farmer T 60a 3h 2c R1 Bowling Green Cen 28.

Simmons, J. (Minnie) farmer O 50a 6h 6c R2 Dunbridge Mid 79 Ind tel.

Simmons, J. A. (Maude) bridge builder O H&L Dowling Mid 76.

Simmons, Marie (dau Del) R3 Perrysburg Pbg 139.

Simmons, Robert (Mary) 1 ch ret O H&L Second St Perrysburg Pbg.

Simmons, Wilbur (Flory M.) farmer O 105a 1h 2c R2 Bowling Green Cen 14.

Simms, F. M. (Aquilla) 4 ch farmer T 111a 5h 4c R4 Bowling Green Cen 109 Ind tel.

Simon. B. T. laborer O H&L R3 North Baltimore Blo.

Simon, Clyde (son M. W.) school teacher R2 Bloomdale Per 26 B & Ind tels.

Simon, Emma J. O H&L Garfield St Bloomdale Blo B & Ind tels.

Simon, Eva (dau M. B.) teacher R1 Bloomdale Blo 122 B & Ind tels.

Simon, E. D. (Sylvia M.) 1 ch farmer T 120a 4h 4c Bloomdale Blo B & Ind tels.

Simon, Mrs. Flora cattle RD Bowling Green Cen.

Simon, Floyd (Ada) 2 ch oil pumper T 5a 1c R1 North Baltimore Hen 69.

Simon, Frank T. RD North Baltimore Hen.

Simon, Fred Corp St Jerry City Por.

Simon, Geo. (Margaret) 1 ch farmer O 11a 2h 1c Jerry City Por.

Simon, Guy (Maude E.) 4 ch laborer & janitor T H&L Factory St Jerry City Por.

Simon, Jess (son Emma J.) blacksmith Garfield St Bloomdale Blo B & Ind tels.

Simon, John H. (Florence M.) 1 ch farmer O 80a 3h 7c R2 Bloomdale Blo 132 B & Ind tels.

Simon, J. W. Corp St Jerry City Por.

Simon, J. W. (Mary) 2 ch postmaster 1h 1c Main St Bloomdale Blo B & Ind tels.

Simon, Levi RD North Baltimore Hen.

Simon, Lloyd E. (son Emma J.) painter Garfield St Bloomdale Blo B & Ind tels.

Simon, L. D. (Lizzie) 1 ch farmer O 60a 3h 5c R3 North Baltimore Blo 40 B & Ind tels.

Simon, Mary ret O H&L West Millgrove Per 70.

Simon, Mrs. Mary O H&L 1c Manor St Bloomdale Blo B & Ind tels.

SIMON, M. B. (Florence) 3 ch farmer O 69a 4h 2c R1 Bloomdale Blo 122 B & Ind tels.

Simon, M. N. ret O H&L Mulbury St Bloomdale Blo B & Ind tels.

Simon, M. W. (Irene) farmer O 34a 2h 4c R2 Bloomdale Per 26 B & Ind tels.

Simon, R. E. RD North Baltimore Blo.

Simon, R. J. Bloomdale Blo.

Simon, Wm. R2 Perrysburg Pbg.

Simon, W. D. RD Hoytsville Jac.

Simon, W. H. Jerry City Blo.

Simond, Vera (dau W. D.) R1 Hoytsville Jac 70.

Simond, W. D. (Carrie) farmer O 80a 3h 5c R1 Hoytsville Jac 70.

Simons, Alfred (Maude) 2 ch laborer O H&L Fifth St Perrysburg Pbg.

Simons, Catherine O H&L Main St Jerry City Por.

Simons, Chas. E. (son J. W.) laborer Jerry City Por 70.

SIMONS, FRANK R1 Millbury.

Simons, James Wesley (Lottie) 3 ch farmer O 11a 3h 2c Jerry City Por 70.

SIMONS, J. L. (Della) 1 ch farmer O 92a 1h 5c R1 Jerry City Blo 69.

Simons, Nellie housekeeper O H&L West Millgrove Per 69.

SIMONS, R. E. (Dottie) 2 ch farmer O 98a 4h 3c R3 North Baltimore Blo 27 Ind tel.

Simpkins, Arthur (Rose) farmer T H&L 4h 4c R3 Bowling Green Cen 85 B tel.

Simpkins, Geo. (Elisa) farmer O 80a 3h 6c R3 Bowling Green Cen 85 B tel.

Sims, F. M. cattle RD Bowling Green Cen.

Sinclair, H. M. (Jeanette) 4 ch manufacturer T 10a 1h 1c R3 Prairie Depot Mon 50.

Sines, C. L. RD Portage Por.

Sines, G. C. (Ethel) 3 ch teamster T 10a 1h 1c North Baltimore Hen 80 Ind tel.

Sinew, Homer (Bertha) farmer T 232a 6h 4c R2 Custar Hen 41.

Singer, W. C. (Anna E.) hardware O H&L Weston Ind tel.

Singer, W. E. (Fern) hardware O H&L Weston Ind tel.

Singleton, Mrs. Bertha housekeeper R1 Tontogany Wash 32.

Sirbrisse, August Prairie Depot Mon.

SITES, D. E. (Mina) 3 ch jewelry & optician H&L Custar Mil Ind tel.

Sites, Esther (dau D. E.) housekeeper Custar Mil Ind tel.

Sites, Mary telephone operator Cygnet Hen 115.

Sites, Philip (Margurite) ret T 1h 1c Cygnet Hen 115.

SKILES, FRANK (Anna) 5 ch farmer T hired man Millbury Lake 76 Ind tel.

Slagle, E. G. (Effie) 2 ch farm laborer 1h 1c R1 Weston Lib 45.

Slagle, E. J. (Ester) 2 ch farmer T 135a 5h 2c R1 Weston Lib 45 Ind tel.

Slagle, Ross cattle RD Bowling Green Cen.

Slagle, W. R. (Lulu) 2 ch farmer T 240a 7h 2c R5 Bowling Green Cen 79 Ind tel.

Slane, L. S. RD North Baltimore Hen.

Slane, Marcus (Beulah) 4 ch tool dresser O H&L R1 Rudolph Por 24½.

Slane, W. RD North Baltimore Hen.

Slater, Joseph (son Wm.) farmer R3 Perrysburg Pbg 140.

Slater, Wm. (Nellie) farmer O 30a 4h 2c R3 Perrysburg Pbg 140 B tel.

Slattery, Dane cement worker Main St Bloomdale Blo.

Slatts, Arthur (May) 2 ch blacksmith O H&L Haskins Mid B tel.

Slaugherback, Herman (Hazel) 1 ch section laborer T H&L Walbridge St Cygnet Blo.

Slaughterback, J. O. (Mary) 1 ch farming T 33a 3h 1c R2 North Baltimore Hen 30 Ind tel.

SLAUGHTERBACK, J. W. (Jennie) 4 ch farmer & road contractor T 25a 6h 2c R2 North Baltimore Hen 30 Ind tel.

Slaughterbeck, Arvel RD North Baltimore Hen.

Slaughterbeck, Grant RD North Baltimore Hen.

Slaughterbeck, J. C. RD North Baltimore Hen.

Slaughterbeck, Winfield (Minnie) 2 ch oil worker O H&L Union St Cygnet Blo.

Slawson, Jas. N. RD Haskins Mid.

Slike, Cornelius (Mary) 4 ch livery O H&L Bradford St Cygnet Blo Ind tel.

Slike, Henry (Jessie) 3 ch farmer O H&L Verango St Cygnet Blo.

SLIKER, MRS. CATHARINE R8 West Toledo.

Slinker, Frank (May) 3 ch laborer T H&L Pine St Perrysburg Pbg.

Sloan, D. J. RD North Baltimore Hen.

Sloan, Judson (Sadie) 1 ch farmer T 5h 2c R1 Weston Pla 12 Ind tel.

Sloan, S. N. (Marie) 3 ch garage O H&L East St Bradner Mon B tel.

Sloan, Will East St Bradner Mon B tel.

Slocum, Charles A. (Sylvia O.) 4 ch farmer & pumper T 80a 4h 4c R3 North Baltimore Blo 24 Ind tel.

Slocum, C. W. oil worker Cygnet Blo 6.

Slocum, Maggie Cygnet Blo.

SLOSSER, OSCAR RD Bloomdale.

SLOTTERBECK, BERT C. (Mary) 1 ch barber O H&L shop Main St Bloomdale Blo.

Slotterbeck, Clayton (son F. D.) R1 Bloomdale Blo 100 B & Ind tels.

Slotterbeck, Dale (son T. A.) R2 Bloomdale Blo 109.

Slotterbeck, E. (Lenna L.) 2 ch automobile factory employee T H&L Harrison St Bloomdale Blo B & Ind tels.

SLOTTERBECK, FRANK D. (Anna B.) 3 ch farmer O 120a 12h 8c R1 Bloomdale Blo 100.

SLOTTERBECK, FRED A. (Lorena B.) 2 ch farmer O 87a 4h 5c R2 Bloomdale Blo 109.

Slotterbeck, Clyde Bloomdale Blo.

Slotterbeck, Geo. W. (Maria) ret farmer O H&L 1c Main St Bloomdale Blo.

Slotterbeck, Ray (Ree) 1 ch laborer Main St Bloomdale Blo.

Slotterbeck, Wm. (Emma) laborer O H&L R1 Bloomdale Blo 112.

Slough, C. G. RD North Baltimore Hen.

Slough, C. L. RD North Baltimore Hen.

Slough, J. E. RD North Baltimore Hen.

Sloyer, Edw. 2 ch ret O H&L East St Bradner Mon.

Sly, E. T. (Lillian) 3 ch farmer O 80a 5h 3c R1 Bowling Green Pla 34 Ind tel.

Sly, Frank (Jessie) farmer T 64a 2h 3c R1 Bowling Green Pla 35 Ind tel.

Sly, Mrs. Katharine ret O 64a R1 Bowling Green Pla 35.

Small, Leslie M. Perrysburg Pbg.

Smalley, A. J. Jerry City Blo.

SMALLEY, HIRTSHIEL Jerry City.

Smalley, W. H. Jerry City Blo.

Smaltz, Claud farmer T 40a 3h R2 Custar Mil 32.

Smaltz, E. J. RD Custar Lib.

Smaltz, Flora A. RD Custar Lib.

Smaltz, Joe 5 ch laborer O 2a 1h R2 Custar Lib 32.

Smaltz, M. C. Custar Milton.

SMEARSOLL, C. H. (Mary) 3 ch farmer T 100a 4h 3c R1 Pemberville Fre 38 B tel.

Smearsoll, H. (Mary) farmer O 54a 3h 7c R1 Pemberville Fre 28.

Smith, Abraham (son Mrs. E.) glass cutter 90 Elm St Rossford Ros.

Smith, Abe N. cattle RD Bowling Green Cen.

Smith, Allen RD Sugar Ridge Mid.

Smith, Alva (son E. J.) farm hand R2 Custar Milton 31.

Smith, Mrs. Anna 1 ch housekeeper O H&L Pemberville Fre.

Smith, Arnold laboring man bds Milton Center Mil. .

Smith, Arthur (Caroline) 5 ch carpenter O. H&L Russ St Weston Ind tel.

SMITH, ASA (Edna) 3 ch farmer T 170a 6h 3c R1 Grand Rapids Gr Rs 11 Ind tel.

SMITH, ALBERT L. (Clara) 2 ch farmer O 40a 1h 2c R1 Rudolph Lib 70 Ind tel.

Smith, A. M. (Elizabeth) 6 ch traveling man T H&L Sixth St Perrysburg Pbg B tel.

Smith, A. M. (Violet) 1 ch farmer O 80a 6h 7c R1 Fostoria Per 16.

Smith, A. W. (Bertha) 7 ch oil worker T H&L Pemberville Fre Ind tel.

Smith, Benedict Geo. (son Mary) laborer R1 Luckey Tro 92.

Smith, Bert Cygnet Blo.

Smith, Bertha (dau T. H.) stenographer R1 Bowling Green Pla 30.

Smith, Bud (Faith) 1 ch farmer O 160a 5h 4c Cygnet Hen 119 B tel.

Smith, Burl (son Arthur) Russ St Weston.

SMITH, B. E. (Grace) 4 ch farmer & school teacher O 40a 4h 6c R1 Fostoria Per 130.

Smith, B. H. (Clemma) 1 ch farmer O 20a 3h 3c R1 Bradner Mon 58.

SMITH, B. J. (Eva) 2 ch blacksmith O H&L Custar Mil.

Smith, Calvin RD North Baltimore Hen.

Smith, Miss Celesta (dau John) housekeeper R2 Haskins Wash 90 B tel.

Smith, Charles (Pearl) 1 ch farmer T 180 4h 3c R1 Fostoria Per 63.

SMITH, CHARLES W. (Gertrude) 4 ch oil roustabout O 2a R1 North Baltimore Hen 123.

Smith, Christopher Cygnet Blo.

Smith, Clarence (Jessie) 2 ch farming T 96a 7h 5c R3 Weston Wes 5.

Smith, Clell (son Samuel E.) N Main St Bloomdale Blo B & Ind tels.

Smith, Cora O H&L Bloomdale Blo 121.

Smith, C. A. (Ida) 1 ch ret O H&L Center St Weston Ind tel.

Smith, C. F. RD North Baltimore Hen.

SMITH, C. J. (Blanche) 2 ch farmer O 66a 2h 3c R2 Custar Lib 34 Ind tel.

Smith, C. L. (E. H.) salesman Pemberville Fre.

A Fine Plow Team.

Smith, C. M. RD Custar Lib.

Smith, C. W. (Florence) 1 ch clerk in grocery store T H&L Garfield St Bloomdale Blo B & Ind tels.

SMITH, C. W. (Hattie) 3 ch farmer O 40a 4h 9c R2 North Baltimore Hen 21 B tel.

Smith, Mrs. C. Z. RD North Baltimore Hen.-

Smith, Daniel (Elizabeth) 2 ch farmer O 50a 2h 7c R1 Luckey Tro 89 B tel.

Smith, Dee (son Lewis) farmer T 1h R4 Bowling Green Por 45 Ind tel.

Smith, Dell (son Wm.) farmer R1 Jerry City Por 74.

Smith, D. A. (Gertrude) 3 ch oil producer O H&L East St Bradner Mon B tel.

SMITH, D. W. (Minnie) 2 ch farmer O 40a 2h 1c R2 Bowling Green Pla 57 B tel.

Smith, Ed. (Lucy) 2 ch farmer T 81a 7h 4c R1 Grand Rapids Wash 66.

SMITH, ED. (Ella) 3 ch farmer O 20a 4h 3c R1 Weston Pla 11.

Smith, Edmund (son Lewis) farmer 1h R4 Bowling Green Por 45 Ind tel.

Smith, Edward D. farmer O 40a R1 Portage Por 120.

Smith, Eldon RD North Baltimore Hen.

Smith, Mrs. Elizabeth ret O H&L 90 Elm St Rossford Ros.

Smith, Elmer (son Daniel farm laborer R1 Luckey Tro 89 B tel.

Smith, Elzy RD North Baltimore Hen.

Smith, Emma housekeeper O 12a 2c R1 Luckey Tro 67.

Smith, Mrs. Emma O. O H&L Center Weston B tel.

Smith, Ephraim farmer O 12a 3h 3c R1 Luckey Tro 67.

SMITH, ERIC N. (Etta M.) 3 ch farmer O 78a 6h 2c Box 74 Hoytsville Jack 113.

Smith, Esta E. Prairie Depot-Mon.

Smith, Ethel (dau J. W.) R2 Bloomdale Blo 120.

Smith, Ezra (Mary) 2 ch thresher and house mover O 2Houses&Lots R1 Hoytsville Jac 116.

Smith, E. B. RD North Baltimore Hen.

Smith, E. J. (Elzira) 6 ch farmer O 81½a 4h 3c R2 Custar Mil B tel.

Smith, E. L. Hoytsville Jac.

Smith, Frank (Maude) 1 ch farmer T 100a 5h 2c R1 Jerry City Portage 75.

Smith, Frank B. (Julia P.) farmer O 55a R1 Bradner Fre 93.

Smith, Frank E. (Lenna) farmer O 15a 2h R2 Bowling Green Pla 92 B tel.

SMITH, FRANK H. care Wm. Ward Walbridge.

Smith, Fred (son J. W.) R2 Bloomdale Blo 120.

Smith, Fred M. (Gertrude) 2 ch oil pumper O H&L Pemberville Fre 40.

Smith, F. E. (Emma E.) farmer T 160a 6h 7c R1 Fostoria Per 60.

Smith, F. L. (Ada) 5 ch farmer O 6a 2h 1c R5 Bowling Green Center 23.

Smith, Geo. laborer Second St Portage Por.

Smith, Grant C. (Ada) 1 ch farmer T 80a H&L 4h 3c R1 Bloomdale Per 15 B & Ind tels.

Smith, Guy (Ida) 1 ch traveling salesman T H&L Fifth & Main Sts Perrysburg Pbg.

Smith, Guy (Lillie) 3 ch farmer O 80a 6h 3c R1 Deshler Jac 25 Ind tel.

Smith, Guy H. (Bertha C.) 1 ch engineer T H&L Hoytsville Jac.

Smith, G. B. RD North Baltimore Hen.

Smith, G. M. (Sarah) 6 ch laborer T H&L Second St Portage Por.

Smith, G. W. (Emma) 2 ch ret O 193a H&L Taylor St Weston Wes Ind tel.

SMITH, G. W. (Annie) 6 ch farmer O 80a 3h 3c R2 Bowling Green Pla 94 B tel.

Smith, Geo. W. (son Lewis) farmer 1h R4 Bowling Green Por 45 Ind tel.

Smith, Harvey N. farmer O 40a R1 Portage Por 102.

Smith, Hazel (dau Lewis) housekeeper R4 Bowling Green Por 45 Ind tel.

Smith, Mrs. Henry ret O 41a R1 Lime City Pbg 51 Ind tel.

Smith, Henry (Mary) farmer T H&L 2h R3 Bowling Green Cen 83 Ind tel.

Smith, Helen L. (dau E. H.) Pemberville Fre.

Smith, Horace (son T. H.) farmer) R1 Bowling Green Pla 80.

Smith, H. farmer bds R1 Luckey Tro 67.

Smith, H. H. (Mabel) 2 ch farmer T H&L 1c R1 Bowling Green Pla 31.

Smith, H. S. (Catherine) general merchandise O 2a & store 1 au R2 Custar Lib 32 Ind tel.

SMITH, H. W. (Geneva) 6 ch farmer O 77a 5h 10c R1 Stony Ridge Tro 81 Ind tel.

Smith, Jacob (Mary) 7 ch farmer T 5a 1h R1 Hoytsville Jac 74.

Smith, Jacob·K. RD North Baltimore Hen.

Smith, Jas. RD North Baltimore Hen.

Smith, Jerome R2 Perrysburg Pbg.

Smith, John (son Mrs. E.) laborer 90 Elm St Rossford Ros.

Smith, Mrs. John ret O H&L West Millgrove Per 68.

Smith, John E. (Cora M.) 7 ch oil pumper O 60a 1c R1 Rudolph Lib 33 Ind tel.

Smith, John H. (Kate) 5 ch carpenter O 5a R2 Haskins Wash 90 B tel.

Smith, Joseph (son Mrs. E.) electric train man 90 Elm St Rossford Ros.

SMITH, JOSEPH (son Mrs. Henry) farmer T 41a 1h R1 Lime City Pbg 51 Ind tel.

SMITH, JOSEPH W. farmer O 40a 1h 1c R1 Portage Por 102.

Smith, Josephine 3 ch farmer O 55a 2h 3c R1 Walbridge Lake 5 Ind tel.

Smith, Josiah (Elmyra) ret O 60a H&L Weston B tel.

SMITH, JULIA P. Bradner.

SMITH, J. D. (Nancy) 5 ch farmer O 53a 1c Sugar Ridge Mid 4 Ind tel.

Smith, J. E. (Clara B.) farmer O 25a 3h 1c East Toledo Ros 20 Ind tel.

Smith, J. E. (Lydia) 5 ch carpenter H&L Loci St Cygnet Blo.

Smith, J. F. (Dillie) farmer O 56a 2h 5c R2 Bloomdale Blo 120 B & Ind tels.

Smith, J. H. (Jennie) 3 ch dry goods store O H&L Custar Mil B & Ind tels.

Smith, J. N. farmer T H&L 2h R1 Fostoria Per 60.

Smith, J. R. RD North Baltimore Hen.

Smith, J. R. (Etta) 3 ch pumper O H&L Bell St Bradner Mon.

Smith, J. W. (Anna) 2 ch 40a 2h 2c R2 Bloomdale Blo 120.

Smith, Mrs. Katharine housekeeper O 80a 2c R1 Perrysburg Pbg 20 B tel.

Smith, Lawrence (son Ed) farmer R1 Grand Rapids Wash 66.

Smith, Mrs. Lena ret Hoytsville Jac B tel.

Smith. Lewis (Mary) stock buyer O 65a 3h 3c R4 Box 18 Bowling Green Por 45 Ind tel.

Smith, Rev. L. B. (Nettie) 1 ch preacher parsonage Pemberville Fre Ind tel.

Smith, L. F. RD North Baltimore Hen.

Smith, Mack W. Bloomdale Blo.

Smith, Margaret Bloomdale Blo.

Smith. Martha ret 1h 1c R1 Deshler Jac 25 Ind tel.

Smith, Mary farmer T 2h 2c R1 Luckey Tro 92 B tel.

Smith, Martin (Sarah) ret O H&L 1h 1c West Millgrove Per 74.

Smith. Matt (Jessie) 1 ch farmer T 80a 4h 5c R1 Custar Jac 39.

Smith, Musie (dau F. H.) housekeeper R1 Bowling Green Pla 80.

Smith, M. D. (Sarah J.) ret O H&L 1c Main St West Millgrove Per.

Smith, Nite (Della) mason O 1a H&L 1c Stony Ridge Tro 3 Ind tel.

Smith, Nora (dau Cora) Bloomdale Blo 121.

SMITH, ORIA (Maude) 2 ch oil worker O H&L 1c S Main St Bradner Mon.

Smith, Orison (Drusilla) 5 ch shoe repairer O H&L Railroad St Bradner Mon.

Smith, Orrin Milton Center Mil.

Smith, O. E. (Blanche) 7 ch farmer O 80a 4h 1c R1 Jerry City Por 29 Ind tel.

SMITH, O. H. R1 Rudolph Lib 105.

SMITH, O. N. (Edith) 2 ch farmer O 30a 3h 2c R3 Bowling Green Cen 87.

Smith, O. W. Risingsun Mon.

SMITH, PETER (Anna B.) 6 ch farmer O 440a 8h 5c Box 74 Hoytsville Jac 113.

SMITH, MRS. RICH'D R1 Bradner.

Smith, Robert (Hattie) farmer T 40a 1h 1c R1 Luckey Web 72 B tel.

Smith, Rollie (Amanda) 3 ch railroader T H&L 2c S Garfield St Bloomdale Blo.

Smith, Rollo (Ida) 1 ch ret T H&L Milton Center Mil.

Smith, Ruth (dau J. F.) Bloomdale Blo 120 B & Ind tels.

Smith, R. D. (son F. E.) farmer R1 Fostoria Per 60.

Smith, R. H. (Mary) farmer T 100a 3h 6c R3 Weston Mil 84 Ind tel.

Smith, Samuel D. (Alta) 5 ch laborer O H&L R2 Custar Lib 32 Ind tel.

SMITH, SAMUEL E. (Edith) 3 ch carpenter O 18a H&L 1c N Main St Bloomdale Blo B & Ind tels.

Smith, Sydney laborer R1 Luckey Web 72 B tel.

Smith. S. (Elenor) farmer O 80a 5h 2c R1 Hoytsville Jac 79.

Smith, Thomas (son Mrs. E.) electrician 90 Elm St Rossford Ros.

Smith, T. H. (Mary) 2 ch farmer T 120a 6h 4c R1 Bowling Green Pla 80 Ind tel.

Smith, Thessa Bloomdale Blo.

Smith, Vern F. Hoytsville Jac.

Smith, Warren H. (Florence) 1 ch bookkeeper T H&L Loci St Cygnet Blo Ind tel.

SMITH, WERD (son Ed) farmer R1 Grand Rapids Wash 66.

SMITH, WILLIAM (Eva) 3 ch farm hand R3 Box 58 Weston Mil 3.

Smith, Wm. (Emma) farmer T 80a 3h 2c R1 Jerry City Por 74.

Smith, Wm. (Mary) farmer O 40a 3h 4c R1 Luckey Web 72 B tel.

SMITH, WM. (Minnie H.) 2 ch blacksmith O H&4Lots & shop Lime City Pbg 121 B tel. See adv.

Smith, Wm. D. 6 ch laborer O Railroad St Custar Lib 37 Ind tel.

Smith, Wm. H. (Mary) 4 ch farmer O 100a 3h 4c R5 Bowling Green Cen 35.

Smith, W. (Carrie) farmer O 81a 3h 6c R2 North Baltimore Hen 84 Ind tel.

Smith, W. C. (Ada) farmer O 40a 3h R2 Bloomdale Blo 120 B & Ind tels.

Smith, W. G. laborer R1 Hoytsville Jac 115.

SMITH, W. H. (Cora) 5 ch hired man T H&L R1 Millbury Lake 105.

Smith, W. P. (Mary) 1 ch ret O H&L Maple St Weston.

Smithers, Geo. (Agnes) farmer O 100a 6h 30c R3 Perrysburg Pbg 79 Ind tel.

Smithers, H. C. (Ruby) farmer T 100a R3 Perrysburg Pbg 77 Ind tel.

Smithers, Robert (Jennie) 3 ch farmer O 40a 3h 4c R3 Perrysburg Pbg 59.

Smithers, Roy (son Geo.) farmer T 100a R3 Perrysburg Pbg 77 Ind tel.

Smithson, Rev. A. L. (Callie) 5 ch T H&L Tontogany Wash Ind tel.

Smock, Mrs. Irvin 6 ch O H&L Rudolph Lib 94 Ind tel.

Snapp, C. E. (Jane) farming O 79a 3h 2c R2 Weston Wes 15 Ind tel.

Snider, Fred farmer O 5a 1c Perrysburg Pbg 118.

Snider, G. W. Bloomdale Blo.

Snider, John (Rose) farmer O H&L Indiana Ave Perrysburg Pbg B tel.

Snider, Martin A. (Emma) 2 ch farmer O 80a 5h 4c R1 Perrysburg Pbg 107 B tel.

Snieder, Stephen (Bertha) laborer O H&L Fifth St Perrysburg Pbg B tel.

Snodgrass, Chas. Perrysburg Pbg.

Snook, Mrs. A. B. Hoytsville Jac.

Snook, Chas. A. (son G. F.) tile burner Hoytsville Jac B tel.

SNOOK, G. F. (Anna B.) 6 ch dray & livery O H&L Hoytsville Jac B tel.

Snyder, Albert M. (Emma) 3 ch farmer O 65a 3h 4c R1 Stony Ridge Tro 10 Ind tel.

Snyder, Alfred O. farmer R3 Prairie Depot Mon 12.

Snyder, Alburtus Grand Rapids Gr Rs.

SNYDER, ANDREW (son W. M.) farmer 2h R2 Haskins Wash 97.

Snyder, Arthur (May) 1 ch laborer O H&L Stony Ridge Tro.

Snyder, Benedict ret R3 Perrysburg Pbg 62.

Snyder, Chas. (Hulda) 1 ch cashier O H&L Fifth St Perrysburg Pbg B tel.

Snyder, Chas. (son Henry) telegraph operator Stony Ridge Tro 2.

Snyder, Chas. (son L.) farm hand 1h R1 Stony Ridge Tro 21 Ind tel.

Snyder, Christ (Clara) 5 ch farmer O 48a 4h 16c R1 Lime City Pbg 54.

Snyder, Cora (dau Ira) 85 Elm St Rossford Ros.

Snyder, C. A. Bloomdale Per.

Snyder, C. E. RD North Batimore Hen.

Snyder, C. N. (Rosa) 20 ch farmer T 80a 7h 3c R1 North Baltimore Hen 56.

SNYDER, C. W. (Alma) 2 ch blacksmith T H&L Stony Ridge Tro Ind tel.

SNYDER, DAVID (Mary) 3 ch farmer O 45a 4h 6c R1 Lime City Web 53 B tel.

Snyder, Dell C. (Anna) 2 ch farmer T 25a 3h 3c R1 Stony Ridge Tro 2 Ind tel.

Snyder, Edwin RD North Baltimore Hen.

Snyder, Mrs. Elizabeth housekeeper O 40a 1h R1 Lime City Pbg 96.

Snyder, Ella (dau Henry) housekeeper Stony Ridge Tro 2.

SNYDER, ELMER (Ethel) 6 ch clerk T H&L Stony Ridge Tro.

Snyder, Elmer (Laura) farmer T 70a 3h 4c R3 Perrysburg Pbg 62 Ind tel.

Snyder, Floyd Grand Rapids Gr Rs.

SNYDER, FRANCIS (Effie) 2 ch farmer 1h R1 Portage Por 87 Ind tel.

SNYDER, FRANK (Mary) 6 ch farmer O 160a 6h 2c R3 Prairie Depot Mon 12.

SNYDER, FRED (Katherine) farmer O 100a 2h 3c R1 Lime City Pbg 43 Ind tel.

Snyder, F. A. (Pearl) 5 ch railroader O H&L Tontogany Wash.

Snyder, F. M. Prairie Depot Mon.

Snyder, F. O. painter & paperhanger Stony Ridge Tro.

SNYDER, GEO. (Alice C.) 3 ch farmer O 40a 2h 2c R1 Walbridge Pbg 64.

Snyder, George (Hazel) 2 ch clerk T H&L Sixth St Perrysburg Pbg B tel.

Snyder, Geo. D. (Ollie) 7 ch machinist T 20a Perrysburg Pbg 141.

Snyder, George F. (Anna) 5 ch farmer T 50a 2h 5c Dowling Pbg 34.

SNYDER, GEO. G. (Eva) 1 ch farmer T 21a 2h 1c R3 Prairie Depot Mon 12.

Snyder, G. F. (Anna) 1 ch farmer O 80a 4h 4c R1 Lime City Pbg 42 B tel.

Snyder, Guy M. (Mabel) 3 ch mail carrier 1h Mulberry St Bloomdale Blo B & Ind tels.

Snyder, Henry R3 Perrysburg Pbg 62.

Snyder, Henry (Mary) 8 ch farmer O 80a Stony Ridge Tro 2,

Snyder, Howard 2 ch farmer T 80a 8h Bowling Green Lib 115 Ind tel.

Snyder, H. L. RD North Baltimore Hen.

Snyder, Ira (Anna) janitor T H&L 85 Elm St Rossford Ros.

Snyder, Ivan (Blanche) 1 ch oil worker T H&L Verango St Cygnet Blo.

Snyder, Jacob R1 Pemberville.

Snyder, Jake (son Mrs. Elizabeth) farmer T 40a 3h 1c R1 Lime City Pbg 96.

Snyder, Jno. RD Hoytsville Jac.

Snyder, John (Annie) 2 ch farmer T 40a 2h 2c R3 Weston Mil 7 Ind tel.

Snyder, John (son W. M.) laborer R2 Haskins Wash 97.

Snyder, John J. (Rosine) 5 ch glass worker O H&5Lots 1h Lime City Pbg 91.

Snyder, John W. (Emma) farmer T 60a 3h 1c R1 Perrysburg Pbg 101 B tel.

Snyder, J. A. RD North Baltimore Hen.

Snyder, J. H. (Caroline) 2 ch farmer O 21a 2h 2c R4 Bowling Green Cen 96 Ind tel.

Snyder, J. L. (Josephine) 2 ch farmer T H&L R1 Haskins Mid 57 Ind tel.

Snyder, Mrs. Lena 2 ch ret O H&L Luckey Tro.

Snyder, Lester clerk T H&L 93 Elm St Rossford Ros.

Snyder, Lucian 2 ch farmer 10a Stony Ridge Tro.

Snyder, Mrs. Lucy RD North Baltimore Lib.

Snyder, L. (Carrie) 2 ch farmer O 50a 2h 7c R1 Stony Ridge Tro 21 Ind tel.

Snyder, L. W. Stony Ridge Tro.

Snyder, Marion RD North Baltimore Hen.

Snyder, Mrs. Mary E. 4 ch housekeeper R1 Luckey Tro 87 Ind tel.

Snyder, Mary M. Pemberville Mon.

Snyder, Oliver H. (Mary D.) 1 ch farmer T 80a 2h 1c Cygnet Blo 67 B & Ind tels.

Snyder, Pearl (dau W. M.) housekeeper R2 Haskins Wash 97.

Snyder, Peter (Lue) 4 ch farmer O H&L 2h Grand Rapids Gr Rs.

Snyder, Rosine Lime City Pbg.

Snyder, Sam (Rose) farmer T 80a 3h R1 Portage Por 102.

Snyder, Samuel H. (Dora) farmer O 80a 7h 5c R1 Pemberville Mon 5 B tel.

Snyder, S. R. (Mary) ret O 70a 1h 3c R1 Walbridge Lake.

Snyder, Mrs. Wm. ret O H&L Millbury Lake.

Snyder, William H. (Cora) 6 ch farmer O 40a 5h 3c R1 Walbridge Lake 18.

Snyder, Wm. Perrysburg Pbg.

Snyder, Wilson (Lily M.) 6 ch farmer T 40a 2h R1 Jerry City Blo 72.

Snyder, W. L. (Clara) 4 ch farmer O 40a 5h 4c R2 Custar Lib 32 B tel.

Snyder, W. M. (Louisa) 2 ch blacksmith O 40a 1c R2 Haskins Wash 97 B tel.

Soash, E. J. (Rosa) 1 ch farmer O 60a 3h 5c R1 Tontogany Wash 10 Ind tel.

Soash, John F. (Anna) farmer O 40a 1h R2 Weston Wash 3 Ind tel.

Soash, Ross (Pearl) 2 ch farmer O 60a 6h 3c R2 Weston Wash 1 Ind tel.

Sober, Chas. R1 Perrysburg.

Sockman, W. L. (Verna) 1 ch farmer T 80a 1h 6c R3 Weston Mil 1 Ind tel.

Sockman, W. W. (Mary E.) 4 ch farmer O 180a 2h 4c R3 Weston Mil 1 Ind tel.

Sole, Sherman 2 ch laborer T H&L Caldwell St Bradner Mon.

Soleman, Hannah O L R1 North Baltimore Hen 123.

Soles, C. H. (Margarite)farmer O 20a 2h 2c R1 Risingsun Mon 81 B tel.

Soles, Homer Risingsun Mon.

Soles, S. S. Risingsun Mon.

Solether, Chas. F. Jerry City Blo.

Solether, C. W. (Elizabeth) 4 ch farmer O 650a 15h 25c Main St Jerry City Blo 78 Ind tel.

Solether, Getta Jerry City Blo.

Solether, Glenn E. (Veta) 1 ch farmer T 160a 3h 3c Jerry City Por 70 Ind tel.

Solether, J. C. RD Jerry City Por.

Sommerlott, W. S. Cygnet Blo.

Sommers, F. H. (Hazel) 1 ch shoe repairing T shop RD Bowling Green Ind tel.

Sommers, Geo. Bradner Mon.

Sommers, H. M. RD North Baltimore Hen.

Sommers, Rebecca North Baltimore Hen.

Souders, John 4 ch barber O H&L Grand Rapids Gr Rs.

Soule, Mrs. Bertha 2 ch O H&L Maple St Bloomdale Blo.

Soule, D. L. farmer T 1a Box 83 Weston Mil 80.

Soule, I. S. Prairie Depot Blo.

Soule, L. K. Jerry City Blo.

Sounsberry, Graham (Inez) insurance man T H&L Second St Perrysburg Pbg B tel.

South, Chas. Dunbridge Web.

South, J. M. (Josephine) farmer T 45a 2h 2c R3 Prairie Depot Por 121.

Southwick, F. (N.) oil worker T H Cygnet Blo 76 Ind tel.

Sowards, M. L. (Roxie) 7 ch clerk O H&L Jerry St Jerry City Blo.

Sowels, Homer (Minnie) 2 ch section hand T H&L Risingsun Mon.

Sowers, Claud laborer T H&L Milton Center Mil.

Sowle, Lydie dressmaker O H&L Risingsun Mon.

Spackey, Adam 3 ch farmer O 40a Jerry City Blo.

Spackey, Elza teacher 1h Jerry City Blo 72 Ind tel.

Spackey, Jacob (Lucy) 9 ch farmer O 60a 4h 2c Jerry City Blo 72 Ind tel.

Spackey, Myron (Alda) farmer O 80a 5h 3c R1 Jerry City Por 73.

Spafford, W. L. RD Haskins Mid.

Spahn, Aug. Pemberville Fre.

Spalelf, J. F. (Florence) farmer O 40a 3h 7c R2 Weston Wes 24.

Spangenberg, Rev. Henry (Rhoda) minister T H&L Millbury Lake.

Spangler, Mrs. Catherine 1c O H&L Second St Portage Mon.

Spangler, Frank (Mary E.) 2 ch farmer O 20a 2h 1c R3 Perrysburg Pbg 130 Ind tel.

Spangler, Geo. (Emma) 1 ch laborer T H&L N Main St Bradner Mon B tel.

Spangler, L. B. Portage.

Sparlin, Bassel Grand Rapids Gr Rs.

Spathalf, Milton (Cora) 1 ch farmer & horse dealer O 40a 7h 4c R1 Grand Rapids Wash 68 Ind tel.

Spathelf, Jno. R2 Weston.

Spathelf, Katherin (wid John) housekeeper T 30a R2 Haskins Wash 98.

Spathelf, Mrs. M. R2 Haskins.

Spaulding, E. (Madora) shoemaker T H&L Haskins Mid 35.

Speaker, H. J. (Velma) 2 ch teamster T H&L 2h Bays Lib 101.

Speaker, Jeff. (Mary) 3 ch farmer T 60a 4h R1 Rudolph Lib.

Speaker, T. J. (Mary) 11 ch farmer T 60a 3h RD Rudolph Lib 71.

Spear, A. B. (Coral) 2 ch oil producer O lease 2h Bowling Green Pla 51.

Specht, Henry Pemberville Fre.

Specht, Herman (Augusta) 5 ch farmer O 80a 3h 2c R4 Bowling Green Cen 72 Ind tel.

Speck, F. H. (Sarah) 2 ch farmer T 140a 6h 5c R2 Dunbridge Mid 79 Ind tel.

Speck, Geo. H. Pemberville Fre.

Speck, Jos. RD Haskins Mid.

Speck, Joseph 1 ch farmer O 245a 1h 1c R2 Dunbridge Pbg.

Speck, J. J. (Jessie) 3 ch farmer T 20a 3h 5c R3 Prairie Depot Mon 16.

Speer, A. B. (Coral) 2 ch oil producer T 40a 1h R1 Bowling Green Pla 33 Ind tel.

Spencer, Geo. telephone operator Main St Jerry City Por Ind tel.

Spencer, H. L. (May) 4 ch telephone mgr & express agt T H&L Main St Jerry City Por Ind tel.

Spencer, H. S. Jerry City Blo.

Spicer, John farmer bds R2 McClure Gr Rs 6.

Spike, Fred H. (Emma) hardware T H&L Milton Center Mil.

Spiker, Clara B. (dau C. H.) 1 ch student R1 Perrysburg Pbg 110.

Spiker, C. H. (Louisa) 1 ch farmer O 108a 7h 3c R1 Perrysburg Pbg 110 B tel.

Spilker, B. F. (Anna) .3 ch farmer O 100a 6h 11c R2 Dunbridge Pbg 23 B tel.

Spilker, Charles P. (Addie A.) farmer O 80a 3h 4c R1 Walbridge Lake 128 B tel.

Spilker, C. E. (son C. H.) farmer R1 Perrysburg Pbg 110.

Spilker, Edna L. (dau C. H.) school teacher R1 Perrysburg Pbg 110.

Spilker, E. J. (Eva) farmer O 100a 5h 6c R1 Dunbridge Web 54 B tel.

Spilker, Ray C. R1 Perrysburg.

Spilker, R. M. (Edna) 2 ch farmer T 115a 5h 3c R2 Dunbridge Mid 84 B tel.

Spilker, W. S. (Alice) farmer O 115a 3h 5c R2 Dunbridge Mid 84.

Spink, A. W. (Ellen) farmer O 85a 5h 7c R3 Prairie Depot Mon 105 B tel.

Spink, J. L. (Harriet) farmer O 80a 4h 8c R3 Prairie Depot Mon 108.

Spink, Mrs. Martha ret Prairie Depot Mon.

Spink, Menerna (dau of A. W.) housekeeper R3 Prairie Depot Mon 108 B tel.

Spink, Wilbur (son J. L.) farmer R3 Prairie Depot Mon 108.

Spirat, Geo. Perrysburg Pbg.

Spitler, Bess (dau Mrs. Lottie) bookkeeper Rudolph Lib 94.

Spitler, Dr. Dan B. (Chloe Dell) 2 ch MD O H&L Hoytsville Jac.

Spitler, F. W. RD North Baltimore Hen.

Spitler, G. M. (Ida) 4 ch farmer T 180a 7h 1c R1 Rudolph Lib 103 Ind tel.

Spitler, Mrs. Lottie 3 ch O H&L Rudolph Lib 94.

Spitler, Vern B. (Ethel M.) 1 ch weigh-
master T H&L Hoytsville Jac.

Spitler, Mrs. W. M. (wid W. M.) housekeeper O 3a 1h R1 Hoytsville Jac 77.

Spitzer, E. B. Perrysburg Pbg.

Spitzer, F. D. (Ora M.) 3 ch president
of bank O H&L Bond St Pemberville
Fre B & Ind tels.

Spitzer, Sidney Perrysburg Pbg.

SPOERL, GEO. (Caroline) 10 ch farmer
O 40a 5h 5c R1 Perrysburg Pbg 30.

Spohn, John (Elizabeth) log cutter T
H&L Pemberville Fre Ind tel.

Sponsler, M. I. RD North Baltimore
Hen.

SPOORES, JOHN W., SR. (Rebecca) 3 ch
farmer O 40a T 40a 4h 5c R2 Custar
Lib 15 Ind tel.

SPOORES, JOHN W., JR. (son John, Sr.)
R2 Custar Lib 15 Ind tel.

SPOORS, E. H. (Dora) 1 ch mgr Milton
Center Grn & Stock Co O H&L Milton Center Mil Ind tel.

Spoors, H. J. (Ruth) 1 ch farm hand
1h 2c Custar Mil 61 Ind tel.

Sprague, Arthur (son LeVina) laborer
Hoytsville Jac.

SPRAGUE, A. L. (Lulu) trucker O 20a
2h 1c R2 Bowling Green Pla 63 B tel.

Sprague, Frank (Bertha) 3 ch laborer
O H&L Main St Perrysburg Pbg.

Sprague, Mrs. LeVina 6 ch ret T H&L
Hoytsville Jac.

Sprague, Wm. (Mabel) 4 ch farmer T
120a 3h 2c R3 North Baltimore Blo
21.

Sprang, Harry (Hattie) 4 ch mail carrier T H&L 1h Seventh & Elm Sts
Perrysburg Pbg B tel.

Sprankel, Chas. RD North Baltimore.

Spratt, Hannah Weston Wes.

Spreng, Harry H. Perrysburg Pbg.

Springer, H. (Bertha) 2 ch glass worker
T H&L 181 Oak St Rossford Ros.

Springer, Jacob gas maker L bds Rossford Ros.

Springer, Japeth (son H.) 181 Oak St
Rossford Ros.

Springer, Philip (Lydia) drill boss O
H&L Rossford Ros.

Sprout, W. F. (Mary) 3 ch farmer T
80a 5h 5c R3 Prairie Depot Mon 96
B tel.

Spurgeon, Frank (Anna) 7 ch laborer
T H&L Risingsun Mon.

Squire, Geo. A. (Lydia A.) 10 ch
farmer O 40 farms 6h 13c R1 Rudolph
Lib 70 Ind tel.

Staads, Oliver (Mattie) 2 ch farmer T
100a 6h 4c R3 Weston Mil 2 B tel.

STAATS, Jos. (Mary) 1 ch farmer 80a
3h 6c R3 Weston Mil 4 B tel.

Stackhouse, Mrs. C. C. Prairie Depot
Mon.

Stackhouse, E. L. (Jennie) concrete
worker O H&L 1h 3c Main St Jerry
City Por.

Stackhouse, J. W. RD North Baltimore
Hen.

STACKHOUSE, RETTIE 3 ch O 17½a Jerry
City Blo 78 Ind tel.

Stackhouse, Wm. T. (May) engineer O
H&L Box 138 Rossford Ros B tel.

Thrashing with Gasoline Power.

Stacy, Mrs. Alice O H&L Garfield & Walnut Sts Bloomdale Blo.

Stacy, Clyde (Loa) farmer T 80a 3h 2c R2 Pemberville Web 28.

Stacy, Curtiss farmer T 50a 2h R4 Bowling Green Cen 68 Ind tel.

Stacy, J. M. (Rosy) 4 ch farmer O 40a 1h 3c R4 Bowling Green Cen 72 Ind tel.

STACY, L. (Lena) farmer O 14a 1h 1c R5 Bowling Green Cen 23 Ind tel.

Stacy, Wallace farmer T 80a 1h R4 Bowling Green Cen 74.

Stacy, Wm. A. (Carrie) 4 ch ret O 15a 1c R4 Bowling Green Cen 68 Ind tel.

STADLER, CHAS. (Sophia) 18 ch farmer T 8a 2h 3c R1 Bowling Green Pla 35.

STAFFORD, EARL (Edith) 8 ch farmer T 240a 11h 4c R1 Hoytsville Jac 109.

STAFFORD, HARRY (Maymie M.) tower operator T H&L 1h R3 North Baltimore Blo.

Stafford, N. E. RD Hoytsville Jac.

Stage, Elizabeth Walnut St Weston.

Stage, James F. (Mary E.) 1 ch farmer O 20a 3h 2c R3 Weston Mil 81 Ind tel.

STAGE, LEO (Daisy) 2 ch farmer T 40a H&L 2h 1c Milton Center Mil 53.

Stage, Lydia O H&L Walnut St Weston.

STAHL, DANIEL (Sarah) 6 ch farmer O 5a 1h Caldwell St Bradner Mon B tel.

Stahl, D. J. (Clo) 2 ch farmer T 77a 4h 5c R1 Risingsun Per 97.

Stahl, Fred laborer Caldwell St Bradner Mon B tel.

Stahl, Harry A. (Helena) 2 ch laborer O H&L Caldwell St Bradner Mon.

STAHL, MRS. J. H. RD North Baltimore.

Stahl, Perry J. (Marsella) 3 ch farmer T H&L 1h 2c R1 Risingsun Mon 71.

Stahl, Roy (Jennie) 1 ch laborer O H&L Risingsun Mon.

Stahl, Samuel (Mary) 2 ch section hand T H&L Risingsun Mon.

Stahl, Wm. 6 ch laborer T H&L Risingsun Mon.

Stahler, S. W. (Lula) hay dealer O H&L 2h Pemberville Fre Ind tel.

STAHR, WM. R1 Custar.

Staid, J. J. (Katharine) 4 ch farmer T 100a 2h 2c R1 Lime City Pbg 52 Ind tel.

Stainbrook, Edgar (Mary M.) 2 ch farmer O 160a 6h 6c R1 Portage Por 88.

Stainbrook, W. O. (Lora E.) 5 ch farmer O 160a 3h 15c R1 Fostoria Per 124 Ind tel.

Stalker, Archie (Addie) farmer O 10a 1h R1 Walbridge Lake 7.

STALL, W. J. (Alice) 7 ch teamster O H&L 4h 1c Hoytsville Jac.

Standering, Charles (Margaret Ellen) 5 ch shoemaker O H&L Luckey Tro.

Standering, Richard (son Charles) laborer Luckey Tro.

Stannard, Clarence 3 ch pumper T H&L Prairie Depot Mon.

Stannard, F. C. (Lena) 5 ch blacksmith T H&L 2h Prairie Depot Mon.

Stark, James (Stella) laborer T H&L Risingsun Mon.

Stark, John butcher O H&L Risingsun Mon.

Starn, Herman (Lavina) 2 ch barber O H&L Indiana Ave Perrysburg Pbg B tel.

Starn, H. C. (Louisa T.) 2 ch barber O H&L Perrysburg Pbg B tel.

Starn, H. M. (Altha Marie) 2 ch bank clerk O H&L East Main St Portage Por 6 Ind tel.

STARR, A. J. (Dorothy) 3 ch farmer T 160a 4h 5c R3 North Baltimore Blo 27 Ind tel.

Starr, J. F. (Edith M.) 2 ch farm laborer T H&L R3 North Baltimore Blo 16.

Stater, Wm. (Hazel) 1 ch laborer O H&L Third St Perrysburg Pbg. .

Stauffer, August H. (son H. J.) farm hand & farmer O 20a R1 Custar Mil 100.

Stauffer, Bertha A. (dau H. J.) housekeeper R1 Custar Mil 100.

STAUFFER, EDWARD (Nellie) 2 ch farmer O 86a 4h 4c R3 Perrysburg Pbg 69 Ind tel.

Stauffer, Elsie (dau H. J.) housekeeper R1 Custar Mil 100.

Stauffer, Eva (dau John) R3 Perrysburg Pbg 139.

Stauffer, Henry W. (son H. J.) farm hand R1 Custar Mil 100.

Stauffer, H. J. (Fannie) 10 ch farmer 120a 6h 20c R1 Custar Mil 100.

Stauffer John (Christiana) farmer O 5a 2h 1c R3 Perrysburg Pbg 139.

Stauffer, Martin T. (son H. J.) farm hand R1 Custar Mil 100.

Stauffer, Mary (dau H. J.) housekeeper R1 Custar Mil 100.

St. Clair, Emma Caldwell St Bradner Mon B tel.

ST. CLAIR, FRED (Verna) 2 ch farmer T H&L 1c R1 Portage Por 87.

St. Clair, J. F. (Cora) 7 ch farmer WOS 80a 2h 2c Bradner Mon 23 B tel.

St. Clair, Mary E. 1 ch ret O H&L Custar Mil.

St. Claire, Thomas (Alice) 1 ch farmer O 40a 2h 3c R2 Weston Pla 3 Ind tel.

Steale, J. W. (Lula) 2 ch teamster RD Rudolph Lib 109.

Steambarge, Ralph RD Haskins Mid.

Stearnes, A. B. (Jennie) 1 ch farmer T 160a 9h 4c R4 Fostoria Per 128 Ind tel.

STEARNES, SAMUEL (Maggie) 2 ch farmer O 50a 2h 3c R1 Fostoria Per 91.

Stearns, Mrs. A. E. 5 ch farmer O 160a 5h 8c R2 Fostoria Per 40 Ind tel.

Stearns, A. J. (Mary) 1 ch farmer O 40a 5h 2c R1 Grand Rapids Gr Rs Ind tel.

Stearns, C. G. Weston Wes.

Stearns, Edna (dau Frank) Taylor St Weston.

Stearns, Frank (Stella) 3 ch ret O 200a 2h 1c Taylor St Weston Ind tel.

Stearns, Geo. (Sarah) ret O H&L 1h West Millgrove Per 68.

. STEARNS, HOWARD (Ada) 1 ch farmer O 85a 4h 4c R2 Fostoria Per 118 Ind tel.

Stearns, Jud (Pearl) 2 ch farmer T 49a 3h 2c R1 Fostoria Per 79.

Stearns, J. A. (Alvira) 4 ch ret O 275a H&L 1h Taylor St Weston B tel.

Stearns, J. J. (Cora) 2 ch farmer O 120a 7h 13c R1 Fostoria Per 128 Ind tel.

Stearns, Kay (son Frank) Taylor St Weston.

STEARNS, LAWRENCE farmer T 170a 4h R1 Weston Pla 10.

Stearns, L. B. (Grace) farmer O 40a 5h 3c R1 Fostoria Per 47.

Stearns, Walter Tontogany Wash.

Stearns, Wm. RD Weston Lib.

Stearns, W. A. (Jennie) 2 ch farmer O 135a 4h 4c R1 Fostoria Per 57 Ind tel.

Stebbins, Samuel RD Bowling Green Por.

Stebealton, E. J. (Elizabeth) ret O H&L 1h Prairie Depot Mon 117.

Stebel, Chas. Luckey Tro.

Stebel, H. M. Dunbridge Web.

Stebel, Jos. A. (Edith) farmer O 114a 4h 8c R1 Dunbridge Web 12 B tel.

Stebel, Loretta Lime City Tro.

Stebel, Ralph (son Wm.) farm laborer Luckey Web 71 B tel.

Stebel, Wm. (Ella) farmer T Luckey Web 71 B tel.

Stebelton, E. J. Prairie Depot Mon.

Stebelton, O. H. (May Belle) restaurant O H&L Prairie Depot Mon.

Stecker, J. M. Bloomdale Blo.

Sted, A. J. Cygnet Blo.

Steele, A. J. RD North Baltimore Blo.

Steele, Jos. RD North Baltimore Hen.

Steele, Mary M. RD North Baltimore Hen.

Steen, C. F. (Martha) 3 ch farmer O 120a 6h 7c R1 Weston Lib 41 Ind tel.

Steensen, Andrew Le Moyne Tro.

Steensen, Mrs. Lucy ret O 15a Latchie Lake 95.

Steffen, C. H. (Bertha) 2 ch lumber company T H&L Pemberville Fre.

Steffen, H. H. (Annie) ret O H&L 1h Pemberville Fre.

Stein, Aug. Pemberville Fre.

Stein, August F. Bradner Fre.

Stein, A. J. 4 ch general merchandise O H&L Walbridge Lake Ind tel.

STEIN, C. F. (Martha) 3 ch farmer O 120a 6h 7c R1 Weston Lib 41 Ind tel.

Stein, George (son A. J.) clerk Walbridge Lake.

STEIN, HENRY (Caroline) 3 ch farmer O 84a 4h 7c R1 East Toledo Lake 70 Ind tel.

Stein, Henry H. (Amy) 1 ch farmer O 27a 2h 2c Station A East Toledo Ros 31.

Stein, H. F. W. Bradner Fre.

STEIN, JOHN bus driver RD Bowling Green.

Stein, John farmer T 40a 2h Walbridge St Walbridge Lake 119.

STEIN, J. G. H. (Anna M.) 2 ch banker & farmer O H&L Pemberville Fre B tel. See adv.

Stein, Rachel O 40a Walbridge St Walbridge Lake 119.

Stein, Velma (dau A. J.) clerk Walbridge Lake.

Stein, Wint (Tillie) farmer O 40a 2h 2c R1 Walbridge Lake 7.

Steiner, M. F. (Lide) 3 ch farmer O 66a 3h 7c R1 Fostoria Per 56 Ind tel.

Steinline, Joe (Mary) 4 ch laborer O H&L Fifth St Perrysburg Pbg B tel.

Steinshauer, Elizabeth O H&L Locust St Weston Ind tel.

Steller, Lloyd cattle RD Portage Por.

Stensen, Andrew (Rosie) 3 ch farmer T 140a 4h 12c R1 Le Moyne Tro 85 B tel.

Stensen, Harry (son Andrew) student R1 Le Moyne Tro 85 B tel.

Stephan, Martin Perrysburg Pbg.

Stephen, D. Bradner Mon.

STEPHENS, J. M. (Ada J.) farmer & stock raiser O 40a 2h 14c R1 Luckey Web 69 B tel. See adv.

Stephenson, Rev. E. N. (Alice) O H&L 1h East St Bradner Mon.

Stepheny, Mrs. Bertha T Wales Road East Toledo Ros 15.

Stephon, Martin Perrysburg Pbg.

STERLING, A. W. (Marguerite) 3 ch oil worker T L 1c R1 North Baltimore Hen 68.

Sterling, B. E. (Iva) 5 ch farmer O 80a 5h 2c R1 North Baltimore Hen 53 Ind tel.

Sterling, Carrie (Sarah) 1 ch traveling man T H&L Grand Rapids Gr Rs Ind tel.

Sterling, C. W. (Clara) farmer O 60a 4h 4c R2 Custar Hen 42.

STERLING, D. W. 2 ch farmer O 200a 8h 2c R2 Custar Lib 34 Ind tel.

STERLING, F. L. (Margaret) physician T H&L Venango St Cygnet Blo Ind tel. See adv.

STERLING, GEO. laborer Loci St Cygnet Blo.

Sterling, H. C. (Cleo) 1 ch farmer T 100a 5h 5c Grand Rapids Gr Rs 45 Ind tel.

Sterling, Joe (Nellie) 1 ch farmer O 80a 6h R1 North Baltimore Hen 71 B & Ind tels.

STERLING, J. E. (Laura) 5 ch laborer T H&L1h 1h Woodside Fre 78.

STERLING, J. H. (Maude) 4 ch farming O 3a 5h 1c R1 North Baltimore Hen 68 Ind tel.

STERLING, LOU A. barber Front St Cygnet Blo. See adv.

Sterling, Owen (Ella) 1 ch ticket agent O H&L Locust St Weston Ind tel.

Sterling, T. S. Grand Rapids Gr Rs.

Sternaman, E. D. Dunbridge Web.

Sternaman, Fred (Katharine) 2 ch farmer O 20a 4h 2c R2 Dunbridge Mid 66 B tel.

STERNAMAN, HENRY (Jane) farmer O 40a 2c R2 Dunbridge Mid 66 B tel.

Sterns, A. A. (Mattie) laborer O 4a H Main St Perrysburg Pbg.

Sterns, Helen (dau Frank) Taylor St Weston.

Sterns, Lloyd (Mary) laborer T H&L Grand Rapids Gr Rs.

Sterns, Wm. (Nell) 1 ch farmer O 40a 7h 7c R1 Weston Lib 2 Ind tel.

Sterritt, J. W. (Alice) canvasser O 2½a H 1h R1 Rudolph Lib 63.

Stevens, A. G. (Mary M.) 3 ch farmer O 60a 4h 4c R2 Bowling Green Cen 6 Ind tel.

Stevens, David 5 ch ret O H&L & store buildings East St Bradner Mon.

Stevens, Elmer B. (son James) student R1 Pairie Depot Mon 115.

Stevens, F. M. (Alice) laborer O H&L 1h Tontogany Wash.

STEVENS, GRANT (Glenn) farmer T 80a 5h 2c R3 North Baltimore Hen 107.

Stevens, H. E., Jr. Cygnet Blo.

STEVENS, JAMES (Mary S.) farmer O 60a 7h 27c R1 Prairie Depot Mon 115. See adv.

Stevens, J. E. (Emma) blacksmith O H&L Grand Rapids Gr Rs Ind tel.

Stevens, J. H. RD North Baltimore Hen.

Stevens, Sylvester (Bird) 1 ch student O H&L Grand Rapids Gr Rs Ind tel.

Stevens, Zahm RD Weston Wash.

Stevenson, E. B. (Iva) 2 ch jeweler O H&L RD North Baltimore Hen.

Stevenson, Frank (Myrtle) saloonkeeper Custar Mil.

Stevenson, Jas. Tontogany Wash.

STEWART, ALEXANDER (Mary) 1 ch farmer O 100a 3h 8c R3 Perrysburg Pbg 141 Ind tel.

Stewart, Anna (dau A.) student R3 Perrysburg Pbg 141 Ind tel.

Stewart, Miss Anna housekeeper R1 Dunbridge Web 52 B tel.

Stewart, A. D. (L. B.) 2 ch farmer O 160a 7h 3c R3 Bowling Green Cen 12 Ind tel.

STEWART, B. B. (Sadie B.) 7 ch field foreman T 20a 2h 1c R1 Rudolph Lib 101 Ind tel.

Stewart, Frank (son A.) collector bds R3 Perrysburg Pbg 141 Ind tel.

Stewart, Hugh farmer O 319a 5h 34c R1 Dunbridge Web 52 B tel.

STEWART, JAMES G. (Metta) 8 ch farmer T 120a R3 Perrysburg Pbg 89 B tel.

Stewart, Joseph (son A.) traveling salesman bds R3 Perrysburg Pbg 141.

Stewart, Lawrence (son A.) farmer R3 Perrysburg Pbg 141.

Stewart, Martin (son A.) student R3 Perrysburg Pbg 141.

Stewart, Mary A. RD North Baltimore Hen.

Stewart, Myra (dau A.) student R3 Perrysburg Pbg 141.

Stewart, S. O. (Lora J.) 1 ch farmer O 146a 5h 7c R4 Fostoria Per 105 B & Ind tels.

Stewart, Wm. (Tiny) 1 ch blacksmith O H&L West Millgrove Per 70.

Stewart, Wm. R1 Rudolph Lib 101 Ind tel.

Stickels, Bob (Etta) blacksmith O H&L 2Lots 1h 1c Locust St Perrysburg Pbg B tel.

Stickels, Edith 8 ch housekeeper T H&L Sycamore St Weston.

Stickels. F. S. (Blanche) 2 ch garage T H&L Hoytsville Jac B tel.

Stickels, John H. (Ida) 3 ch farmer O 40a 3h 3c R4 Bowling Green Cen 101 Ind tel.

Stickels, J. S. Perrysburg Pbg.

Stickels, Wallace (son Edith) laborer Sycamore St Weston.

Stiffler, R. F. 2c Bradner Mon.

Stifler, Clel. (Minnie) 2 ch farmer .O H&L 2h Stahl St Bradner Mon.

Stiger, A. A. (Mattie) 3 ch mill manager T H&L East St Bradner Mon.

Stiger, I. (Phoebe) 1 ch ret O H&L W Crocker St Bradner Mon 28.

STIGER, J. W. (Ida) 4 ch lumber dealer O H&L 2h N Main St Bradner Mon B tel.

Stiger, Ruth N Main St Bradner Mon B tel.

STILLWELL, ABRAHAM (Mary J.) farmer O 40a 2h 3c R2 Bloomdale Per 24 B tel.

Stillwell, Wm. Perrysburg Pbg.

STILWELL, J. M. (Jessie M.) 2 ch painter O H&L Harrison St Bloomdale Blo.

Stilwell, Rosa Bloomdale Blo.

Stilwell, Samuel (Melissa) ret O H&L Main St Bloomdale Blo.

Stimmel, Clark W. Hoytsville Jac.

Stimmel, E. M. 3 ch laborer O H&L 1h 1c Hoytsville Jac B tel.

STIMMEL, ISAAC (Lottie) farmer T 80a 4h 3c R1 Hoytsville Jac 83.

Stimmel, Vern (soh E. M.) student Hoytsville Jac.

Stine, E. M. ret O H&L Indiana Ave Perrysburg Pbg B tel.

Stine, F. W. (Minnie) 1 ch farmer O 76a 2h 8c R1 Bradner Fre 91 B tel.

Stine, Gerath farmer T 3h 4c R1 Bradner Fre 96 B tel.

Stine, Wm. 2 ch ret O 100a R1 Bradner Fre 94 B tel.

Stinehart, P. A. (Sarah) 2 ch farmer T 160a 7h 5c R1 Hoytsville Jac 93 B tel.

Stinger, Isaac (Martha) 1 ch saw mill merchant T H&L Weston Ind tel.

Stinger, Robert (Alice) 1 ch saw mill man O 40a H&L 2h Walnut St Weston B tel.

Stininger, Isaac Weston.

Stininger, Robt. Weston Wes.

Stitt, James (son Wm.) RD Rudolph Lib 39 Ind tel.

Stitt, John (son Wm.) RD Rudolph Lib 39 Ind tel.

Stitt, Lydia (dau Wm.) R1 Rudolph Lib 39 Ind tel.

Stitt, Wm. (Mary) 3 ch oil producer O 200a 1h 1c R1 Rudolph Lib 39 Ind tel.

Stiwell, A. RD Bloomdale Per.

Stock, Benjamin Bradner Mon.

Stock, Edward RD Rudolph Lib.

Stockdill, R. D. (Elizabeth) ret O H&L Bell St Bradner Mon.

Stocker, D. B. farmer T 120a 5h 2c R1 Weston Mil 60 Ind tel.

Stocker, G. W. Weston Wes.

Stocker, John D. (Jennie) 2 ch farmer T 40a 1h 1c R1 Grand Rapids Gr Rs 13.

Stockwell, A. C. (Rosa) 6 ch laborer T Lot R1 North Baltimore Hen 69.

STOCKWELL, A. F. (Grace) 5 ch farmer O 280a 11h 2c R1 Rudolph Lib 75 Ind tel.

Stockwell, Eli farmer RD Rudolph Lib 83 Ind tel.

STOCKWELL, GRACE R1 Rudolph.

Stockwell, Ross (Thressie) 1 ch farmer O 80a 6h 2c R1 Rudolph Lib 70 Ind tel.

Stockwell, Mrs. R. V. RD North Baltimore Hen.

Stoddard, Ada (dau Elinor) Clark St Weston.

Stoddard, D. D. (Josephine) farmer T H&L Broadway St Weston Wes Ind tel.

Stoddard, Elenor 5 ch Clark St Weston.

Stoddard, L. C. farmer O 16a H&L 2h 1c Clark St Weston.

Stoffer, Alex. RD North Baltimore Hen.

Stoffer, Alice RD North Baltimore Hen.

Stoltz, L. R. (Crystal) 4 ch railroader T 6a R3 Prairie Depot Mon 50.

Stolz, N. Prairie Depot Mon.

Stolz, P. O. Prairie Depot Mon.

Stondinger, L. F. Prairie Depot Mon.

Stone, Mrs. Anna 2 ch housekeeper T H&L Risingsun Mon.

Stone, B. F. Luckey Web.

Stone, Frank farmer R2 Perrysburg Mid 14.

STONE, F. C. (Rosa) 5 ch oil pumper T 7a 3c Risingsun Mon 71.

STONE, F. H. (Alice) 2 ch ret T H&L Perry St Pemberville Fre.

Stone, L. C. (Clara) 1 ch safe decorator T H&L Pemberville Fre 80.

Stone, Mrs. Margaret ret Risingsun Mon 71.

STONE, THOMAS (Florence E.) tiling business O H&L Millbury Lake 54 Ind tel.

Stonebrook, Lorenzo Dunbridge Mid.

Stoner, Noah Walbridge Lake.

Stoner, William farm hand R1 Stony Ridge Tro 31.

Stoner, Wm. A. (Maud) 3 ch railroader O H&L Walbridge Lake.

Stoots, F. C. (Ruth) 2 ch farmer T 40a 2h 2c R1 Bowling Green Pla 39 Ind tel.

Stoots, Jos. Weston Mil.

Stoots, Oliver Weston Mil.

Storeholder, Edward (Mary) 4 ch farmer T 80a 3h 4c R3 Bowling Green Cen 47.

Stormer, Fredrick farmer O 20a R1 Walbridge Lake 101.

Story, Martin RD North Baltimore Hen.

Stott, William (Lula) farm laborer R1 Hoytsville Jac 94.

Stoudinger, Caroline farmer O 19a 1h R1 Prairie Depot Mon 85 B tel.

Stoudinger, Clyde (son C. W.) farmer 1h R1 Prairie Depot Mon 118 B tel.

Stoudinger, C. W. (Clara) farmer T 155a 5h 2c R1 Prairie Depot Mon 118 B tel.

Stoudinger, Elizabeth 5 ch farmer O H&L Prairie Depot.

Stoudinger, Lewis farmer T 40a 3h 3c R1 Prairie Depot Mon 84 B tel.

Stoudinger, L. F. (May) farmer T 40a 3h 3c R1 Prairie Depot Mon 84 B tel.

Stouffer, Alice L. RD North Baltimore Hen.

Stouffer, H. D. RD North Baltimore Hen.

Stouffer, J. (Almeda) shoes & gents' furnishings 1h Main St Bloomdale Blo B & Ind tels.

Stouffer, Myrt (dau J.) clerk Main St Bloomdale Blo B & Ind tels.

Stout, H. RD Bowling Green Pla.

Stove, E. L. Bloomdale Blo.

Stover, Chester (Imo) 1 ch school teacher T H&L Prairie Depot Mon.

Strail, Edward (Sophia) 1 ch farmer T 90a 4h 6c R1 Stony Ridge Tro 9 Ind tel.

Strail, Fred (Lena) 6 ch farmer 18a 1h 1c R1 Le Moyne Tro 85 B tel.

Straley, W. H. RD North Baltimore Hen.

Strasburger, Jacob gen mdse T H&L Risingsun Mon B tel.

Stratton, B. P. RD Weston Pla.

Stratton, Fred (son F. W.) clerk E Main St Portage Por 6 B tel.

Stratton, F. W. (Hattie) genl store O H&L farm 1h E Main St Portage Por 6 B & Ind tels.

Stratton, H. L. Corp St Portage Por.

Strawbridge, Mrs. D. C. Bloomdale Blo.

Strawn, C. E. (Dora) 4 ch farmer T 160a 5h 21c R1 Custar Jac 43 B tel.

Strawser, H. G. Weston Wes.

Strayer, Jessie 3 ch clerk R2 Weston Wash 51.

Streeter, Mary E. housekeeper O H&L Tontogany Wash.

Streeter, Sam Tontogany Wash.

Stretchbury, Fred. (E. F.) 5 ch farming O 22a 3h 2c R3 Weston Wes 56.

Stretchbury, James farming O 28a R3 Weston Wes 56.

Stretsberry, Wm. (Rebecca) 3 ch ret O H&L Main St Weston B tel.

Stricker, Philip (Margaret) 3 ch laborer O H&L Box 78 Rossford Ros.

Stricker, William, Jr. (son Philip) Box 78 Rossford Ros.

Stricklen, C. (Nellie) 1 ch laborer O H&L Stony Ridge Tro.

Striff, Wm. Prairie Depot Mon.

Stroble, Mrs. Fred ret O 73a 1c R1 Stony Ridge Pbg 52.

Stroble, F. L. (Anna) farmer T 73a 3h 2c R1 Stony Ridge Pbg 52.

Strock, Guy P. (Mabel) 1 ch produce dealer T H&L Front St Pemberville Fre 40 Ind tel.

Strohl, J. B. (Bertha) contractor 1c Custar Mil 45 B tel.

Strohl, Mrs. Sarah Custar Mil.

Strohl, Wm. (Florence) 1 ch pumper T H&L Risingsun Mon.

Strohl, W. B. (Geneva) 4 ch painter & paperhanger O H&L Custar Mil.

Strock, W. H. (Drusilla) 2 ch farmer O 80a 6h 5c R1 Jerry City Blo 66 Ind tel.

Strong, Lyman (son T. D.) supt architect work RD Bowling Green Pla.

Strow, Earnest (son Lee) farmer R2 Custar Mil 48.

Strow, Elsie B. Milton Center Mil.

Strow, H. L. Custar Mil.

Strow, Lee (Nellie) 3 ch farmer O 160a 11h 11c R2 Custar Mil 48 Ind tel.

Strow, Dr. R. M. (Elsa B.) 2 ch MD O H&L Milton Center Mil B & Ind tels.

Struble, Chas. (Rosa) farmer O 80a 8h 14c R2 McClure Gr Rs 3 Ind tel.

Struble, Hazel (dau Chas.) housekeeper R2 McClure Gr Rs 3.

Struck, H. W. Walbridge Lake.

Stubbins, Wm. Cygnet Blo.

Stuchell, Dr. A. (Kit) T Luckey Tro Ind tel.

Stucker, G. W. (Belle) ret O 80a H&L Oak St Weston Ind tel.

Studer, Francis (Etta) 2 ch farmer T 60a R1 Haskins Mid 43.

Stuller, Lloyd (Maggie) farmer & horse breeder T 267a 25h 6c R1 Portage Por Ind tel.

Stump, A. A. (Nellie) 3 ch insurance agt O H&L Bell St Bradner Mon B tel.

Stump, C. H. (Blanche) banker O H&L 1c Caldwell St Bradner Mon B tel.

Stump, C. W. (Zella) 2 ch laborer O H&L N Main St Bradner Mon.

208

Stump, D. F. (Angeline) miller O H&L 1h Grand Rapids Gr Rs Ind tel.

Stump, Frank (Angeline) miller O H&L 1h Grand Rapids Gr Rs Ind tel.

Stump, Frank 5 ch farmer O 40a 4h 4c R1 Risingsun Mon 78.

Stump, Herbert (Ella) 2 ch miller O H&L Grand Rapids Gr Rs Ind tel.

Stump, J. F. Risingsun Mon.

Stump, Mary E. Grand Rapids Gr Rs.

Stump, S. B. ret O 5a R1 Risingsun Mon 75.

Stump, W. H. Grand Rapids Gr Rs.

STYER, C. (Cora) 3 ch farmer T 80a 4h 4c R1 Dunbridge Web 3.

STYER, HARLEY farm laborer 1h R1 Dunbridge Web 5 B tel.

STYER, JACOB B. (Lymire) 2 ch farmer T 60a 5h 4c R2 Haskins Mid 89 B tel.

Styer, Minnie (dau C.) housekeeper 1c R1 Dunbridge Web 3.

Styer, Myrtle (dau C.) housekeeper 1c R1 Dunbridge Web 3.

Styers, David (Martha) 3 ch farmer O H&L Custar Mil B tel.

Suder, H. J. Walbridge Lake.

Sudholtz, Anna Hoytsville Jac.

Suger, Adam (Frederick) 5 ch dairy farmer O 113a 6h 25c R1 Stony Ridge Tro 31 Ind tel.

Sugg, Chas. (Grace) 2 ch farmer T 80a 3h 1c R2 North Baltimore Hen 32 Ind tel.

Suind, George V. (Catherine) 13 ch farmer thrashing & general store O 200a 11h 5c R2 Perrysburg Pbg 5 B tel. ·

Sullivan, Ed. RD Dunbridge Mid.

Sullivan, Frank V. (Clara) 3 ch farmer T 70a 4h 2c R2 Perrysburg Mid 3 B tel.

SULLIVAN, GEO. (Katie) 3 ch contractor O H&L Dowling Mid.

Sullivan, Mrs. Martha cattle RD Bowling Green` Cen.

Sullivan, Martin (Mildred) 5 ch oil man T H&L Risingsun Mon.

Sullivan, Robert Argo (son Frank) farmer Perrysburg Mid 3.

Sullivan, Wm. RD Dunbridge Mid.

Sullivan, W. O. (Ruth) farmer T 50a 3h 4c R5 Bowling Green Cen 65 Ind tel.

Sullwold, Louise (dau R.) housekeeper R1 Lime City Pbg 56 Ind tel.

Sullwold, Reiner ret O 113a 5h 3c R1 Lime City Pbg 56 Ind tel.

Sullwold, Wm. (son R.) farmer R1 Lime City Pbg 56 Ind tel.

Summer, John carpenter O 7a 1h R3 Perrysburg Pbg 157.

Summerlot, Sherman oil worker H&L 1h Claron St Cygnet Blo 6.

Summers, G. M. (Artie) 3 ch carpenter O H&L East St Bradner Mon.

SUMMERS, JACOB R1 North Baltimore Hen 8.

Calf in a Modern Shipping Crate.

SUMMERS, WM. A. (Mary) 8 ch farmer T 80a 4h 4c Bradner Mon 23.

·Sundemeir, Laura (dau Henry) housekeeper Luckey Tro Ind tel.

Sundemyer, Henry (Anna) 4 ch farmer T 80a 4h 3c R1 Stony Ridge Lake 86 B tel.

Sundy, Fred (Lulu) 2 ch farmer O 80a 5h 6c R3 Bowling Green Pla 87 B tel.

Surplus, Jas. RD North Baltimore Hen.

Suter, Floyd R1 Perrysburg Pbg.

Suter, George (Katherine) 2 ch farmer O 40a 5h 4c R1 Walbridge Lake 20 B tel.

Suter, Mrs. Harry F. housekeeper 1h R1 Walbridge Lake.

Suter, H. J. (Maud) 3 ch H&L Walbridge Lake.

Suter, Jacob (Anna) ret O 2a 1h 1c R1 Walbridge Lake 18 Ind tel.

Sutter, P. C. (Helen) 5 ch salesman T H&L Front St Perrysburg Pbg.

Sutton, Celina RD Bowling Green Wash.

SUTTON, MRS. FRANCES 4 ch O 1a Cygnet Blo 6.

Sutton, Frank RD Tontogany Wash.

SUTTON, FRED (Carrie) 1 ch farmer T 40a 2h 2c R2 Bowling Green Pla 44 Ind tel.

Sutton, Geo. (Jennie) 2 ch farmer O 74a 1h 3c R1 Haskins Mid 50 B tel.

Sutton, Miss Hazel school teacher R1 Haskins Mid 50.

Sutton, Isaac RD Dowling Mid.

Sutton, I. I. (Florence) 1 ch farmer T 2a 1h R1 Tontogany Wash 21 Ind -tel.

Sutton, J. V. (Alice) 3 ch farmer O 70a 3h 2c R1 Tontogany Wash 20 Ind tel.

Sutton, Louisa Dunbridge Mid.

Sutton, R. H. (Libbie E.) 4 ch farmer O 80a 5h 1c R1 Tontogany Wash 20 Iud tel.

SUTTON, W. L. (Caroline) 3 ch farmer T 20a 3h 1c R2 Bowling Green Pla 62 Ind tel.

Swan, F. W. (Margaritte) hardware T H&L Pemberville.

Swan, H. C. (Susan R.) hardware store O H&L Pemberville.

Swan, James (Edna) 2 ch hardware T H&L Pemberville Fre.

Swane, Henry farmer O 70a 1h R2 Pemberville Fre 46.

SWANSON, J. F. (Julia) 3 ch laborer 1h R1 Bloomdale Blo 122 B & Ind tels.

Swarm, J. H. Weston Mil.

Swartz, Alfred H. (Mary) 1 ch farmer O 40a 3h 3c R3 Perrysburg Pbg 65 Ind tel.

Swartz, Andrew (Lena) farmer O 80a 2h 6c RD Dunbridge Web 57 B tel.

Swartz, Arthur (Beatrice) dis supt T H&L Walbridge Lake.

SWARTZ, AUGUST (Ethel) 1 ch farmer T 40a 3h 2c R1 Lime City Pbg 53.

SWARTZ, A. jeweler Losee St Cygnet Blo.

SWARTZ, CHARLES (Lottie) 3 ch farmer O 40a 4h 3c R3 Perrysburg Pbg 69 Ind tel.

Swartz, Chas. (Carrie) 1 ch farmer O 50a 2h 2c R1 Walbridge Lake 25 Ind tel.

Swartz, Clarence 2 ch carpenter T H&L Pemberville Fre.

Swartz, Clarence (son Geo.) farm laborer R1 Dunbridge Web 54 B tel.

Swartz, C. R. (son S. L.) farmer O 40a R1 Jerry City Blo 65 B & Ind tels.

Swartz, Dora (dau Geo.) dressmaker R1 Dunbridge Web 54 B tel.

Swartz, Edward C. (son Frank L.) farm hand R1 Luckey Tro 19 Ind tel.

Swartz, Elma (dau J. G.) R3 Perrysburg Pbg 69 Ind tel.

Swartz, Elmer (son Fred) ret Stony Ridge Tro.

Swartz, Elmer F. (Amy) 2 ch farmer T 80a 3h 3c R3 Perrysburg Pbg 87.

Swartz, Elmer J. (son Frank L.) farm hand R1 Luckey Tro 19 Ind tel.

Swartz, Esther (dau Frank L.) housekeeper R1 Luckey Tro 19 Ind tel.

Swartz, Floyd S. (son S. L.) farmer T 185a 1h 4c R1 Jerry City Blo 65 B & Ind tels.

Swartz, Frank (Katie) 1 ch farmer O 47a 5h 3c R1 Lime City Pbg 45 Ind tel.

SWARTZ, FRANK L. (Anna) 4 ch farmer O 68a 4h 4c R1 Luckey Tro 19 Ind tel.

Swartz, Fred (Louisa) 8 ch ret O 80a H&L Stony Ridge Tro.

Swartz, F. G. (Mary) 2 ch farmer O 160a 4h 2c R1 Walbridge Lake 24 Ind tel.

SWARTZ, GEORGE (Elizabeth) 2 ch farmer O 86a 4h 4c R1 Dunbridge Web 54 B tel.

Swartz, Geo. E. (Clara) 2 ch farmer O 40a 1h 1c R1 Stony Ridge Lake 87 B tel.

SWARTZ, G. W. farmer O 60a 2h 3c R1 Lime City Pbg 94.

Swartz, Henry (son Andrew) farm laborer 2h R1 Dunbridge Web 57 B tel.

Swartz, Henry M. (Carry) 6 ch farmer O 120a 3h 2c R1 Lime City Pbg 47 Ind tel.

SWARTZ, ISAAC A. (Lizzie) 1 ch farmer O 60a 3h 7c R1 Stony Ridge Lake 31 Ind tel.

SWARTZ, ISAAC H. (Carrie) 2 ch farmer T 116a 2h 4c Lime City Pbg 91 B tel.

Swartz, Isaac O. Bloomdale Blo.

Swartz, Jacob (Dora) 4 ch farmer O 80a 6h 5c Lime City Pbg 40 B tel.

SWARTZ, JOHN R3 Perrysburg.

SWARTZ, JOHN H. (Rosie) 1 ch farmer O 50a 4h 5c R1 Stony Ridge Lake 31.

Swartz, J. B. 3 ch ret R1 Deshler Jac 6 B tel.

Swartz, J. G. farmer O 100a 5h 3c R3 Perrysburg Pbg 69 Ind tel.

Swartz, J. L. (Mary) 1 ch farmer O 47a 3h 3c R1 Lime City Pbg 54 Ind tel.

Swartz, Katherine farmer O R1 Luckey Tro 20 Ind tel.

Swartz, Mabel (dau Malinda) housekeeper R1 Lime City Pbg 53 Ind tel.

Swartz, Mrs. Malinda housekeeper O 52a 2h 1c R1 Lime City Pbg 53 Ind tel.

Swartz, Maretta O H&L R3 North Baltimore Blo 16.

Swartz, Mary E. housekeeper T H&L 1c R1 Lime City Pbg 52.

Swartz, Mearl L. (son S. L.) farmer T 185a 1h 4c R1 Jerry City Blo 65 B & Ind tels.

SWARTZ, OLIVER I. farmer O 80a 7h R2 Bloomdale Blo 106 B & Ind tels.

Swartz, O. F. (Anna) farmer O 60a 7h 7c R1 Weston Mil 57 Ind tel.

SWARTZ, SILAS S. (Etta) farmer O 185a 5h 20c R1 Jerry City Blo 65 B & Ind tels.

Swartz, S. H. Jerry City Blo.

Swartz, S. H. (Kate) 7 ch farming T 40a 4h 2c R3 Weston Wes 52.

Swartz, Walter (son Geo.) ditcher R1 Dunbridge Web 54 B tel.

Swartz, Wm. Latchie Lake.

SWARTZ, W. J. farmer O 3h 20c R1 Luckey Tro 20 Ind tel.

Swartz, W. L. Walbridge Lake.

Swartz, W. S. Cygnet Blo.

Swartz, W. W. (Ethel) farmer T 90a 2h 5c R1 Bloomdale Per 18 B & Ind tels.

Swartz, W. Wm. (Susan) 3 ch farmer O 79a 6h 4c Lime City Pbg 120.

Swebey, Lester farmer R4 Deshler Jac 13.

Sweebe, Amos (Bertha) 1 ch farmer O 40a 6h 1c R1 Rudolph Lib 33 B & Ind tels.

Sweebe, Clarence Custar Hen.

Sweebe, Edward teamster R1 Rudolph Lib 33 B & Ind tels.

SWEEBE, J. E. (Mary) 5 ch farmer O 160a 2h 10c R1 Rudolph Lib 33 B & Ind tels.

Sweebe, Mrs. Lulu Custar Hen.

SWEEBE, SAM (Estella) 1 ch farmer T 54a 2h 2c R2 Custar Lib 27 B tel.

Sweebe, Mrs. Sarah O H&L R7 Custar Lib 33 Ind tel.

Sweebe, Wm. (Bertha) 3 ch farmer T 80a 3h 3c R3 North Baltimore Hen 100 Ind tel.

Sweede, C. (Lulu) farmer T 93a 4h 5c R2 Custar Hen 62.

SWEET, D. E. (Mary) 5 ch farmer T 80a 3h 4c R1 Weston Lib 45 Ind tel.

SWEET, FLORENCE (dau D. E.) R1 Weston Lib 45 Ind tel.

Sweet, Herriot ret O H&L Mulberry St Perrysburg Pbg B tel.

Sweet, Jno. Walbridge Lake.

Sweet, J. A. RD North Baltimore Hen.

SWEET, J. M. (Ardie) 3 ch farmer O 70a 2h 4c R1 Rudolph Lib 99 Ind tel.

Sweger, A. H. RD North Baltimore Hen.

Swerlein, Chalmer J. (son W. R.) farm hand R3 Weston Mil 88.

Swerlein, Ellen Weston Wes.

Swerlein, Harmon (Ellen) ret O 180a H& 12Lots 3h 2c Elm & Ash Sts Weston Ind tel.

Swerlein, Roena (dau W. R.) R3 Weston Mil 88.

Swerlein, W. R. (Esther Jane) 6 ch farmer O 40a 6h 2c R3 Weston Mil 88 Ind tel.

Swigart, B. F. Perrysburg Pbg.

Swin, Wm. P. (Anna) 2 ch restaurant & pool room Luckey Tro.

Swindler, Chas. (Rose) 2 ch farmer T H&L R1 Bowling Green Pla 76.

Swindler, J. L. (Edna) 4 ch farmer O 40a 5h 5c R3 Bowling Green Cen 47 Ind tel.

SWINEHART, C. H. farmer T 159a 11h 5c R1 Bloomdale Blo 110.

Swinehart, G. J. (Samantha) 4 ch farmer O 39a 4h 1c RD North Baltimore Hen 98 Ind tel.

Swinehart, Noah farmer T 40a 2h 1c R1 Bloomdale Blo 128.

SWINEHART, O. A. farmer T 159a 11h 5c R1 Bloomdale Blo 110.

Swinehart, S. R. cattle RD Bowling Green Center.

Swinehart, S. W. (Bertha) farmer O 24a 2h 3c R1 Deshler Jac 23 Ind tel.

Swingruber, Jacob (Lizzie) laborer T Second St Grand Rrapids Gr Rs.

SWISHER, WM. E. (Clara) farmer O 83a 5h 7c R1 Weston Mil 76 Ind tel.

Switzer, C. P. (Mollie) 4 ch pumper 1c R1 Rudolph Lib 70 Ind tel.

Switzer, Fred M. (son Nancy) farmer T 5h 20a Longley Per 103 Ind tel.

Switzer, Manerva (dau Nancy) house-keeper Longley Per 103 Ind tel.

Switzer, Nancy farmer O 307a Longley Per 103 Ind tel.

Swope, Mrs. Abraham O H&L Main St Jerry City Por.

Swope, Albert E. (son Enos) student R1 Jerry City Por 74 Ind tel.

Swope, A. C. (Drucilla) 1 ch farmer T 77a 6h 6c R1 Rising Sun Per 96 B tel.

SWOPE, A. T. (Lottie M.) farmer O 80a 4h 4c R1 Jerry City Por 74 Ind tel.

Swope, C. C. (Beatrice) R1 North Baltimore Hen 49.

Swope, C. C. (Harriet) 2 ch farmer O 60a 3h 6c R1 North Baltimore Hen 49.

Swope, Drucilla RD Rising Sun Per.

Swope, D. H. (Caroline) 3 ch farmer O 80a 3h 6c R1 North Baltimore Hen 49.

Swope, Enos (Emma) 4 ch ice dealer & farmer O 40a 2h 3c R1 Jerry City Por 74 Ind tel.

Swope, E. A. (Elizabeth A.) 1 ch farmer O 10a 1h 3c R1 Bradner Mon 61.

Swope, E. L. (Myrtle) 3 ch farmer O 40a 5h 12c R1 North Baltimore Hen 50.

Swope, Guy H. (Faye) farmer T H&L Bronson St Jerry City Por.

SWOPE, H. W. (Bessie) 2 ch tinner & painter O H&L Jerry City Por Ind tel.

Swope, Neil (son A. C.) farmer Rising Sun Per 96 B tel.

Swope, W. A. (Minnie) 2 ch farmer O 80a 2h 8c R1 North Baltimore Hen 48 B tel.

Symmes, C. D. (Rose) 1 ch farmer O 40a 3h 1c R1 Jerry City Por 28 Ind tel.

Symonds, Cora (Nona) 1 ch pumper O H&L 1h 1c Mermill Por 19 Ind tel.

Symonds, Harvey (son Wm.) farmer Mer-Mill Por 13.

Symonds, Roy (son Wm.) teamster Mermill Por 13.

Symonds, Wm. (Helena) farmer T 77a 3h 2c Mermill Por 13.

SYNINGTON, MRS. M. R3 Box 61 Perrysburg.

TABERN, DONALEE Box 236 Portage.

Tabern, Mrs. Louise 1 ch farmer O 80a Portage Por 2 Ind tel.

Taburn, Geo. RD Bowling Green Lib.

Tacker, Frank (Mary) railroad man O H&L Walbridge Lake.

Taft, A. L. Perrysburg Pbg.

Taft, Mrs. Nancy 1 ch ret O H&L Milton Center Mil.

Tague, C. A. (Grace) telegraph operator O H&L Front St Cygnet Blo Ind tel.

Tait, Frank (Margaret) 1 ch farmer T 5a R3 Perrysburg Pbg 124.

Talmage, Clyde L. (son Joe N.) laborer R1 Bloomdale Blo 57 B & Ind tels.

Talmage, Joe N. (Eliza M.) 1 ch oil man pumping 1c R1 Bloomdale Blo 57 B & Ind tels.

Talmage, Martha L. (dau Joe N.) R1 Bloomdale Blo 57 B & Ind tels.

Talmage, Merl C. (son Joe N.) laborer R1 Bloomdale Blo 57 B & Ind tels.

Talmage, W. P. RD North Baltimore Hen.

Talor, Roy drayman & marshal T H&L 1h Fifth St Perrysburg Pbg B tel.

Tanner, Anna RD Dunbridge Mid.

Tanner, Sophia Grand Rapids Gr Rs.

Tape, Amelia Luckey Tro.

Tape, Jno. Luckey Tro.

Tarleton, Bertha boarding house T H&L R3 Pemberville Fre 24.

Tarr, Hallie RD North Baltimore Hen.

Tarr, I. N. RD North Baltimore Hen.

Tarr, J. W. RD North Baltimore Hen.

Taulker, F. H. (Anna K.) garage O H&L Pemberville Fre 40 Ind tel.

Taulker, H. F. (Caroline) ret O H&L Pemberville Fre 60 B tel.

Taulker, Wm. Nellie 2 ch salesman T H&L 1h Pemberville Fre B tel.

Tavenier, George (Frances) 2 ch farmer T 83a 4h 4c R1 Bowling Green Pla 72 Ind tel.

Tavenier, Jacob Portage Lib.

Taverner, Fred Weston Lib.

Taverner, Isaac Weston Lib.

Taylor, Adison (Lena) 7 ch farmer T H&L 1c Jerry City Por 70.

Taylor, Albert (Ruth) 1 ch operator T H&L Walbridge Lake.

TAYLOR, A. (Cora) 3 ch farmer T H&L 3h 1c Millbury Lake 54.

Taylor, A. A. Risingsun Mon.

Taylor, Chas. 1 ch laborer T H&L Sixth St Perrysburg Pbg.

Taylor, George (Jennie) 3 ch civil engineer O 7a R1 Sta A R1 East Toledo Lake 116.

Taylor, Jas. G. RD North Baltimore Hen.

Taylor, J. R. RD North Baltimore Hen.

Taylor, Mary A. RD North Baltimore Hen.

TAYLOR, OSCAR (Helen) 1 ch farmer T 40a 2h 2c R1 Millbury Lake 68 Ind tel.

Taylor, Ray (Sofie) oil worker 2½a H 1h 1c Cygnet Blo 14 Ind tel.

Taylor, Ralph (Cora) 1 ch laborer T H&L Millbury Lake.

Taylor, Rhoda B. RD North Baltimore Hen.

Taylor, Sherman (Dollie) 3 ch maintainer T H&L Millbury Lake.

Taylor, Warren laborer O H&L Rising Sun Mon.

Taylor, Wm. (Mable) 2 ch oil man teamster 2h R1 Jerry City Blo 20 B & Ind tels.

Taylor, Wm. (Ruth) farmer 6h 2c Sandusky St West Millgrove Per.

Taylor, Wm. 4 ch mail carrier T H&L Walbridge Lake.

Teatsorth, Bert (Jane) 1 ch farmer O 40a 5h 5c R1 Hoytsville Jac 64.

Teatsorth, Charley RD North Baltimore Hen.

Teatsorth, Ethel (dau James) housekeeper Hoytsville Jac.

TEATSORTH, FRANK (Lillie) 1 ch farmer O 80a 6h 5c R1 Hoytsville Jac 107 Ind .tel.

Teatsorth, Guy Franklin (son Frank) farm hand R1 Hoytsville Jac 107 Ind tel.

Teatsorth, James (Effie) 1 ch teamster & farmer O H&L 2h Hoytsville Jac.

Tebeau, Eli (Jennie) 4 ch farmer T 78a 3h 1c Bradner Mon 20.

Teegordin, Chas. (Jennie) farmer T 226a 3h 3c Waterville Mid 3 B tel.

Teeple, B. L. (Katherine) 3 ch driller O H&L East St Bradner Mon.

Teeple, C. L. (Pearl) oil man O H&L S Main St Bradner Mon.

Teeple, Mrs. E. J. (Mary) 6 ch O H&L N Main St Bradner Mon.

Tefft, Byron (son R. G.) farmer R2 Prairie Depot Por 118.

Tefft, Ruby (dau R. G.) housekeeper R2 Prairie Depot Por 118.

Tefft, R. G. (Dorcas) 3 ch pumper & farmer O 5a 1h R2 Prairie Depot Por 118.

Teitjen, Fred RD Perrysburg Cen.

Telfer, J. A. (Emly) 2 ch farmer O 20a 2h 2c Prairie Depot Mon 110.

Teller, Chas. (Maggie) 2 ch farmer O 75a 3h 7c Portage Lib 113.

Teller, C. O. (Merta) 3 ch farmer T 40a 2h 1c R1 North Baltimore Hen 47.

Teller, Francis RD Portage Por.

Teller, Jennie (dau Chas.) Portage Lib 113.

Temple, Edward (Charlotte) 1 ch gardening Center St Weston.

Ten Eyck, S. P. (Adaline) 4 ch farmer T 50a 2h 4c R2 North Baltimore Hen 31.

Tennis, Dan (Ollie) carpenter T Grand Rapids Gr Rs.

Tennor, Dale (Elta) 1 ch teamster T H&L Rudolph Lib 96.

Tenny, T. H. Lime City Pbg.

TENPENY, D. A. (Agnes) 1 ch farmer T H&L R1 Weston Pla 10 Ind tel.

THACKER, C. D. 2 ch newstand T H&L Main St Weston.

THAISS, CHAS., JR. (Emma) 2 ch farmer O 78a 3h 4c R1 Perrysburg Pbg 101 Ind tel.

THAISS, JACOB (Sophia) 2 ch farmer O 40a 3h 3c R1 Walbridge Lake 94.

Thaiss, Karl, Sr. R3 Perrysburg Pbg.

Thatcher, Frank R. Walbridge Lake.

THATCHER, H. E. (Effie) 3 ch oil worker T 170a 5h 4c R1 Rudolph Lib 76.

Thatcher, Jess (Bertha) 1 ch farmer O 67a 4h 4c Jerry City Por 73.

Thatcher, S. B. (Neomi Luvern) 1 ch farmer T 105a 4h 2c R1 Deshler Jac 6.

Thatcher, W. S. (Julia) 9 ch farmer T 110a 6h 4c R2 Deshler Jac 4.

THAXTON, MRS. J. R. West Millgrove.

Theis, Jacob Walbridge Lake.

Theise, Jno. F. RD North Baltimore Hen.

Thielen, Barney (Ruth) 1 ch farmer T 80a 3h 2c R1 Weston Mil 71 Ind tel.

Thielen, H. (Gertrude) 2 ch cement works O H&L Custar Mil.

Thielen, Mrs. J. 7 ch ret O H&L Custar Mil.

Thielen, Lena (dau Mrs. J.) asst postmistress Custar Mil.

Thirbly, B. F. (Jessie E.) 4 ch motorman T H&L Front St Perrysburg Pbg.

Thomas, A. A. (Amanda) 4 ch farmer T 77a 5h 2c R1 Hoytsville Jac 124.

THOMAS, A. H. (Gertrude) 1 ch farmer O 20a 4h 7c R2 Fostoria Per 36 Ind tel.

Thomas, C. W. RD Bowling Green Pla.

Thomas, G. J. RD Bowling Green Pla.

Thomas, Harry (Emma) 2 ch glass blower O 2a H Pine St Perrysburg Pbg B tel.

Thomas, Jay W. farmer T 4a R2 Bowling Green Pla 92.

THOMAS, O. W. 2 ch farmer T 82a 4h 1c R2 Bowling Green Pla 63 B & Ind tels.

Thomas, Percy (Nina) mail clerk T H&L Pine St Perrysburg Pbg B tel.

Thomas, W. H. RD North Baltimore Hen.

Thomas, W. T. RD North Baltimore Hen.

213

Thome, Jacob RD North Baltimore Hen.

Thomkins, Mathis (Delia) farmer O 55a 2h 1c R2 Weston Wash 51.

Thompson, Alva (Catherine) 1 ch farmer O 5a 1h 1c R5 Bowling Green Cen 61 Ind tel.

Thompson, Amanda RD North Baltimore Hen.

Thompson, Chas. oil worker Main St Jerry City Por.

Thompson, Clarence W. (Cecile M.) 2 ch farmer T 90a 2h R1 Millbury Lake 120.

Thompson, C. E. (Jennie) 1 ch general store O 70a 1c Main St Jerry City Blo 78 Ind tel.

THOMPSON, EARL R3 Bowling Green.

THOMPSON, EDW. (Pearl) 2 ch farmer T 40a 3h 4c R1 Dunbridge Mid 67 B tel.

Thompson, Eliza ret O H&L Fifth St Perrysburg Pbg.

Thompson, Erwin Dowling Mid.

THOMPSON, E. A. R3 Perrysburg Pbg 157.

THOMPSON, MRS. F. H. farming O 80a 3h 1c R3 Perrysburg Pbg 157.

THOMPSON, H. K. (Della) 1 ch farmer T 154a 5h 10c R1 Rudolph Lib 39 Ind tel.

THOMPSON, JESSE (son Lee T.) RD Bloomdale Blo 115 B & Ind tels.

Thompson, John (Mary) 1 ch laborer O H&L Indiana Ave Perrysburg Pbg.

Thompson, John ret O H&L Fifth St Perrysburg Pbg.

Thompson, J. B. RD North Baltimore Hen.

Thompson, J. H. (Emma) motorman T H&L Main St Jerry City Por.

Thompson, J. J. oil pumper Dunbridge Mid.

THOMPSON, J. L. (Cascindia) 5 ch farmer O 24½a 3h 3c R1 Rudolph Lib 96 Ind tel.

Thompson, Lee (Isa M.) 4 ch farmer T 50a 4h R2 Bloomdale Blo 115 B & Ind tels.

Thompson, L. (Emma) farmer O 90a 4h 3c Woodside Fre 78 Ind tel.

Thompson, L. E. carpenter bds Luckey Tro.

Thompson, L. H. (Etta) 5 ch oil man O Lot 1h 1c R1 North Baltimore Hen 68.

THOMPSON, L. L. (May) 2 ch laborer O H&L Third St Perrysburg Pbg B tel.

THOMPSON, MORRIS (Sarah J.) carpenter O H&L 1c Dunbridge Mid 69.

Thompson, Mrs. Ruth 1 ch T H&L R2 Prairie Depot Por 114.

Thompson, Robt. H. RD North Baltimore Hen.

Thompson, R. C. (Luella) oil pumper T H&L Woodside Fre 78.

Thompson, S. G. RD North Baltimore Hen.

Thompson, T. B. (Lizzie) 4 ch laborer O H&L 1c Maple St Bloomdale Blo.

THOMPSON, WILLIAM (Ellen) 4 ch farmer T H&L R1 Walbridge Lake 4.

Thompson, Worthy (Alice) 6 ch farmer T 100a 5h 1c R4 Bowling Green Cen 96 Ind tel.

THOMPSON, W. L. (Edith) farmer T 100a 4h 3c Woodside Fre 78 Ind tel.

Thorley, T. F. (Anna) 3 ch janitor O H&L Oak & Clark Sts Weston B tel.

Thorlough, William (Leah) 2 ch farmer T 20a 2h 2c R1 Walbridge Lake 99 Ind tel.

THORUS, R. L. (Gertrude) 2 ch telegraph operator O 2a R1 Genoa Lake 84 B tel.

Thornton, Art (Rosalia) 3 ch bakery O H&L Perrysburg Pbg Ind tel.

Thornton, Ben S. Perrysburg Pbg.

Thornton, Mrs. B. ret O 44a R1 Stony Ridge Lake 91 Ind tel.

Thornton, Chester (Cora) ret O H&L Indiana Ave Perrysburg Pbg B tel.

Thornton, Claud (Elizabeth) 1 ch bricklayer T H&L 128 Oak St Rossford Ros.

Thornton, Edward (Minnie) 1 ch mason O H&L Second St Perrysburg Pbg B tel.

Thornton, Elmer (Carrie) 1 ch railroader T H&L Walbridge Lake.

Thornton, Esther (dau John) housekeeper Le Moyne Tro 29 Ind tel.

Thornton, E. C. (Dell) farmer O 80a 5h 5c R2 Haskins Mid 37 B tel.

Thornton, Geo. H. (Loretta) 1 ch farmer T 80a R2 Haskins Mid 37.

Thornton, Halstead farming O 30a 1h 2c R3 Perrysburg Pbg 136.

Thornton, Harry (Cora) 1 ch bricklayer O H&L Indiana Ave Perrysburg Pbg B tel.

Thornton, Hazel (dau John) housekeeper Le Moyne Tro 29 Ind tel.

Thornton, Henry (Emma) 1 ch brick mason O H&L 176 Oak St Rossford Ros.

Thornton, James, Jr. brick mason Box 24 Rossford Ros.

Thornton, James, Sr. (Matilda) brick mason O H&L 176 Oak St Rossford

Thornton, John (Victoria) 10 ch farms & section foreman 3a H&L 1h 1c Le Moyne Tro 29 Ind tel.

Thornton, J. H. 1 ch mason O H&L Front St Perrysburg Pbg B tel.

Thornton, Margaret E. housekeeper T Perrysburg St Perrysburg Pbg 136.

Thornton, Rodger (Mary) 3 ch contractor T 38a 1h 1c R3 Perrysburg Pbg 137.

Thornton, Wm. (Emma) 1 ch hostler T H&L Walbridge Lake.

Thorton, Benjamin (Carrie) 4 ch mason O H&L Sixth St Perrysburg Pbg.

Thorton, Henry (Dora) 4 ch carpenter T H&L Walbridge Lake.

Thoxton, J. R. (May) 1 ch farmer T 200a 2h 2c West Millgrove Per 69.

Thrailkill, J. W. RD North Baltimore Hen.

Thrush, Frank (Lizzie) farmer O 160a 6h 14c R2 North Baltimore Hen 28 Ind tel.

Thurlow, Wm. Walbridge Lake.

Thurman, Gladys (dau I. R.) R1 Rudolph Lib 109 Ind tel.

Thurman, J. R. (Mary) 8 ch farmer T 80a 4h 10c R1 Rudolph Lib 109 Ind tel.

Thurman, Roscoe (son J. R.) R1 Rudolph Lib 109 Ind tel.

Thurston, Mrs. 7 ch ret O H&L 1h Second St Grand Rapids Gr Rs Ind tel.

Thurston, Athun 1 ch president bank O H&L Second St Grand Rapids Gr Rs.

Thurston, Azor (Lulu) 7 ch banker O H&L Grand Rapids Gr Rs B tel.

Tice, J. F. (Susanna) shoe shop O H&L North Baltimore Hen Ind tel.

Tienarend, Fred (son Louis) farm hand Le Moyne Tro 31 Ind tel.

Tienarend, Henry (son Louis) farm hand Le Moyne Tro 31 Ind tel.

Tienarend, Louis (Mary) 7 ch farmer 105a 5h 15c Le Moyne Tro 31 Ind tel.

Tienarend, Louise (dau Louis) housekeeper Le Moyne Tro 31 Ind tel.

Tienarend, Minnie (dau Louis) housekeeper Le Moyne Tro 31 Ind tel.

Tietzen, Fred R3 Perrysburg Pbg.

Tighe, Lucy J. Cygent Blo.

Tilliston, James ret O 15a East St Bradner Mon.

Tillitson, M. E. Bradner Mon.

Tilton, S. E. (Mary) hardware O H&L Prairie Depot Mon B tel.

Tilton, W. R. Prairie Depot Mon.

Timmons, Lemuel Bradner Mon.

TINKCOM, J. J. oil man & pumping T H&L 1h 2c R1 Bloomdale Blo 58 B & Ind tels.

Tinkebinder, Chris (Martha) furniture store O H&L Front St Perrysburg Pbg B tel.

TINNEY, ARTHUR (Sadie) 1 ch engineer T H&L Lime City Pbg 92 B tel.

Tinney, Chas. (Mable) oiler T H&L Lime City Pbg 92 B tel.

Tinney, T. H. (Amelia) farmer O 42a 3h 2c Lime City Pbg 92 B tel.

Tiplady, Robert (Ellen) 1 ch farmer O 60a 4h 8c R1 Millbury Lake 80.

Tippie, Emily Perrysburg Pbg.

Tippie, George W. (Eva) 3 ch laborer T H&L Sycamore St Weston Wes.

Tippin, James (Rosa) 3 ch farmer T 275a 8h 4c R2 Perrysburg Pbg 6.

Tipton, A. E. (Phoebe) 4 ch farmer T 151a 5h 4c R3 Bowling Green Cen 42 Ind tel.

Tipton, Stanley farmer R3 Bowling Green Cen 42 B tel.

Tirk, Estella RD North Baltimore Hen.

TIRK, JESSIE M. RD North Baltimore.

Tirk, Mrs. M. C. RD North Baltimore Jac.

Titkemeier, Anna Pemberville Fre.

Titkemier, Fred (Elizabeth) 2 ch confectionery T H&L Pemberville Fre 40 B tel.

Titkemier, Henry (Nora) 1 ch confectionery T H&L Pemberville Fre 40 B tel.

Tittle, Irwin 2 ch elevator man T H&L Risingsun Mon.

TITUS, O. D. (Belle) 2 ch orange grower O H&L Front St Pemberville Fre 40 Ind tel.

Tober, Henry (Alga) 6 ch farmer O 80a 3h 4c R1 Walbridge Lake 11.

Tobin, D. C. (Mary) manager O H&L Loci St Cygnet Blo.

Todd, Ben L. RD North Baltimore Hen.

Todd, C. W. RD Custar Lib.

TODD, FRANK L. (Gertrude) farmer T 80a 4h 4c R2 Custar Mil 52.

Todd, J. B. Weston Wes.

Todd, Lott (Lucinda) 6 ch T H&L 1c R1 Rudolph Lib 33.

Todd, M. G. RD North Baltimore Hen.

Tolles, A. G. (Laura) 7 ch farmer & thrasher O H&L 3h Silver St Weston.

Tolles, Burt (Flossie) 1 ch farmer T 40a 2h R2 Weston Wash 6 Ind tel.

Tolles, Jay (son A. G.) Silver St Weston.

Tomb, J. (Mary) oil pumper T 39a 1h 2c R1 North Baltimore Hen 109 Ind tel.

Tompkins, Arthur (Lena) 3 ch farmer O 158a 6h 4c R2 Weston Wes 50.

Toole, Walter (Ruth) chemist T H&L 174 Oak St Rossford Ros.

Tooth, Sarah J. ret R1 Box 15 East Toledo Ros 26.

Topel, Albert (Margaret) 2 ch farmer hired man R1 Haskins Mid 54.

Tompkins, A. M. R3 Perrysburg Pbg.

Tompkins, M. RD Weston Wash.

Tonges, Geo. Grand Rapids Gr Rs.

Topping, Charles V. (Carrie A.) 3 ch laborer R1 Bloomdale Blo 61.

Topping, W. S. (Nellie) farmer T 142a 5h 7c R1 Jerry City Blo 62 B & Ind tels.

Toth, Stephen (Trecia) 1 ch bricklayer O H&L 214 Maple St Rossford Ros.

Townsbury, John B. ret T H&L Second St Perrysburg Pbg B tel.

Townsberry, John G. (Florence) shoe clerk T H&L Fourth St Perrysburg Pbg.

TOWNSEND, E. S. (Amelia) farmer O 20a 2h 4c R1 Perrysburg Pbg 103.

Tracy, Ethel Perrysburg St Perrysburg Pbg 135.

Tracy, Laura Perrysburg St Perrysburg Pbg 135.

Tracy, Tom 4 ch blacksmith H&L Union St Cygnet Blo.

Tracy, T. H. (Laurra E.) 1 ch lawyer O 20a Perrysburg St Perrysburg Pbg 135.

Tracy, W. E. (Eva) 3 ch farmer O 172a 7h 45c R1 Millbuty Lake 105 B tel.

Trapp, Geo. Luckey Tro.

Trapp, Henry Luckey Tro.

Trapp, John Luckey Tro.

Trask, C. R. (Grace) 1 ch farmer O 15a 1h 2c R3 Weston Mil 91 Ind tel.

Trauer, Chas. (Elizabeth.) 1 ch farmer T 80a 3h 2c R1 Millbury Lake 112.

Trautman, G. W. (Sadie) 1 ch oil pumper T L R3 North Baltimore Hen 111.

Trautman, Jacob (Barbara) 2 ch ret O H&L Hoytsville Jac.

Traver, Chas. Millbury Lake.

Traver, Edw., Sr. Millbury Lake.

Traver, E. A. Millbury Lake.

Traver, Frank Millbury Lake.

· TRAVER, J. J. (Minnie) 2 ch farmer O 20a 3h 2c R1 Millbury Lake 117.

Traver, Lydie 9 ch housekeeper R1 East Toledo Ros 28 Ind tel.

Treft, Elizabeth RD North Baltimore Hen.

Trembly, Miss Edith bookkeeper bds with Z. V. Blain R1 Box 25 East Toledo Ros 30 Ind tel.

Trenh, Louis (Henrietta) 2 ch laborer 8a H 2h 1c Cherry St Perrysburg Pbg B tel.

Trepanier, L. A. Dunbridge Mid.

Trepanier, P. D. Dunbridge Mid.

Tresher, Laura ret O H&L Fifth St Perrysburg Pbg.

Treuschal, C. W. R1 Perrysburg Pbg.

Trombly, Ed. (Emily) laborer O H&L Main St Perrysburg Pbg.

Trowbridge, Geo. M. (Barbara) 2 ch farmer O 80a 3h 8c R1 Lime City Pbg 50 Ind tel.

Trowbridge, Mrs. Sarah Lime City Pbg.

Troxel, H. W. Bloomdale Blo.

Troy, Thos. H. Perrysburg Pbg.

Troyier, J. A. (Myrtle) 2 ch collector T H&L Main & Sixth Sts Perrysburg Pbg B tel.

Trudeau, C. B. (Myra) barber O H&L Front St Perrysburg Pbg B tel.

Trudel, John, Jr. (Flossie M.) 1 ch farmer T 106a 4h 3c R2 Prairie Depot Por 1.

Truman, E. A. (Clara) farmer O 215a 5h 28c R1 Stony Ridge Tro 31 Ind tel.

Truman, Frank carpenter T H&L Le Moyne Tro.

Truman, Geo. E. (Susan) 5 ch farmer O 80a 2h 3c R1 Le Moyne Tro 32.

Truman, J. D. (Lora) 2 ch farmer O 60a 4h 6c R1 Le Moyne Lake 85 B tel.

Truman, J. D. Stony Ridge Lake.

Truman, Mrs. Mary ret R1 Stony Ridge Tro 31 Ind tel.

Trumbull, C. E. (Mabel) 3 ch prop blacksmith shop O H&L Milton Center Mil.

Trumbull, C. R. (Blanch) 3 ch blacksmith O H&L Silver St Weston.

Trump, Amos (Agnes) furniture clerk O furniture store Box 441 Rossford Ros B tel.

Trumpy, Frank (Hattie) 3 ch ditcher O H&L Seventh & Pine Sts Perrysburg Pbg B tel.

Trup, Geo. (Mary) 1 ch laborer O H&L Luckey Tro Ind tel.

Trutt, J. A. (Ellen) 3 ch farmer & contractor O 40a 1h 7c R1 Deshler Jac 45 B tel.

Tubbs, Howard oil worker R1 Bowling Green Lib 51 B tel.

Tucker, Homer Tontogany Wash.

TUCKER, RAY (Bertha) 4 ch farmer hired man R3 Perrysburg Pbg 74.

Tuller, Charlie (Elizabeth) laborer O 2H&L Grand Rapids Gr Rs.

Tuller, Joe (Mary) plumber O H&L Sixth St Perrysburg Pbg B tel.

Turley, H. W. (R. N.) 1 ch farmer O 120a 3h 2c R2 Bloomdale Per 59.

Turley, J. W. (Jennie) 4 ch farmer O 80a 4h 3c R2 Fostoria Per 40.

Turner, A. W. RD North Baltimore Hen.

Turner, Columbus (Minnie) 1 ch school teacher T H&L Maple St Bloomdale Blo B & Ind tels.

Turner, Geo. (Ella) 3 ch farmer T 80a 4h 4c R2 Prairie Depot Por 83.

TURNER, H. H. electrical engineer bds Custar Mil.

Turner, Raymond art student Maple St Bloomdale Blo B &Ind tels.

Turton, Mordecai RD Rudolph Lib.

Tuttle, Bradford (Emma) 4 ch laborer O H&L 1c R1 Prairie Depot Mon 111.

Tuttle, Ben B. (Minnie) boot & shoe repairing Main St Bloomdale Blo.

Tuttle, Emma Prairie Depot Mon.

Tuttle, F. L. (Ennia) 5 ch oil worker T H&L Rudolph Lib 94.

Tuttle, Ralph laborer R1 Prairie Depot Mon 111.

Twining, Edith Haskins Mid.

TWINING, G. R. (Luella) 2 ch farmer T 104a 5h 3c R1 Perrysburg Pbg 103 B tel.

TYLER, A. (May) general merchandise O H&L 2h Walbridge Lake. See adv.

Tyler, Charles (Anna) 1 ch farmer O 78a 4h 3c R2 Bowling Green Wash 34 Ind tel.

Tyler, Chas. H. Weston Mil.

Tyler, E. J. RD North Baltimore Hen.

Tyler, Geo. 1 ch farmer O 170a 6h 3c R1 Bowling Green Pla 54 Ind tel.

Tyler, Mary A. O 40a Walbridge St Walbridge Lake 119.

Tyler, Mrs. P. E. Dunbridge Mid.

Tyler, Wm. (Belle) 2 ch farmer O 40a 2h 10c R2 Bowling Green Pla 49 Ind tel.

Tyner, A. R. (Christina) 4 ch clerk in store O H&L Hoytsville Jac.

Tyner, Cathryn Corp St Portage Por.

Tyner, Clyde (O l a) mason O H&L Hoytsville Jac.

TYNER, DAVID (Mary) farmer T 120a 1h R1 Hoytsville Jac 58.

Tyner, Harl (Annie) 1 ch farmer T 40a 2h 1c R3 North Baltimore Blo 20 B & Ind tels.

Tyner, Leroy V. (May) laborer O H&L Findlay St Portage Por 2.

Tyner, Mary Hoytsville Jac.

Tyner, Mrs. Myrtle Hoytsville Jac.

Tyner, Wm. (Mary) 3 ch laborer O H&L Hoytsville Jac.

Tyson, Almina (dau Wm.) teacher R3 Prairie Depot Por 115.

Tyson, Calvin (Marie) 1 ch laborer O H&L 1h 1c R2 Prairie Depot Por 114.

Tyson, C. D. (Lillian D.) 6 ch painter O H&L 1h 1c Prairie Depot Mon B tel.

Tyson, D. K. (Angeline) 10 ch rct O H&L 1h R2 Prairie Depot Mon 99.

Tyson, Floyd (Edith) 2 ch contractor T H&L 1h Prairie Depot Mon.

Tyson, Geo. K. (Maggie A.) 2 ch carpet weaver O H&L 1h 1c R3 Prairie Depot Por 111.

Tyson, Geo. W. RD Rudolph Lib.

Tyson, H. H. (Mary L.) 3 ch thrasher O 12a 2h 1c R3 Prairie Depot Mon 99.

Tyson, H. L. (Rosella) 4 ch farmer T 50a 3h 5c R3 Prairie Depot Mon 94.

Tyson, L. W. (Bessie) 3 ch oil worker O H&L 1h 1c Rudolph Lib 81.

Tyson, Milo A. (son Wm.) student R3 Prairie Depot Por 115.

Tyson, O. J. oil worker 2h R2 Prairie Depot Mon 99.

TYSON, S. E. Bradner.

TYSON, WM. (Eliza) 3 ch farmer O 60a 7h 5c R3 Prairie Depot Por 115.

Tyson, W. F. (Mary) 1 ch pumper T H&L Stahl St Bradner Mon.

Uhlman, F. W. RD North Baltimore Hen.

Uhlman, H. C. Weston Wes.

Ulis, Pert (Mary) farmer T 104a 3h 2c R1 Portage Por 91.

Ulis, Wm. F. (Mary) 1 ch farmer O 40a 2h 3c R1 Portage Por 91.

Ulrich, Frank (Ida) 5 ch laborer O H&L Sixth St Perrysburg Pbg B tel.

Ulsh, Claud (Maggie) 2 ch oil man O H&L Risingsun Mon.

Ulsh, L. F. RD North Baltimore Hen.

Underhill, Mary ret O H&L Front St Perrysburg Pbg B tel.

Underwood, A. (Eula) farmer 120a R1 Weston Lib 3 Ind tel.

Underwood, H. A. (Emma) 2 ch farmer O 40a 2h 4c R4 Bowling Green Cen 33 Ind tel.

Underwood, Irwin Weston Wes.

Underwood, J. L. (Adella) farmer & elevator manager O 16a 1h 1c Center Wes Ind tel.

Underwood, Sam (Mabel) 1 ch section hand T H&L Custar Mil.

Unkart, Geo. Weston Wash.

Unkart, W. M. RD Weston Wash.

Updegraff, C. J. (Hattie) carpenter O 80a 3h 2c R3 Prairie Depot Por 119 Ind tel.

UPDEGRAFF, J. R. (Bertha) 1 ch farmer T 83a 2h 3c R3 Prairie Depot Por 119 Ind tel.

UPDEGRAFF, O. W. (Ida) farmer T 23a 1h 1c R1 Jerry City Por 76.

Updike, Dan Cygnet Blo.

URBAN, W. M. (Myrtle) 5 ch farmer T 140a 4h 1c RD North Baltimore Hen 65.

Urie, Geo. W. Bloomdale Blo.

Urie, Mrs. Lizzie Bloomdale Blo.

Urie, M. T. (Della) ret O H&L Main St Bloomdale Blo B & Ind tels.

Urshalk, Peter (Sarah) 5 ch ret O H&L 1h 3c Risingsun Mon.

Uthoff, Henry (Alta) 4 ch cigar manufacturer O H&3Lots 1c Main & Sixth Sts Perrysburg Pbg B tel.

Uthoff, Henry (Martha) farmer T 59a R1 Luckey Tro 68 Ind tel.

Uthoff, Wm. (Martha) 2 ch cigarmaker O 1a H Walnut St Perrysburg Pbg B tel.

Utter, Jesse (Alta) chauffeur R1 East Toledo Ros 26 Ind tel.

Utter, Ralph Hoytsville Jac.

Vail, S. (Lucy) 3 ch carpenter O 5a 1c R5 Bowling Green Cen 23 Ind tel.

Vail, T. H. (Emma) 3 ch farmer O 115a 9c R1 Bradner Fre 92.

Valentine, Amos (son Etta Irene) clerk Second St Portage Por.

Valentine, Susie (dau Etta Irene) housekeener Second St Portage Por.

Valerius, Nick (Clara) 4 ch garage T H&L Grand Rapids Gr Rs Ind tel.

VAN BRIMER, C. L. RD North Baltimore.

Van Buskirk, N. T. (Edith) 3 ch conductor T H&L Elm St Perrysburg Pbg.

Van Camp, Abner (Nellie) 1 ch barber T Luckey Tro.

Van Camp, Fred (Emma) 8 ch farmer O 30a 3h 10c R1 Le Moyne Tro 85 B tel.

VAN CAMP, L. (Bertha) 2 ch laborer T H&L Luckey Web 91.

Van Camp, Merril (son Fred) farm hand R1 Le Moyne Troy 85 B tel.

Van Camp, R. L. (Elizabeth) 8 ch O 31a H&L 1c Le Moyne Tro.

Vance, L. W. (Florence) 1 ch oil worker T H&L 1h 1c R1 Portage Lib 59.

Vancodter, Clay (Katie) 8 ch laborer T H&L Hoytsville Jac.

Vancodter, Garrett Francis (son Clay) laborer Hoytsville Jac.

Vancodter, Wm. C. (son Clay) laborer Hoytsville Jac.

Vandala, Mrs. O H&L Grand Rapids Gr Rs.

Vanderbrook, A. L. (Reva) foreman T H&L Second St Perrysburg Pbg.

Vandersall, H. E. Hoytsville Hen.

Vandersoll, C. H. Perrysburg Pbg.

Vandorf, Julius 6 ch farmer T 77a 4h 1c R2 Perrysburg Mid 5 B tel.

Van Dorn, G. M. (Elsba) 4 ch farmer T 120a 4h 6c Hoytsville Jac 114 Ind tel.

Van Dorn, Ruth (dau G. M.) student Hoytsville Jac 114 Ind tel.

Van Eman, John ret O H&L Main St Bloomdale Blo B & Ind tels.

Van Ewegan, Gilbert RD Dunbridge Mid.

Van Ewegan, Jno. RD Dunbridge Mid.

VanGycke, Chas. laborer R1 Walbridge Lake 18.

Van Helen, C. H. Perrysburg Pbg.

Van Horn, Austin RD Bowling Green Jac.

Van Horn, Isaac (Elizabeth) O 55a 1h 2c R1 Grand Rapids Gr Rs 9 Ind tel.

Van Horn, J. A. (Ida I.) 4 ch farmer T 27a 6h 2c R1 Deshler Jac 12 B tel.

Van Norman, Chas. (Clara) 1 ch traveling man O H&L Third St Perrysburg Pbg B tel.

Van Norman, Harry Perrysburg Pbg.

Van Pelt, Dr. H. F. (Ella) 3 ch O H&L East St Bradner Mon B tel.

Van Pelt, Leslie clerk bds at S. Dacen 183 Oak St Rossford Ros.

Vanschooter, W. H. laborer T Haskins Mid.

Van Scoder, Elzada (dau Wm.) housekeeper Haskins Wash 95.

Van Scoder, Wm. (Mary) 4 ch laborer O H&L Haskins Wash 95.

Van Tassel, Laura (dau Martha) nurse R2 Wes Wash 53 Ind tel.

Van Tassel, Lula (dau Martha) housekeeper R2 Weston Wash 53 Ind tel.

VAN TASSEL, MARTHA H. O 30a R2 Weston Wash 53 Ind tel.

Van Tine, C. H. East Toledo Lake.

Vanvalkenberg, Ethel Bell Perrysburg St Perrysburg Pbg 135.

Vanvalkenberg, Isabelle V. Perrysburg St Perrysburg Pbg 135 B tel.

Vanvalkenberg, J. B. (R. L.) stonemason O 2a 1c Perrysburg St Perrysburg Pbg 135.

VAN VALKENBERG, J. M. (Minnie) restaurant & millinery O H&L Grand Rapids Gr Rs Ind tel.

Van Voorhis, I. N. Prairie Depot Mon.

Vanvorce, C. B. (Elizabeth) 2 ch farmer T 160a 3h 2c R1 North Baltimore Hen 118.

Van Vorce, J. R. (Ida) 5 ch ret O 122a H&3Lots 1c Ash St Weston Ind tel.

Van Vorhis, A. Weston Wes.

Van Vorhis, I. N. (Lucy) 7 ch farmer O 100a 8h 3c R3 Prairie Depot Mon 4.

Van Wagoner, W. I. Tontogany Wash.

Varague, F. A. Millbury Lake.

Vedder, A. C. (Lucy) 2 ch ret O H&L Taylor St Weston B tel.

Veitch, Anna artist O H&L Fourth St Perrysburg Pbg.

VEITCH, W. J. (Gertrude) 1 ch dry goods store O H&L Perrysburg Pbg B tel.

Venia, Harvey (Lyda) 5 ch gardener O 20a 1217 Miami St East Toledo Ros 14.

Veour, Nic RD Haskins Mid.

Vermilya, Miss Bertha (dau H. A.) school teacher R1 Haskins Mid 57.

VERMILYA, H. A. (Emma) 2 ch farmer O 170a 7h 5c R1 Haskins Mid 57 Ind tel.

Vermilya, L. W. (Ethel) 1 ch cashier T H&L 1h Haskins Mid 25.

VESTAL, CHAS. W. (Agnes) 1 ch hired man R3 Perrysburg Pbg 74.

Vetter, Arthur (son Geo.) farmer R1 Perrysburg Pbg 96.

Vetter, F. E. (Anna) 1 ch farmer O 75a 3h 3c R2 Dunbridge Mid 61 B tel.

Vetter, Geo. (Caroline) 1 ch farmer O 80a 4h 5c R1 Perrysburg Pbg 96.

Vetter, William (Nellie) 2 ch farmer T 160a 4h 2c R1 Walbridge Lake 134 B tel.

Vickers, Geo. H. Walbridge Lake.

Vincent, Sam'l Pemberville Fre.

Vine, James (Mary) 2 ch farmer O 60a 2h 6c R1 Millbury Lake 80.

Vinyard, A. E. (Mary I.) 1 ch barber O shop H&L Main St West Millgrove Per.

Vogel, Geo. (Susan D.) 3 ch ret O H&L Custar Mil.

Vogel, V. V. RD Rudolph.

Vogelsong, A. W. (Jane) 2 ch carpenter O H&L Prairie Depot Mon.

Vogelsong, Henry (Elizabeth) 2 ch painter & paperhanger O H&L Risingsun Mon.

VOGLE, V. V. (Allie) 2 ch farmer O 40a 4h 7c R1 Rudolph Lib 70 Ind tel.

Vogt, Sam'l Pemberville Fre.

VOLAND, C. (Ada) 5 ch farmer O 90a 4h 3c R1 Perrysburg Pbg 103 B tel.

Voland, Lou Hoytsville Jac.

Vollmar, Annie C. Grand Rapids Gr Rs.

Vollmar, Chas. RD Haskins Mid.

Volhmar, Don (Glenna) laborer T H&L Haskins Mid.

VOLLMAR, E. R1 Tontogany.

Vollmar, Fred RD Haskins Mid.

Vollmar, Henry (Annie) 3 ch farmer T 80a 5h 7c R1 Grand Rapids Gr Rs 33 Ind tel.

Vollmar, Jake (Elizabeth) farmer O 110a 3h 10c R2 Haskins Wash 78 B tel.

Vollmer, Bertha housekeeper R2 Haskins Wash 78..

Vollmer, Fred (Phoebe) 7 ch farmer O 60a 4h 2c R1 Tontogany Wash 80.

Vollmer, Geo. (Mary) ret O 200a R1 Tontogany Wash 81 Ind tel.

VOLLMER, JOHN (Elizabeth) thresher T 20a R1 Tontogany Wash 80.

Vollmer, Lew (Louisa) 7 ch farmer T H&L 6h 7c R1 Tontogany Wash 81.

Vollmer, Roy farmer R2 Haskins Wash 78.

Von Ahrens, Geo. RD North Baltimore Hen.

Vonderkall, Gilbert (Helen) 1 ch glass worker T H&L 246 Maple St Rossford Ros.

Von Vallsenberg, R. L. Perrysburg Pbg.

Vosburg, Irvin (Mina) 2 ch farmer T H&L 1h 1c R1 Portage Por 83 Ind tel.

Vosburg, John (Mary) farmer O 100a 2h 2c R1 Portage Por 55 Ind tel.

Wachter, Chas. F. (Grace C.) clerk T 1h 1c East Toledo Ros 18 Ind tel.

Wachter, Mrs. Clara F. ret O 7a East Toledo Ros 18 Ind tel.

Wachter, Harvey C. (Hazel) 2 ch draftsman East Toledo Ros 18 Ind tel.

Wade, Abbey (wife Wilson) 20a R1 Grand Rapids Wash 52.

Wade, Alva (Minnie) 2 ch farmer O 64a 2h R2 Weston Wes 32 Ind tel.

Wade, E. E. (Maud) 2 ch farmer O 58a 3h 3c R2 Weston Wes 24 Ind tel.

WADE, F. J. (Olive) 5 ch farming O 70a 2h 3c R2 Weston Wes 22.

WADE, I. N. (Cassandra) 1 ch farmer O 50a 4h 10c R1 Grand Rapids Wash 63 Ind tel.

Wade, James (Maude) 1 ch farmer O 37a 3h 2c R1 Grand Rapids Wash 58 Ind tel.

Wade, J. K. (Nellie) 1 ch oil pumper O 3a 2h 2c R1 North Baltimore Hen 124.

Wade, J. P. (Cathern) farmer O 10a 2h 3c R2 Weston Wes 31.

Wade, J. W. Grand Rapids Gr Rs.

Wade, Leroy (Frances) 2 ch farmer T 80a 3h 6c R1 Fostoria Per 122.

Wade, Louisa (wid J. I.) 1 ch farming O 73a 4h 9c R2 Weston Wes 32 Ind tel.

Wade, M. H. RD Rudolph Lib.

WADE, O. G. (Sally) farming O 60a 1h 2c R2 Weston Wes 46 Ind tel.

Wade, Wilson (Abbey) 1 ch farmer O 40a 2h 2c R1 Grand Rapids Wash 52 Ind tel.

Wadsworth, Katy ret O 160a H&L Hoytsville Jac B tel.

Waegman, Lucy housekeeper O H&L R2 Pemberville Web 30.

Waffle, LeRoy (Bessie) 1 ch motorman T H&L Front St Perrysburg Pbg.

Waggoner, Corvin 1c farmer & merchant O 50a 3h R1 Stony Ridge Tro 7 Ind tel.

WAGGONER, FRANK (Estella) 7 ch farmer T 97a 5h 1c R1 Walbridge Lake 11 Ind tel.

Waggoner, Velma (dau Frank) teacher R1 Walbridge Lake 11 Ind tel.

Waggoner, W. H. (Rachel) 4 ch farmer O 55a 3h 4c R3 Perrysburg Pbg 87 Ind tel.

Waggoner, W. W. (Minnie) oil man O L R1 North Baltimore Hen 69 B tel.

Wagler, Lawrence A. (son L. A.) farm hand R1 Deshler Jac 37 B tel.

Wagler, Lima A. (dau L. A.) music teacher R1 Deshler Jac 37 B tel.

Wagler, L. A. (Augusta E.) 6 ch farmer T 120a 5h 3c R1 Deshler Jac 37 B tel.

Wagner, A. (Alta) 2 ch farmer T 45a 2h 1c R2 Bowling Green Cen 5.

Wagner, A. C. (Ellie) 3 ch farmer O 80a 7h 4c R2 Custar Mil 48 Ind tel.

Wagner, C. F. RD Portage Lib.

Wagner, C. M. (May) 7 ch farmer T 160a 8h 3c R1 Portage Lib 83 Ind tel.

WAGNER, DELL harnessmaker O RD North Baltimore Ind tel. See adv.

WAGNER, EDWARD (Alice) farming O 96a H&L Hoytsville Jac.

Wagner, Fletch (Nettie) 7 ch farmer T 15h 5c R2 Pemberville Web 44 B tel.

Wagner, F. J. (Ottilie) 3 ch farmer O 160a 8h 2c R2 Dunbridge Mid 82.

Wagner, Hamly (Estella) 3 ch farmer O 40a 2h 1c R1 Hoytsville Jac 70 Ind tel.

Wagner, John H. (Lydia) boarding House O H&L 1c Main St Bairdstown Blo B & Ind tels.

Wagner, J. (Mary) 3 ch laborer O H&L R1 Rudolph Lib 77.

Wagner, Mat Custar Mil.

Wagner, Mike (Annie) 8 ch farmer & thresher T 95a 5h 5c R1 Custar Mil 19 B tel.

Wagner, Peter farm hand R1 Custar Mil 19.

WAGNER, RAY (Alta) 1 ch farmer T 40a 2h R1 Hoytsville Jac 75.

Wagner, Volney (May) 1 ch railroad man T H&L Walbridge Lake.

Wagoner, Alfred laborer Stony Ridge Tro.

Wagoner, Alice T H&L Stony Ridge Tro.

WAGONER, ANTHONY (Addie) farmer O 60a 1h R1 Walbridge Lake 10 Ind tel.

Wagoner, Audrey E. (dau S. E.) R1 Lime City Pbg 54.

Wagoner, Chas. E. (Mary) farmer & agent 1a H&L R1 Stony Ridge Tro 7 Ind tel.

Wagoner, Clarence (Edith) 2 ch farmer O 64a 2h 6c R1 Le Moyne Tro 82 Ind tel.

Wagoner, Earl F. (Celeste) farmer O 16a 1h R1 Walbridge Lake 3.

Wagoner, Geo. Stony Ridge Lake.

Wagoner, Harrison bartender Stony Ridge Tro.

Wagoner, Henry (Rosie) 4 ch farmer O 45a 3h 4c R1 Walbridge Lake 100 Ind tel.

Wagoner, Ira B. farmer O 47a 2h 3c R1 Walbridge Lake 25.

Wagoner, Jake RD Bowling Green Web.

WAGONER, JAMES (Frances) 2 ch carpenter O Stony Ridge Tro.

Wagoner, Lester (son W. W.) R1 Stony Ridge Lake 31 Ind tel.

Wagoner, Mrs. Lizzie ret O 110a R1 Walbridge Lake 27 B tel.

Wagoner, Lola F. (dau W. W.) R1 Stony Ridge Lake 31 Ind tel.

Wagoner, Mary Stony Ridge Tro.

Wagoner, Melvin (Rose) farmer T 4h 10c R1 Walbridge Lake 27 B tel.

Wagoner, Merle (son Mrs. Lizzie) carpenter R1 Walbridge Lake 27 B tel.

Wagoner, S. E. (Correl E.) 2 ch farmer O 30a 2h 2c R1 Lime City Pbg 59 Ind tel.

Wagoner, W. W. (Ella) 1 ch farmer O 84a 4h 6c R1 Stony Ridge Lake 31 Ind tel.

Wahler, W. E. RD North Baltimore Hen.

Wakeman, H. C. (Bessie) 1 ch school teacher T H&L Hatton Per 84.

Walbolt, H. G. (son S. B.) traveling salesman Waterville Mid 20.

WALBOLT, JNO. G. (Anna) 2 ch farmer T 100a 6h 2c R2 Haskins Mid 19 B tel.

Walbolt, S. B. (Elizabeth) 1 ch farmer O 108a 4h 15c Waterville Mid 20 B tel.

Walden, Elmer (Gertrude) 2 ch farmer T 80a 5h 7c R1 Deshler Jac 35.

Walden, Ollie (Pearl) 2 ch stone road worker T H&L Custar Mil.

Walden, Mrs. Sarah 3 ch farmer O 80a R1 Deshler Jac 35.

Walden, Wesley W. Weston Lib.

Walerius, Eva housekeeper R2 Deshler Jac 1.

Walerius, Peter (Barbara) 10 ch farmer O 67a 5h 5c R2 Deshler Jac 1.

Walerius, William (Eva) 8 ch farmer 42a 1h 2c Custar Mil 18.

Wales, J. W. (Clara) 2 ch machinist O H&L Verango St Cygnet Blo.

Wales, W. H. (Anna) 3 ch oil producer O oil wells R1 Rudolph Lib 70.

Walk, A. J. Corp St Jerry City Por.

Walker, Clayton (Alta) 2 ch oil worker T H&L R1 Rudolph Por 24½.

WALKER, C: S. 5 ch farmer T 160a 7h 4c R1 Haskins Mid 51 B tel.

Walker, Ethel housekeeper R1 Rudolph Por Ind tel.

WALKER, JAMES (Celia) 1 ch farmer T 140a 7h 2c R1 Haskins Mid 53 B tel.

Walker, James (Sofarona) pumper O 2a H&L R1 Rudolph Por 24½ Ind tel.

Walker, Mrs. Jennie ret T H&L Pemberville Fre.

Walker, John (Iola) 1 ch lineman T H&L Evans St Bradner Mon.

Walker, J. B. (Amanda) 1 ch laborer O 2a H 1c Pine St Perrysburg Pbg B tel.

Walker, Lillian H. housekeeper Grand Rapids Gr Rs Ind tel.

Walker, Mrs. Louise Perrysburg Pbg.

Walker, Mattie 4 ch T H&L Second St Portage Por.

Walker, Mrs. Rachel T H&L Main St Weston B tel.

Walker, Weldon carbon worker Evans St Bradner Mon.

Walker, Wm. (Martha) 4 ch farmer O 40a 2h 1c R3 Bowling Green Cen 17.

Wall, Arnold RD Hoytsville Jac.

Wall, F. M. (Hattie L.) 5 ch grocery & meats O H&L Hoytsville Jac B tel.

Wall, George (Mary) 2 ch farmer T 80a 4h 2c Tontogany Wash 43 Ind tel.

Wall, H. E. Hoytville Jac.

Wall, Parley H. Hoytsville Jac.

Wallace, A. E. (Mabel) farmer O 103a 4h 6c R2 Pemberville Web 31 & 34.

WALLACE, CHAS. 1 ch blacksmith O H&L Front St Perrysburg Pbg B tel.

WALLACE, FRANK (Gertrude) 3 ch elevator man T H&L 1c Sugar Ridge Mid 63 Ind tel.

WALLACE, FRED W. (Alma) 4 ch farmer T 100a 4h 3c Mermill Por 20.

Wallace, Geo. laborer T H&L R1 Genoa Lake 45.

Wallace, George ret R2 Pemberville Web 31 & 34.

Wallace, James (Mary) 3 ch farmer T H&L R1 Walbridge Lake 8.

Wallace, Marjorie housekeeper R2 Pemberville Web 31 & 34.

Wallace, Ralph farmer R2 Pemberville Web 31 & 34.

Wallace, Wm. (Mamie) ret O 100a 1h 2c R1 Fostoria Per 91.

Walling, S. B. (M. M.) farming O 2a 1h R2 Weston Wes 24.

Walling, William (Adaline) 4 ch ret O 46a H&L Main St Wes Ind tel.

Walsh, M. J. Cygnet Blo.

WALSTON, PERRY (Tekla) 4 ch farmer O 198a 4h 9c R1 Pemberville Fre 55 B tel.

WALSWORTH, EARL laborer T H&L 1h R1 Tontogany Wash 22 & 23 Ind tel.

Walter, Carl Pemberville Fre.

Walter, G. Perrysburg Pbg.

Walter, J. F. (Edith) 5 ch station agent T H&L Hoytsville Jac B tel.

Walters, Elizabeth dry goods & notions O H&L Grand Rapids Gr Rs Ind tel.

Walters, Joe (Daisy) 3 ch oil worker T H&L Portage Lib 113.

Walters, Joseph laborer R1 Stony Ridge Tro 31 Ind tel.

WALTERS, J. M. (Donna) 1 ch driller T H&L 1h Water St Portage Por.

Walters, Mary ret O H&L Sixth St Perrysburg Pbg.

Walters, Michael (Sarah) ret T H&L Rising Sun Mon.

Walters, T. C. (Ida) 4 ch farmer T 58a 3h 8c R3 Prairie Depot Mon 12.

Walters, Mrs. Violet 1 ch dry goods & notions O H&L Grand Rapids Gr Rs Ind tel.

Walters, Wm. laborer H&L Hatton Per 84.

Walters, Wm. (Emma) farmer O 2a 1c R1 Fostoria Per 91.

Waltz, Jay A. (Eva A.) 1 ch abstracter O H&L Main St Weston.

Wan, Helen (dau T. F.) teacher R2 Bowling Green Web 20.

Wan, Howard (son T. F.) farmer R5 Bowling Green Web 20.

Wan, Ronald (son T. F.) farmer R5 Bowling Green Web 20.

Wan, T. F. (Martha) farmer O 200a 14h 2c R5 Bowling Green Web 20 B tel.

Wansetler, John (Mary) 12 ch farmer T 160a 6h 2c Cygnet Blo 19 Ind tel.

Wansitler, Elias M. (Murrel A.) 1 ch farmer T 80a 2h 2c Cygnet Blo 60 B & Ind tels.

Ward, C. E. (Ella) 3 ch confectionery & barber shop O H&L Walbridge Lake.

Ward, D. A. farmer T 41½a 3h 1c R1 Prairie Depot Mon 35.

WARD, ERWIN, SR. Box 88 Perrysburg.

Ward, Floyd (Effie) 1 ch farmer O 40a 2h 3c R1 Jerry City Por 62.

WARD, DR. HARLEY E. (Jennie T.) 5 ch physician O H&L 1c Pemberville Fre 4 B tel. See adv.

Ward, Hiram RD Bowling Green Cen.

Ward, I. E. RD Dunbridge Mid.

Ward, L. A. RD Dunbridge Mid.

Ward, Mary A. Perrysburg Pbg.

WARD, O. W. (Flora) 3 ch farmer O 80a 6h 4c R4 Bowling Green Cen 114 Ind tel.

Warden, Delbert truck farmer O 3a Caldwell St Bradner Mon B tel.

Warden, G. S. Pemberville Fre.

Warden, M. W. (Dora) 2 ch gardener O 5a 1h E Caldwell St Bradner Mon 23.

Warden, Ruth H. Bradner Mon.

Warden, Samuel RD Portage Por.

Warder, W. O. (Effie) 4 ch laborer RD Rudolph Lib 37.

Warner, Chas. (Louisa) 1 ch pumper T H&L Findlay St Portage Por.

Warner, C. C. (Mary Florence) 3 ch farmer O 50a 3h 3c R4 Deshler Jac 19 Ind tel.

Warner, Edgar Grand Rapids Gr Rs.

Warner, Edward (Nettie) photographer O 4a Grand Rapids Gr Rs Ind tel.

Warner Elliot M. ret O 3a Rossford Ros.

Warner, Herbert (Cora) 1 ch pumper T H&L Prairie Depot Mon.

Warner, H. A. Bloomdale Blo.

Warner, H. H. (Estella) 4 ch farmer O 860a 5h 6c R1 Grand Rapids Gr Rs 17 Ind tel.

Warner, Otis A. (Priscilla) 1 ch glass worker O H&L 213 Maple St Rossford Ros.

Warner, Peter (Mary) oil worker O H&L Rudolph Lib 94 Ind tel.

Warns, Anna C. (dau B. F.) housekeeper R1 Lime City Pbg 55.

Warns, Antone J. (Sophia) 3 ch farmer O 82a 5h 9c R1 Perrysburg Pbg 28 B tel.

WARNS, A. (Carrie) 3 ch farmer O 30a 3h 1c R1 Lime City Pbg 54 B tel.

Warns, B. F. (Catharine) ret O127a 2h 2c R1 Lime City Pbg 55.

Warns, B. M. Lime City Pbg.

Warns, Ivan (Mabel) 1 ch stock dealer O 50a 1h 10c Lime City Pbg 121.

Warns, John F. (Amelia) 5 ch farmer O 80a 2h 18c R1 Stony Ridge Tro 31 Ind tel.

Warns, Katharine D. (dau B. F.) housekeeper R1 Lime City Pbg 55.

Warns, Reuben Dunbridge Web.

Warns, W. P. (Dora) 7 ch farmer O 53a 6h 4c R1 Lime City Pbg 55.

Warren, H. R. (Maude) 1 ch barber O H & shop Front St Pemberville Fre.

Warren, Thomas (Sarah) farmer T H&L 1h 1c R1 Lime City Pbg 116.

Wasserman, Fred (Carrie) 2 ch farmer O 60a 4h 8c Station A East Toledo Ros 31.

Wasserman, William (son Fred) 2h Station A East Toledo Ros 31.

Wasso, Louie fireman Luckey Tro Ind tel.

Waters, Sylvester (Chloe) 5 ch farmer T 140a 4h 19c R1 Prairie Depot Mon 83

Watkins, Gackel Weston Wes.

WATKINS, W. C. (Maude M.) 1 ch furniture & undertaking T H&L Weston Wes B & Ind tels. See adv.

Watson, C. C. (Laura) 4 ch oil pumper T R1 Rudolph Hen 64.

WATSON, FINLEY Cygnet.

Watson, Fred (Mary) genearl T H&L Second St Portage Por.

Watson, F. H. (Cora) 3 ch carpenter T H&L 1h 1c R2 Bowling Green Cen 11 Ind tel.

Watson, Wm. (Mary) blacksmith O Second St Portage Por.

Watson, Wm. (Sadie) 3 ch laborer O H&L Prairie Depot Mon.

WATSON, W. E. (Lizzie) 5 ch farm foreman O 17a 2h 3c R3 Prairie Depot Mon 50 B tel.

Watt, John farmer T 120a 4h 4c R1 Prairie Depot Mon 44.

Watters, S. M. Prairie Depot Mon.

Watts, C. A. (Kitty) 2 ch contractor O H&L Haskins Mid 35 B tel.

Watts, Ellen Haskins Mid B tel.

Watts, J. R. Haskins Mid.

Watts, W. A. (Katie) 3 ch farmer T 160a 3h 8c R2 Fostoria Per 117.

Waugh, Harold W. (son Wm.) farmer Portage Por 5 Ind tel.

Waugh, Herbert Weston Wes.

Waugh, J. A. (Mercy) farmer O 80a 2h 4c R5 Bowling Green Web 20.

Waugh, R. D. (Gleen) traveling man T H&L Tontogany Wash Ind tel.

Waugh, Thos. RD Bowling Green Web.

Waugh, Wm. (Maggie) farmer O 120a 16h 5c Portage Por 5 Ind tel.

Weagley, Geo. S. RD North Baltimore Hen.

Weagley, Jannett RD North Baltimore Hen.

Weak, S. W. (Mary) carpenter T H&L Pemberville Fre 40.

Weaks, S. P. Pemberville Fre.

Weaver, Albert P. Perrysburg Pbg.

Weaver, Andes W. RD Bowling Green Pla.

Weaver, Andrew R1 Bowling Green Por.

Weaver, B. W. (Anna) motorman T H&L Pemberville Fre 40.

Weaver, Catherine RD Bowling Green Pla.

Weaver, Clement Haskins Mid.

Weaver, Cyrus (son J. D.) machinist R1 Stony Ridge Lake 92 Ind tel.

Weaver, F. V. RD North Baltimore Hen.

Weaver, G. (Cora) 1 ch farmer T 261a 1c R2 Weston Wes 24.

Weaver, Henry farmer O 40a 4h 3c R1 Haskins Mid 50 B tel.

Weaver, Irvin (Bertha) 1 ch railroad man T H&L Walbridge Lake.

Weaver, James (Mary) 6 ch mail carrier O 1a R1 Walbridge Lake 15 Ind tel.

Weaver, John (Mary) 4 ch section foreman O 1½a Custar Mil 44.

WEAVER, J. D. (Susan) machinist O 55a 1h 1c R1 Stony Ridge Lake 92 Ind tel.

WEAVER, J. J. (Jennie) 2 ch farmer O 80a 3h 1c R1 Deshler Jac 46 B tel.

WEAVER, J. R. (Elibeth) 2 ch farming O 80a 6h 4c R2 Weston Wes 34.

Weaver, Leona (dau John) Custar Mil 44.

Weaver, Louis (son John) timekeeper bds Custar Mil 44.

Weaver, L. J. (Florence) timekeeper T H&L Custar Mil.

Weaver, Margaret Grand Rapids Gr Rs.

Weaver, Miss Mary housekeeper R1 Haskins Mid 50.

WEAVER, MICHAEL (Anna) farmer O 10a 2h 1c R3 Perrysburg Pbg 136.

Weaver, Nancy RD North Baltimore Hen.

Weaver, Norma (dau S. M.) Pemberville Fre.

Weaver, Ollie Hoytsville Jac.

WEAVER, ORVILLE concrete mixer Vine St Pemberville Fre.

Weaver, O. RD Rudolph Lib.

Weaver, Romaine RD North Baltimore Hen.

Weaver, Roy (Bertha) hostler T H&L Walbridge Lake.

Weaver, Susan Stony Ridge Lake.

Weaver, S. M. (Hattie) 1 ch laborer O H&L Pemberville Fre.

Weaver, Urban (Edith) 1 ch farmer T 10a R3 Perrysburg Pbg 136.

· Weaver, Webster laborer T H&L Woodside Fre 78.

Webb, A. W. (Ella) 7 ch teamster T 74a 3h 4c Caldwell St Bradner Mon.

Webb, A. W. telegraph operator T H&L Le Moyne Tro.

Webb, Bert (Bertha) 3 ch farmer T 80a 3h 7c R1 Bloomdale Blo 53 B & Ind tels.

Webb, B. J. (Victoria) 4 ch high school principal T H&L Pemberville Fre 40.

Webb, Mrs. Corwin 1 ch ret O H&L Second St Perrysburg Pbg B tel.

Webb, Henry E. (Eva) farmer & ditcher O 5a 1c Luckey Tro 90 B tel.

Webb, John (Mary) ret 80a R1 Bloomdale Blo B & Ind tels.

Webb, J. E. (Nora) 2 ch farmer O 80a 4h 6c R2 North Baltimore Hen 23 Ind tel.

WEBB, W. M. R1 Bloomdale Blo 53.

Weber, Charles (Cora) 4 ch oil man pumping T H&L Vine St Bloomdale Blo.

Weber, F. H. (Anna) 2 ch gardener T Wales Road East Toledo Ros 15.

Weber, J. Geo. A. (son Louisa) rate clerk bds Walbridge Lake.

Weber, Louisa C. housekeeper O H&L Walbridge Lake.

Weber, Wiliam (Margaret) 5 ch glass worker O H&L Box 147 Rossford Ros.

Weber, Wm. G. (son Louisa) paper & tinsel bds Walbridge Lake.

Weddell, Bell Pemberville Fre.

Weddell, Wm. (Cora) 3 ch farmer O 80a 5h 15c R2 Pemberville Web 38 & 67 B tel.

WEDDLE, WILL RD Luckey.

Wedell, Mrs. Isabelle ret O 109a R2 Pemberville Fre 1 B tel.

Weeber, F. Richard (Lena) 3 ch works in garage O H&L R3 Perrysburg Pbg 82.

Weeker, Adam (Catherine) 1 ch harness maker T H&L Luckey Tro.

Weeks, Henry H. (Sarah) 2 ch ret O 55a 1h 2c R3 Weston Mil 6.

Wegman, Alfred (son Lizzie) carpenter R3 Pemberville Fre 16.

WEGMAN, CARL H. (Helen) 1 ch farmer T 156a 6h 10c R1 Le Moyne Tro 81 Ind tel.

Wegman, Clarence W. farmer O 63a 3h 4c R3 Pemberville Fre 16.

Wegman, H. H. (Anna) farmer O 76a 4h 4c R3 Pemberville Fre 23 B tel.

Wegman, Julia farmer O 192a 7h 2c R3 Pemberville Fre 23 B tel.

Wegman, Lizzie housekeeper R3 Pemberville Fre 16.

Wegner, George (son John) farmer R1 Pemberville Fre 53.

Wegner, John (Lina) farmer O 80a 3h 4c R1 Pemberville Fre 53.

Wegner, John H. (Clara) 3 ch farmer T 160a 4h 11c R2 Pemberville Web 39 Ind tel.

Weide, R. B. Cygnet Blo.

Weidner, Amelia (dau Chas.) artist R2 Perrysburg Mid 10.

Weidner, Chas. (Philipine) 1 ch farmer O 80a 2h 3c R2 Perrysburg Mid 10.

Weidner, Homey (son Chas.) farmer R2 Perrysburg Mid 10.

Weigman, Fred Pemberville Fre.

Weigman, Mary Louise Pemberville Fre.

WEIHL, F. J. farmer T 80a 3h 7c R2 Bowling Green Mid 45 B tel.

Weihl, Geo. Grand Rapids Gr Rs.

Weihl, Wm. (Caroline) 4 ch farmer O 80a 3h 5c R1 Haskins Mid 90 B tel.

Weiker, Alonzo (Ila L.) 1 ch laborer T H&L 1h R1 Bloomdale Blo 112.

Weiker, Catherine Bloomdale Blo.

Weiker, C. D. RD Risingsun Per.

WEIKER, CHARLES S. (Anna M.) 2 ch farmer O 30a 3h 2c R1 Bloomdale Blo 99.

Weiker, Daniel (Catherine E.) farmer O 80a 3h R2 Bloomdale Blo 110.

Weiker, David Bloomdale Blo.

Weiker, Elma (dau D.) 1h R2 Bloomdale Bl 111.

Weiker, I. E. Bloomdale Blo.

WEIKER, I. M. (Minerva J.) 1 ch farmer T 80a 2h Cygnet Blo 15.

Weiker, I. N. Cygnet Blo.

Weiker, Jess (Amy) 2 ch farmer O 20a 3h 1c R1 Rudolph Lib 29.

Weiker, Simon W. (son David) laborer 1h R2 Bloomdale Blo 111.

WEIL, WM. H. (Pronie) farmer O 60a 2h R2 Perrysburg Mid 14 B tel.

Weiland, Christ (Maggie) farmer O 14a 2h 1c Station A East Toledo Ros 31.

Weiland, Geo. Perrysburg Pbg.

Weiland, Henry Dunbridge Web.

Weiland, Herman (Frances) farmer 1h R1 Dunbridge Web 53 B tel.

WEIMAR, FRED. (Minnie) 2 ch farmer O 100a 4h 5c R1 Haskins Mid 48 B tel.

Weimar, Oswald (son Fred.) farmer R1 Haskins Mid 48.

Weimer, Charley Weston Mil.

Weimer, Mrs. Elizabeth 2 ch farmer O 37a 1h 2c R2 Bowling Green Mid 47 B tel.

Weimi, Charley (Annie) 3 ch farmer O 80a 5h 5c R3 Weston Mil 90 Ind tel.

Weimi, May (dau Charley) R3 Weston Mil 90 Ind tel.

Weimi, Nora (dau Charley) R3 Weston Mil 90 Ind tel.

Weimi, Paud (son Charley) farmer R3 Weston Mil 90 Ind tel.

Wein, A. E. Prairie Depot Mon.

Weinert, Frank (Mary) 1 ch T H&L Rossford Ros.

Weirich, John (Pearl) mason O H&L Second St Grand Rapids Gr Rs.

Weirough, Jacob RD North Baltimore Hen.

Welch, Chas. (Lura) 2 ch farmer O 120a 4h 8c R3 Bowling Green Cen 46 Ind tel.

WELCH, H. (Lettie) farmer T 80a 3h 2c R1 Tontogany Pla 22.

Welch, Jim boilermaker Cygnet Blo.

Welch, Sarah E. O H&L Main St Bairdstown Blo.

Welchoff, Nick Perrysburg Pbg.

Weller, Delphas (Clara) 2 ch farmer O 50a 4h 4c R1 Jerry City Portage 62.

Wellhiser, Jno. RD Mermill Por.

Welling, Arnold (Emma) carpenter R1 Luckey Tro 75.

Welling, Arthur G. Lime City Pbg.

Welling, Charley (son Geo.) farmer 2h R1 Lime City Pbg 58 Ind tel.

WELLING, FRANK (son Mrs. Fred) cream business O Luckey Tro Ind tel.

Welling, Mrs. Fred 8 ch farmer O 75a Luckey Tro Ind tel.

Welling, George (Mary) 1 ch farmer T 80a 4h 1c R1 Walbridge Lake 97 B tel.

Welling, Geo. (Sophia) farmer O 60a 2h 2c R1 Lime City Perrysburg 58 Ind tel.

Welling, Harley (son Henry) R1 Dunbridge Web 49 B tel.

Welling, Harvey (son Henry) R1 Dunbridge Web 49 B tel.

WELLING, HENRY (Carrie) farmer O 130a 4h 6c R1 Dunbridge Web 49 B tel.

WELLING, JOHN (Sophia) 3 ch farmer O 58a 2h 2c R1 Lime City Pbg 59 Ind tel.

WELLING, J. GEO. (Ida A.) 5 ch saloonkeeper O H&L Luckey Tro Ind tel.

Welling, J. H. Dunbridge Web.

Welling, Wm. (Mary) 4 ch farmer O 55a 4h 5c R3 Pemberville Tro 63 Ind tel.

Welling, Wm. (Oma) 2 ch carpenter T H&L 1h R1 Dunbridge Web 59 B tel.

Wells, Benjamin (Sarah) 1 ch farmer O 60a 3h 3c R2 North Baltimore Jac 119 Ind tel.

Wells, F. E. (Fannie) harnessmaker O H&L Third St Perrysburg Pbg.

Wells, Harly (Lizzie) painter O H&L Indiana Ave Perrysburg Pbg.

Wells, H. S. (Mary) 2 ch farmer O 40a 2h 6c R1 Rising Sun Pbg 99 Ind tel.

WELLS, JOSEPH (Alda) 1 ch engineer T H&L Woodside Fre 78.

224

WELLS, LOUIS (Maude) 3 ch farmer T H&L R4 Bowling Green Cen 111.

Wells, U. T. (Lucy) farmer T 80a 3h 3c R1 Rudolph Hen 44.

WELLSTEAD, FRED C. R1 Perrysburg.

Wellstead, M. J. O H&L Sixth St Perrysburg Pbg.

WELLSTEAD, WM. (Rose) 1 ch farmer T 186a 5h 4c R1 Perrysburg Pbg 12 Ind tel.

Welsh, Lawrence (Bernice) farm laborer R1 Deshler Jac 34 B tel.

Welson, C. C. (son J. H.) R1 Rudolph Lib 77 Ind tel.

WELSON, J. H. (Jennie) 4 ch farmer T 35a 3h 4c R1 Rudolph Lib 77 Ind tel.

Welson, M. C. (Nellie) 1 ch thrasher & laborer T H&L R1 Rudolph Lib 77.

Wenig, Gust (Sophia) 1 ch farmer O 100a 4h 8c R1 Bowling Green Pla 53 Ind tel.

WENIG, HARRY K. (Elsie) farmer T 50a 2h 1c R2 Bowling Green Pla 52 Ind tel.

WENIG, HENRY (Anna) 7 ch farmer O 160a 5h 5c R2 Haskins Mid 32 B tel.

WENIG, JOHN (Lizzie) 3 ch farmer O 105a 9h 5c R1 Tontogany Wash 71 Ind tel.

Wensel, Henry Prairie Depot Mon.

Wensel, Ira farmer T 75a 4h R2 Prairie Depot Mon 9.

WENSEL, J. H. (Elizabeth) 7 ch farmer O 180a 5h 5c R3 Prairie Depot Mon 4 B tel.

WENSEL, MAMIE R3 Prairie Depot Mon 4 B tel.

Wensel, Rolla (Luella) 2 ch farmer T 80a 3h 3c R3 Prairie Depot Mon 7 Ind tel.

Wensink, John (Gertrude) 1 ch farmer O 80a 7h 5c R2 Deshler Jac 3 B tel.

Wensink, William (Bessie) farmer O 93½a 6h 3c R2 Deshler Jac 2.

Went, F. L. (Matilda) 2 ch railroad man O H&L R3 North Baltimore Blo.

Wenton, G. L. Corp St Portage Por.

Wentz, A. H. (Pauline) 2 ch butcher shop O H&L Custar Mil B & Ind tels.

Wentz, A. R. (Lou) 3 ch butcher shop O H&L Custar Mil B & Ind tels.

Wentz, Ed (Effie) 2 ch farmer T 52a 4h 2c R5 Bowling Green Cen 60 Ind tel.

Wenz, Ed Perrysburg Pbg.

Wenz, Fred Perrysburg Pbg.

Wenz, R. C. Perrysburg Pbg.

Werick, John (Pearl) laboring man O H&L Grand Rapids Gr Rs.

Werner, F. W. dentist bds RD North Baltimore Hen Ind tel.

Werner, H. A. Prairie Depot Mon.

Werner, I. W. (Emma) farmer O 37a 6h 4c R1 Fostoria Per 77.

Werner, Peter (Margerth) 1 ch farmer O 30a 2h 3c R2 Custar Mil 50.

Wershing, Peter (Lena) 4 ch farmer O 40a 6h 4c R2 Perrysburg Mid 13.

WESEMAN, A. H. (Emma) farmer O 65a 3h 4c R3 Perrysburg Pbg 77 Ind tel.

WESEMAN, E. H. (Clara) 1 ch farmer O 63a 4h 4c R3 Perrysburg Pbg 62 Ind tel.

Weseman, Harry (son A. H.) farmer R3 Perrysburg Pbg 77.

Weseman, Pearl (son A. H.) R3 Perrysburg Pbg 77.

Wessler, Frederick (Mary) ret O H&L Locust St Perrysburg Pbg.

West, E. K. RD North Baltimore Hen.

West, G. L. (son H. E.) bookkeeper Prairie Depot Mon.

West, H. E. (Cora) 1 ch tinner O H&L 2c Prairie Depot Mon.

WESTENBERGER, CHAS. (Lillie) 1 ch farmer O 80a 4h 6c R1 Prairie Depot Mon 35 B tel.

Westenhaver, Mrs. A. E. RD Hoytsville Jac.

Westenhaver, Mrs. Ersula ret O H&L Hoytsville Jac.

Westerfield, Harmon 2 ch farmer O 40a 2h 5c R1 Bradner Mon 23.

Westerfield, J. H. Bradner Mon.

Westerfield Wm. farmer O 60a 2h Bradner Mon 17 B & Ind tels.

Westerhaus, Emma R1 Pemberville Cen 114 Btel.

Westerhaus, Frank (Carrie) 3 ch farmer O 80a 4h 5c R1 Pemberville Cen 114 B tel.

Westerhaus, Henry R1 Pemberville Cen 114 B tel.

WESTERHAUS, L. H. (Julia) 1 ch farmer O 73a 2c R1 Pemberville Fre 66 B tel.

Westerhouse, H. W. (Sophia) farmer O 66a 4h 7c R1 Pemberville Fre 70 B tel.

Westerhouse, Minnie (dau H. W.) housekeeper R1 Pemberville Fre 70.

Westerfield, J. H. (Ella) 5 ch farmer 120a 3h 7c Bradner Mon 23 B tel.

WETCH, M. J. Perrysburg.

WETHERHOLTER, F. E. (Adaline) 6 ch oil man T L 1h R1 North Baltimore Hen 123 Ind tel.

Wetherill, J. C. (Bertha) 1 ch physician H&L Weston Wes B & Ind tels.

Wetzel, Philip Perrysburg Pbg.

Weyker, Clarence (Gladys) farmer T 80a 3h 3c R1 Rising Sun Per 95.

Whalem, C. H. Bradner Mon.

Wheeler, Mrs. E. S. housekeeper O H&L Lime City Pbg 121.

WHEELER, HARVEY (Emma) 3 ch laborer T H&L 1h Woodside Fre 78.

15   225

Wheeler, J. W. Weston Lib.

WHEELER, NOAH (Alice) 4 ch farmer O 1a 1h 1c R2 Custar Hen 1½.

Whelan, C. H. (Ella) 2 ch oil producer O H&L Evans St Bradner Mon.

Whelan, Edw. oil producer Evans St Bradner Mon.

Whelan, Oliver Evans St Bradner Mon.

Whitacre, Alice (dau R. M.) R1 Rudolph Lib 5 Ind tel.

Whitacre, Albert H. (Irinea) 6 ch carpenter O 2a T H Jerry & Union Sts Jerry City Blo 74 Ind tel.

WHITACRE, ARTHUR 5 ch farmer O 80a 5h 4c Cygnet Blo 15 Ind tel.

Whitacre, Calvin (Addie) 1 ch farmer T H&L 3h 3c R1 Portage Por 50.

Whitacre, C. E. Cygnet Blo.

WHITACRE, D. L. (Amanda) 10 ch farmer O 276a 5h 2c R1 Rudolph Lib 104 Ind tel.

WHITACRE, E. M. (Laura) 1 ch farmer O 35a 1h R1 Jerry City Blo 78.

Whitacre, Fannie student Cygnet Blo 15 Ind tel.

Whitacre, Frank farmer Cygnet Blo 5 Ind tel.

Whitacre, Harry farmer Cygnet Blo 15 Ind tel.

WHITACRE, H. D. (Dolla) farmer T 110a 4h 1c R1 Rudolph Lib 104 Ind tel.

Whitacre, H. W. (Ella) 2 ch farmer O 75a 3h 4c R4 Bowling Green Cen 73.

WHITACRE, J. H. (Mary J.) 7 ch laborer O H&L Jerry St Jerry City Blo Ind tel.

Whitacre, Levi L. (Mary J.) 1 ch farmer O 135a 3h 16c Washington St Cygnet Blo 5 Ind tel.

Whitacre, L. S. Cygnet Blo.

Whitacre, Mary J. Jerry City Blo.

Whitacre, Reason farmer Cygnet Blo Ind tel.

Whitacre, R. F. (Rose) 2 ch physician O H&L 3h Prairie Depot Mon B tel.

WHITACRE, R. H. (Flora) 1 ch farmer T 50a 3h 1c Rudolph Lib 99 Ind tel.

WHITACRE, R. M. (Altha) 2 ch farmer T 100a 6h 10c R1 Weston Lib 5 Ind tel.

WHITACRE, THOMAS J. (Weamettie) 5 ch farmer O 160a 8h 16c R1 Rudolph Lib 104 Ind tel.

WHITACRE, WARREN R. Box 102 Cygnet.

WHITACRE, W. J. Bays.

White, Albert (Jennie) 3 ch section worker O H&L Hoytsville Jac.

White, Alva (Bessie) 3 ch quarry T H&L Water St Portage Por.

White, Mrs. Annie 1 ch O H&L cor Evans & Leightner Sts Bradner Mon.

White, A. M. (Elmira) 5 ch ret O 120a 1h Taylor St Box 141 Weston Mil Ind tel.

White, Chas. E. Weston Mil.

White, Clarence cor Leightner & Bell Sts Bradner Mon.

White, Clarence (Mable) 2 ch oil worker T H&L Rudolph Lib 94 Ind tel.

White, Everett (Bess) clerk O H&L Rudolph Lib 81 Ind tel.

White, E. E. (Ida) 3 ch druggist O H&L Risingsun Mon B tel.

White, Geo. (Anna) 5 ch oil worker O H&L Rudolph Lib 94 Ind tel.

White, G. C. Pemberville Fre.

White, Mrs. H. ret O H&L Prairie Depot Mon.

WHITE, H. M. mail carrier 3h bds Grand Rapids Gr Rs 2 Ind tel.

White, J. C. (Grace) cashier O H&L Maple St Weston Ind tel.

White, P. L. (Ellen) 2 ch farmer O 80a 1h 1c R1 Deshler Jac 36.

White, Raymond A. cor Leightner & Bell Sts Bradner Mon.

White, Thos. Prairie Depot Mon.

White, W. (Jeannette) 5 ch station agent O H&L cor Leightner & Bell Sts Bradner Mon B tel.

White, Mrs. W. H. O H&L Rudolph Lib 81 Ind tel.

White, Zella cor Leightner & Bell Sts Bradner Mon.

Whitehead, D. C. (Mary E.) grocery & drugs O H&L Perrysburg Pbg B tel.

Whiteman, A. T. (Lena) 1 ch farmer O 60a 4h 8c West Millgrove Per 73 Ind tel.

Whiteman, E. T. West Millgrove Per.

Whitker, Jno. Weston Wes.

Whitker, J. H. (Liza) 8 ch ret O 80a H&L Main St Weston Ind tel.

Whitker, Margaret (dau J. H.) clerk Main St Weston.

Whitker, May (dau J. H.) Main St Weston.

Whitman, B. (Callie) 2 ch gas pumper H&L West Millgrove Per 68.

Whitman, C. E. Prairie Depot Mon.

Whitman, Ed 5 ch farmer T 40a 4h 6c R1 Risingsun Mon 77.

Whitman, Mrs. Elizabeth 2 ch housekeeper O H&L West Millgrove Per 69.

Whitman, Mary 3 ch ret O H&L Sixth St Perrysburg Pbg.

Whitman, Merrill (Anna) miller O H&L 1h 1c West Millgrove Per 70 B tel.

Whitman, Norman L. (Dessie) 1 ch farmer O 40a 4h 5c Prairie Depot Blo 85 Ind tel.

Whitman, Orrin RD Prairie Depot Por.

Whitman, Sarah E. West Millgrove Per.
Whitman, S. L. Prairie Depot Mon.
Whitman, Willis A. West Millgrove Per.
Whitman, W. H. West Millgrove Per.
Whitmer, C. J. (Lydia C.) 2 ch farmer O 50a 4h 2c R2 Bowling Green Cen 5 Ind tel.
Whitmer, F. B. (Margaret) 1 ch farmer O 80a 3h 3c R3 Bowling Green Cen 41 Ind tel.
Whitmer, Orrin L. (Florence) 1 ch farmer T 40a 2h 2c R2 Prairie Depot Por 82.
Whitmill, Earl (Edith) laborer T H&L R5 Bowling Green Web 20.
Whitmill, H. E. (Lydia) 5 ch farmer T 80a 2h 5c R3 Bowling Green Cen 44.
Whitmore, Chas. A. (Dortas) 1 ch dairyman O 125a 6h 60c 1716 Oak St East Toledo Ros 18 B tel.
Whitmore, Chas. W. (Ethel) dairyman T 1716 Oak St East Toledo Ros 18.
Whitmore, J. D. Perrysburg Pbg.
Whitmore, Louise O 20a 1705 Oak St East Toledo Ros 18 B tel.
Whitmore, Sophie O 24a 1705 Oak St East Toledo Ros 18 B tel.
Whitmore, S. W. O H&L Tontogany Wash.
Whitney, Albert (Jennie) 4 ch ret O H&L Center St Weston Ind tel.
Whitney, Bert (Nancy) blacksmith O H&L West Millgrove Per 69.
Whitney, Mrs. Flora dressmaker Center St Weston.
Whitney, Fred (Noma) 4 ch farmer T 40a 4h 3c R1 Grand Rapids Gr Rs 6 Ind tel.
WHITNEY, F. R. (Eliza) 4 ch ret O H&L Milton Center Mil Ind tel.
Whitney, Gertrude (dau F. R.) dressmaker Milton Center Mil Ind tel.
Whitney, Walter J. (Emma) 1 ch drayman O H&L 3h Sycamore St Weston Wes.
Whitson, Geo. (Cora) 2 ch farmer T 60a 4h 3c R1 Lime City Pbg 94 B tel.
WHITSON, ISAAC (Lovina) ret O 120a 1h 1c R1 Lime City Pbg 93 B tel.
WHITSON, WM. J. (Jennie) 1 ch farmer T 60a 4h 3c R1 Lime City Pbg 95 B tel.
WHITTENMYER, JOHN F. (Flossie) 5 ch farmer T 110a 3h 1c R1 Rudolph Lib 63.
Whittmore, James (Clara) 1 ch laborer T H&L Second St Perrysburg Pbg B tel.
Wice, B. R. Pemberville Fre.
Wice, Chas. A. Pemberville Fre.

Wice, C. A. (Myrtle) 3 ch auto salesman T H&L Pemberville Fre.
Wice, Wm. Pemberville Fre.
Wickam, Earl (Leta) 3 ch clerk T H&L Haskins Mid B tel.
WICKARD, CLEO (dau Wm. W.) R1 Rudolph Lib 66 Ind tel.
Wickard, L. (Jennie) 2 ch laborer O H&L Factory St Jerry City Por.
Wickard, Martin laborer Factory St Jerry City Por.
Wickard, Maude housekeeper Factory St Jerry City Por.
Wickard, Miles laborer Factory St Jerry City Por.
Wickard, Wm. (Bessie) 1 ch section T H&L Jerry St Jerry City Blo.
WICKARD, WM. W. (Sada) 5 ch farmer T 40a 3h 2c R1 Rudolph Lib 66 Ind tel.
Wickham, W. M. (Florence) real estate & ins O H&L Prairie Depot Mon B tel.
Wickman, Henry (Sophia) 3 ch salesman O H&L Pemberville Fre B tel.
Wicks, Seth (Lucie) farmer O 5a 1h R1 Walbridge Lake 2 Ind tel.
Widmer, Lewis J. (Susie) 5 ch laborer T H&L Millbury Lake 80.
Wiebeck, Otto (Anna) 10 ch section foreman T H&L Hoytsville Jac.
Wiechman, Fred H. Luckey Tro.
Wiechman, Herman (Anna) 5 ch farmer O 118a 4h 8c R3 Bowling Green Web 14.
Wiegman, Lucy Pemberville Web.
Wiegman, Mrs. Wm. 4 ch farmer O 69a 3h 6c R3 Pemberville Fre 3.
Wieland, John W. (Cordelia) gardener O 20a 3h R1 East Toledo Ros 28.
WIELAND, WILLIAM G. (Hannah) 4 ch carpenter O 2a R1 Rudolph Lib 104.
Wight, Henry Pemberville Fre.
WIGHT, H. E. (Anna S.) 2 ch farmer O 218a 16h 42c Millbury Lake 54 Ind tel.
Wight, L. E. Pemberville Web.
Wight, S. E. Pemberville Web.
Wight, Wm. Pemberville Fre.
Wihl, Geo. (Jessie B.) 2 ch farmer O 40a 5h 4c R2 Weston Gr Rs 31 Ind tel.
Wilber, Bird (Gusta) farmer T 13a 1h 1c R3 Perrysburg Pbg 81.
WILBER, E. cattle R4 Bowling Green Cen.
WILBER, GEO. R4 Box 97 Bowling Green.
Wilcox, Chas. E. (Maude N.) 1 ch farmer 40a 4h 3c R1 Deshler Jac 27 Ind tel.

227

Wilcox, Clyde (Mary) 2 ch farmer T 80a 4h 2c R1 Bowling Green Pla 76 Ind tel.

Wilcox, Elizabeth ret O 80a R4 Deshler Jac 30 Ind tel.

Wilcox, E. B. RD Bowling Green Pla.

Wilcox, Hugh H. (Alice) laborer T H&L R1 Rudolph Lib 62 Ind tel.

Wilcox, Roy (Nettie) farmer T 60a 3h 2c R1 Bowling Green Cen 28.

Wilcox, Robt. N. RD Bowling Green Pla.

WILCOX, R. J. (Evvie) 2 ch farmer T 80a 4h 5c R1 Hoytsville Jac 30 Ind tel.

WILCOX, S. H. farmer O 111a 4h R2 Bowling Green Pla 63.

WILCOX, S. O. RD Hoytsville Jac.

Wilcox, William (Sarah) 1 ch ret O H&L Russ St Weston Ind tel.

Wilderson, S. E. RD North Baltimore Hen.

Wilds, Henry (Mary) painter O H&L Fifth St Perrysburg Pbg B tel.

Wiley, Ned (Rose) 4 ch railroad man T H&L Walbridge Lake.

Wilford, W. T. (Martha) 3 ch farmer O 60a 4h 3c R3 Bowling Green Cen 82.

Wilhelm, Flory (Mary) 4 ch farmer O 80a 5h 6c R1 Hoytsville Mil 28.

Wilhelm, John (Helena) 7 ch farmer O 160a 4h 3c R1 Custar Mil 40 B tel.

Wilhelm, John W. (son John) farmer T 100a 3h R1 Custar Mil 40 B tel.

Wilhelm, Lewis (Mary) farmer T 80a 3h 3c R2 Custar Mil 29 B tel.

Wilhelm, Martin (Rosa) 2 ch farmer T 80a 4h 4c R1 Weston Mil 71 B tel.

WILKERHOLT, J. E. R1 North Baltimore Hen 123.

Wilkinson, G. W. (Ella M.) 4 ch printer O H&L RD North Baltimore Hen Ind tel.

Wilky, Minnie ret O H&L Fifth St Perrysburg Pbg.

Will, G. W. (Lizzie) farmer O 40a 2h 2c Main St Bloomdale Blo B & Ind tels.

Willacker, John (Katy) 1 ch bricklayer T H&L Box 682 Rossford Ros.

Willford, Opal (dau Sam) housekeeper R1 Deshler Jac 9 B tel.

Willford, Sam (Daisy) 8 ch farmer 1c R1 Deshler Jac 9 B tel.

Williams, Antone RD Tontogany Wash.

Williams, Art (Minnie) 3 ch painter O H&L Second St Perrysburg Pbg B tel.

Williams, A. G. (Minnie) 3 ch real estate O H&L Perrysburg Pbg B tel.

Williams, A. R. (Clora) 7 ch grocer O H&L Fifth St Perrysburg Pbg B tel.

Williams, Carleton 1h R2 Custar Lib 32 Ind tel.

Williams, Mrs. Charlotte 1 ch O H&L Grand Rapids Gr Rs.

WILLIAMS, CHARLES W. (Margret C.) engineer T 20a 2h R3 Perrysburg Pbg 158.

Williams, C. H. Risingsun Perry.

WILLIAMS, C. R. (Edith) gen store O H&L Pemberville Fre 40 B tel.

Williams, David (Lillie) 2 ch oil worker O H&L Walbridge St Cygnet Blo.

WILLIAMS, D. (Elizabeth) ret O 127a 2c R1 Prairie Depot Mon 89 B tel.

Williams, Elda (dau Dr. J. N.) school teacher Main St Weston.

Williams, Enoch farmer R1 Portage Por 102.

Williams, Elias A. (Emma F.) 2 ch farmer T 100a 5h 3c R3 North Baltimore Blo 20 B & Ind tels.

Williams, Mrs. Erma 1 ch farmer O 73a 1h 1c R2 Bowling Green Mid 47.

WILLIAMS, FRANK (Edithe) 2 ch farmer T 160a 5h 1c R3 North Baltimore Hen 112.

WILLIAMS, FRANK (Rosena) 3 ch farmer T 57a 7h 6c Tontogany Wash 42½.

Williams, George (Mary) 5 ch cement worker O H&L Fifth St Perrysburg Pbg B tel.

Williams, Geo. F. (Lena) farmer T 73a 3h 2c R2 Bowling Green Mid 47 B tel.

Williams, Henry farmer R2 Prairie Depot Por 77.

WILLIAMS, JAMES (Ida) 2 ch oil pumper 1h 1c R2 Custar Lib 32 Ind tel.

WILLIAMS, J. B. (Minnie) 6 ch farmer O 80a 8h 12c RD Weston Wes 17 Ind tel.

WILLIAMS, J. L. (Dottie G.) 4 ch blacksmith O H&L Findlay St Portage Por 10 Ind tel.

Williams, Dr. J. N. (DeVella) 5 ch physician O H&L Main St Weston B tel.

Williams, Lewis (Lizzie) 7 ch farmer T 80a 4h 9c Tontogany Wash.

Williams, Liza Tontogany Wash.

Williams, May M. (dau Dr. J. N.) clerk Main St Weston.

Williams, Nehemiah Starr (son Dr. J. N.) Main St Weston.

Williams, N. C. (Frances) 8 ch farming O 80a 3h 4c R1 Deshler Jac 9 B tel.

WILLIAMS, N. K. farmer T 106a 2h 4c R3 Prairie Depot Mon 47 B tel.

Williams, Peter (Jennie) 3 ch farmer O 13a 1c R1 Walbridge Lake 10.

Williams, Ruth (dau Dr. J. N.) Main St Weston.

Williams, Sarah E. (dau Dr. J. N.) seamstress Main St Weston.

Williams, S. R. (Ida M.) 2 ch bank cashier O H&L Pemberville Fre 40 B tel.

Williams, Thomas (Gertrude) farmer T 60a 2h 1c R1 Walbridge Lake 6.

Williams, W. A. (Mary) 1 ch real estate O 5a 1h Rossford Pbg 80.

Williamson, A. A. 2 ch oil worker T H&L R1 Rudolph Lib 98.

Williamson, Bell housekeeper O 62a 5h R1 Hoytsville Jac 86 B tel.

Williamson, B. A. (Lina) 7 ch farmer T 80a 4h 4c R2 Prairie Depot Por 80.

Williamson, Catherine RD Hoytsville Jac.

Williamson, Clayton (Anna) farmer T 2h 2c R2 Dunbridge Pbg 22 B tel.

WILLIAMSON, MRS. ELLA housekeeper O 53a 4h 6c R1 Dunbridge Web 49 B tel.

Williamson, E. E. (Gertrude) 2 ch general merchandise T H&L 1h Prairie Depot Mon B tel.

WILLIAMSON, H. H. (Altha) garage O H&L Luckey Tro Ind tel.

Williamson, H. L. (Jeannette) 2 ch general merchandise O H&L 2h Prairie Depot Mon.

Williamson, J. L. (Hattie) 3 ch carpenter O H&L Prairie Depot Mon B tel.

Williamson, Perry (Bertha) 4 ch laborer T H&L 1h R2 Prairie Depot Por 114.

Williamson, R. C. (son Mrs. Ella) farmer R1 Dunbridge Web 49 B tel.

Williamson, R. C. (Edith) 5 ch farmer T 60a 3h R1 Portage Lib 91.

Williamson, F. W. (Mary) 1 ch laborer O H&L 1c Rose St Bloomdale Blo.

Willis, R. H. Luckey Tro.

Willman, John F. (Anna) 1 ch farmer O 90a 4h 9c R1 Luckey Tro 86 B tel.

Willman, L. A. grocery store O H&L 1h 1c R1 Jerry City Blo 60.

Willstead, Fred R1 Perrysburg Pbg.

WILSON, ALLIE R1 Walbridge.

Wilson, Catherine RD Bowling Green Gr Rs.

WILSON, ELI (Marie) farmer O 40a 4h 3c R1 Jerry City Por 69 Ind tel.

Wilson, Elmer E. (Leotia) 3 ch farmer T 100a 5h 2c R2 North Baltimore Hen 58.

Wilson, Emery (Maud) 2 ch porter T H&L Sixth St Perrysburg Pbg.

Wilson, E. D. (Anna E.) 5 ch physician O H&L 1c Haskins Mid B tel.

WILSON, E. J. (Emma) 2 ch electric repair shop T H&L Pemberville Fre.

WILSON, E. J. (Mary) farmer T 40a 4h 4c R1 Grand Rapids Gr Rs 9 Ind tel.

Wilson, F. C. (Clide) 5 ch farmer O 110a 4h 13c R2 North Baltimore Hen 81 Ind tel.

Wilson, G. D. (Phoebe) 1 ch blacksmith O 2a 1h R2 Bowling Green Pla 60 B tel.

Wilson, G. R. (Bertha C.) building contractor T H&L Rudolph Lib 81 Ind tel.

Wilson, Hamilton (Della) 4 ch farmer O 80a 3h 13c R2 Custar Lib 24 Ind tel.

Wilson, Howard (Katherine) 1 ch laborer T H&L Rossford Ros.

Wilson, Jim 1 ch ret O H&L Sixth St Perrysburg Pbg B tel.

Wilson, John (Myrtle) 1 ch farmer O H&L 2h 1c Third St Portage Por.

Wilson, John (Maggie) 7 ch tile man O H&L Second St Perrysburg Pbg B tel.

WILSON, MRS. J. B. Pemberville.

Wilson, J. F. Prairie Depot Mon.

Wilson, J. L. (Mary L.) moving buildings O H&L Haskins Mid.

Wilson, Lester (Allie) 3 ch railroad man T H&L R1 Walbridge Lake 11 B & Ind tels.

Wilson, L. C. (Julia A.) farmer O 40a 2c R1 Haskins Mid 47 Ind tel.

Wilson, Maria RD Jerry City Por.

Wilson, Merit 2 ch auto salesman H&L Loci St Cygnet Blo.

WILSON, N. G. Stony Ridge.

Wilson, Roy (Minnie) 2 ch laborer O H&L Fifth St Perrysburg Pbg.

Wilson, S. R. (Helen) ret R1 Prairie Depot Mon 35 B tel.

Wilson, Thomas mason bds Perrysburg Pbg.

Wilson, Wm. P. (Ruby) 3 ch meat cutter 1c R1 East Toledo Lake 112 Ind tel.

Wilson, W. M. Cygnet Blo.

WILSON, W. R. (Rose) farmer T 20a 2h 1c R3 North Baltimore Hen 102 Ind tel.

Wilt, Amos (Lena) 1 ch hired man T H&L R1 Prairie Depot Mon 114.

Wilt, John (Maud) 1 ch clothing O H&L RD North Baltimore Hen Ind tel.

Winans, Mrs. Albert RD North Baltimore Hen.

Winchel, Mrs. Lusinda ret O H&L Risingsun Mon.

Winchell, Leister (Dora) 2 ch ret O H&L 1h Risingsun Mon.

Windisaman, Adolph (Ida) 2 ch machinist O 3a R1 East Toledo Lake 112.

Windland, Lesley (Vella) painter O H&L Maple St Bloomdale Blo.

Windsor, I. W. (Marie) 2 ch farmer T 160a 5h 16c R4 Fostoria Per 108 B tel.

Wineland, E. (Vera) farmer O 10a 1h 2c R3 Bloomdale Blo 120 B & Ind tels.

Wineland, Franklin B. (Samentha) stationary engineer O H&L S Main St Bloomdale Blo.

Wineland, Fred E. (son T. E.) laborer Mulberry St Bloomdale Blo B & Ind tels.

Wineland, L. Bloomdale Blo.

Wineland, Mabel (dau T. E.) Mulberry St Bloomdale Blo B & Ind tels.

Wineland, T. E. (Alla B.) 6 ch drayman moving picture O H&L 2h Mulberry St Bloomdale Blo B & Ind tels.

Wing, Mead (Fannie) 3 ch pumper O 118a 3c Rudolph Lib 77 Ind tel.

Wingart, Mary A. Bays Lib.

Wingart, William H. laborer O 3Lots Bays Lib.

WINKELMAN, FRED (Louise) 8 ch farmer O 35a 7h R1 Hoytsville Jac 56.

Winkelman, Fred, Jr. (son Fred, Sr.) farm hand R1 Hoytsville Jac 56.

WINKLE, ROBERT (Mary) 1 ch farmer O 140a 5h 4c R1 Pemberville Fre 59 B tel.

Winkleman, John (Christina) 4 ch carpenter O H&L Milton Center Mil.

Winner, I. S. (Verne) supt of schools T H&L Pembervillge Fre 40 B tel.

Winner, Verne Pemberville Fre.

Winnup, J. T. Weston Wes.

Winnup, Taylor (Ellen) farmer T 80a 3h 4c R2 Weston Wes 23 Ind tel.

Winter, A. H. Grand Rapids Gr Rs.

Winterhoff, E. H. D. (Etta) 1 ch minister T H&L Pemberville Fre 40 B tel.

Winterholder, Martin RD North Baltimore Hen.

Winters, A. H. (Thressa) carpenter O H&L Grand Rapids Gr Rs.

WINTERS, A. J. (Zora) 1 ch farmer T 120a 5h 1c RD North Baltimore Hen 93 B tel.

Winters, J. R. (Ettie) 6 ch farmer O 80a 4h 5c R1 Hoytsville Jac 44.

Winters, W. A. RD North Baltimore Blo.

Winton, Geo. L. (Celestia) janitor O H&L Findlay St Portage Por.

Winzeler, J. F. (Anna) clerk O H& 3Lots Lime City Pbg 91.

Wirebaugh, Amanda Bradner Mon.

Wirebaugh, Mrs. Celia 2 ch housekeeper O H&L Prairie Depot Mon B tel.

Wirebaugh, E. L. (Hazel) farmer & cattle breeder T 120a 4h 15c R3 Prairie Depot Por 111 B tel.

Wirebaugh, Ladora E. housekeeper O H&L Prairie Depot Mon.

Wirebaugh, Miranda 1 ch O H&L 1c W Crocker St Bradner Mon.

Wirebaugh, Margaret E. RD Prairie Depot Por.

Wirebaugh, Mrs. N. J. ret O H&L Prairie Depot Mon.

Wires, John (Mary) 1 ch farmer T 47a 3h 6c R1 Grand Rapids Wash 68 Ind tel.

Wires, Mrs. Mary Grand Rapids Wash.

Wirick, J. E. RD North Baltimore Hen.

Wirick, Marie RD North Baltimore Blo.

Wirick, O. E. Bairdstown Blo.

Wirt, A. J. (Katie) farmer T 40a 2h 2c Jerry City Blo 78 Ind tel.

Wirt, J. E. West Millgrove Per.

Wirt, O. D. (Lucy) 2 ch farmer O 102a 6h 10c West Millgrove Per 72 Ind tel.

Wirt, Wm. RD North Baltimore Hen.

Wisar, Joseph (Alice) 4 ch gardener O H&L Indiana Ave Perrysburg Pbg.

Wise, A. C. (Hazel) traveling man T H&L Hickory St Pemberville Fre Ind

Wise, B. R. (Josephine) blacksmith T H&L Pemberville Fre 40.

Wise, Fred (son P.) farmer R1 Perrysburg Pbg 16.

Wise, Levi Bradner Mon.

Wise, P. J. (Carrie) 1 ch farmer O 80a 4h 4c R1 Perrysburg Pbg 16 B tel.

WISE, WESLEY (Minnie) 6 ch farmer O 50a 3h 4c R1 Prairie Depot Mon 115.

WISE, W. A. (Ester) 4 ch farmer T 120a 4h 4c R1 Rudolph Lib 76 Ind tel.

WISE, W. T. (Nellie) 2 ch blacksmith O H&L 1h Pemberville Fre 40 B tel.

Wiseley, Walter G. (son Mrs. C. A.) school teacher Center St Weston.

Wiseley, Mrs. S. A. O H&L Rose St Bloomdale Blo.

WISELY, GEORGE W. oil man Rose St Bloomdale Blo.

Wiseman, E. E. (Lesta) 3 ch carpenter T H&L 1h 2c R4 Bowling Green Cen 36 Ind tel.

Wismar, Albert RD Rudolph Lib.

Wismar, Chas. (Elizabeth) 6 ch postmaster O H&L Milton Center Mil Ind tel.

Wismar, Chas. Milton Center Mil.

Wismar, Mrs. Hannah 10 ch ret O H&L Custar Mil.

WISMAR, T. C. (Dela) 1 ch farmer T 80a 2h 7c R1 Custar Mil 101 Ind tel.

Wismer, Barney (Blanche) oil worker O 1h 1c R1 Portage Lib 83 Ind tel.

WISMER, FRED (Eva) 10 ch farmer O 40a 2h 3c R1 Custar Mil 101 B tel.

Wisner, T. E. general store T H&L Main St Jerry City Por.

Wisner, W. N. (Abbie) farmer T 20a 2h Main St Prairie Depot Mon 52.

Wisterman, G. J. (Laura A.) 3 ch oil worker & barber O H&L Rudolph Lib 94 Ind tel.

Witherell, O. O. (Minnie P.) ret T H&L R1 Genoa Lake 42.

WITHERHOLT, F. E. R1 North Baltimore Hen 123.

WITHERUP, M. D. R2 North Baltimore.

Withrow, C. F. RD North Baltimore Hen.

Withrow, F. E. (Julia) 2 ch farmer T 80a 3h 3c R2 North Baltimore Hen 56.

Withrow, O. A. (Agnes) 2 ch farmer T 110a 3h 3c R3 Bowling Green Pla 90 Ind tel.

Wither, Albert (son F. W.) farmer R3 Pemberville Tro 60.

Witker, Chas. F. Pemberville Fre.

Witker, Ernest Pemberville Tro.

WITKER, F. W. (Anna) farmer O 78a 3h 7c R3 Pemberville Tro 60 B tel.

WITKER, J. F. (Mary Ann) 1 ch farmer O 93½a 4h 8c R1 Bradner Fre 92 B tel.

Witker, Wm., Jr. (Anna) 1 ch farmer T 80a 3h 15c R3 Pemberville Tro 58.

Witmore, J. H. (Nettie) 2 ch farmer T 160a 5h 4c R1 Risingsun Per 97 Ind tel.

Witmore, Mary A. Perrysburg Pbg.

Witte, Harold F. laborer 2h 1c R2 Pemberville Web 34½.

Witte, Henry (Savilla) 6 ch farmer T 2h 1c R2 Pemberville Web Ind tel.

Witte, R. F. Scotch Ridge Web.

Witten, Bishop RD North Baltimore Hen.

Wittenmyer, Jno. F. RD Rudolph Lib.

WITTENMYER, WALDO (Mary E.) 6 ch farmer T 30a R1 Portage Por 39.

Witter, Chas. (Della) 1 ch oil worker O H&L Rudolph Lib 95 Ind tel.

Witters, Bishop RD North Baltimore Hen.

Witters, Frank, Jr. (Rosa) 1 ch farmer T 226a 3h 2c Waterville Mid 3 B tel.

Witzler, A. J. (Bertha) 1 ch furniture & undertaking O H&L 3h Perrysburg Pbg Ind tel.

Witzler, Emma ret O H&L Second St Perrysburg Pbg.

Witzler, Ed. J Marie Louise) 1 ch electrician T H&L Second St Perrysburg Pbg B tel.

WITZLER, F. A. (Edith) 6 ch manufacturer boxes O H&L Fourth St Perrysburg Pbg B tel.

Witzler, Julius (Anna) 2 ch laborer O H&L Fourth St Perrysburg Pbg B tel.

Witzler, Margaret ret O H&L Second St Perrysburg Pbg B tel.

Witzler, Wm. ret O H&L Fourth St Perrysburg Pbg.

Wlecke, E. Henry Pemberville Fre.

Woelke, Edward Dunbridge Web.

Woessner, J. J. (Emma) 5 ch oil worker O H&L 1c R1 Rudolph Lib 77 Ind tel.

Wohlgamut, Clarence (Gertrude) 5 ch town marshal T H&L Box 165 Rossford Ros.

Wohlgamuth, A. F. (Ida) field foreman T H&L Washington St Cygnet Blo Ind tel.

Wohlgamuth R. J. Portage Lib.

Wolenbecker, Henry RD Dunbridge Mid.

Wolf, Alfred (Helen) 1 ch electrical worker O H&L Indiana Ave Perrysburg Pbg B tel.

Wolf, Ambrose Millbury Lake.

Wolf, Bert (Mabel) 3 ch farmer T 50a 3h 3c R3 Perrysburg Pbg 88.

Wolf, Berl 4 ch teamster O H&L Second St Perrysburg Pbg.

Wolf, Chas. F. (Ida) 4 ch farmer O 80a 3h 4c R1 Hoytsville Jac 64 Ind tel.

Wolf, C. E. (Sherlot) 4 ch oil worker T H&L Walbridge St Cygnet Blo Ind tel.

Wolf, D. C. (Bertha Pearl) 1 ch mail carrier O H&2Lots Locust St Weston Wes Ind tel.

Wolf, Fred R3 Perrysburg Pbg.

Wolf, Geo. J. Perrysburg Pbg.

Wolf, Harry (Bertha) carpenter O H&L Sixth St Perrysburg Pbg.

Wolf, Jos R3 Perrysburg Pbg.

Wolf, P. J. RD North Baltimore Hen.

Wolfe, Chas. Prairie Depot Mon.

Wolfe, Glenn RD Haskins Mid.

Wolfe, H. H. (Mary) sexton O 6a Portage Por 6.

WOLFE, RALPH bakery & restaurant Cygnet Front St Blo B & Ind tels. See adv.

WOLFF, MRS. EMMA Box 47 Millbury.

Wolford, Robt. RD North Baltimore Hen.

Wollam, C. F. (Mary E.) farmer O 247a 3h 11c R1 Risingsun Mon 61 B tel.

Wollam, Geo. RD Prairie Depot Por.

WOLLAM, J. F. (Nettie) 2 ch drug store O H&store 1h Main St Jerry City Por Ind tel.

WOLLAM, J. H. county commissioner O 98a 2h R1 Risingsun Mon B tel.

Wollam, J. W. farmer O 120a 5h 15c R1 Bradner Mon 82.

Wollam, R. H. farmer O 98a 1h 9c R1 . Risingsun Mon 69.

Wollam, W. M. Risingsun Mon.

Wommer, J. Q. RD North Baltimore Hen.

WOOD, ARTHUR (Alice R.) 3 ch farmer T 125a 4h 2c R2 Bowling Green Pla 52.

WOOD, B. T. (Maud) 1 ch farmer T 80a 4h 3c R3 Weston Mil 70 Ind tel.

WOOD, E. (Ella) fruit grower O 10¾a 1h 1c Weston Wes 48 B & Ind tels. See adv.

Wood, E. (Dora E.) farmer O 40a 3h 2c R3 North Baltimore Blo 27 Ind tel.

Wood, E. D. (Martha J.) farmer T 160a 9h 8c R1 North Baltimore Hen 72.

Wood, F. T. (Bessie) 1 ch home bakery T H&L RD North Baltimore ‚Hen B tel.

Wood, Harry (son R. R.) R1 Grand Rapids Gr Rs 11.

Wood, Mrs. H. A. Weston Wes.

Wood, James E. (Blanche) farmer T 160a 5h 7c R3 North Baltimore Hen 114 Ind tel.

Wood, Martha J. North Baltimore Hen.

WOOD, R. R. (Jane) farmer T 105a 6h 3c R1 Grand Rapids Gr Rs 11 Ind tel.

Wood, S. O. (Lucy R.) 2 ch dentist O H&L Weston B tel.

WOOD, T. H. (Mary) 5 ch farmer T 120a 4h 3c R3 North Baltimore Hen 107 Ind tel.

Woodacre, Geo. Hoytsville Jac.

Woodard, Mrs. M. 1 ch housekeeper 189 Superior St Rossford Ros.

Woodbury, Earnest (Bessie) farmer T 60a 2h 4c R2 Bowling Green Mid 42.

Woodbury, Harold (Hazel) 1 ch farmer T 132a 3h 4c R1 Grand Rapids Gr Rs 46 Ind tel.

Woodbury, J. P. (Mary J.) farmer O 60a 4h 15c R1 Tontogany Pla 18 Ind tel.

Woodbury, M. E. (Martha) farmer O 60a 2h 8c R1 Bowling Green Pla 24.

Woodbury, Ray RD Tontogany Pla.

WOODBURY, W. R. farmer T 120a 4h 8c R1 Tontogany Pla 19 Ind tel.

Wooden, F. A. (Christiana) artist O H&L Fourth St Perrysburg Pbg B tel.

WOODLIEF, FRANCES B. Perrysburg.

Woodruff, Ezra (Sarah) 7 ch farmer O H&L 2h Risingsun Mon.

Woodruff, E. W. Risingsun Mon.

WOODRUFF, FLOYD (Edna) 1 ch farmer T 108a 3h R2 Prairie Depot Mon 10.

Woodruff, Jacob (Minnie) 5 ch laborer T H&L Risingsun Mon.

Woodruff, J. P. (Minnie) 5 ch blacksmith O H&L 1c Prairie Depot Mon.

Woodruff, J. W. Bradner Mon.

Woodruff, Marion (Idie) 4 ch laborer T H&L Portage Lib 113.

Woodruff, Richard (Martha) 3 ch laborer O H&L Risingsun Mon.

Woodruff, Richard (Florence) 1 ch section hand T H&L Risingsun Mon.

Woodruff, T. E. (Mary) 1 ch sta agt T H&L Pemberville Fre 40 B tel.

Woodruff, Walter RD North Baltimore Hen.

WOODS, HARRY (Mable) 2 ch section foreman T H&L Union St Cygnet Blo 6.

Woods, Jonathan R1 Rudolph Lib 36 Ind tel.

Woodward, Geo. (Nora) 2 ch farming O H&L Hoytsville Jac.

Woolf, Fred W. (Mabel) laborer T H&L 2h R1 Lime City Pbg 55.

Woolf, John (Mary) ret O 85a R3 Perrysburg Pbg 121.

Woolf, Joseph (Martha) 2 ch farmer O 20a 2h 6c R3 Perrysburg Pbg 121 B tel.

Woolley, C. W. (Bertha) 2 ch farmer O 76a 5h 4c R2 Dunbridge Mid 70 Ind tel.

Wooster, Helen W. RD Bowling Green Mid.

Worine, Peter (Matilda) 5 ch farmer T 70a 4h 3c R1 East Toledo Ros 38.

Worley, C. B. RD North Baltimore Hen.

Worley, David H. (Cora B.) farmer O 46a 2h 3c RD North Baltimore Hen 88 Ind tel.

Woyame, Charles (son Margurette) T 65a 5h 2c R1 East Toledo Lake 116 lnd tel.

WOYAME, JOSEPH (Emily) 2 ch farmer O 18a 3h 3c R1 East Toledo Lake 70 Ind tel.

Woyame, Margurette O 65a R1 East Toledo Lake 116.

Wrede, A. RD North Baltimore Hen.

Wright, Adron (Blanche) laborer T R1 North Baltimore Hen 46.

Wright, A. F. (Blanch) farmer O H&L 3h 3c R3 Weston Wes Ind tel.

WRIGHT, A. H. (Nora E.) farmer O 50a 3h 2c R1 Bloomdale Blo 95 B & Ind tels.

Wright, Brainard (Frances) 4 ch carpenter T H&L Prairie Depot Mon.

Wright, B. O. (Sadie) 2 ch laborer T H&L Findlay St Portage Por.

WRIGHT, C. W. (Millie) 2 ch farmer O 108a 2h 6c Scotch Ridge Web 29 B tel.

Wright, Dean (son Elza) R1 Jerry City Blo 70.

Wright, Ed. (Carrie D.) 1 ch farmer O 200a 3h 3c R1 Grand Rapids Wes 5 Ind tel.

Wright, Eddie H. (Bertha E.) farmer O 80a 3h 5c R1 Bloomdale Blo 129 B & Ind tels.

WRIGHT, ELMER (Gemima) 1 ch farmer T 130a 4h 9c R1 Tontogany Pla 1 Ind tel.

WRIGHT, ELZA S. (Florence) 6 ch farmer T 80a 5h 4c R1 Jerry City Blo 70.

Wright, E. P. (Anna) laborer O H&L Wall St Tontogany Wash.

Wright, Glada E. (dau Elza) R1 Jerry City Blo 70.

Wright, Jas. Cygnet Blo.

Wright, Jasper (Mary Jane) 5 ch farm O H&L Milton Center Mil.

Wright, J. H. Weston Wes.

Wright, J. M. Weston Wes.

Wright, Levern J. (Verda) farmer O 60a 3h R2 Weston Pla 3 Ind tel.

Wright, S. E. (Margaret) 2 ch farmer O 4h 9c R2 Pemberville Web 65 B tel.

Wright, W. M. Freeport Mon.

Wright, W. S. Tontogany Wash.

Wyant, H. L. (Daisy) 1 ch hardware & furniture O Main St Bloomdale Blo B & Ind tels.

Wyant, Mrs. J. W. O H&L N Main St Bradner Mon B tel.

Wyant, Lucretia Bradner Mon.

Wyer, R. M. Risingsun Mon.

Wyers, Olive Custar Lib.

Wygant, Charles (Daisy) laborer T R3 Perrysburg Pbg 134.

Wygant, John H. (Genett) glass worker T Perrysburg Pbg 134.

Wygant, Letta R3 Perrysburg Pbg.

Wygant, Martin (Clara) 3 ch gardner O 5a 1h Rossford Pbg 83.

Wymer, Chas. E. (Clara) 7 ch farmer T 87a 5h 2c R3 North Baltimore Blo 29 B & Ind tels.

Wynn, Carl E. farmer R3 Prairie Depot Mon 13.

Wyrick, Otis (Mary) T H&L 1h Bairdstown Blo B & Ind tels.

Yambert, A. H. (Diana) 2 ch clerk O H&L Risingsun Mon.

Yambert, E. M. (Emma E.) 2 ch farmer T 100a 2h 4c R1 Risingsun Mon 61.

Yambest, A. H. Risingsun Mon.

Yambest, Mabel Risingsun Mon.

Yant, C. W. Bradner Mon.

Yantis, F. W. Bloomdale Blo.

Yarger, W. O. (Effie) 4 ch oil pumper T H&L R1 Rudolph Lib 68 Ind tel.

Yarnell, David carpenter bds 118 Oak St Rossford Ros.

YARNELL, JOHN (Sarah E.) carpenter & joiner T 12a R1 Bradner Fre 79.

Yates, James (Sarah) ret O H&L 1h 1c West Mill Grove Per 68.

Yates, Mrs. John 2 ch farmer O 120a 1h 7c R1 Fostoria Per 48 Ind tel.

Yates, J. A. (Sarah E.) ret O 160a 1h 2c West Millgrove Per 68.

Yates, J. C. (Nebraska) 7 ch farmer O 80a 5h 5c R2 Prairie Depot Per 7 B & Ind tels.

Yates, J. E. (Sylvia) 2 ch farmer T 87a H&L 4h 3c R1 Bloomdale Per 8 B & Ind tels.

Yates, L. L. (Martha E.) ret O 160a 2h 2c West Millgrove Per 10 B & Ind tels.

Yates, Rachael ret O H&L West Millgrove Per 69.

Yates, T. H. (Carrie E.) 7 ch farmer T 154a 6h 4c Prairie Depot Per 2 B & Ind tels.

YATES, VIRGLE W. (son J. E.) laborer 3h 1c R1 Bloomdale Per 8 B & Ind tels.

Yeager, A. J. RD North Baltimore Hen.

Yeager, C. M. (Retta) 1 ch farmer O 80a 5h 8c RD Custar Lib 23 Ind tel.

Yeager, Fred (Sidelia) ret O H&L Second St Perrysburg Pbg.

Yeager, Geo. L. Freeport Mon.

Yeager, John (Sara) 2 ch ret O H&L Fourth St Perrysburg Pbg.

Yeager, J. A. RD North Baltimore Hen.

Yeager, W. O. Rudolph Lib.

Yeagle, Rev. Michael (Lucy May) 1 ch minister H&L Cor Silver & Walnut Sts Weston B tel.

Yealey, Lee oil worker Rudolph Lib 81.

Yetter, Caroline 2 ch ret O 60a H&L Grand Rapids Gr Rs Ind tel.

Yochum, Henry RD North Baltimore Hen.

Yochum, Peter barber O H&L Bradner Mon.

Yoder, H. F. (Anna) 3 ch laborer O H&L Longley Per 103 B tel.

Yoder, Joe (Bessie) 1 ch foreman T H&L Pemberville Fre B tel.

Yoeder, John (Mary) 3 ch auto salesman T H&L Pemberville Fre.

Yont, C. W. (Nellie) 2 ch confectionery T H&L East St Bradner Mon B tel.

Yont, J. T. (son Willard) farmer Sugar Ridge Mid 61.

York, Wm. (Wilhelmina) 2 ch farmer O 40a 4h 6c R1 Genoa Lake 49 B tel.

Youud, Jno. RD Rudolph Lib.

Young, A. B. (Mariah Jane) 3 ch watchmaker T H&L 1166 Oak St East Toledo Ros 19.

Young, Christina 4 ch farmer O 40a R1 Deshler, Jac 36.

YOUNG, C. A. (Estella) station agent T H&L Haskins Mid B tel.

Young, C. A., Jr. (son C. A.) manager of theatre Haskins Mid.

Young, C. E. (Mary) merchant O H&L 1h Findlay St Portage Por 2 Ind tel.

Young, C. M. (son C. A.) manager Lyric Theatre Haskins Mid.

Young, C. R. (son C. A.) school teacher Haskins Mid.

Young, Frank teaming O H&L 2h Cherry St Weston Ind tel.

Young, Mrs. Geo. 3 ch farmer O 40a 3h 4c R1 Deshler Jac 6 B tel.

Young, H. W. (Mabel) 3 ch hired man T H&L R1 Millbury Lake 105.

Young, Jacob Millbury Lake.

Young, Jesse (son A. B.) 1166 Oak St East Toledo Ros 19.

YOUNG, JNO. Millbury.

Young, J. A. (Nellie) 2 ch pumper O 40a 1c R1 Rudolph Lib 70.

Young, J. W. (Rose) 2 ch pumper T H&L Findlay St Portage Por.

Young, Kate Perrysburg Pbg.

YOUNG, NELLIE R1 Rudolph.

Young, Philip H. (Caroline) ret O 60a H&L Clark St Weston Ind tel.

Young, Richard (son Christina) laborer R1 Deshler Jac 36.

YOUNG, ROBERT A. (Adelaide) farmer T 12a 1h R1 Tontogany Wash 12 Ind tel.

Young, R. E. (son C. A.) operator Haskins Mid.

YOUNG, WM. W. (Carrie) 4 ch farm manager T 2c R2 Deshler Jac 8.

Young, W. J. (Elizabeth A.) ret blacksmith O 2a R2 Pemberville Web 34½.

Youngs, A. E. (Mary) 1 ch baker T H&L Church St Bradner Mon.

Youngs, Carrie R1 Weston Lib 1 Ind tel.

Youngs, Grace R1 Weston Lib 1 Ind tel.

YOUNGS, H. A. (Mertie) 2 ch oil producer O H&L cor Crocker & Bell Sts Bradner Mon B tel.

Youngs, Robert R1 Weston Lib 1 Ind tel.

Youngs, Mrs. Sarah O 147a 10h 6c R1 Weston Lib 1 Ind tel.

Youngs, Walter (Estella) farmer T 20a 3h 2c R1 Weston Pla 12.

Youngs, William R1 Weston Lib 1 Ind tel.

Youngs, W. C. (Ida) 3 ch grocer O H&L Evans St Bradner Mon B tel.

Younkin, Jess (Laura) 5 ch farmer T 40a 3h 2c R3 Bowling Green 13 Ind tel.

YOUNKIN, P. F. R1 Haskins Has 43.

Younkin, P. F. (Elsie) 1 ch farmer T 64a 4h 1c RD Haskins Mid 43 B tel.

YOUNT, WILLARD (Mary) farmer O 40a 4h 3c Sugar Ridge Mid 61 B tel.

Zaenger, Christian (Sophia) 2 ch ret O H&L Indiana Ave Perrysburg Pbg.

Zauger, Chris ret O H&L Sixth St Perrysburg Pbg.

Zauger, Fred ret O H&L Sixth St Perrysburg Pbg.

Zeigler, E. (Ella) 1 ch farmer T 40a 3h 2c R1 Portage Por 59 Ind tel.

Zeigler, Fred (Bessie) farmer T 40a 3h 4c R2 Prairie Depot Por 123.

Zeigler, John L. (Euphia) 1 ch farmer O 80a 4h 4c R2 Prairie Depot Por 78.

Zeigler, J. L. (Verna) 4 ch farmer T 40a 3h 4c R3 North Baltimore Hen 108 Ind tel.

Zeigler, J. O. (Matilda) 3 ch farmer O 119a 3h 5c R2 Prairie Depot Por 78.

Zellers, T. H. farm hand R1 Luckey Tro 69 Ind tel.

Zeltner, Mrs. Margaret Hoytsville Jac.

Zender, Peter Rising Sun Mon.

Zepernick, C. E. (Lora) 3 ch farmer T 60a 2h 5c R1 Pemberville Fre 66.

Zepernick, F. W. (Wilda) 2 ch farmer O 120a 7h 5c R1 Fostoria Per 49 Ind tel.

Zepernick, Ira ret O 60a R1 Pemberville Fre 68.

Zepernick, Laura Pemberville Fre.

Zepernick, Thos. Pemberville Fre.

Zeigler, Mrs. Ella RD Portage Por.

Zeigler, Elzie RD Portage Por.

Zeigler, Emma Bloomdale Blo.

Zeigler, Fred RD Prairie Depot Por.

Zeigler, Jno. M. Pemberville Fre.

Zeigler, J. L. RD North Baltimore Hen.

Zeigler, J. O. RD Prairie Depot Por.

Zeltner, John H. (Margaret) 3 ch farmer O 80a 4h 6c R1 Hoytsville Jac 47.

Zeltner, Louisa K. (dau John H.) housekeeper R1 Hoytsville Jac 47.

Zeltner, Otto J. (son John H.) farm hand R1 Hoytsville Jac 47.

Zeltner, Paul G. farming R1 Hoytsville Jac 47.

Zesing, Chas. (May) thresher T 2h 1c R1 Genoa Tro.

Zesing, Oscar (Susie) 1 ch thresher O H 3h 1c R1 Genoa Tro 42 Ind tel.

Zeternick, Thomas (Mary) farmer O 145a 3h 15c R1 Pemberville Fre 62.

Zetle, Susan Second St Portage Por.

ZIEGLER, CHARLES F. (Sadie J.) 1 ch farmer O 55a 4h 3c R1 Bloomdale Blo 112 B & Ind tels.

Ziegler, Martin 2 ch laborer O H&L Pemberville Fre 40 B tel.

Ziegler, Milo C. farmer 80a R1 Bloomdale Blo 61 B & Ind tel.

Ziegman, Geo. (Elizabeth) 6 ch farmer O 40a 5h 6c R1 Fostoria Per 116 Ind tel.

Ziems, F. D. R3 Perrysburg Pbg.

Ziessler, S. E. (Emma) 3 ch farmer O 80a 5h 5c R1 Deshler Jac 38 B tel.

Zigler, Albert (Iola) 2 ch stone contractor O H&L Front St Pemberville Fre 40 Ind tel.

Zigler, H. T. (Mary A.) general store O L R1 Bloomdale Blo 112 B & Ind tels.

Zigler, Mike RD Rudolph Lib.

Zihlman, Fred RD North Baltimore Hen.

Zimmerly, Mrs. Ellen 1 ch O H&L East St Bradner Mon B tel.

Zimmerman, Asher cattle RD Bowling Green Cen.

Zimmerman, Bert (Francis) farmer O 20a 2h 4c R5 Bowling Green Web 19 Ind tel.

Zimmerman, C. D. cattle RD Bowling Green Cen.

Zimmerman, E. S. (Emma) 6 ch laborer O 65a R1 Rudolph Lib 70 Ind tel.

Zimmerman, G. H. (Emma) 1 ch painter O H&L Perry St Pemberville Fre.

ZIMMERMAN, H. W. (Lucy) farmer T 119a 4h 8c R1 Pemberville Fre 51.

Zimmerman, John (Jennie) farm manager 290a R2 Deshler Mil 15 B tel.

Zimmerman, J. W. (Violet) 2 ch farmer T 80a 3h 3c R2 Dunbridge Cen 54.

Zimmerman, Mrs. Lizzie 2 ch ret O H&L Milton Cen Mil.

ZIMMERMAN, NATHAN 7 ch ret O H&L Sycamore St Weston.

ZIMMERMAN, R. O. (Ethel) 2 ch farmer O 40a 3h 2c R3 Weston Mil 4 Ind tel.

ZIMMERMAN, S. W. (Elsie) 4 ch oil well driller T H&L Bradford St Cygnet.

Zindler, A. (A.) 2 ch storekeeper O H&L Pemberville Fre 40 B tel.

Zindler, F. W. (Minna) 1 ch storekeeper O H&L Pemberville Fre 40 B tel.

Zingg, Catherine Lime City Pbg.

ZINGG, CHAS. (Ida) 4 ch farmer O 80a 4h 15c R1 Lime City Pbg 93 B tel. See adv.

Zingg, Frank (Matilda) plumber O H&L Indiana Ave Perrysburg Pbg B tel.

Zingg, John (Caroline) 2 ch farmer O 61a 3h 5c R1 Perrysburg Pbg 32 B tel.

Zingg, Wm. (Maggie) farmer O 60a 4h 4c R1 Perrysburg Pbg 95 B tel.

Zink, H. G. (Anna) 2 ch oil worker O H&L 1h Union St Cygnet Blo 6.

ZINK, O. J. (Cannon B.) 3 ch farmer T 80a 4h 3c R3 North Baltimore Blo 18 B & Ind tels.

Zinn, Bert (Jenny) 2 ch laborer T H&L Sixth St Perrysburg Pbg B tel.

Ziss, E. G. (Hazel) 1 ch farmer T 155a 2c R1 Haskins Mid 83 B tel.

Ziss, G. O. (Cora) 1 ch farmer T 155a 3c R1 Haskins Mid 83.

Ziss, P. A. (Sophia) O 315a 12h 5c R1 Haskins Mid 56 B tel.

ZISSLER, JOHN (Annie) 5 ch section foreman T H&L Tontogany Wash.

ZORN, MRS. C. F. RD North Baltimore.

Zuch, A. W. (Ellen) 3 ch motorman O H&L Pemberville Fre 40.

Zulch, G. J. (Nora) 2 ch farmer T 80a 4h 4c R2 Weston Wes 52 Ind tel.

Zurcher, Geo. (son G.) farmer R1 Tontogany Wash 75.

Zurcher, Fred (son G.) farmer R1 Tontogany Wash 75.

Zurcher, Margaret 3 ch farmer T 88a 4h 4c R1 Tontogany Wash 75 Ind tel.

Zwefil, Bettina ret O H&L Freemont Pike Perrysburg Pbg B tel.

Zwefil, Salome 2 ch ret caretaker Perrysburg Pbg B tel.

Zweifel, George farmer Freemont Pike Perrysburg Pbg B tel.

ZWEIFEL, GEO. farmer T 22a 1h 7c Perrysburg. Pbg 141 Ind tel.

Securing Orders for the Wood County Directory.

Main Street looking South, Bowling Green, Ohio.

NORTH BALTIMORE

ABBREVIATIONS.—a, means acres; bds, boards; B tel, Bell telephone; 4 ch, 4 children; H&L, house and lot; O, owns; R1, Rural Route No. 1; ret, retired; T, tenant; 4h, 4 horses; 2c, 2 cattle.

Abbott, D. C. (Louise) 3 ch hay baler T H 424 Poplar St Ind tel.
Abbott, F. M. (Anna M.) carpenter O L 413 Pamett Ave Ind tel.
Abbritson, S. B. (Mina) carpenter O L Broadway Ind tel.
Adams, A. W. (Minnie K.) ret O L N Main St Ind tel.
Adams, H. A. (Fay) T Central Ave Ind tel.
AIKEN, J. A. grocer N Main St. See adv.
Alexander, C. A. (Lillie) 3 ch teamster Ind tel.
Apple, Cora 1 ch dressmaker O L Central Ave.
Apple, Margurite O Central Ave.
Archer, Henry (Jennie) school janitor O L W Water St Ind tel.
Archer, John (Louise) doctor O L Broadway B & Ind tels.

Archer, Marion W Water St.
Babbock, W. C. (Melissia) farmer Central Ave.
Bachman, J. W. (Grace) fruit farm O 15a S Summit St Ind tel.
Backer, J. H. (Emma) novelty store O L S Second St.
Baker, Anna sugar maker Central Ave.
Baker, Frank electrician Central Ave.
Baker, J. (Cathrine) oil man T L S Tarr St Ind tel.
Baker, Ralph tailor Central Ave.
Baker, T. C. (Anna) 1 ch oil pumper T L Central Ave Ind tel.
Baldwin, John ret T L W Water St.
Baldwin, J. A. (Delia) carpenter O L E Water St Ind tel.
Baldwin, L. J. (Jessie A.) 1 ch traveling man T L N Second St.
Barber, T. C. blacksmith Central Ave.

237

Barger, Jacob (Anna) ret O L W Broadway Ind tel.

Barker, Geo. (Catherine) grocery delivery O L 419 N Third St.

Barlow, A. M. (Jennie) laborer S Tarr St.

Barn, C. F. 1 ch dairyman S Tarr St.

Barnard, E. H. (Rosa) 3 ch oil driller O L 558 Belmont St.

Bartz, John (Amelia) stone mason O L W Broadway Ind tel.

Basler, Anna M. school teacher S Main St.

Baty, Harriet housekeeper T L N Main St.

Beard, Nick (Adda) 2 ch laborer T L East St.

Beck, William (Lillie) 3 ch carpenter O L East St.

BECKETT, J. W. (Nannie) oil business O H&L S Main St B & Ind tels.

Behler, Alta housekeeper O L E Maple St.

Bell, G. L. (Nana) 2 ch carpenter O L Jewett Ave.

Bell, Jennie M. nurse O L N Tarr St.

Bender, J. W. (Elmira) drayman O 311 S Second St.

Bender, J. W. decorator 311 S Second St Ind tel.

Bennett, G. F. (Lillie B.) oil driller O L N Third St Ind tel.

Bernard, Charles sign painter S Main St.

Biehler, L. W. (Hilda) clerk N Main St.

Billhermer, Meta 5 ch housekeeper Marguret Ave.

Blackall, M. J. (Elizabeth C.) 1 ch oil gauger O L E Walnut St B tel.

Blackley, Christ (Kate) 2 ch carpenter L East St Ind tel.

Blair, C. B. (Alice) laborer O L 793 Poplar St.

Bobb, D. H. (Alice) carpenter O L 782 Poplar St.

Bobb, J. H. 3 ch barber O 805 Poplar St.

Boltz, Abner (Tryhena) 2 ch engineer O L 316 Railroad St B tel.

Boltz, Phoebe housekeeper O L 219 Marguret Ave.

Bond, John (Bertha) 1 ch oil pumper T L N Second St Ind tel.

Bond, W. E. (Minnie) 1 ch oil pumper 233 Central Ave.

Bordman, H. H. ret O L Railroad St.

Bordman, W. H. (Edna) 3 ch water well O Railroad St.

Bosler, A. D. (Augusta K.) 1 ch ret S Main St.

Botz, Ray (Katy) 1 ch laborer Marguret Ave.

Bovey, Rev. J. B. (Ida) minister T L N Second St.

Bowers, Mary 1 ch housekeeper O L S Main St Ind tel.

Brager, H. J. (Anna) engineer O L Water St Ind tel.

Brennard, Mary housekeeper O L S Main St Ind tel.

Bretz, C. L. (Florence) 1 ch laborer T L.

Briant, Mary 1 ch housekeeper W Walnut St.

Briget, William (Lottie) 1 ch teamster T L.

Britten, G. W. (Mary) carpenter O L W Water St Ind tel. ·

Brobes, C. F. (Mary) barber O L Beecher St Ind tel.

Brobest, L. (Louisa) ret O L S Summet St.

Brooks, Charley oil driller S Tarr St.

Brooks, E. C. (Corine) 1 ch sawer O L S Tarr St.

BROWN, MARGARET E. real estate & ins S Main St. See adv.

Brown, R. E. (Lesta) 1 ch bartender T L N Taylor St.

Bucher, H. J. (Rosa) carpenter O Central Ave.

Bufington, I. P. (Estella) 2 ch carpenter T Maple St.

Burton, I. M. (Mary) 3 ch salesman T Central Ave Ind tel.

Bushey, J. P. (Lizzie) 6 ch teamster T Frazier St Ind tel.

Bushy, David (Osyth) 1 ch oil man S Main St Ind tel.

Butler, A. C. (Bertha) 2 ch laborer W Walnut.

Butler, E. F. (Pearl) 2 ch oil worker O L S Tarr St Ind tel.

Buzzo, Steve (Mary) 1 ch laborer O L N Second St.

Caldwell, W. A. (Lena) 1 ch oil pumper T L W Water St Ind tel.

Cameron, Mary housekeeper O L N Third St.

Camfield, W. M. (Eliza) 5 ch laborer T L Taylor St.

Campbell, Cowen (May) 1 ch plumber O L E Water St Hen Ind tel.

Campbell, James (Kate) druggist O L E Water St Ind tel.

Campbell, J. P. (Mary) 3 ch garage man O L E Walnut St B tel.

CAMPBELL, PARK (Mary) 3 ch garage O H&L E Walnut St B & Ind tels.

Carn, Minnie housekeeper N Second St.

Carks, Chas. laborer O L Beecher St.

Carnahan, Sadie housekeeper O L N Third St.

Carnicun, Enos (Laura) 5 ch teamster N Third St Ind tel.

Carr, W. E. (Grace) jitney driver T L Broadway Ind tel.

Cathery, Fred oil driller N Main St.

Cathery, Jas. (Harriett) rig contr N Main St Ind tel.

Cathery, Ray carpenter N Main St.

Chapman, L. C. (Sarah) farm hand T L.

Chase, Geo. (Mary) farmer O L Walnut St Ind tel.

Clark, John (Nellie) housekeeper N Main St.

Clark, John (Elizabeth) 1 ch oil business T N Main St B tel.

Clark, John barber N Main St.

Coats, Rebecca O L Central Ave.

Cole, Mary housekeeper N Tarr St Ind tel.

Colman, D. K. (Margaret) blacksmith O Broadway. Ind tel.

Conner, John (Mina) engineer Broadway St Ind tel.

Cooper, Harriet housekeeper O L W Water St.

Cooper, V. W. (Ethel) mail carrier O L 317 Railroad St.

Cope, J. W. (Nora) 1 ch manager lumber yard T L E Water St.

Cramp, Ed (Rose) tinner & plumber T W Water St.

Crane, James (Mary) laborer 539 N Third St.

Crist, John (Christena) 1 ch laborer O L Margaret Ave.

Culver, A. (Susie) fireman T L N Third St.

Culver, F. E. (Ellie) 4 ch brick mason T L East St.

Culver, J. bookkeeper N Third St Ind tel.

Davis, Nort oil man T L S Main St Ind tel.

Decker, Edward (Mary) 1 ch carpenter S Main St Ind tel.

Decter, J. W. (Saphrona) 4 ch grocery O L W Water St Ind tel.

Deroder, J. E. (Lillian) 1 ch oil worker O W Water St Ind tel.

De Rose, Effie 2 ch agent O L S Tarr St.

Deter, Madison (Elizabeth) farmer O L Frazier St Ind tel.

Dewalt, Paul (Gidas) 2 ch thrasher. T L Margaret Ave.

Diebley, W. E. (Jessie I.) 2 ch undertaker O H&L 6h N Tarr St B & Ind tels.

Dirk, John (Amy) fruit manager O L W Broadway.

Dirk, M. E. (Alice) fruit manager O L W Broadway.

Dodson, Geo. C. (Cora) clothing clerk Ind tel.

Doil, Ellen housekeeper 424 N Third St.

Downs, S. E. (Elizabeth) 5 ch laborer T L Taylor St.

Drayton, Elizabeth O 407 Central Ave.

Dubbs, Henry (Alice) carpenter Beecher St.

Ducat, Geo. (Zoe) 2 ch oil pumper O N Main St.

Ducat, Mrs. G. W.

Eberle, Catherine housekeeper O L N Main St Ind tel.

Ebersole, J. A. farmer 1a N Main St B tel.

Elliott, Frank (Julia) oil pumper O L East St B tel.

Elliott, John (Minnie) 3 ch laborer T L N Third St.

Elliott, Mary housekeeper O L.

English, Frank (Grace) 3 ch laborer O L Margaret Ave.

Enninger, Ed (Hazel) 1 ch delivery man T L E Water St.

Everbon, P. O. (Cassie) 3 ch laborer Taylor St.

Evertts, Henry (Mary) lumberman O L E Water St.

Ewing, Jennie housekeeper S Main St.

Ewing, L. E. (Hazel M.) 2 ch salesman S Main St.

Exline, Adam (Flora) machinist O L N Tarr St Ind tel.

Exline, Will machinist N Tarr St.

Fausnauge, K. W. (Henrietta) 2 ch bakery O L S Tarr St Ind tel.

Fellers, R. M. (May) 1 ch painter & decorator O L 306 Railroad St.

Ferguson, A. B. (Inia) 2 ch section hand O L S Tarr St Ind tel.

Pilsan, Elizabeth housekeeper O L N Water St.

Fisher, Harry (Catherine) ticket agent T L S Tarr St.

Fitspatrick, J. J. (Arma) oil pumper S Second St.

Flagg, W. M. (Gladys) 1 ch baker T S Second St.

Flickner, B. A. housekeeper O L S Tarr St.

Foley, Ida school teacher 798 Poplar St.

Foley, S. (Lena) 1 ch machinist O L 798 Poplar St.

Foltz, Carl (Florence) 2 ch oil worker O N Main St.

Foltz, Grace school teacher Box 444.

Foltz, H. Central Ave.

Foltz, H. A. (Mary) 2 ch oil pumper O L Central Ave B tel.

Foster, J. (Eliza) 3 ch lumberman T L Bates St.

Foust, O. (Bessie) druggist T L N Tarr St. Ind tel.

Fowell, Mark (Jennie) machinist O L E Water St Ind tel.

Frank, Mary A. housekeeper O L 325 N Third St Ind tel.

Franks, A. J. (Olive) farmer O L N Maple St.

Franks, Birdie housekeeper O L N Tarr St Ind tel.

Franks, John farmer O L N Tarr St Ind tel.

Francisca, B. S. (Hazel) 3 ch insurance agent O L 298 Railroad St.

Fredrick, Erastus farmer T L Taylor St.

Freece, Delia housekeeper O Central Ave.

Freeman, A. E. (Effie) 1 ch superintendent O L 286 Railroad St.

Fromer, John (Jeannette) grocery clerk O W Broadway.

Fromer, L. (Barbara) oil pumper O L 425 N Third St.

Frost, Clyde (son Jacob) student 799 Poplar St.

Frost, Jacob (Vernona) 1 ch blacksmith O L 799 Poplar St Ind tel.

Fuller, Oliver (Edith) 4 ch electrician T L East St.

Gaush, Susa 3 ch housekeeper O L E Water St Ind tel.

Gear, M. N. (Carrie) master mechanic T L N Third St.

Gear, William (Amanda) carpenter T L N Third St.

George, David (Catherine) miller O L 300 Water St.

George, Eliza A. O N Third St.

Gilmore, Henry (Catherine) ret S Tarr St.

Girdman, L. C. (Margaret) 2 ch real estate T L N Main St.

Glick, H. T. (Lelia V.) shoes & tailoring O H&L.

Goble, Charles 2 ch minister T L N Third St Ind tel.

Goldner, Frank (Bell) 4 ch ret O L N Second St.

Grant, Charles (Grace) painter O L Beecher St Ind tel.

Green, S. F. (Elizabeth) 2 ch machinist T L S Tarr St Ind tel.

Griner, J. O. (Belle) 1 ch school superintendent T L S Second St.

Grow, Bertha (dau Henry) housekeeper 299 Railroad St.

Grow, Henry ret O L 299 Railroad St B tel.

Halberth, Henry (Augusta) farmer O L N Tarr St.

Hall, Frank (Mary) 1 ch farmer T L.

Haman, Charles (Mary) ret O N Tarr St.

Hamon, Amanda housekeeper O L N Tarr St.

Hampshire, Geo. S. (Freda) clerk T L W Broadway.

Harder, Ed (Rufena) 3 ch laborer T L Broadway.

Hardman, Earl (Fern) 1 ch ticket agent T L S Tarr St.

Hartman, Catherine housekeeper O N Third St.

Hasbrook, A. (Helen C.) blacksmith N Tarr St.

Hasting, Fannie 1 ch housekeeper Broadway Ind tel.

Hathaway, Almina housekeeper O L Margaret Ave.

Hawk, James L. gardener O L W Broadway.

Hawk, J. W. (Mary) 1 ch master mechanic O L W Broadway B tel.

Helfrich, Frank (Mary M.) laborer S Main St.

Henning, Ellen J. housekeeper O L 190 Railroad St.

Henning, R. E. (Maude) 5 ch tailor T Central Ave.

Henning, W. B. (Jennie) telephone clerk O L 333 N Second St.

Heton, Al. (Helen) carpenter O L Beecher St.

Hichmond, F. (Minnie) 3 ch car brakeman N Main St.

Hill, G. A. (Helen) 3 ch deliveryman T L Broadway.

Hiller, S. R. (Sarah) ret O N Second St.

Hillery, Geo. canvasser O L N Second St.

Hillery, Jane housekeeper N Second St.

Hindle, B. J. bricklayer O L Frazier St.

Hoffes, Clara housekeeper 314 N Tarr St.

Hoffsis, W. M. (Anna) 4 ch laborer O L Smith St.

Hogen, Jack (Daisy) 1 ch blacksmith.

Houge, Beatrice housekeeper O L W Broadway.

HOUGH, E. W. (Phoebe) bakery T H&L Box 962 Ind tel.

Hough, J. A. (Abbia) farmer O 130a 3h 8c N Third St B tel.

House, G. O. (Catherine) 2 ch oil worker 409 S Second St.

Howard, E. L. (Nellie) craneman 121 N Third St.

Hubbell, F. S. (Leidy) oil gauger O E Walnut St B & Ind tels.

Hubber, Alida housekeeper E Walnut St.

Huber, F. R. (Sola) insurance agent. O 520 Railroad St.

Hughes, B. J. (Carrie C.) storekeeper T H&L Ind tel.

Hughs, C. W. teamster N Third St.

Hughs, J. M. laborer O N Third St. Ind tel.

Hulse, E. G. (Mary A.) general repair business O L S Main St.

Hulse, L. J. (Elsie) blacksmith T L S Main St.

Hunt, C. G. (May) telephone manager T S Second St Ind tel.

Irwin, Elizabeth housekeeper O L 800 Poplar St.

Irwin, Ernest clerk 800 Poplar St.

Ish, John (Etta) section hand N Tarr St.

Jimeson, P. H. (Laura) 6 ch machinist O L Railroad St.

Johnson, Almira housekeeper O S Second St.

Johnson, Bruce laborer S Second St.

Johnson, C. G. (Bertha) 5 ch O L N Third St.

Johnson, G. W. (Jennie C.) 2 ch section hand O L 794 Poplar St.

Johnson, H. C. (Belle) 2 ch tool dresser T L 403 N Third St.

Jones, L. D. (Jennie) ret T L S Main St Ind tel.

Josett, Frank (Josephine) foreman E Water St Ind tel.

Julis, Elmer (Alice) plumber E Walnut St.

Kakensparger, John (Mabel) 2 ch laborer T L Broadway.

Kakensparger, Sam (Emma) carpenter O L Broadway.

KALMBACH, FRED grain & coal S Second St B & Ind tels. See adv.

Kardatzke, Fred (Orpha) 2 ch section foreman E Walnut St.

KELLER, C. A. (Louise) 1 ch florist O Belmont St B & Ind tel.

Keller, Frances housekeeper Belmont St.

Kerns, Harry (Millie) miller T L S Main St Ind tel.

Kingsley, Ida 3 ch O L Central Ave.

Kissel, Aaron (Mary L.) 1 ch laborer T L. E Walnut St.

Kissel, Aaron ret T L N Tarr St.

Kissell, Chas. laborer N Tarr St.

Kissell, Dorlan N Tarr St.

Kissell, Ethel N Tarr St.

Kissell, Minnie N Tarr St.

Kleckner, Harry (Sarah) laborer N Third St Ind tel.

Kline, Anna housekeeper O L N Second St.

Klinger, Dan gardener.

Knisley, Clarence (Emma) machinist O L Broadway Ind tel.

Knodle, Edgar (Stella) 2 ch grocery store O H&L N Main St B & Ind tels.

Koaerk, Gabriel (Anna) 2 ch section hand O 1a Central Ave.

Laney, J. W. (Bessie) 3 ch electrician T L W Water St.

Lano, Charles (Mary) policeman O L 365 Railroad St.

Lawrence, Cras. electric engineer N Main St.

Lawrence, Nellie G. O L N Main St.

Leatherman, Jim (Carrie) 2 ch sugar salesman O L Broadway Ind tel.

Leathers, G. B. (Vera) 1 ch garage.

Leathers, J. C. (Alice) 1 ch carpenter O L 829 Water St Ind tel.

Lee, Walter (Jenney) 2 ch junk dealer T L Taylor St.

Lehr, J. C. (Clara) 1 ch laborer T L N Third St.

Lenert, Mana (Ada) 2 ch farmer T L East St.

Leoman, Thomas (Eva) engineer T L Broadway Ind tel.

Lewis, Cras. engineer O 789 Poplar St.

Lewis, Cleo (Della) decorator O 300 Railroad St.

Lewis, Edward (Jessie) teamster T L 328 Railroad St.

Link, T. A. (Anna) teamster O L.

Lingmad, L. D. (Carrie) 1 ch oil producer O L N Tarr St B & Ind tels.

Long, Mary housekeeper T L N Second St.

Lotzenhiser, E. B. (Bessie) laborer O L Margaret Ave.

Lowry, W. J. (Lillian) brakeman E Walnut St.

Lybarger, Frank (Gurne) 2 ch boiler maker T L N Third St.

Lyons, Lewis (Maggie) ret.

McCormic, C. D. (Roslie) 1 ch veterinary T L Broadway B & Ind tels.

McCoy, Leroy. grocery deliveryman N Tarr St.

McCoy, WILLIAM (Minnie) 2 ch oil driller O L N Tarr St.

McDonald, J. R. (Delia) oil man T L Broadway Ind tel.

McEvoy, Elmer (Wildia) oil pumper T L N Second St.

McEwen, Julie E. housekeeper O L N Third St.

McGann, C. F. (Esther) 2 ch oil driller O L W Water St.

McGann, Geo. W Water St.

McGann, Harold tool dresser W Water St.

McGuire, Adam (Ellen) 1 ch section foreman O L Beecher St.

McKee, Armed housekeeper O N Main St.

McKee, Elden L N Main St.

McKee, L. (Ida) 5 ch T L Smith St Ind tel.

McMan, Frank (Elizabeth) 2 ch oil pumper N Third St.

McMan, John 1 ch farmer O L N Second St.

McMan, Susan housekeeper T L Railroad St.

McMILLEN, W. H. (Minnie C.) 2 ch attorney-at-law O H&L S Main St B tel. See adv.

McPhale, Meta housekeeper S Main St.

McVitty, M. C. (Laura) oil worker O L N Tarr St Ind tel.

MacCormack, C. D. (Rosalie) 1 ch veterinarian T H&L N Tarr St B & Ind tels.

Mackley, G. V. (Hallie) 2 ch tool driller T W Water St.

Maden, Tom (Laura) tool dresser N Third St.

Madox, Anna L N Third St.

Magill, A. (Delia R.) painter S Main St.

Maid, Emma housekeeper N Second St.

Marona, Delia canvasser O L East St Ind tel.

Martin, B. O. (Anna C.) 1 ch traveling salesman S Main St.

Martin, Isabelle housekeeper O L N Tarr St.

Marvel, Fred (Dora) painter T L N Third St.

Mathile, C. B. (Dora) 2 ch oil pumper O L Broadway Ind tel.

Matter, Rev. W. W. (Pearl) 2 ch M E Minister T L S Second St.

Mays, Grant tool dresser S Second St.

Mays, Gravel (Ida) oil contractor T L S Second St Ind tel.

Merritt, D. C. (Laurantha) 4 ch laborer T 303 Railroad St.

Mesmore, Leizia 1 ch housekeeper T L N Third St.

Messer, Frank (Gabby) 1 ch RR operator T L 216 S Second St.

Miles, Patrick ret N Tarr St.

Miller, A. A. (Florence) 6 ch butcher O L Railroad St.

Miller, Emma housekeeper O L Beecher St.

Miller, E. E. (Mary) 1 ch restaurant O H&L N Main St B & Ind tels.

Miller, Ray (Beulah) laborer T Summet St.

Miller, W. F. (Clara) 1 ch oil well driller T L N Second St.

Miller, W. H. (Catharine) ret preacher O L Railroad St.

Mitchell, Edward (Julie) laborer T L Railroad St.

Monasmith, Henry (Lena) ret O L Beecher St Ind tel.

MONASMITH, W. S. (Jennie) cemetery sexton N Tarr St.

Moore, C. L. (Minnie) 3 ch laborer N Third St.

Moore, W. D. (Blanche) 4 ch engineer T L N Maple St.

Morehead, Fred (Ethel) bartender S Main St.

Morehead, Isaac (Hattie) carpenter Broadway Ind tel.

Mosie, James laborer N Third St.

Mullholand, C. E. (Nellie) 4 ch bookkeeping T L W Broadway.

Murphey, Dennis (Mary) RR fireman N Tarr St.

Musser, Charley housekeeper Marguret Ave.

Musser, Mary housekeeper O L Marguret Ave.

NEIL, JOHN (Sarai) oil man O L N Second St.

Neisley, Harold (Laura) laborer T L Broadway.

Niceley, Jennie 4 ch housekeeper O L Beecher St.

Nigh, C. G. (Lottie) 5 ch clerk in bank O 80a S Main St Ind tel.

Nigh, Roy farmer O 80a S Main St Ind tel.

Nigh, R. G. (Mary A.) laborer O L Gater St.

Noble, F. H. (Phoebe) engineer O.

Noble, Mollie Frazier St.

Northrup, C. M. (Blanche) 2 ch butcher T L Railroad St.

Ody, George (Catharine) 2 ch brick mason T 1a N Main St.

Oxenrider, Howard (Daisy) 2 ch driller O L 797 Poplar St.

Painter, Ida 1 ch housekeeper O L W Walnut St.

Palmerie, Mike (Cora) oil pumper L N Tarr St Ind tel.

Parke, George oil worker O L 322 S Tarr St.

Parker, Phila housekeeper S Tarr St Ind tel.

Parson, A. R. (Arken) 5 ch farmer O L Marguret Ave.

Parson, S. N. ret Marguret Ave B tel.

Parsons, R. J. (Wilda) foreman T L 298 Railroad St.

Patterson, Elmer (Ethel) 3 ch teamster N Tarr St.

Peirce, Cora housekeeper E Walnut St.

242

Perry, Ray (Nina) 1 ch laborer O L N Third St.

Persing, R. L. (Jennie) shoemaker.

Peters, Clel (Olie) 2 ch farmer O 2a Broadway Ind tel.

Peters, D. W. (Marie) 2 ch dairyman T L Broadway Ind tel.

Philips, Joe (Nellie) 4 ch laborer O L.

Pisor, G. H. butcher O L S Second St Ind tel.

Pisor, G. W. bookkeeper S Second St Ind tel.

Pollock, Ed. (Vergia) 1 ch engineer T N Main St.

Powers, H. E. (Maggie) oil worker L Broadway.

Presler, Hattie housekeeper O L E Water St Ind tel.

Priddy, J. L. (Hattie L.) 1 ch music store T H&L S Main St Ind tel.

Purdue, A. J. (Ora) machinist O L S Tarr St B tel.

Radabaugh, Jay (Emma) 1 ch rural carrier O L N Third St.

Ramsey, Chas. (Elmira) B&O gateman.

Reed, Dora 2 ch housekeeper O L Marguret Ave.

Reed, John (Martha) engineer O L E Walnut St.

Reedy, A. A. (Minnie) grocer clerk O L N Second St Ind tel.

Reedy, Fred painter N Second St.

Rensch, J. A. (May) driller 408 Railroad St Ind tel.

Rich, Charles (Rebecca) laborer T L N Third St.

Richmond, Orland (M a r i l l i a) T L Broadway.

Ritter, C. L. (Nary) 1 ch monument salesman 217 S Second St.

Roache, M. (Anna) oil gauger N Tarr St Ind tel.

Rockwell, C. J. (Nellie E.) cashier National Bank O H&L E Main St Ind tel.

Rockwell, Fred (Effie) 1 ch miller O H&L E Railroad St Ind tel.

Rockwell, G. G. (Hannah) ret O H&L & mill E Railroad St Ind tel.

Rockwell, Quin (Rose) miller S Tarr St Ind tel.

Rogers, Naomi housekeeper O L 223 N Third St.

Rogers, Scott (Amanda) farmer O L N Main St.

Rogers, W. P. (Lottie) implement dealer O H&L S Main St B & Ind tel.

Rose, F. H. (Mary) farmer T L W Broadway.

Ruch, D. R. (Dorleska) oil pumper Ind tel.

Ruffner, Jim (Bertha) 2 ch oil business T L N Tarr St.

Safford, Matilda housekeeper E Water St.

Swartz, Geo. (Margarite) 2 ch oil driller E Walnut St.

Savage, Geo. (Barbara) druggist T L E Walnut St.

Savage, Will (Orpha) 1 ch laborer T L 304 Railroad St.

Sayre, C. G. (Emma) 2 ch preacher T L.

Scirage, H. W. (Minnie) 2 ch blacksmith O L Water St.

Sciroll, H. D. (Anna M.) 1 ch Central Hardware Co O H&L N Main St Ind tel.

Schultz, H. A. (Maude) oil driller O L 403 S Second St.

Scott, Geo. (Lillie) butcher S Second St.

Scott, G. F. (Ella L.) 1 ch traveling salesman O L N Second St Ind tel.

Seymore, Sam clerk in grocery O L S Second St.

Sharp, Floyd W. (Helen) salesman N Main St.

Sharp, H. L. (Grace) laborer T L W Broadway.

Siarp, John F. (Della) salesman O L N Main St Ind tel.

Shaufler, Dave contractor O Central Ave.

Sherman, A. L. (Estella) 2 ch carpenter O L Railroad St.

Siuler, L. A. (Edith) 3 ch drayman 232 N Third St.

Shuler, P. P. (Lydia) drayman O L Central Ave Ind tel.

Simmons, Geo. (Elsie) 4 ch farm hand T Railroad St.

Simons, Levi ret.

Slaire, W. M. (Mary) 1 ch farmer O Central Ave.

Slaughterback, B. F. laborer Frazer St.

Slaughterback, C. B. (Ola) 1 ch laborer O L 124 S Frazer St.

Slaughterback, G. A. (Rose) 6 ch laborer Frazer St.

Slaughterback, Jacob (Etta) ret O L Broadway.

Slough, C. L. (Helen) 1 ch oil producer O L 238 Central Ave Ind tel.

Slougi, I. N. (Maria) ret T L Central Ave.

Slough, J. E. (Hattie) 1 ch conductor T L Central Ave Ind tel.

Smith, Calvin (Ella) drayman S Main St.

Smith, C. F. (Alwild) 2 ch music teacher O L S Main St Ind tel.

Smith, C. Z. (Agnes) 3 ch boiler maker T L E Broadway B tel.

Smith, Edson (Gertrude) 1 ch oil pumper O E Walnut St.

Smith, Elden (Bessie) oil pumper T L Taylor St.

Smith, E. J. decorator T L Beecher St.

Smith, G. B. (Barbara) mechanic O L S Second St.

Smith, J. (Bertha) field boss T L N Second St Ind tel.

Smith, J. G. (Belle) field boss O L 330 N Third St Ind tel.

Smith, J. K. (Rae) 1 ch O L E Water St.

Smith, J. R. (Gaily) 1 ch traveling salesman T L N Second St.

Smith, L. F. (Martha M.) field boss S Main St.

Smith, W. H. teamster T East St.

Snyder, Charles (Anna) 3 ch oil pumper O L N Third St Ind tel.

Snyder, Ed Caroline) 1 ch ret O L N Tarr St Ind tel.

Snyder, Harry (Mary) laborer T L Taylor St.

Snyder, H. L. (Myrtle) 7 ch oil pumper T L N Second St.

Snyder, Lucy housekeeper O N Tarr St Ind tel.

Snyder, Marion (Anna) farmer O L 245 Central Ave. Ind tel.

Sommers, H. M. (Lulu A.) 1 ch druggist O H&L S Main St Ind tel.

Spergin, G. R. (Belle) 1 ch laborer O L.

Spitler, A. R. (Melissia) tile setter O L 796 Poplar St Ind tel.

Spitler, T. A. 2 ch painter & decorator T L 796 Poplar St Ind tel.

Spitler, W. F. (Laura) farmer W Broadway Ind tel.

Sprangler, Chas. fireman N Third St.

Sprankle, C. A. (Viola) laborer T L N Third St.

Stackhouse, John (Bertha) oil pumper N Third St Ind tel.

Starkey, Dave (Frances) teamster T L East St.

Steel, Joe (Mary) farmer 408 S Second St.

Stouffer, W. L. general store O H&L S Main St. B & Ind tels.

Stradley, S. O. (Elizabeth) oil pumper T L N Second St.

Stull, Jane housekeeper O L 808 Poplar St.

Swanson, Alice M. 3 ch housekeeper O L Belmont St.

Swanson, Fina Belmont St.

Swanson, J. R. (Myrtle) 1 ch barber O H&L.

Swartz, Harry (Leah) 2 ch bartender E Walnut St.

Swartz, Joe (Maggie) oil man O L East St Ind tel.

Sweet, Roy (Cecil) 3 ch oil pumper T L Broadway.

Swiger, Adam (Alice) painter O L W Broadway Ind tel.

Swoh, Fannie housekeeper S Main St Ind tel.

Swoh, Rosa housekeeper N Tarr St.

Swonson, J. R. (Myrtle) 1 ch barber T L Broadway.

Tarr, Haley school teacher N Main St.

Tarr, J. W. (Elizabeth) oil pumper O L N Main St Ind tel.

Tarr, Nute (Etta) 2 ch butcher S Main St. Ind tel.

Taylor, Ethel housekeeper.

Taylor, Freda oil pumper.

Taylor, Gladwin R. carpenter N Tarr St.

Taylor, Harry oil worker.

Taylor, J. G. (Marinda E.) carpenter & contractor O L N Tarr St Ind tel.

Taylor, Roda housekeeper O L Ind tel.

Taylor, Thomas oil pumper O L N Third St.

Teatsorth, Charlie (Jennie) 2 ch driller O L Jewett Ave Ind tel.

Thomas, Lucy housekeeper O L Margaret Ave.

Thomas, W. H. (Vina) 1 ch oil driller E Walnut St.

Thomas, Dr. W. T. (Flora) physician O 213 Railroad St.

Thompson, J. B. (Anna) milk man O L 329 N Third St.

Thompson, Mack (Manda) 1 ch housekeeper N Third St.

Thompson, Robert (Zeta) farmer E Walnut St.

Thompson, Sam (Tursey) 1 ch oil & tool dresser O L E Walnut St Ind tel.

Thrailgull, J. W. (Anna) 7 ch hay baler O 3Lots S Second St Ind tel.

Timmus, Ethel housekeeper Margaret Ave.

Timmus, Sara housekeeper Margaret Ave.

Todd, Charley Todd (Alice) laborer T L Central Ave.

Todd, J. L. (Frances) laborer L 340 Railroad St.

Todd, M. G. (Bertie) boiler maker O L 804 Poplar St Ind tel.

Tracy, J. P. (Della) 2 ch barber O H&L E Walnut St Ind tel.

Treft, William (Luella) laborer T L 781 Poplar St.

Trout, L. L. (Dollie B.) 3 ch furniture & carpet & stoves O H&L Ind tel.

Vogelsong, Mary housekeeper O L W Walnut St.

WAGNER, DELL (Jennie L.) harness maker O H&L 424 N Third St Ind tel. See adv.

Warner, S. (Mary) oil man O L N Second St.

Watters, H. M. (Viola) 1 ch engineer T L N Second St.

Weaver, Eckard (Nancy) 3 ch farmer Jewett Ave.

Weber, Perry painter N Main St.

Weeter, J. H. (Sarah) laborer T L Frazier St.

West, E. K. (Emma) 1 ch clerk O Railroad St Ind tel.

West, W. H. (Margaret) carpenter Railroad St Ind tel.

Wetzel, Erna (Tharl) 3 ch laborer T L Beecher St.

Wetzel, J. M. (Frances) laborer East St.

White, T. J. (Lucy C.) 1 ch evangelist S Main St Ind tel.

Whitten, Elizabeth T L Broadway.

Wicher, Clara 1 ch housekeeper O L N Second St.

Wigley, George (Hattie May) butcher O L Margaret Ave.

Wigley, Jeannette housekeeper O L S Tarr St.

Wilderson, S. E. (Laura) oil driller O N Main St.

Wiley, Haley dressmaker O L N Second St.

Winks, Olwen (Frona) ret O L Smith St.

Winterholte, Mat glassblower O L Margaret Ave Ind tel.

Winterhotter, Clara sugar maker Margaret Ave Ind tel.

Wirick, Ira (Mary) 2 ch butcher T L E Walnut Ind tel.

Wirries, Henry (Anna) 3 ch section hand O L E Walnut St Ind tel.

Wirt, William (Clara) 3 ch oil contractor O L N Second St.

WITHROW, C. F. (Carrie) 2 ch restaurant O H&L W Railroad St B tel.

Withrow, John (Alice) laborer O Belmont St.

Withrow, Lulu 1 ch.

Witten, Bishop farmer Second St.

Wolf, P. J. (Hattie) farmer E Walnut St.

Wolford, Robert (Darly) 1 ch mill man T L Railroad St.

Womer, Willis (Eliza) laborer O L Beecher St.

Wrensch, Hershel (son H. A.) laborer 408 Railroad St.

Yager, Alva (Jennie) 2 ch laborer O L N Tarr St.

Yates, P. K. (Ruth) 1 ch druggist L E Water St.

Yeager, J. A. (Lucy) 1 ch machinist O L N Main St Ind tel.

Young, Josie 1 ch housekeeper T L N Tarr St.

Young, Washington ret O L N Second St.

ZORN, C. J. telephone operator S Tarr St.

WOOD COUNTY BUSINESS DIRECTORY

S. W. BOWMAN
ATTORNEY

Nos. 1, 2 & 3 MERCER BLOCK
BOWLING GREEN, OHIO

BOTH PHONES ·

EARL D. BLOOM
LAWYER

Reference
THE FIRST NATIONAL BANK

Reed and Merry Block
P. O., BOWLINGGREEN, OHIO

BELL PHONE 16-K

HOME PHONE 91-B
RES. HOME PHONE 11-A

WM. DUNIPACE
LAWYER
124½ North Main St., Bowling Green, Ohio

ATTORNEY FOR
Business Men's Credit Association
Wood County Jersey Cattle Breeders' Association
R. G. Dun & Co.

A Thoroughly Equipped Collection
Department in Connection with
General Practice. ·

EDWARD M. FRIES

C. S. HATFIELD

FRIES & HATFIELD
ATTORNEYS-AT-LAW

OFFICE OVER LINCOLN'S DRUG STORE

BOTH PHONES

BOWLING GREEN, OHIO

C. R. PAINTER
Attorney-at-Law

FIRST DOOR SOUTH FIRST NATIONAL BANK

BᶜLL PHONE
THE WOOD COUNTY PHONE

BOWLING GREEN, OHIO

J. E. KELLY   L. D. HILL

KELLY & HILL
ATTORNEYS-AT-LAW

129 EBERLY BLOCK, SOUTH MAIN STREET
BOWLING GREEN, OHIO

NEWTON R. HARRINGTON   ROBERT C. DUNN

HARRINGTON & DUNN
ATTORNEYS-AT-LAW

Exchange Bank Building   Bowling Green, Ohio

I. A. GORRILL
ATTORNEY-AT-LAW

Office over Lincoln's Drug Store
Both Phones

Associated with
FRIES & HATFIELD
Attorneys-at-Law

BOWLING GREEN, OHIO

AGRICULTURAL IMPLEMENTS
—Continued.

CUSTER—Bickmyer, Geo. B.
Engesser, F. J.
LE MOYNE—Christen, E. R., & Co.
MILLBURY—**BAILEY, W. J.** See adv.
NORTH BALTIMORE—Rogers, Wm. P.
PERRYSBURG—Bayer, Chas.
PORTAGE—Richardson, C. C.
WESTON—DeWeese, B.
Pugh & Jones
WEST TOLEDO—**MARLEAU, DAVID.**
See adv.

ARCHITECTS.

BOWLING GREEN—Stewart, S. P., & Son

ATTORNEYS.

BOWLING GREEN—**B E V E R S T O C K, EDWARD.** See adv.
BLOOM, EARL D., 141 S Grove St.
See adv.
BOWMAN, S. W., 1-2-3 Mercer
Block. See adv.
CAMPBELL, A. R., 175 N Main St.
See adv.

Conley, Thos. F.
DUNIPACE, WM. See adv.
FRIES & HATFIELD. See adv.
GORRILL, I. A. See adv.
HARRINGTON & DUNN, Exchange
Bank Bldg. See adv.
JAMES, BENJAMIN F., 307 N
Church St. See adv.

Jones, Datus R.
KELLY & HILL. See adv.

LADD & JAMES. See adv.

BOWLING GREEN—McClelland & Bowman
Moore, R. B.
Nearing, G. C.
PAINTER, C. R. See adv.
REID, FRANK A., 220 Pike Ave.
See adv.

RIEGLE & AVERY. See adv.
SHATZEL, J. E. See adv.

NORTH BALTIMORE—**McMILLEN, W. H.**
See adv.
PEMBERVILLE—Hoyman, John S.

AUCTIONEERS.

GRAND RAPIDS—Lybarger, M. M.
TONTOGANY—**SCHALLER, J. H.** See
adv.
WESTON—**LANG NELSON CO.** See
adv.

AUTOS AND AUTOMOBILE SUPPLIES.

BLOOMDALE—Van Eman & Butler
BOWLING GREEN—Aller & McCrory
Bowling Green Motor Truck Co., The
LUCKEY—Williamson, H. H.
PORTAGE—Killian & Darrow
RISINGSUN—Sun Auto Agency

AUTOS AND AUTOMOBILE SUP- PLIES—Continued.

RUDOLPH—Carnicom, Ray

TOLEDO—**LANCASHIRE, H. W.** See adv.

TONTOGANY—Gill H. E.
Johnston & Robertson

WEST MILLGROVE—Ascess Auto Co.

BAKERS.

BOWLING GREEN—Ellsworth Bakery
Miller Bros.
Randall, A. R.
Sanitary Bakery
SHEPHERD, W., 165 N Main St. See adv.

BRADNER—Youngs, A. E.

CYGNET—**WOLF, RALPH W.** See adv.

GRAND RAPIDS—**GIERKE, PAUL.** See adv.

NORTH BALTIMORE—Home Bakery
Hough Bros.
Wilt, Will
Wood & Fleck

PEMBERVILLE—Goeckerman, C. F.
Johnson, R. M.

PERRYSBURG—Davidson, R. T.
Thornton, Arthur

PRAIRIE DEPOT—Weber & Messer

RISINGSUN—**SASS, H. C.**

ROSSFORD—Mierzejewski, C.
Nelles, Henry

RUDOLPH—Regal, Roy

WALBRIDGE—Baker & Bahnsen

WESTON—Hill, D. E.

BANKS.

BLOOMDALE—Campbell, T. J., & Sons
Exchange Bank

BOWLING GREEN—**COMMERCIAL BANK & SAVINGS CO., THE.** See adv.

FIRST NATIONAL BANK. See adv.

WOOD CO. SAVINGS BANK CO., THE. See adv.

BRADNER—Mechanics' Banking Co.

CYGNET—Cygnet Savings Bank Co.

HASKINS—**FARMERS SAVINGS BANK CO., THE.** See adv.

HOYTSVILLE—Hoytsville Bank

LUCKEY—Exchange Bank
Rees, A. D.

BANKS—Continued.

NORTH BALTIMORE—Hardy Banking Co.

PEMBERVILLE—**CITIZENS SAVINGS BANK, THE.** See adv.

PERRYSBURG—**CITIZENS BANKING CO., THE.** See adv.

FERRYSBURG BANKING CO., THE. See adv.

PRAIRIE DEPOT—Farmers Banking Co.

RISINGSUN—**Sun Savings Bank Co., The**

STONY RIDGE—Stony Ridge Bank

TONTOGANY—**TONTOGANY BANKING Co.** See adv.

BARBERS.

BOWLING GREEN—Ducat & Wales
Gokey, George
Gray, J. C.
Model Barber Shop
Plotner, J. A.
Up-to-Date Barber Shop
Zeller, C. P.

CYGNET—**STERLING, LON A.,** Front St. See adv.

GRAND RAPIDS—Roberts, John M.

PORTAGE—Bavis, H. H.

BARBERS—Continued.

RISINGSUN—Ireland; J. M.

WEST MILLGROVE—Teets, Walter

BICYCLES AND MOTORCYCLES.

BOWLING GREEN——**BALDWIN'S,** 175-177 S Main St. See adv.

Binkley, D. D.

Ducat & Walker

Long, J. W., Co.

FOSTORIA—**BIKE SHOP, THE,** 132 E Center St. See adv.

GRAND RAPIDS—Sherwood, Gill & Gray

NORTH BALTIMORE—Becker, W. A.

Sponsler, M. I.

PERRYSBURG—National Wheel Co., The

BICYCLE REPAIRS.

BLOOMDALE—Strawbridge, G. C.

BOWLING GREEN—Walker, James E.

BRADNER—Sloan, S. N.

PRAIRIE DEPOT—Hawkins, L.

TONTOGANY—Phillips, Jay

BILLIARDS.

BOWLING GREEN—Branigan Bros.

Brunswick Billiard Parlors

BILLIARDS—Continued.

BOWLING GREEN—Grames & Maynard
  Tuller & Forbes
BRADNER—Horner, J. L.
CUSTER—Raney, John
CYGNET—Stevens, H. E.
NORTH BALTIMORE—Bechtel, M. (Mrs. H.)
  Fauhnaugh, K. W.
  Monthaven, A. G.
PEMBERVILLE—Lehman, Grover
PERRYSBURG—Harper, Z. Q.
  Rossbeck, Fred P.
RUDOLPH—Aldrich, Clyde T.

BLACKSMITHS.

BAYS—**GORDON, THOMAS C.** See
  adv.
BOWLING GREEN—Bishop, J. E.
  Gustin, F.
  HARTMAN, W. W. See adv.
  Hopkins Bros.
  Petty, O. J.
BRADNER—Egbert, Claud
  Robinson, Geo. W.
CUSTAR—Bamberger, Geo.
CYGNET—Anderson, W. A.
  Oats, Riley

BLACKSMITHS—Continued.

DUNBRIDGE—Goodell, John
GRAND RAPIDS—Long, John E.
  Stevens, John E., & Son
HASKINS—Champion, Benjamin F.
JERRY CITY—Frankfother Bros.
LE MOYNE—Miller, J. B.
LIME CITY—**SMITH, WM.** See adv.
LUCKEY—Buck, Henry
MILLBURY—Munch, John
MILTON CENTER—Trumble Bros.
NORTH BALTIMORE—Coleman, D. K.
  Hasbrook, A. H.

Hogan, J.
Schrage, H. W.
Ulch, L. F.
PEMBERVILLE—Seik, W. H.
  Wice Brothers
PERRYSBURG—Stickles, Robert
  Wallace, Charles T.
PORTAGE—Watson, Wm.
  Williams, J. L.
PRAIRIE DEPOT—Fields, Bert
RISINGSUN—Reese, J. A.
RUDOLPH—Hathaway, J. B.
  Rechert, Frank
SCOTCH RIDGE—Grimer, C. W.

BLACKSMITHS—Continued.
SUGAR RIDGE—Elliott, R. B.
TONTOGANY—Foster, Edwin M.
RICKARD, I. E. See adv.
WEST MILLGROVE—King, John
WESTON—Abbott, Leander

BOOKS AND STATIONERY.
ROSSFORD—Juhoz, Chas. C.

BOTTLERS.
BOWLING GREEN—Bowling Green Bottling Works
Rapp & Bysel

BOXES.
RUDOLPH—T. & W. Stuffing Box Co., The

BRICK AND TILE MANUFACTURERS.
BLOOMDALE—Bloomdale Brick & Tile Co., The
HOYTSVILLE—Hoytsville Brick & Tile Co.
MILLBURY—Diefenthaler Co.
PEMBERVILLE—Buckeye Tile Co.
PERRYSBURG—Moser, Wm.

BRICK AND TILE MANUFACTUR-ERS—Continued.

PERRYSBURG—Perrysburg Tile & Brick Co., The

ROSSFORD—Rossford Brick & Tile Co., The

BROKERS.

PORTAGE—Munn, G. C., & Co.

BUILDERS AND CONTRACTORS.

BOWLING GREEN—Campbell, W. V.
Long & Ketchum
Maurer, Adolf
Moree, C. E.
Veber, Chas.
WESTON—Bortel, Allen

BUILDERS' SUPPLIES.

CUSTER—Thielen, H.

PERRYSBURG—Elks Builders Supply Co., The

BUILDING AND LOAN ASSOCIATION.

BLOOMDALE—Bloomdale Building Loan Co., The

CARRIAGES AND WAGONS.

BOWLING GREEN—**BALDWIN'S**, 175-177 S Main St. See adv.

CARRIAGES AND WAGONS
—Continued.

BRADNER—Hutchinson, John
GRAND RAPIDS—**SHERWOOD & GRAY.**
See adv.
PERRYSBURG—Hagermaster, Herman
RISINGSUN—Notestine, Henry

CATTLE, HORSE AND SWINE BREEDERS.

AMSDEN—**MOWRY & AUMAUGHER.**
See adv.
BOWLING GREEN—**BENDER, JOSEPH.**
See adv.

DUNNIPACE, ROBT. L. See adv.
LeGALLEY, CHARLEY. See adv.
DUNBRIDGE—**BRINKMEIER, C. L.**
GRAND RAPIDS—**PETTEYS, D. J.** See adv.
Spathelf, Milton
HASKINS—**LAHMAN, CHAS. E.** See adv.
LIME CITY—**ZINGG, CHAS.** See adv.
LUCKEY—**GLENWOOD FARM, THE.**
See adv.
PEMBERVILLE—**HESS, MRS. N. O.** See adv.
PERRYSBURG—**ACKLIN, DONALD R.**
See adv.

CATTLE, HORSE AND SWINE BREEDERS—Continued.

PRAIRIE DEPOT—**STEPHENS, JAMES.** See adv.

RUDOLPH—**POTTER, CLARENCE.** See adv.

TIFFIN—**KNEPPER, W. I.** See adv.

WESTON—**PETTEYS, L. A.** See adv.

CARPET CLEANING.

BOWLING GREEN—Rosenthal, Chas.

CARPET WEAVING.

WESTON—Morgan, J. J.

CEMENT, CONCRETE AND LIME.

BOWLING GREEN—Bowling Green Cement Block & Brick Co.

Carl & Culver Cement Co.

GRAND RAPIDS—Gill, J. F.

HATTON—Bradner, A. J.

LUCKEY—Keppler, F. J.

Ohio & Western Lime Co.

MILTON CENTER—Rummell, I. E.

PRAIRIE DEPOT—German, Fred C.

RISINGSUN—Goudy & Ousel Bros.

STONY RIDGE—Beauregard, Fred

CHIROPODIST.
BOWLING GREEN—McCarty, Mary E.

CHIROPRACTORS.
BOWLING GREEN—NORRIS, C. E., Suite No 9, Whitker Furniture Bldg. See adv.

Rutledge, C. C.
CUSTAR—NESMITH, REV. DR. L. M. See adv.

CIGARS AND TOBACCO.
BOWLING GREEN—Branigan & Sullivan
Coleman, J. N.
Ducat & Wales
Gribben, Q. N.
Hale, Fred
Loew, Frank
Noble Grand Cigar Factory
Smith, C. A.
Zuch, A. F.

BRADNER—Yaut, C. W.

CIGARS AND TOBACCO—Continued.

GRAND RAPIDS—Backus, Howard R.
 Souders, John A.
JERRY CITY—Kidd, L. A.
LUCKEY—Goodell, C. E.
NORTH BALTIMORE—Robinson, Thos. A.
 Romey, R.
PEMBERVILLE—Warren, H. R.
PERRYSBURG—Baird, Geo. W.
 Phillips, S. T.
 Rossbach, Geo.
 Shepherd, S. L.
 Whoff, II.

PORTAGE—Hyte, S. A.
ROSSFORD—Martin, Chas. E.
WESTON—French, J. F.

CLAY MANUFACTURERS.

HATTON—National Clay Co., The

CLEANING AND DYEING.

BOWLING GREEN—**BOWERS, E. J.,** 109
 N Main St. See adv.
Keyes, R. D.
Norris, C. M.
Sanitary Dry Cleaning Co.

CLOTHING.

BLOOMDALE—Stouffer, Josiah

BOWLING GREEN—Donahey & Co.
Riess, A.

NORTH BALTIMORE—Fleckner Clothing Co.
Lamfrom, M.

PRAIRIE DEPOT—Brentgarten, Chas.

WESTON—Powell, Mrs. E.

COAL.

BAYS—Robinson, James

BLOOMDALE—**GOOD, L. R.** See adv.

BOWLING GREEN—**AVERY, A. E.** See adv.

Central Coal Co.

DAVIDSON, P. M. See adv.

Keil, F. A.

STRONG, T. D. See adv.

Sutton, Mrs. O. B.

Sutton, R. A.

BRADNER—Silverwood, F. A.

CUSTER—Leiter, Andrew

CYGNET—Slike, C.

GRAND RAPIDS—Hutchinson, H. W.

Miller, Geo. H.

COAL—Continued.

Le Moyne—King, A. H.
Longley—Brant, Frank
Millbury—Martin, Christian
North Baltimore—Arnold, L. D.
Fulton, G. B., & Co.
KALMBACH, FRED. See adv.
Portage—Amos, C. J.
Prairie Depot—Tilton, S. E., & Son
Rossford—Gampher & Enis
Walbridge—**BRIM, OTTO R.** See adv.
Weston—Chapman, A. M.

Oswald Bros.
Smith, C. A.

CONFECTIONERY AND ICE CREAM.

Bowling Green—Anthony, P.
Calomiras, N.
Chroms, Thos.
DAVIDSON, P. M. See adv.
Howard, Solomon
Ichroni, T.
Custer—Ohlrich, F. W.
Cygnet—Lloyd, Harry

CONFECTIONERY AND ICE CREAM
—Continued.

GRAND RAPIDS—Ducat, D. L.
  Tanner, Mrs. A.
HASKINS—Vollmer, C. H.
JERRY CITY—Spencer, H. L.
MILTON CENTER—Filiere, Geo. F.
NORTH BALTIMORE—Giha, Michael
PEMBERVILLE—Titkemeier Bros.
PERRYSBURG—VanNorman, Harry
PORTAGE—Ray, Miss E. A.
PRAIRIE DEPOT—Baker, B. C.
  Crimer, Chas.

Feltman, Mary S. (Mrs. Geo.)
ROSSFORD—Tuller, C. A.
  Weber, S. (Mrs. Frank)
WALBRIDGE—Rhodes, Chas. W.
WESTON—Keep, R.
  Laba & Howard
  Thacker, C. D.

DAIRIES.

LIME CITY—Alexander, R. F.
ZINGG, CHAS. See adv.
MILLBURY—Knndson Bros.

DENTISTS.

DR. F. A. ELSON
DENTIST
PHONES:
OFFICE: BELL & U. S.   BOWLING GREEN, O.
RESIDENCE: BELL

Frowine, E. J.
Gernert, W. H.
LEA, THOMAS W. See adv.
TABER, C. M. See adv.
Yonker, E. L.
NORTH BALTIMORE—Milbourn, R. E.
PEMBERVILLE—McCormick, Dr. A. C.

DEPARTMENT STORES.

BOWLING GREEN—FORNEY, A., & CO. See adv.
LADD, FRANK H. See adv.

C. M. TABER
DENTIST
BOWLING GREEN, OHIO

Hours by Appointment   Both Phones

DR. THOMAS M. LEA
DENTIST

134 Reed and Merry Block   BOWLING GREEN, OHIO

THE GLENWOOD FARM
RAISER OF
Registered Jersey Cattle, Duroc-Jersey Swine, R. C. Brown Leghorn Chickens
Bell Phone   **J. M. STEPHENS, R. D. 1 LUCKEY, O.**

DRUGS.

BAYS—**CHAMBERS, J. W.** See adv.
BLOOMDALE—Butler, E. M.
BOWLING GREEN—**BOLLES DRUG STORE**, 108 S Main St. See adv.
Palace Pharmacy
LINCOLN & DIRLAM. See adv.
Rogers Bros.
SARGENT, ED. O. See adv.
YEAGER & STARN. See adv.
BRADNER—Bryan, Wm. L.
Leopold, H. L., & Son
CUSTER—Custar Drug Co.
CYGNET—Draper, M. C.

GRAND RAPIDS—Agner, H. M.
JERRY CITY—Wollam, J. F.
LUCKEY—Goetz & Babione
MILTON CENTER—Leaming, Wm. M.
NORTH BALTIMORE—Hoffman, J. T., Jr.
Sommers, H. M.
PEMBERVILLE—Fehr, Chas. A.
PERRYSBURG—Champney, C. P.
PORTAGE—Young, Chas. E.
PRAIRIE DEPOT—Messer, H. L.
Yeager, Geo. L.
RISINGSUN—White, E. E.
RUDOLPH—Jones, F. M.

DRUGS—Continued.

TONTOGANY—Eddmon, Mrs. A.
WEST MILLGROVE—Risser, Chas. E.
WESTON—White & Patterson

DRY GOODS AND NOTIONS.

BOWLING GREEN—"**CLEVENGER STORES, THE.**" See adv.
  Levine, Ellis
  Uhlman, Fred W.
GRAND RAPIDS—**BLACKBURN, W. R.** See adv.
  Bortel, Lewis
  Kerr & Shaffner

Walters & Co.
JERRY CITY—Wisner, Mrs. T. E.
LUCKEY—Meyers, F. W., & Son
NORTH BALTIMORE—Schmidt, A. P.
  Uhlman, Fred W.
PERRYSBURG—Fuller, A. C., & Son
  Veitch, W. J.
PRAIRIE DEPOT—Fike, L. M. (Mrs. F. H.)
ROSSFORD—Wilusz, Jos.
  Zion, Alex. A.
WALBRIDGE—Doughty, D. D.
WEST MILLGROVE—Chase, Mrs. Ella

ELECTRICIANS AND ELECTRICAL SUPPLIES.

BOWLING GREEN—**LOCKWOOD ELECTRIC SHOP.** See adv.
Electric Light Office
PEMBERVILLE—Stone, F. H.
Wilson, E. J.

FERTILIZERS.

GRAND RAPIDS—Donald, Watson
Stevens, Zahm

FISH.

BOWLING GREEN—Orwig, T. C.

FIVE- AND TEN-CENT STORE.

BOWLING GREEN—McDowell's

FLORISTS AND NURSERYMEN.

BOWLING GREEN—**MILNOR, W. W.** See adv.
NORTH BALTIMORE—**Keller Floral Co.**
PERRYSBURG—Hufford, J. Henry
WESTON—**WOOD, E.** See adv.

The Sunnyside Dairy Farm
Owned by
JAMES STEPHENS, Prairie Depot, Wood Co., Ohio
BUYER AND SELLER OF LIVE STOCK
Milk Cows and Draft Colts a Specialty
All stock guaranteed. PRAIRIE DEPOT, OHIO

Where Your Money Buys the Most
What Do You Want? We Have It
OUR REPUTATION IS BUILT ON LOW PRICES
MAKE US PROVE IT
W. R. BLACKBURN Grand Rapids, Ohio

BOTH PHONES "EVERYTHING ELECTRICAL"
LOCKWOOD ELECTRIC SHOP
C. R. LOCKWOOD
Fixtures, Wiring, Lamps, Etc., Automobile Storage
Batteries, Self Starters and Generators Repaired
250 No. Main St. - Bowling Green, Ohio
AGENT—EVER-READY STORAGE BATTERY

FLOUR, FEED AND GRAIN.

BLOOMDALE—**GOOD, L. R.** See adv.
BOWLING GREEN—**REIDERS MILL.** See adv.
    ROYCE & COON GRAIN CO., THE. See adv.
    Whitker, F. E.
BRADNER—Kortier, Chas. H.
CUSTER—Krohn & Deckrosh
CYGNET—**CYGNET GRAIN & HAY CO., THE.** See adv.
DUNBRIDGE—Trepauier, L. A.
GRAND RAPIDS—Grand Rapids Farmers' Elevator Co., The

Pilliod, Aug.
Stump, D. F.
HASKINS—Haskins Farmers' Grain Co., The
HATTON—Ash & Shaw
HOYTSVILLE—Hoytsville Grain Co., The
LATCHIE—Christiansen, Frank
LONGLEY—Sneath & Cunningham Co., The
LUCKEY—Luckey Elevator Co.
MILLBURY—McDougal, Adrian F.
MILTON CENTER—Garrison Grain Co.
    Milton Center Stock & Grain Co., The

FLOUR, FEED AND GRAIN
—Continued.

NORTH BALTIMORE — **KALNBACH, FRED**. See adv.

Rockwell Milling Co.

PEMBERVILLE—Bushman Bros.

PERRYSBURG—Devore Grain Co., H. W. Maddy, C. L., Co., The

PRAIRIE DEPOT—Cruikshank, J. L., & Co.

RISINGSUN—Farmers' Commercial Grain & Seed Co.

ROSSFORD—Larrowe Milling Co., The

RUDOLPH—Kinney, Mark

STONY RIDGE—**ELLIOTT & BEASLEY.** See adv.

TONTOGANY—Phillips, J. S.

WEST MILLGROVE—Whitman Milling Co.

WESTON—Cass, L. L.

Dirk, John V.

KEENER, MRS. JENNIE L. See adv.

Rural Grain Co., The

WESTON ELEVATOR & MILLING CO. See adv.

FURNITURE.

BOWLING GREEN—**COEN BROS.** See adv.

Whitker, J. W., & Co.

FURNITURE—Continued.

GRAND RAPIDS—**LAWRENZ, O. R.** See adv.

NORTH BALTIMORE—Trout, L. L.

PERRYSBURG—**MAHR, F. L.** See adv.

PRAIRIE DEPOT—Goodrich, J. M.

WESTON—**RAUBENOLT & LANCE.** See adv.

WATKINS, MR. & MRS. W. C. See adv.

GARAGES.

BOWLING GREEN—Bascom, Chas.
Bishop, Jas. E.
CALDWELL, C. W. See adv.
Court Street Garage
Gauder & Son
Loomis, L. C.
Miller Bros.
Smith, John

CYGNET—Slike & Hetter

FOSTORIA—**ADAMS, HENRY J.** See adv.

275

GARAGES—Continued.

GRAND RAPIDS—**GORSUCH, N. N., & SON.** See adv.

GRAND RAPIDS GARAGE. See adv.

HOYTSVILLE—Dellinger, H. H.
Dick & Raugler
Hoytsville Garage

LUCKEY—Luckey Garage

MILTON CENTER—**LONGBRAKE, W. A.** See adv.

NORTH BALTIMORE—Campbell's Garage
FULTON & BECKETT. See adv.

Leiter, H.
North Side Garage

PEMBERVILLE—Taulker, Fred H.

PERRYSBURG—Moser, Geo. W.

PRAIRIE DEPOT—**HOILS, C. H.** See adv.
STANDARD GARAGE, THE. See adv.

ROSSFORD—Henderson & Harter
. Rossford Garage

WALBRIDGE—**WALBRIDGE GARAGE.** See adv.

WESTON—Roe, Chas.

GENERAL STORES.

BAIRDSTOWN—Ensininger, F. G.
Hollinger, J. W.
BAYS—Wing, Lloyd
BLOOMDALE—Rearick, Frank
BOWLING GREEN—Belleville, L. E.
FORNEY, A., & CO. See adv.
Lenine, E.
McClay, D. W.
BRADNER—Fairbanks & Kortier
Riley, Chas. L.
CUSTAR—Claggett & Knapp
Sites, Daniel E.

Smith, Bennett, & Son
CYGNET—Grant, Geo. E.
Hudson, Harry P.
Mike, T. C.
Myers, L. (Mrs. S. M.)
DOWLING—Berry, H. E.
DUNBRIDGE—Current, John
Hale, A. G.
Hite, James A.
HASKINS—Browne, Earl
Rupp, David
Twining & Challen
Watts Store
HATTON—Elarton, T. J.

GENERAL STORES—Continued.

HOYTSVILLE—Dishong, U.
  Sawyer, F. T., & Co.
JERRY CITY—Jones, S. E.
LATCHIE—Bahnsen, Bahne
LE MOYNE—Brough, John R.
LIME CITY—**HALL, EDWARD D.** See
  adv.
LUCKEY—Current, John
  Goertz & Babeyone
  Myers, Frederick W., & Son
  Samson & Hoelter
MILLBURY—**MARTIN, PETER.** See adv.
MILTON CENTER—Blasius, John M.

MERMILLE—Rowland, J. A.
NEW ROCHESTER—Stewart & Brander-
  berry
NORTH BALTIMORE—Knodle Store Co.
  Sloan, D. J., & Co.
PEMBERVILLE—Hobart-Bowlus Co.
  Taulker & Williams
  Zindler Bros.
PORTAGE—Stratton, H. L. (Mrs. F. W.)
PRAIRIE DEPOT—Basey, A. F.
  McAlpine, Geo. A.
  Rogers & Frisbie
  Sage, Chas. S.
  Williamson Bros.

GENERAL STORES—Continued.

RISINGSUN—Home Bakery & Supply Co.

Strasberger, Jacob

ROSSFORD—Frautch, S., & Sons Co., The

Zion, John

RUDOLPH—Cupp, Lydia A. (Mrs. C. C.)

Schondelmyre & Co.

SCOTCH RIDGE—Davidson Bros.

STONY RIDGE—Shook, Ira E.

Waggoner, Corwin

SUGAR RIDGE—Reed, J. H.

TONTOGANY—Foote, A. D.

Gill, E. G., & Co.

WALBRIDGE—**GILBERT & TYLER.** See adv.

MILLER, G. F. See adv.

Stein, A. J.

WEST MILLGROVE—Bennett, W. S.

Shanks, Samuel L.

WESTON—Gould, W. T.

Uhlman, H. C., & Co.

WOODSIDE—**HELLE, H. W.** See adv.

GLOVE MANUFACTURER.

BRADNER—Bradner Manufacturing Co.

GROCERS.

BAIRDSTOWN—Bronson, C. D.
BAYS—Wingart & Hussey
BLOOMDALE—Hatfield, Ralph D.
  Mackey, John F.
  Markle, Wm. T.
  Willman, L. A.
BOWLING GREEN—Bradbrook, E. J.
  (Mrs. Samuel)
  Bradbrook, S.
  Coen, Frank M.
  Cook, Wm. A.
  English Bros., & Co.

Hodgson, Geo., & Co.
Kurrley, A. L.
McCrory & Munn
Maas Bros.
Red Front Grocery
South, Geo.
Underwood & Son
West End Grocery
BRADNER—Hoxworth, Frank L.
  Youngs Bros.
CUSTAR—Kistner Bros.
  Mahnen, C. F.
CYGNET—Bachman, John

GROCERS—Continued.

GRAND RAPIDS—Blackburn, W. R.
  Gill, Frederick
  Heeter, Fred
  Huffman, E. E.
  Long, Clarence
HASKINS—Bemis, Fred
HOYTSVILLE—Otto, E. P.
  Wall, F. M.
JERRY CITY—Cornwell, Levi
  Thompson, C. E.
LIME CITY—Hall, E. D.
  Lintner, Frank E.
LONGLEY—Huffman, D. B.

MERMILLE—Bortel, F. L.
MILTON CENTER—DePoy, B.
  Schunyer, John
NORTH BALTIMORE—**AIKEN, J. A.** See adv.
  Deter Bros.
  Heminger, M. T., & Son
  Peters, B. H.
  Poulson, C. A.
  Straley, W. H.
PEMBERVILLE—Prante, Fred
PERRYSBURG—Eckel, L. E.
  Hazmaier, R. F.
  Hoffman, Geo. Frederick

GROCERS—Continued.
PERRYSBURG—Jezzard, Frederick
Roberts, S. A.
Whitehead, D. C.
Williams, A. R.
PORTAGE—Sargent, A. C.
PRAIRIE DEPOT—Rogers, Thomas
Stolz & Franklin
RISINGSUN—Sass, H. C.
ROSSFORD—DeSheltler, Edwin B.
Harris, Chas. W.
Kusner, J.
STONY RIDGE—Haag, Grover C.

TONTOGANY—Roberson, Ross
Stevenson, James
WESTON—Pennock, G. W.
Saxby, Chas. B.
Shafer, H. T.
Vedder, A. C.

HARDWARE.

BOWLING GREEN—**CAMPBELL BROS.**
See adv.
Hopper Hardware Co.
PRIEUR, F. H. See adv.
BRADNER—Phister, J. C.

HARDWARE—Continued.

CUSTAR—**BRINK, GEO.** See adv.
  Drummer, Joseph
  Meurer, Henry
CYGNET—**EIDSON, J. W.** See adv.
GRAND RAPIDS—Digby, Fred
  Evans, W. K., & Son
HASKINS—**HASKINS HDWE. CO.** See adv.
HOYTSVILLE—Gottschalk, D. N.
  Herringshaw, Samuel
  Layton, A. E.
  Rader, W. C.
JERRY CITY—Frankfather, Orville

LIME CITY—Rider, C. F.
LUCKEY—Goodell, Sanford E.
  Krane Hardware Co.
  Luckey Hardware Co.
  Overmyer, Chas.
MILLBURY—**BAILEY, W. J.** See adv.
MILTON CENTER—Banks, F. J.
NORTH BALTIMORE—Central Hardware Co.
  Priebe, H. D.
  Ralston, Thomas
  Stouffer, W. L.
PEMBERVILLE—Keil, Wm., & Son
  Swan, H. C., & Sons

HARDWARE—Continued.
PERRYSBURG—Amon, John J.
  Davis, Jacob, & Son
PORTAGE—Saylor, W. H.
PRAIRIE DEPOT—Allen, F. S.
  Gibson & Reichelberger
  Tilton, S. E.
RISINGSUN—Brandeberry, F. E.
ROSSFORD—Algyre, A. J.
  Kotowiez, Paul
RUDOLPH—Shuler Hardware Co.
TONTOGANY—Irwin, H. P. (Mrs. S. L.)
WEST MILLGROVE—Miller, J. W.
WEST TOLEDO—**MARLEAU, DAVID.**
  See adv.

SCHUNK HARDWARE CO., THE.
  See adv.
WESTON—Singer, W. C., & Son
  **WESTON HARDWARE & IMPLE-
  MENT CO.** See adv.

HARNESS.
BLOOMDALE—Bryan, J. H.
BOWLING GREEN—**BALDWIN'S,** 175-
  177 S Main St. See adv.
  Darr, Frank
  Taggart, W. A.
BRADNER—DeBrandt, R.
  Kirk, E. R.

HARNESS—Continued.
CYGNET—Frederick, S. E.
GRAND RAPIDS—Adams, Frank A.
JERRY CITY—Page, T. O.
NORTH BALTIMORE—**WAGNER, DELL.**
 See adv.
PEMBERVILLE—Offerman, J. H.
PERRYSBURG—Enich, A. J.
 Schlecht, Wm.
PRAIRIE DEPOT—Janney, Wm. P.
RISINGSUN—Shirk, W. S.
RUDOLPH—Henning, C. E.

HOOPS AND STAVES.
PEMBERVILLE—Colvin Stave Co., The
 Jacob Lapp Cooperage Co., The

HOTELS.
BLOOMDALE—**RAGER, ALF**, Main St.
 See adv.
BOWLING GREEN—Brown Hotel
 Milliken, W. H.
 Ross, Mrs. R. J.
BRADNER—O'Bryan, Mrs. I. E.
CUSTAR—Custar House
HASKINS—Garrett, W.
 Vollmars' Park Hotel

HOTELS—Continued.

LUCKEY—Goodell, Malinda (Mrs. Marion)

NORTH BALTIMORE—Steele, A. J.

PERRYSBURG—Herman & Mary Harper

ROSSFORD—Felzer, Henry J.

WALBRIDGE—Scott Bros.

WESTON—Hotel Gayso

HOUSE FURNISHINGS.

BLOOMDALE—Wyant, Harry L.

WEST TOLEDO—**MARLEAU, DAVID.** See adv.

HOUSE MOVER.

WESTON—Irwin, Wm.

ICE.

BOWLING GREEN—**DAVIDSON, P. M.** See adv.

NORTH BALTIMORE—Laney & Adams Ice Co.

INSURANCE.

BLOOMDALE—**PELTON, S. S.** See adv.
BOWLING GREEN—Barr & Snyder
DANFORTH, H. J. See adv.

EBERLY, C. B., 133 E Wooster St. See adv.

LENHART & EASLEY, 110 W Wooster St. See adv.
Loomis, Roy E.
Miller & Bachman
NEARING & SEARS. See adv.
Stahl, Harry J.
WILSON, MILO D. See adv.
WOOD CO. INSURANCE AGENCY. See adv.
YONKER, C. D., 327 W Wooster St. See adv.
CYGNET—**HOWE, RAYMOND R.** See adv.
McSTAY, JAMES. See adv.

INSURANCE—Continued.
FREMONT—**FARMERS LIGHTNING PROTECTED MUTUAL INSURANCE CO., THE.** See adv.
NORTH BALTIMORE—**BROWN, MARGARET E.** See adv.
Francisco, B. S.
FULTON & BECKETT. See adv.
WESTON—**CONKLIN, J. D.** See adv.

JEWELRY.
BLOOMDALE—Blair, D. L.
BOWLING GREEN—Cornell, E. E.

Hunter, Chas. E.
VanKanel, Mrs. Fred
BRADNER—Cunningham, M. L.
Leggett, D. E.
DUNBRIDGE—Stonebrook, L. D.
GRAND RAPIDS—Nyswander, E.
HASKINS—North, F. H.
NORTH BALTIMORE—Stevenson, Ernest B.
Tyler, Elmer J.
PERRYSBURG—Clark, E. E.
PRAIRIE DEPOT—Gilson, W. W.
RISINGSUN—Myers, Miss Herma
WESTON—Strawser, H. G.

JUNK.

BOWLING GREEN—**KANDER, H.** See adv.

KRAUT MANUFACTURER.

WESTON—Clyde Kraut Co., The

LAUNDRIES.

BOWLING GREEN—Buckeye Laundry Agency
Capen, N. Lea
Home Steam Laundry

Model Laundry Agency

LIGHT AND POWER.

BLOOMDALE—Bloomdale Electric Light Co.

BOWLING GREEN—City Water Co., The Northwestern Ohio Natural Gas Co., The

NORTH BALTIMORE—North Baltimore Water & Electric Co., The

PRAIRIE DEPOT—Prairie Depot Electric Light & Power House

LIVERY.

BLOOMDALE—Henry, O. W.
BOWLING GREEN—**WILSON, GEORGE F.** See adv.
BRADNER—O'Bryan, S. C.
CUSTAR—Durliat, L. M.
   Thielen, B.
GRAND RAPIDS—Nye, E. D.
HOYTSVILLE—Snook, Geo. F.
NORTH BALTIMORE—Diebley, Wm. E.
   Jordan, D. B.
   SHROLL, WM. See adv.
PEMBERVILLE—Biddle, A. J., & Co.
PERRYSBURG—Cook, James
   Shepard, Geo. J.
PORTAGE—Hudson, T. A.
PRAIRIE DEPOT—King, Frank P.
RISINGSUN—Henry, P. C.
RUDOLPH—Ray, James H.
WEST MILLGROVE—Brandeberry, C. W.
WESTON—Murphy, J. M.

LOAD BINDER MANUFAC-TURER.

BLOOMDALE—Goodyear, A. B., & Co.

LUMBER.

BLOOMDALE—**LINHART, S. A.** See adv.
BOWLING GREEN—Bigelow Bros.
   HANKEY LUMBER CO., THE. See adv.
   Keil Lumber & Builders Supplies
BRADNER—Stiger, J. W.
CUSTAR—Hopkins Lumber Co.
DUNBRIDGE—Trepanier Lumber Co., The
GRAND RAPIDS—Hersh, G. E.
HASKINS—Watts, C. A.
HOYTSVILLE—Lytle Lumber Co., The
LE MOYNE—Andrews, Mrs. Laura
NORTH BALTIMORE—Everett Lumber & Supply Co., The
PEMBERVILLE—Pemberville Lumber Co.
   Steffen, H. F.
PERRYSBURG—**CHAS. L. KOCH CO., The.** See adv.
   Witzler, Fred A.
PRAIRIE DEPOT—Hoiles, C. H.
RISINGSUN—Myers, G. G.
RUDOLPH—Mercer Lumber Co.
TONTOGANY—Gill, E. G.
WESTON—Oswald Bros.

292

MACHINERY AND MACHINISTS.

BOWLING GREEN—CARR, E. T. See adv.
Luck, Geo. F.
National Supply Co., The
Universal Machine Co., The
Walker, J. E.
BRADNER—Heckert, Wm.
CYGNET—Walsh, M. J.
GRAND RAPIDS—Valerius, Nick

NORTH BALTIMORE—Exline & Son
Hardy Machine Co., The
Todd, M. G.
PERRYSBURG—Emch, Nicholas
Leydorf, Henry C.
Small, L. M.
PORTAGE—Laramore, O. O.
RUDOLPH—Osborne, H.
WEST TOLEDO—BANTING MACHINE CO., THE. See adv.

293

METAL SPECIALTIES.
FOREST—**DICKELMAN MFG. CO.** See adv.

MANICURING AND HAIR DRESSING.
BOWLING GREEN—Ducat, Mrs. Napoleon
Fryberger, Miss Erma
McCarty, Miss Mary E.
Turritin, Mrs. W. E.

MARBLE AND GRANITE.
BOWLING GREEN—**CRAMER, C. M.** See adv.

Smith, Frank E.
NORTH BALTIMORE—Ritter, Chas.
WESTON—Caldwell, W. N.

MEATS.
BLOOMDALE—Himlock, W. L.

BOWLING GREEN—Lehmann Bros.
Mertel, Geo. J.
Schlicher, Jacob
Witmer, Frederick
CUSTAR—Wentz, Aug. R.

MEATS—Continued.

CYGNET—Apple, W. E.
  Boudrie, Jeff
NORTH BALTIMORE—Hughes, C. J.
  Tarr, Isaac N.
  Yocum, Henry
PEMBERVILLE—Murphey & Hacker
PERRYSBURG—Kazmaier, H. A.
  Leydorf, C. C.
  Munger Bros.
PORTAGE—Schweckheimer, G.

PRAIRIE DEPOT—Ory & Lombard
RISINGSUN—Zender, P.
ROSSFORD—Holefka, W. L.
WESTON—Knauss, G. F.
  Shipman, C. L.

MEN'S FURNISHINGS.

BOWLING GREEN—**BOWERS, E. J.,** 109
N Main St. See adv.
HOYTSVILLE—Butler, Jos. B.

MILLINERY.

BLOOMDALE—Leathers, Miss B.
BOWLING GREEN—Collins & Aldrich
OTT, MRS. E. A. See adv.
Ott, G. P.
McMillan, Miss Mary
WARD, MRS. L. See adv.
CUSTAR—Ireland, Miss B.
GRAND RAPIDS—Mahler, Mrs. E.
 Van Valkenberg, M. (Mrs. L. M.)

HOYTSVILLE—Sudholtz, Miss Anna
MILTON CENTER—Bright, Miss M.
NORTH BALTIMORE—Edsall & Edsall
 Eiting, Miss B. M.
PEMBERVILLE—Gerding Sisters
 Stearns & Fisher
PERRYSBURG—Emch, Miss Lina
RISINGSUN—Howey, Mrs. B. F.
WESTON—**GINDER, MRS. MAY.** See adv.

NEWSPAPERS.

BLOOMDALE—Derrick

BOWLING GREEN—Sentinel-Tribune
Thomas, Frank W.
WOOD COUNTY DEMOCRAT, 210
N Main St. See adv.

BRADNER—**Advocate, The**

CUSTAR—News, The

CYGNET—**REVIEW, THE.** See adv.

NORTH BALTIMORE—Becon, The
Times, The

PEMBERVILLE—**P E M B E R V I L L E
LEADER.** See adv.

PERRYSBURG—Leader, The

PRAIRIE DEPOT—**OBSERVER, THE.** See
adv.

RISINGSUN—**Unique Weekly**

WESTON—**HERALD, THE.** See adv.

NOTARY PUBLIC.

BOWLING GREEN—**COMSTOCK, ABEL,**
134 W Wooster St. See adv.

OILS.

BRADNER—Van Vlick & Stowe Oil Co.

JERRY CITY—**ALLER, E. L.** See adv.

NORTH BALTIMORE—Standard Oil Co.

PRAIRIE DEPOT—Ohio Oil Co., The

RISINGSUN—Ulsh, C. A.

OSTEOPATHIST.

BOWLING GREEN—COLE, DR. E. A. See adv.

PAINT MANUFACTURER.

TOLEDO—**BUCKEYE PAINT VARNISH CO.** See adv.

PAINTS AND PAINTERS.

BOWLING GREEN—Hollinger, L. J.
Kenower, F. D.
Kenower, J. S.
West, Chas.
West, Clint.
Wilkens, J. H.
WEST TOLEDO—**MARLEAU, DAVID.** See adv.
WESTON—Rosencrantz, Jay

PHOTOGRAPHERS.

BOWLING GREEN—Sweet, J. A.
  Walker, J. A.
  White, Bert
NORTH BALTIMORE—Sweet, Jas. A.
PEMBERVILLE—Nobis, F. W.
PRAIRIE DEPOT—Callihan, Chas.

PHYSICIANS.

BAYS—**CHAMBERS, J. W.** See adv.
BOWLING GREEN—**Boyle, F. V.**
  COLE, E. A., 163 S Main St. See
  adv.

GORSUCH, DR. G. A., 110 S Main
  St. See adv.
Halleck, F. D.
Harrison, A. M.
McKendree, Lydia
McKENDREE, M. A., & L., 14 Reed
  and Merry Block. See adv.
Powel, H. J.
RAE, JAMES W., 123½ S Main St.
  See adv.
Schrader, C. O.
Schrader, I. M.

CYGNET, OHIO

F. L. STERLING, M.D.

OFFICE HOURS:
  9.00 to 11.00 A. M.
  2.00 to 4.00 P. M.
  6.30 to 8.00 P. M.

PHONE 10

WOMEN'S AND CHILDREN'S DISEASES
A SPECIALTY

DR. HARLEY E. WARD

PHYSICIAN AND SURGEON

X-RAY WORK. MICROSCOPIC AND CHEMICAL ANALYZER
JUST THINK A MOMENT WHAT THIS MIGHT MEAN TO YOU

PEMBERVILLE, OHIO

BELL PHONE { Res. 31-R
         { Office 31-M

OFFICE HOURS 12 TO 2 P. M.

J. E. BURNHAM

PHYSICIAN AND SURGEON

PRAIRIE DEPOT

OHIO

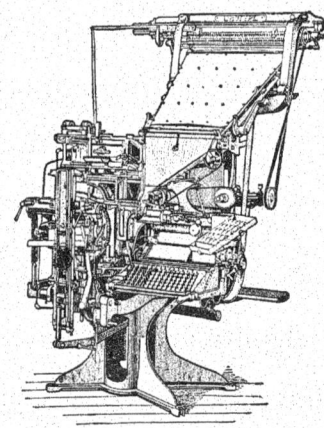

PHYSICIANS—Continued.

BOWLING GREEN—Snyder, J. C.
St. John, C. S.
Stove, F. A.
Thomas, E. P.
Trichler, W. S.
Whitacre, Thomas
CUSTAR—Maunhardt, Walter
CYGNET—**STERLING, FRANK L.** See
adv.
GRAND RAPIDS—Mercer, E. H.
HASKINS—Carter, Dr.
Johnston, Dr.

HOYTSVILLE—Salisbury, J. W.
LUCKEY—Smith, J. M.
MILTON CENTER—Strow, R. M.
NORTH BALTIMORE—Archer, J. H.
Campbell, J. A.
Cavett, C. S.
Foltz, G. W.
Henry, A. G.
MacCormack, C. D.
Powell, E. A.
Reddin, D. W.
Thomas, W. T.

PHYSICIANS—Continued.
PEMBERVILLE—Cline, C. A.
Collier, E. M.
Greiner, C. C.
Peabody, G. F.
Richardson, S. G.
WARD, DR. HARLEY E. See adv.
PRAIRIE DEPOT—BURNHAM, J. E. See adv.
WESTON—Aurand, G. C.
Williams, J. W.

PIANOS AND MUSICAL INSTRUMENTS.

BOWLING GREEN—CRANE'S MUSIC STORE, 235 N Main St. See adv.
Doane, E. G.
LADD, FRANK H. See adv.
LUCKEY—Greiner, Chas. F.
NORTH BALTIMORE—Lathrop, C. L.
Priddy, John L.

PIPE LINES.

HASKINS—Buckeye Pipe Line Co.
NORTH BALTIMORE—National Pipe Line Co.

PLATE GLASS MANUFACTURERS.

ROSSFORD—Edward Ford Plate Glass Co., The

PLUMBERS.

BOWLING GREEN—**CAMPBELL & COLLER**, S Main St. See adv.

Gillespie, W. J.
Ridenour, Daniel
THOMPSON, CHAS. R., 143 S Prospect St. See adv.
WIGGINS PLUMBING CO. See adv.
NORTH BALTIMORE—Moore, C. A.
PERRYSBURG—Braun, Chas. A.
PRAIRIE DEPOT—Harman, John H.

POULTRY.

BOWLING GREEN—**LeGALLEY, CHARLEY.** See adv.

POULTRY—Continued.

DUNBRIDGE—**BRINKMEIR, C. L.** See adv.

NORTH BALTIMORE—Hammond, C. G.

WESTON—**KEENER, MRS. JENNIE L.** See adv.

POULTRY MEDICINES.

TIFFIN—**SENECA COMPANY, INC., THE.** See adv.

POWDER MANUFACTURERS.

PRAIRIE DEPOT—De-Nemour Powder Co., The

PRINTERS AND PUBLISHERS.

BLOOMDALE—Hurrell, W. A.

BOWLING GREEN—**Bigelow, J. Harvey**
Campbell & Coller
Commercial Printing Co.
Democrat Co., The
Hubbard, E. M.
Sentinel Co., The
VanVoorhis & Thomas

BRADNER—Maurer, E. W.

CUSTER—Norcross & Son

CYGNET—Phillips, J. S.

GRAND RAPIDS—Lisemer, L. J.

PRINTERS AND PUBLISHERS
—Continued.

NORTH BALTIMORE—Beacon Publishing & Job Printing
Huddle, S. (Mrs. C. L.)
Rockwell, C. K.
Wilkinson, Geo. W.
PEMBERVILLE—**SPECK, GEO. H.** See adv.
PERRYSBURG—Blue, E. L.
PRAIRIE DEPOT—Hodges, H. L.
RISINGSUN—Myers, Calvin C.
RUDOLPH—Berry, C. R. F.
TONTOGANY—Crown Publishing Co.
WESTON—Coward, W. W.
Herald Office

PRODUCE.

PEMBERVILLE—Elmore Produce Co., The
WESTON—Miller Bros. Co., The

REAL ESTATE.

BOWLING GREEN—**BARR & SNYDER.** See adv.
Black, F. F.
EBERLY, C. B., 133 E Wooster St. See adv.

Miller & Bachman
Miller, T. J.
NEARING & SEARS. See adv.
Underwood, J. W.
LANSING, MICH.—**YOUNG BROS. REALTY CO.,** 536 E Michigan St. See adv.
NORTH BALTIMORE—**BROWN, MARGARET E.** See adv.
PERRYSBURG—**PERRYSBURG REALTY CO.** See adv.
WESTON—**SIBERT, F. M. G.** See adv.

RESTAURANTS.

BLOOMDALE—**RAGER, ALF.,** Main St. See adv.
BOWLING GREEN—College Inn
Davenport & Son
Davis, E. C.
Ireland's Restaurant
Yonker, E. E.
BRADNER—Tillotson, M. E.
CYGNET—**WOLF, RALPH W.** See adv.
HASKINS—Bernthisel, W. H.
HOYTSVILLE—Tyner, H.
JERRY CITY—Lee, Chas. C.

RESTAURANTS—Continued.

LUCKEY—Berning, Clem
Swin, W. P.

MILTON CENTER—Gribben, J. P.

NORTH BALTIMORE—Grimes, W. N.
Miller, E. E.
Withrow, C. F.

PEMBERVILLE—Carroll, C. R.
Goodell, M. C.

PERRYSBURG—Benton, Fred
Keifer, Miss G. A.

PORTAGE—Richmond, C. G.
Shuler, Wm.

PRAIRIE DEPOT—Stebeleton, O. H.

RISINGSUN—Hill, Chas. H.

RUDOLPH—Raney, Chas. A.

TONTOGANY—Carpenter, C. L.
Huston, J. I.
Pauff, John F.

WALBRIDGE—Ward, C. E.

WESTON—Bash, J. C.

ROOFERS.

CUSTER—Older, S. S., & Son

FOREST—**DICKELMAN MFG. CO.** See adv.

RUBBER MANUFACTURERS.

BOWLING GREEN—Bowling Green Rubber Co.

SALOONS.

BRADNER—Errett, Henry B.
CUSTER—Kistner & Stevenson
LUCKEY—Schifferd, Chas.
  Welling, J. Geo.
NORTH BALTIMORE—Ellis, Clarence W.
  Feese, Samuel F.

Hahn, C. O.
Monthaven, E. II.
Wahler, Wm. E.

PEMBERVILLE—Foster & Schwane
  Rolf Bros.

ROSSFORD—Gates, Jos.
  Gladish, John
  Holmes, Howard L.
  Manning, Wm. O.
  Mathias, J. J.

STONY RIDGE—Davis, Wm. A.

SANITARIUMS.

Bowling Green—**BOWLING GREEN SANITARIUM.** See adv.

SECOND-HAND GOODS.

Bowling Green—Huber, P. C.

SEEDS.

Toledo—**PAGE-PHILIPPS SEED CO., THE.** See adv.

PHILLIPS, WM. T., & CO. See adv.

SHOE REPAIRING.

Bowling Green—English, C. W.
Kehler, Jacob F.
Sommers, F. H.
Woodson, Chester
Woodson, H. A.

Custer—Nagel, J. P.

North Baltimore—Persing, R. L.
Tice, J. F.

Rossford—Toth, John P.

Weston—May, C. A.

SHOES.

BOWLING GREEN—Bourquin, E. P., & Co.
    Eberly & Son
    Gaines, J. L.
    Ketchum, A. B.
BRADNER—Wear-U-Well Shoe Co.
    Young, Wm. C., & Son
LUCKEY—Claus, G. F., & Son
NORTH BALTIMORE—Lamfrom, Rudolph
PEMBERVILLE—Schroeder Bros.
PERRYSBURG—Eberly, Frederick C.
    Shoemaker, John
TONTOGANY—Haffner, Casper

SIGN PAINTERS.

BOWLING GREEN—Kenower & Bros.

SPRAYING FLUID MANUFAC-TURER.

NORTH BALTIMORE—Sharp, John F.

SUGAR MANUFACTURERS.

ROSSFORD—Toledo Sugar Co., The

STONE.

BOWLING GREEN—France Stone Co., The
    Wood County Stone & Construction
    Co., The

STONE—Continued.

HAMMANSBURG—France Balast Co.

LIME CITY—Mercer, Geo. E.

LUCKEY—Doherty Lime & Stone Co., The

NORTH BALTIMORE—N. Baltimore Stone Co., The

TAILORS.

BOWLING GREEN—Bartlett, C. E.
Greiner, Michael
Neiman, H., & Son
Renz, Lawrence
Riess, A.
WILLIAMS, H. B., 142 W Wooster St. See adv.

CYGNET—Carson, Wm. H.

NORTH BALTIMORE—Fleck, Theo.
Harvey, J. T.
Henning, R. E.

PEMBERVILLE—Hollman, H. H.

ROSSFORD—Paul, Andrew

TELEPHONES.

BOWLING GREEN—Wood County Telephone Co., The

BRADNER—Bradner Telephone Co., The

DOWLING—Webster Telephone Co., The

GRAND RAPIDS—Crescent Telephone Co., The

Grand Rapids Mutual Telephone Co., The

HASKINS—Haskins Bell Telephone Co., The

LE MOYNE—Le Moyne Telephone Co., The

LUCKEY—Webster Telephone Co., The

MILLBURY—New Ottawa County Telephone Co., The

NORTH BALTIMORE—Wood County Telephone Co., The

PEMBERVILLE—New Ottawa County Telephone Co., The

PERRYSBURG—Northern Ohio Telephone Co., The

PRAIRIE DEPOT—New Ottawa County Telephone Co., The

RISINGSUN—Rising Sun Bell Telephone Co., The

TONTOGANY—Tontogany Telephone Co., The

WESTON—Crescent Telephone Co., The
Weston Home Telephone Co., The

THEATERS.

Bowling Green—**CHIDESTER THE-ATER.** See adv.
Everybody's 5 & 10 cent
Lyric, 5 & 10 cent
People's 5 cent

TIN AND TINNERS.

Bowling Green—**BARACKMAN, W. R.** See adv.
GOEBEL, GUS, 128 W Wooster St. See adv.
Fredeking, Lee
Grand Rapids—Winters, Andrew H.
Jerry City—Swope, H. W.
Pemberville—Dean, W. H.
Prairie Depot—West, H. E.
Rossford—Munding, Adolph

TRACTORS.

Bowling Green—**CARR, E. T.** See adv.

UNDERTAKERS.

Bloomdale—Adams, H. M.
Leathers, E. O.
Bowling Green—**DECK, J. F.,** 170 E Wooster St. See adv.
Hill, J. L.
Young, Carl H.
YOUNG, D. W., 306 Haskins St. See adv.
Bradner—Sage, O. O.
Custer—Gottemoller, F. H.
Cygnet—Goodwin, G. R.
Grand Rapids—Croll & Heyman
LAWRENZ, O. R. See adv.
Jerry City—Adams, M.
Luckey—Schwan, W. H.
North Baltimore—Chandler, M. R., & Son
Pemberville—Nieman, Henry
Perrysburg—Barton, Russell P.
Witzler, Alfred J.
Prairie Depot—**GOODRICK, JOHN M.** See adv.
Sage, O. O.
Williamson Bros.
Risingsun—Eby, Clifford B.
Weston—**WATKINS, MR. & MRS. W. C.** See adv.
RAUBENOLT & LANCE. See adv.

UNDERWEAR MANUFAC-TURERS.

BOWLING GREEN—Monarch Underwear Co., The

VARIETIES.

BLOOMDALE—Emerson, Ralph W.
BOWLING GREEN—Ladd & Adams
Rust, W. W.
NORTH BALTIMORE—Baker, John H.
Perry, M. H.
WESTON—Rust, W. W.

VETERINARIANS.

BAYS—Conkey, W. G.
BOWLING GREEN—Bailey, J. W.
Bailey, S. W.
Barker, F. A.
FOSTORIA—**ROSSITER, J. W.** See adv.
PRAIRIE DEPOT—**CONN, G. H.** See adv.
Wirebaught, V. I.

RUDOLPH—**CONKEY, DR. W. G.** See adv.
WESTON—Lanier, W. C.
Rosenberger, R. W.

WALL PAPER.

RUDOLPH—Hanna, M. L.
TONTOGANY—Baker, J. M.

WOMEN'S WEAR.

BOWLING GREEN—**DICUS LADIES' FURNISHING CO.** See adv.
NORTH BALTIMORE—Hughes, B. J.

WOODENWARE MANUFAC-TURERS.

PERRYSBURG—Chapman Sargent Co., The

WOOLENS.

PRAIRIE DEPOT—Garber Wool Co.
WESTON—Baldwin, E., & Co.

Poultry Diseases and Enemies

(From the Biggle Poultry Book)

Many of the ills that poultry flesh is heir to are directly traceable to bad breeding and treatment. In-and-inbreeding is practiced and the law of the survival of the fittest is disregarded until the stock becomes weak and a prey to disease.

Yards and runs occupied for any considerable time become covered with excreta and a breeding ground for all manner of disease germs.

Dampness from leaky roofs or from wet earth floors, and draughts from side cracks, or from overhead ventilation slay their thousands yearly.

A one-sided diet of grain, especially corn, moldy grain or meal, decayed meat or vegetables, filthy water, or the lack of gritty material are fruitful sources of sickness.

In the treatment of sick birds much depends on the nursing and care. It is useless to give medicine unless some honest attempt be made to remove the causes that produce the disturbance. Unless removed the cause will continue to operate and the treatment must be repeated.

It is an excellent plan to have a coop in some secluded place to be used exclusively as a hospital. If cases cannot be promptly treated it is better to use the hatchet at once and bury deeply, or burn the carcasses. This is the proper plan in every case where birds become very ill before they are discovered.

Sick birds should in no case be allowed to run with the flock and to eat and drink with them.

In giving the following remedies we make no pretence to a scientific handling of the subject.

FEVERS, from colds, fighting of cocks, etc. Symptoms: unusual heat of body, red face, watery eyes and watery discharge from nostrils.

Give dessertspoonful citrate of magnesia and, as a drink, ten drops of nitre in half a pint of water.

APOPLEXY AND VERTIGO, from overfeeding or fright. Symptoms: unsteady motion of the head, running around, loss of control of limbs. Give a purgative and bleed from the large veins under wing.

PARALYSIS, from highly seasoned food and over stimulating diet. Symptoms: inability to use the limbs, birds lie helpless on their side. Treatment—The same as for apoplexy.

LEG WEAKNESS occurs in fast-growing young birds, mostly among cockerels. A fowl having this weakness will show it by squatting on the ground frequently and by a tottering walk. When not hereditary it usually arises from a diet that contains too much fat and too little flesh and bone-making material, such as bread, rice, corn and potatoes. To this should be added cut green bone, oats, shorts, bran and clover, green or dry. Give a tonic pill three times a day made of sulphate of iron, 1 grain; strychnine, 1 grain; phosphate of lime, 16 grains; sulphate of quinine, $\frac{1}{2}$ grain. Make into thirty pills.

CANKER OF THE MOUTH AND HEAD.— The sores characteristic of this disease are covered with a yellow cheesy matter which, when it is removed, reveals the raw flesh. Canker will rapidly spread through a flock, as the exudation from the sores is a virulent poison, and well birds are contaminated through the soft feed and drinking water. Sick birds should be separated from the flock and all water and feed vessels disinfected by scalding or coating with lime wash. Apply to sores with a small pippet syringe or dropper the peroxide of hydrogen. When the entire surface is more or less affected, use a sprayer. Where there is much of the cheesy matter formed, first remove it with a large quill before using the peroxide. A simple remedy is an application to the raw flesh of powdered alum, scorched until slightly brown.

SCALY LEG, caused by a microscopic insect burrowing beneath the natural scales of the shank. At first the shanks appear dry, and a fine scale like dandruff forms. Soon the natural scale disappears and gives place to a hard, white scurf. The disease passes from one fowl to another through the medium of nests and perches, and the mother-hen infecting her brood. To prevent its spread, coat perches with kerosene and burn old nesting material and never use sitting hens affected by the disease. To cure, mix $\frac{1}{2}$ ounce flowers of sulphur, $\frac{1}{4}$ ounce carbolic acid crystals and stir these into 1 pound of melted lard. Apply with an old tooth brush, rubbing in well. Make applications at intervals of a week.

WORMS in the intestines of fowls indicate disturbed digestion. Loss of appetite and lack of thrift are signs of their presence. Give santonin in 2-grain doses

317

six hours apart. A few hours after the second dose give a dessertspoonful of castor oil. Or, put 15 drops of spirits of turpentine in a pint of water and moisten the feed with it.

BUMBLE-FOOT, caused by a bruise in flying down from perches or in some similar manner. A small corn appears on the bottom of the foot, which swells and ulcerates and fills with hard, cheesy pus. With a sharp knife make a cross cut and carefully remove all the pus. Wash the cavity with warm water, dip the foot in a solution of one-fourth ounce sulphate of copper to a quart of water and bind up with a rag and place the bird on a bed of dry straw. Before putting on the bandage anoint the wound with the ointment recommended for scaly leg or coat it with iodine.

GAPES, caused by the gape-worm, a parasite that attaches itself to the windpipe, filling it up and causing the bird to gasp for breath. The worm is about three-fourths of an inch long, smooth and red in color. It appears to be forked at one end, but in reality each parasite is two worms, a male and female, firmly joined together. This parasite breeds in the common earth worm. Chicks over three months old are seldom affected. If kept off of the ground for two months after hatching, or on perfectly dry soil, or on land where affected chicks have never run, chicks will seldom suffer from the gapes. Old runs and infested soil should have frequent dressings of lime.

In severe cases the worms should be removed. To do this put a few drops of kerosene in a teaspoonful of sweet oil. Strip a soft wing feather of its web to within an inch of the tip, dip in the oil, insert feather in windpipe, twirl and withdraw. Very likely some of the parasites and mucus will come with it. The rest will be loosened or killed, and eventually thrown out. It may be necessary to repeat the operation.

To kill the worm in its lodgment, gum camphor in the drinking water or pellets of it as large as a pea forced down the throat is recommended. Turpentine in the soft feed, as advised in the treatment for worms in the intestines, is said to be fective. Pinching the windpipe with .ie thumb and finger will sometimes loosen the parasite.

When broods are quartered on soil known to be infested, air-slacked lime should be dusted on the floor of the .oop, and every other night, for two or three weeks, a little of the same should be dusted in the coop over the hen and her brood. To apply, use a dusting bellows and only a little each time.

CHOLERA is due to a specific germ, or virus, and must not be confounded with common diarrhœa. In genuine cholera digestion is arrested, the crop remains full, there is fever and great thirst. The bird drinks, but refuses food and appears to be in distress. There is a thickening of the blood, which is made evident in the purple color of the comb. The discharges from the kidneys, called the urates, which in health are white, become yellowish, deep yellow, or, in the final stages, a greenish-yellow. The diarrhœa grows more severe as the disease progresses. A fowl generally succumbs in two days. The virus of cholera is not diffusible in the air, but remains in the soil, which becomes infected from the discharges, and in the body and blood of the victims. It may be carried from place to place on the feet of other fowls or animals. Soil may be disinfected by saturating it with a weak solution of sulphuric acid in water. Remove at once all well birds to new and clean quarters and wring the necks of all sick birds and burn their carcasses and disinfect their quarters.

For cases not too far gone to cure give sugar of lead, pulverized opium, gum camphor, of each, 60 grains, powdered capsicum (or fluid extract of capsicum is better, 10 drops), grains, 10. Dissolve the camphor in just enough alcohol that will do so without making it a fluid, then rub up the other ingredients in the same bolus, mix with soft corn meal dough, enough to make it into a mass, then roll it and divide the whole into one hundred and twenty pills. Dose, one to three pills a day for grown chicks or turkey, less to the smaller fry. The birds that are well enough to eat should have sufficient powdered charcoal in their soft feed every other day to color it slightly, and for every twenty fowls five drops of carbolic acid in the hot water with which the feed in moistened.

ROUP.—The first symptoms are those of a cold in the head. Later on the watery discharge from the nostrils and eyes thickens and fills the nasal cavities and throat, the head swells and the eyes close up and bulge out. The odor from affected fowls is very offensive. It is contagious by diffusion in the air and by contact with the exudations from sick fowls. To disinfect houses and coops burn sulphur and carbolic acid in them after turning the fowls out and keep closed for an hour or two. Pour a gill of turpentine and a gill of carbolic acid over a peck of lime and let it become slaked, then scatter freely over the interior of houses and coops and about the yards.

For the first stages spray the affected flock while on the roost or in the coop with a mixture of two tablespoonfuls of carbolic acid and a piece of fine salt as big as a walnut in a pint of water. Repeat two or three times a week. Or, if a dry powder is preferred, mix equal parts of sulphur, alum and magnesia and dust this in their nostrils, eyes and throat with a small powder gun. The nasal cavities should be kept open by injecting with a glass syringe or sewing machine oil-can a drop or two of crude petroleum. A little should be introduced also through the slit in the roof of the mouth. Give sick birds a dessertspoonful of castor oil two nights in succession, and feed soft food of bran and corn meal seasoned with red pepper and powdered charcoal. A physician advises the following treatment: hydrastin, 10 grains; sulph. quinine, 10 grains; capsicum, 20 grains. Mixed in a mass with balsam copaiba and made into twenty pills; give one pill morning and night; keep the bird warm and inject a saturated solution of chlorate potash in nostrils and about 20 drops down the throat.

PIP, so-called, is not a disease but only a symptom. The drying and hardening of the end of the tongue in what is called "pip" is due to breathing through the mouth, which the bird is compelled to do because of the stoppage of the nostrils. By freeing the natural air passages the tongue will resume its normal condition.

DIPHTHERIA is a contagious disease. The first symptoms are those of a common cold and catarrh. The head becomes red and there are signs of fever, then the throat fills up with thick, white mucus and white ulcers appear. The bird looks anxious and stretches its neck and gasps. When it attacks young chicks it is frequently mistaken for gapes. When diphtheria prevails, impregnate the drinking water with camphor, a teaspoonful of the spirits to a gallon of water, and fumigate the house as recommended for roup.

Spray the throat with peroxide of hydrogen or with this formula: 1 ounce glycerine, 5 drops nitric acid, 1 gill water. To treat several birds at once with medicated vapor, take a long box with the lid off, make a partition across and near to one end and cover the bottom with coal ashes. Mix a tablespoonful each of pine tar, turpentine and sulphur, to which add a few drops, or a few crystals, of carbolic acid and a pinch of gum camphor. Heat a brick very hot, put the fowls in the large part and the brick in the other, drop a spoonful of the mixture on the brick and cover lightly to keep the fumes in among the patients. Watch carefully, as one or two minutes may be all they can endure. Repeat in six hours if required.

CROP-BOUND.—The crop becomes much distended and hard from obstruction of the passage from the crop to the gizzard by something swallowed; generally, it is long, dried grass, a bit of rag or rope. Relief may sometimes be afforded by giving a tablespoonful of sweet oil and then gently kneading the crop with the hand. Give no food, except a little milk, until the crop is emptied. Wet a tablespoonful or more of pulverized charcoal with the milk and force it down the throat. Should the crop not empty itself naturally pluck a few feathers from the upper right side of it and with a sharp knife make a cut about an inch long in the outer skin. Draw this skin a little to one side and cut open the crop. Remove its contents, being careful not to miss the obstruction. Have a needle threaded with white silk ready, and take a stitch or two in the crop skin first, then sew up the outer skin separately. Put the patient in a comfortable coop, and feed sparingly for a week on bran and meal in a moist state, and give but little water.

SOFT OR SWELLED-CROP arises from lack of grit, or from eating soggy and unwholesome food. The distended crop contains water and gas, the bird is feverish and drinks a great deal. By holding it up with its head down the crop will usually empty itself. When this is done give teaspoon doses of charcoal slightly moistened twice at intervals of six hours. Restrict the supply of water and feed chopped onions and soft feed in moderation.

EGG-BOUND, DISEASES OF THE OVIDUCT Overfat hens are often troubled in this way. Forcing hens for egg production will sometimes break down the laying machinery. Give green food, oats, little corn, and no stimulating condiments. Let the diet be plain and cooling in its nature. To relieve hens of eggs broken in the oviduct, anoint the forefinger with sweet oil and deftly insert and draw out the broken parts. When the hen is very fat and the egg is so large it cannot be expelled, the only way to save the hen is to break the egg and remove it as above directed.

WHITE-COMB OR SCURVY, caused by crowded and filthy quarters and lack of green food. The comb is covered with a white scurf. This condition sometimes extends over the head and down the neck, causing the feathers to fall off.

Change the quarters and diet, give a dose of castor oil and follow this with a half a teaspoonful of sulphur in the soft food daily.

RHEUMATISM AND CRAMP caused by cold and dampness. Chicks reared on bottom-heat brooders are particularly subject to these troubles. Damp earth floors and cement floors in poultry houses produce it in older birds.

Give dry and comfortable quarters, feed little meat, plenty of green food, and soft feed seasoned with red pepper.

DIARRHŒA of chicks with clogging of the vent. Remove the hardened excre-

tion and anoint the parts. Chamomilla is useful in this complaint, a few drops in drinking water.

FROSTED COMB AND WATTLES.—As soon as discovered bathe with compound tincture of benzoin.

FOR LICE on perches, walls and coops, use kerosene or lime wash. To make the lime-wash more effective, pour a little crude carbolic acid on the lime before slaking or mix with plenty of salt.

For use in nests, pour crude carbolic acid on lime and allow it to air-slake. Put one or two handfuls of the carbolized lime dust in the nest box.

Pyrethrum powder kills by contact and is effective for dusting in nests, and through the feathers of birds. Its judicious use in the plumage and nests of sitting hens will insure immunity from lice for the hen and her young brood.

Chicks and poults are often killed by large lice that congregate about the head, throat, vent and wings. To destroy them, soak fish berries in alcohol, take the birds from under the mothers at night and slightly moisten the down of the infested parts with the poison.

How to Preserve Eggs

Now that eggs are dearer as a rule than they have been for years, many people are inquiring about the methods of preserving them. The old way was to pack them in salt or lime. This served the purpose, but it gave the eggs a very strong taste.

The approved method now is the one which calls for the use of "water glass," or silicate of soda. This is a thick, syrupy liquid which can be had at most drug stores for about 10 cents a pound, and a pound is enough to treat five dozen eggs, so that the cost of preserving is about two cents a dozen.

There are several grades of water glass, and it is wise to get the best. To prepare the solution, stir one part of the silicate of soda into sixteen parts of water which has been boiled, cooled and carefully measured.

It is essential to have the eggs fresh, or the experiment will not be a great success. Those over three days old should not be used, as the air has already had a chance to penetrate them. The very best way is to keep the solution made up ready and put the eggs into it just as soon as they are brought in from the nests, if you have your own chickens.

It is worse than useless to try to preserve eggs that are not fresh or that have been cracked or washed.

Incubation and Gestation Tables

Chickens	20-22 days
Geese	28-34 days
Ducks	28 days
Turkeys	27-29 days
Guinea fowls	28 days
Pheasants	25 days
Ostriches	40-42 days

The period of gestation in animals varies considerably, but the following is an average period based on a long series of observations:

Elephant	2 years
Camel	11-12 months
Ass	12 months
Mare	11 months
Cow	9 months
Sheep	5 months
Goat	5 months
Pig	3½ months
Bitch	9 weeks
Cat	8 weeks
Rabbit	30 days
Guinea pig	65 days

The Wood County Savings Bank Co.

Bowling Green, Ohio

OFFICERS

E. M. FRIES	- - -	President
W. M. TULLER	- -	- Vice-President
J. H. LINCOLN	- - -	Cashier
S. R. CASE -	- -	Assistant Cashier

DIRECTORS

FRANK KABIG   A. C. McDONALD

E. M. FRIES   J. C. LINCOLN

C. B. EBERLY   C. W. LENHART

WM. R. HOPPER   S. R. CASE

ED. O. SARGENT   N. R. HARRINGTON

W. M. TULLER

4 per cent. paid on time deposits

Solicit Commercial Business and give
Special Attention to those engaged
in Agricultural Pursuits   :   :   :   :

2260

Lightning Source UK Ltd.
Milton Keynes UK
UKHW021825080119
335203UK00008B/344/P